NAVAL FORCES OF THE WORLD

NAVAL FORCES OF THE WORLD

CHRISTOPHER CHANT

COLLINS WILLOW

ISBN 0 00 218113 4

Published by William Collins Sons & Co Ltd,
8, Grafton Street,
London W1X 3LA

Produced by Winchmore Publishing Services
Limited
40 Triton Square, London NW1 3HG

Edited by Sue Butterworth
Designed by Brian Benson
Picture Research by Jonathan Moore

Printed in Yugoslavia

CONTENTS

Introduction

This volume is intended to provide the reader with a comprehensive but yet readable and easily assimilated account of the world's navies (but only incidentally their coast guards and other maritime forces) in the first half of 1984. The subject matter is divided into three major groupings: *Naval Forces, Warships* and *Ship-Launched Missiles*.

The *Naval Forces* section is arranged alphabetically by country, and aims to give the reader a useful pen-picture of the general organization, objectives and capabilities of the world's various naval forces, together with a listing of the major types, classes and numbers operated by each navy. It should be noted that in the tabular sections the ship types are arranged broadly within the role sub-groups used for the *Ships* section, and that in the numbers column the first figure indicates ships in service (as of July 1984), the second figure ships under construction, the third figure ships ordered, and the occasional fourth figure ships projected: thus a column reading 7+3+4+2(?) would indicate that as of July 1984 the relevant navy had of the class in question seven ships in commission, with three more building, four more ordered and a possible two units projected for future order.

The *Warships* section is arranged alphabetically by

class name within each basic type. These basic types are missile-armed submarines (with a strategic capability against land or ship targets), nuclear-powered fleet (or attack) submarines, conventionally-powered patrol submarines, aircraft-carriers, heavy cruisers (including the world's sole battleship and battle-cruiser classes), cruisers, destroyers, frigates, corvettes (including large patrol ships), fast attack craft (missile-, gun- and torpedo-armed, all capable of a maximum speed of 25 kts or more), assault ships, landing ships, and minesweepers. It is worth noting that though the ships are classified quite categorically, this categorization is somewhat arbitrary: ships over 5,000

tons displacement are generally regarded as cruisers, though there is a case (for example) for the assessment of the Soviet 'Sovremenny' and 'Udaloy' class as destroyers. As a rule only those classes likely to be in service by 1990 have been included. It should also be noted that in the case of 'guided-missile' classes, the designation indicates that the ships in question have a missile fit of offensive or operational (but not local) defence capability.

The *Ship-Launched Missiles* section is arranged alphabetically by manufacturer, and provides the reader with details of the most important guided weapons used by the vessels in the Ships section.

Naval forces of the world

Albania

The navy of Albania has a personnel strength of some 3,200 including about 300 coastal frontier guards. Of this total about 1,000 are conscripts, who do a three-year stint in the service, and the breakdown of the 2,900 naval personnel is some 1,500 afloat, 500 under training and 900 ashore.

The navy is structured purely for local defence, and is based at Duressi, Vlora, Sazan Island, Sarande, Shingjin and Pasa Liman with a not very effective mixture of Soviet and Chinese ships. The Soviet-supplied vessels were all delivered before the break with the USSR in 1962, and must now be of limited operational capability as a result of spares shortages: of the three submarines, for example, one is used only for harbour training. A similar situation is probably arising with the Chinese-supplied craft, for an ideological rift opened with this ally in the later 1970s. The two operational submarines and two large patrol craft are sufficient to provide a longer-range warning and attack capability, while the real defensive strength, such as it is, lies with the 44 torpedo-armed fast attack craft of the 'Huchuan' and 'P 4' classes. The mine warfare force is adequate, but in general the Albanian navy must be categorized as capable of meeting only the most limited of threats.

type	number	class
patrol submarine	3	'Whiskey'
FAC (gun)	6	'Shanghai II'
FAC (torpedo)	32	'Huchuan'
	12	'P 4'
patrol craft	2	'Kronshtadt'
minesweeper (ocean)	2	'T 43'
minesweeper (inshore)	6	'T 301'
	9	'PO 2' mine-sweeping boat
other	about 24	

Algeria

Though geographically a large country, Algeria has only a relatively small seaboard, and only limited political involvement in the Mediterranean. However, the area abounds with ambitious nations, and the country has a fairly large merchant marine, so the navy is larger than one might expect, with a personnel strength of about 8,000, all of them volunteers. The Algerian bases are at Algiers, Annaba and Mers el Kebir.

The main strength of the Algerian navy lies with Soviet-supplied vessels, and the country is still maintaining close links with the USSR. However, since 1980 the Algerian navy has sought to diversify its suppliers, as evidenced by the placing of orders in British and Italian yards (the former for fast attack

craft and logistic landing ships, and the latter for coast guard patrol craft). This may see a gradual development towards Western-designed vessels of a more capable variety, but may run into political opposition from the USSR. The current balance of the Algerian navy is swung towards coastal defence, with useful numbers of missile-armed fast attack craft available for the task, though longer-range operations are possible with the navy's 'Nanuchka II' class missile corvettes supported by the 'Koni' class SAM-armed frigates. Further evidence of Algeria's increasing interest in longer-range operations is provided by probable training of submariners, preparation for the possible delivery later in this decade of Soviet 'Foxtrot' class boats.

As well as the navy, Algeria has a small coast guard force with 18 small patrol craft, 16 of them supplied by Italy.

Algerian navy ship strength

type	number	class
patrol submarine	(?)	?
frigate	2	'Koni'
corvette	4	'Nanuchka II'
FAC (missile)	9	'Osa II'
	3	'Osa I'
	6	'Komar'
FAC (gun)	2	Brooke Marine 'Trident'
FAC (torpedo)	4	'P 6'
patrol craft	6	'SO I'
	1	'Zhuk'
landing ship	2	Brooke Marine L5 Logistic
landing craft	1	'Polnochny'
other	13	

Angola

Angola secured its independence from Portugal in 1975, and with independence received a substantial number of ex-Portuguese vessels which were either abandoned or more formally handed over to the new government. Angola has a long coastline liberally provided with good natural harbours, but the main naval bases are Luanda (with headquarters on the Ila de Luanda, where a fortified base is being established), Lobito and Mocamedes. Personnel strength is about 1,000, probably all volunteers, and this factor conditions the overall efficiency of this coastal-defence force: trained personnel are wholly inadequate for the task of manning and operating the ex-Portuguese vessels and the various Soviet-supplied craft that have been received since 1975. Therefore, the numerical strength of the fleet (whose precise details are unknown) is little indication of the effectiveness of the Angolan navy. Training is a primary consideration for the force, which has readily accepted offers of help from Portugal, Nigeria, Cuba and the USSR. A single Fokker F.27 is operated by the Angolan navy for maritime surveillance, and a number of coastal merchantmen have been impressed for naval support.

Angolan navy ship strength

type	number	class
FAC (missile)	4	'Osa II'
FAC (torpedo)	4	'Shershen'
patrol craft	5	'Argos'
	1	'Zhuk'
	2	'Poluchat I'
	2	'Jupiter'
	4	'Bellatrix'
landing craft	3	'Polnochny' LCT
	1	'Alfange' LCT
	14	LCU
other	8	

Anguilla

This small Caribbean island has been administered by the British since its separation from St Christopher and Nevis in 1971, and operates two small craft, a Fairey Marine 'Huntsman' class craft for police duties, and a Fairey Marine 'Interceptor' class craft for rescue. This latter is associated with the island's airport, and carries rafts for the rescue of 200 survivors.

Argentina

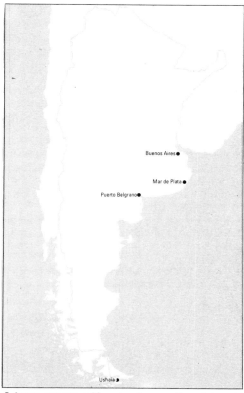

A large country with extensive maritime interests and potential threats, Argentina is currently undergoing a combined political and military revision following the catastrophic defeat in the Falkland Islands'/Malvinas' campaign of 1982 and the removal of the military administration that launched the war. The Argentine navy did not shine in this conflict, and practical experience of the Royal Navy's far greater strategic, tactical and technical superiority is reflected in the Argentine navy's current programme of revision and accelerated purchase of modern equipment. Current personnel strength is 36,900 including the marine corps and 12,000 12-month conscripts. The marine corps totals 6,000 officers and men, and the regular strength of the navy comprises 2,900 officers plus 16,000 petty officers and other ranks. There are five main naval bases: Buenos Aires (complete with drydocks and floating docks), Rio Santiago (complete with a building yard and a slipway), Mar de Plata (a submarine base with slipway), Puerto Belgrano (the main naval base with schools, two drydocks and one floating dock) and Ushaia (only a small base). The naval organization divides the country's coastal and offshore waters into three sections: Naval Area North (HQ at Rio Santiago) is concerned with the area as far south as the River Plate and including the Parana and Uruguay rivers; Naval Area Centre (HQ at Puerto Belgrano) deals with the area between the Plate estuary and the Valdes peninsula; and Naval Area South (HQ at Ushaia) covers the area from the Valdes peninsula to Cape Horn.

The current fleet is equipped largely with war-ships of British and US origins, and these are now showing their age. Spares from the UK have been halted, and those from the USA curtailed, so far with little operational effect, but Argentina has increasingly turned to West Germany for the supply (or licence production) or more modern vessels, notably patrol submarines, destroyers and frigates of superior anti-submarine and anti-air capabilities. There are also three French 'A 69' class general-purpose frigates, and France is the major supplier of surface-to-surface missiles. Italy is the primary source for guns (DP and AA) and surface-to-air missiles, and it can be concluded that the Argentine navy is moving away from its old mix of carrier airpower/gun-armed cruisers and destroyers towards a more modern mix of carrier airpower/missile- and DP gun-armed destroyers and frigates, with modern patrol submarines providing long-range capability. The constant factor in these equations is the elderly but useful carrier *Veinticinco de Mayo*, which operates a useful mix of fixed-wing strike and anti-submarine aircraft, and of rotary-wing anti-sub-marine and utility aircraft. Naval task forces can be provided with additional air support from five naval air bases. Total naval air strength is some 75 aircraft, of which 22 (18 fixed- and four rotary-wing aircraft) can be deployed aboard the *Veintincinco de Mayo*, which has fairly modern aircraft and electronics, though possibly unreliable machinery.

The Argentine coast guard (*Prefectura Naval Argentina*) operates two elderly and five modern patrol ships (with five more of the Spanish-built and helicopter-equipped 'Halcon' class on order), eight large patrol craft and 33 small patrol craft.

Argentine navy ship strength

type	number	class
patrol submarine	1+2+3	'TR 1700'
	2	'Type 209' or 'Satta'
	1	'Guppy IA'
aircraft-carrier	1	'Colossus'
destroyer	4	'Meko 360' or 'Almirante Brown'
	2	'Type 42'
	1	'Fletcher'
	2	'Allen M. Sumner (FRAM II)'
	1	'Allen M. Sumner'
	1	'Gearing (FRAM II)'
frigate	2+4	'Meko 140' or 'Espora'
	3	'A 69'
FAC (gun)	2	'Lürssen TNC 45'
FAC (torpedo)	2	'Higgins'
patrol craft/vessel	2	'Cherokee'
	2	'King'
	2	'Sotomoyo'
	1	'Surubi'
	4	'Dabur'
minesweeper (coastal)	6	'Ton'
landing ship	1	'Cabo San Antonio' LST
landing craft	12+	LCM & LCVP
other	32+1	

Australia

Australia and her armed forces are one of the most stabilizing factors in a potentially unstable east Asia/Pacific area, and the Royal Australian Navy is the country's most effective means of projecting long-range military muscle. Yet in a general area notable for its small defence expenditures and largely obsolescent equipment, the Royal Australian Navy can remain relatively small so long as its training and equipment are of the highest possible standards. This explains in part the small personnel strength of the Royal Australian Navy, some 17,600 volunteers

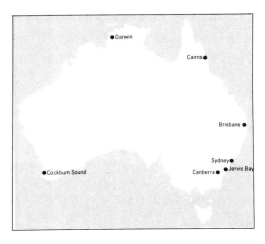

including 1,150 members of the Women's Royal Australian Naval Service. Given the vast size of the country, there are remarkably few bases available for the Royal Australian Navy, namely Sydney and Jervis Bay in New South Wales, Brisbane and Cairns in Queensland, Darwin in the Northern Territory, and Cockburn Sound in Western Australia. The bases in Queensland and the Northern Territory are used mainly for patrol craft and amphibious warfare forces.

In a highly controversial move during 1982, the carrier *Melbourne* was paid off, and though it was at one time decided to buy a British 'Invincible' class carrier as a replacement, this plan has been abandoned for financial and political reasons, leaving task groups of the Royal Australian Navy totally devoid of organic air support/cover on long-range deployments. Yet even without air support from such a platform, the Royal Australian Navy remains a potent force centred on six submarines for long-range operations, and a mixed complement of three 'Perth' class missile destroyers and an increasing number of 'Oliver Hazard Perry' class missile frigates. The balance of these two types has been nicely judged to provide powerful task groups with capabilities against air, surface and underwater targets, and recent developments in equipment procurement and training have been designed to promote more effective use of these assets. Further missile procurement is also enhancing the Royal Australian Navy's ability to deal with potential threats at long range, well beyond those possible with the missiles likely to be used by theatre opponents. There are also some older but still useful frigates.

Mine warfare has been somewhat neglected, but the Royal Australian Navy is now pressing ahead with a new class of catamaran minehunters to supplement the present strength of three coastal minesweepers. Patrol forces are small, but the arrival of growing numbers of 'Fremantle' class large patrol craft has permitted the secondary deployment and local sale of the smaller and less capable 'Attack' class craft. Amphibious and service force vessels are adequate for their tasks, and the stump of a Fleet Air Arm keeps naval aviation in being for the possible reversal of the decision to abandon seaborne airpower.

Australian navy ship strength

type	number	class
patrol submarine	6	'Oberon'
destroyer	3	'Perth'
frigate	4+6	'Oliver Hazard Perry'
	6	'River'
patrol craft	15+5	'Fremantle'
	10	'Attack'
minelayer	—	—
minesweeper (ocean)	—	—
minesweeper (coastal)	0+2+4	'MHCAT'

	3	'Ton'
landing ship	1	'Sir Bedivere'
landing craft	6	'Balikpapan' LCH
	17	'LCM Mk 8'
	4	LCVP
other	65+	

Austria

Austria has a small riverine 'navy' administered as part of the engineer corps, a personnel strength of about 30 manning one large and one small river patrol craft, and also 10 ex-US patrol craft that are also part of the Austrian army's bridging equipment.

Bahamas

Based at New Providence Island as part of the Royal Bahamian Defence Force, the Bahamian navy operates a few patrol craft for coastal operations. The largest craft is the 109-ton Vosper-build *Marlin*, complemented by five Vosper-built 30-ton craft and four Phoenix Marine-built inshore craft. There are also two floating base craft, the *Fort Montague* and the *Fort Charlotte*.

Bahrain

Using a small part of the oil wealth that has also made the country worthy of attack in a highly volatile region, Bahrain has a small navy manned by some 300 volunteer personnel, the two original Lürssen 'FPB 38' class gun-armed fast attack craft being supplemented recently by two missile-armed Lürssen 'TNC 45' class fast attack craft. This force is controlled as part of the Bahrain Defence Force by the Ministry of Defence, while the 150-man coast guard falls under the aegis of the Ministry of the Interior. This force currently comprises 20 craft including one hovercraft and one tug, and is scheduled for considerable enlargement in the near future.

Bahrain navy ship strength

type	number	class
FAC (missile)	2	Lürssen 'TNC 45'
FAC (gun)	2	Lürssen 'FPB 38'

Bangladesh

Impoverished, beset by social and political problems, and lacking any real or potential enemy, Bangladesh maintains only a small navy whose major units are of British origins. The country's relatively close relationship with India and China is reflected in the provision of patrol craft and fast attack craft respectively by those two countries. Manpower strength is 5,800 volunteers (400 officers and 5,400 petty officers and other ranks), and the Bangladesh navy's principal bases are Chittagong, Dacca, Khulna and Kaptai. Three ex-British frigates provide the sea-going force, but most important also is the light force strength of fast attack craft and patrol craft, which provide protection for the vulnerable Mouthes of the Ganges area that forms Bangladesh's coastline. Given the vulnerability of this economically vital area, it is hardly understandable that Bangladesh has no mine warfare capability whatsoever.

Bangladesh navy ship strength

type	number	class
frigate	1	'Salisbury'
	2	'Leopard'
FAC (gun)	1+3(?)	'Hainan'
	8	'Shanghai II'
patrol craft	2	'Kraljevica'
	2	'Akshay'

	1	'River'
	5	'Pabna'
other	4	misc

Barbados

Manned by 124 volunteers, the naval arm of the integrated Barbados defence forces operates as a coast defence and coast guard force from its base at Bridgetown. The force's main asset is the 37.5-m Brooke Marine large patrol craft *Trident*, which is backed by five coastal patrol craft (one 'Guardian I' class, two 'Guardian II' class and two 'Enterprise' class).

Belgium

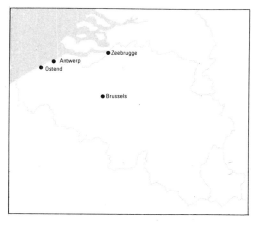

Belgium has only a small navy devoted entirely to the support of NATO objectives in the North Sea, English Channel and eastern Atlantic. Personnel strength is 4,725 including 1,350 men doing a 10-month national service period, and the main bases are Zeebrugge (frigates and one ocean minesweeper squadron), Ostend (one coastal minehunter squadron and one inshore minesweeper squadron), and Kallo near Antwerp (one inshore minesweeper squadron, reserve inshore minesweepers and river patrol craft). The three helicopters operated by the Belgian navy are based at Coxyde.

Up to the late 1970s the Belgian navy was concerned almost exclusively with mine warfare in Belgium's coastal and estuarine waters, but the building of the four 'Wielingen' class missile frigates has given the force a more wide-ranging capability, these frigates offering an excellent balance of surface-to-surface, surface-to-air and anti-submarine capabilities in conjunction with other NATO surface forces. However, the capital cost of these fine vessels has meant the postponement of urgently-required mine warfare vessels, and for the next few years Belgium will concentrate naval efforts on the planned 15 units of the 'Tripartite' type minesweeper/minehunter being produced in collaboration with France and the Netherlands, the completion of the Belgian units allowing the retirement of the now-elderly mine warfare stalwarts of the 'Aggressive' and 'Adjutant' classes.

Belgian navy ship strength

type	number	class
frigate	4	'Wielingen' or 'E-71'
patrol craft	8	'Leie'
minesweeper (ocean)	0+10+5	'Tripartite'
	7	'Aggressive'
minesweeper (coastal)	6	'Adjutant'
minesweeper (inshore)	14	'Herstal'
other	16	misc

Belize

Based at Belize, the 50 volunteers of the Belize naval unit have a single coastal patrol craft commissioned in 1972 after building at the Brooke Marine yard at Lowestoft. The operating agency is the office of the Comptroller of Customs.

Benin

The small West African state of Benin has a small naval force with a personnel strength of about 200. Operating from the base at Cotonou, this force has two 'P 4' class fast attack craft (torpedo) and four 'Zhuk' class coastal patrol craft, more than adequate for the defence needs of this country.

Bermuda

Under the control of the Bermudian Police, Bermuda operates five inshore patrol craft from the base at Hamilton.

Bolivia

Though completely landlocked, the South American state of Bolivia has a small navy independent of the other services, and intended mainly for service on Lake Titicaca and four principal river systems (the Beni, Madre de Dios, Mamore and Paraguay). The force is allocated to four naval districts, and the 4,000 personnel (including a marine battalion) have bases at Guayaramerin, Puerto Busch, Puerto Horquilla, Puerto Suarez, Puerto Villaroel, Riberalta, Tiquina and Trinidad. Apart from some 36 lake and river patrol craft, the Bolivian navy operates one 6,400-ton freighter on Lake Titicaca for commercial purposes, and also two hospital ships.

There is also a small naval air arm with one Cessna U206 utility aircraft and two North American AT-6C trainers. The 600-man marine battalion is based at Tiquina.

Brazil

Currently the most powerful navy in South America, the Brazilian navy operates a balanced force of surface and underwater vessels suitable for ocean and coastal operations. Manpower strength is about 46,000 including a small number doing 12 months of national service, and this figure comprises 4,100 officers and 41,900 petty officers and other ranks of the navy proper, fleet air arm and marines (the last comprising 14,500 officers and men). The Brazilian navy is divided into naval districts: I Naval District has its headquarters at Rio de Janeiro, II Naval District at San Salvador, III Naval District at Recife, IV Naval

District at Belem, V Naval District at Florianopolis, VI Naval District at Sao Paulo, and VII Naval District at Brasilia. The navy's main bases are Rio de Janeiro, where there are graving docks, floating docks and drydocks; Aratu near Bahia; Belem; Natal, which is being transformed into a major base; and Ladario, which is home for the Mato Grosso flotilla of riverine craft. There is also a small naval air arm based at Sao Pedro. This operates only helicopters, of which current strength is 45 for anti-submarine and utility purposes.

The core of the Brazilian navy's surface strength is the carrier *Minas Gerais*. She is currently configured for the anti-submarine role, but Brazilian plans call for her development as a multi-role carrier for service well into the 1990s. This carrier is supported by 12 ex-US destroyers of the 'Gearing', 'Fletcher' and 'Allen M. Sumner' classes, though these are limited by modern standards in terms of electronics and missiles, most of the ships carrying no missile armament and the others only self-defence surface-to-air missiles. More capable by a considerable degree are the six 'Niteroi' class destroyers (a seventh is being fitted out as a training ship). Four of these are optimized for anti-submarine warfare with the Ikara missile system, and the remaining two as general-purpose ships with Exocet surface-to-surface missiles in addition to the Sea Cat point-defence missiles carried by all 'Niteroi' class destroyers. Surface capabilities will be much enhanced by the delivery of possible 12 of a new type of multi-role frigate being designed by Brazil with West German aid: the first pair were ordered in 1982, and the type features advanced anti-submarine capability combined with four Exocet surface-to-surface missiles. Further expansion of the surface force, including a new carrier, is planned when finances permit.

Though Brazil still deploys five obsolescent 'Guppy' type submarines alongside three more advanced 'Oberon' class boats, two 'Type 209' boats are on order for yet greater capability, and further development of the submarine arm is envisaged if resources are available. Amphibious forces are well supplied with the relevant vessels, and the rest of Brazil's navy is formed of significant river and coastal patrol forces, service vessels and a mine warfare force that is small but probably adequate given the minimal threat faced by Brazil in this respect.

Brazilian navy ship strength

type	number	class
patrol submarine	0+2	'Type 209'
	3	'Oberon'
	2	'Guppy III'
	3	'Guppy II'
aircraft-carrier	1	'Colossus'
destroyer	2	'Gearing (FRAM II)'
	5	'Fletcher'
	1	'Allen M. Sumner'
	4	'Allen M. Sumner (FRAM II)'
	6	'Niteroi'
frigate	0+4+8	new construction
patrol craft	10	'Imperial Marinheiro'
	2	'Pedro Teixeiro'
	1	Thornycroft type
	3	'Roraima'
	6	'Piratini'
minesweeper (coastal)	6	'Aratu' or 'Schütze'
landing ship	1	'De Soto County' LST
	1	'LST 511-1152' LST
landing craft	35	LCU & EDVP
other	90+	misc

Brunei

Oil-rich and potentially vulnerable, Brunei has sensibly invested in a small navy that could inflict serious damage on a would-be aggressor. This force is administered as the Royal Brunei Malay Regiment Flotilla, and is based at Muara. Personnel are all volunteers, and total 446 (42 officers and 404 other ranks) including a commando unit and river division. The 'teeth' of the force are three powerful fast attack craft (missile), backed by three coastal patrol craft and a number of river patrol/amphibious craft.

Brunei navy ship strength

type	number	class
FAC (missile)	3	'Waspada'
patrol craft	3	'Perwira'
	3	Rotork type
landing craft	2	'Cheverton Loadmaster'
	24	'Rigid Raider' assault boat

Bulgaria

A component of the Warsaw Pact military forces, the Bulgarian navy is designed for operations in the Black Sea, and has a strength of some 10,000 personnel, of whom 6,000 are conscripts undergoing a 3-year period of military service. Of this overall strength, some 4,000 are afloat, 3,000 ashore, 1,000 undergoing training and the balance of 2,000 allocated to two coastal artillery regiments with 150- and 100-mm (5.9- and 3.9-in) guns. A small number of personnel are on the strength of the naval air arm, which has eight Mil helicopters. The main bases are Varna, Burgas, Sozopol and Atiya.

Bulgarian navy ship strength

type	number	class
patrol submarine	2	'Romeo'
frigate	2	'Riga'
corvette	3	'Poti'
FAC (missile)	2	'Osa II'
	3	'Osa I'
FAC (torpedo)	6	'Shershen'
	4	'P 4'
patrol craft	6	'SO I'
	5	'Zhuk'
minesweeper (ocean)	2	'T 43'
minesweeper (coastal)	4	'Vanya'
minesweeper (inshore)	4	'Yevgenya'
landing craft	19	'Vydra' LCU
	11	'MFP C-3'
other	25	miscs

Burma

The navy of the Union is relatively obsolete, but adequate for its limited tasks, which include the prevention of infiltration by anti-government forces of men and matériel. Personnel strength is some 10,000 volunteers, including about 800 marines, and these operate a mixed fleet of four corvettes, 43 river patrol boats, a number of gunboats and the various ancillary vessels. The main bases are Bassein, Mergui, Moulmein, Rangoon, Seikyi, Sinmalaik, Sittwe and Zadet, allowing extensive riverine and coastal patrols, but it is clear that the force needs to replace some of its larger vessels with comparable units of modern construction with better sensors.

Burma navy ship strength

type	number	class
corvette	1	'PCE 827'
	1	'Admirable'
	2	'Nawarat'
patrol craft	76	misc
other	2	misc

Cameroun

The navy of Cameroun is based at Douala, and is a strongly unbalanced coastal defence force with a personnel strength of 350. Apart from a wide miscellany of coastal patrol and comparable craft, the Cameroun navy operates two ex-Chinese 'Shanghai II' class fast attack craft (gun) and the prodigiously well-armed single 'P 48S' class fast attack craft (missile) from France, with no fewer than eight Exocet surface-to-surface missiles.

Cameroun navy ship strength

type	number	class
FAC (missile)	1	'P 48S'
FAC (gun)	2	'Shanghai II'
patrol craft	1	'PR 48'
	9	misc
landing craft	1	LCM
	1	LCU
	11	LCVP
other	5	misc

Canada

The Canadian navy is an intrinsic part of the Canadian Armed Forces formed as a unified service in 1968. The navy (Maritime Command) has a personnel strength of about 8,700, all volunteers, and is concerned primarily with anti-submarine warfare in the North Atlantic, though a useful detachment is located in the Pacific. The two main bases are Halifax and Esquimault respectively, and here the bulk of the Maritime Command's anti-submarine destroyers and frigates are deployed for task group and convoy protection within the context of a war between the NATO and Warsaw Pact blocs.

In the Pacific, centred on the replenishment ship *Provider*, are the 2nd Destroyer Squadron and the Training Squadron. The former comprises the four 'Improved Restigouche' class frigates, which are officially classed as destroyers and are currently being upgraded with improved electronics and Mk 32 anti-submarine torpedo tubes to improve on the current fit, which includes an octuple ASROC launcher. The type's main failing is lack of an embarked helicopter for longer-range search. Also classed officially as destroyers are the four 'Mackenzie' class frigates that make up the strength of the Training Squadron. These would require considerable modification to become first-line anti-submarine escorts, but are being improved with new sonar.

Again, the ships' main failing is lack of an embarked helicopter, compounded by lack of long-range anti-submarine weapons of the ASROC type.

In the Atlantic are based the Maritime Command's primary assets in the anti-submarine sphere. Here too are located the Canadians' only three patrol submarines, which are being upgraded with more advanced sonar and fire-control systems as part of the SOUP (Submarine Operational Update Programme) modernization. Also in the Atlantic are the 1st and 5th Destroyer Squadrons, the former comprising two 'Iroquois' class destroyers and four 'St Laurent' class frigates, and the latter two 'Iroquois' class destroyers, two 'St Laurent' class frigates and two 'Annapolis' class frigates. These are all based on the replenishment ships *Protecteur* and *Preserver*. All these Atlantic-based primary assets are fitted with at least one embarked helicopter, and are being modernized under the DELEX (Destroyer Life Extension) programme with Sea Sparrow point-defence missile systems, improved sensors and enhanced communications, but it is clear that new construction is the only answer to the Maritime Command's increasingly obsolescent force of frigates. The first steps have thus been taken towards replacement of the 'St Laurent' class by a new class of advanced anti-submarine destroyer: the first six were ordered in 1983, though the programme might be stretched slightly to make possible the eventual purchase of 12 units.

Other Maritime Command assets are secondary vessels such a survey and research vessels, and patrol craft. There is also a large coast guard organization (icebreakers and navigation/rescue vessels) and a fishery protection force with 22 ships and more than 750 smaller ships.

Canadian navy ship strength

type	number	class
patrol submarine	3	'Oberon'
	0+6	Canadian
destroyer	4	'Iroquois'
frigate	2	'Annapolis'
	4	'Mackenzie'
	4	'Improved Restigouche'
	6	'St Laurent'
patrol craft	6	'Bay'
	1	'Fort'
	5	'Porte'
	6	'Adversus'
other	39	misc

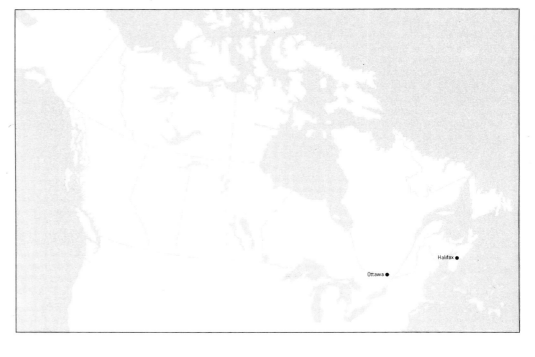

Canadian coast guard strength

type	number	class
icebreaker	25	misc
tenders	14	misc
patrol and rescue cutters	45	misc
other	61	misc

Cape Verde

The island state of Cape Verde has fallen into the Soviet sphere of influence since independence from Portugal, and now boats a small navy with some 75 personnel, three 'Shershen' class fast attack craft (torpedo) and two 'Zhuk' class coastal patrol craft. These vessels use the ports being built (with Soviet assistance) at Palmeira on de Sal island, Salrei on Boa Vista island, Tarrafa on Sao Nicolau island and Janela on Santo Antao island. The force's sole responsibility is coastal defence and patrol.

Chile

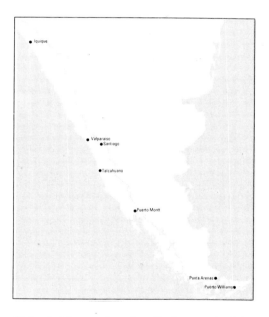

Chile stretches north and south along much of the southern part of the coastal strip to the west of the Andes, and thus possesses a very long and dangerously exposed coast, possible threats coming from most of the country's neighbours. Chile thus needs and maintains a strong navy whose major failing is a steady maintenance of now-obsolete gun- rather than missile-armed heavy warships. Personnel strength is 28,600, including 3,000 1-year conscripts. This total includes 2,000 officers, 23,900 petty officers and other ranks, and 2,700 marines. The main bases are at Talcahuano (schools, repair yard, drydocks and floating docks), Valparaiso (schools, repair yard and floating dock), Puerto Montt (small base), Punta Arenas (small base with repair yard), Puerto Williams (small base), Iquique (small base) and Vina del Mar (small base). The Chilean navy is disposed into four commands: the Northern Naval District has its headquarters at Iquique and is reponsible for the coast as far south as 26° S; the 1st Naval Zone is headquartered at Vina del Mar with responsibility from 26° S to 33° S; the 2nd Naval Zone is based at Talcahuano with an area of responsibility stretching from 33° S to 47° S; and the 3rd Naval District has its headquarters at Punta Arenas with responsibilities stretching from 47° S to the South Pole.

Chile's easier political and economic relationship with the West has in recent years allowed a certain modernization of her naval forces. In the underwater field this is epitomized by the introduction of two 'Type 209' class patrol submarines to complement the indifferent mix of two 'Oberon' and one 'Balao' class boats previously used. Surface forces have also been revitalized: the 'Brooklyn' class cruiser *Prat* has been replaced with an ex-British 'County' class missile light cruiser, with a second 'County' class unit to follow. Whereas the 'Brooklyn' class ship was a useful gun cruiser, the two 'County' class units offer a modern combination of gun, surface-to-surface, surface-to-air and helicopter armament suitable for anti-ship, anti-aircraft and anti-submarine warfare. The purchase of the second 'County' class ship will free the second 'Brooklyn' class cruiser for retirement, to be followed later by the ex-Swedish 'Göta Lejon' class gun cruiser, possibly when Chile manages to acquire the light carrier it is currently considering. The main surface force currently comprises a mix of old and slightly less old destroyers, though it seems likely that the two 'Fletcher' and two 'Allen M. Sumner' class gun destroyers will be retired, leaving the two missile-armed 'Almirante' class destroyers complemented by two (with two more to follow) missile- and helicopter-armed 'Leander' class frigates.

Chilean navy ship strength

type	number	class
patrol submarine	2	'Type 209'
	2	'Oberon'
	1	'Balao'
cruiser	1+1	'County'
	1	'Göta Lejon'
	1	'Brooklyn'
destroyer	2	'Almirante'
	2	'Allen M. Sumner (FRAM II)'
	2	'Fletcher'
frigate	2+2(?)	'Leander'
	2	'Charles Lawrence'
FAC (missile)	2	'Saar 4'
FAC (torpedo)	4	'Guacolda'
	2	'Sotomoyo'
patrol craft	1	'Cherokee'
	1	'PC 1638'
	24	misc
landing ship	2	'Batral' LST
	2	'LST 511-1152' LST
landing craft	2	LCU
	11	LCVP
other	17	misc

China

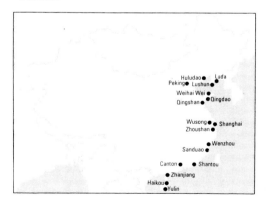

The navy of the People's Republic of China is one of the largest in the world in terms of manpower and vessels, but is shrouded in secrecy as to precise details, and is of uncertain technological capability in an era of fast development. Yet there can be little doubt that since China's partial thaw of relations with the West there has been a rapid evolution in the capabilities of China's armed forces, and that the modernization of her shipyards coupled with pro-gress in the nuclear and missile fields will permit the rapid evolution of the Chinese navy into a far more capable force than it is now. Current preoccupations are purely defensive, and within this of a generally coastal nature, while longer-term planning is certainly gearing the Chinese navy towards a more ambitious offensive capability of strategic proportions.

The current manpower strength of the Chinese navy is just under 360,000 men, most of them conscripts involved in the 6-year national service programme. Of the total manpower strength some 38,000 are allocated to the powerful naval air arm, and another 38,000 to the coast defence forces, which are deployed in regimental-sized units for the defence of naval bases, strategic offshore islands and other vulnerable points with 85-, 100- and 130-mm (3·35-, 3·9- and 5·1-in) artillery and HY-2 surface-to-surface missiles. This latter is a Chinese-developed version of the Soviet SS-N-2 'Styx'. The organization of the Chinese navy is into three main fleets, the most important of which is the North Sea Fleet, with bases at Qingdao (its headquarters), Lushun, Weihaiwei, Qingshan, Luda, Huludao and Xiaopingdao. The other two fleets are the East Sea Fleet and the South Sea Fleet. The former has its headquarters at Shanghai, with other bases at Zhoushan, Zhenjiangguan, Wusong, Xinxiang, Wenzhou and Sanduao; and the latter is commanded from Zhanziang, with other bases at Yulin, Haikou, Huangfu, Canton and Shantou. Technical training plays a great part in the life of the Chinese navy, and major schools and colleges are on the strength of these and other bases. This technical training is seen as a major part of the modernization of the Chinese navy, and also in the technological education of the whole country.

The Chinese navy's strategic ambitions are reflected in the slow but persevering attempts to develop a submarine-launched nuclear missile system, now beginning to bear fruit with the 'Xia' class of nuclear-powered ballistic missile submarine. Displacing about 8,000 tons dived, the sole 'Xia' class boat is probably fitted with 14 or 16 launch tubes for the CCS-NX-3 missile, which was fired first in 1982 over a range of some 3,350 km (2,080 miles). The combination of boat and missile is new, so production will initially be slow, but it must be anticipated that this marks the real beginning of Chinese strategic capabilities at sea. This offensive capability is currently exceeded by a nuclear-powered defensive capability in the form of six or more 'Han' class fleet submarines, which are being supplemented in a continuing programme to replace the current force of 'Romeo' and 'Whiskey' class boats, which are obsolete by modern submarine standards. It is likely, though that China will develop an indigenous patrol submarine type to complement the nuclear-powered fleet submarines, which are not as effective as smaller diesel-electric boats for operations in shallow waters.

Surface forces are currently in a parlous state, with wholly inadequate numbers of destroyers and frigates in service, and these lacking many of the modern sensors and armament fits that would make them effective. It is believed that British electronics and the Lightweight Sea Dart surface-to-air missile system will eventually be fitted to the 'Luda' class destroyers and 'Jiangnan' class frigates, but the programme seems bedevilled by political hesitations. Otherwise, the Chinese destroyers and frigates are fitted with capable DP guns and HY-2 surface-to-surface missiles. Also available to the Chinese navy are some 14 escort vessels inherited from the Nationalists, Japanese, British and Australians. These are truly venerable in age, and have been considerably modernized for service mainly with the East Sea and South Sea Fleets.

The coastal preoccupation of the Chinese navy is reflected in the huge and widely diverse numbers of fast attack craft operated in conjunction with extensive coastal patrol forces. These are backed by a small but effective minesweeping force, and a large amphibious warfare capability of indigenous and foreign manufacture. There are also large numbers of service and research ships, while the naval air force of some 700 aircraft offers useful coastal reconnaissance and strike capability.

Chinese navy ship strength

type	number	class
nuclear-powered ballistic missile submarine	1+?	'Xia'
ballistic missile submarine	1	'Golf'
nuclear-powered fleet submarine	6(?)+?	'Han'
patrol submarine	2	'Ming'
	94	'Romeo'
	16	'Whiskey'
	1	'S-1'
destroyer	14+2	'Luda'
	4	'Anshan' or 'Gordy'
frigate	14+3	'Jianghu'
	3+2(?)	'Jiangdong'
	5	'Jiangnan'
	4	'Chengdu'
corvette (escort vessel)	1	'Kamishima'
	1	'Ukuru'
	1	'Etorofu'
	1	'Hashidate'
	5	'Kaikoban'
	1	'Castle'
	1	'Bathurst'
	1	'Ming'
	2	'Hai Tse'
FAC (missile)	1	'Haidau'
	115	'Osa' or 'Huangfen'
	97	'Komar' or 'Hegu'
FAC (gun)	10	'Shanghai I'
	310	'Shanghai II'
	3	'Haikou'
	50	'Shantou'
FAC (torpedo)	140	'Huchuan'
	65	'P 6'
	55	'P 4'
patrol craft	20	'Kronshtadt'
	32	'Hainan'
	1	'173-ft'
	4	'Taishan'
	30	'Beihai' or 'Wuhsi'
	30	'Fujian'
	40	'Huangpu'
	40	'Yulin'
minesweeper (ocean)	23	'T 43'
minesweeper (coastal)	60	misc
minesweeper (inshore)	20	'Fushun'
landing ship	5+2	'Yukan' LST
	2	'Yuling' LSM
	1	'Yudao' LSM
	15	'LST 1-511' LST
	14	'LSM 1' LSM
	6	LSIL
landing craft	300	'Yunnan' LCU
	150	US/British LCM
	10	US/British LCU
other	426+12	misc

Colombia

The naval defence requirements of Colombia are made particularly difficult by the fact that the country has seaboards on the Pacific and in the Caribbean, and also an extensive network of major rivers that require patrol forces. The two-front sea problem is not helped by the fact that one front can only be reinforced from the other via the Panama Canal.

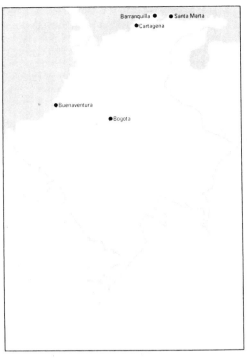

Basic naval personnel strength is 7,200 (700 officers and 6,500 petty officers and other ranks, many of them 2-year conscripts), as well as some 2,500 marines. The organization of the Colombian navy inevitably reflects the peculiar defence needs of the country. Headquartered at Cartagena is the Caribbean Coast Command, which is also the area's main training base and repair/maintenance facility; at Buenaventura is the headquarters of the Pacific Coast Command, which has lesser bases at Palanquero, Santa Marta and Barranquilla; the riverine forces are divided into two, those allocated to the Putumayo river system (Western River Forces Command) being based at Puerto Leguizama, and those allocated to the Meta river system (Eastern River Forces Command) being based at Puerto Orocue.

Useful offensive capability is bestowed by the two 'Type 209' class patrol submarnes, the other two units of the submarine force being a pair of 'Type SX-506' class midget submarines able to deliver underwater demolition teams (eight attack swimmers per boat) and explosives. The surface forces are somewhat weaker, with three elderly gun destroyers currently being supplemented by a planned four (three delivered) 'Type FS 1500' class frigates. It is planned to dispose of one of the two 'Modified Halland' class destroyers, this loss being more than balanced by the considerably more versatile sensor and armament fit of the new frigates, which each carry surface-to-surface and surface-to-air missiles in addition to guns, anti-submarine torpedoes and a light helicopter.

Colombian navy ship strength

type	number	class
patrol submarine	2	'Type 209'
	2	'Type SX-506'
destroyer	2	'Halland (Modified)'
	1	'Allen M. Sumner (FRAM II)'
frigate	3+1	'FS 1500'
	1	'Courtney'
FAC (gun)	2	'Asheville'
patrol craft	4	'Cherokee'
	3	'Arauca'
	1	'Baranquilla'
	10	misc
other	22	misc

Comores

Based at Moroni, the navy of the Comores islands operates one ex-British LCT Mk 8 supplied by the French after the islands' unilateral declaration of independence in 1975, and two 'Yamayuri' class patrol craft supplied by Japan.

Congo

Based at Pointe Noire, the navy of the People's Republic of the Congo has a volunteer strength of about 250 men, and operates a variety of patrol craft, the most capable of which are the three 'Pirana HS' class craft derived from the Spanish 'Barcelo' class.

Congolese navy ship strength

type	number	class
FAC (gun)	3	'Pirana HS'
	1	'Shershen'
	3	'Shanghai II'
patrol craft	4	'Yulin'
	4	'Arco'
	12	riverine
other	2	misc

Costa Rica

Based at the civil ports of Limon, Golfito, Puntarenas and Puerto Somon, the Costa Rican navy's 90 volunteers operate one 105-ft (32-m) and five 65-ft (19.9-m) US-supplied Swift patrol craft, and three smaller patrol craft for what are really coast guard duties.

Cuba

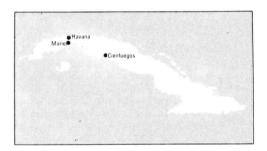

The navy is the smallest of the three Cuban services, but is a highly proficient coastal defence force which, with the support of Soviet advisers and vessels, is beginning to emerge as a strategic force of some import in the Caribbean. Personnel strength is in the order of 6,000 (380 officers and 5,620 petty officers and men), and the main bases are at Canasi, Cienfuegos, Havana, Mariel and Punta Ballenatos.

Until recently the Cuban navy was nothing more than a coastal defence force, well equipped with Soviet-supplied large patrol craft and fast attack craft, this capability being reinforced in the late 1970s and early 1980s by the development of a mine warfare branch centred on the 'Sonya' class minesweepers/minehunters and the 'Yevgenya' class inshore minesweepers. However, the arrival at much the same time of three submarines (of which the 'Whiskey' class boat is now probably non-operational) and a 'Koni' class frigate marked a considerable departure.

Cuban navy ship strength

type	number	class
patrol submarine	2	'Foxtrot'
	1	'Whiskey'
frigate	1	'Koni'
FAC (missile)	13	'Osa II'

	9	'Osa I'
	10	'Komar'
FAC (gun)	4	'Komar'
	6	'Turya'
FAC (torpedo)	2	'Shershen'
	6	'P 6'
	12	'P 4'
patrol craft	9	'SO I'
	4	'Kronshtadt'
	22	'Zhuk'
minesweeper (coastal)	2	'Sonya'
minesweeper (inshore)	9	'Yevgenya'
	1	'K 8'
landing ship	3	'Polnochny' LSM
landing craft	7	'T 4' LCM
other	22	misc

Cyprus

The small island republic of Cyprus, divided between the Greek and Turkish communities, operates only the smallest of navies, comprising one '32 L' class 96-ton coastal patrol craft and two smaller craft also built in French yards.

Czechoslovakia

The Czech river patrol force numbers some 1,200 personnel, who operate about 20 river patrol craft.

Denmark

Though a small country, Denmark operates a moderate-size navy tasked with coastal defence plus more ambitious anti-submarine and anti-ship operations in the Baltic, North Sea and North Atlantic within the framework of NATO maritime strategy. Denmark also operates an extensive force of fishery protection 'frigates' and smaller craft. Personnel strength is about 5,860, including 1,370 officers and 1,270 conscripts doing a 9-month national service term, and the principal bases for the Royal Danish navy are Arhus (headquarters), Copenhagen, Korsør, Frederikshavn, Thorshavn in the Faeroes and Grønnedal in Greenland, and the service also mans two forts (equipped with 150-mm/5·9-in guns) on the approaches to the sound and the Great Belt.

For underwater defence of Denmark's extensive coastline the navy operates five submarines. The two 'Narhvalen' class boats are still relatively effective, but the three 'Delfinen' class boats are reaching the ends of their lives, and will during the later 1980s be replaced by three new boats. Apart from these craft, Danish coastal defence is tasked to the 10 'Willemoes' class fast attack craft (missile) and six 'Søløven' class fast attack craft (torpedo). The latter

are now in reserve, but their importance is attested by the navy's decision to update them. Advance warning of any incursion into Danish waters would be provided by aircraft, operating in conjunction with the eight units of the 'Daphne' class patrol craft.

Longer-range capabilities are entrusted to the two 'Peder Skram' and three 'Nils Juel' class frigates, for their size particularly well armed vessels with adequate anti-aircraft, excellent surface-to-surface and good anti-submarine fits of weapons and sensors. Though rated as frigates, the units of the 'Hvidbjørnen' and 'Hvidbjørnen (Modified)' classes are really large fishery protection vessels with only limited armament.

Also worth noting is the good minelaying and minesweeping capability of the Royal Danish navy, centred on one small, two medium and four large minelayers and six 'Sund' class coastal minesweepers. The large minelayers of the 'Falster' class double up in peace as depot and training ships.

Danish navy ship strength

type	number	class
patrol submarine	2	'Narhvalen'
	3	'Delfinen'
frigate	2	'Peder Skram'
	3	'Nils Juel'
	1	'Hvidbjørnen (Modified)'
	4	'Hvidbjørnen'
FAC (missile)	10	'Willemoes'
FAC (torpedo)	6	'Søløven'
patrol craft	8	'Daphne'
	3	'Agdlek'
	2	'Maagen'
	9	'Barsø'
	28	misc
minelayer	4	'Falster'
	2	'Lindormen'
	1	'Langeland'
minesweeper (coastal)	6	'Adjutant' or 'Sund'
other	8	misc

Djibouti

This small Red Sea state began to form a small navy after independence from France in 1977, and currently operates a small force of one patrol craft and three landing craft. Real defence is undertaken by France.

Dominican Republic

Operating from Santo Somingo, Las Calderas and Haina, the small navy of the Dominican Republic has a manpower strength of 4,050 including marines, and operates solely as a coastal defence force with a small number of obsolescent vessels, their flagship being the frigate *Mella* which doubles as a presidential yacht.

Dominican navy ship strength

type	number	class
frigate	1	'River'
corvette	3	'Cohoes'
	2	'Admirable'
patrol craft	3	'Argo'
	1	'PGM 71'
	12	misc
landing ship	1	'LSM 1' LSM
landing craft	2	LCU
other	19	misc

Ecuador

Sandwiched between Colombia and Peru, Ecuador until recent times rested content with a small navy

equipped with obsolescent destroyers and frigates of US origins. In recent years considerable developments have taken place, transforming the Ecuadorean navy into a powerful though short-range force. The main bases are at Guayaquil, Manta and San Lorenzo on the mainland, and a small base is also maintained in the Galapagos Islands in the Pacific. The personnel strength is some 4,500 including 700 marines, while of the navy proper's 3,800 men some 300 are officers. There are a small number of 2-year conscripts in the navy.

The older type of equipment still used by the Ecuadorean navy is epitomized by the single examples of the 'Gearing' and 'Charles Lawrence' classes, while the shift towards more modern vessels of European manufacture is shown by the navy's most powerful strike elements, namely two 'Type 209' class patrol submarines and six 'Esmeraldas' class missile corvettes, bought from West Germany and Italy respectively. The corvettes are ably backed by six fast attack craft (missile), and it is believed that consideration is being given to further development with the purchase of 'Descubierta' class frigates from Spain. All these vessels are or would be armed with Exocet or Gabriel anti-ship missiles, the larger ships also having surface-to-air point-defence missiles and useful anti-submarine capability.

Ecuadorean navy ship strength

type	number	class
patrol submarine	2	'Type 209'
destroyer	1	'Gearing (FRAM I)'
frigate	1	'Charles Lawrence'
corvette	6	'Esmeraldas'
FAC (missile)	3	'Lürssen TNC 45'
	3	'Manta' or 'Guacolda'
patrol craft	7	misc
landing ship	1	'LST 511-1152' LST
	1	'LSM 1' LSM
landing craft	6	Rotork type
other	15	misc

Egypt

Egypt is still in the technical throes of extricating her armed forces from Soviet influence and equipment, and her navy reflects the change in emphasis to Western sources of supply, the older Soviet-built vessels being re-equipped where necessary with Western sensors and weapons while more modern equipment is building. Manpower strength is some 20,000, and the technical problems are no doubt exacerbated by the fact that 15,000 of these are 3-year conscripts with little or no technical capability. The Egyptian navy's main bases are Alexandria, Port

minesweeper (inshore)	2	'T 301'
landing ship	3	'Polnochny-A' LSM
landing craft	10	'Vydra' LCU
	4	'SMB 1' LCU
	10	LCM
other	24	misc

Eire

The Irish naval service is concerned with coastal patrol and fishery protection, and operates its small fleet from a base at Haulbowline Island near Cork. Current strength is 1,105 volunteers (137 officers, 505 petty officers and 463 ratings), and plans call for the supplementing of the present four 'P 22' and 'Deidre' class patrol ships (Corvettes) with a single 'P 31' class ship early in 1984. The new class introduces an embarked helicopter.

Irish navy ship strength

type	number	class
corvette	0+1	'P 31'
	3	'P 22'
	1	'Deidre'
patrol craft	3	'Ton'
other	6	misc

El Salvador

The navy of El Salvador is a small coast guard service, with a strength of 130 volunteers manning four patrol craft, one tug and some 25 launches operating from the ports of Acajutla, La Libertad and La Union.

Equatorial Guinea

With the aid of Chinese and Spanish training teams, the small navy of Equatorial Guinea operates from Bata in Rio Muni and Malabo in Fernando Po exclusively for coastal protection. The current manpower strength is about 100, and these men operate one 'P 6' class fast attack craft (torpedo), one 'Poluchat I' Class patrol craft and two small inshore patrol craft.

Ethiopia

Ethiopia is heavily embroiled in external excursions together with a vicious civil war, and also lacks the finance for a substantial navy. However, the country faces no real naval threat, and is currently switching over to Soviet-supplied fast attack craft (missile and torpedo) in place of the earlier US-supplied vessels, for which spares cannot now be obtained as a result of the regime's communist affiliations. Strength is about 1,500 officers and men, most of the latter 30-month conscripts. The main operating bases are Massawa and Assab, while there is a Soviet-built forward base in the Dahlak Islands and a commando training establishment at Embaticalla.

Ethiopian navy ship strength

type	number	class
FAC (missile)	3	'Osa II'
FAC (torpedo)	3	'Mol'
patrol craft	1	'Barnegat'
	1	'Wildervank'
	4	'Swift 105-ft'
	1	'Kraljevica'
	4	'PGM 53' or 'Cape'
	2	'Zhuk'
	4	'Sewart'
landing ship	1	'Polnochny-C' LSM
	2	'EDIC' LSM
landing craft	4	'T 4' LCVP
	2	LCM
	2	LCVP

Fiji

The navy of Fiji is more properly the Naval Division of the Royal Fiji Military Forces, and has a strength of 170 volunteers. Based at Suva, the force operates three 'Redwing' class minesweepers converted for inter-island patrol and fisheries protection, plus two survey craft.

Finland

As part of the settlement of Finland's part in World War II by the Treaty of Paris in 1947, the Finnish navy is restricted to maxima of 10,000 tons of vessels and a manpower strength of 4,500; submarines and torpedo craft are prohibited by the treaty, whose main purpose was to assure the USSR free access into the Baltic from the main base at Leningrad in the Gulf of Finland. Current manpower strength is 2,500, including some 1,500 conscripts doing an 8/11-month period of service and 600 coast guard personnel.

During the 1970s it was planned to develop the navy into a more capable force with six frigate/corvette types, two minelayers, 14 inshore minesweepers and 24 fast attack craft. Financial problems have led to the rethinking of this programme, which is now fixed at the current pair of 'Turunmaa' class corvettes, three minelayers, six inshore minesweepers and a larger force of fast attack craft based on the 'Helsinki' class of fast attack craft (gun), with provision for missiles on these latter in the future. The emphasis of the Finnish navy is thus strongly towards coastal defence with fast attack craft and mines.

The navy's two main bases are Turku, on the northern shore of the Gulf of Finland where it debouches into the Baltic, and Helsinki. The former is the home of the Gunboat Flotilla ('Turunmaa' and 'Nuoli' classes), the Missile Flotilla ('Tuima' class and the experimental missile craft *Isku*) and the Mine Warfare Flotilla of layers and sweepers, while Helsinki is home for the Patrol Craft Flotilla ('Ruissalo' and 'Rihtniemi' classes). There is also a considerable amphibious capability, with alternative equipment fits to suit individual craft as gunboats or minelayers, and the coast guard (Frontier Guard) operates five large patrol craft and 43 coastal patrol craft. It is worth noting that while most hulls and machinery are of Finnish construction, the country's location on the border between East and West is reflected in a studied policy of equal purchase of sensors and armament.

Said and Mersa Matruh on the Mediterranean, and Bur Taufiq, Safaqa and Hurghada on the Red Sea. The northern and southern ends of the vital Suez Canal are guarded respectively by Port Said and Bur Taufiq.

Current submarine strength is ten 'Romeo' and six 'Whiskey' class boats, though the operational viability of some of these submarines must be suspect. China is helping with the maintenance of the boats, and supplied the last two 'Romeo' class units during 1982. Greater long-term importance is attached to the four 'Agosta' class boats building in Spain for delivery in the later 1980s, when the obsolescent Soviet-designed boats will be phased out of service.

The same situation prevails with the larger surface combatants, namely four 'Skory' class destroyers, one ex-British destroyer and three ex-British frigates. These are either lacking spares or lacking modern capability, and will be phased out or into secondary tasks once the two 'Descubierta' class frigates on order from Spain are delivered in 1984.

Light forces currently feature a preponderance of Soviet-designed craft (including the Egyptian-built 'October' class using the 'Komar' class hull), and are kept operational with Western technical assistance and spares. The shift in emphasis towards Western sources has already started, the six current 'Ramadan' class fast attack craft (missile) being of British manufacture with Italian weapons, while the six 'Cormoran' class fast attack craft (missile) on order from Spain for delivery in the mid-1980s will have Italian guns and French Exocet missiles.

Egyptian navy ship strength

type	number	class
patrol submarine	0+4	'Agosta'
	10	'Romeo'
	6	'Whiskey'
destroyer	4	'Skory'
	1	'Z'
frigate	1+1	'Descubierta'
	1	'Black Swan'
	1	'River'
	1	'Hunt'
FAC (missile)	0+6	'Cormoran'
	6	'Ramadan'
	6	'October'
	8	'Osa I'
	4	'Komar'
FAC (gun)	4	'Shershen'
FAC (torpedo)	2	'Shershen'
	20	'P 6'
	4	'P 4'
patrol craft	12	'SO I'
	6+6	'Timsah'
minesweeper (ocean)	6	'T 43'
	4	'Yurka'

Finnish navy ship strength

type	number	class
corvette	2	'Turunmaa'
FAC (missile)	4	'Tuima'
	1	experimental
FAC (gun)	1+3+4	'Helsinki'
	10	'Nuoli'
patrol craft	3	'Ruissalo'
	2	'Rihtniemi'
	1	experimental
minelayer	1	'Pohjanmaa'
	1	'Riga'
	1	'Keihässalmi'
minesweeper (inshore)	6	'Kulia'
landing craft	3	'Kampela' LCU
	6	'Kala' LCU
	5	'Kave' LCU
other	30	misc

France

France has three maritime frontiers (the Mediterranean, the Atlantic and the English Channel) and an extensive interest in maritime trade and in overseas dependencies and allies. For this and other reasons, therefore, France maintains a large and modern navy, which can fairly claim to be the only European navy with a truly balanced composition in terms of ship types and capabilities. The Fench navy has powerful anti-ship, anti-submarine and anti-aircraft capabilities backed by strong defensive submarine forces, good amphibious capacity, a powerful ship-borne air arm for the projection of long-range sea-power, rapidly growing mine warfare capability, useful fast attack craft forces, and a semi-independent but formidable strategic missile force based on nuclear-powered submarines. Manpower strength is 69,130 including 4,230 officers, 27,750 petty officers, 18,850 regular ratings and 18,300 12-month conscript ratings. Of these men (there are only 800 women in naval service) 49,000 are allocated to surface forces and shore support, 3,950 to the submarine force and 9,150 to the fleet air arm. The French navy is divided into four main operational commands: the Mediterranean Fleet based on Toulon, the Atlantic Fleet based on Brest (with its submarines at Lorient), the Channel Squadron based on Cherbourg, and the Strategic Ocean Force (missile-carrying nuclear submarines) based on Brest as part of the Atlantic Fleet. There are also smaller commands in the Pacific (three frigates, one landing ship, dock and five patrol craft), the Indian Ocean (tanker/command ship *Var*, one patrol submarine, one destroyer, three frigates, one landing ship, tank, one patrol craft and two support ships, usually supported by an extra two frigates and other ships from home commands), the West Indies (one ship), and for training (*Jeanne d'Arc*

and *Doudart de Lagrée*).

Of the major home commands, the Mediterranean Fleet has as its flagship the *Colbert*, its general composition being eight patrol submarines, two aircraft-carriers, one missile cruiser, six destroyers, six frigates, three ocean minesweepers, two landing ships, tank and support forces; the Atlantic Fleet disposes of five nuclear-powered missiles submarines, one nuclear-powered fleet submarine, seven patrol submarines, 10 destroyers, six frigates, seven ocean minesweepers, 18 other mine countermeasures vessels, two landing ships, dock, one landing ship, tank and support forces; and the Channel Squadron has three frigates and support forces.

The French navy's main striking capability comes from its five 'Le Foudroyant' class SSBNs, soon to be joined by the sole example of the improved 'L'Inflexible' class. Further construction has not been fixed, but a new class will begin construction in about 1990 at the new yard being built at the moment in Cherbourg, where current SSBNs and SSNs have and are being built. France was late to the building of nuclear-powered fleet submarines, but the new 'Rubis/SNA 72' class is now entering service as a complement to the SSBNs. Patrol submarine capability rests with the excellent 'Agosta' and 'Daphné' class boats.

Alone amongst European navies, that of France maintains two multi-role aircraft carriers, the 'Clemenceau' class ships. These are still capable units, thanks to the provision of new or updated aircraft and advanced electronics, but are clearly approaching the ends of their useful lives. France has therefore decided on the bold and extremely expensive step of replacement by a pair of nuclear-powered carriers, the 'PA 88' class to be laid down in the mid-1980s. These 35,000-ton carriers will be capable of 27 kts, carry a defensive armament of point-defence missiles and be fitted for heavy fighter/attack aircraft in addition to helicopters and anti-submarine aircraft. The carriers are used mainly in the Mediterranean, where area defence can be provided by the Masurca surface-to-air missiles of the cruiser *Colbert*, which also possesses extensive command capability in terms of accommodation and communications. Further anti-air capacity comes from the pair of 'Suffren' class light cruisers, also armed with the Masurca SAM and Exocet anti-ship missile. The role of the *Colbert* and the two 'Suffren' class units is undertaken for the Atlantic Fleet by the three 'Type F 67' class destroyers which are, however, optimized for the anti-submarine and anti-ship role rather than air defence. Further anti-air and anti-submarine warfare capability is offered by the 'Type T 56', 'Type T 53', 'Type T 47' and 'Type C 65' class destroyers, but these are becoming obsolete and will be replaced as the full numbers of 'Type C 70' destroyers come into service. Twelve of these are planned, eight optimized for anti-submarine operations and the other four for anti-air warfare.

These larger units are backed by a powerful force of frigates, in the form of the 17 'Type A 69' coastal ships optimized for anti-submarine warfare, and the nine 'Commandant Rivière' class ships designed for worldwide anti-ship and anti-submarine warfare. The 'Commandant Rivière' design incorporates provision for command facilities and for troop accommodation to provide maximum operational flexibility.

Amphibious warfare capability is well provided by a carefully considered mix of 'TCD', 'Batral' and 'BDC' class ships, backed by 'EDIC' class landing craft, tank and some 40 LCMs. This force would be supplemented in war by the training ship *Jeanne d'Arc*, which can carry a battalion of marines and the helicopters for their assault landing.

Light Forces, in the shape of the 'P 400' and 'Patra'

classes, offers a limited but useful coast defence capacity, but is designed more to keep France up to the 'state of the art' than to offer real fast attack craft capability, a role which France feels is better undertaken by larger and more capable (albeit more expensive) ships. Mine warfare is adequately covered by current forces, but will be improved qualitatively with the delivery of the 15 planned 'Eridan' class minehunters, the French part of the 'Tripartite' minehunter programme shared with Belgium and the Netherlands. The French navy is well supplied with ancillaries and support forces, and maintains a capable service force for its world-wide deployment needs.

France's fleet air arm has some 270 aircraft of all types, these operating from ships and 11 naval air bases.

French navy ship strength

type	number	class
nuclear-powered ballistic missile submarine	0+1	'L'Inflexible'
	5	'Le Foudroyant'
experimental ballistic missile submarine	1	'Gymnote'
nuclear-powered fleet submarine	2+4	'Rubis' or 'SNA 72'
patrol submarine	4	'Agosta'
	9	'Daphné'
aircraft-carrier	0+2	'PA 88'
	2	'Clemenceau'
helicopter carrier	1	'Jeanne d'Arc'
cruiser	1	'Colbert'
destroyer	2	'Suffren'
	4+2+2	'Type C 70 ASW'
	0+2+2	'Type C 70 AA'
	3	'Type F 67'
	1	'Type T 56'
	1	'Type T 53 (Modified)'
	2	'Type T 47 AA'
	5	'Type T 47 ASW'
	1	'Type C 65'
frigate	9	'Commandant Rivière'
	17	'Type A 69'
FAC (missile)	0+4+4	'P 400'
	4	'Patra'
	1	'La Combattante I'
patrol craft 5, 1,	1	'Sirius'
	4	'La Dunkerquoise'
	1	'Tourmaline'
minesweeper (ocean)	3+7+5	'Eridan' or 'Tripartite'
minesweeper (coastal)	5	'Circé'
	10	'Aggressive'
	4	'Adjutant'
	5	'Sirius'
assault ship	2	'TCD'
landing ship	4+2	'Batral' LSM
	5	'BDC' LST
landing craft	12+1	'EDIC' LCT
	40	LCM
other	233	misc

Gabon

Gabon operates a small coast defence force from the base at Port Gentil, manpower strength comprising 170 volunteers. The primary assets of this force are one well-armed fast attack craft (missile) and two fast attack craft (gun), backed by a number of less capable craft. There is also a coast guard with some 10 craft.

Gabonese navy ship strength

type	number	class
FAC (missile)	1	'President el Hadj

FAC (gun)	1	'Omar Bongo'
	1	'Ngolo'
patrol craft	1	'Swift 105-ft'
		'Colonel Djoué
		Dabony'
	1	'President Leon
		M'ba'
landing craft	3	LCM

East Germany

The East German navy operates under close Soviet control, and is designed solely for operations in the Baltic and southern portion of the North Sea. The navy proper works closely with the *Grenze Brigade Kuste* (coastal frontier brigade), the craft operated by the two services often being of common design, and the combined total strength of the two services is some 16,000 men (1,800 officers and 14,200 petty officers and ratings), 3,000 of these being border guards. About half of the manpower strength is formed of conscripts, who do either 3 years or 18 months in the service depending on whether they have volunteered for the navy or merely been conscripted into the forces and then allocated to the navy. The main bases are Rostock (headquarters), Peenemünde (1st Flotilla), Warnemunde (4th Flotilla) and Dranske-Bug (6th Flotilla), with smaller bases at Sassnitz, Wolgast and Tarnewitz.

The main offensive power of the East German navy is formed by its two 'Koni' class frigates and the 'Parchim' class corvettes, of which a total of 18 is expected. The 'Parchim' class is very similar to the Soviet 'Grisha' class, and its light gun and missile armament is optimized for protection of surface units against air attack, while a useful anti-submarine armament is also fitted. These larger units are backed by a mixed complement of missile- and torpedo-armed fast attack craft.

East German navy ship strength

type	number	class
frigate	2	'Koni'
corvette	9+9	'Parchim'
FAC (missile)	15	'Osa I'
FAC (torpedo)	18	'Shershen'
	31	'Libelle'
patrol craft	9	'Hai III'
minesweeper (coastal)	27	'Kondor II'
landing ship	12	'Frosch' LST
other	84	misc

Ghana

Beset by drastic economic problems, the continued viability of the Ghanaian navy's relatively advanced equipment must be problematical, reducing the effectiveness of what was one of the most capable navies in West Africa. Based at Sekondi (Western Naval Command) and Tema (Eastern Naval Command), the Ghanaian navy has a personnel strength of about 1,350 volunteers, and is concerned with off-shore and coastal patrol with two British-built corvettes, four fast attack craft (gun) and various patrol craft.

Ghanaian navy ship strength

type	number	class
corvette	2	'Vosper Mk 1' or
		'Kromantse'
FAC (gun)	2	'Lürssen PB 57'
	2	'Lürssen FPB 45'
patrol craft	2	'Dela'
	2	'Ford'
	4	'Spear 2'
other	2	'Rotork

Greece

In common with her rival Turkey, Greece has been a recipient of vessels discarded by more advanced and more prosperous NATO partners, and has also instituted a belated policity of outside contracting and indigenous production to alleviate the matériel shortfalls of this important Mediterranean and Aegean power. From NATO's standpoint, it is a considerable problem that the current (1984) Greek government's socialist platform has combined with fears of Turkish ambitions in the Aegean and Cyprus to divert attention away from the two countries' ideal position to block Soviet and other Warsaw Pact egress through the Darndanelles into the Aegean and Mediterranean. Current Greek naval strength is 19,500 (2,500 officers and 17,000 petty officers and ratings) including 12,000 2-year conscripts. The main bases are Salamis just off the mainland, and Suda Bay in Crete.

Although the Greek Navy possesses 12 ex-US destroyers of World War II vintage (some of them modified with more modern guns, anti-submarine armament, sensors and occasionally a helicopter), the main strength of the navy lies with its eight 'Glavkos' (or 'Type 209') class patrol submarines, two 'Kortenaer' class missile frigates and extensive fast attack craft force. The 'Glavkos' class boats are supplemented by two 'Guppy' class submarines, but these latter are of use only for training. The two 'Kortenaer' class ships are well-suited to Aegean operations, being handy and good sea boats, and

well provided with sensors and armament, including Harpoon medium-range anti-ship missiles, a point-defence surface-to-air missile system, good anti-submarine armament and two organic helicopters.

The Greek light forces are particularly strong, with 14 powerful fast attack craft (missile) backed by a number of capable torpedo craft. The missile deployed to the FAC(M)s is the French Exocet anti-ship missile, which would be highly effective in the Aegean, where the launch craft could make good use of the cover provided by prolific islands. The amphibious capability offered by a mass of specialized ships and craft is obsolescent but considerable, and these units are well deployed in peace for a host of inter-island tasks. Mine warfare of an offensive nature is entrusted to a pair of converted 'LSM 1' class landing ships, but the defensive task is inadequately handled by obsolete types of American origins. The naval air arm provides helicopters for embarkation of surface combatants, and provides a proportion of the crews in the mixed navy/air force search-and-rescue squadron based at Elefsis. There is also a small coast guard operating some 80 patrol craft.

Greek navy ship strength

type	number	class
patrol submarine	8	'Type 209' or
		'Glavkos'
	1	'Guppy III'
	1	'Guppy IIA'
destroyer	1	'Allen M. Sumner
		(FRAM II)'
	1	'Gearing
		(FRAM II)'
	6	'Gearing
		(FRAM I0'
	6	'Fletcher'
frigate	2	'Katenaer'
	4	'Cannon'
FAC (missile)	10	'La Combattante III'
	4	'La Combattante II'
FAC (gun)	2	'Diopos Antoniou'
FAC (torpedo)	5	'Nasty'
	5	'Zobel'
	6	'Jaguar'
patrol craft	11	misc
minelayer	2	'LSM 1'
minesweeper (coastal)	9	'MSC 294'
	5	'Adjutant'
landing ship	1	'Cabildo' LSD
	2	'Terrebonne
		Parish' LST
	5	'LST 1-510' & 'LST
		511-1152' LST
	5	'LSM 1' LSM
landing craft	2	British LCT
	8	LCT Mk 6 LCU
	13	LCM
	34	LCVP
	14	LCP
	7	LCA
other	43	misc

Grenada

A small coastal defence force based at St George's operates one Brooke Marine 40-ft (12·2-m) coastal patrol craft for local duties round the island of Grenada.

Guatemala

Lying astride Central America, Guatemala has coast-lines on the Pacific Ocean and Caribbean, but operates only relatively small coastal patrol forces for local defence. Manpower strength is 600 (made up of 100 officers and 500 men) including 210 marines (10 officers and 200 other ranks), many of these being

2-year conscripts. The Guatemalan navy's two principal bases at Santo Tomas de Castillas and Sipacate allow operations in the Pacific and Caribbean respectively.

Guatemalan navy ship strength

type	number	class
patrol craft	2	'Broadsword'
	5	'Cutlass'
	35	misc
landing craft	1	LCM Mk 6 LCM
other	9	misc

Guinea

Based at Conakry and Kakanda, the small Guinean navy is designed solely for coastal patrol and defence, though the influx of Soviet and Chinese equipment has given the force a capability beyond its real needs. Manpower strength, including 2-year conscripts, is about 600. These man a small but nicely balanced force of minesweepers, attack craft and patrol craft.

Guinean navy ship strength

type	number	class
FAC (missile)	6	'Shanghai II'
patrol craft	2	'Shershen'
	4	'P 6'
	2	'Poluchat I'
	2	'MO VI'
minesweeper (ocean)	1	'T 58'
landing craft	2	LCU
other	1	'Almamy Bocar'

Guinea-Bissau

Based at Bissau with some 250 volunteers as its personnel strength, the navy of Guinea-Bissau concerns itself solely with coastal patrol and internal transport, and relies mainly on equipment of Soviet origins, with the exception of two French and seven Spanish coastal patrol craft.

Guinea-Bissau navy ship strength

type	number	class
patrol craft	2	'Shershen'
	1	'P 6'
	1	'Poluchat I'
	5+4	misc
landing craft	2	'T 4' LCVP
	?	LCU
other	several	misc

Guyana

Based at Georgetown and New Amsterdam, the navy of Guyana is part of the integrated Guyana Defence Force, and has a volunteer strength of about 150 men. Tasks are coastal patrol and internal security and transport, the latter being effected with the aid of one Dutch-built landing craft, tank. Other forces are dependent on equipment for the UK and North Korea, though there is a is a trio of ex-US coastal patrol craft.

Guyanese navy ship strength

type	number	class
patrol craft	1	'Peccari'
	2	'Sin Hung'
	3	'Jaguar'
	4	'45-ft'
landing craft	1	LCT
other	2	misc

Haiti

The island dictatorship of Haiti operates no navy as such, but rather a 300-volunteer coast guard based on Port au Prince. Apart from 14 coastal patrol types, the Haitian force also operates two 'Sotomoyo' class vessels, one for coast guard duties and the other for ocean research.

Honduras

The navy of Honduras is a small coastal patrol force based at Puerto Cortes and manned by 100 personnel, most of them 8-month conscripts. The force's principal vessels are two 105-ft (31·5-m) and five 65-ft (21·3-m) patrol craft built by Swiftships in the USA. These are complemented by one ex-US buoy tender, one survey launch and a small number of locally built craft (three coastal patrol craft and six stores vessels).

Hong Kong

With a personnel strength of 111 officers, 450 non-commissioned officers and 1,952 constables, the Marine District of the Royal Hong Kong Police Force operates from Kowloon for policing and coastal patrol duties. An important part of the force's task is the prevention of illegal immigration from mainland China, and an extensive number of patrol craft (48 supported by 13 logistic craft) is operated for this difficult role, the on-water direction of which is entrusted to the two 'Sea' class command vessels, each of 220 tons and able to carry two platoons of men in addition to their normal complement of 25.

Hungary

Hungary has no navy as such (it was disbanded in 1968), but the army currently operates a thriving maritime wing for service on the Danube. Strength is about 500, including a number of 2-year conscripts, and the force operates several riverine minesweepers, 10 patrol craft, a number of troop transports (up to 1,000 tons displacement), five landing craft, and support forces in the form of tugs, barges and river icebreakers.

Iceland

Iceland has no formally constituted armed forces, the nearest to such being the coat guard used for local patrol and fishery protection. Based at Reykjavik, this coast guard has a strength of 120 volunteers who operate vessels specifically constructed for operations in icy northern waters.

Icelandic coast guard ship strength

type	number	class
patrol craft	2	'Aegir'
	1	'Odinn'
	1	'Thor'
	1	'Arvakur'

India

India occupies a dominant population, political and economic position in the Indian Ocean area, and this is reflected in her armed services, which are the most powerful in the theatre, and also the world's largest all-volunteer forces. Current personnel strength is about 47,000 including the naval air arm, and the Indian navy operates from main bases at Bombay (headquarters of the Western Fleet), Vishakapatnam (headquarters of the Eastern Command), Cochin (headquarters of the Southern Area), Calcutta, Goa and Port Blair. India has a lengthy coastline, perpetual problems with neighbours, and extensive overseas interests combined with a substantial mercantile marine, and must therefore

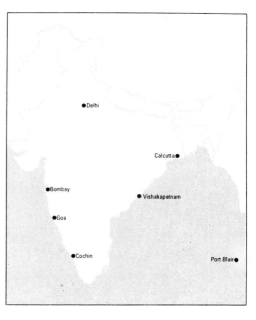

operate widely diverse coastal and blue-water forces for offensive and defensive roles. Western and Soviet equipment is widely used, but the Indian navy is increasingly able to draw upon local resources for the construction of new vessels, which are then fitted with Soviet armament and Western (or Western-derived) electronics.

The current core of the Indian navy's strength is the carrier *Vikrant*, which has recently been refurbished and upgraded electronically. Her aircraft complement offers excellent versatility, anti-submarine types (both fixed- and rotary-wing) being complemented by BAe Sea Harrier V/STOL strike fighters. A new light carrier and/or sea-control ship will probably be ordered in the near future.

Escort for the *Vikrant* is provided by the three 'Kashin' class destroyers supplied from the USSR. Apart from a useful surface-to-surface missile capability, these three ships have good anti-aircraft and anti-submarine weapons and sensors. Further upgrading of this capability may come later in the decade, for it is reported that during 1982 the Indian navy may have ordered three 'Kresta II' class cruisers from the USSR.

Underwater support for these forces is currently the responsibility of eight 'Foxtrot' class patrol submarines bought new from the USSR, with a further three or four to follow. However, considerably improved types are scheduled for service in the second half of the decade with the delivery of the first of four 'Type 209' class boats. The first two of these are building in West Germany, while the second pair is to be constructed in India from knock-down components supplied by the Howaldtswerke.

Anti-submarine warfare is the primary responsibility of six 'Leander' class frigates and 12 'Petya II' class frigates, supplemented by a number of older types and the new-construction 'Godovari' class of Indian manufacture. These last are multi-role ships based on the 'Leander' class but stretched overall and fitted with Soviet armament and Indian electronics. It is reported that the Indian navy is seeking assistance from Dutch design sources in the preparation of gas turbine-powered frigates of more modern capability.

More local defence is the task of various Soviet-supplied craft, notably the three 'Nanuchka II' class missile corvettes (to be supplemented later in the decade by another three or four of the same type) and 16 'Osa' class fast attack craft (missile). Though the SS-N-2 'Styx' surface-to-surface missiles used by the Indian navy is obsolescent by Western standards, it is more than adequate for the threats likely to be encountered in the Indian Ocean theatre. Other forces include a small amphibious warfare strength, and small but adequate mine warfare forces of a defensive nature. These are backed by the normal support and service forces, plus a coast guard which operates two 'Blackwood' class frigates and a planned total of 19 large and small patrol craft. The naval air arm is undergoing a much-needed modernization programme, and may now be regarded as an effective force with coastal and offshore reconnaissance aircraft in addition to the fixed- and rotary-wing assets deployed aboard warships.

Indian navy ship strength

type	number	class
patrol submarine	0+2+2	'Type 209'
	8+4	'Foxtrot'
aircraft-carrier	1	'Majestic'
destroyer	3	'Kashin'
frigate	1+2+3	'Godavari'
	6	'Leander'
	12	'Petya II'
	2	'Whitby'
	3	'Leopard'
	1	'Black Swan'
corvette	3+3	'Nanuchka II'
FAC (missile)	8	'Osa II'
	8	Osa I
patrol craft	1	'Abhay'
	3	'SDB Mk 2'
minesweeper (ocean)	6	'Natya'
minesweeper (coastal)	4	'Ton'
minesweeper (inshore)	4	'Ham'
landing ship	1	LST Mk 3
landing craft	6	'Polnochny' LCT
	4	LCU
other	41	misc

Indonesia

A vast island archipelago with important economic assets, Indonesia was for long reliant on Soviet equipment and doctrines, but broke from this allegiance long enough ago for most Soviet ships to have been deleted or rendered inoperative for lack of spares. The navy of Indonesia is thus largely of Western construction at present, and is designed to ensure the security of the archipelago with a small but technically advanced mix of patrol submarines, anti-submarine frigates and fast attack craft. Personnel strength is about 35,800 including the marine corps and naval air arm, and this total includes a number of national servicemen. The naval air arm has about 1,000 personnel, and the marine corps numbers 5,000. Future plans call for the maintenance of the marine corps and naval air arm at current manpower levels, but to reduce the purely naval strength to about 25,000 by the adoption of warships of a more automated type. The Indonesian navy's main bases are Gorontalo, Jakarta and Surabaya.

The submarine strength of the Indonesian navy was at one time 14 'Whiskey' class boats, but of these only two now survive, and these are hardly operational as they are limited to a diving depth of 100 ft (30 m). A new construction programme has already seen the delivery of three 'Type 209' class sub-

marines from West Germany, and a total of six is planned by the end of the decade, though only the fourth unit has so far been ordered.

Long-term plans for a force of six fast anti-submarine frigates, the most modern ships currently in service being a trio of Dutch-built 'Fatahillah' class frigates, which have good anti-submarine and anti-ship armament, but which with the exception of *Nala* lack an embarked helicopter.

Short-range defence and patrol is the task of the light forces. There are a useful number of patrol craft, which are being bolstered by the receipt of ex-Australian 'Attack' class craft, but greater striking power rests with the fast attack craft. It is planned to have eight 'PSMM Mk 5' fast attack craft (missile), and these are supplemented by two 'Lürssen PB 57' class fast attack craft (gun), with another six possibly to be built under licence in Indonesia.

Indonesian navy ship strength

type	number	class
patrol submarine	3+1+2	'Type 209'
	2	'Whiskey'
frigate	3	'Fatahillah'
	4	'Claud Jones'
	2	'Riga'
FAC (missile)	4+4	'PSMM Mk 5'
FAC (gun)	2+6	'Lürssen PB 57'
FAC (torpedo)	2	'Lürssen TNC 45'
patrol craft	4	'Kronshtadt'
	4	'Kraljevica'
	4	'Attack'
	6	'Carpentaria'
	2	'Spear'
minesweeper (ocean)	4	'T 43'
landing ship	9	'LST 1-511' & 'LST 512-1152' LST
	5	'Tacoma' LST
	1	Japanese LST
landing craft	2	LCU
	38+	LCM
	20+	LCVP
other	45	misc

Iran

Iran came under revolutionary Islamic sway in the midst of a major re-equipment programme, and her navy is thus highly unbalanced, often lacking the weapons to go with various ships classes, the Harpoon anti-ship missile being the most significant of these. Moreover, the war that broke out with Iraq in 1980 has made matériel and training problems considerably more acute, so the nominal and actual strengths of the Iranian navy must inevitably be radically different, recent estimates putting the operational strength as low as two frigates and 10 fast

attack craft (missile). The value of these latter must also be doubted given the US embargo on the supply of missiles since 1979: it is reported that only nine Harpoons had been delivered up to that time. Another vital factor in the Iranian navy's effectiveness is manpower, and it is believed that only 10,000 personnel (many of them 2-year conscripts of little technical capability) are currently available compared with an establishment of 20,000. The main bases operated by the Iranian navy are Bandar Abbas, Bushire, Kharg Island and Khorramshar in the Persian Gulf, Chah Bahar under slow construction on the Indian Ocean, and Bandar-Pahlavi on the Caspian Sea. The last is used mainly for training, leaving the strength of the Iranian navy in the Persian Gulf.

The three old destroyers operated by the Iranian navy must be little more than training ships or in reserve for lack of spares by now, leaving four 'Saam' class frigates and four 'PF 103' class corvettes as the major surface vessels possibly available for operations. Other than these there are 12 'Kaman' class fast attack craft, which probably lack the missiles for any effective use, and a number of patrol craft, amphibious warfare vessels, mine warfare ships and service/support forces.

Iranian navy ship strength

type	number	class
destroyer	1	'Battle'
	2	'Allen M. Sumner (FRAM II)'
frigate	4	'Saam'
corvette	4	'PF 103'
FAC (missile)	12	'La Combattante II' or 'Kaman'
patrol craft	3	'PGM 71 (Improved)'
	4	'Cape'
	6	'Wellington' hovercraft
	8	'Winchester' hovercraft
minesweeper (coastal)	3	'MSC 292'
minesweeper (inshore)	2	'Cape'
landing ship	4	'Hengam' LS Logistic
other	50+	misc

Iraq

Iraq is currently fighting a decimating war of attrition with Iran for control of the Shatt-al-Arab waterway and for ideological reasons, and is receiving much matériel help from France and the USSR. Hitherto little more than an estuarine and coastal defence force, the Iraqi navy is thus being developed into a potentially powerful multi-role force, with particular emphasis on Persian Gulf operations dictating relatively light vessels of speed and manoeuvrability. Manpower strength is about 3,000 officers and men (including a proprotion of 2-year conscripts), and the main bases are at Basra and Umm Qasr.

The changing nature of the Iraqi navy is indicated by the fact that whereas the main strength currently lies with a single 'Ibn Khaldoum' class frigate (very similar to the Indonesian training ship *Hadjar Dewantoro* built by the same Yugoslav yard), by the end of the decade it will rest with this unit and four 'Lupo' class frigates plus six 'Assad' class corvettes. These 10 powerful combatants will be armed with eight and six Otomat anti-ship missiles respectively, though two of the 'Assad' class will have only two Otomats when fitted with helicopters. The 'Lupo' class has already proved its value, and the 'Assad' class is also in service with the Libyan navy.

Light forces operate mainly Soviet craft, in the form of 12 'Osa' class fast attack craft (missile) and 12 'P 6' class fast attack craft (torpedo). There are also a number of patrol craft, and a useful amphibious capability is bestowed by four 'Polnochny' class landing craft, tanks, which are being supplemented by three Danish-built LCTs. There are small mine warfare forces, but the coastal nature of the Iraqi navy's purview renders all but superfluous any support and service forces. Further capability is offered, however, by a small but potent naval air arm equipped with Aérospatiale Super Frelon helicopters armed with AM.39 Exocet anti-ship missiles.

Iraqi navy ship strength

type	number	class
frigate	1	'Ibn Khaldoum'
	0+4	'Lupo'
corvette	1+5	'Assad'
FAC (missile)	8	'Osa II'
	4	'Osa I'
FAC (torpedo)	12	'P 6'
patrol craft	3	'SO I'
	2	'Poluchat I'
	5	'Zhuk'
	4	'Nyryat II'
	3	'PO 2'
	8	'Thornycroft 36-ft'
	4	'Thornycroft 21-ft'
minesweeper (ocean)	2	'T 43'
minesweeper (inshore)	3	'Yevgenya'
	2	'Nestin'
landing craft	4	'Polnochny' LCT
	1+2	Danish LCT
other	9	misc

Israel

The small state of Israel operates a small but extremely powerful navy designed for coastal operations in conjunction with land forces, and for the protection of Israeli shipping and mercantile interests in the eastern Mediterranean. Naval manpower strength is about 6,600 (800 officers and 5,800 men) including a 300-man naval commando unit. Some 3,500 of this peacetime total are 3-year conscripts, and in war mobilization increases the total to 11,600 by the rapid recall of reservists. Israel has two maritime frontiers, and this is reflected in the location of bases at Haifa and Ashdod on the Mediterranean, and of Eilat on the Gulf of Aqaba at the head of the Red Sea.

Long-range striking power is vested in the three 'Type 206' class patrol submarines, but greater emphasis is placed on the various 'Saar' class missile craft, most of which can carry a varying number of missiles depending on the gun armament fitted. The use of Gabriel and Harpoon anti-ship missiles offers the possibility of short- and intermediate-range engagement respectively. The smallest of the 'Saar' classes are the basically similar 'Saar 2' and 'Saar 3' classes, each six strong and equipped with 40-mm AA guns and Gabriel missiles. These are supported by the larger 'Saar 4' class craft, which have more powerful gun armament and a mix of Gabriel and Harpoon missiles. Seven of the eight 'Saar 4' class craft are deployed in the Red Sea and fitted with sonar for anti-submarine operations in conjunction with the 'Saar 2' class, which carry sonar of a less capable type but also an anti-submarine armament of four Mk 46 torpedoes. Even with Gabriel missiles, however, these craft are limited by the relatively short range of their targeting radars, and this has prompted the development of the 'Saar 4.5' class with an embarked helicopter for mid-course missile guidance, plus guns and missiles as before. This wealth of attack craft has also decided the Israelis to develop an indigenous 'Saar 5' class corvette for command purposes. The 'Saar 5' class is being produced in general-purpose and anti-submarine forms: each has a helicopter and 76-mm (3-in) gun armament, and while the general-purpose version additionally accommodates eight Harpoon anti-ship and several surface-to-air missiles, the anti-submarine model has four Gabriel anti-ship missiles, a Bofors rocket-launcher and six anti-submarine torpedoes. Further anti-ship capability of a short-range/high-speed type is provided by the growing force of 'Flagstaff' class hydrofoils and the two semi-experimental 'Dvora' classs craft.

Israeli navy ship strength

type	number	class
patrol submarine	3	'Type 206'
corvette	0+2+?	'Saar 5'
FAC (missile)	6	'Saar 4.5'
	8	'Saar 4'
	6	'Saar 3'
	6	'Saar 2'
	2+10	'Flagstaff 2'
	2	'Dvora'
patrol craft	37	'Dabur'
	3	'Yatush'
	4	'Kedma'
	1	'Firefish'
landing ship	3	'LSM 1' LSM
landing craft	3	'Ash' LCT
	3	'LC' LCT
	3	LCM
other	6	misc

Italy

Italy is a key component of NATO's southern flank, and together with the French Mediterranean and US 6th Fleets offers the greatest possibility of denying

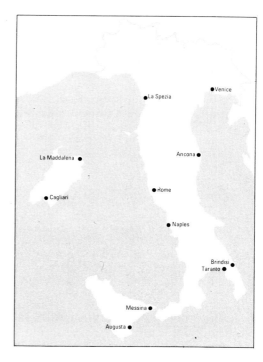

the USSR's Black Sea Fleet access to and use of the Mediterranean. Manpower strength is 41,900, including 1,500 in the naval air arm and 750 marines, of whom some 23,500 are 18-month conscipts. The Italian navy has major bases at La Spezia, Taranto and Ancona, with subsidiary bases located at Augusta, Brindisi, Cagliari, La Maddalena, Messina, Naples and Venice.

The submarine arm of the Italian navy currently comprises eight patrol submarines: four small 'Toti' class coastal boats and four larger 'Sauro' class open-water boats. Another two 'Sauro' class boats are to be built later in this decade to provide the Italian navy with enhanced long-range strike power.

The surface combatants of the Italian navy are optimized as dual-capable anti-ship/anti-submarine ships for the most part, though the largest ships are basically anti-submarine vessels. These are currently the light carrier *Vittorio Veneto* and the two helicopter cruisers of the 'Andrea Doria' class. The latter proved slightly too small for the proposed helicopter complement, leading to the slightly larger and considerably more capable *Vittorio Veneto*, whose success paved the way for the still larger *Giuseppe Garibaldi*, with 18 Agusta (Sikorsky) SH-3 Sea King helicopters in place of the *Vittorio Veneto*'s nine Agusta (Bell) AB.212ASW helicopters. And whereas the three older ships have area-defence capability in the form of Terrier and Standard surface-to-air missiles, the *Giuseppe Garibaldi* has only point-defence SAM capability, but also an anti-ship punch in the form of 62 Otomat Mk 2 anti-ship missiles launchable from six launchers. Like *Vittorio Veneto*, the *Giuseppe Garibaldi* is slated for comprehensive and advanced electronics and communications.

Protection of these major assets from air, surface and underwater attack is currently entrusted to the two 'Audace' and two 'Impavido' class guided-missile destroyers. These carry powerful armaments, but suffer in the anti-air role from having only single launchers, with consequent inability to cope with saturation air attacks. Further strength may come in the late 1980s with the currently deferred 'Improved Audace' class guided-missile destroyers. These should replace the two 'Impetuoso' class destroyers deleted in 1982, and have a versatile multi-role armament combining embarked helicopters, area-defence surface-to-air missiles, point-defence surface-to-air missiles, anti-ship missiles, guns and effective anti-submarine armament, all combined with advanced sensors and other electronics.

Smaller surface vessels are designed principally for anti-submarine operations with secondary anti-ship capability. Thus the 'Alpino', 'Lupo' and 'Maestrale' classes all carry helicopters, the definitive 'Maestrale' class (eight units planned) having two Agusta (Bell) AB.212ASWs to be used in conjunction with an anti-submarine suite that includes variable-depth sonar, and two types of anti-submarine torpedo. Other weapons include a quartet of Otomat anti-ship missiles, an octuple point-defence surface-to-air missile launcher, radar-controlled AA guns and a 127-mm (5-in) main gun. As the later units of the 'Maestrale' class became available, the 'Centauro' and 'Bergamini' class frigates are being phased out. Extra capability comes from the corvette force, where the older 'Albatros' and 'De Cristofaro' class units will be phased out as the new and as yet unnamed 1,025-ton multi-role corvette class begins to enter service at the end of the decade. It is planned that 12 of the type be built for a diversity of tasks such as fishery protection, training and anti-submarine warfare.

The naval air arm operates the large number of helicopters embarked on surface combatants, and also a modest maritime patrol force of three squadrons, two of them equipped with the Dassault-Breguet Atlantic and one with the Grumman S-2F Tracker.

Italian navy ship strength

type	number	class
patrol submarine	4+2	'Sauro'
	4	'Toti'
aircraft-carrier	0+0+1	'Garibaldi'
	1	'Vittorio Veneto'
cruiser	2	'Andrea Doria'
destroyer	0+2	'Audace (Improved)'
	2	'Audace'
	2	'Impavido'
frigate	8	'Maestrale'
	4	'Lupo'
	2	'Alpino'
	2	'Bergamini'
	1	'Centauro'
corvette	0+0+12	new construction
	4	'De Cristofaro'
	4	'Albatros'
FAC (missile)	7	'Sparviero'
FAC (gun)	2	'Freccia'
	2	'Lampo'
patrol craft	2	'Higgins'
minesweeper (ocean)	0+4+6	'Lerici'
	4	'Aggressive'
minesweeper (coastal)	9	'Adjutant'
	14	'Agave'
minesweeper (inshore)	5	'Aragosta'
landing ship	2	'De Soto County' LST
landing craft	7	LCVP
other	97	misc

Ivory Coast

With a strength of 550 men, the navy of the Ivory Coast operates from the ports of Abidjan, San Pedro, Sassandra and Tabou for coastal defence purposes, with a limited offshore capability as further units of the 'Patra' class come into service. The purchase of light patrol craft and small amphibious vessels permits the force to operate in the riverine role for patrol and transport purposes.

Ivory Coast navy ship strength

type	number	class
FAC (missile)	2+2	'Patra'
patrol craft	2	'Franco-Belge'

	6	'Arcoa'
	3	misc
landing ship	1	'Batral' LSM
landing craft	2	LCVP
	10	Rotork
other	1	Japanese training ship

Japan

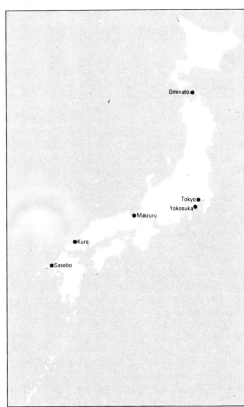

Since her defeat in World War II Japan has been prohibited by her constitution and by treaty from possessing armed force with any offensive capability, and the Japanese Maritime Self-Defense Force is thus structured only for the defence of Japanese territorial waters and maritime interests. Current manpower strength is 46,390 volunteers, including about 11,000 in the powerful naval air arm. And that this is none too much is indicated by the size of Japan's merchant marine, with 10,650 ships totalling over 41·5 million tons, and the fact that Japan is an archipelago nation whose first line of defence is the sea. The task facing the JMSDF is thus a difficult one, and is tackled by carefully balanced forces operating from naval bases at Kure, Maizuru, Oominato, Sasebo and Yokosuka, and from air bases located at Atsugi, Hachinobe, Iwakuni, Kanoya, Komatsujima, Okinawa, Ozuku, Oominato, Oomura, Shimofusa, Tateyama and Tokushima. The main strength of the naval air arm is currently 14 anti-submarine squadrons with a secondary maritime reconnaissance role, thus offering local protection against Soviet submarine threats and also warning of the approach of hostile forces; however, Japan has become increasingly aware of the threat posed by the Soviet Far East Fleet, and is in the process of bolstering its maritime reconnaissance/anti-submarine capability with a fleet of Lockheed P-3C Orion aircraft, multi-role platforms with a potent anti-ship capability in the form of Harpoon air-to-surface missiles.

The JMSDF has a useful anti-ship and anti-submarine capability in its patrol submarine force, with 15 boats currently in service (five 'Yuushio', seven 'Uzushio' and three 'Asashio' class submarines), soon to be joined by a further two 'Yuushio'

class boats; an eighth 'Yuushio' is also planned. The completion of the 'Yuushio' class will permit the phasing out of the elderly 'Asashio' class.

On the surface the main strength of the JMSDF lies with its substantial destroyer force, which is largely optimized for the anti-submarine role with a wide diversity of weapons (including ASROC missiles) and specialized anti-submarine helicopters, notably the Sikorsky SH-3 Sea King series. It is realized that an improved anti-aircraft and anti-missile capability is essential if these ships are to survive in a modern naval confrontation, and Sea Sparrow SAM systems and Phalanx CIWS mountings are being retrofitted to several existing classes. Where possible, an anti-ship capability is also being provided with the introduction of Harpoon surface-to-surface missiles. New construction, notably the two entirely new destroyers planned and the single 'Hatsuyuki (Improved)' class ship, features improved anti-air capability and enhanced anti-ship capabilities.

Backing for the destroyer force is provided by a small frigate arm, the most important of whose members are the 11 units of the 'Chikugo' class, the smallest warships in the world to mount ASROC armament. Light forces are small, and devoted largely to inter-island patrol and the maintenance of torpedo-attack doctrines, but oddly enough the JMSDF has undertaken little work with fast attack craft (missile), which could offer a useful capability in Japan's confined waters. The amphibious forces are also small, in keeping with Japan's defensive military posture, and its six LST's are intended primarily for the movement between islands of Japan's armoured forces.

There is also a Japanese Maritime Safety Agency (coast guard) with a personnel strength of some 12,000. This extensive force operates a large number of patrol ships and patrol craft, as well as survey and navigation aid craft, plus relatively small complements of fixed- and rotary-wing aircraft.

Japanese ship strength

type	number	class
patrol submarine	4+3+1	'Yuushio'
	7	'Uzushio'
	3	'Asashio'
destroyer	0+1+1	'Japanese'
	2	'Shirane'
	2	'Haruna'
	0+1	'Hatsuyuki (Improved)'
	2+5+5	'Hatsuyuki'
	3	'Tachikaze'
	4	'Takatsuki'
	6	'Yamagumo'
	3	'Minegumo'
	1	'Amatsukaze'
	2	'Akizuki'
	3	'Murasame'
	7+4	'Ayanami'
frigate	1+1	'Yubari'
	1	'Ishikari'
	11	'Chikugo'
	4	'Isuzu'
FAC (torpedo)	5	'PT 11'
patrol craft	3	'Mizutori'
	2	'Umitaka'
	9	'PB 19'
minelayer	1	'Souya'
minesweeper (coastal)	11+4	'Hatsushima'
	19	'Takami'
	3	'Kasado'
minesweeper (inshore)	6	'Nana-Go'
landing ship	3	'Miura' LST
	3	'Atsumi' LST
	2	'Yura' LSU
landing craft	15	LCM
	22	LCVP
other	119+1	misc

Jordan

The Hashemite kingdom of Jordan operates no formal navy as such, but rather a Jordan Coastal Guard based at Aqaba, patrol forces on the Dead Sea having been discontinued. Personnel strength is about 300 volunteers, and the force operates purely for coastal patrol, the current strength of 15 small craft being supplemented in the near future by six planned fast attack craft (patrol).

Kampuchea

Given the extraordinary tribulations through which this hapless cocountry has gone, and continues to go, in the period since World War II, it is difficult to establish with any kind of certainty the extent of any of the Kampuchean forces. The latest year for which relatively accurate figures are available is 1975, when the Kampuchean navy numbered some 11,000 including a marine force of 4,000 officers and men; at that time conscription of 18 months was the norm. The strength is now far less certain, and it seems that although a potentially useful coastal force is available on paper, less than one-third of this is likely to be operational.

Kampuchean ship strength

type	number	class
patrol craft	9	'Swift'
	2	'AVR'
	25	'PBR Mk 1' & 'PBR Mk 2'
	3	'Yulin'
	1	'HDML'
other	6	misc

Kenya

Based at Mombasa, the Kenyan navy is designed solely for the coastal patrol of territorial waters, though these have been extended to 200 miles (322 km) seawards. The current force is just about adequate for the role, but future plans will probably call for an increase in strength by the purchase of corvette-type vessels to replace the ageing members of the present force. Manpower strength is 350 volunteers.

Kenyan ship strength

type	number	class
FAC (missile)	3	'Madaraka'
patrol craft	1	'Mamba'
	3	'Simba'

Kuwait

Kuwait is a stable oil-rich country in an area of extraordinary volatility, and her potential vulnerability to others and to circumstances is evidenced by the current Gulf War between Iraq and Iran, and by the threatened closure of the Straits of Hormuz by Iran. Despite its small population, therefore, Kuwait has come to the eminently sensible decision that continued stability and prosperity can only be bolstered by the possession of small but qualitatively advanced armed forces. The Kuwaiti navy is constituted as a coast guard under the control of the Ministry of the Interior, and has a manpower strength of 1,100 volunteers; it operates from Kuwait at the moment, though a new and larger base is being built by a Japanese consortium to cater for the increased size of the navy envisaged.

The main strength of the Kuwaiti navy lies in equipment of French and West German manufacture, namely Lürssen fast attack craft armed with Exocet anti-ship missiles supported by French electronics. Current plans call for a total of two 'FPB 57' and six

'TNC 45' class craft, though the continuing unrest in the area may well lead to a further increase in this strength, together with a mine countermeasures force. This latter would be a very sensible purchase given the ease with which the Persian Gulf and its approaches can be mined. Other plans call for the delivery of six SR.N6 hovercraft.

Kuwaiti ship strength

type	number	class
FAC (missile)	3+3	'Lürssen TNC 45'
	2	'Lürssen FPB 57'
patrol craft	10	'Thornycroft 78-ft'
	5	'Thornycroft 56-ft'
	1	'Halter 61-ft'
	7	'Thornycroft 50-ft'
	1	'Thornycroft 46-ft'
	14	'Thornycroft 36-ft'
	7	'Magnum Sedan'
	3	'Vosper 39-ft'
landing ship	3	Vosper LSS
landing craft	3	Vosper LCU
other	2	misc

Laos

Like Kampuchea, Laos is in a state of turmoil, and the current status of her small riverine navy is uncertain. It is believed that manpower strength is about 550, most of them 18-month conscripts, and that the nominal strength of 42 river patrol craft and transports comprise only 22 operational vessels.

Lebanon

Based at Beirut and Jounieh, the small Lebanese navy has a strength of some 400 officers and men, and its equipment comprises one large and three coastal patrol craft. There is also a customs service with eight coastal patrol craft, but the parlous condition of Lebanon as a whole is reflected in the sorry state of these small forces.

Liberia

Liberia operates only a coast guard service in the way of maritime forces, six coastal patrol craft and one light aircraft being operated by a complement of 445 volunteers from bases at Monrovia, Bassam Sinoe and Cape Palmaa.

Liberian ship strength

type	number	class
patrol craft	3	'Karlskrona TV 103'
	2	'Sewart 65-ft'
	1	'Swift 42-ft'

Libya

Libya is one of the most ambitious nations in Africa, and led by a dominant leader has devoted much of its oil wealth to the building up of powerful communist-influenced forces organized along Soviet lines. The Libyan navy is expanding rapidly, and its position in the central Mediterranean makes it a factor of vital importance to southern Europe and North Africa. Equipment is drawn from Soviet and Western sources, and an ambitious training programme is proceeding alongside the development of new and larger bases to provide this technically-advanced navy with the necessary manpower and maintenance infrastructures. Current manpower level, all volunteers, is about 4,000. The main bases are Tripoli, Derna and Benghazi, while the base at Tobruk is being expanded considerably and new bases are being established at Homs and Ras Hilal, the latter for submarines. A small naval air arm is operated from Misurata, the Aérospatiale SA.321G Super Frelons being used for search-and-rescue, and the Mil Mi-14 'Hazes' for anti-submarine warfare.

Libya currently operates six ex-Soviet 'Foxtrot' class patrol submarines, an obsolescent design whose main uses are training and, in time of war, mining. Libya is believed to have approached West Germany for 'Type 209' submarines of a more capable nature than her present 'Foxtrots', but it is highly unlikely that West Germany would seriously consider such an order. Other submarine assets currently operated by Libya are two ex-Yugoslav 'Mala' class submersibles, whose only real use would be underwater delivery of demolition teams.

Libya's sole frigate, a 'Vosper Thornycroft Mk 7' class ship, is currently being refitted at Genoa after a disastrous fire, leaving the Libyan navy with a major surface ship force of two 'Nanuchka II' class and four 'Assad' class corvettes, the former each with four SS.N-2 'Styx' missiles and the latter each with four Otomat missiles. This useful anti-ship force is to be supplemented by another two 'Nanuchka II' class corvettes, providing a formidable leader and support capability for the fast attack craft (missile) force, which comprises 10 'La Combattante IIG', 12 'Osa II' and three 'Susa' class craft. The last are of little value, being capable only of short-range attacks with SS.12 wire-guided missiles, but the fast attack craft force is being bolstered by 12 'SAR 33' class craft from Turkey: of West German design, the 'SAR 33' class craft are dual-role vessels that can be fitted with a 76-mm (3-in) gun, anti-ship missiles and twin 35-mm AA cannon.

Libyan ship strength

type	number	class
patrol submarine	6	'Foxtrot'
	1+1	'Mala'
frigate	1	'Vosper Thornycroft Mk 7'
corvette	2+2	'Nanuchka II'
	4	'Assad'
	1	'Tobruk'
FAC (missile)	10	'La Combatante IIG'
	12	'Osa II'
	2+10	'SAR 33'
	3	'Susa'
patrol craft	4	'Garian'
	3	'Benin'
	1	'Thornycroft 78-ft'
minesweeper (ocean)	4	'Natya'
landing ship	1	'Zeltin' LSD
	2	'PS 700' LST
landing craft	3	'Polnochny' LCT
	20+30(?)	'C107' LCT
other	10	misc

Madagascar

Operating from a number of ports around the coast of this large island (Diego Suarez, Fort Dauphin, Majunga, Manakara, Nossi-Be, Tamatave and Tulear), the Madagascar navy has a personnel strength of some 600 (many of them 18-month conscripts) to operate one large and five coastal patrol plus eight amphibious vessels. The latter are intended mainly for transport rather than genuine amphibious warfare.

Madagascan ship strength

type	number	class
patrol craft	2	'PR 48'
	5	small patrol craft
landing ship	1	'Batram' LSU
landing craft	4	'Nampo' LCU
	3	LCM
other	1	training ship

Malawi

Operating as part of the army, the naval arm of Malawi has some 100 personnel and four small patrol craft deployed on Lake Nyasa.

Malaysia

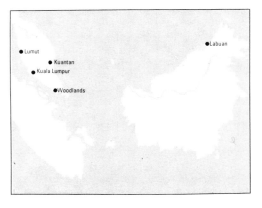

Malaysia has a very long coastline in a region disturbed by communist aggression, and must therefore maintain a strong navy for local and external security. The problem is exacerbated by the fact that the country is divided into two portions, West Malaysia occupying the southern part of the Malay peninsula and East Malaysia covering large portions of north-west Borneo, where during the 1960s considerable pressure was exerted by Indonesia. Current manpower strength is about 11,000 volunteers, and the main bases of the Royal Malaysian navy are at Lumut (fleet headquarters and main base, taking over these roles from Woodlands in the Johore Strait during 1984), Kuantan (as an advanced base in mainland Malaysia) and Labuan (the main base in East Malaysia).

Given the fairly enclosed nature of the waters to be protected, and the relative shortage of funds available, the Malaysian navy has pinned much of its faith in fast attack craft, with a small but increasing complement of frigates for more serious threats and as back-up for the attack craft. There are currently two British-built frigates in service, but these are obsolescent in terms of anti-ship and anti-submarine armament, and will be supplemented by two (possibly four) 'Type FS 1500' frigates from West Germany. These will have considerably superior electronics, and will also have useful anti-ship armament in the form of four Exocet surface-to-surface missiles. The gun armament is also interesting, for it is planned that each of the ships will have one 100-mm (3·9-in) DP gun, one 57-mm gun with

which to engage fast attack craft, and two twin 30-mm AA cannon mountings.

Light forces comprise 14 fast attack craft, soon to be increased to 18 as the current four 'Spica-M' fast attack craft (missile) are joined by another four Swedish-built craft. Also fitted with four Exocet anti-ship missiles apiece are the four 'Perdana' class craft, and these FAC(M)s are backed by the six 'Jerong' class fast attack craft (gun), each armed with the same type of powerful 57-mm gun that will be fitted in the 'Type FS 1500' frigates for FAC engagements. This fast attack capability is backed by a substantial force of patrol craft, currently 22 strong in three major classes, with six more patrol craft in Sabah.

Other ships are used for survey and other services, and there is also a useful martime component of the Royal Malaysian Police, which operates no fewer than 51 substantial patrol craft.

Malaysian ship strength

type	number	class
frigate	0+2	'Type FS 1500'
	1	'Rahmat'
	1	'Type 41/61'
FAC (missile)	8	'Spica-M'
	4	'Perdana'
FAC (gun)	6	'Jerong'
patrol craft	4	'Kedah'
	4	'Sabah'
	14	'Kris'
minesweeper (ocean)	0+4	'Lerici'
landing ship	2	LSS
	2	'LST 511-1152'
landing craft	5	LCM
	15	LCP
	9	RCP
other	3+1	misc

Maldives

A scattered series of atolls in the Indian Ocean, the Maldives operates six patrol craft for inter-island communications, plus four ex-Royal Air Force general-purpose landing craft for inter-island transport.

Mali

The landlocked state of Mali in West Africa operates a riverine force of three patrol craft on the Upper Niger, some 50 men being based at Bamako, Mopti, Segou and Timbuktu.

Malta

Operated as the maritime wing of the Maltese Regiment, the navy of Malta is designed solely for coastal operations and deploys some 15 patrol craft from sources as diverse as the UK, USA, Libya and Yugoslavia.

Maltese ship strength

type	number	class
patrol craft	2	'Yugoslav Type 131'
	2	'Swift 50-ft'
	2	'Libyan 103-ft'
	1	'German 97-ft'
	2	'Libyan 100-ft'
	2	'RTTL Mk 2'
	1	'RAF 1300'
	1	'RRSL'
	2	'Couacher'

Mauritania

Lacking the finance and ambitions for more than a

small coastal patrol navy, Mauritania operates only a limited number of craft in this role from its bases at Port Etienne and Nouadhibou. Personnel strength is about 320 volunteers, and consideration is being given to the slight expansion of this strength to allow an increase in large patrol craft from five to eight with an additional three 'Barcelo' class craft.

Mauritanian ship strength

type	number	class
FAC (gun)	1	'Auroux 40·4-m'
	3	'Barcelo
patrol craft	2	'CNE 32-m'
	2	'CNE 18·2-m'
	1	'Chinguetti'
landing craft	0+2(?)	'Batral' LCT

Mauritius

This diminutive island state operates only a single craft, an ex-Indian 'Abhay' class large patrol craft.

Mexico

Mexico possesses extensive coastlines on the Pacific and along the Gulf of Mexico in the Caribbean. However, the country faces little or no external threat given the proximity of the USA to the north, and thus maintains relatively small armed forces. The principal task of the Mexican navy is this coastal patrol and the protection of Mexican mercantile interests. Personnel are all volunteers, and number some 23,625 including the small naval air arm (fixed- and rotary-wing aircraft for search-and-rescue, patrol, transport and utility purposes) and 3,810 marines divided into 19 marine security companies. The main bases of the Mexican navy are at Acapulco, Ciudad del Carmen, Guaymas, Manzanillo, Salina Cruz, Tampico and Veracruz. Because the country has two unconnected coastlines, the naval command structure is divided into the Pacific and Gulf Areas, each subdivided into naval zones and subordinate naval sectors.

The major surface assets of the Mexican navy are all obsolete, and comprise three destroyers (two 'Gearing' and one 'Fletcher' class) and six frigates (one 'Edsall', four 'Charles Lawrence/Crossley' and one 'Durango' class). The most important task of the Mexican navy is reflected in the number of patrol ships and craft used: 41 patrol ships and 31 large patrol craft.

Mexican ship strength

type	number	class
destroyer	2	'Gearing (FRAM I)'
	1	'Fletcher'
frigate	1	'Edsall'
	4	'Charles Lawrence/ Crossley'
	1	'Durango'
corvette (patrol ship)	6	'Halcon'

type	number	class
	18	'Auk'
	1	'Guanajuato'
	16	'Admirable'
patrol craft	31	'Azteca'
	5	'Polimar'
	2	'Azueta'
	11+?	river patrol craft
landing ship	1	'De Soto County' LST
	2	'LST 511-1152'
landing craft	6	'Pegasos' LCP
other	33	misc

Montserrat

From its base at Plymouth, the Montserrat police force operates a single Brooke Marine 15-ton patrol craft.

Morocco

Morocco has seaboards in the Mediterranean and on the Atlantic, and faces the possible threats of Soviet-urged Algeria and Libya, two countries which have of late shown an increased desire to bolster their long-range offensive naval forces. Thus the Royal Moroccan navy has launched a small but important modernization and expansion programme, its primary source being Spain, though weapons and electronics are generally of French and Italian origins. Manpower strength is 1,800, including some 500 marines, and this total includes a number of men undergoing an 18-month national service obligation. All the main bases are on the Atlantic coast, namely Agadir, Safi, Casablanca, Kenitra and Tangier, though the position of the last on the southern side of the Strait of Gibraltar opens the possibility of operations in the Mediterranean.

Whereas the Moroccan navy has hitherto restricted its ambitions to coastal operations with gun-armed fast attack craft ('PR 72' class), heightened tensions in the area were reflected first by the purchase of 'Lazaga' class fast attack craft (missile), and now by the order placed with Bazán in Spain for a 'Descubierta (Modified)' class missile frigate, and by discussions currently taking place with a Dutch builder for five missile-armed corvettes. Apart from their missiles (Exocet anti-ship and, in the frigate, Aspide surface-to-air missiles), these new ships are notable for their anti-submarine capabilities. Other than these units, the Moroccan navy operates only patrol craft and a small amphibious force.

Moroccan ship strength

type	number	class
frigate	o+1	'Descubierta (Modified)'
corvette	0+0+5	Dutch
FAC (gun)	2	'PR 72'
	4	'Lazaga'
patrol craft	1	'Sirius'
	1	'Lieutenant Riffi'
	1	'Al Bachir'
	1	'VC'
	6	'P 32'
	3	coastal patrol craft
landing ship	3	'Batral' LSU
landing craft	1	'EDIC' LCT
other	2	logistic support

Mozambique

Since independence from Portugal was gained in 1975, Mozambique has set up with the aid of Soviet and Tanzanian training teams a small coastal patrol navy with a personnel strength of 700 volunteers and a complement of 16 small patrol craft, one landing craft, tank and two landing craft, utility, and one survey vessel. The main bases are at Maputo, Nacala, Beira and Pemba, and the waters of Lake Nyassa are patrolled from Metangula.

Mozambiquan ship strength

type	number	class
patrol craft	5	'Zhuk'
	1	'Poluchat'
	2	'Bellatrix'
	3	'Jupiter'
	1	'Autares'
landing craft	1	LCT
	2	LCU
other	1	survey ship

Netherlands

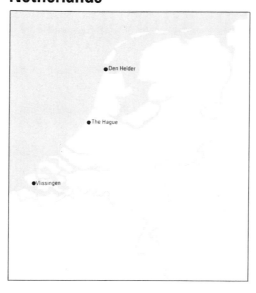

The Royal Netherlands navy operates within the structure of NATO's eastern Atlantic and North Sea command structure, providing multi-role task forces of surface ships optimized for anti-submarine and anti-ship operations. Current manpower strength is 16,800 including the naval air arm and marines; of this total some 1,250 are conscripts undertaking a period of national service varying from 14 to 17 months in length. There are also 410 women personnel. The principal naval base is Den Helder, and there are minor bases at Vlissengen (Flushing) in The Netherlands and on Curacao in the Dutch Antilles. The naval air arm, with a strength of about 1,700 personnel, operates from Valkenburgh and De Kooy, the former accommodating Lockheed P-3C Orion and Dassault-Breguet Atlantic maritime reconnaissnce/anti-submarine aircraft, and the latter Westland UH-14A utility helicopters; another squadron, equipped with SH-14B/C Lynxes, operates as embarked detachments on Dutch warships for anti-submarine warfare.

Long-range underwater power is currently entrusted to six patrol submarines (two 'Zwaardvis', two 'Potvis' and two 'Dolfijn' class boats). Currently building are two 'Walrus' class boats, to a design improved from that of the 'Zwaardvis' boats. Their commissioning in the mid-1980s will allow the deletion of the two 'Dolfijn' class submarines, while the proposed construction of another pair later in the decade will permit the retirement of the two 'Potvis' class boats.

The currently available surface forces comprise two 'Tromp' class guided-missile destroyers (officially rated as frigates, but having the size plus anti-ship and anti-aircraft capabilities to be regarded as destroyers), 10 'Kortenaer' class guided-missile frigates, six 'Van Speijk' class guided-missile frigates and four elderly 'Wolf' class corvettes. These last are being retired as the last of the 'Kortenaer' class come into service, further strength being planned with the current programme, which sees the launch of two 'Jacob van Heemskerck' class anti-aircraft frigates in 1984, and the laying down of the first of five 'M' class general-purpose guided-missile frigates in the second half of the decade. The 'M' class will not begin to enter service until the early 1990s, so Dutch naval plans for this decade envisage the operation of three surface ship groups. Operating in the eastern Atlantic will be ASW Groups I and II: when at full strength the former is to consist of the destroyer Tromp, one air-defence frigate of the 'Jacob van Heemskerck' class, three 'Kortenaer' class ASW frigates, two 'Van Speijk' class ASW frigates and the fast combat support ship Zuiderkruis; and at full strength the latter is to comprise the destroyer De Ruyter, four 'Kortenaer' class ASW frigates, two 'Van Speijk' class ASW frigates and the fast combat support ship Poolster. Operating area for the ASW Group III is the English Channel and southern portion of the North Sea, and at full strength this group will be made up of one air-defence frigate of the 'Jacob van Heemskerck' class, three 'Kortenaer' class ASW frigates, two 'Van Speijk' class ASW frigates and a new fast combat support ship of the 'Poolster' class. It should be noted that although the 'Kortenaer' and 'Van Speijk' classes are designed primarily for ASW operations, they are now multi-capable ships, with eight Harpoon anti-ship missiles and useful point-defence missile systems (Sea Sparrow in the 'Kortenaer' class and Sea Cat in the 'Van Speijk' class derived from the British 'Leander' class).

The Dutch navy also operates five 'Balder' class large patrol craft for local patrol, and is building up an effective mine countermeasures force, the previous 18 units of the 'Dokkum' class being supplemented by a planned total of 15 'Tripartite' class minehunters produced in collaboration with France and Belgium.

Netherlands ship strength

type	number	class
patrol submarine	0+2+2	'Walrus'
	2	'Zwaardvis'
	2	'Potvis'
	2	'Dolfijn'
destroyer	2	'Tromp'
frigate	0+2	'Jacob van Heemskerck'
	0+0+5	'M'
	10	'Kortenaer'
	6	'Van Speijk'
corvette	4	'Wolf
patrol craft	5	'Balder'
minesweeper (ocean)	4+11	'Tripartite'
minesweeper (coastal)	18	'Dokkum'
landing craft	10+12	LCU
other	32	misc

New Zealand

Operating from a base at Auckland, the Royal New Zealand Navy makes up in skill and advanced equipment for its relative lack of size, and thus plays an important part in the maintenance of stability in the southern Pacific and parts of South-east Asia. Personnel strength is made up of 2,760 volunteers, backed by 445 reservists, and these man and support a primary force of five British-designed frigates. These are multi-role vessels with adequate point-defence missile armament but superior anti-submarine armament, the two 'Leander (Broad-beam)' class ships having a Westland Wasp helicopter and Ikara missile-launcher apiece. Other than these five well-armed ships, the Royal New Zealand Navy operates a small force of survey vessels, four large patrol craft, four coastal patrol craft and some auxiliaries.

New Zealand ship strength

type	number	class
frigate	2	'Leander'
	2	'Leander (Broad-beam)'
	1	'Rothesay'
patrol craft	4	'Lake'
	4	'HDML'
other	6	misc

Nicaragua

Operating from the ports of Carinto, Puerto Somoza and San Juan del Sur on the Pacific coast, and from Puerto Cabezas on the Caribbean coast, the Nicuaraguan navy's 200 men operate a small force of coastal patrol craft for local defence. The most significant of these 16 patrol craft are four 'Dabur' class craft obtained from Israel, and two French-built craft. There is also one LCM Mk 6 utility landing craft.

Nicaraguan ship strength

type	number	class
patrol craft	4	'Dabur'
	2	'CNE 28-m'
	1	'Sewart 85-ft'
	9	misc
landing craft	1	LCM Mk 6

Nigeria

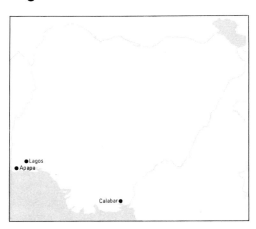

Despite recent political and religious disturbances, Nigeria remains one of the most stable states in West Africa, and has devoted a not inconsiderable portion of its wealth, derived largely from the export of oil, to the building up of effective armed forces. After a flirtation with the USSR Nigeria has once again returned to the Western fold, and this is fully evident in the current composition of the Nigerian navy, which has a volunteer personnel strength of 550 officers and 3,500 other ranks. The Nigerian navy operates in two commands, the Western Naval Command being based at Apapa near Lagos, and the Eastern naval command having its headquarters at Calabar.

Nigeria has no need of submarines, and the main strength of her navy is thus centred on a judicious blend of heavier and lighter surface combatants. Largest of these are one 'Meko 360' class destroyer and one 'Obuma' class frigate. Of these the former is now the Nigerian navy's most powerful warship, with advanced sensors and a potent mix of anti-ship, anti-aircraft and anti-submarine armament; the latter, with the delivery of the *Meko 360* in 1982, became a training ship with limited armament and sensors. There are also four British-built corvettes, in the form of two 'Vosper Thornycroft Mk 9' and two 'Vosper Thornycroft Mk 3' ships. The latter Mk 9 series is the more effective of the classes, for whereas the Mk 3s have a gun armament only, the Mk 9s have guns, limited anti-submarine capability is added by six fast attack craft (missile), namely three 'Lürssen FPB 57' and three 'La Combattante IIIB' class craft. All carry the useful 76-mm (3-in) OTO-Melara Compact gun, and the former also has four Otomat anti-ship missiles whereas the latter operates four Exocet anti-ship missiles. Given the fact that Sea Cat and Aspide surface-to-air missiles are also used by the Nigerian navy, this must pose something of a maintenance and spares nightmare for the service, which lacks a large pool of skilled manpower on which to draw.

Nigerian ship strength

type	number	class
destroyer	1	'Meko 360'
frigate	1	'Obuma'
corvette	2	'Vosper Thornycroft Mk 9'
	2	'Vosper Thornycroft Mk 3'
FAC (missile)	3	'Lürssen FPB 57'
	3	'La Combattante IIIB'
patrol craft	4	'Makurdi'
	2	'Ford'
	4	'Abeking & Rasmussen'
	15	'Intermarine'
	41	misc
landing ship	2	'Type Ro-Ro 1300' LST
landing craft	2	LCU
other	64	misc

North Korea

The hard-line communist state of North Korea lives in a condition of total war-preparedness, the anticipated opponent being South Korea and her American ally. It is hardly surprising, therefore, that North Korea maintains exceptionally strong armed forces, the North Korean navy having a strength of 31,000 men (many of them conscripts undergoing a 5-year period of national service) for a fleet that is designed only for coastal operations. The manpower pool can also be bolstered in time of emergency by some 40,000 reservists. As might be expected of a large coastal navy, the North Korean navy operates from a large number of relatively small bases, many of them outfitted with underground berthing and maintenance facilities to ensure their survival in the face of air and surface bombardment. On the east coast of the country the main base is Wonsan, with secondary bases at Mayang-do and Cha-ho, and minor bases at Najin, Sanjin-dong, Kimchaek, Yohori, Songjon, Pando, Munchon-up, Namae-ri and Konsong-up. The same pattern is followed on the west coast, with the major base at Nampo supported by a secondary base at Pipa-got and minor bases at Yogampo-ri, Tasa-ri, Sohae-ri, Chodo, Sunwi-do, Pupo-ri and Sagon-ri. In general, the major bases accommodate the more important surface forces, the secondary bases the patrol submarine force, and the minor bases the North Korean light forces.

North Korea boasts a relatively large patrol submarine force, though the boats themselves are somewhat elderly. However, the South Korean navy boasts only a small submarine arm, and given the size of the South Korean surface forces these North Korean boats would probably prove quite effective in time of war. The 'Romeo' class boats are based on the west coast for operations in the Yellow Sea, while the 'Whiskey' class boats are based on the east coast for operations in the Sea of Japan.

Major surface units are restricted to four, the frigates of the 'Najin' class, which would probably operate as flotilla leaders for the powerful light forces operated by North Korea. These latter are centred on ex-Soviet craft and their North Korean-developed versions: thus the eight 'Osa I' class fast attack craft (missile) are complemented by the eight (four built and four building) units of the enlarged 'Soju' class, while the four 'Komar' class craft are completed by the 10 (six built and four building) units of the 'Sohung' class.

North Korean ship strength

type	number	class
patrol submarine	15	'Romeo'
	4	'Whiskey'
frigate	4	'Najin'
FAC (missile)	4+4	'Soju'
	8	'Osa I'
	6+4	'Sohung'
	4	'Komar'
FAC (gun)	15	'Shanghai I'
	8	'Shanghai II'
	4	'Chodo'
	8	'Shantou'
	4	'K 48'
	20	'MO IV'
	66	'Chaho'
	38	'Chong-Jin'
FAC (torpedo)	4	'Shershen
	40	'P 6'
	8	'Sinpo'
	10	'P 4'
	15	'Iwon'
	6	'An Ju'
	72	'Ku Song' and 'Sin Hung'
patrol craft	2	'Tral'
	4	'Sariwan'
	6(?)	'Hainan'

	15	'SO I'
	2(?)	'Artillerist'
	10	'Taechong'
	10	'KM 4'
landing ship	4	'Nantae' LSM
landing craft	80	'Nampo' LCP
other	about 110	misc

North Yemen

The North Yemen navy operates from Hodeida as a coastal patrol force, and has a manpower strength of about 600, most of them conscripts undergoing a 3-year period of national service. Indoctrination and practice are of Soviet origins, and this is reflected in the make-up of the navy's blend of fast attack craft, patrol craft and inshore minesweepers, together with a small amphibious capability.

North Yemeni ship strength

type	number	class
FAC (missile)	2	'Osa II'
FAC (torpedo)	4	'P 4'
patrol craft	4	'Zhuk'
	4	'Poluchat'
	12	misc
minesweeper (inshore)	2	'Yevgenya'
landing craft	two	'T 4' LCU

Norway

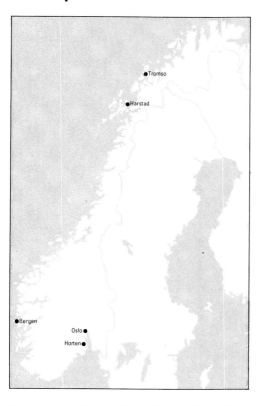

The kingdom of Norway faces a formidable maritime defence problem given its relatively small population and small defence budget, for the country has an extremely long and vulnerable coastline, is adjacent to the USSR in its northern reaches, and with Denmark controls the Soviet Union's exit from the Baltic at its southern tip. The Royal Norwegian navy thus plays a vital part in NATO defence planning, and operates as two interlinked parts, the conventional navy being supplemented by a coastal artillery arm that absorbs some 1,600 personnel from the Norwegian navy's total strength of 8,500. Some 6,000 of this strength is found by conscripts undergoing a national service obligation varying in length from 12 to 15 months. Reserves total 16,000, and there is also a naval home guard of some 6,000 personnel.

Norway's first line of defence is her submarine arm, currently composed of 14 'Type 207' class coastal submarines developed from the West German 'Type 205' class. These are now beginning to show the basic age of their design, and plans are in hand for their eventual replacement by the much more capable 940-ton being designed by Thyssen Nordseewerke in West Germany for service in the 1990s. This class (of which six have been ordered, with options for another two units) will deploy the Seal wire-guided torpedo in association with an advanced Kongsberg-developed fire-control system.

Surface strength is provided by the five 'Oslo' class frigates and two 'Sleipner' class corvettes. Both types have useful anti-submarine capability, but the frigates also have an anti-ship role with six Penguin surface-to-surface missiles. The 'Oslo' class frigates can also operate in a hostile air environment thanks to the provision of Sea Sparrow point-defence surface-to-air missiles.

Given the nature of Norway's cliff-ridden and fjord-indented coastline, the navy has made the sensible decision to devote a considerable proportion of its assets to a powerful missile-armed fast attack force: 14 'Hauk', 19 'Storm' and six 'Snögg' class craft, all equipped with the Penguin anti-ship missile. These are backed by eight 'Tjeld' class fast attack craft (torpedo) currently in reserve. Further coastal defence is afforded by three coastal minelayers, while continued operability of Norwegian ports is promoted by the availability of 10 'Adjutant' class coastal minesweepers, though in the near future the Norwegians must give careful attention to the replacement of these old vessels.

Norwegian ship strength

type	number	class
patrol submarine	0+6+2	West German
	14	'Type 207'
frigate	5	'Oslo'
corvette	2	'Sleipner'
FAC (missile)	14	'Hauk'
	19	'Storm'
	6	'Snögg'
FAC (torpedo)	8	'Tjeld'
patrol craft	1	'Vädso'
	2	'Fjellstrand 16·3-m'
minelayer	2	'Vidar'
	1	'Borgen'
minesweeper (coastal)	10	'Adjutant'
landing craft	5	'Reinøysund' LCT
	2	'Kvalsund' LCT
other	17	misc

Oman

The maritime defence problem faced by the Sultanate of Oman is similar to that of other states bordering the Persian Gulf: lack of large numbers of trained personnel within a small propulation, vital but vulnerable oil-production assets, and unstable and/or ambitious neighbours in the region. Oman's problem is exacerbated by the fact that she lies on the opposite shore of the strategic Straits of Hormuz from volatile Iran. Personnel comprise 2,000 volunteers, and the Omani navy has three bases, the principal one being located in the port of Muscat with advanced bases available at Mina Raysut and Jazirat Ghanam.

Manpower and tactical considerations have made it inevitable that the Omani navy should concentrate its efforts on light forces, though the largest vessel in the fleet is the training vessel *Al Mabruka*, a 900-ton British-built ship that doubles as a royal yacht. The British link is maintained with the light forces, whose major strength lies with five fast attack craft (missile). The three largest of these are the 'Province' class

craft, each armed with six Exocet anti-ship missiles and also with useful anti-FAC and anti-aircraft gun armament (one 76-mm/3-in OTO-Melara Compact for the former and one twin 40-mm Breda mounting for the latter). The 'Province' class craft are backed by two smaller 'Al Mansur' class craft, equipped with only two Exocets each. Also available are four 'Al Wafi' class fast attack craft (gun), based on the same design as the 'Al Mansur' class craft but fitted with a 76-mm (3-in) gun instead of missiles. Four Vosper boats provide a coastal patrol capability.

Omani ship strength

type	number	class
FAC (missile)	3	'Province'
	2	'Al Mansur'
FAC (gun)	4	'Al Wafi'
patrol craft	4	'Vosper 83-ft'
landing ship	0+1	'Brooke 305-ft' LSL
	1	'Al Munassir' LSL
landing craft	3	LCM
	4	LCU
other	3	misc

Pakistan

Pakistan has for long faced pressure from India, her eastern neighbour, and has fought several short wars with her since independence from the UK in 1947; now, however, Pakistan faces pressure on two fronts, for in the east a vicious war is being fought inside Afghanistan while the Gulf War between Iran and Iraq is also destabilizing the area. Most obviously, these pressures demand powerful Pakistani land and air forces, but just as important for the long-term stability of the country (under its present dictatorial military leadership or under a democratically-elected government) is an effective navy.

Current personnel strength is 1,250 officers and 14,550 other ranks, all of them volunteers, operating from bases at Karachi and Gwadar a powerful mix of surface and sub-surface forces, supported by a useful air arm of maritime reconnaissance aircraft and anti-submarine helicopters. The main strike component of the submarine arm is of French origins, and comprises two 'Agosta' class and four 'Daphné' class patrol submarines, all of them qualitatively superior to the Soviet-supplied 'Foxtrot' class boats operated by India. Pakistan also operates five Italian-supplied 'SX 404' class midget submarines, which carry no offensive armament but can deliver special demolition teams up to 12-men strong.

The ex-British 'Dido (Modified)' class cruiser *Jahangir* (ex-*Babur*) is no longer operational, so the largest ship operated by the Pakistani navy is the 'County' class light cruiser *Babur*, previously HMS

London, which operates as a gun cruiser now that her Sea Slug long-range surface-to-air missiles have been removed, leaving only Sea Cat SAMs as point-defence weapons. Other major surface assets (though lacking in modern sensors and armament) are five 'Gearing' and one 'Battle' class destroyer. More effective, perhaps, are the Chinese-supplied light forces, whose primary strength lies with four 'Hegu' class fast attack craft (missile) and four 'Huchuan' class fast attack Hydrofoils (torpedo), backed by 12 'Shanghai II' class fast attack craft (gun) and four 'Hainan' class large patrol craft.

Pakistani ship strength

type	number	class
patrol submarine	2	'Agosta'
	4	'Daphné'
	5	'SX 404'
cruiser	1	'Dido (Modified)'
	1	'County'
destroyer	5	'Gearing (FRAM I)'
	1	'Battle'
FAC (missile)	4	'Hegu'
FAC (gun)	12	'Shanghai II'
FAC (torpedo)	4	'Huchuan'
patrol craft	1	'Town'
	4	'Hainan'
minesweeper (coastal)	6	Adjutant'
landing craft	2	LCU
other	14+1	misc

Panama

Operating from bases at the ends of the Panama Canal, the Panamanian coast guard's 500 volunteers have a force of two 'Vosper 103-ft' large patrol craft and four coastal patrol craft at their disposal, together with some amphibious vessels used for transport purposes and a few auxiliaries.

Papua New Guinea

Formerly a territory mandated to Australia after World War I, Papua New Guinea still relies on the erstwhile colonial power for external protection, the naval arm of the Papua New Guinea Defence Force having a volunteer strength of 410 for its fleet of large patrol craft and amphibious craft, the latter being used for transport in an area poorly provided with roads. The main bases are Port Moresby and Lombrum in the Admiralty Islands.

Papua New Guinea ship strength

type	number	class
patrol craft	4	'Attack'
landing craft	2	'Salamaua' LCH
	4	'500-ton' LCU
	4	'260-ton' LCU
other	1	tug

Paraguay

The Paraguayan navy is a riverine force operating mainly on the Paraguay and Pilcomayo rivers of this landlocked country, and its ships can only be regarded as antiquated. Manpower strength is 2,000 and there are also 500 marines; conscription accounts for about 25 per cent of the total, national servicemen undergoing an 18-month period of conscription. The main base is at Puerto Sajonia at Asuncion, with the base for the small naval air arm opposite it on Chaco Island in the Paraguay river; a minor base is maintained at Bahia Negra on the upper Paraguay.

Paraguayan ship strength

type	number	class
frigate (river defence ship)	2	'Humaita'

corvette	3	'Bouchard'
patrol craft	9	misc
other	19	misc

Peru

Peru lies at a hub of South America's conflicts, political and economic, and has in recent years turned to the USSR for the modern equipment needed by her army and air force. However, the same situation has not prevailed with the Peruvian navy, by South American standards an exceptionally capable force equipped with ships from a variety of Western sources. Current manpower strength is 2,000 officers and 18,500 other ranks including the naval air arm (useful fixed- and rotary-wing anti-submarine capability as well as utility aircraft), of whom some 7,000 are 2-year national servicemen; many of the conscripts are allocated to the 2,500-strong marine brigade. The Peruvian navy operates from three main bases: Callao, headquarters of the Pacific Naval Force; Iquitos, headquarters of the Amazon River Force; and Puno, headquarters of the Lake Titicaca Patrol Force. Other bases are to be found at San Lorenza (submarines), Talara (light forces) and Madre de Dios (river forces).

The main 'punch' of Peru's large submarine arm is undoubtedly packed by the six boats of the 'Type 209' class, all commissioned during the 1970s and early 1980s, and clearly a force without equal in South America. These modern boats are backed up by two 'Guppy IA' and four 'Dos de Mayo' class boats, previously American submarines of the 'Balao' and 'Mackerel' class modernized in the 1950s and 1960s respectively.

Peru also commands a large and potentially devastating force of surface combatants, the two largest of which are the ex-Dutch 'De Ruyter' class cruisers. Of these *Almirante Grau* remains a conventional gun cruiser with good radar, and the *Aguirre* has been converted into a hybrid gun/anti-submarine cruiser, her main armament being reduced from eight to four 152-mm (6-in) guns to allow the installation of a hangar aft for three Sikorsky SH-3D Sea King anti-submarine helicopters. Back-up for these two cruisers is provided by 10 destroyers: the seven ex-Dutch 'Friesland' class ships and one ex-Dutch 'Holland' class ship remain virtually as built, namely gun destroyers of the type finalized in World War II, but the two ex-British 'Daring' class destroyers have been upgraded with eight Exocet anti-ship

missiles apiece as well as provision for an anti-submarine helicopter.

Perhaps more useful in modern naval affairs are the four 'Lupo (Modified)' class guided-missile frigates, two built in Italy and the other two in Peru. These carry the full range of modern sensors and armament, the latter including Otomat anti-ship missiles, Aspide point-defence surface-to-air missiles, anti-submarine torpedoes and an anti-submarine helicopter in addition to DP and AA guns. And offering only slightly less offensive power are six 'PR 72P' fast attack craft (missile), each armed with four Exocet anti-ship missiles and a useful gun armament of one 76-mm (3-in) OTO-Melara Compact DP and one twin 40-mm Breda AA mounting.

Riverine forces comprise five river gunboats, and there are also four lake patrol craft. Other maritime assets are three landing ships, tank and two landing ship, medium, plus the normal miscellany of service and support forces. Also available is a coast guard organization which operates 13 large patrol craft, seven coastal patrol craft and three river patrol craft.

Peruvian ship strength

type	number	class
patrol submarine	6	'Type 209'
	2	'Guppy IA'
	4	'Dos de Mayo'
cruiser	2	'De Ruyter'
destroyer	2	'Daring'
	7	'Friesland'
	1	'Holland'
frigate	3+1	'Lupo (Modified)'
FAC (missile)	6	'PR 72P'
patrol craft	2	'Maranon' river gunboat
	2	'Loreto' river gunboat
	1	'America' river gunboat
	4	lake patrol craft
landing ship	1	'LST 1-510'
	2	'LST 511-1152'
	2	'LSM 1'
other	34	misc

Philippines

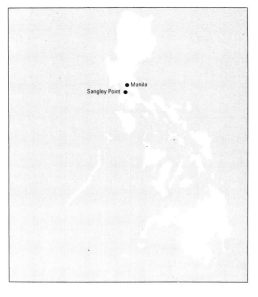

The Philippines face no serious exterior threat, and the Filipino navy is thus devoted more to internal security and inter-island patrol throughout the 7,000 or more islands that form the republic. The navy has a strength of 1,600 officers and 13,060 men, all of them volunteers, and there are in addition 6,840 marines and 2,000 coast guard personnel. The Filipino navy's main base is Sangley Point, and there are smaller bases at Cavite and Zamboanga. Little is currently being procured as new equipment for the Filipino forces, the navy being restricted at the moment to the construction of one training ship and the provision of Otomat anti-ship missiles on existing vessels.

Although the Filipino navy hopes in the near future to order three 1,500-ton frigates of modern capability, the current force of seven old vessels seems certain to remain in service for some time to come. These ex-US ships are one 'Savage' class and two 'Cannon' class units, and four ex-US Coast Guard 'Casco' class cutters. None of them could operate in conditions of modern naval warfare, and the same applies to the corvette force, currently made up of two 'Auk' class ex-fleet minesweepers, seven 'PCE 827' class ex-patrol ships, and one 'Admirable' class ex-mine-sweeper.

The Philippines also operate a very large amphibious capability, largely for transport within the island republic and to provide the army with tactical mobility in its guerrilla war with Moslem guerrillas. Some 24 landing ships, tank, and four landing ships, medium, form the backbone of the force, and there are also a useful variety and number of smaller types. Service force vessels are few in number but adequate for the task in hand. The coast guard operates a number of coastal patrol craft (the total is uncertain) plus three large patrol craft.

Filipino ship strength

type	number	class
frigate	1	'Savage'
	2	'Cannon'
	4	'Casco'
corvette	2	'Auk'
	7	'PCE 827'
	1	'Admirble'
FAC (missile)	3	'PSMM Mk 5'
patrol craft	4+6	'Hamelin 30·6-m'
	2	'PC 461'
	2	'Vosper 124-ft'
	5	'PGM 39' & 'PGM 71'
	31	'de Havilland'
	25+13	'Swift (Improved)'
	13	'Swift'
	3	'72-ton'
landing ship	4	'LSM 1'
	6	'LST 1-510'
	18	'LST 511-1152'
	3	'LSSL 1'
landing craft	0+1	LCT
	61	LCM
	3	LCU
	7	LCVP
other	33	misc

Poland

The Polish navy is closely subordinated to Soviet plans for operations in the Baltic, and is concerned with coastal matters (attack, minesweeping and amphibious warfare) under the umbrella of a dedicated air arm. To this end the Polish navy is a relatively small but effective force with a personnel strength of some 22,500, only 5,000 of whom are 3-year national servicemen. Of the navy's total manpower, only 7,500 are afloat, 5,000 others being allocated to coastal defence, 2,000 to the naval air arm (one attack regiment, one helicopter regiment and one reconnaissance squadron) and the balance to other shore postings. The main bases used by the Polish navy are Gdynia, Hel and Swinoujscie, with minor bases at Kolobrzeg and Ustka.

There can be little purpose served by the Polish navy's submarine arm, which consists only of four 'Whiskey' class patrol boats of limited capability, and the same could be said of the navy's largest com-batant, one 'SAM Kotlin' class anti-aircraft destroyer, whose single twin launcher for SA-N-1 missiles (20 missiles) would be wholly inadequate in the event of a war between NATO and the Warsaw Pact.

The main effective strike power of the Polish navy thus rests with 13 'Osa I' class fast attack craft (missile) and 10 'Wisla' class fast attack craft (torpedo), though the real use of even the latter is suspect. Other assets are a considerable patrol force, which with the coast guard service operates 23 large patrol craft and 45 coastal patrol craft. Great importance is attached to mine warfare, as can be gauged from the fact that the Polish navy possesses no fewer than 24 ocean minesweepers and 23 'K 8' class minesweeping boats, and has recently launched the lead ship of a new coastal minesweeper class.

Polish ship strength

type	number	class
patrol submarine	4	'Whiskey'
destroyer	1	'SAM Kotlin'
FAC (missile)	13	'Osa I'
FAC (torpedo)	10	'Wisla'
patrol craft	8	'Obluze (Modified)'
	21	'K 8'
minesweeper (ocean)	12	'Krogulec'
minesweeper (coastal)	1+?	'Notec'
minesweeper (inshore)	23	'K 8'
landing craft	23	'Polnochny' LCT
	4	'Marabut' LCM
	15	'Eichstaden' LCP
other	53	misc

Portugal

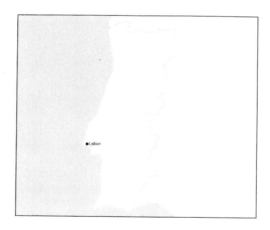

Since the loss of the last portions of her overseas empire in the 1970s, Portugal has become a fuller member of the NATO alliance despite the emergence of several socialist governments in place of the previous authoritarian regime. However, financial resources are not sufficient for the modernization scheme that the Portuguese navy needs, and plans have thus been made for a joint NATO funding for the proposed new frigate programme, for a derivative of the Dutch 'Kortenaer' design to be built to the extent of five units, three in The Netherlands and two in Portugal. Manpower strength is 14,000 including 2,000 marines, 5,200 of the total being 2-year national servicemen. The navy's main base is Alfeite near Lisbon.

For longer-range operations Portugal maintains three 'Daphné' class patrol submarines, the fourth unit of this French-built class having been transferred to Pakistan in 1975. The most advanced surface ships operated by the Portuguese navy are the four 'Commandante Joao Belo' class frigates, built in France to a variation of the 'Commandant Riviere' design. These attractive ships are optimized for the anti-submarine role, and their most serious deficiency has been the lack of an embarked helicopter; this deficiency is now being remedied in a modernization programme, which is also updating the sensor fit and other weapons, in which there is a superfluity of guns and shortage of missiles for anti-ship and anti-aircraft operations. Also in service are three 'Almirante Pereira da Silva' class frigates, modelled on the US 'Dealey' class and suffering the same failings as the 'Commandante Joao Belo' class units. It had until recently been planned to update the class considerably, but a constant string of problems has persuaded the authorities to opt instead for new-construction frigates. Also in Portugal are four 'Baptista de Andrade' class frigates, relatively modern in design and construction, which were sold to Colombia in 1977; the deal fell through and the four ships still await a buyer. Finally, in the frigate bracket, there are six 'Joao Coutinho' class ships. Worthy enough in basic concept, these ships lack the armament to be effective in modern war, though a considerable updating programme is planned in the near future as part of an effort to upgrade the Portuguese navy effectively.

Portuguese ship strength

type	number	class
patrol submarine	3	'Daphné'
frigate	0+5	'Kortenaer (Modified)'
	4	'Commandante Joao Belo'
	3	'Almirante Pereira da Silva'
	4	'Baptista de Andrade'
	6	'Joao Coutinho'
patrol craft	10	'Cacine'
	2	'Dom Aleixo'
	14	'Albatroz'
	4	'Cheverton 39-ft'
minesweeper (coastal)	4	'Sao Roque'
landing craft	2	'Bombarda' LCT
	10	LCM
	1	LCA
other	9	misc

Qatar

Yet another country that has profited from the oil wealth of the Persian Gulf but has recently realized its vulnerability to the ambitions of its larger neighbours in the region, Quatar has no navy organized formally as such, but has been developing the Marine Police division of the Qatari police. Operating from a base at Doha, the 400 volunteer personnel operate a small but formidable light navy. The core of this force is represented by three 'La Combattante IIIM' fast attack craft, each armed with eight Exocet anti-ship missiles in addition to a capable gun armament optimized for defence against light craft and aircraft. Back-up is provided by six 'Barzan' class large patrol craft, 36 assorted coastal patrol craft, two assault and rescue craft, and a single workboat.

Qatari ship strength

type	number	class
FAC (missile)	3	'La Combattante IIIM'
patrol craft	6	'Barzan'
	31	misc
other	1	workboat

Romania

Romania is a staunch but not unquestioning member of the Warsaw Pact organization, and follows a fairly orthodox Soviet line in naval matters, though she has imported numbers of Chinese craft to supplement local and Soviet-supplied vessels. The Romanian navy is designed largely for operations in the Black Sea, but also operates a substantial riverine force on the lower reaches of the Danube. Manpower levels are relatively high (10,500 including about 3,500 2-year conscripts), but of these only 4,500 are afloat; about 2,000 others are allocated to coastal defence units, which are headquartered in Constanta and operate 18 artillery batteries with approximately 110 130-mm (51·12-in), 150-mm (5·9-in) and 152-mm (6-in) guns. Reserves amount to about 20,000, and a sizable proportion of these would form two naval infantry regiments on mobilization. Of the remaining regular strength, a certain part is allocated to training and shore support, with the balance allocated to quasi-military labouring tasks such as canal digging. The ship assets of the Romanian navy are divided into the Black Sea Fleet and Danube Squadron, the former with bases at Mangala and Constanta on the coast, and the latter with bases at Tulcea, Braila, Giorgiou and Sulina on the Danube.

Romania has for some time built smaller vessels, but has recently begun to develop an indigenous warship capability, with evidence suggesting that currently on the stocks are one destroyer and one frigate, with two more frigates to follow. Details of these two new classes are not available, but it is thought that both ships were begun in 1981. The Black Sea fleet is configured largely for coastal operations, with its main strength lying with its light forces. However, the navy operates three ex-Soviet 'Poti' class corvettes as flotilla leaders and anti-submarine vessels. The strength and diversity of the light forces available are odd, with relatively few missile craft backed by large numbers of torpedo craft.

The Danube Squadron has some 40 river patrol craft of four classes, the largest being the 'VB' class displacing 85 tons and each carrying an 85-mm (3·35-in) gun and two twin 25-mm AA mountings; this class continues in production at the rate of two units per year.

Mine warfare is also important to Romania, a small but useful sweeping force being complemented by the sole 'Cosar' class minelayer and mine counter-measures support ship. Amphibious capability rests with eight LCUs, and there are a few auxiliaries and support vessels.

Romanian ship strength

type	number	class
destroyer	0+1	?
frigate	0+1+2	?
corvette	3	'Poti'
FAC (missile)	5	'Osa I'
FAC (gun)	19	'Shanghai'
FAC (torpedo)	20	'Huchuan'
	6	'P 4'
	8+?	'Epitrop'
patrol craft	3	'Kronshtadt'
	40	river patrol craft
minelayer	1	'Cosar'
minesweeper (ocean)	—	—
minesweeper (coastal)	4	'M 40'
minesweeper (inshore)	20	'VD 141'
	12	'T 301'
	8	'TR 40' boats
landing ship	—	—
landing craft	8	'Braila' LCU
other	8+1	misc

St Kitts

Based at Basseterre, the maritime wing of the St Kitts police force operates a single Fairey 'Spear' class coastal patrol craft.

St Lucia

Based at Castries, the St Lucian customs service operates one Buhler-built coastal patrol craft.

St Vincent & The Grenadines

Like those of several other Caribbean island states, the 'Navy' of St Vincent and The Grenadines is con-trolled by the police force, and from its base at Kings-town operates one Vosper Thornycroft 75-ft coastal patrol craft and two locally-built 27-ft inshore patrol craft.

Saudi Arabia

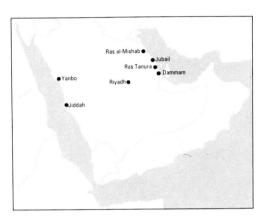

The underpopulated but immensely wealthy king-dom of Saudi Arabia has become the major factor in stabilizing the Middle East since the overthrow of the Shah of Iran in the late 1970s, and the country has undertaken this burden with great willingness, bolstering its small armed forces with some of the most advanced equipment available while building major bases and establishing mammoth training schemes to provide the skilled manpower neces-sary. So far as the Royal Saudi navy is concerned, this development programme has seen the emergence of the force from a small but powerful coastal-defence navy into the chrysalis of a sophisticated blue-water navy. Manpower is small in numbers, with only 4,500 volunteers, and the main naval bases are located at Jiddah on the Red Sea (headquarters of the Western Fleet) and Jubail on the Persian Gulf (headquarters of the Eastern Fleet); subsidiary bases are in existence at Dammam, Ras al Mishab, Ras Tanur and Yanbo. This is a fairly scattered deploy-ment, made inevitable by the geography of the country and the small manpower available, and greater potency is given to the navy by the establish-ment of a small naval air arm equipped with 24 of the powerful Aérospatiale AS.365 Dauphin II helicopter, some equipped with the AS.15TT anti-ship missile.

The growth of the Saudi navy is based on the delivery, expected in the second half of this decade, of four 'Type F 2000' class guided-missile frigates from France. These will provide the Saudi navy with an offensive punch unmatched locally, for each ship carries one helicopter, eight Otomat anti-ship missiles, 26 Crotale Naval surface-to-air missiles, torpedoes, one 100-mm (3·9-in) DP gun and two twin 40-mm AA mountings. These frigates will match well the present four 'Badr' class guided-missile corvettes delivered from the USA in the early 1980s and carry-ing a smaller armament without a helicopter but with eight Harpoon anti-ship missiles apiece. Also missile-armed are the nine 'Al Siddiq' class fast attack craft built in the USA: each of these carries four Harpoon missiles and a useful gun armament.

There is also a Saudi coast guard, which operates some 450 craft on coastal and inshore patrol duties from bases at Ruwais and Aziziyah (main bases), and at As Sharmah, Haqi and Qizan (minor bases). Most of these craft are small, but the coast guard is planning a force of large patrol craft.

Saudi Arabian ship strength

type	number	class
frigate	0+4	'Type F 2000'
corvette	4	'Badr'
FAC (missile)	9	'Al Siddiq'
FAC (torpedo)	3	'Jaguar'
patrol craft	8	'P 32'
	12	'Rapier'
	15	'Skorpion'
	16	'SR.N6'
	0+8	'BH.7'
	3	misc
minesweeper (coastal)	4	'MSC 322'
landing craft	8	LCM
	8	LCU
other	14+1	misc

Senegambia

Formed as a federated state in 1982, Senegambia is in the process of developing unified armed forces and foreign policy, while retaining the civil admini-strations of its to components (Senegal and The Gambia). The Senegambian navy is small and devoted to coastal patrol and internal security, with about 350 men (including some 2-year conscripts) operating from the bases at Dakar and Banjul. Most of the federation's naval equipment was provided by Senegal, an ex-French colony that used largely French craft. The most powerful of these is a single 'PR 72M' class fast attack craft (gun), backed by three 'P 48' class large patrol craft. There are also a few coastal patrol craft and a small amphibious force. The customs service operates a few coastal patrol craft.

Senegambian ship strength

type	number	class
FAC (gun)	1	'PR 72M'
patrol craft	3	'P 48'
	3	'Interceptor'
	2	'Fairey'
landing craft	1	'EDIC' LCT
	2	LCM
other	2	misc

Seychelles

Operated as part of the army, the Seychelles navy has about 150 men and operates a small force of patrol craft and one landing craft, tank, from Port Victoria on Mahe island. The LCT is generally operated for commercial purposes.

Seychellois ship strength

type	number	class
patrol craft	0+1+1	'Inma 42-m'
	1	'Sirius'
	2	'Zhuk'
	1	'Tyler 60-ft'
landing craft	1	LCT
other	—	—

Sierra Leone

Small and impoverished, the West African state of Sierra Leone operates a small coastal patrol navy from its base at Freetown. Manpower strength is some 150 volunteers, and marine assets currently comprise one coastal patrol craft and three small landing craft, with one 'Shanghai II' class fast attack craft (gun) held in reserve.

Singapore

Wealthy, technologically advanced and strategically placed, the Republic of Singapore maintains a small but potent local-defence navy at its base of Paulau Brani on Singapore island. The manpower strength available is about 3,000 including about 1,800 conscripts undergoing a 24- or 30-month national service obligation.

Core of the Singapore navy is the fast attack craft (missile) strength, comprising six 'Lürssen TNC 45' units, each armed with Gabriel Mk 2 anti-ship missiles. These are backed by nine fast attack craft (gun), in the form of three 'Lürssen FPB 57', three 'Vosper Type A', and three 'Vosper Type B' units. The first and last of these carry a 76-mm (3-in) gun apiece, while the 'Vosper Type A' carries one 40-mm Bofors as its primary weapon. Local patrol is provided by 12 'Swift 75-ft' class craft, and there are also minesweeping and amphibious forces. The Singapore police also has a marine arm, with 49 assorted patrol craft.

Singaporean ship strength

type	number	class
FAC (missile)	6	'Lürssen TNC 45'
FAC (gun)	3	'Lürssen FPB 57'
	3	'Vosper Type A'
	3	'Vosper Type B'
patrol craft	12	Swift 75-ft'
minesweeper (coastal)	2	'Redwing'
landing ship	6	'LST 511-1152'
landing craft	6	LCU
other	6	misc

Solomon Islands

Operating from Honiara under the control of the ministry of transport are one 'de Havilland' class coastal patrol craft and two small research vessels.

Somalia

Somalia has recently moved out of the Soviet orbit and into that of the USA, but her navy is still equipped exclusively with Soviet vessels. This must inevitably cause problems with serviceability, and it is expected that Somalia will shift slowly towards Western sources of supply, while retaining only a coastal-defence capability comparable with the current situation. The Somali navy is thus small, with only 600 volunteer personnel, and operates from bases at Berbera, Kismayu and Mogadishu.

Somali ship strength

type	number	class
FAC (missile)	2	'Osa II'
FAC (torpedo)	4	'P 6'
patrol craft	4	'Mol'
	5	'Poluchat'
landing craft	1	'Polnochny-A' LCT
	4	'T 4' LCM

South Africa

Occupying a strategic but troublesome location on the southern tip of Africa, South Africa is by far the most powerful military force in the region, but operates only a relatively small and old-fashioned navy given the naval ineffectiveness of neighbouring Black African countries. However, the country is becoming increasingly worried about the vulnerability of the trade routes round the Cape of Good Hope, and the next few years could well see an expansion of the South African navy's surface and mine countermeasures forces. One of the most important parts of any such programme must include

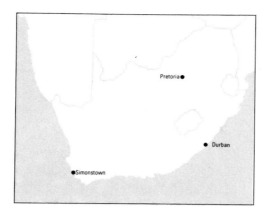

the replacement of the two obsolete 'President' class frigates, probably with a new class of frigate built in South Africa, possibly to an imported design. There would also seem to be a need for missile-armed corvettes as flotilla leaders for the fast attack craft (missile) force, which is growing steadily. Other aspects of the modernization programme should include the manufacture within South Africa of modern submarines, and the development in the 1990s of an effective mine warfare force. Current manpower strength is 6,760 including 1,575 conscripts doing a 2-year period of national service, and there are some 2,000 reservists. Only two naval bases are maintained, that at Simonstown catering for the larger surface combatants and submarines, and that at Salisbury Island, Durban, for fast attack craft and other units of the Strike Craft Flotilla.

South Africa deploys three 'Daphné' class patrol submarines as her longer-range strike force, but these are essentially coastal submarines which are now beginning to show their age. The same factor applies to the two 'President' class frigates, originally British 'Rothesay' class ships and lacking modern weapons for anti-ship and anti-submarine operations.

More capable by a considerable degree are the light forces, centred on the nine units of the 'Mod' class currently in service. These fast attack craft (missile) are fitted with the Skorpioen anti-ship missile based on the Israeli Gabriel, as befits a craft designed and first built in Israel to a design modelled closely on that of the 'Saar 4' class. Another three 'Mod' class units are building in South Africa, and it seems likely that three completed units plus the production facilities for the Israeli 'Dvora' class FAC(M) have been transferred to South Africa. Only small patrol forces complement the FAC(M) units and, apart from auxiliaries and support vessels, South Africa's only other surface assets are 10 obsolescent 'Ton' class coastal minesweepers.

South African ship strength

type	number	class
patrol submarine	3	'Daphné'
frigate	2	'President'
FAC (missile)	9+3	'Mod'
	(3+6	'Dvora')
patrol craft	4	'Ford'
	1	'29·5-m'
minesweeper (coastal)	10	'Ton'
other	47	misc

South Korea

Given the nature and magnitude of the threat she faces from North Korea, South Korea has to maintain powerful armed forces, but whereas those of the likely opponent are characterized by massive manpower and limited technical quality, the South Korean forces are relatively smaller and rely more heavily on technological factors. Total manpower

strength of the navy is about 47,000, but of these some 20,000 are in the marine corps, and of the total about 35,000 conscripts undergoing a 3-year period of national service. The South Korean navy's main base is at Chinhae, with smaller bases at Cheju, Inchon, Mokpo, Mukho, Pohang and Pusan. There is also a small naval air arm with limited anti-submarine capability from 16 Grumman S-2 Tracker aircraft, and this force is based at Chinae and Pohang together with a number of utility aircraft and helicopters.

South Korea is particularly sensitive about national building programmes, and it is difficult to establish the truth of certain reported details. However, it is fairly clear that a limited submarine-building capability has been established, with the first of four 175-ton coastal submarines commissioned in 1983. It is also reported that a much smaller type is under construction, and it is tempting to believe that this constitutes an effort to develop a means of delivering underwater demolition and sabotage teams, with submarines possibly akin to the Italian SX-506 type.

The above notwithstanding, the real strength of the South Korean navy lies with its large surface forces, comprising 11 destroyers, eight frigates and four corvettes. The destroyers are all elderly ex-US types, but have been considerably modernized in their electronics suites and anti-submarine capability, thus posing a considerable threat to the North Korean submarine arm. Anti-ship capability is limited in these 'Gearing', 'Allen M. Sumner' and 'Fletcher' class destroyers, though Harpoon surface-to-surface missiles have been fitted in some units, but the 5-in (127-mm) guns sported by these destroyers would be vitally important in stemming any North Korean advance through the region along South Korea's east and west coasts. Frigate support is more nominal than real, for only the one 'Ulsan' an one 'Rudderow' class ship could truly be used in the intended role. The 'Ulsan' class is of local design and manufacture, and particularly well armed for the anti-ship, anti-aircraft and anti-submarine roles. It was expected that this would be the lead ship of a new class, but costs were so high that the South Korean navy decided to abandon further building plans, at least for the moment. The six units of the 'Charles Lawrence' and 'Crosley' classes are relatively lightly armed, and are really high-speed transports, with accommodation for 160 troops and four LCVPs. The four 'KCX' class corvettes are also available, though these well armed and fast ships are better used as flotilla leaders and support ships for the useful missile-armed fast attack craft force of eight 'PSMM Mk 5' units and one similar 'Asheville' class unit. Also available is a substantial force of patrol craft with the speed and armament to deal with North Korean fast attack craft.

Amphibious forces are quite large, though this factor reflects South Korea's appreciation of the need for amphibious operations within South Korea rather than any intention of offensive operations against North Korea. The South Korean coast guard operates about 25 small ships and craft.

South Korean ship strength

type	number	class
patrol submarine	1+5	'South Korean'
	0+?	midget
destroyer	2	'Gearing (FRAM II)'
	5	'Gearing (FRAM I)'
	2	'Allen M. Sumner (FRAM II)'
	2	'Fletcher'
frigate	0+0+1	'2,000-ton'
	0+0+3	'1,600-ton'
	1	'Ulsan'
	1	'Rudderow'
	2	'Charles Lawrence'
	4	'Crosley'
corvette	0+0+3	'1,000-ton'
	0+0+3	'600-ton'
	4	'KCX'
FAC (missile)	8	'PSMM Mk 5'
	1	'Asheville'
FAC (gun)	6	'CPIC'
patrol craft	?	'Sea Falcon'
	?	'Sea Dolphin'
	8	'Cape'
	?	'Sea Hawk'
	?	'Sea Snake'
	3	misc
minesweeper (coastal)	8	'MSC 268'
assault ship	0+0+2	LSL
landing ship	3	'LST 1-510'
	5	'LST 511-1152'
	1	'Elk River' LSMR
	8	LSM 1
landing craft	10	LCU
	10	LCM
other	about 56	misc

South Yemen

Like North Yemen, South Yemen has also fallen into the Soviet sphere of influence, but her navy is considerably larger though still devoted largely to coastal operations from bases at Aden, Mukalla, Perim and Socotra. Manpower strength is about 1,000, most of them 2-year conscripts. The blend of vessels, again mostly of Soviet origins, is fairly standard. The main offensive force comprises fast attack craft (missile) and fast attack craft (torpedo), supported by patrol craft, a useful amphibious capability and a small but vital minesweeping force.

South Yemeni ship strength

type	number	class
FAC (missile)	7	'Osa II'
FAC (torpedo)	2	'P 6'
patrol craft	2	'SO I'
	1	'Poluchat'
	2	'Zhuk'
	6	'Fairey'
minesweeper (ocean)	1	'T 58'
minesweeper (inshore)	3	'Ham'
landing ship	1	'Ropucha' LST
landing craft	3	'Polnochny-B' LCT
	3	'T 4' LCVP
other	1	lighter

Spain

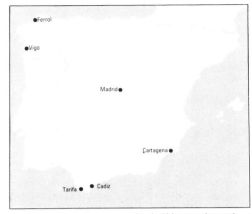

Spain is a recent but somewhat half-hearted member of the NATO alliance, and operates a relatively large navy with important responsibilities in the southern half of the North Atlantic as well as in the Mediterranean. For many years the Spanish were content to operate a moderately obsolete mix of surface warships, but in recent times a considerable modernization and new-construction programme has been pursued. Financial problems have meant a curtailment in this programme, but the Spanish navy hopes by the 1990s to be able to operate two carrier groups with effective anti-ship, anti-aircraft and anti-submarine escort (destroyers and frigates) plus smaller fast attack craft (missile) task groups with corvette support. Other projected improvements will add to the effectiveness of the mine countermeasures and amphibious forces, the former receiving four 'Tripartite' class minehunters and eight new minesweepers, and the latter one amphibious transport dock and four landing ships, tank.

Manpower strength is 4,215 officers and 37,865 ratings in the navy proper, plus a marine corps of 700 officers and 11,500 other ranks. Of this total of 54,280 some 44,000 are conscripts undergoing an 18-month national service obligation. The Spanish navy is broken down into five operational and four regional support commands, deployed to Spain's major naval bases. The Naval Air Group consists of the light carrier Dedalo (to be replaced by the Principe de Asturias) with escorts as appropriate and based at Rota; the Escort Command operates as three squadrons, the 11th Squadron being based at Ferrol with one 'Roger de Lauria' and five 'Gearing' or 'D 60' class destroyers, the 21st Squadron at Cartagena with two 'Fletcher' or 'D 20' class destroyers and four 'Descubierta' class frigates, and the 31st Squadron at Ferrol with five 'Baleares' class frigates; the Amphibious Command controls all such assets but LCT 2-5 and is based at Puntales near Cadiz; the Mine Countermeasures Command has four ocean and eight coastal minesweepers at Palma de Mallorca; and the Submarine Flotilla controls all underwater assets from the base at Cartagena. These are the operational commands, and the support commands are those of the Cantabrian Zone (headquarters at Ferrol), the Straits Zone (headquarters at Cadiz), the Mediterranean Zone (headquarters at Cartagena) and the Canaries Zone (headquarters at Las Palmas). Each of these zones has an allocation of support vessels plus one or two destroyers and/or frigates.

Patrol submarine strength is marginal, with only the four 'Daphné' and four 'Agosta' class boats (the latter to be commissioned in 1985) truly effective. More can be expected from this force if the SM.39 underwater-launched version of the Exocet anti-ship missile is provided for the 'Agosta' class. The two 'Guppy IIA' class boats are of little use but for training.

Much the same can be said of the carrier strength, in which the V/STOL ship Dedalo (with BAe Harrier aircraft and 20 helicopters) will shortly, but not before time, be replaced by the Principe de Asturias sea-control carrier. Spanish longer-term plans call for the construction of another sea-control ship as the core of a second carrier group.

The destroyer force of five 'Gearing (FRAM I)', five 'Fletcher' and one 'Roger de Lauria' class destroyers, can only be regarded as obsolete, and the proposed construction of at least two new destroyers is long overdue. The frigate situation is more promising, however, for the older 'Atrevida' class is being phased out as newer ships are commissioned, and the five 'Baleares' and six 'Descubierta' class frigates can be regarded as adequate multi-role types despite the fact that they lack embarked helicopters. Considerably more capable are the five 'Oliver Hazard Perry' class guided-missile frigates currently proposed. Three of these are building, but the programme has been delayed to allow the rapid completion of the Principe de Asturias. Further frigate construction will probably be of a 'Descubierta (Modified)' class, with CODAG propulsion for a longer hull to provide greater speed and area for the fitting of a helicopter hangar.

Spanish ship strength

type	number	class
patrol submarine	3+1	'Agosta' or 'S 70'
	4	'Daphné' or 'S 60'
	2	'Guppy IIA' or 'S 30'
aircraft-carrier	1	'Independence'
	0+1	'Principe de Asturias'
destroyer	1	'Roger de Lauria' or 'D 40'
	5	'Gearing (FRAM I)' or 'D 60'
	5	'Fletcher' or 'D 20'
frigate	0+3+2	'Oliver Hazard Perry' or 'F 80'
	6	'Descubierta' or 'F 30'
	5	'Baleares' or 'F 70'
	4	'Atrevida' or 'PA 60'
corvette	—	—
FAC (missile)	6	'Lazaga'
FAC (gun)	6	'Barcelo'
patrol craft	10	'Anaga'
	3	'Adjutant'
	70	misc
minesweeper (ocean)	4	'Aggressive'
minesweeper (coastal)	8	'Adjutant'
assault ship	2	'Paul Revere' LPA
	1	'Cabildo' LSD
landing ship	3	'Terrebonne Parish' LST
landing craft	7	LCT
	2	LCU
	8+6	LCM
	0+9	LCPL
other	144	misc

Sri Lanka

The Sri Lanka navy is a small coastal patrol force with a manpower strength of 2,960 volunteers, with a main base at Trincomalee and smaller bases at Colombo, Kalpitiya, Karainagar, Tangale and Welisara. Only patrol forces are operated, and the current Soviet and Chinese craft are being supplemented by locally-built large patrol craft for operations in the 200-mile (322-km) Sri Lankan economic zone.

Sri Lankan ship strength

type	number	class
FAC (gun)	7	'Shanghai II' or 'Sooraya'

	1	'Mol'
patrol craft	0+2	'330-ton'
	7+4	'40-ton'
	2	'36-ton'
	2	'21-ton'
	5	'Cheverton 56-ft'
	10	'Thornycroft 45·5-ft'
other	1	lighthouse tender

Sudan

Sudan is a large but impoverished country that faces trouble on two fronts: from Ethiopia and Ethiopian guerrillas in the east, and from Libya in the west. Though the country has only a relatively short seaboard on the Red Sea, it also possesses a considerable riverine requirement on the River Nile. Manpower strength amounts to some 2,000 volunteers, and the two primary bases are Port Sudan on the Red Sea and Khartoum on the Nile. Coastal patrol forces constitute the bulk of the Sudanese navy's forces, though these are of limited capability because of spares shortages.

Sudanese ship strength

type	number	class
patrol craft	1	'Kraljevica'
	4	'PBR'
	3	'Abeking & Rasmussen 23-m'
	4	'Sewart 40-ft'
landing craft	2	'DTM 221' LCT
other	3	misc

Surinam

Based at Paramaribo, the 160-man navy of this former Dutch colony operates a small number of coastal patrol craft and auxiliaries.

Sweden

The Royal Swedish navy faces an extremely difficult problem in ensuring the integrity of Sweden's coastline and territorial waters without vast expense, and to this end has concentrated its efforts on highly effective coastal submarines and light forces operating from well protected underground pens dotted along Sweden's vulnerable coast. Dedicated to a deterrent neutrality between the ambitions of the Warsaw Pact and NATO, the country has developed its own specialist philosophy and a largely indigenous manufacturing capability. The navy proper has a manpower strength of 14,200, and also controlled by the navy is the coastal artillery arm of 3,700 regulars, 7,000 national servicemen and 3,500 reservists for times of crisis. Major bases are maintained at Göteborg, Karlskrona and Stockholm, with minor bases at Härnösand and Farosund, and small operating bases located at secret spots.

The submarine arm is vitally important to Sweden, and the current force consists of four 'Draken', five 'Sjöormen' and three 'Näcken' class boats. The first class is now reaching obsolescence, and will be replaced in the late 1980s by the new 'Västergötland' class operating the latest wire-guided torpedoes with the aid of an advanced locally-developed fire-control system.

Sweden still boasts two destroyers of the 'Halland' class, but these no longer serve any real purpose, the *Halland* having been put into reserve in 1983.

More faith is pinned in the considerable fast attack force, currently composed of 16 'Hugin' class fast attack craft (missile), 12 'Spica II' class FAC(M)s and six 'Spica I' class fast attack craft (torpedo). All these craft carry a 57-mm Bofors gun for use against opposing FACs, and the primary missile and torpedo armaments are highly advanced thanks to the use of radar-directed fire-control systems. A serious deficiency in the light forces is being remedied by the building of two 'Stockholm' class FAC(M)s, each based on the hull of the 'Spica II' class and fitted with six RB15 anti-ship missiles, but having the extra length and displacement for superior radar and the installation of command facilities. With these two units built, Karlskrona Varvet will turn its attentions to a six-unit replacement class for the 'Spica I' class FAC(T)s. Patrol is entrusted to 35 coastal patrol craft.

Mine warfare is also a feature of Sweden's coast defence planning, the navy operating no fewer than three large and 10 (to be increased to 13) coastal minelayers in addition to 16 small minelayers operated by the coastal artillery arm. On the other side of the coin there are 10 coastal and 18 inshore minesweepers, now somewhat outdated and to be complemented in the second half of the 1980s by 6 'Landsort' class minehunters able to operate an unmanned demolition catamaran.

Swedish ship strength

type	number	class
patrol submarine	0+4	'Västergötland'
	3	'Näcken'
	5	'Sjöormen'
	4	'Draken'
destroyer	1	'Halland'
	(1 reserve)	
FAC (missile)	0+2	'Stockholm'
	16	'Hugin'
	12	'Spica II'
FAC (torpedo)	6	'Spica I'
patrol craft	1	'Jägaren'
	4	'Hanö'
	1	'V'
	4	'SVK'
	8	'Skanor'
	17	misc
minelayer	1	'Carlskrona'
	2	'Alvsborg'
	1+3	'MUL 20'
	8	'MUL 10'
	1	'MUL 11'
	16	small minelayers
minesweeper (coastal)	2+4	'Landsort'
	10	'Arkö'
minesweeper (inshore)	3	'M 47'
	4	'M 43'
	3	'M 31'
	8	'M 15'
landing craft	11	LCM
	81	LCU
	54	LCA
other	52	misc

Switzerland

Switzerland operates 11 5·9-ton patrol boats on its lakes.

Syria

Syria is an implacable foe of Israel and staunch ally of the USSR, and has thus thought fit and been able to develop a navy out of all proportion to the country's real needs, and modelled closely on Soviet practice. Bases are maintained at Al Mina al Bayda, Baniyas, Latakia and Tartous, and current manpower strength is 2,500 including a proportion of 18-month conscripts, and there are reserves of another 2,500. A small naval air arm operates about 10 Kamov Ka-25 'Hormone' anti-submarine helicopters.

Though Syria's relationship with the USSR guarantees low-cost purchases of any ships she might need, it is reported that Syria is beginning to look to the West for new ship purchases, possibly because of the lack of operational flexibility and performance displayed by many smaller Soviet ship designs. What these purchases might be is as yet uncertain.

The main strength of the Syrian navy, as with most small navies supported by the USSR, lies with its missile-armed fast attack craft. However, Syria has in service two 'Petrya II' class frigates, which differ from their Soviet counterpart in having different torpedo and anti-submarine fits. This pair of ships will be joined in the near future by four 'Nanuchka II' class missile corvettes currently building in Leningrad. These latter are effective dual-role anti-ship and anti-aircraft vessels, carrying SS-N-2 and SA-N-4 missiles. This combination of 'Petya' and 'Nanuchka' class ships will dovetail nicely with Syria's light forces, comprising as they do eight 'Osa II', six 'Osa I' and six 'Komar' class fast attack craft (missile), backed by eight 'P 4' class fast attack craft (torpedo) and a number of patrol craft.

Syrian ship strength

type	number	class
frigate	2	'Petya II'
corvette	0+4	'Nanuchka II'
FAC (missile)	8	'Osa II'
	6	'Osa I'
	6	'Komar'
FAC (torpedo)	8	'P 4'
patrol craft	3	'CH'
	3	'Zhuk'
minesweeper (ocean)	1	'T 43'
minesweeper (coastal)	2	'Vanya'
minesweeper (inshore)	1	'Yevgenya'
other	1	diving ship

Tahiti

Operating from the port of Papeete is a sole 'EDIC' class landing craft, tank.

Taiwan

Beset by fears of communist Chinese aggression, the island republic of Taiwan commands one of the strongest navies in Asia, it being realized that such a force is a massive deterrent towards invasion from the mainland. However, the American diplomatic rapproachment with communist China has threatened to terminate US supplies to the island, and the nationalist Chinese government is now seeking to widen its supply base with extensive purchases from other Western countries, and with the development of an indigenous design, construction and equipment capability. Some 35 of Taiwan's primary ships and submarines date form the period immediately after World War II, so it is essential that a new construction programme be put in hand shortly if the island's navy is to match the new construction beginning to pour from mainland yards. This might mean an indigenous programme of smaller ships (frigates replacing destroyers, and corvettes replacing frigates) with powerful missile armament and advanced sensors, or the procurement of advanced foreign types. This latter course has already, however, run into serious political opposition from communist China. Taiwan's only current submarines, for example, are two 'Guppy II' class boats built in 1943 and 1944; but their planned replacement by two Dutch-built 'Zwaardvis (Improved)' class boats has been jeopardized by Chinese pressure on the government of The Netherlands.

Current Taiwanese naval strenth is 7,100 officers and 28,000 men (including a large number of 3-year conscripts), plus a marine corps of 3,000 officers and 26,000 men in two divisions. The naval forces operate from two main and one subsidiary base: Tsoying is the headquarters of the 1st Naval District, covering southern Taiwan and island groups to the south that are claimed by Taiwan; Chi-lung is the headquarters of the 3rd Naval District, covering northern Taiwan and the Matsu island group; and Makung in the Pescadores is the headquarters of the 2nd Naval District, covering the Pescadores, Quemoy and Wu Ch-iu islands, and home of the light forces. A small naval air arm operates 12 Hughes Model 500MD Defender helicopters for anti-submarine strike.

As noted above, the destroyer arm, though large, is antiquated thanks to its retention of 'Allen M. Sumner', 'Fletcher' and 'Gearing' class ships. These have been modernized in electronics and in parts of their armament (some units being fitted with the Hsiung Feng Taiwanese version of the Israeli Gabriel anti-ship missile), but are ripe for replacement. The same verdict must be passed on the frigate force, whose 'Charles Lawrence', 'Crosley' and 'Rudderow' class ships are of real use only as high-speed transports for marines. Though only three 'Auk' class ships strong, the corvette arm is in the same state, but it is reported that a new corvette is under construction by Vosper (Pte) of Singapore, perhaps as the lead ship for a new class. Details are not available for any worthwhile assessment.

The contrast of these elderly ships with the new units of the fast attack craft force is considerable. It was at first proposed to produce some 15 of the 'PSMM Mk 5' class fast attack craft (missile), but problems with the first two units, only partially remedied in the two succeeding half-sister craft, have led to the alteration of plans to substitute the 'Hai Ou' class fast attack craft (missile), derived from the Israeli 'Dvora' class and carrying two Hsiung Feng anti-ship missiles. It is expected that 34 'Hai Ou' class units will be built. These offensive assets are backed by 28 coastal patrol craft and an unknown number of harbour-defence motor launches.

Taiwnese ship strength

type	number	class
patrol submarine	0+2	'Zwaardvis (Improved)'
	2	'Guppy II'
destroyer	13	'Gearing (FRAM I/II)'
	1	'Gearing (FRAM II)'
	2	'Allen M. Sumner (FRAM II)'
	6	'Allen M. Sumner'
	4	'Fletcher'
frigate	0+0+?	'US'
	3	'Charles Lawrence'
	6	'Crosley'
	1	'Rudderow'
corvette	0+1	'Vosper'
	3	'Auk'
FAC (missile)	4	'PSMM Mk 5'
	34	'Hai Ou'
patrol craft	28+?	misc
minesweeper (coastal)	13	'Adjutant'
minesweeper (inshore)	1	minesweeping boat
	8	minesweeping launches
assault ship	1	'Ashland' LSD
	1	'Cabildo' LSD
landing ship	2	'LST 1-510'
	20	'LST 511-1152'
	4	'LSM 1'
landing craft	22	LCU
	258	LCM
	150	LCVP
other	62	misc

Tanzania

The influence of communist China is very strong in Tanzania, the manpower strength of about 700 volunteers being trained in Chinese tactical doctrines at the main base built by China at Dar es Salaam. Equipment is derived from Chinese, East German and North Korean sources for the most part, and the Tanazanian navy is equipped for the coastal role with relatively unsophisticated fast attack and patrol craft.

Tanzanian ship strength

type	number	class
FAC (gun)	7	'Shanghai II'
	4	'P 6'
FAC (torpedo)	4	'Huchuan'
patrol craft	1	'Poluchat'
	4	'Nampo'
	4	'Vosper 75-ft'
	2	'Schwalbe'
	4	'Yulin'
	2	'GDR 24-m'
landing craft	2	LCM
other	1	research vessel

Thailand

Already beset by the threat of Vietnamese operations in Kampuchea spilling over the border into eastern Thailand, the Thai kingdom has recently suffered the additional economic blow of being deleted from the USA's list of countries eligible for military aid at advantageous rates. Despite this setback, the Thai government has realized that long-term stability can only be ensured by moderate-sized but well-equipped armed forces, and has decided to build up the Thai navy with a view to containment of the border war and the protection of Thai interests in the Gulf of Siam and Andaman Sea. The main bases for the Royal Thai navy are thus at Bangkok, Paknam, Sattahip and Songhkla on the country's eastern seaboard, and a new base at Phang-Nga on the western seaboard. Manpower amounts to 7,000 officers and 23,000 other ranks, though this total includes 1,000 officers and 20,000 other ranks of the marine corps. A fairly high proportion of the total is found by 2-year conscripts, though most of these are allocated to the marine corps. There is also a small naval air arm concerned mostly with maritime patrol and anti-submarine warfare.

In contrast with several other Asian navies, that of Thailand is notable for its balance, though no submarines are operated. Though there remain in service one 'Cannon' and two 'Tacoma' class frigates of venerable vintage, Thailand also disposes of three more modern frigates, namely one British 'Makut Rajakumarn' and two US 'PF 103' class ships; these lack missile armament, but are moderately well off in terms of radar, gun armament and anti-submarine capability. This force will be enhanced considerably with the delivery of two 825-ton missile corvettes (one building in the USA and the other to be built in Thailand); precise details are lacking, but it seems likely that the design will be based on that of the Saudi Arabian 'Badr' class, with eight Harpoon anti-ship missiles.

Light forces are well suited to the waters and operational conditions prevailing around Thailand, and the Thai navy dispose of nine such craft, six armed with anti-ship missiles (three 'Ratcharit' class each with four Exocets and three 'Lürssen TNC 45' class each with five Gabriels) and three 'MV 400' class units with two 76-mm (3-in) OTO-Melara Compact guns for the engagement of hostile fast attack craft. Local patrol and early warning is provided by a substantial patrol force with indigenously- and US-built vessels.

Thai ship strength

type	number	class
frigate	1	'Makut Rajakumarn'
	2	'PF 103'
	1	'Cannon'
	2	'Tacoma'
corvette	0+2	'825-ton'
FAC (missile)	3	'Ratcharit'
	3	'Lürssen TNC 45'
FAC (gun)	3	'MV 400'
patrol craft	4	'Scattahip'
	6	'PC 461'
	3	'Cape'
	6	'PGM 71'
	7	'RTND 31·8-m'
	12	'Swift'
	12	'Thai 19·5-m'
	37	'PBR Mk II'
	3	'RPC'
minesweeper (coastal)	0+4	?
minesweeper (inshore)	4	'Bluebird'
	5	minesweeping boats
landing ship	1	'LST 1-510'
	4	'LST 511-1152'
	3	'LSM 1'
	2	'LSIL 351'
landing craft	11	LCU
	26	LCM
	12	LCVP
	4	LCA
other	21	misc

Togo

With 105 men and a base at Tome, the Togolese navy is a small force dedicated solely to coastal defence with two 'CNE 32-m' coastal patrol craft and (possibly) two other craft.

Tonga

The island kingdom of Tonga formed its navy in 1973, and now operates a small force of two 'Brooke 45-ft' coastal patrol craft and one Australian LCM from Touliki Base at Nuku'alofa. There is also a very small 'royal yacht'.

Trinidad & Tobago

The coast guard of Trinidad & Tobago has a personnel strength of 585 volunteers, and from its base at Staubles Bay operates a fleet of six large and seven coastal patrol craft plus a sail-training ship and two survey launches. And from a base at Chaguaramas, the Trinidad & Tobago police force operate six coastal patrol craft.

Trinidad & Tobago ship strength

type	number	class
patrol craft	2	'Type CG 40'
	2	'Chaguaramas'
	2	'Trinity'
	4	'Wasp 17-m'
	3	misc
other	3	misc

Trinidad & Tobago police strength

type	number	class
coastal patrol craft	2	'Wasp 20-m'
	1	'Wasp 14-m'
	2	'Fairey Sword'
	1	'Watercraft 45-ft'

Tunisia

With a strength of 2,600 including some 500 1-year conscripts, the Tunisian navy operates a small but relatively obsolescent navy from bases at Susa and Tunis. The largest ship in commission is a 'Savage' class frigate, for which a replacement is being considered if finances permit, but the main strength of the fleet lies with three 'La Combattante IIIM' class fast attack craft (missile). These are scheduled for delivery by the end of 1984, and each carry eight Exocet anti-ship missiles. Other assets are a variety of patrol craft.

Tunisian ship strength

type	number	class
frigate	1	'Savage'
FAC (missile)	2+1	'La Combattante IIIM'
FAC (gun)	2	'Shanghai II'
patrol craft	1	'Le Fougeux'
	2	'Tazarka'
	3	'P 48'
	2	'Adjutant'
	4	'CNE 31·5-m'
	6	'CNE 25-m'
	2	'Aresa 23-m'
other	1	tug

Turkey

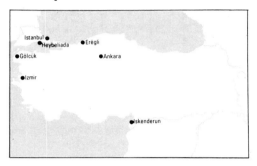

In naval and well as in other respects, Turkey is one of the most important members of the NATO alliance, as she straddles the only waterway by which the Soviets can bring their Black Sea Fleet into the Mediterranean. To this end the Turks maintain a large and relatively efficient Turkish navy, though the overall capability of the force is subject to considerable speculation because of the age and relative obsolescence of many combatant warships. Turkey's strategic attentions are also divided by the venerable dispute with Greece in the Aegean and Cyprus, the former problem assuming increasingly serious overtones as the economic value of the disputed sea bed becomes increasingly apparent. The current manpower strength of the Turkish navy is 45,000 including 5,000 officers and men of the marine corps; of this total some 36,000 are conscripts fulfilling a 20-month national service obligation. There is also a small naval air arm that operates helicopters for anti-submarine and utility roles, and also 20 Grumman S-2 Tracker aircraft for maritime patrol and anti-submarine warfare. The main naval base is at Gölcük, with other bases at Istanbul, Eregli, Izmir and Iskenderun.

The balance of the Turkish navy is somewhat old fashioned, largely because of the elderly ships operated as major component of the fleet. Much should be expected from a patrol submarine force of 17 boats, but of these only the current six 'Type 209' class units can be regarded as truly effective, the various 'Guppy' submarines and the single 'Tang' class boat on loan from the USA being more useful for show and training than for operations. Improvements are in hand, however, for another six 'Type 209' class boats are to be built under licence in Turkey, complementing the three already built at Gölcük, to permit the retirement of the obsolescent American boats.

The suface force comprises a main strength of destroyers backed by a few frigates. But of the 13 ex-US destroyers currently in service, only the seven 'Gearing (FRAM I)' class ships can be considered to be of any real value, and then only because they are fitted with ASROC missile launchers. None of the ships have modern anti-aircraft armament (missiles of CIWS mountings), so their survivability against modern air attack must be highly doubtful. It is worth noting that the sole 'Robert H. Smith' class destroyer has been converted for minelaying.

Better things can be expected of the frigate arm, for Turkey has launched a programme of four 'Meko 200' class frigates (two to be built in West Germany and the other pair at Gölcük) supplementing the two 'Köln' class frigates received from West Germany and the two 'Berk' class ships built indigenously. The two Turkish-built ships are to a design modified from that of the US 'Claud Jones' class, and could profitably be modernized with a sensible anti-aircraft defence.

Considerably more can realistically be expected of the Turkish light forces, for in recent years the service has received a number of useful fast attack craft, notably five 'Lürssen FPB 57' and nine 'Kartal' class fast attack craft (missile), the former each carrying eight Exocet anti-ship missiles and the latter each armed with four Penguin Mk 2 anti-ship missiles. There are also four ex-West German 'Jaguar' class fast attack craft (torpedo), each fitted with four 533-mm (21-in) tubes. This offensive force is backed by a substantial fleet of large patrol craft.

Given the importance of the Bosphorus, the Turkish navy has wisely invested in both offensive and defensive mine warfare force. In addition to the converted 'Robert H. Smith' class destroyer mentioned above, there is also on strength one 'Falster' class minelayer and five 'LSM 1' class landing ships converted into coastal minelayers; mine defence of harbours is entrusted to a single 'YMP' class coastal minelayer. Defensive mine warfare forces are not as capable, the complement of 22 coastal minesweepers, four inshore minesweepers and nine minehunting boats being perhaps adequate in numbers but inadequate in modernity and sensor capability for all but conventional sweeping against 'unintelligent' mines.

Also available in relatively large numbers in the Turkish navy are amphibious vessels which, though in part elderly, have recently been improved by the injection of modern Turkish-built ships.

Turkish ship strength

type	number	class
patrol submarine	5+1+6	'Type 209'
	2	'Guppy III'
	7	'Guppy IIA'
	1	'Guppy IA'
	1	'Tang'
destroyer	2	'Gearing (FRAM II)'
	7	'Gearing (FRAM I)'
	2	'Carpenter (FRAM I)'
	1	'Allen M. Sumner (FRAM II)'
frigate	0+4	'Meko 200'
	2	'Köln'
	2	'Berk'
FAC (missile)	5	'Lürssen FPB 57'
	9	'Kartal'
FAC (gun)	1	'Girne'
	2	'Asheville'
FAC (torpedo)	4	'Jaguar'
patrol craft	12	'AB 25'
	6	'PCE 1638'
	4	'PGM 71'
	4	'USCG 83-ft'
minelayer	1	'Robert H. Smith'
	1	'Falster'
	5	'LSM 1 (Modified)'
	1	'YMP'
minesweeper (coastal)	12	'Adjutant'
	4	'MCB'
	6	'Vegesack'
minesweeper (inshore)	4	'Cape'
	9	minehunting boats
landing ship	2	'Terrebonne Parish' LST
	2	'LST 511-1152'
	2+1	LST
landing craft	13	LCT
	16	LCU
	20	LCM
other	100	misc

UK

The Royal Navy is the only world-power navy to have been involved in combat in recent years, during the 1982 conflict with Argentina for possession of the Falkland Islands (Malvinas), and is currently re-evaluating its tactics and ships in the light of experience in the South Atlantic. The problem is made the more difficult by the fact the Royal Navy is designed essentially for anti-submarine operations in the North Atlantic in collaboration with other NATO navies, and that though some modern weapons were employed by Argentina, the Falklands war was atypical. Several important lessons were learned, however, and these included the need for better damage-control conditions, more reliable electronics, the provision of an airborne early-warning capability, and provision of better and more numerous point-defence weapons for engagement of aircraft and sea-skimming anti-ship missiles. Also fully vindicated was the utility of even small aircraft-carriers able to operate V/STOL aircraft as well as helicopters. The task now faced by the Royal Navy is the integration of these lessons into the overall scheme of the British maritime task, which centres on the nuclear-missile ballistic-missile submarine force as the UK's strategic deterrent force, and the provision of anti-submarine task forces with adequate air protection for the security of convoys crossing the North Atlantic in time of war. The current strength of the fleet, which must also have a capability for excursions such as that into the South Atlantic, is hardly adequate by modern standards, but growth and the replacement of older ships is made very difficult by rising costs and relative shortage of finance for matériel and manpower.

The current manpower strength of the Royal Navy is 68,200 volunteers, comprising 9,800 officers plus 58,400 ratings and Royal Marines, supplemented by 3,500 members of the Women's Royal Naval Service. Reserves amount to 25,800 regular reserves and 4,300 volunteer reserves. The Royal Marines are organized as a single brigade of three Royal Marine Commandos plus support services, and the Fleet Air Arm operates three fighter/light attack squadrons, eight helicopter anti-submarine flights, two commando assault helicopter squadrons and their associated utility and training components.

The organization of the fleet is into three surface-force flotillas, the Submarine Command and the Mine Countermeasures Command of four squadrons. The 1st Flotilla consists of one 'County' class cruiser, one destroyer squadron and three frigate squadrons; the 3rd Destroyer Squadron is made up of HMS *Newcastle*, three destroyers and three frigates; the 1st Frigate Squadron is made up of HMS *Ajax* and seven frigates; the 6th Frigate Squadron is made up of HMS *Plymouth* and seven frigates; and the 7th Frigate Squadron is made up of HMS *Cleopatra* and six frigates. The 2nd Flotilla consists of two 'County' class cruisers, HMS *Battleaxe*, one destroyer squadron and three frigate squadrons. The 5th Destroyer Squadron has HMS *Exeter* and four destroyers; the 2nd Frigate Squadron has HMS *Broadsword* and two

frigates; the 4th Frigate Squadron has HMS *Avenger* and five frigates; and the 8th Frigate Squadron has HMS *Andromeda* and five frigates. The 3rd Flotilla has the Royal Navy's aircraft-carrier and amphibious assets, plus HMS *Bristol* and the antarctic patrol ship HMS *Endurance*. The Submarine Command has four squadrons, the 1st Squadron with eight patrol submarines, the 2nd Squadron four fleet submarines, the 3rd Squadron three fleet submarines and two patrol submarines, and the 10th Squadron three ballistic-missile submarines. Finally, the Mine Counter-measures command has its four subordinate MCM squadrons.

British ship strength

type	number	class
nuclear-powered ballistic-missile submarine	0+0+4 or 5	?
	4	'Resolution'
nuclear-powered fleet submarine	1+4+1	'Trafalgar'
	6	'Swiftsure'
	3	'Churchill'
	2	'Valiant'
patrol submarine	0+0+?	'Type 2400'
	13	'Oberon'
	2	'Porpoise'
aircraft-carrier	2	'Invincible'
cruiser	1	'Type 82'
	3	'County'
destroyer	9+3	'Sheffield'
frigate	5+3+5	'Broadsword'
	6	'Amazon'
	24	'Leander'
	8	'Rothesay'
patrol craft	0+5	'Peacock'
	2	'OPV Mk 2'
	7	'Island'
	4	'Bird'
	5	'Ton (Modified)'
	1	'Ford'
	1	'Z 28'
minelayer	1	'Abdiel'
minesweeper (coastal)	6+5	'Hunt'
	28	'Ton'
	1	'Wilton'
	2	'Venturer'
assault ship	2	'Fearless'
	5	'Sir Bedivere' (RFA)
	2	LLS (RFA)
landing craft	2	LCL
	2+3+4	'Mulberry' LCR
	13	'LCM Mk 9'
	8	'Avon' RPL

	26	LCVP
	3	LCPL
other	222+5	misc

Uruguay

Given that her two neighbours are both considerably larger, more populous and wealthy than she is, Uruguay has concluded sensibly not to try to match the naval power of Argentina and Brazil, so the Uruguayan navy is a small and not particularly advanced force operating a mix of elderly surface combatants leavened with more advanced light forces. Naval manpower is 5,000 including the naval air arm and marine corps, all of them volunteers. The main naval base is Montevideo, and considerable emphasis is place on the air arm, with fixed-wing maritime patrol and anti-submarine aircraft complemented by utility helicopters and a light attack capability.

Uruguayan ship strength

type	number	class
destroyer	1	'Gearing'
frigate	1	'Dealey'
	2	'Cannon'
corvette	1	'Auk'
patrol craft	3	'Vigilante'
	1	'Adjutant'
	1	'CNRA 41·8-m'
	3	misc
landing craft	2	LCM
	5	LCU
other	7	misc

USA

The US Navy is the largest and most powerful navy the world has yet seen, possessing truly global capability for the protection of the USA and its interests, and for the projection of American power. The three principal components of the US Navy are its submarine arm, heavily biased in favour of nuclear-powered boats; its maritime air arm, centred on multi-role aircraft-carriers carrying a diversity of ffensive/defensive aircraft and protected by missile-armed cruisers and detroyers; and its amphibious arm, dedicated to the carriage and shoreward delivery of the US Marine Corps, and usually protected by frigates. The submarine arm is being rationalised at the moment, with heavy emphasis on the rapid construction of the 'Ohio' class SSBN and 'Los Angeles' class SSN to allow the retirement of older classes. The SSBNs are being equipped with the Trident I C4 strategic missiles as a replacement for the older Poseidon C3, and will soon begin to receive the definitive Trident II D5; combined with improved communications capability for submerged submarines (thanks to the development of ELF and new TACAMO systems), greater reliance can be placed on the rapid and accurate response capabilities of the SSBN force, helping to promote it towards the primary position amongst the elements of the US offensive strategic triad (land-based missiles, air-released bombs and missiles and submarine-launched missiles). The SSN force is designed for two offensive/defensive functions, namely the defence of the USA by attacks on Soviet missile-carrying submarines, and the defence of carrier task groups by attacks on Soviet submarines equipped with torpedoes (of which about half are nuclear-tipped). But while in theory the concentration on the 'Ohio' and 'Los Angeles' classes is excellent, offering the possibility of large standardized forces, the pro-

Treasure Island
Longbeach
San Diego
Coronado
Bangor
Boston
New London
Brooklyn
Philadelphia
Washington, DC
Little Creek
Newport
Charleston
Mayport

gramme has run into immense problems of cost escalation and production slippages, requiring the retention of older vessels as a stop-gap. Moreover, while the capability of the new classes is unquestionable, so too is their vulnerability, for both classes are extremely large and relatively noisy. And the very size of the 'Los Angeles' class raises another problem, for it makes it difficult for the boats of the class to operate in the shallow waters of the large continental shelf areas, where Soviet boats could well lurk for some time. It would seem sensible, therefore, for the US Navy to develop a new class of diesel-electric hunter-killer submarine for this specific purpose, but so entrenched is the position of the nuclear-boat lobby that this seems impossibly difficult to achieve.

Naval aviation in the US Navy rests with the aircraft-carrier force, planned at 15 carrier air wings (one per carrier) but currently operational as only 12 carrier air wings. This is still a formidable capability, given that each carrier air wing can muster up to 80 or more aircraft (usually two fighter squadrons, one medium attack squadron, one light attack squadron and two anti-submarine squadrons, plus support aircraft) of the US Navy and US Marine Corps, but leave the US Navy with little reserve capacity. Four more of the massive nuclear-powered 'Nimitz' class carriers are planned or building, which will improve matters considerably, but in the short term the deficiency is being made good in an alternative fashion by the reactivation and modernization (with missiles and modern sensors) of two (possibly four) 'Iowa' class battleships. Though these cannot carry the aircraft of a carrier air wing (though a complement of V/STOL strike aircraft is planned when the ships are modernized yet further), they do have formidable gun and missile firepower. Escort of each carrier task group is theoretically entrusted to two missile-armed cruisers (nuclear-powered in groups which are centred on a nuclear carrier) plus a number of missile-armed destroyers. A shortfall in numbers has often meant, however, that frigates have to be included in the escort force as part of the outer screen. The situation should be improved greatly with the delivery of additional 'Ticonderoga' class cruisers, with their highly capable AEGIS analysis and control functions, and with the first arrivals of the 'Arleigh Burke' class destroyers at the end of the decade. Hand-in-hand with this ship and sensor modification programme goes a constant upgrading of the vital Standard missile, designed

principally as an air-defence weapon but possessing a limited anti-ship capability and being developed into a longer-range and more accurate weapon system. Other missile developments centre on the widespread deployment of the medium-range Harpoon anti-ship missile, and the installation on larger ships of the Tomahawk cruise missile for long-range anti-ship defence. Close-range air-defence remains a problem, the Sea Sparrow system being too slow in launch, and the Phalanx 20-mm CIWS mounting lacking sufficient punch for last-ditch defence against sea-skimming anti-ship missiles. It is anticipated that the capability and versatility of shipboard missile systems will be much enhanced later in the decade by the adoption of vertical-launch systems capable of handling anti-ship, anti-aircraft and anti-submarine missiles of several types.

Amphibious forces are in something of a quandary at the moment, for the precise role of the US Marine Corps remains uncertain. Amphibious operations are clearly important, but their precise nature (and perhaps their vulnerability) remains open to question. Nevertheless their ships are being developed and built as a matter of urgency as the need to replace older units becomes more apparent. One of the problems is that these large and lightly defended targets require extensive escort protection from frigates armed with anti-ship and anti-aircraft missiles, and that the frigates are in short supply because of the need for their deployment in carrier task group escort forces.

The US Navy has an all-volunteer personnel strength, this amounting at the moment to some 569,000 including 42,700 women. Naval air power, which has about 1,450 combat aircraft and 160 combat helicopters, is included in this total, and operates 24 fighter squadrons, 12 medium attack squadrons, 24 light attack squadrons, 11 shipboard anti-submarine squadrons, 11 fixed- and 17 rotary-wing anti-submarine squadrons, 12 airborne early warning squadrons, 24 land-based maritime reconnaissance and anti-submarine squadrons, two mine countermeasures helicopter squadrons, 22 operational conversion units, 18 training squadrons and 17 miscellaneous squadrons.

Operationally, the US Navy is divided into four fleets controlled by two command organizations: headquartered at Norfolk, Virginia, the Atlantic Fleet controls the 2nd Fleet (headquarters in Norfolk) and the 6th Fleet (headquarters at Gaeta in Italy) for

operations in the Mediterranean; and head-quartered at Pearl Harbor, Hawaii, the Pacific Fleet controls the 3rd Fleet (headquarters at Pearl Harbor) and the 7th Fleet (headquarters at Yokohama in Japan for operations in the western Pacific with detachments into the Indian Ocean and Persian Gulf areas). With other continental bases at Bangor, Boston, Brunswick, Charleston, Jacksonville, Kings Bay, New London, New Orleans and Newport, the 2nd Fleet has overseas bases at Guantanamo Bay (Cuba), Holy Loch (UK), Keflavik (Iceland) and Roosevelt Roads (Puerto Rico), and generally deploys 31 SSBNs, 41 SSNs, 76 surface combatants and 27 amphibious warfare vessels. Apart from its base at Gaeta, the 6th Fleet has a base at La Rota in Spain and at La Maddalena, Naples and Sigonella in Italy, and usually musters some two SSNs, one or two aircraft-carriers and about 38 other surface combatants and amphibious warfare vessels. The 3rd Fleet has additional bases at Adak, Long Beach, San Diego, San Francisco and Whidbey Island, and has a typical strength of two SSBNs, 30 SSNs, three carriers, one battleship and about 44 other surface combatants plus 31 amphibious warfare vessels. And the 7th Fleet, with additional bases at Agena and Apra Harbor on Guam, Midway Island, Subic Bay in the Philippines and forward facilities in the Indian Ocean at Diego Suarez, operates a few SSNs on temporary assignment, plus some 45 surface combatants including three or four carriers; the detachments in the Indian Ocean and Persian Gulf, often suported by vessels from the 6th Fleet, generally comprise a carrier task group with five escorts in the former, and two destroyers plus a command ship in the latter.

US Navy Reserves amount to an extra 87,900 men, and these man a varying number of ships, normally about three destroyers and six frigates, and also provide the manpower strength for two additional carrier air wings, two maritime reconnaissance wings and one tactical support wing (all with fixed-wing aircraft), plus one helicopter wing.

The US Coast Guard service is administered by the Department of Transportation, but in war comes under the operational control of the US Navy as part of the armed forces. Regular strength is 38,800 including 1,800 women, and there are 11,800 reservists. Ship assets comprise 17 high-endurance cutters (small destroyers), 28 medium-endurance cutters (lightweight frigates), six icebreakers, 76 patrol craft, and 118 other craft. The US Coast Guard also possesses a small air arm with 41 fixed- and rotary-wing aircraft, most of them dedicated to patrol and search-and-rescue.

US ship strength

type	number	class
nuclear-powered ballistic-missile submarine	5+5+14	'Ohio'
	12	'Benjamin Franklin'
	19	'Lafayette'
nuclear-powered fleet submarine	30+4+	
	7+21	'Los Angeles'
	1	'Glenard P. Lipscomb'
	1	'Narwhal'
	37	'Sturgeon'
	3 (1)	'Ethan Allen'
	2 (1)	'George Washington'
	13	'Thresher'
	1	'Tullibee'
	5	'Skipjack'
	4	'Skate'
	1	'Seawolf'

patrol submarine	3	'Barbel'
	1	'Darter'
	1	'Grayback'
	1 (1)	'Tang'
	1	'Dolphin'
nuclear-powered multi-role aircraft-carrier	3+3+2	'Nimitz'
	1	'Enterprise'
	3	'Kitty Hawk'
	1	'John F. Kennedy'
multi-role aircraft-carrier	3 (1)	'Forrestal'
	2	'Midway'
aircraft-carrier	1 (1)	'Hancock'
	(1)	'Intrepid'
anti-submarine aircraft-carrier	(2)	'Essex (Modernized)'
battleship	1+1 (2)	'Iowa'
nuclear-powered guided-missile cruiser	4	'Virginia'
	2	'California'
	1	'Truxtun'
	1	'Bainbridge'
	1	'Long Beach'
guided-missile cruiser	2+8+14	'Ticonderoga'
	9	'Belknap'
	9	'Leahy'
	(2)	'Albany'
gun cruiser	(2)	'Des Moines'
guided-missile destroyer	0+0+60	'Arleigh Burke'
	4	'Kidd'
	10	'Coontz'
	23	'Charles F. Adams'
	(2)	'Forrest Sherman (Converted)'
	(2)	'Hull (Converted)'
destroyer	31+1	'Spruance'
	(9)	'Forrest Sherman'
	(5)	'Hull'
	(2)	'Gearing FRAM I'
guided-missile frigate	39+2+9	'Oliver Hazard Perry'
	6	'Brooke'
	46	'Knox'
	10	'Garcia'
	1	'Glover'
	2	'Bronstein'
FAC (missile)	6	'Pegasus'
FAC (gun)	(4)	'Asheville'
patrol craft	(1)	'High Point'
	19	'PB Mks 1 and 2'
inshore patrol craft	5	'PCF' class
river patrol craft	37	'PBR Mks 1 and 2'
	22	small troop carriers
minesweeper (ocean)	0+2+19	'Avenger'
	(2)	'Acme'
	3 (16)	'Aggressive'
minesweeper (coastal)	0+0+17	'MSH'
minesweeper (inshore)	7	minesweeping boats
amphibious command ship	2	'Blue Ridge'
assault ship	0+0+12	'LHD'
	5	'Tarawa'
	7	'Iwo Jima'
amphibious transport dock	0+0+1	'LPD 71'
	12	'Austin'
	2	'Raleigh'
landing ship, dock	0+2+10	'Whidbey Island'
	5	'Anchorage'
	8	'Thomaston'
landing ship, tank	18 (2)	'Newport News'
	(3)	'De Soto County'
amphibious cargo ship	5	'Charleston'
landing craft, air cushion	9+99	'LCAC' air-cushion
	51	'LCU 1610'
	4	'LCU 1466'
	?	LCM
other	about 1,200	misc
	(about 1,250)	misc

Note: numbers in brackets refer to ships in reserve or attached to the Naval Reserve Force.

USSR

The Soviet Navy is a truly formidable force, which since World War II and under the long-term professional leadership of Admiral S. G. Gorshkov has emerged from third-rate status as an obsolescent coastal defence force into a true blue-water navy of enormous power and capability. It must still protect the integrity of the USSR against amphibious and air (aircraft and missile) attack, but is also one of the mainstays of the Soviet strategic nuclear capability and has recently emerged as a proper instrument of 'power projection' in any part of the world thanks to the development of capable aircraft-carriers and escorts backed by highly effective support forces. For long the chief threat posed by the US Navy to the USSR lay in its carrier groups and nuclear-powered missile submarines, and the USSR has devoted enormous effort into the development of weapons and tactics to counter these two strategic threats, often relying on numbers rather than quality in ships designed largely for a single highly specific role. But in recent years the Soviets have made great qualitative advances, allowing the development and production in useful numbers of true multi-role types; this has, in turn, allowed a shift in strategic doctrine away from the previously-established strategic defensive undertaken by offensive tactical forces towards multi-role strategies undertaken in a spirit always of the offensive. Further evidence of the Soviets' desire for the true strategic offensive coupled with worldwide 'power-projection' capability is provided by the constant updating of ships with sensors and weapons in no real way inferior to those of the NATO forces, by the rapid evolution of Soviet tactical expertise, and by the willingness of the Soviet Navy to 'show the flag' in any part of the world. Such capability inevitably destabilizes portions of the world conidered vital to Western security, and also poses a genuine threat to NATO sea communications.

It is believed that the manpower strength of the Soviet Navy is about 500,000 officers and men; of these about 90,000 are long-term regulars (both officers and petty officers) while the balance of 410,000 is found by conscripts, who do a 3-year period of service if afloat and a 2-year period if ashore. At any one time the Soviet Navy has 200,000 men afloat, 65,000 allocated to the naval air arm, 55,000 involved in training, 15,000 deployed in naval infantry units and 18,000 devoted to coastal defence. The balance of 157,000 men is devoted to shore support functions. Of the subsidiary arms already mentioned, the naval infantry (marine) corps is divided into five brigades and one naval infantry division, the latter allocated to the Pacific Fleet. The coast defence force is designed to provide cover for the approaches to main naval bases, and operates heavy guns and perhaps 100 SS-C-1b 'Sepal' surface-to-surface missiles based on the SS-N-3 anti-ship missile. Considerably more important, however, is the naval air arm, which is organized as four air forces, one allocated to each of the main fleets. Each of these air forces is organized in the same way as the conventional air arm into divisions, regiments and squadrons, and has at least 775 combat aircraft and 300 combat helicopters plus about 450 non-combat fixed- and rotary-wing aircraft. The roles undertaken by the naval air arm

include maritime reconnaissance, maritime strike, electronic warfare, anti-submarine warfare and mine countermeasures from land bases, and light attack, anti-submarine warfare and electronic warfare from ship platforms. It is worth noting that an increasingly large proportion of Soviet ships (excluding the aircraft-carriers now in service and under construction) is fitted for the operation of helicopters.

The Soviet Navy is organized into four large fleets. The Northern Fleet has about 118,000 men and has bases at Severomorsk (headquarters), Motovsky Gulf, Polyarny and Severodvinsk. This fleet controls most of the USSR's nuclear-powered submarines, generally deploying 45 SSBNs, two SSBs, 28 SSGNs, eight SSGs, 40 SSNs, 55 SSs and one aircraft-carrier plus about 275 other surface combatants and support ships. The Baltic Fleet has about 105,000 men and has bases at Baltiisk (headquarters), Kronshtadt, Kalingrad, Liepaja, Riga and Tallinn. The fleet has relatively few submarines, usually about six SSBs, five SSGs and 23 SSs complemented by about 405 surface combatants and support ships. The Black Sea Fleet controls about 105,000 men and has bases at Sevastopol (headquarters), Balaklava, Nikolayev, Odessa, Poti and Tuapse. Submarine assets for this fleet are normally one SSG and about 22 SSs, while the surface forces comprise one aircraft-carrier and about 390 other surface combatants and support ships. And finally there is the Pacific Fleet, with about 121,000 men and bases at Vladivostok (headquarters), Komsomolsk, Magadan, Petropavlovsk and Sovetskaya Gavan. This fleet disposes of the second largest number of submarines, namely 24 SSBNs, seven SSBs, 20 SSGNs, four SSGs, 22 SSNs and 50 SSs, plus one aircraft-carrier and 465 other surface combatants and support ships. Within these allocations of surface forces, it is worth noting that the Baltic and Pacific Fleets have a higher proportion of light forces than either the Northern or Black Sea Fleets, as well as larger mine countermeasures and amphibious forces. The Northern Fleet has the greatest number of submarines, and also particularly powerful long-range surface forces in the form of the single 'Kirov' class nuclear-powered battle-cruiser plus missile-armed escorts of all sizes and the relevant underway replenishment assets to give them worldwide operational capability. This latter is promoted by the availability of overseas bases in Africa, the Middle East, the Far East and the Caribbean. Supply and service bases have been established in such areas, together with the airfields that permit Soviet naval aircraft to undertake exceptionally long reconnaissance flights before returning to the USSR.

Soviet ship strength

type	number	class
nuclear-powered ballistic-missile submarine	2+?	'Typhoon'
	14+1	'Delta III'
	4	'Delta II'
	18	'Delta I'
	25	'Yankee'
	1	'Hotel III'
	5	'Hotel II'
ballistic-missile submarine	1	'Golf III'
	13	'Golf II'
	1	'Golf V'
nuclear-powered cruise-missile submarine	1+?	'Oscar'
	1	'Papa'
	8	'Charlie II'
	11	'Charlie I'
	29	'Echo II'
cruise-missile submarine	16	'Juliett'

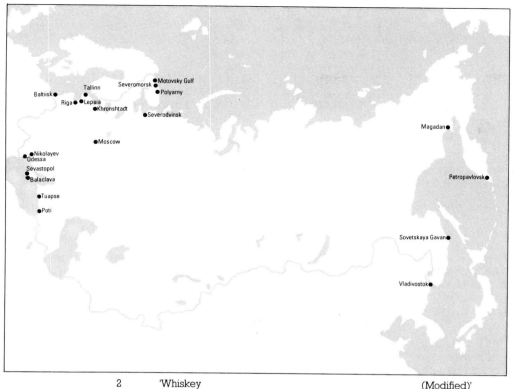

type	number	class
	2	'Whiskey Long-Bin (Modified)'
nuclear-powered fleet submarine	6+?	'Alfa'
	9	'Yankee'
	16+?	'Victor III'
	7	'Victor II'
	16	'Victor I'
	5	'Echo I'
	12	'November'
patrol submarine	4+1	'Kilo'
	18+2	'Tango'
	60	'Foxtrot'
	4 (+5 reserve)	'Zulu IV'
	12	'Romeo'
	50 (+80 reserve)	'Whiskey'
nuclear-powered aircraft-carrier	0+1+?	?
aircraft-carrier	3+1	'Kiev'
nuclear-powered battle-cruiser	1+1	'Kirov'
helicopter cruiser	2	'Moskva'
cruiser	1+2	'Krasina'
	7	'Kara'
	10	'Kresta II'
	4	'Kresta I'
	4	'Kynda'
	12	'Sverdlov'
destroyer	2+4	'Sovremenny'
	2+4	'Udaloy'
	6	'Kashin (Modified)'
	13	'Kashin'
	3	'Kildin (Modified)'
	1	'Kildin'
	8	'Kanin'
	8	'SAM Kotlin'
	12	'Kotlin (Modified)'
	6	'Kotlin'
	10 (+10 reserve)	'Skory'
frigate	11	'Krivak II'
	21+?	'Krivak I'
	1	'Koni'
	47	'Riga'
	31	'Grisha III'
	6	'Grisha II'
	15	'Grisha I'
	9	'Mirka II'
	9	'Mirka I'
	1	'Petya II'
	25	'Petya II'
	11	'Petya I (Modified)'
	7	'Petya I'
corvette	5+1	'Nanuchka III'
	17	'Nanuchka I'
	1	'Tarantul II'
	4+3	'Tarantul I'
patrol ship	1	'Purga'
	18	'T 58'
radar picket	2	'Whiskey Canvas Bag'
	2	'T 58/AGR'
	11	'T 43/AGR'
FAC (missile)	1	'Sarancha'
	15+1	'Matka'
	50	'Osa II'
	70	'Osa I'
FAC (torpedo)	17	'Shershen'
	30	'Turya'
FAC (patrol)	10+?	'Pauk'
	59	'Poti'
	1	'Babochka'
	30	'SO I'
	90	'Stenka'
	1	'Slepen'
	8	'Pchela'
coastal patrol craft	30	'Zhuk (KGB)'
river patrol craft	80	'Schmel'
	0+15	misc
minelayer	3	'Alesha'
minesweeper (ocean)	1	'Natya II'
	34	'Natya I'
	45	'Yurka'
	65	'T 43'
	2	'Andryusha'
minesweeper (coastal)	42	'Sonya'
	3	'Zhenya'
	3	'Vanya (Modified)'
	69	'Vanya'
	10	'Sasha'
minesweeper (inshore)	45	'Yevgenya'
	10	'Ilyusha'
	7	'Olya'
minesweeping boat	10	'TR 40'
	40	'K 8'
assault ship	2	'Ivan Rogov'
landing ship	16+1	'Ropucha' LST
	14	'Alligator' LST
	50	'Polnochny' LSM
	5	'MP 4' LSM
landing craft	20	'Vydra' LCU
	15	'SMB I' LCU
	6	'Ondatra' LCM
	?	'T 4' LCM
hovercraft	60	misc
other	600+?	misc

Venezuela

In recent years the Venezuelan economy has been buoyed by considerable oil wealth, but a decline in oil price coupled with political indiscretions has led to a curtailment in Venezuela's ability to import modern naval craft. This notwithstanding, the Venezuelan navy may be reckoned the most formidable in the southern half of the Caribbean, with a nicely balanced force of underwater and surface forces backed by an effective naval air arm (including fixed-wing anti-submarine aircraft and rotary-wing anti-submarine machines for embarkation) and marine corps. Manpower strength is some 9,000 including a proportion of 18-month conscripts, and of this total 4,000 are absorbed by the three battalions of the marine corps. The Venezuelan navy's main base is at Puerto Cabello, with a smaller base at La Guaira and lesser facilities at Falcon and Puerto de Hierro.

The 'Type 209' submarine designed and produced in West Germany has proved very popular in South America, and two boats of this class form the main operational strength of the Venezuelan navy's submarine arm, a single 'Guppy II' class boat being used mainly for training.

Major surface combatants are all of Italian origins, the most formidable grouping in the area being Venezuela's six 'Lupo' class frigates. Equipped with varied gun armament, Otomat surface-to-surface missiles, Aspide surface-to-air missiles and an embarked multi-role helicopter, these vessels are genuine multi-role types. They are backed by two older 'Almirante Clemente' class frigates built in the 1950s in Italy and now beginning to reveal their obsolescence, and the surface force will be considerably bolstered with the purchase of four 'Assad' class misile corvettes from Italy, bridging the gap between the frigates and the six 'Constitucion' class fast attack craft built by Vosper-Thornycroft: three of these are gun craft with the excellent 76-mm (3-in) OTO-Melara Compact gun, and the other three missile craft each with two Otomat anti-ship missiles.

Venezuelan ship strength

type	number	class
patrol submarine	2	'Type 209'
	1	'Guppy II'
frigate	6	'Lupo'
	2	'Almirante Clemente'
corvette	0+0+4	'Assad'
FAC (missile)	3	'Constitucion'
FAC (gun)	3	'Constitucion'
landing ship	1	'Achelous' LSR
	1	'LSM 1'
	0+4	LST
landing craft	12	LCVP
other	17	misc

Vietnam

It is difficult to gauge the size and effectiveness of the Vietnamese navy, for this force inherited an enormous number of vessels from the Americans and South Vietnamese, many of which have since been rendered non-operational by lack of need or lack of spares. With bases at Cam Ranh Bay, Can Tho, Chuhai, Haiphong, Hue, Quang Khe Qui Nhon and Vinh Long, the Vietnamese navy is designed principally for coastal patrol and the riverine support of the

Vietnamese forces operating in Kampuchea. Personnel strength is about 4,000, a proportion of them specialists conscripted for 3- or 4-year terms. The list below is believed to represent a fairly accurate assessment of the Vietnamese navy's operational strength, which is a tithe of the nominal strength.

Vietnamese ship strength

type	number	class
frigate	4	'Petya II'
	1	'Barnegat'
	1	'Savage'
corvette	2	'Admirable'
FAC (missile)	8	'Osa II'
FAC (torpedo)	12	'Shershen'
patrol craft	6	'SO I'
	7	'PGM 71'
	11	'PGM 59'
	6	'Zhuk'
	3	'PO 2'
minesweeper (ocean)	1	'Yurka'
landing ship	3	'Polnochny' LSM
	1	'LST 1-510'
	2	'LST 511-1152'
	3	'LSM 1'
other	2	misc

Virgin Islands

The navy of the Virgin Islands is part of the police force, and is based at Road Town on Tortola with one 'Brooke 40-ft' coastal patrol craft and two 'Coloso 23-ft' launches.

West Germany

The West German navy is tasked with the prevention of amphibious landings along the north German coastline, and with the protection of the approaches to West German ports within the overall NATO maritime strategy for the western Baltic, North Sea and North Atlantic. The tasks are major, and entrusted to an organization that encompasses a large force of patrol submarines, a useful number of powerful missile-armed destroyers and frigates, a very effective force of missile-armed fast attack craft, and a thoroughly modern air arm well integrated with the activities of the surface forces and also prepared for longer-range activities into the Baltic. Including the naval air arm, the West German navy has some 38,500 personnel (5,640 officers and 32,860 petty officers and ratings), 11,000 of them national servicemen undergoing a 15-month period of conscription. The main bases are at Flensburg, Wilhelmshaven, Kiel, Olpenitz and Eckernforde, and there are lesser bases at Neustadt and Borkum.

The West German navy operates a force of 24 coastal submarines for essentially defensive purposes, six of these being the older and less capable 'Type 205' class boats, but the remainder of the highly effective 'Type 206' class. The earlier boats are nearing the ends of their effective lives, and Ingenieurkontor Lübeck is developing a new and advanced 'Type 208' design for construction in the 1990s. A key feature of the new design is the use of fuel cells in place of the conventional diesel-electric arrangement.

Longer-range anti-ship operations are the responsibility of the 'Type 103A' or 'Charles F. Adams (Modified)' class destroyer and 'Hamburg' class destroyers. These carry Harpoon and Exocet anti-ship missiles respectively, and the 'Type 103A' class ships also have a powerful anti-air armament of Standard surface-to-air missiles. Both classes carry a useful anti-submarine fit. Better anti-submarine performance is available from the planned total of six 'Bremen' class frigates, which are built to a design adapted from that of the Dutch 'Kortenaer' class as a replacement for the 'Köln' class. The 'Bremen' class

frigates have a capable multi-role armament of guns, surface-to-surface and surface-to-air missiles, anti-submarine weapons and also an anti-submarine helicopter. Further capability is added to this lighter type of major surface combatant by the availability of five 'Thetis' class corvettes and 10 'Rhein' class depot ships; the latter are generally used in support of the submarine, light and minesweeping forces, but have frigate-type performance and armament.

The light forces are now entirely missile-armed, the current strength of 40 fast attack craft (missile) having been achieved by the delivery of the last 'Type 143A' class craft during 1983 and 1984. All the craft are armed with Exocet anti-ship missiles, and form one of the most capable light forces in the world, particularly so as plans are in hand for their updating with improved electronics and new point-defence surface-to-air missile systems as these become available during the decade.

The amphibious warfare force comprises 28 landing craft, medium (22 of them in reserve) and 22 landing craft, utility. These are used for a miscellany of service tasks in peace, but would provide a useful if limited amphibious capability in war. Another force of substantial numbers is that concerned with mine warfare, namely 39 coastal minesweepers and minehunters plus 20 inshore minesweepers.

There are the usual service and support forces, and the strong naval air arm is being updated as Panavia Tornado strike aircraft replace ageing Lockheed F-104G Starfighters, and as the Dassault-Breguet Atlantic maritime reconnaissance/electronic warfare force is upgraded with more advanced avionics.

West German ship strength

type	number	class
patrol submarine	0+0+?	'Type 208'
	18	'Type 206'
	6	'Type 205'
destroyer	3	'Charles F. Adams (Modified)'
	4	'Hamburg'
frigate	6	'Bremen'
	3	'Köln'
	(10	'Rhein')
corvette	5	'Thetis'
	1	'Hans Bürkner'
FAC (missile)	10	'Type 143A'
	20	'Type 148'
	10	'Type 143'
patrol craft	6	'KW 15'
minelayer	0+0+10	'Type 343'
minesweeper (coastal)	21	'Schütze'
	18	'Lindau'
	0+0+?	'Type 332'
minesweeper (inshore)	10	'Frauenlob'
	8	'Adriadne'
	1	'Niobe'
landing craft	6 (+22 reserve)	'Type 521' LCM
	22	'Type 520' LCU
other	100	misc

Yugoslavia

Sandwiched as a committed neutral between the European powers of the NATO and Warsaw Pact alliances, Yugoslavia maintains a small but moderately effective navy that has been considerably strengthened in recent years by a judicious policy of indigenous construction with imported specialized equipment. The Yugoslav navy is intended only for coastal protection, and has a strength of 14,000 (1,500 officers and 12,500 ratings) including about 6,000 conscripts fulfilling a 15-month national service obligation. Of the total there are about 6,000 afloat and 1,500 ashore in training pro-

grammes. A small naval air arm provides liaison and transport capability, while one specialist squadron of Kamov Ka-25 'Hormone' helicopters from the USSR provides anti-submarine capacity. The Yugoslav navy is divided operationally into the Split Naval Region (divided into the Fleet, Pula Naval District, Sibenik Naval District and Boka Naval Sector) and the River Flotilla controlled by the Belgrade Army Region. The main base is Split, and there are smaller bases at Dubrovnik, Kardeljevo, Kotor, Pula and Sibenik.

Yugoslavia maintains a relatively small submarine-construction facility, and this has permitted the development of four local submarine classes, three of them built to the extent of two units each. Yugoslavia has also the 'Mala' class midget, whose precise function remains obscure but is probably clandestine. All the submarine classes use Soviet armament and electronics.

The largest surface combatants deployed at present are two 'Koni' class missile frigates obtained from the USSR in the early 1980s to complement the two locally-built 'Mornar' class corvettes with Western machinery and Soviet armament plus sensors.

Greater punch is packed by the light forces, which currently operate 16 fast attack craft (missile) and 15 fast attack craft (torpedo). The FAC(T)s are Soviet 'Shershen' class craft, while the mix in the FAC(M)s is six Yugoslav-built 'Koncar' class craft based on the Swedish 'Spica' design but fitted with Soviet armament and sensors, and 10 'Osa I' class craft. This strength is about to be increased by 10 new-construction FAC(M)s being built in Yugoslavia with French diesels and (possibly) Norwegian Penguin anti-ship missiles.

Yugoslav ship strength

type	number	class
patrol submarine	2	'Sava'
	2	'Heraj'
	2	'Sutjeska'
	?	'Mala'
frigate	2	'Koni'
corvette	2	'Mornar'
FAC (missile)	0+0+10	?
	6	'Koncar'
	10	'Osa I'
FAC (torpedo)	15	'Shershen'
patrol craft	1	'Fougeux'
	10	'Kraljevica'
	8	'Type 131'
	6+?	'Mirna'
minesweeper (coastal)	4	'Vukor Klanac'
minesweeper (inshore)	6	'M 117'
	4	'Ham'
	6	'Nestin'
	14	'M 301'
landing craft	13	'DTM 211' LCT
	?	river LCT
	18	'Type 601' LCU
other	40	misc

Zaire

The Zairean navy is firmly committed to communist ideals and Chinese equipment, and operates in three flotillas: a lake flotilla on Lake Tanganyika, a river flotilla on the River Congo, and a coastal flotilla on Zaire's very short seaboard. The bases for these forces are Banana, Kalemie, Kinshasa and Matadi.

Zairean ship strength

type	number	class
FAC (gun)	4	'Shanghai II'
patrol craft	4	'Huchuan'
	6	'Sewart 65-ft'
	3	'P 4'
	36	misc

The 'Los Angeles' class of nuclear-powered fleet (or attack) submarines is one of the most important projects in the US Navy's current programme, plans calling for a force of 60+ such boats. The design is quiet, fast and deep-diving, and can carry a powerful mix of weapons and sensors. Seen here is a 'Los Angeles' class boat built by the Electric Boat Division of General Dynamics.

The US Navy's main surface strength lies in its considerable force of aircraft-carriers, both conventional- and nuclear-powered. Seen here in the Arabian Sea during January 1980 is Task Force 70, deployed around three carriers – one old, one middle-aged and one young. Supported by replenishment ships and escorting warships, the carriers are the USS *Kitty Hawk* (CV 63), the USS *Midway* (CV 41) and USS *Nimitz* (CVN 68), all multi-purpose carriers.

Inset left: Under way off southern California, the nuclear-powered USS *Enterprise* (CVN 65) shows off her remarkable island superstructure festooned with antennae, and the angled flight-

deck. The ship has four C13 catapults (two on the angled deck and the other pair in the bows) and four deck-edge lifts (one to port and the other three to starboard). Since this aerial photograph was taken in 1978 the *Enterprise* has been modernized, the most notable difference being to the superstructure, which now resembles that of the 'Nimitz' class.

Inset right: A distinctive feature of aircraft-carriers such as the USS *Dwight D. Eisenhower* (CVN 69) is the need to accommodate a considerable portion of the carrier air wing's aircraft strength on deck, the hangar being too small to hold any but aircraft under maintenance or overhaul.

The Swedish 'Näcken' class of patrol submarine is notable for its high beam-to-length ratio, the forward portion of the hull being devoted to the armament, the midships portion to the control room with the accommodation spaces abaft it, and the stern portion to the machinery spaces. Illustrated is the *Najad*, the second of the three 'Näcken' class boats.

Seen running on the surface below a Westland Sea King Mk 41 search-and-rescue helicopter of the West German Marineflieger is the *Casma* (S 31), the third of six Type 1200 patrol submarines built for the Peruvian navy by Howaldtswerke of Kiel. The bulbous fairing over the bow houses the sonar gear.

Now obsolescent but still in relatively widespread service, the Soviet 'Whiskey' class of patrol submarine was built in substantial numbers between 1951 and 1957 and was heavily influenced by the excellence of German U-boats in the latter half of World War II.

The Japanese 'Uzushio' class of patrol submarine, seen in the form of the lead boat *Uzushio* (SS 566) built by Kawasaki Heavy Industries at Kobe, is of teardrop hull design for high submerged speed and relative quietness.

The USSR's first aircraft-carrier, the elegant *Kiev*, passes through the Bosporus, a vital bottleneck in the deployment of Soviet warships from the Black Sea into the Mediterranean.

The *Kiev* and her sisters are essentially development ships, able to operate a useful number of Kamov Ka-25 'Hormone' anti-submarine helicopters and a few Yakovlev Yak-36 'Forger' VTOL light strike aircraft, but lack the flexibility of full carrierborne airpower as exercised by the US Navy with its highly developed catapult-equipped carriers. In peace the class could be used for intervention in overseas squabbles, with excellent communications for control from Moscow, and in war would form the basis of effective anti-submarine task groups.

The *Kiev*'s flight deck is intended for VTOL operations only, with helicopters and VTOL fixed-wing aircraft embarked, while the foredeck is given over to armament: one twin 76-mm (3-in) mounting, eight SS-N-12 container-launchers, one SA-N-3 twin-rail launcher, one SUW-N-1 twin-rail launcher and two MBU 6000 launchers.

In recent years few countries other than the USA and USSR have been able to countenance the construction of large multi-role carriers, but the smaller carrier dedicated to a single main role has undergone something of a renaissance. In Italy, for example, 1982 saw the launch (*left*) of the *Giuseppe Garibaldi* (C 551), scheduled to enter service in 1985 as an anti-submarine carrier with a complement of 18 Agusta (Bell) Sea King helicopters. The British HMS *Invincible* (R 05) was rushed into service in 1982 in time for the Falklands campaign, in which she operated Westland Sea King helicopters and BAe Sea Harrier V/STOL multi-role fighters to good effect, the latter type using the 7° ski jump at the forward end of the flight deck for greater payload after a short take-off. France, on the other hand, still operates a multi-role carrier force centred on the *Foch* (*below*) and her sister ship *Clemenceau*. These two units are to be replaced in the 1990s by two nuclear-powered multi-role carriers.

One of the most remarkable reappearances of modern times has been that of the battleship, seen here in the form of the USS *New Jersey* (BB 62) during reactivation trials off southern California during October 1982. The four battleships of the class are being successively modernized, not for superpower confrontation but rather for the support of US forces operating in secondary theatres, where the battleship's guns, missiles, aircraft (both fixed- and rotary-wing), communications and general facilities will expedite the implementation of US policies.

The Soviet anti-submarine helicopter-carrier *Moskva* is the lead ship of a planned class of 16 that was curtailed to two so as to allow the building of the 'Kiev' class carriers on the slips that would otherwise have been occupied by the 'Moskva' class ships.

The major weakness in US carrier task groups has generally been the lack of adequate escort: where theory called for an escort of missile-equipped cruisers and destroyers, practice generally allowed an escort of missile-armed destroyers and frigates, occasionally supplemented by a cruiser. The arrival of the USS *Ticonderoga* (CG 47) missile-armed cruiser and her class marks a new era, however, for the phased-array radar, extensive threat-analysis and communications equipment, and improved missile armament of each of these AEGIS ships allows a more effective defence of the carrier over all ranges and at all heights.

Key to the 'Ticonderoga' class cruisers' ability to control the defence of a carrier task group from air, surface and underwater threats is the lavishly-equipped Combat Information Center, the heart of the AEGIS Weapons Control System Mk 7 which co-ordinates the detection, analysis, tracking and destruction of multiple threats by the use of advanced sensors and data-processing equipment.

Above: The USS *Ticonderoga* (CG 47) is seen on her sea trials during May 1982. The design is based on that of the 'Spruance' class destroyer, with the hull lengthened and a new superstructure provided for the accommodation of the special phased-array radar and associated equipment.

Left: An overhead view of the USS *Ticonderoga* reveals salient features such as the after pair of antennae for the AN/SPY-1A surveillance radar, the paired exhausts for the four gas turbines, the gun armament of two 5-in (127-mm) guns, the two twin-rail launchers for Standard MR missiles, the helicopter platform and hangar, and the two 20-mm Phalanx CIWS mountings with their white domes on each beam between the masts.

HMS *Glasgow* (D 88) was the third unit of the 'Type 42' class of guided-missile destroyer. Key features are the single 4·5-in (114-mm) gun, the twin launcher with two Sea Dart missiles visible, the Type 965R search radar with double AKE-2 arrays, the domed Type 909 Sea Dart control radars above the bridge and above the helicopter hangar aft, and the Type 992Q surveillance and target-indication radar on top of the tower mast.

Georges Leygues (D 640) is the lead ship of the planned eight-strong anti-submarine version of the 'C 70' class. She has a flush deck with cutaway stern for the DUBV 43 variable-depth sonar, and the substantial deckhouse aft of the funnel accommodates a helicopter hangar and also supports four container-launchers for MM.38 Exocet surface-to-surface missiles and an octuple launcher for Crotale Naval surface-to-air missiles.

The pennant number F 810 identifies this 'Kortenaer' class guided-missile frigate as the *Banckert*, the fourth of 10 vessels planned for the Dutch navy. The tower-head dome houses the WM-25 fire-control radar, and the parabolic dish aft is the antenna for the LW-08 air-search radar.

Numerically the most important US destroyer type is the 'Spruance' class, with 31 ships afloat and another unit planned. The entire class was entrusted to Ingalls Shipbuilding, and individual ships were built from prefabricated modules each weighing from 1,500 to 2,100 tons and extensively fitted out before assembly of the modules to produce a vessel some 92 per cent complete before 'launch' (immersion on a submersible pontoon). The programme suffered considerable slippage, but there is little doubt that the class is a significant portion of the US Navy's current anti-submarine strength. The box launcher just aft of the single 5-in (127-mm) gun on the USS *Elliott* (DD 967) is for ASROC missiles, and the dome above the bridge covers the antenna for the AN/SPQ-9A radar that works in conjunction with the AN/SPG-60 radar just above it as part of the Mk 86 fire-control system.

'Benjamin Franklin' class nuclear-powered ballistic missile submarine
USA

Displacement: 6,650 tons light, 7,250 tons surfaced and 8,250 tons dived
Dimensions: length 425ft (129.5m); beam 33ft (10.1m); draught 31.5ft (9.6m)
Gun armament: none
Missile armament: vertical launch tubes for 16 submarine-launched ballistic missiles (UGM-93A Trident I C4 in SSBNs 640, 641, 643, 655, 657 and 658, and UGM-73A Poseidon C3 in the others)
Torpedo armament: four 21-in (533-mm) Mk 65 tubes (all bow)
Anti-submarine armament: UUM-44A SUBROC tube-launched missiles
Electronics: SSBN sonar, Mk 84 tactical computer, three Mk 2 Ship's Inertial Navigation System units, Mk 113 torpedo fire-control system, WSC-3 satellite communications transceiver and a navigational satellite receiver
Propulsion: one Westinghouse S5W pressurized-water cooled reactor supplying steam to two geared turbines delivering 15,000shp (11,185kW) to one shaft

Performance: maximum speed 20kts surfaced and about 30kts submerged; diving depth more than 1,000ft (305m)
Complement: 20+148

The 'Benjamin Franklin' class Simon Bolivar (SSBN 641) is seen running at speed on the surface. Aft of the sail are the hatches covering the 16 tubes for Poseidon missiles, replaced in 1980 by Trident I C4 missiles.

Remarks: The 19 'Lafayette' and 12 'Benjamin Franklin' class boats are currently the mainstay of the US Navy's strategic missile arm. The later 'Benjamin Franklin' class differs from the 'Lafayette' class only in having quieter machinery. As built the boats were outfitted with the Polaris A3 missile, replaced from 1970 with the Poseidon C3. From 1979 six SSBNs of the 'Benjamin Franklin' class (SSBNs 640, 641, 643, 655, 657 and 658) were modified to take the Trident I C4, this requiring the addition of extra ballast in the nose and the total revision of the fire-control systems.

Class
1. USA (12)

Name	No.	Builders	Laid down	Commissioned
BENJAMIN FRANKLIN	SSBN 640	GD (EB Div)	May 1963	Oct 1965
SIMON BOLIVAR	SSBN 641	Newport News S.B.	Apr 1963	Oct 1965
KAMEHAMEHA	SSBN 642	Mare Island NY	May 1963	Dec 1965
GEORGE BANCROFT	SSBN 643	GD (EB Div)	Aug 1963	Jan 1966
LEWIS AND CLARK	SSBN 644	Newport News S.B.	July 1963	Dec 1965
JAMES K. POLK	SSBN 645	GD (EB Div)	Nov 1963	Apr 1966
GEORGE C. MARSHALL	SSBN 654	Newport News S.B.	Mar 1964	Apr 1966
HENRY L. STIMSON	SSBN 655	GD (EB Div)	Apr 1964	Aug 1966
GEORGE WASHINGTON CARVER	SSBN 656	Newport News S.B.	Aug 1964	June 1966
FRANCIS SCOTT KEY	SSBN 657	GD (EB Div)	Dec 1964	Dec 1966
MARIANO G. VALLEJO	SSBN 658	Mare Island NY	July 1964	Dec 1966
WILL ROGERS	SSBN 659	GD (EB Div)	Mar 1965	Apr 1967

'Charlie I' class nuclear-powered cruise-missile submarine
USSR

Displacement: 4,000 tons surfaced and 5,000 tons dived
Dimensions: length 93.9m (308ft); beam 9.9m (32.5ft); draught 7.5m (24.6ft)
Gun armament: none
Missile armament: eight launch tubes for SS-N-7 underwater-to-surface cruise missiles and two tube-launched SS-N-15 A/S missiles
Torpedo armament: six 533-mm (21-in) tubes (all bow) for 12 torpedoes
Anti-submarine armament: six A/S torpedoes and missiles (see above)
Electronics: one 'Snoop Tray' surface-search radar, one sonar fitted in the fin, and computer-assisted command centre

Propulsion: one nuclear reactor supplying steam to two turbines delivering 14,915kW (20,000shp) to one shaft
Performance: maximum speed 20kts surfaced and 27kts submerged; diving depth 400m (1,325ft) operational and 600m (1,970ft) maximum
Complement: 90

Class
1. USSR (11)
11 boats

'Charlie II' class nuclear-powered cruise-missile submarine
USSR

Displacement: 4,400 tons surfaced and 5,500 tons dived
Dimensions: length 102.9m (337.5ft); beam 9.9m (32.5ft); draught 7.8m (25.6ft)
Gun armament: none
Missile armament: eight launch tubes for SS-N-7 underwater-to-surface or SS-N-9 'Siren' surface-to-surface cruise missiles, and provision for SS-N-16 underwater-to-underwater missiles fired from the torpedo tubes
Torpedo armament: six 533-mm (21-in) tubes (all bow) for 12 torpedoes
Anti-submarine armament: SS-N-16 missiles (see above) and six A/S torpedoes
Electronics: on 'Snoop Tray' surface-search radar, one low-frequency sonar

array, one 'Stop Light' ECM suite and one computer-assisted command centre
Propulsion: one nuclear reactor supplying steam to two turbines delivering 14,915kW (20,000shp) to one shaft
Performance: maximum speed 28kts submerged
Complement: 90

Class
1. USSR (6)
6 boats

'Delta I' class nuclear-powered ballistic-missile submarine
USSR

Displacement: 10,000 tons dived
Dimensions: length 136.0m (446.1ft); beam 11.6m (38ft); draught 10.0m (32.8ft)
Gun armament: none
Missile armament: 12 launch tubes for SS-N-8 underwater-to-surface ballistic missiles
Torpedo armament: six 533-mm (21-in) tubes (all bow) for 18 torpedoes
Anti-submarine armament: A/S torpedoes
Electronics: one 'Snoop Tray' surface-search radar, one low-frequency bow-array sonar, and a computer-assisted command centre
Propulsion: two nuclear reactors supplying steam to two sets of turbines delivering 22,370kW (30,000shp) to two shafts
Performance: maximum speed 25kts submerged
Complement: 120

Class
1. USSR (18)
18 boats

Remarks: Built from 1972, the 'Delta I' class could carry only 12 instead of 16 SLBMs because of the SS-N-8's greater length and diameter.

Built at Severodvinsk and Komsomolsk, the 'Delta I' class SSBNs superseded the 'Yankee' class, the greater length of the SS-N-8 missiles requiring a heightened casing on the after section carrying the 12 launch tubes.

'Delta II' class nuclear-powered ballistic-missile submarine

USSR

Displacement: 11,000 tons dived
Dimensions: length 152·7m (500·9ft); beam 11·8m (38·7ft); draught 10·2m (33·5ft)

The 'Delta II' class SSBN lacks the after-casing 'kink' of the 'Delta I'.

Gun armament: none
Missile armament: 16 launch tubes for SS-N-8 underwater-to-surface ballistic missiles
Torpedo armament: six 533-mm (21-in) tubes (all bow) for 18 torpedoes
Anti-submarine armament: A/S torpedoes (see above)
Electronics: one 'Snoop Tray' surface-search radar, one low-frequency bow-array sonar, and a computer-assisted combat centre
Propulsion: two nuclear reactors supplying steam to two geared turbines delivering 22,370kW (30,000shp) to two shafts
Performance: 25kts submerged
Complement: 132
Class
1. USSR (4)
4 boats

'Delta III' class nuclear-powered ballistic-missile submarine

USSR

Displacement: 11,000 tons dived
Dimensions: length 150·0m (492ft); beam 12·0m (39·4ft); draught 10·2m (33·4m)
Gun armament: none
Missile armament: 16 launch tubes for SS-N-18 underwater-to-surface ballistic missiles
Torpedo armament: six 533-mm (21-in) tubes (all bow) for 18 torpedoes
Anti-submarine armament: A/S torpedoes (see above)
Electronics: one 'Snoop Tray' surface-search radar, one low-frequency bow-array sonar, and a computer-assisted combat centre
Propulsion: two nuclear reactors supplying steam to two geared turbines delivering 22,370kW (30,000shp) to two shafts
Performance: maximum speed 24kts submerged
Complement: 132

Class
1. USSR (14+1)
14+1 boats

Further heightening of the missile-section casing marks the 'Delta III' design.

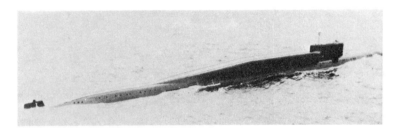

'Echo II' class nuclear-powered cruise-missile submarine

USSR

Displacement: 4,800 tons surfaced and 5,800 tons dived
Dimensions: length 117·3m (384·7ft); beam 9·2m (30·2ft); draught 7·8m (25·5ft)
Gun armament: none
Missile armament: eight launch tubes for SS-N-3A 'Shaddock' surface-to-surface missiles, or for SS-N-12 'Sandbox' surface-to-surface missiles
Torpedo armament: six 533-mm (21-in) tubes (all bow) for 24 torpedoes
Anti-submarine armament: two 406-mm (16-in) tubes (both stern) for two A/S torpedoes, plus 16 A/S torpedoes in total above
Electronics: one 'Snoop Tray' surface-search and navigation radar, one 'Front Piece' and one 'Front Door' SS-N-3 mid-course guidance radars, one *Herkules* sonar, one *Feniks* sonar, one 'Stop Light' electronic countermeasures system, and a computer-assisted command centre
Propulsion: two nuclear reactors supplying steam to two sets of geared turbines delivering 22,370kW (30,000shp) to two shafts
Performance: maximum speed 25 knots submerged; diving depth 300m (985ft) operational and 500m (1,640ft) maximum

Complement: 100
Class
1. USSR (29)
29 boats

The 'Echo II' class SSGN carries eight angled tubes for SS-N-3A (23 boats) or SS-N-12 (six boats) cruise missiles, and was built in the first half of the 1960s for attacks on US carrier forces.

'Golf' class ballistic-missile submarine

USSR/China

Displacement: 2,350 tons surfaced and 2,850 tons dived
Dimensions: length 98·0m (321·4ft); beam 8·5m (27·9ft); draught 6·4m (21ft)
Gun armament: none
Missile armament: three launch tubes for ballistic underwater-to-surface missiles
Torpedo armament: six 533-mm (21-in) tubes (all bow) for 12 torpedoes
Anti-submarine armament: none
Electronics: surface-search radar and sonar
Propulsion: diesel-electric arrangement, with three diesels delivering 4,475kW (6,000hp) and three electric motors delivering 8,950kW (12,000hp) to three shafts
Fuel: diesel oil
Performance: maximum speed 17kts surfaced and 14kts submerged; range 42,000km (26,100 miles) at cruising speed
Complement: 12+74
Class
1. China (1)
1 boat

Three launch tubes are carried in the long sail of the 'Golf' class.

'Golf II' class ballistic-missile submarine
USSR

Displacement: 2,600 tons surfaced and 3,000 tons dived

Dimensions: length 98·0m (321·4ft); beam 8·5m (27·9ft); draught 6·4m (21ft)

Gun armament: none

Missile armament: three launch tubes for SS-N-5 'Serb' underwater-to-surface ballistic missiles

Torpedo armament: six 533-mm (21-in) tubes (all bow) for 12 torpedoes

Anti-submarine armament: A/S torpedoes (see above)

Electronics: one 'Snoop Tray' or 'Snoop Plate' surface-search and navigation radar, *Herkules* sonar and *Feniks* sonar

Propulsion: diesel-electric arrangement, with three diesels delivering 4,470 kW (6,000 hp) and three electric motors delivering 11,930 kW (16,000 hp) to three shafts

Fuel: diesel oil

Performance: maximum speed 17 kts surfaced and 14 kts submerged; range 42,000 km (26,100 miles) at cruising speed; endurance 70 days

Complement: 12+75

Class
1. **USSR** (13)   13 boats

Remarks: The 'Golf II' class resulted from a simple conversion of 13 'Golf I' class boats, the launch tubes in the sail being modified to accept three of the SS-N-5 'Serb' missiles in place of the shorter-range SS-N-4 'Sark' first deployed in the 'Golf I' class.

'Hotel II' class nuclear-powered ballistic-missile submarine
USSR

The 'Hotel II' class can launch its SS-N-5 'Serb' missiles underwater.

Displacement: 4,500 tons surfaced and 5,500 tons dived

Dimensions: length 115·2m (377·2ft); beam 9·1m (29·8ft); draught 7·6m (25ft)

Gun armament: none

Missile armament: three launch tubes for SS-N-5 'Serb' underwater-to-surface ballistic missiles

Torpedo armament: six 533-mm (21-in) tubes (all bow) for a maximum of 20 torpedoes

Anti-submarine armament: two 406-mm (16-in) tubes (both stern) for A/S torpedoes included in the total above

Electronics: one 'Snoop Tray' surface-search radar, one *Herkules* sonar and one *Feniks* sonar

Propulsion: two nuclear reactors supplying steam to two sets of geared turbines delivering 22,370 kW (30,000 shp) to two shafts

Performance: maximum speed 26 kts submerged

Complement: 90

Class
1. **USSR** (5)
5 boats

'Hotel III' class nuclear-powered ballistic-missile submarine
USSR

Displacement: 5,000 tons surfaced and 6,000 tons dived

Dimensions: length 115·2m (377·2ft); beam 9·1m (29·8ft); draught 7·6m (25ft)

Gun armament: none

Missile armament: six launch tubes for SS-N-8 underwater-to-surface ballistic missiles

Torpedo armament: six 533-mm (21-in) tubes (all bow) for a maximum of 20 torpedoes

Anti-submarine armament: two 406-mm (16-in) tubes (both stern) for A/S torpedoes included in the total above

Electronics: one 'Snoop Tray' surface-search radar, one *Herkules* sonar and one *Feniks* sonar

Propulsion: two nuclear reactors supplying steam to two sets of geared turbines delivering 22,370 kW (30,000 shp) to two shafts

Performance: maximum speed 26 kts submerged

Complement: 90

Class
1. **USSR** (1)
1 boat

'Juliett' class cruise-missile submarine
USSR

Displacement: 3,000 tons surfaced and 3,800 tons dived

Dimensions: length 86·7m (284·4ft); beam 10·1m (33·1ft); draught 7·0m (22·9ft)

Gun armament: none

Missile armament: four launch tubes for SS-N-3A 'Shaddock' surface-to-surface missiles

Torpedo armament: six 533-mm (21-in) tubes (all bow) for 18 torpedoes

Anti-submarine armament: A/S torpedoes (see above)

Electronics: 'Front Piece' and 'Front Door' missile-control radars, one 'Snoop Slab' surface-search and navigation radar, one *Herkules* sonar, one *Feniks* sonar, and one 'Stop Light' electronic countermeasures system

Propulsion: diesel-electric arrangement, with three diesels delivering 5,965 kW (8,000 bhp) and three electric motors delivering 4,475 kW (6,000 hp) to two shafts

Performance: maximum speed 19 kts surfaced and 14 kts submerged; range 27,800 km (17,275 miles) at surfaced cruising speed

Complement: 79

Class
1. **USSR** (16)
16 boats

The 'Juliett' class SSG has an unmistakably massive casing and short sail.

'Lafayette' class nuclear-powered ballistic-missile submarine

USA

Displacement: 6,650 tons light, 7,250 tons surfaced and 8,250 tons dived

Dimensions: length 425ft (129·5m); beam 33ft (10·1m); draught 31·5ft (9·6m)

Gun armament: none

Missile armament: vertical launch tubes for 16 submarine-launched ballistic missiles (UGM-93A Trident I C4 in SSBNs 627, 629, 630, 632 and 634, and UGM-73A Poseidon C3 in the others)

Torpedo armament: four 21-in (533-mm) Mk 65 tubes (all bow)

Anti-submarine armament: UUM-44A SUBROC tube-launched missiles

Electronics: SSBN sonar, Mk 84 tactical computer, three Mk 2 Ship's Inertial Navigation System units, Mk 113 torpedo fire-control system, WSC-3 satellite communications transceiver and a navigational satellite receiver

Propulsion: one Westinghouse S5W pressurized-water cooled reactor supplying steam to two geared turbines delivering 15,000shp (11,185kW) to one shaft

Performance: maximum speed 20kts surfaced and about 30kts submerged; diving depth more than 1,000ft (305m)

Complement: 20+148

Class

1. USA (19)

Name	No.	Builders	Laid down	Com-missioned
LAFAYETTE	SSBN 616	GD (EB Div)	Jan 1961	Apr 1963
ALEXANDER HAMILTON	SSBN 617	GD (EB Div)	June 1961	June 1963
ANDREW JACKSON	SSBN 619	Mare Island Navy Yard	Apr 1961	July 1963
JOHN ADAMS	SSBN 620	Portsmouth Navy Yard	May 1961	May 1964
JAMES MONROE	SSBN 622	Newport News S.B.	July 1961	Dec 1963
NATHAN HALE	SSBN 623	GD (EB Div)	Oct 1961	Nov 1963
WOODROW WILSON	SSBN 624	Mare Island Navy Yard	Sep 1961	Dec 1963
HENRY CLAY	SSBN 625	Newport News S.B.	Oct 1961	Feb 1964
DANIEL WEBSTER	SSBN 626	GD (EB Div)	Dec 1961	Apr 1964
JAMES MADISON	SSBN 627	Newport News S.B.	Mar 1962	July 1964
TECUMSEH	SSBN 628	GD (EB Div)	June 1962	May 1964
DANIEL BOONE	SSBN 629	Mare Island Navy Yard	Feb 1962	Apr 1964
JOHN C. CALHOUN	SSBN 630	Newport News S.B.	June 1962	Sep 1964
ULYSSES S. GRANT	SSBN 631	GD (EB Div)	Aug 1962	July 1964
VON STEUBEN	SSBN 632	Newport News S.B.	Sep 1962	Sep 1964
CASIMIR PULASKI	SSBN 633	GD (EB Div)	Jan 1963	Aug 1964
STONEWALL JACKSON	SSBN 634	Mare Island Navy Yard	July 1962	Aug 1964
SAM RAYBURN	SSBN 635	Newport News S.B.	Dec 1962	Dec 1964
NATHANAEL GREENE	SSBN 636	Portsmouth Navy Yard	May 1962	Dec 1964

Seen slowly under way in Roosevelt Roads, Puerto Rico, is the 'Lafayette' class submarine Daniel Boone (SSBN 629).

Remarks: The 'Lafayette' and basically identical 'Benjamin Franklin' class SSBNs were the largest underwater craft built by the Western alliance during the 1960s, and still constitute the most formidable portion of its submarine-launched missile deterrent capability pending the arrival of the vast 'Ohio' class boats. Each boat is assigned two crews, one manning the boat during a 70-day patrol and then helping the alternate crew during the 32-day refit before the next patrol, which is manned by the second crew. Every six years the boats each undergo a major refit lasting just under two years. The nuclear cores fitted in the late 1960s and early 1970s provide energy for about 400,000 miles (643,720km), and the 'Lafayette' class boats currently fitted with the Trident I C4 missiles are SSBNs 627, 629, 630, 632, 633 and 634. All the boats of the 'Lafayette' and 'Benjamin Franklin' classes are currently operational with the Atlantic Fleet.

'L'Inflexible' class nuclear-powered ballistic-missile submarine

France

Displacement: 8,080 tons surfaced and 8,920 tons dived

Dimensions: length 128·7m (422·2ft); beam 10·6m (34·7ft); draught 10·0m (32·8ft)

Gun armament: none

Missile armament: vertical launch tubes for 16 M4 submarine-launched ballistic missiles, and ? tube-launched SM.39 Exocet anti-ship missiles

Torpedo armament: four 533-mm (21-in) tubes (all bow) for ? L5 torpedoes

Anti-submarine armament: L5 torpedoes (above)

Electronics: one Thomson-CSF Calypso surface-search and attack radar, one passive ECM suite, one missile fire-control system, one torpedo fire-control system, one inertial navigation system, one CIT/Alcatel DUUX 2 ranging sonar, and one DSUX 21 multi-role sonar

Propulsion: one pressurized-water cooled reactor supplying steam to two sets of geared steam turbines powering two turbo-alternators/one electric motor delivering ?kW (?shp) to one shaft; auxiliary diesel-electric arrangement

Performance: maximum speed about 25kts dived

Complement: 15+44+68

Class

1. France (0+1)

Name	Builders	Laid down	Com-missioned
L'INFLEXIBLE	Cherbourg ND	Mar 1980	1984

'Le Redoutable' class nuclear-powered ballistic-missile submarine

France

Displacement: 8,045 tons surfaced and 8,940 tons dived

Dimensions: length 128·7m (422·1ft); beam 10·6m (34·8ft); draught 10·0m (32·8ft)

Gun armament: none

Le Foudroyant (S610) was the second completed unit of the 'Le Redoutable' class.

Remarks: The last four boats will be fitted with the M4 missile later in the 1980s. Operational planning calls for four boats in service and the fifth refitting at any one time, with two crews for each in-service boat for the maximum possible patrol time. The SM.39 submarine-launched version of the Exocet anti-ship missile will soon be carried for tube-launching.

Missile armament: launch tubes for 16 MSBS M-20 underwater-to-surface ballistic missiles

Torpedo armament: four 533-mm (21-in) tubes for 18 torpedoes

Anti-submarine armament: A/S torpedoes carried as part of the total above

Electronics: one Thomson-CSF Calypso surface-search and navigation radar, one DSUX 21 multi-role sonar, one CIT/Alcatel DUUX 2 passive ranging sonar, inertial navigation system, torpedo fire-control system, missile fire-control system, and passive electronic countermeasures systems

Propulsion: one pressurized-water cooled nuclear reactor supplying steam to two sets of geared turbines driving two turbo-alternators providing current to one electric motor delivering 11,930kW (16,000hp) to one shaft; there is also an auxiliary powerplant comprising two diesels delivering 975kW (1,307hp)

Performance: maximum speed 20+kts surfaced and 25kts submerged; range 9,250km (5,750 miles) on auxiliary diesels; diving depth more than 300m (985ft)

Complement: 15+120

Class

1. France (5)

Name	No.	Builders	Laid down	Operational
LE FOUDROYANT	S 610	Cherbourg ND	Dec 1969	June 1974
LE REDOUTABLE	S 611	Cherbourg ND	Mar 1964	Dec 1971
LE TERRIBLE	S 612	Cherbourg ND	June 1967	Dec 1973
L'INDOMPTABLE	S 613	Cherbourg ND	Dec 1971	Dec 1976
LE TONNANT	S 614	Cherbourg ND	Oct 1974	May 1980

'Ohio' class nuclear-powered ballistic-missile submarine
USA
Displacement: 16,600 tons surfaced and 18,700 tons dived
Dimensions: length 560ft (170·7m); beam 42ft (12·8m); draught 35·5ft (10·8m)
Gun armament: none
Missile armament: 24 launch tubes for UGM-94A Trident I (C-4) underwater-to-surface ballistic missiles
Torpedo armament: four 21-in (533-mm) Mk 68 tubes (all bow)
Anti-submarine armament: A/S torpedoes
Electronics: one Hughes/General Electric/IBM/Raytheon BQQ-5 sonar system without active units, Mk 118 torpedo fire-control system, two Mk 2 Ship's Inertial Navigation Systems, and WSC-3 satellite communications transceiver
Propulsion: one pressurized-water cooled General Electric S8G nuclear reactor supplying steam to two geared turbines delivering 60,000shp (44,740kW) to one shaft
Performance: maximum speed 25-30kts; diving depth 985ft (300m)
Complement: 16+117

Class

1. USA (5+5+14)				Com-
Name	No.	Builders	Laid down	missioned
OHIO	SSBN 726	GD (EB Div)	Apr 1976	Nov 1981
MICHIGAN	SSBN 727	GD (EB Div)	Apr 1977	Sep 1982
FLORIDA	SSBN 728	GD (EB Div)	June 1977	July 1982
GEORGIA	SSBN 729	GD (EB Div)	Apr 1979	Feb 1984
RHODE ISLAND	SSBN 730	GD (EB Div)	Jan 1981	Oct 1984
ALABAMA	SSBN 731	GD (EB Div)	Apr 1981	July 1985
ALASKA	SSBN 732	GD (EB Div)	—	Mar 1986
—	SSBN 733	GD (EB Div)		
—	SSBN 734	GD (EB Div)		
—	SSBN 735	GD (EB Div)		
—	SSBN 736	Proposed FY 1984 programme		
—	SSBN 737	Proposed FY 1985 programme		
—	SSBN 738	Proposed FY 1986 programme		
—	SSBN 739	Proposed FY 1987 programme		
—	SSBN 740	Proposed FY 1988 programme		

Remarks: The vast size of the 'Ohio' class boats (exceeded only by the Soviet 'Typhoon' class) is demanded by the need to carry 24 launch tubes for the large Trident missile, and the massive reactor system needed to provide adequate performance. Great hopes are entertained for the class, despite delays and cost overruns attendant on political vacillation and production problems. Major refits will be needed at nine-year intervals, and the use of alternating crews permits 70-day patrol broken by 25-day refit periods. SSBN 734 onwards will carry the Trident II D5 missile.

The Michigan (SSBN 727) is the second of the 'Ohio' class boats.

'Oscar' class nuclear-powered cruise-missile submarine
USSR
Displacement: 10,000 tons surfaced and 15,000 tons dived
Dimensions: length 150·0m (491·2ft); beam 18·3m (60ft); draught 11·0m (36·1ft)
Gun armament: none
Missile armament: 24 launch tubes for SS-N-19 surface-to-surface missiles and two launch tubes for two SS-N-16 A/S missiles
Torpedo armament: six 533-mm (21-in) tubes for 28 torpedoes
Anti-submarine armament: 14 A/S torpedoes carried as part of the total above

Electronics: surface-search radar, and sonar
Propulsion: possibly two nuclear reactors supplying steam to two sets of geared turbines delivering about 44,740kW (60,000shp) to two shafts
Performance: maximum speed 20kts surfaced and 35kts submerged; diving depth 500m (1,640ft) operational and 830m (2,725ft) maximum
Complement: about 130
Class
1. USSR (1+?)
1 boat plus ? others on order

'Papa' class nuclear-powered cruise-missile submarine
USSR
Displacement: about 6,100 tons surfaced and 7,000 tons dived
Dimensions: length 150·0m (492·1ft); beam 11·5m (37·7ft); draught 7·6m (24·9ft)
Gun armament: none
Missile armament: 10 launch tubes for 10 SS-N-9 'Siren' anti-ship missiles
Torpedo armament: six 533-mm (21-in) tubes (all bow) for 12 torpedoes
Anti-submarine armament: six A/S torpedoes (see above) and two SS-N-15 missiles
Electronics: one 'Snoop Tray' surface-search radar, one 'Stop Light' E electronic

countermeasures system, and one sonar
Propulsion: two nuclear reactors supplying steam to two sets of geared turbines delivering 29,830kW (40,000shp) to two shafts
Performance: maximum speed 20kts surfaced and 40kts submerged; diving depth 400m (1,325ft) operational and 600m (1,970ft) maximum
Complement: 90

Class
1. USSR (1)
1 boat

'Resolution' class nuclear-powered ballistic-missile submarine
UK
Displacement: 7,500 tons surfaced and 8,400 tons dived
Dimensions: length 425ft (129·5m); beam 33ft (10·1m); draught 30ft (9·1m)
Gun armament: none
Missile armament: launch tubes for 16 UGM-27C Polaris A-3 underwater-to-surface ballistic missiles
Torpedo armament: six 21-in (533-mm) tubes (all bow)
Anti-submarine armament: A/S torpedoes fired from the tubes above
Electronics: one surface-search radar, one Type 2001 long-range active/passive

sonar, one GEC Type 2007 long-range passive sonar, and inertial navigation systems
Propulsion: one pressurized-water cooled Rolls-Royce nuclear reactor supplying steam to one set of English Electric geared turbines delivering 15,000shp (11,185kW) to one shaft
Performance: maximum speed 20kts surfaced and 25kts submerged
Complement: 13+130

Class				
1. UK (4)				Com-
Name	No.	Builders	Laid down	missioned
RESOLUTION	S 22	Vickers (Shipbuilding)	Feb 1964	Oct 1967
REPULSE	S 23	Vickers (Shipbuilding)	Mar 1965	Sep 1968
RENOWN	S 26	Cammell Laird	June 1964	Nov 1968
REVENGE	S 27	Cammell Laird	May 1965	Dec 1969

Remarks: In common with other navies' SSBNs, the 'Resolution' class boats have two crews for maximum patrol time. The class will be replaced in the 1990s by a new class with Trident ballistic missiles.

The Resolution (S22) was the lead ship of her class.

'Typhoon' class nuclear-powered ballistic-missile submarine

USSR

Displacement: about 30,000 tons dived
Dimensions: length 183·0m (600·4ft); beam 22·9m (75·1ft); draught 15m (49·2ft)
Gun armament: none
Missile armament: launch tubes for 20 SS-N-20 underwater-to-surface ballistic missiles
Torpedo armament: six or eight 533-mm (21-in) tubes
Anti-submarine armament: A/S torpedoes
Electronics: surface-search radar, navigation radar, sonar, inertial navigation systems, missile fire-control system, and torpedo fire-control system
Propulsion: two nuclear reactors supplying steam to two sets of geared turbines delivering about 89,500kW (120,020shp) to two shafts
Performance: maximum speed about 24kts submerged
Complement: about 150

Class
1. USSR (2+?)
2 boat plus ? on order

Artist's impression of a 'Typhoon' class SSBN.

Remarks: The 'Typhoon' class SSBNs are the largest submarines ever built. The construction features twin outer hulls, and the forward-located launch tubes leave the after section free for a twin-reactor powerplant.

'Yankee' and 'Yankee II' class nuclear-powered ballistic-missile submarines

USSR

Displacement: 9,300 tons dived
Dimensions: length 129·5m (424·6ft); beam 11·6m (38ft); draught 7·8m (25·6ft)
Gun armament: none
Missile armament: 16 launch tubes for SS-N-6 underwater-to-surface ballistic missiles ('Yankee' class) or SS-N-17 underwater-to-surface ballistic missiles ('Yankee II' class)
Torpedo armament: six 533-mm (21-in) tubes for 18 torpedoes
Anti-submarine armament: A/S torpedoes carried as part of the total above
Mines: up to 36 in place of the torpedoes
Electronics: one 'Snoop Tray' surface-search radar, and one bow-mounted low- or medium-frequency sonar array
Propulsion: two nuclear reactors supplying steam to two sets of geared turbines delivering 22,370kW (30,000shp) to two shafts
Performance: maximum speed 30kts submerged
Complement: 120

Class
1. USSR (24+8 'Yankee' and 1 'Yankee II' class)
24 'Yankee' class missile boats
8 'Yankee' class fleet boats
1 'Yankee II' class boat

The 'Yankee' class design incorporates 16 missile launch tubes.

Remarks: The 'Yankee' class was the first Soviet SSBN class, and seems to have been based on the design of the 'Ethan Allen' class of the US Navy. Built at Severodvinsk and Komsomolsk, the boats were deployed operationally off the eastern coast of the USA from 1968. The class is notable for its high speeds, prompting the conversion of obsolescent hulls into iterim fleet submarines.

'Xia' class nuclear-powered ballistic-missile submarine

China

Displacement: about 8,000 tons dived
Missile armament: vertical launch tubes for either 14 or 16 CSS-NX-3 underwater-to-surface ballistic missiles
Complement: about 84

Remarks: Very little is known with certainty of the Chinese SSBN programme,

which has undergone a slow and uncertain development with the aid of the country's sole 'Golf' class SSB. It seems likely that the only boat so far in service was laid down in 1978 and launched in 1981. The exact status of the CSS-NX-3 missile is also uncertain: the first and second underwater test firings took place from a pontoon in the Yellow Sea during 1982, and a range of 3,350km (2,080 miles) is believed possible with a 200-kiloton warhead. As both the missile and submarine are new and present the Chinese with novel problems of integration, it seems likely that only cautious progress will be made with additional boats within the foreseeable future.

'Alfa' class nuclear-powered fleet submarine

USSR

Displacement: 2,800 tons surfaced and 3,680 tons dived
Dimensions: length 81·0m (265·75ft); beam 9·5m (31·2ft); draught 8·0m (26·25ft)
Gun armament: none
Missile armament: two SS-N-15 A/S missiles
Torpedo armament: six 533-mm (21-in) tubes for 18 wire-guided torpedoes, or SS-N-15 rocket-assisted torpedo-launchers, or 36 mines
Anti-submarine armament: up to 10 A/S torpedoes (see above)
Electronics: one 'Snoop Tray' surface-search radar and one low-frequency bow-array sonar; the hull may be coated with 'Cluster Guard'
Propulsion: one nuclear reactor providing steam to two turbines delivering 29,825kW (40,000shp) to one shaft; there is also an auxiliary diesel
Performance: maximum speed 20kts surfaced and 45kts submerged; diving depth 600m (1,970ft) operational and 1,000m (3,280ft) maximum
Complement: 60

Class
1. USSR (6+?)
6 boats (plus ? building)

Remarks: The new 'Alfa' class of Soviet SSN marks a decisive turning point in the East/West balance of maritime power, for the 'Alfa' class boats have speed and diving capabilities far beyond those of Western contemporaries. These factors result from the use of a liquid metal-cooled reactor, permitting greater power from a smaller reactor system, and of titanium alloy for the hull. It has been reported reliably that an 'Alfa' class boat showed a clean pair of heels to a shadowing 'Los Angeles' class SSN of the US Navy (albeit very noisily), while the estimated diving depth renders the 'Alfa' class boats safe from any current anti-submarine torpedo operated by the Western alliance. The class was designed with the aid of two now-dismantled prototypes, and now that the concept has been proved it is to be expected that the construction programme will see the fairly rapid construction of a fairly large fleet of the type.

'Churchill' and 'Valiant' class nuclear-powered fleet submarines

UK

Displacement: 4,000 tons light, 4,400 tons standard and 4,900 tons dived
Dimensions: length 285ft (86·9m); beam 33·2ft (10·1m); draught 27ft (8·2m)
Gun armament: none
Missile armament: six Sub-Harpoon anti-ship missiles
Torpedo armament: six 21-in (533-mm) tubes (all bow) for 26 torpedoes
Anti-submarine armament: torpedoes (see above)
Electronics: one Kelvin Hughes Type 1006 surface-search radar, one Type 2001 active/passive sonar, one GEC Type 2007 long-range passive sonar, one Type 197

sonar and one Type 2019 sonar, and one Type 2024 towed sonar
Propulsion: one pressurized-water cooled reactor supplying steam to two English Electric geared turbines delivering 20,000shp (14,915kW) to one shaft
Performance: maximum speed 28kts submerged
Complement: 13+90

Class
1. UK (3 'Churchill' class)

Name	No.	Builders	Laid down	Com-missioned
CHURCHILL	S 46	Vickers (Shipbuilding)	June 1967	July 1970
CONQUEROR	S 48	Cammell Laird	Dec 1967	Nov 1971
COURAGEOUS	S 50	Vickers (Shipbuilding)	May 1968	Oct 1971

2. UK (2 'Valiant' class)

Name	No.	Builders	Laid down	Com-missioned
VALIANT	S 102	Vickers (Shipbuilding)	Jan 1962	July 1966
WARSPITE	S 103	Vickers (Shipbuilding)	Dec 1963	Apr 1967

Remarks: Derived from the design of the 'Dreadnought' class with an all-British reactor system, the 'Valiant' class of the late 1960s was bolstered by the three improved 'Churchill' class boats of the early 1970s, these differing from their predecessors by the installation of quieter machinery.

Churchill (S46) was the lead craft of a sub-class of the 'Valiant' class.

'Echo I' class nuclear-powered fleet submarine

USSR

Displacement: 4,300 tons surfaced and 5,200 tons dived
Dimensions: length 114·0m (373·9ft); beam 9·1m (29·8ft); draught 7·3m (23·9ft)
Gun armament: none
Missile armament: none (originally carried six launchers for the SS-N-3 'Shaddock' surface-to-surface missiles)
Torpedo armament: six 533-mm (21-in) tubes (all bow) for 24 torpedoes
Anti-submarine armament: two 406-mm (16-in) tubes (both stern) for 2 A/S torpedoes plus 16 A/S torpedoes (see above)

Electronics: one 'Snoop Tray' surface-search radar, one *Herkules* sonar, one *Feniks* sonar, and one 'Stop Light' electronic countermeasures system
Propulsion: two nuclear reactors supplying steam to two sets of turbines delivering 22,370kW (30,000shp) to two shafts
Performance: maximum speed 20kts surfaced and 28kts submerged; diving depth 300m (985ft) operational and 500m (1,640ft) maximum
Complement: 12+80

Class
1. USSR (5)
5 boats

'Ethan Allen' class nuclear-powered fleet submarine

USA

Displacement: 6,955 tons surfaced and 7,880 tons dived
Dimensions: length 410ft (125·0m); beam 33ft (10·1m); draught 32ft (9·8m)
Gun armament: none
Missile armament: 16 launch tubes for UGM-27 Polaris submarine-launched ballistic missiles; when the boats were converted from SSBNs to SSNs these tubes were filled with cement as ballast, the associated fire-control system and one SINS (Ship's Inertial Navigation System) being removed at the same time
Torpedo armament: four 21-in (533-mm) tubes (all bow) for eight torpedoes
Anti-submarine armament: four A/S torpedoes carried as an alternative to the four reloads for the bow tubes
Electronics: one multi-function sonar, one Mk 2 SINS, and one WSC-3 satellite communications transceiver
Propulsion: one pressurized-water cooled Westinghouse S5W nuclear reactor supplying steam to two sets of General Electric geared turbines delivering 15,000shp (11,185kW) to one shaft
Performance: maximum speed 20kts surfaced and 30kts submerged
Complement: 15+127

Class
1. USA (4)

Name	No.	Builders	Laid down	Com-missioned
SAM HOUSTON	SSN 609	Newport News S.B.	Dec 1959	Mar 1962
THOMAS A. EDISON	SSN 610	GD (EB Div)	Mar 1960	Mar 1962
JOHN MARSHALL	SSN 611	Newport News S.B.	Apr 1960	May 1962
THOMAS JEFFERSON	SSN 618	Newport News S.B.	Feb 1961	Jan 1963

Remarks: The 'Ethan Allen' class of nuclear-powered ballistic-missile submarine was designed in the late 1950s as successor to the 'George Washington' class, with greater size and improved layout to offer enhanced operational performance and increased diving depth. The latter is comparable with that of the contemporary 'Thresher' class fleet submarine thanks to the use of HY-80 steel as the primary structural medium. When the Poseidon SLBM was introduced it was decided not to convert this class for the new weapon, and with the phasing out of the Polaris SLBM the units of this class were modified as fleet submarines, largely as training boats. SSBNs 609 and 610 were reclassified as SSNs in 1980, SSBNs 611 and 618 following in 1981. The other units were scrapped, and the *Thomas A. Edison* (SSN 610) has since been laid up in reserve.

'George Washington' class nuclear-powered fleet submarine

USA

Displacement: 6,020 tons standard and 6,890 tons dived
Dimensions: length 381·7ft (116·3m); beam 33ft (10·1m); draught 29ft (8·8m)
Gun armament: none
Missile armament: 16 launch tubes for UGM-27 Polaris submarine-launched ballistic missiles; when the boats were converted from SSBNs to SSNs these tubes were filled with cement as ballast, the associated Mk 84 missile fire-control systems and two SINS (Ship's Inertial Navigation Systems) being removed at the same time
Torpedo armament: six 21-in (533-mm) Mk 59 tubes (all bow)
Anti-submarine armament: A/S torpedoes (see above)
Electronics: one multi-function sonar, one Mk 2 SINS, and one WSC-3 satellite communications transceiver
Propulsion: one pressurized-water cooled Westinghouse S5W nuclear reactor supplying steam to two sets of General Electric geared turbines delivering 15,000shp (11,185kW) to one shaft
Performance: maximum speed 20kts surfaced and 31kts submerged
Complement: 12+100

Class
1. USA (3)

Name	No.	Builders	Laid down	Com-missioned
GEORGE WASHINGTON	SSN 598	GD (EB Div)	Nov 1957	Dec 1959
PATRICK HENRY	SSN 599	GD (EB Div)	May 1958	Apr 1960
ROBERT E. LEE	SSN 601	Newport News S.B.	Aug 1958	Sep 1960

Remarks: The 'George Washington' class was the Western world's first submarine class fitted with underwater-launched ballistic missiles, in the form of 16 Polaris SLBMs. The origins of the class lie with the SSN *Scorpion*, which was modified while under construction to become the SSBN *George Washington* (SSGN 598, later SSBN 598). The conversion included an increase of 130ft (39·62m) in length, the addition of a pronounced dorsal 'hump' to accommodate the upper ends of the missile tubes, and the installation of the relevant navigation and fire-control systems. In later 1981 and early 1982 the last three survivors were reclassified as SSNs, though *Robert E. Lee* (SSN 601) is now in reserve; the other two boats serve with the Pacific Fleet, and have been much simplified in their systems.

'Glenard P. Lipscomb' class nuclear-powered fleet submarine

USA

Displacement: 5,815 tons standard and 6,480 tons dived
Dimensions: length 365 ft (111·3 m); beam 31·7 ft (9·7 m); draught 31 ft (9·5 m)
Gun armament: none
Missile armament: four Sub-Harpoon anti-ship missiles
Torpedo armament: four 21-in (533-mm) tubes (all amidships) for 15 torpedoes
Anti-submarine armament: four tube-launched UMM-44A SUBROC missiles and A/S torpedoes
Electronics: one BPS-15 surface-search radar, one BQQ-2/5 sonar suite, one Mk 117 torpedo fire-control system, one Mk 2 Ship's Inertial Navigation System, and one WSC-3 satellite communications transceiver
Propulsion: one pressurized-water cooled Westinghouse S5Wa nuclear reactor delivering steam to one General Electric turbo-electric drive delivering ?hp (?kW) to one shaft
Performance: maximum speed 25+ kts submerged

Complement: 12+108

Class

Name	No.	Builders	Laid down	Commissioned
1. USA (1)				
GLENARD P. LIPSCOMB	SSN 685	GD (EB Div)	June 1971	Dec 1974

Remarks: The origins of the 'Glenard P. Lipscomb' class design can be traced back to 1964, when the US Navy was expressing considerable dissatisfaction with the high underwater noise levels of contemporary fleet submarines, which stemmed largely from their steam turbine powerplants. Experiments had already been undertaken with the turbo-electric driven *Tullibee* (SSN 597), prototype for the 'Thresher' class with the sonar allocated the prime bow position and the torpedo tubes relegated to the amidships position, and this was taken a step further with the *Glenard P. Lipscomb* (SSN 685), which unfortunately suffered from excessive powerplant size and weight, which reduced performance.

'Los Angeles' class nuclear-powered fleet submarine

USA

Displacement: 6,000 tons standard and 6,900 tons dived
Dimensions: length 360 ft (109·7 m); beam 33 ft (10·1 m); draught 32·3 ft (9·9 m)
Gun armament: none
Missile armament: tube-launched RGM-84A Harpoon underwater-to-surface missiles, and BGM-109 Tomahawk underwater-to-surface missiles; of the latter type, SSNs 688-720 will each carry 12 for tube-launching, while remaining boats will have two vertical banks of 15 missile-launch tubes in the VLS arrangement
Torpedo armament: four 21-in (533-mm) tubes (all amidships) for 26 weapons
Anti-submarine armament: Mk 48 A/S torpedoes and UUM-44 SUBROC missiles
Electronics: one BPS-15 surface-search radar, one Hughes/General Electric/IBM/Raytheon BQQ-5 multi-function attack sonar (including EDO BQR-7 passive sonar and Raytheon BQS-13 active/passive search sonar), one BQS-15 close-range sonar, and one Western Electric BQR-15 towed passive sonar all used in conjunction with the Mk 113 torpedo fire-control system (to be replaced by Mk 117 torpedo fire-control system, which will be fitted from SSN 700 onwards) with the aid of an UYK-7 computer, and WSC-3 satellite communications transceiver
Propulsion: one pressurized-water cooled General Electric S6G nuclear reactor supplying steam to two sets of geared turbines delivering about 35,000 shp (26,100 kW) to one shaft
Performance: maximum speed 31 kts submerged; diving depth 1,475 ft (450 m) operational and 2,460 ft (750 m) maximum
Complement: 12+115

The pennant number 714 identifies this sleek submarine as the Norfolk (SSN 714), a fleet submarine of the large 'Los Angeles' class.

Remarks: The 'Los Angeles' class of fleet submarines is planned as the US Navy's standard attack boat into the 21st century, and marks a considerable advance in underwater capability by combining the weapons and sensors of the 'Thresher' and 'Sturgeon' classes with a more refined hull form and greatly improved powerplant, reportedly based on the General Dynamics D2G reactor used in the 'Truxtun' class guided-missile cruiser. Thus power has been more than doubled in comparison with that of the 'Sturgeon' class, but only at the expense of size and weight, which have partially offset the advantages that would otherwise have accrued from the use of the more powerful propulsion system. Even so, the 'Los Angeles' class boats are the only US Navy SSNs able to match the speed of carrier task groups, allowing them to be deployed with such groups as counters to Soviet SSNs and SSGNs. The sensor fit is admirable, but the first 33 boats are having their complement of ASW torpedoes cut to permit the carriage of 12 tube-launched BGM-109 Tomahawk cruise missiles with anti-ship warheads. From the 34th boat onward 15 vertical launch tubes for Tomahawks will be fitted between the pressure and outer hulls in the area of the sonar dome in the bows, returning ASW weapon strength (torpedoes and SUBROC missiles) to 26. Sensor improvements are also on the way, for later boats will replace the clip-on towed-array sonar with a retractable towed-array sonar system. Apart from its lack of speed in comparison with the Soviet 'Alfa' class boats, the main failing of the 'Los Angeles' class is its size, which precludes operations over the continental shelf.

Class

Name	No.	Builders	Laid down	Commissioned
1. USA (30+11+21)				
LOS ANGELES	SSN 688	Newport News S.B.	Jan 1972	Nov 1976
BATON ROUGE	SSN 689	Newport News S.B.	Nov 1972	June 1977
PHILADELPHIA	SSN 690	GD (EB Div)	Aug 1972	June 1977
MEMPHIS	SSN 691	Newport News S.B.	June 1973	Dec 1977
OMAHA	SSN 692	GD (EB Div)	Jan 1973	Mar 1978
CINCINNATI	SSN 693	Newport News S.B.	Apr 1974	June 1978
GROTON	SSN 694	GD (EB Div)	Aug 1973	July 1978
BIRMINGHAM	SSN 695	Newport News S.B.	Apr 1975	Dec 1978
NEW YORK CITY	SSN 696	GD (EB Div)	Dec 1973	Mar 1979
INDIANAPOLIS	SSN 697	GD (EB Div)	Oct 1974	Jan 1980
BREMERTON	SSN 698	GD (EB Div)	May 1976	Mar 1981
JACKSONVILLE	SSN 699	GD (EB Div)	Feb 1976	May 1981
DALLAS	SSN 700	GD (EB Div)	Oct 1976	July 1981
LA JOLLA	SSN 701	GD (EB Div)	Oct 1976	Oct 1981
PHOENIX	SSN 702	GD (EB Div)	July 1977	Dec 1981
BOSTON	SSN 703	GD (EB Div)	Aug 1978	Jan 1982
BALTIMORE	SSN 704	GD (EB Div)	May 1979	Feb 1982
CORPUS CHRISTI	SSN 705	GD (EB Div)	Sep 1979	1982
ALBUQUERQUE	SSN 706	GD (EB Div)	Dec 1979	1983
PORTSMOUTH	SSN 707	GD (EB Div)	May 1980	1983
MINNEAPOLIS-ST PAUL	SSN 708	GD (EB Div)	Jan 1981	1984
HYMAN G. RICKOVER	SSN 709	GD (EB Div)	July 1981	1984
—	SSN 710	GD (EB Div)	Mar 1982	1985
SAN FRANCISCO	SSN 711	Newport News S.B.	May 1977	Apr 1981
ATLANTA	SSN 712	Newport News S.B.	Aug 1978	Feb 1982
HOUSTON	SSN 713	Newport News S.B.	Jan 1979	1982
NORFOLK	SSN 714	Newport News S.B.	Aug 1979	1983
BUFFALO	SSN 715	Newport News S.B.	Jan 1980	1983
SALT LAKE CITY	SSN 716	Newport News S.B.	Aug 1980	1983
OLYMPIA	SSN 717	Newport News S.B.	Mar 1981	1984
—	SSN 718	Newport News S.B.	Nov 1981	1984
—	SSN 719	GD (EB Div)	1982	1985
—	SSN 720	GD (EB Div)	1983	1985
—	SSN 721	Newport News S.B.	—	1986
—	SSN 772	Newport News S.B.	—	1987
—	SSN 723	Newport News S.B.	—	1987
—	SSN 724	GD (EB Div)	—	—
—	SSN 725	GD (EB Div)	—	—
NEWPORT NEWS	SSN 750	Newport News S.B.	—	—
—	SSN 751	GD (EB Div)	—	—
—	SSN 752	GD (EB Div)	—	—
—	SSN 753-5	Proposed FY 1984	—	—
—	SSN 756-9	Proposed FY 1985	—	—
—	SSN 760-3	Proposed FY 1986	—	—
—	SSN 764-8	Proposed FY 1987	—	—
—	SSN 769-73	Proposed FY 1988	—	—

'Narwhal' class nuclear-powered fleet submarine

USA

Displacement: 4,450 tons standard and 5,350 tons dived
Dimensions: length 314·6ft (95·6m); beam 37·7ft (11·5m); draught 27ft (8·2m)
Gun armament: none

Missile armament: to be fitted with RGM-84A Harpoon and BGM-109 Tomahawk underwater-to-surface missiles
Torpedo armament: four 21-in (533-mm) tubes (all amidships)
Anti-submarine armament: A/S torpedoes and UUM-44 SUBROC missiles
Electronics: one Raytheon BQQ-2 attack sonar system with BQS-6 active and BQR-7 passive units, and used in conjunction with the Mk 113 torpedo fire-control system (to be replaced by Mk 117 torpedo fire-control system), one EDO/Hazeltine BQS-8 upward-looking sonar for under-ice operations, and WSC-3 satellite communications transceiver
Propulsion: one pressurized-water cooled General Electric S5G nuclear reactor supplying steam to two sets of geared turbines delivering 17,000shp (12,675kW) to one shaft
Performance: maximum speed 20+ kts surfaced and 30+ kts submerged
Complement: 12+95

Class
1. USA (1)

Name	No.	Builders	Laid down	Commissioned
NARWHAL	SSN 671	GD (EB Div)	Jan 1966	July 1969

*The **Narwhal** (SSN 671) uses a natural-convection powerplant in an effort to reduce machinery noise (circulation pumps) at low speeds.*

'November' class nuclear-powered fleet submarine

USSR

Displacement: 4,200 tons surfaced and 5,000 tons dived
Dimensions: length 109·7m (359·8ft); beam 9·1m (29·8ft); draught 6·7m (21·9ft)
Gun armament: none
Missile armament: none
Torpedo armament: eight 533-mm (21-in) tubes (all bow) for 24 torpedoes
Anti-submarine armament: two 406-mm (16-in) tubes (stern) for two A/S torpedoes plus A/S torpedoes (see above)
Electronics: one 'Snoop Tray' surface-search radar, one 'Stop Light' electronic countermeasures system, one *Herkules* sonar, and one *Feniks* sonar
Propulsion: two nuclear reactors supplying steam to two sets of geared turbines delivering 22,370kW (30,000shp) to two shafts
Performance: maximum speed 20kts surfaced and 30kts submerged; diving depth 300m (985ft) operational and 500m (1,640ft) maximum
Complement: 86
Class
1. USSR (12)
12 boats

'Rubis' class nuclear-powered fleet submarine

France

Displacement: 2,385 tons surfaced and 2,670 tons dived
Dimensions: length 72·1m (236·5ft); beam 7·6m (24·9ft); draught 6·4m (21ft)
Gun armament: none
Missile armament: SM.39 Exocet underwater-to-surface missiles to be fitted when developed

Torpedo armament: four 533-mm (21-in) tubes (all bow) for 14 torpedoes
Anti-submarine armament: A/S torpedoes carried as part of the total above
Mines: up to 14 in place of torpedoes
Electronics: one surface-search radar, one DSUV 22 passive listening sonar, one CIT/Alcatel DUUA 2B active sonar, one CIT/Alcatel DUUX 2 passive detection and ranging sonar, one TUUM 1 underwater telephone, and extensive electronic countermeasures systems
Propulsion: one nuclear reactor supplying steam to two turbo-alternators delivering current to one electric motor driving one shaft
Performance: maximum speed 26kts submerged
Complement: 9+35+22

Class
1. France (2+4)

Name	No.	Builders	Laid down	Commissioned
RUBIS	S 601	Cherbourg ND	Dec 1976	July 1982
SAPHIR	S 602	Cherbourg ND	Sep 1979	July 1984
—	S 603	Cherbourg ND	Sep 1981	mid-1986
—	S 604	Cherbourg ND	Oct 1982	1987
—	S 605	Cherbourg ND	—	1988

The 'Rubis' class SSN has smaller dimensions than any other fleet submarine.

'Skate' class nuclear-powered fleet submarine

USA

Displacement: 2,310 tons light and 2,360 tons full load (SSNs 578 and 579) or 2,385 tons light and 2,545 tons full load (SSNs 583 and 584)
Dimensions: length 267·7ft (81·5m); beam 25ft (7·6m); draught 22ft (6·7m)
Gun armament: none
Missile armament: none
Torpedo armament: six 21-in (533-mm) tubes (all bow)
Anti-submarine armament: two 21-in (533-mm) tubes (both stern) for short A/S torpedoes
Electronics: one Raytheon/EDO/Honeywell BQS-4 active/passive sonar used in conjunction with the Mk 101 torpedo fire-control system
Propulsion: one pressurized-water cooled nuclear reactor (Westinghouse S3W in SSNs 578 and 583, and Westinghouse S4W in SSNs 579 and 584) supplying steam to two sets of Westinghouse geared turbines delivering 6,600shp (4,920kW) to two shafts

Performance: maximum speed 20+ kts surfaced and 25+ kts submerged
Complement: 11+76

Class
1. USA (4)

Name	No.	Builders	Laid down	Commissioned
SKATE	SSN 578	GD (EB Div)	July 1955	Dec 1957
SWORDFISH	SSN 579	Portsmouth Navy Yard	Jan 1956	Sep 1958
SARGO	SSN 583	Mare Island Navy Yard	Feb 1956	Oct 1958
SEADRAGON	SSN 584	Portsmouth Navy Yard	June 1956	Dec 1959

Remarks: The 'Skate' class SSNs were the world's first production fleet submarines, and the design was modelled on that of the pioneering *Nautilus* (SSN 571) though with a smaller and more maintainable reactor system of which two variants were built by Westinghouse under the designations S3W and S4W, both equally successful. *Seadragon* (SSN 584) is now in reserve.

'Skipjack' class nuclear-powered fleet submarine
USA
Displacement: 3,075 tons surfaced and 3,515 tons dived
Dimensions: length 251·7ft (76·7m); beam 31·5ft (9·6m); draught 29·4ft (8·9m)
Gun armament: none
Missile armament: none
Torpedo armament: six 21-in (533-mm) Mk 59 tubes (all bow) for 24 torpedoes
Anti-submarine armament: A/S torpedoes included in the total above
Electronics: one Raytheon/EDO/Honeywell BQS-4 active/passive sonar used in conjunction with the Mk 101 torpedo fire-control system
Propulsion: one pressurized-water cooled Westinghouse S5W nuclear reactor supplying steam to two sets of geared turbines (Westinghouse in SSN 585 and General Electric in others) delivering 15,000shp (11,185kW) to one shaft
Performance: maximum speed 16+ kts surfaced and 30+ kts submerged; diving depth 985ft (300m) operational and 1,640ft (500m maximum
Complement: 8+85

Class
1. USA (5)

Name	No.	Builders	Laid down	Commissioned
SKIPJACK	SSN 585	GD (EB Div)	May 1956	Apr 1959
SCAMP	SSN 588	Mare Island NY	Jan 1959	June 1961
SCULPIN	SSN 590	Ingalls Shipbuilding	Feb 1958	June 1961
SHARK	SSN 591	Newport News S.B.	Feb 1958	Feb 1961
SNOOK	SSN 592	Ingalls Shipbuilding	Apr 1958	Oct 1961

Remarks: Despite their age, the five units of the 'Skipjack' class are still considered to be first-line assets of the US Navy's fleet submarine strength, largely for their high underwater speed, unexcelled in a Western boat until the advent of the 'Los Angeles' class. The class originally numbered six boats, but the *Scorpion* (SSN 589) was lost with all hands in the Atlantic in May 1968. Notable features of the design were the adoption of the Westinghouse S5W reactor, which became standard on all American nuclear-powered boats up to the 'Glenard P. Lipscomb' class, and the use of a full-teardrop hull design for maximum underwater speed. The S5W reactor was used in conjunction with fully duplicated engine-room machinery (with the exception of the turbines) to reduce the chances of breakdown, and the long taper of the after section of the hull necessitated the adoption of a single-shaft propulsion scheme and the elimination of the stern torpedo tubes previously standard. At the same time the diving planes were relocated from the hull to the sail in a successful attempt to improve underwater manoeuvrability. With the advent of the 'Los Angeles' class, it is to be expected that the 'Skipjack' class boats (of which one serves with the Pacific Fleet and the other four with the Atlantic Fleet) will be relegated to secondary tasks; the role of high-speed underwater ASW target looks most suitable for these still-speedy boats. The boats each carry a normal load of 24 Mk 48 torpedoes, or alternatively a load of 48 Mk 57 moored mines. The submarine-launched Mk 48 torpedo is the US Navy's standard heavyweight weapon for this role, and is a wire-guided weapon with active/passive acoustic homing suitable for the anti-submarine and anti-ship roles. The Mk 48's maximum speed is 50kts and its range 29 miles (47km).

'Sturgeon' class nuclear-powered fleet submarine
USA
Displacement: 3,640 tons standard and 4,640 tons full load
Dimensions: length 292·2ft (89·0m); beam 31·7ft (9·5m); draught 26ft (7·9m)
Gun armament: none
Missile armament: four tube-launched Sub-Harpoon underwater-to-surface missiles in SSNs 638, 639, 646, 649, 652, 660, 662, 665, 667-670, 679, 681, 684, 686 and 687; tube-launched BGM-109 Tomahawk underwater-to-surface missiles in all but SSNs 637, 647, 650, 651, 653, 661, 664, 666, 674-678, 680 and 683
Torpedo armament: four 21-in (533-mm) Mk 63 tubes (all amidships) for 15 torpedoes
Anti-submarine armament: A/S torpedoes and four UUM-44A SUBROC missiles
Electronics: one BPS-15 surface-search radar, one Raytheon BQQ-2 sonar system with BQS-6 active and BQR-7 passive sonars used in conjunction with the Mk 117 underwater weapons fire-control system, EDO/Hazeltine BQS-8 under-ice navigation sonar, Raytheon BQS-12 (SSNs 637-639, 646-653 and 660-664) or Raytheon BQS-13 (SSNs 665-670, 672-684 and 686-687) active/passive search sonar, and WSC-3 satellite communications transceiver
Propulsion: one pressurized-water cooled Westinghouse S5W nuclear reactor supplying steam to two sets of geared turbines delivering 15,000shp (11,185kW) to one shaft
Performance: maximum speed 20+ kts surfaced and 30+ kts submerged; diving depth 1,320ft (400m) operational and 1,985ft (600m) maximum
Complement: 12+95

Class
1. USA (37)

Name	No.	Builders	Laid down	Commissioned
STURGEON	SSN 637	GD (Quincy)	Aug 1963	Mar 1967
WHALE	SSN 638	GD (Quincy)	May 1964	Oct 1968
TAUTOG	SSN 639	Ingalls Shipbuilding	Jan 1964	Aug 1968
GRAYLING	SSN 646	Portsmouth NY	May 1964	Oct 1969
POGY	SSN 647	Ingalls Shipbuilding	May 1964	May 1971
ASPRO	SSN 648	Ingalls Shipbuilding	Nov 1964	Feb 1969
SUNFISH	SSN 649	GD (Quincy)	Jan 1965	Mar 1969
PARGO	SSN 650	GD (Quincy)	June 1964	Jan 1968
QUEENFISH	SSN 651	Newport News S.B.	May 1964	Dec 1966
PUFFER	SSN 652	Ingalls Shipbuilding	Feb 1965	Aug 1969
RAY	SSN 653	Newport News S.B.	Apr 1965	Apr 1967
SAND LANCE	SSN 660	Portsmouth NY	Jan 1965	Sep 1971
LAPON	SSN 661	Newport News S.B.	July 1965	Dec 1967
GURNARD	SSN 662	Mare Island NY	Dec 1964	Dec 1968
HAMMERHEAD	SSN 663	Newport News S.B.	Nov 1965	June 1968
SEA DEVIL	SSN 664	Newport News S.B.	Apr 1966	Jan 1969
GUITARRO	SSN 665	Mare Island NY	Dec 1965	Sep 1972
HAWKBILL	SSN 666	Mare Island NY	Sep 1966	Feb 1971
BERGALL	SSN 667	GD (Quincy)	Apr 1966	June 1969
SPADEFISH	SSN 668	Newport News S.B.	Dec 1966	Aug 1969
SEAHORSE	SSN 669	GD (Quincy)	Aug 1966	Sep 1969
FINBACK	SSN 670	Newport News S.B.	June 1967	Feb 1970
PINTADO	SSN 672	Mare Island NY	Oct 1967	Sep 1971
FLYING FISH	SSN 673	GD (Quincy)	June 1967	Apr 1970
TREPANG	SSN 674	GD (Quincy)	Oct 1967	Aug 1970
BLUEFISH	SSN 675	GD (Quincy)	Mar 1968	Jan 1971
BILLFISH	SSN 676	GD (Quincy)	Sep 1968	Mar 1971
DRUM	SSN 677	Mare Island NY	Aug 1968	Apr 1972
ARCHERFISH	SSN 678	GD (Quincy)	June 1969	Dec 1971
SILVERSIDES	SSN 679	GD (Quincy)	Oct 1969	May 1972
WILLIAM H. BATES	SSN 680	Ingalls Shipbuilding	Aug 1969	May 1973
BATFISH	SSN 681	GD (Quincy)	Feb 1970	Sep 1972
TUNNY	SSN 682	Ingalls Shipbuilding	May 1970	Jan 1974
PARCHE	SSN 683	Ingalls Shipbuilding	Dec 1970	Aug 1974
CAVALLA	SSN 684	GD (Quincy)	June 1970	Feb 1973
L. MENDEL RIVERS	SSN 686	Newport News S.B.	June 1971	Feb 1975
RICHARD B. RUSSELL	SSN 687	Newport News S.B.	Oct 1971	Aug 1975

The evolution of the 'Sturgeon' class nuclear-powered fleet submarine from the 'Thresher' class can be distinguished in the type's alteration from the pure teardrop shape of the 'Albacore' type of hull, with a cylindrical section inserted aft of the taller sail. Seen here is the Drum (SSN 677) running on the surface off San Diego, California. In this class the optimum bow position is reserved for sonar, the four torpedo tubes being angled outwards, two on each beam, in the midships section.

Remarks: The 'Sturgeon' class of 37 boats was the world's most prolific single class of nuclear-powered vessel until the advent of the 'Los Angeles' class, and was essentially a development of the 'Thresher' class with additional noise-reduction features and extra electronics. The last nine units are 10ft (3·05m) longer than their predecessors to permit the installation of additional electronics. The bow position is reserved for the sonar, the torpedo tubes comprising a pair angled out on each beam abaft the sail, which is taller than that of the 'Thresher' class, with the diving planes set lower to improve control when the submarine is at periscope depth. Some 22 of the boats are allocated to the Atlantic Fleet and the other 15 to the Pacific Fleet, these groups including respectively five and four 'Holy Stone' boats, with special electronic equipment for use by the National Security Agency in sensitive areas.

'Swiftsure' class nuclear-powered fleet submarine

UK

Displacement: 4,200 tons standard and 4,500 tons dived
Dimensions: length 272ft (82·9m); beam 32·3ft (9·8m); draught 27ft (8·2m)
Gun armament: none
Missile armament: five Sub-Harpoon underwater-to-surface missiles

Swiftsure (S 126) on the surface.

Torpedo armament: five 21-in (533-mm) tubes (all bow) for 20 torpedoes
Anti-submarine armament: A/S torpedoes included in the total above
Electronics: one Kelvin Hughes Type 1006 surface-search radar, one Type 2019 sonar, one Type 197 sonar, one Type 2001 active/passive sonar, one GEC Type 2007 passive long-range sonar, and one Type 2024 towed sonar
Propulsion: one pressurized-water cooled Rolls-Royce nuclear reactor supplying steam to one set of General Electric geared turbines delivering 15,000shp (11,185kW) to one shaft; there is also an auxiliary Paxman diesel delivering 4,000hp (2,985kW)
Performance: maximum speed 28kts surfaced and 30+ kts submerged; diving depth 1,325ft (400m) operational and 1,985ft (600m) maximum
Complement: 12+85

Class

1. UK (6)				
Name	No.	Builders	Laid down	Commissioned
SWIFTSURE	S 126	Vickers (Shipbuilding) Ltd	June 1969	Apr 1973
SOVEREIGN	S 108	Vickers (Shipbuilding) Ltd	Sep 1970	July 1974
SUPERB	S 109	Vickers (Shipbuilding) Ltd	Mar 1972	Nov 1976
SCEPTRE	S 104	Vickers (Shipbuilding) Ltd	Feb 1974	Feb 1978
SPARTAN	S 105	Vickers (Shipbuilding) Ltd	Apr 1976	Sep 1979
SPLENDID	S 106	Vickers (Shipbuilding) Ltd	Nov 1977	Mar 1981

Remarks: The 'Swiftsure' class is the Royal Navy's second-generation SSN, with a larger hull than the 'Valiant' class for greater internal volume and deeper diving capability combined with higher speed. Each of the five torpedo tubes can be reloaded in only 15 seconds. Type 2020 multi-role sonar is to be retrofitted in place of the current Type 2001 during normal refits.

'Thresher' class nuclear-powered fleet submarine

USA

Displacement: 3,750 tons standard or 3,800 tons standard (SSNs 613-615) and 4,300 tons dived or 4,470 tons dived (SSN 605) or 4,245 tons dived (SSNs 613-615)
Dimensions: length 278·5ft (84·9m) or 297·4ft (90·7m) for SSN 605 or 292·2ft (89·1m) for SSNs 613-615; beam 31·7ft (9·6m); draught 28·4ft (8·7m)
Gun armament: none
Missile armament: four Sub-Harpoon underwater-to-surface missiles
Torpedo armament: four 21-in (533-mm) Mk 63 tubes (amidships) for 15 torpedoes
Anti-submarine armament: A/S torpedoes and four UUM-44A SUBROC missiles
Electronics: one Raytheon BQQ-2 sonar system with BQS-6 active and BQR-7 passive sonar elements, used in conjunction with the Mk 117 underwater weapons fire-control system, WSC-3 satellite communications transceiver
Propulsion: one pressurized-water cooled Westinghouse S5W nuclear reactor supplying steam to two sets of geared turbines delivering 15,000shp (11,185kW) to one shaft, except in SSN 605 which has an ungeared contra-rotating turbine driving co-axial contra-rotating propellers

Performance: maximum speed 20+ kts surfaced and 30+ kts submerged; diving depth 1,325ft (400m) operational and 1,985ft (600m) maximum
Complement: 12+91

Class

1. USA (13)				
Name	No.	Builders	Laid down	Commissioned
PERMIT	SSN 594	Mare Island NY	July 1959	May 1962
PLUNGER	SSN 595	Mare Island NY	Mar 1960	Nov 1962
BARB	SSN 596	Ingalls Shipbuilding	Nov 1959	Aug 1963
POLLACK	SSN 603	New York Shipbuilding	Mar 1960	May 1964
HADDO	SSN 604	New York Shipbuilding	Sep 1960	Dec 1964
JACK	SSN 605	Portsmouth NY	Sep 1960	Mar 1967
TINOSA	SSN 606	Portsmouth NY	Nov 1959	Oct 1964
DACE	SSN 607	Ingalls Shipbuilding	June 1960	Apr 1964
GUARDFISH	SSN 612	New York Shipbuilding	Feb 1961	Dec 1966
FLASHER	SSN 613	GD (EB Div)	Apr 1961	July 1966
GREENLING	SSN 614	GD (EB Div)	Aug 1961	Nov 1967
GATO	SSN 615	GD (EB Div)	Dec 1961	Jan 1968
HADDOCK	SSN 621	Ingalls Shipbuilding	Apr 1961	Dec 1967

'Trafalgar' class nuclear-powered fleet submarine

UK

Displacement: 4,700 tons surfaced and 5,200 tons dived
Dimensions: length 85·4m (280·1ft); beam 9·8m (32·1ft); draught 8·2m (26·9ft)
Gun armament: none
Missile armament: up to five tube-launched Sub-Harpoon anti-ship missiles
Torpedo armament: five 21-in (533-mm) tubes (all bow) for 20 Mk 8 and Mk 24 Tigerfish torpedoes, or 50 Mk 5 Stonefish and Mk 6 Sea Urchin mines
Anti-submarine armament: torpedoes (above)
Electronics: one Kelvin-Hughes Type 1006 surface-search radar, one Type 2020 multi-role sonar, one Type 2024 towed-array sonar, one BAC Type 2007 long-range passive sonar, one Type 2019 sonar, one passive ESM suite, one DCB missile and torpedo fire-control system, and navigation systems
Propulsion: one pressurized-water cooled reactor supplying steam to two sets of

General Electric geared turbines delivering 15,000shp (11,185kW) to one shaft; one 4,000-hp (2,983-kW) Paxman auxiliary diesel
Performance: maximum speed 20kts surfaced and 32kts submerged; diving depth 1,315ft (400m) operational and 1,970ft (600m) maximum
Complement: 12+85

Class

1. UK (2+3+1)			
Name	Builders	Laid down	Commissioned
TRAFALGAR	Vickers Ltd	1978	Mar 1983
TURBULENT	Vickers Ltd	1979	1984
TIRELESS	Vickers Ltd	1981	—
TORBAY	Vickers Ltd	1982	—
TALENT	Vickers Ltd	1983	—

'Tullibee' class nuclear-powered fleet submarine

USA

Displacement: 2,315 tons standard and 2,640 tons dived
Dimensions: length 273ft (83·2m); beam 23·3ft (7·1m); draught 21ft (6·4m)
Gun armament: none
Missile armament: none
Torpedo armament: four 21-in (533-mm) Mk 64 tubes (all amidships)
Anti-submarine armament: A/S torpedoes
Electronics: one Raytheon BQQ-2 sonar system with BQS-6 active and BQR-7 passive sonars, and one Sperry/Raytheon BQG-4 Passive Underwater Fire-control Feasibility System (PUFFS), both systems used in conjunction with the Mk

112 torpedo fire-control system
Propulsion: one pressurized-water cooled Combustion Engineering S2C nuclear reactor supplying steam to one Westinghouse turbo-electric drive unit delivering 2,500shp (1,865kW) to one shaft
Performance: maximum speed 15+ kts surfaced and 20+ kts submerged
Complement: 6+50

Class

1. USA (1)				
Name	No.	Builders	Laid down	Commissioned
TULLIBEE	SSN 597	GD (EB Div)	May 1958	Nov 1960

'Victor I' class nuclear-powered fleet submarine
USSR
Displacement: 4,200 tons surfaced and 5,200 tons dived
Dimensions: length 93·9m (307·7ft); beam 10·0m (32·8ft); draught 7·3m (23·9ft)
Gun armament: none
Missile armament: none
Torpedo armament: six 533-mm (21-in) tubes (all bow) for 18 torpedoes
Anti-submarine armament: 10 A/S torpedoes, and two SS-N-15 underwater-to-underwater missiles
Electronics: one 'Snoop Tray' surface-search radar, one bow-mounted low-frequency sonar array, and one hull-mounted medium-frequency fire-control sonar array
Propulsion: two nuclear reactors supplying steam to two sets of geared turbines delivering 22,370kW (30,000shp) to one main and two auxiliary shafts
Performance: maximum speed 20kts surfaced and 32kts submerged; diving depth 400m (1,325ft) operational and 600m (1,970ft) maximum
Complement: 90

Part of the crew of a 'Victor I' class SSN enjoy themselves in the sun of the Malacca Strait while being photographed in 1974.

Class
1. USSR (16)
16 boats

'Victor II' class nuclear-powered fleet submarine
USSR
Displacement: 4,800 tons surfaced and 5,800 tons dived
Dimensions: length 100·0m (328·1ft); beam 10·0m (32·8ft); draught 7·3m (23·9ft)
Gun armament: none
Missile armament: none
Torpedo armament: six 533-mm (21-in) tubes (all bow) for 20 torpedoes
Anti-submarine armament: 10 A/S torpedoes and two SS-N-16 missiles
Electronics: one 'Snoop Tray' surface-search radar, one bow-mounted low-frequency sonar array, one hull-mounted medium-frequency fire-control sonar array, and one 'Brick Group' electronic support measures system with 'Brick Spit' passive intercept and 'Brick Pulp' threat-warning systems

Propulsion: two nuclear reactors supplying steam to two sets of geared turbines delivering 22,370kW (30,000shp) to one main and two auxiliary shafts
Performance: maximum speed 20kts surfaced and 31kts submerged; diving depth 400m (1,325ft) operational and 600m (1,970ft) maximum
Complement: 90
Class
1. USSR (7)
7 boats
Remarks: The 'Victor' classes still form the main strength of the Soviet fleet submarine strength. The 'Victor I' appeared in 1967 and introduced teardrop shape to the Soviet navy, 'Victor II' in 1972 and 'Victor III' in 1976.

'Victor III' class nuclear-powered fleet submarine
USSR
Displacement: 5,000 tons surfaced and 6,000 tons dived
Dimensions: length 104·0m (341·2ft); beam 10·0m (32·8ft); draught 7·3m (23·9ft)
Gun armament: none
Missile armament: none
Torpedo armament: six 533-mm (21-in) tubes (all bow) for 20 torpedoes
Anti-submarine armament: A/S torpedoes, and SS-N-16 underwater-to-underwater missiles
Electronics: one 'Snoop Tray' surface-search radar, one bow-mounted low-frequency sonar array, one hull-mounted medium-frequency fire-control sonar

array, (possibly) one towed-array sonar, and one 'Brick Group' electronic support measures system with 'Brick Spit' passive intercept and 'Brick Pulp' threat-warning systems
Propulsion: two nuclear reactors supplying steam to two sets of geared turbines delivering 22,370kW (30,000shp) to one main and two auxiliary shafts
Performance: maximum speed 20kts surfaced and 30kts submerged; diving depth 400m (1,325ft) operational and 600m (1,970ft) maximum
Complement: 90
Class
1. USSR (16+?)
16 boats plus ? building

'Agosta' class patrol submarine
France
Displacement: 1,200 tons standard, 1,450 tons surfaced and 1,725 tons dived
Dimensions: length 67·6m (221·7ft); beam 6·8m (22·3ft); draught 5·4m (17·7ft)
Gun armament: none
Missile armament: none
Torpedo armament: four 550-mm (21·65-in) tubes (all forward) and 20 torpedoes
Anti-submarine armament: A/S torpedoes (see above)
Electronics: one Thomson-CSF Calypso II surface-search and navigation radar, one DSUV 2 passive sonar, one DUUA 1 active sonar, one DUUA 2 active search and attack sonar and one DUUX 2 passive ranging sonar
Propulsion: diesel-electric arrangement, with two SEMT-Pielstick A 16 PA4 185 main diesels delivering 2,680kW (3,600hp), one cruising diesel engine delivering 23kW (31hp), and one electric motor delivering 3,500kW (4,695hp) to one shaft
Performance: maximum speed 12kts surfaced and 20kts submerged; range 15,750km (9,785 miles) at 9kts schnorkelling and 400km (249 miles) at 3·5kts submerged; endurance 45 days
Complement: 7+45

The French navy's 'Agosta' class Ouessant (S 623) on the surface.

Class

1. France (4)

Name	No.	Builders	Laid down	Commissioned
AGOSTA	S 620	Cherbourg ND	Nov 1972	July 1977
BÉVÉVIERS	S 621	Cherbourg ND	May 1973	Sep 1977
LA PRAYA	S 622	Cherbourg ND	1974	Mar 1978
OUESSANT	S 623	Cherbourg ND	1974	July 1978

2. Pakistan (2)

Name	No.	Builders	Laid down	Commissioned
HASHMAT	S 135	Dubigeon-Normandie	Sep 1976	Feb 1979
HURMAT	S 136	Dubigeon-Normandie	—	Feb 1980

3. Spain (4)

Name	No.	Builders	Laid down	Commissioned
GALERNA	S 71	Bazán	Sep 1977	June 1982
SIROCO	S 72	Bazán	1978	May 1983
MISTRAL	S 73	Bazán	May 1980	June 1984
TRAMONTANA	S 74	Bazán	Dec 1981	June 1985

Remarks: Highly capable boats for continental-shelf operations, the 'Agosta' class patrol submarine was designed for minimum internal and external noise, the latter being promoted particularly by a clean casing. These were the first French patrol submarines fitted with 533- rather than 550-mm (21- rather than 21.7-in) torpedo tubes, and these can be operated at all speeds right down to maximum depth, with a rapid-reload capability installed. The two Pakistani boats were built originally for South Africa, but were embargoed by the UN Organization while building. The Spanish boats have a different electronics fit, this including DRUA 33C radar, plus two DUAA-21 active sonars, one DSUV 2H passive sonar and one DUUX-2A ranging sonar; it is also likely that SM.39 Exocet underwater-launched missiles may be carried.

'Asashio' class patrol submarine

Japan
Displacement: 1,650 tons standard
Dimensions: length 88·0m (288·7ft); beam 8·2m (26·9ft); draught 4·9m (16·2ft)
Gun armament: none
Missile armament: none
Torpedo armament: six 21-in (533-mm) tubes (bow) for 16 torpedoes
Anti-submarine armament: two 12·75-in (324-mm) tubes aft for swim-out A/S torpedoes
Electronics: one ZPS-3 surface-search radar, one JQS-3A sonar, one JQS-2A sonar, and one UQS-1 sonar
Propulsion: diesel-electric, with two Kawasaki diesels delivering 2,165kW

(2,900shp) and two electric motors delivering 4,700kW (6,300hp) to two shafts
Performance: maximum speed 14kts surfaced and 18kts submerged
Complement: 80

Class
1. Japan (3)

Name	No.	Builders	Laid down	Commissioned
HARUSHIO	SS 563	Mitsubishi	Oct 1965	Dec 1967
MICHISHIO	SS 564	Kawasaki	July 1966	Aug 1968
ARASHIO	SS 565	Mitsubishi	July 1967	July 1969

Remarks: The 'Asashio' class was the first truly modern submarine evolved in Japan after World War II, and by comparison with earlier boats was enlarged to make possible a larger torpedo complement and sensor fit, coupled with greater seaworthiness and a double hull for improved diving depth. There was little remarkable in the design, though a distinctive recognition feature is the 'step' in the leading edge of the sail. It is likely that from the mid-1980s the boats will be relegated to secondary tasks as more of the 'Yuushio' class boats become available. An obsolescent feature was the use of swim-out stern tubes for anti-submarine torpedoes.

'Asashio' class patrol submarine on the surface.

'Balao' class patrol submarine

USA
Displacement: 1,815 tons surfaced and 2,425 tons dived
Dimensions: length 311·6ft (95·0m); beam 27ft (8·2m); draught 17ft (5·2m)
Gun armament: one 5-in (127-mm) L/25
Missile armament: none
Torpedo armament: eight 21-in (533-mm) tubes (six bow and two stern)
Anti-submarine armament: none
Electronics: one SPS-2 air-search, one BQR passive sonar, one BQS active sonar and Mk 106 fire-control system
Propulsion: diesel-electric arrangement with four General Motors diesels delivering 6,500hp (4,850kW) and two electric motors delivering 4,610bhp (3,440kW) to two shafts
Performance: maximum speed 20kts surfaced and 10kts dived
Complement: 80

Class
1. Chile (1)

Name	No.	Builders	Laid down	Commissioned
SIMPSON	21	Mare Island Navy Yard	1943	Aug 1944

Remarks: The *Simpson* (21) was transferred to Chile in 1961, and then paid off in 1975. However, after a major refit in 1977 she was recommissioned as an interim first-line but longer-term training boat. The 'Balao' class was a variant of the mass-produced 'Gato' class with a hull strengthened to permit greater diving depth, and represents the culmination of US experience with patrol submarines in the years up to 1939. The design is characterized by good finish and careful attention to detail, with considerable cruising range thanks to the provision of substantial bunkerage and food storage.

'Barbel' class patrol submarine

USA
Displacement: 1,740 tons standard, 2,145 tons surfaced and 2,895 tons dived
Dimensions: length 219·1ft (66·8m); beam 29ft (8·84m); draught 19ft (5·8m)
Gun armament: none
Missile armament: none
Torpedo armament: six Mk 58 21-in (533-mm) tubes (all bow)
Anti-submarine armament: none
Electronics: one Raytheon/EDO/Honeywell BQS-4 active sonar and one Mk 101 Model 20 torpedo-control system
Propulsion: diesel-electric arrangement with three Fairbanks-Morse diesels delivering 4,800bhp (3,580kW) and one Westinghouse electric motor delivering 3,150shp (2,350kW) to one shaft
Performance: maximum speed 15kts surfaced and 21kts submerged
Complement: 8+69

Class
1. USA (3)

Name	No.	Builders	Laid down	Commissioned
BARBEL	SS 580	Portsmouth Navy Yard	May 1956	Jan 1959
BLUEBACK	SS 581	Ingalls Shipbuilding	Apr 1957	Oct 1959
BONEFISH	SS 582	New York Shipbuilding	June 1957	July 1959

Remarks: The three 'Barbel' class patrol submarines were the last non-nuclear submarines built for the US Navy, and as such represent a peak of their type. The class was authorized in 1956, and represents something of a hybrid design, with the 'Albacore' teardrop hull and centralized attack/control centre of nuclear-powered boats, and the diesel-electric drive plus hull-mounted diving planes of earlier designs. After the boats' construction, however, the diving planes were shifted to the current position on the sail. The boats are still in the active list, two with the Pacific Fleet and one with the Atlantic Fleet, and it is arguable that the US Navy should show a renewed interest in such boats, which have the relatively small size and quietness to operate effectively in the continental-shelf waters of the USA, which are otherwise unprotected by US submarines but accessible to Soviet attack and cruise-missile submarines, which could thus play havoc with major surface and sub-surface combatants of the US Navy as they approached or left their bases in the continental USA. The fact has been appreciated by the USA's NATO allies in Europe (and by the USSR), all of whom maintain a patrol submarine capability if they operate submarines at all.

*The **Barbel (SS 580)** shows off her hybrid lines while running on the surface. The bow planes were originally located on the hull, and were relocated to the sail only after the boat had been launched.*

'Daphné' class patrol submarine

France

Displacement: 700 tons standard, 860 tons surfaced and 1,040 tons dived
Dimensions: length 57·75 m (189·5 ft); beam 6·76 m (22·2 ft); draught 4·62 m (15·2 ft)
Gun armament: none
Missile armament: none
Torpedo armament: 12 550-mm (21·7-in) tubes (eight bow and four stern)
Anti-submarine armament: none
Electronics: one Thomson-CSF Calypso II search and navigation radar, one DSUV 2 passive search sonar, one DUUA 1 active sonar, one DUUA 2A active search and attack sonar, and one DUUX 2 passive ranging sonar
Propulsion: diesel-electric arrangement with two SEMT-Pielstick diesels delivering 915 kW (1,225 bhp) and two electric motors delivering 1,940 kW (2,600 bhp) to two shafts
Performance: maximum speed 13·5 kts surfaced and 16 kts submerged; range 18,500 km (11,495 miles) at 7 kts surfaced, or 5,560 km (3,455 miles) at 7 kts snorting; diving depth 300 m (985 ft) operationally, and 575 m (1,885 ft) maximum
Complement: 6+39

Daphné (S 641) was the lead craft of her class, which has proved highly successful for coastal operations, and has been built extensively for the export market. The sonar installation above the bow is of the old type that has now been replaced by a considerably more bulbous dome just aft of the bow. This reduces performance somewhat, but has considerably superior performance in the all-important underwater acquisition and tracking roles.

Remarks: Nine 'Daphné' class boats are still operational with the French navy, offering a useful capability in the protection of France's Atlantic and Mediterranean coasts and ports. Pakistan operates four boats of the class, three bought directly from France and the *Cachalote* from the Portuguese navy and renamed *Ghazi*. The boats are essentially similar to the French boats, but have been modified internally to suit them to Pakistan's particular operational requirement and climatic conditions. Portugal's surviving three boats are also modified only marginally from the French norm, the same applying to the three boats in South

Class				
1. France (9)				*Com-*
Name	*No.*	*Builders*	*Laid down*	*missioned*
DAPHNÉ	S 641	Dubigeon-Normandie	Mar 1958	June 1964
DIANE	S 642	Dubigeon-Normandie	July 1958	June 1964
DORIS	S 643	Cherbourg ND	Sep 1958	Aug 1964
FLORE	S 645	Cherbourg ND	Sep 1958	May 1964
GALATÉE	S 646	Cherbourg ND	Sep 1958	July 1964
JUNON	S 648	Cherbourg ND	July 1961	Feb 1966
VENUS	S 649	Cherbourg ND	Aug 1961	Jan 1966
PSYCHÉ	S 650	Brest Naval Dockyard	May 1965	July 1969
SIRÉNE	S 651	Brest Naval Dockyard	May 1965	Mar 1970
2. Pakistan (4)				*Com-*
Name	*No.*	*Builders*	*Laid down*	*missioned*
HANGOR	S 131	Arsenal de Brest	Dec 1967	Jan 1970
SHUSHUK	S 132	C. N. Ciotat (Le Trait)	Dec 1967	Jan 1970
MANGRO	S 133	C. N. Ciotat (Le Trait)	July 1968	Aug 1970
GHAZI	S 134	Dubigeon-Normandie	May 1967	Oct 1969
3. Portugal (3)				*Com-*
Name	*No.*	*Builders*	*Laid down*	*missioned*
ALBACORA	S 163	Dubigeon-Normandie	Sep 1965	Oct 1967
BARRACUDA	S 164	Dubigeon-Normandie	Oct 1965	May 1968
DELFIN	S 166	Dubigeon-Normandie	May 1967	Oct 1969
4. South Africa (3)				*Com-*
Name	*No.*	*Builders*	*Laid down*	*missioned*
MARIA VAN RIEBEECK	S 97	Dubigeon-Normandie	Mar 1968	June 1970
EMILY HOBHOUSE	S 98	Dubigeon-Normandie	Nov 1968	Jan 1971
JOHANNA VAN DER MERWE	S 99	Dubigeon-Normandie	Apr 1969	July 1971
5. Spain (4 'S 60' class)				*Com-*
Name	*No.*	*Builders*	*Laid down*	*missioned*
DELFIN	S 61	Bazán	Aug 1968	May 1973
TONINA	S 62	Bazán	1969	July 1973
MARSOPA	S 63	Bazán	Mar 1971	Apr 1975
NARVAL	S 64	Bazán	1971	Nov 1975

African service. These latter constitute the country's main offensive naval force, and must in the near future be supplemented or replaced by larger boats, possibly of local construction. Spain, in keeping with her policy of local construction of imported designs, has built four of the class with considerable French assistance, differing from the French boats only in their radar, which is Thomson-CSF DRUA 31 or 33 with ECM equipment.

'Darter' class patrol submarine

USA

Displacement: 1,590 tons standard, 1,720 tons surfaced and 2,390 tons dived
Dimensions: length 284·5 ft (86·7 m); beam 27·2 ft (8·3 m); draught 19 ft (5·8 m)
Gun armament: none
Missile armament: none
Torpedo armament: eight 21-in (533-mm) tubes (six bow and two stern)
Anti-submarine armament: A/S torpedoes (see above)
Electronics: one Sperry/Raytheon BQG-4 PUFFS passive fire-control sonar used in conjunction with the Mk 106 torpedo fire-control system
Propulsion: diesel-electric arrangement, with three Fairbanks-Morse diesels delivering 4,500 bhp (3,355 kW) and two Elliott electric motors delivering 5,500 shp (4,100 kW) to two shafts

Performance: maximum speed 19·5 kts surfaced and 14 kts submerged
Complement: 8+75

Class				
1. USA (1)				*Com-*
Name	*No.*	*Builders*	*Laid down*	*missioned*
DARTER	SS 576	GD (EB Div)	Nov 1954	Oct 1956

Remarks: The *Darter* (SS 576) was planned as lead craft of a class of at least three, but *Growler* and *Grayback* (SS 574) were completed as missile-launching boats and additional construction was foregone in favour of nuclear-powered submarines. The design is almost identical with that of the 'Tang' class, and the *Darter* is homeported at Sasebo in Japan, being active with the Pacific Fleet.

'Delfinen' class patrol submarine

Denmark

Displacement: 595 tons surfaced and 645 tons dived
Dimensions: length 54·0 m (177·2 ft); beam 4·7 m (15·4 ft); draught 4·2 m (13·8 ft)
Gun armament: none
Missile armament: none
Torpedo armament: four 21-in (533-mm) tubes (all bow)
Anti-submarine armament: A/S torpedoes
Electronics: active and passive sonars
Propulsion: diesel-electric arrangement, with two Burmeister & Wain diesels delivering 895 kW (1,200 bhp) and two electric motors delivering 895 kW (1,200 hp) to two shafts
Performance: maximum speed 16 kts surfaced and submerged; range 7,400 km (4,600 miles) at 8 kts surfaced
Complement: 33

Class				
1. Denmark (3)				*Com-*
Name	*No.*	*Builders*	*Laid down*	*missioned*
DELFINEN	S 326	Royal Dockyard	June 1954	Sep 1958
SPAEKHUGGEREN	S 327	Royal Dockyard	Nov 1954	June 1959
SPRINGEREN	S 329	Royal Dockyard	Jan 1961	Oct 1964

Remarks: Now reaching the ends of their useful lives, the three 'Delfinen' class patrol submarines are typical of the Danish defence policy, which emphasizes the importance of coastal patrol, with a view particularly to the closing in wartime of the exit from the Baltic Sea. The replacements for these three boats will be either the Swedish A17 design from Kockums or a West German design, the type selected to be known in Danish service as the 'UB 80' class.

'Dolfijn' and 'Potvis' class patrol submarine
Netherlands

Displacement: 1,140 tons standard, 1,495 tons surfaced and 1,825 tons dived
Dimensions: length 79·5m (260·9ft); beam 7·8m (25·8ft); draught 5·0m (16·4ft)
Gun armament: none
Missile armament: none
Torpedo armament: eight 21-in (533-mm) tubes (four bow and four stern)
Anti-submarine armament: A/S torpedoes
Electronics: one Type 1001 surface-search radar, sonar, and one Hollandse

Signaalapparaten WM-8 fire-control system
Propulsion: diesel-electric arrangement, with two MAN diesels delivering 2,310kW (3,100bhp) and two electric motors delivering 3,130kW (4,200hp) to two shafts
Performance: maximum speed 14·5kts surfaced and 17kts submerged; diving depth 300m (985ft)
Complement: 67

Class
1. The Netherlands (2 'Dolfijn' class)

Name	No.	Builders	Laid down	Commissioned
DOLFIJN	S 808	Rotterdamse Droogdok Mij	Dec 1954	Dec 1960
ZEEHOND	S 809	Rotterdamse Droogdok Mij	Dec 1954	Mar 1961

2. The Netherlands (2 'Potvis' class)

Name	No.	Builders	Laid down	Commissioned
POTVIS	S 804	Wilton-Fijenoord	Sep 1962	Nov 1965
TONIJH	S 805	Wilton-Fijenoord	Nov 1962	Feb 1966

Remarks: The 'Potvis' and 'Dolfijn' classes are almost identical thanks to the latter's modernization to the former's standard. The combined class is to be replaced by the 'Walrus' class, and the *Dolfijn* (S 808) is now in reserve.

'Draken' class (Type A11) patrol submarine
Sweden

Displacement: 770 tons standard, 835 tons surfaced and 1,110 tons dived
Dimensions: length 69·0m (226·4ft); beam 5·1m (16·7ft); draught 4·6m (15·1ft)
Gun armament: none
Missile armament: none
Torpedo armament: four 533-mm (21-in) tubes (all bow) for 12 torpedoes
Anti-submarine armament: A/S torpedoes (see above)
Electronics: sonar
Propulsion: diesel-electric arrangement, with two Pielstick diesels and one electric motor delivering 1,240kW (1,660bhp) to one shaft
Performance: maximum speed 17kts surfaced and 20kts submerged
Complement: 36

Class
1. Sweden (4)

Name	No.	Builders	Laid down	Commissioned
DELFINEN	Del	Karlskrona Varvet	1959	June 1962
NORDKAPAREN	Nor	Kockums	1959	Apr 1962
SPRINGAREN	Spr	Kockums	1960	Nov 1962
VARGEN	Vgn	Kockums	1958	Nov 1961

'Dos de Mayo' class patrol submarine
USA

Displacement: 825 tons standard and 1,400 tons dived
Dimensions: length 243ft (74·1m); beam 22ft (6·7m); draught 14ft (4·3m)
Gun armament: one 5-in (127-mm) L/25
Missile armament: none
Torpedo armament: six 21-in (533-mm) tubes (four forward and two aft)
Anti-submarine armament: none
Electronics: ?
Propulsion: diesel (surface) and electric (submerged), with two General Motors 278A diesels or two electric motors delivering 2,400bhp (1,791 kW) to two shafts
Performance: maximum speed 16kts surfaced and 10kts submerged; range 5,750 miles (9,255km) at 10kts surfaced
Complement: 40

Class
1. Peru (4)

Name	No.	Builders	Laid down	Commissioned
DOS DE MAYO	S 41	GD (EB Div)	May 1952	June 1954
ABTAO	S 42	GD (EB Div)	May 1952	Feb 1954
ANGAMOS	S 43	GD (EB Div)	Oct 1955	July 1957
IQUIQUE	S 44	GD (EB Div)	Oct 1955	Oct 1957

'Foxtrot' class patrol submarine
USSR

Displacement: 1,950 tons surfaced and 2,500 tons dived
Dimensions: length 91·5m (300·1ft); beam 8·0m (26·2ft); draught 6·1m (20ft)
Gun armament: none
Missile armament: none
Torpedo armament: six 533-mm (21-in) tubes (all bow)
Anti-submarine armament: four 406-mm (16-in) tubes (all stern) for A/S torpedoes carried among the total torpedo capacity of 22
Mines: 44 launched through the torpedo tubes as an alternative to torpedoes
Electronics: one 'Snoop Tray' surface-search radar, one *Herkules* sonar, one *Feniks* sonar, and one 'Stop Light' electronic countermeasures system
Propulsion: diesel-electric arrangement, with three diesels delivering 4,475kW (6,000bhp) and three electric motors delivering 4,475kW (6,000bhp) to three shafts
Performance: maximum speed 18kts surfaced and 16kts submerged; range 37,000km (22,990 miles) at low cruising speed; endurance 70 days
Complement: 8+67

Class
1. Cuba (2)
2 boats

2. India (8+4)

Name	No.
KURSURA	S 20
KARANJ	S 21
KANDERI	S 22
KALVARI	S 23
VELA	S 40
VAGIR	S 41
VAGLI	S 42
VAGSHEER	S 43

3. Libya (6)

Name	No.
AL BADR	311
AL AHAD	313
AL FATEH	312
AL MATREGA	314
plus 2 more	

4. USSR (60)
60 boats

Remarks: The 'Foxtrot' has been a considerable success for the Soviet navy, despite the fact that only 62 out of a planned 160 units were built at the Sudomekh Yard between 1958 and 1971, the curtailment in production being caused by a decision to concentrate on nuclear-powered boats. The type is a hybrid design, combining the hull of the 'Zulu' class with the powerplant of the 'Golf' class.

'Grayback' class transport/patrol submarine

USA

Displacement: 2,670 tons standard and 3,650 tons dived
Dimensions: length 334ft (101·8m); beam 27·2ft (8·3m); draught 19ft (5·8m)
Gun armament: none
Missile armament: none
Torpedo armament: six 21-in (533-mm) Mk 52 tubes (all bow) and two 21-in (533-mm) Mk 53 tubes (both stern)
Anti-submarine armament: A/S torpedoes (see above)
Capacity: 7+60 troops plus landing craft, swimmer delivery vehicles and the like
Electronics: one Sperry/Raytheon BQG-2 passive fire-control sonar and one Raytheon/EDO/Honeywell BQS-4 active/passive underwater fire-control system used in conjunction with the Mk 106 torpedo fire-control system
Propulsion: diesel-electric arrangement, with three Fairbanks-Morse diesels delivering 4,500bhp (3,355kW) and two Elliott electric motors delivering 5,500shp (4,100kW) to two shafts
Performance: 20kts surfaced and 16·7kts submerged
Complement: 12+77

Class

1. USA (1)				Com-
Name	No.	Builders	Laid down	missioned
GRAYBACK	SS 574	Mare Island Navy Yard	July 1954	Mar 1958

Remarks: Though classified officially as a patrol submarine, the *Grayback* (SS 574) is almost unique in the world's modern navies in being a transport submarine for clandestine operations and the delivery of underwater demolition teams. The *Grayback* and her near-sister *Growler* were originally to have been conventional patrol submarines of the 'Darter' class, but were completed as missile-launch submarines each carrying two Regulus I strategic cruise missiles in paired forward hangars. In May 1964 the *Grayback* was taken in hand by Mare Island Naval Shipyard for conversion into a troop transport, the hull being lengthened by 11ft 8in (3·56m) and modified for the sleeping accommodation of 67 troops, and the missile hangars adapted for the carriage of six swimmer delivery vehicles, which can be launched and recovered underwater together with scuba-equipped divers. The boat is based at Subic Bay in the Philippines.

'Guppy IA' class patrol submarine

USA

Displacement: 1,870 tons standard and 2,440 tons dived
Dimensions: length 308ft (93·8m); beam 27ft (8·2m); draught 17ft (5·2m)
Gun armament: none
Missile armament: none
Torpedo armament: 10 21-in (533-mm) tubes (six bow and four stern)
Anti-submarine armament: none
Electronics: navigation/surface-search radar, and sonar
Propulsion: diesel-electric arrangement, with three diesels delivering 4,800hp (3,580kW) and two electric motors delivering 5,400shp (4,025kW) to two shafts
Performance: maximum speed 17kts surfaced and 15kts dived
Complement: 84

Remarks: The GUPPY (Greater Underwater Propulsion Project) programme was launched in the 1950s to improve radically the underwater capabilities of the diesel-electric boats then used in considerable numbers by the US Navy. With the advent of nuclear-powered fleet submarines the programme was curtailed after only 52 boats had been modernized, and these have all been phased out of service with the US Navy, many being transferred to the navies of the USA's principal allies not in a position to afford (and in many cases to need) highly advanced underwater attack craft. Argentina originally received two 'Guppy IA'

Class

1. Argentina (1)				Com-
Name	No.	Builders	Laid down	missioned
SANTIAGO DEL ESTERO	S 22	Electric Boat	Feb 1944	Apr 1945

2. Peru (2)				Com-
Name	No.	Builders	Laid down	missioned
PACOCHA	S 48	Portsmouth NY	Dec 1943	June 1944
LA PEDRERA	S 49	Portsmouth NY	Feb 1944	July 1944

3. Turkey (1)				Com-
Name	No.	Builders	Laid down	missioned
DUMLUPINAR	S 339	Electric Boat	Oct 1943	July 1944

class boats modified from 'Balao' class submarines, and the *Santa Fe* was lost in the Falklands War of 1982, becoming the first submarine destroyed by a missile. Peru received two comparable boats at about the same time, ex-*Tench* (SS 417) also being bought for cannibalization to keep the two current boats operational. Turkey operates its single 'Guppy IA' class boat with seven 'Guppy IIA' boats.

'Guppy II' class patrol submarine

USA/Taiwan

Displacement: 1,870 tons standard and 2,420 tons dived
Dimensions: length 307·5ft (93·6m); beam 27·2ft (8·3m); draught 18ft (5·5m)
Gun armament: none
Missile armament: none
Torpedo armament: 10 21-in (533-mm) tubes (six bow and four stern)
Anti-submarine armament: none
Electronics: navigation/surface-search radar, and sonar
Propulsion: diesel-electric arrangement, with three Fairbanks-Morse diesels delivering 4,800bhp (3,580kW) and two Elliott electric motors delivering 5,400shp (4,025kW) to two shafts
Performance: maximum speed 18kts surfaced and 15kts submerged
Complement: 7+68

Class

1. Brazil (3)				Com-
Name	No.	Builders	Laid down	missioned
GUANABARA	S 10	Electric Boat Co	June 1944	Apr 1946
BAHIA	S 12	Portsmouth Navy Yard	Nov 1944	June 1945
CEARÁ	S 14	Boston Navy Yard	Feb 1944	Mar 1946

2. Taiwan (2)				Com-
Name	No.	Builders	Laid down	missioned
HAI SHIH	736	Portsmouth Navy Yard	July 1944	Mar 1945
HAI PAO	794	Federal S.B. and D.D. Co	Aug 1943	Apr 1946

3. Venezuela (1)				Com-
Name	No.	Builders	Laid down	missioned
PICUA	S 22	Boston Navy Yard	Feb 1944	Feb 1951

Brazil operates three 'Guppy II' class boats, all bought from the USA in the first half of the 1970s. This is the Bahia (S 12), previously the Sea Leopard (SS 483) of the US Navy's 'Tench' class.

Remarks: In addition to Brazil, which operates three 'Guppy II' class patrol submarines, the type is also used by Taiwan, whose two ex-'Tench' class boats have Italian torpedoes received three years after the boats, which were handed over in 1973. Apart from their normal sonar and radar suites, these Taiwanese boats have WLR-1 and WLR-3 passive ESM suites, and French DUUG 1B sonar. Venezuela's sole 'Guppy II' class boat was bought in 1973, and was extensively refitted in Argentina during 1979-80, but has relatively little operational value.

'Guppy IIA' class patrol submarine

USA/Turkey

Displacement: 1,850 tons surfaced and 2,440 tons dived
Dimensions: length 306ft (93·2m); beam 27ft (8·2m); draught 17ft (5·2m)
Gun armament: none
Missile armament: none
Torpedo armament: 10 21-in (533-mm) tubes (six bow and four stern) for 24 torpedoes
Anti-submarine armament: A/S torpedoes carried as part of the 24 above
Mines: 40 carried as an alternative to torpedoes
Electronics: surface-search/navigation radar, one EDO BQR-2 passive sonar, one BQS-2 active sonar and one GQR-3 passive tracking sonar, all used in conjunction with the Mk 106 A/S torpedo fire-control system
Propulsion: diesel-electric arrangement, with three General Motors diesels delivering 4,800hp (3,580kW) and two electric motors delivering 5,400hp (4,025kW) to two shafts
Performance: maximum speed 17kts surfaced and 15kts submerged; range 13,800 miles (22,210km) at 10kts surfaced
Complement: 82

Remarks: The sole example of the 'Guppy IIA' class in service with the Greek navy was bought in 1972 from the USA, and is now used only as a training boat. Spain, having received three 'Guppy IIA' class boats in the earlier part of the 1970s, now operates only two such craft under the local designation 'S 30'; these are of decreasing significance as further units of the 'Agosta' class are commissioned as 'S 70' class boats. The largest operator of the 'Guppy IIA' class is Turkey, which received no fewer than seven of the type during the early 1970s. These still play an important part in Turkish naval planning despite their obsolescence in the face of modern threats posed by the USSR and her Warsaw Pact allies in the Black

Class

1. Greece (1)

Name	No.	Builders	Laid down	Commissioned
PAPANIKOLIS	S 114	Manitowoc S.B.	July 1943	Apr 1944

2. Spain (3 'S 30' class)

Name	No.	Builders	Laid down	Commissioned
ISAAC PERAL	S 32	Portsmouth NY	Sep 1943	Apr 1944
COSME GARCIA	S 34	Portsmouth NY	Apr 1943	Dec 1943
NARCISO MONTURIOL	S 35	Manitowoc S.B.	Sep 1943	July 1944

3. Turkey (7)

Name	No.	Builders	Laid down	Commissioned
BURAKREIS	S 335	Portsmouth NY	Nov 1943	June 1944
MURATREIS	S 336	Portsmouth NY	Sep 1943	Apr 1944
ORUÇREIS	S 337	Portsmouth NY	July 1943	Feb 1944
ULUÇALIREIS	S 338	Portsmouth NY	Apr 1944	Oct 1944
ÇERBE	S 340	Portsmouth NY	Dec 1943	Nov 1944
PREVEZE	S 345	Electric Boat Co	Feb 1944	Apr 1945
BIRINCI INÖNÜ	S 346	Portsmouth NY	Mar 1944	Aug 1944

Sea; however, the increasing availability of 'Type 209' class boats from West Germany and from local production means that at last these venerable boats can be retired or used for secondary tasks such as training. Though the 'Guppy' boats carry adequate sensors and armament, they are very noisy by modern standards, making it difficult for them to avoid detection, and their diving depth is totally inadequate to provide them with any real measure of protection.

'Guppy III' class patrol submarine

USA/Turkey

Displacement: 1,975 tons standard and 2,450 tons dived
Dimensions: length 326·5ft (99·4m); beam 27ft (8·2m); draught 17ft (5·2m)
Gun armament: none
Missile armament: none
Torpedo armament: 10 21-in (533-mm) tubes (six bow and four stern) for 24 torpedoes
Anti-submarine armament: A/S torpedoes carried as part of the 24 above
Mines: 40 carried as an alternative to torpedoes
Electronics: surface-search/navigation radar, and Sperry/Raytheon BQG-4 passive underwater fire-control sonar used in conjunction with the Mk 106 A/S torpedo fire-control system
Propulsion: diesel-electric arrangement, with four diesels delivering 6,400shp (4,770kW) and two electric motors delivering 5,400bhp (4,025kW) to two shafts
Performance: maximum speed 17·5kts surfaced and 15kts submerged

Remarks: The ultimate stage in the GUPPY programme produced the 'Guppy III' class in the early 1960s with much-improved sonar equipment in comparison with earlier boats; the most characteristic feature of this capability was the BQG-4 PUFFS (Passive Underwater Fire-control Feasibility System) tracking and ranging sonar with three fins spaced along the length of the upper casing. Brazil currently operates two such boats, both bought from the USA in 1973. Greece also operates the 'Guppy III' class, one boat being used for training. This was originally

Complement: 8+78

Class

1. Brazil (2)

Name	No.	Builders	Laid down	Commissioned
GOIÁZ	S 15	Cramp S.B. Co	Aug 1943	Jan 1946
AMAZONAS	S 16	Electric Boat Co	June 1944	June 1946

2. Greece (1)

Name	No.	Builders	Laid down	Commissioned
KATSONIS	S 115	Portsmouth Navy Yard	Mar 1945	Jan 1946

3. Turkey (2)

Name	No.	Builders	Laid down	Commissioned
ÇANAKKALE	S 341	Electric Boat Co	Apr 1944	Aug 1945
IKINCI INONÜ	S 333	Electric Boat Co	Apr 1944	Nov 1945

a 'Guppy II' unit but was modified, like the Brazilian boats, with the BQR-4 PUFFS and also the BQR-2 passive sonar array. The last operator of the 'Guppy III' class is Turkey, which has two such boats. Part of the type's continued though limited operational value stems from the fact that 40 mines can be carried as an alternative to the normal complement of 24 torpedoes. This is particularly important for Turkey, which lies astride the USSR's only exit from the Black Sea into the Mediterranean.

'Heroj' class patrol submarine

Yugoslavia

Displacement: 1,070 tons standard, 1,170 tons surfaced and 1,350 tons dived
Dimensions: length 64·0m (210ft); beam 7·2m (23·6ft); draught 5·0m (16·4ft)
Gun armament: none
Missile armament: none
Torpedo armament: six 533-mm (21-in) tubes (all bow)
Anti-submarine armament: A/S torpedoes
Electronics: Soviet sonar
Propulsion: diesel-electric arrangement, with two diesels and two electric motors delivering 1,790kW (2,400hp) to one shaft
Performance: maximum speed 16kts surfaced and 10kts submerged; range 11,175km (6,945 miles) at 10kts surfaced
Complement: 55

Class

1. Yugoslavia (2)

Name	No.	Builders	Laid down	Commissioned
JUNAK	822	S. and D.E. Factory	1965	1969
USKOK	823	Uljanik Shipyard	1966	1970

Remarks: The two 'Heroj' class patrol submarines operated by the Yugoslav navy are relatively modern boats, and were designed during the 1960s with the aid of the USSR, which supplied the torpedo armament, underwater sensors and the relatively primitive torpedo fire-control system. The boats are designed for coastal protection duties along Yugoslavia's highly complex and island-studded coastline, and thus were designed with greater emphasis on manoeuvrability and quietness than on great diving depth and endurance. As with much of the equipment operated by the Yugoslav forces, these submarines show the country's desire for local production coupled with the purchase from abroad of advanced components, the balance between sources in the East and West being maintained as part of Yugoslavia's strongly neutral stance between the communist and non-communist power blocs.

'IKL/Vickers Type 206' class patrol submarine

West Germany

Displacement: 420 tons surfaced and 600 tons dived
Dimensions: length 45·0m (146·7ft); beam 4·7m (15·4ft); draught 3·7m (12ft)
Gun armament: none
Missile armament: may have SLAM launcher for Blowpipe surface-to-air missiles
Torpedo armament: eight 533-mm (21-in) tubes (all bow) for 10 torpedoes
Anti-submarine armament: A/S torpedoes carried as part of the total above
Electronics: surface-search radar, and sonar
Propulsion: diesel-electric arrangement, with two MTU 12V493 TY60 diesels powering AEG generators supplying current to one electric motor delivering 1,345 kW (1,800hp) to one shaft
Performance: maximum speed 11 kts surfaced and 17 kts submerged
Complement: 22

Class
1. Israel (3)

Name	No.	Builders	Laid down	Commissioned
GAL	—	Vickers Shipbuilding Ltd	1973	Jan 1977
TANIN	—	Vickers Shipbuilding Ltd	1974	1977
RAHAV	—	Vickers Shipbuilding Ltd	—	Dec 1977

Remarks: Currently forming Israel's sole submarine strength, the three 'Type 206' class boats are similar to the West German 'Type 206' boats, but could not be built in the latter country for political reasons and so were contracted from Vickers Ltd at Barrow-in-Furness in April 1972. The *Gal* was badly damaged when she ran aground during her delivery voyage, but has since been repaired. It is believed (though no official confirmation has ever been forthcoming) that the three boats carry the SLAM remotely-controlled launcher for Blowpipe SAMs.

'Kilo' class patrol submarine

USSR

Displacement: 2,500 tons surfaced and 3,200 tons dived
Dimensions: length 70.0m (229·7ft); beam 9·0m (29·5ft); draught 7·0m (23ft)
Gun armament: none
Missile armament: probably tube-launched SS-N-15 A/S missiles
Torpedo armament: eight 533-mm (21-in) tubes (all bow) for ? torpedoes
Anti-submarine armament: A/S torpedoes (above) and SS-N-15 missiles (above)
Electronics: one surface-search and navigation radar, a comprehensive assortment of sonar systems, one ESM suite and one torpedo fire-control system
Propulsion: diesel-electric arrangement, with ? diesels and ? electric motors delivering ?kW (?shp) to one shaft
Performance: maximum speed 16 kts submerged
Complement: about 55

Class
1. USSR (5+?)
5+? boats   built at Komsomolsk from 1979 in a continuing programme

Remarks: This class is building in Siberia to replace the 50 or so elderly diesel-electric boats currently in service with the Pacific Fleet. It is uncertain why the 'Tango' class boat building for and in service with the Northern and Black Sea Fleets has not been introduced at Komsomolsk, though the hull form of the 'Kilo' class suggests that it may be considerably deeper-diving than the 'Tango' design, with obvious advantages in the Pacific.

'Ming' class patrol submarine

China

Displacement: about 1,500 tons surfaced and 1,900 tons dived
Dimensions: length about 76·0m (249·3ft); beam and draught figures not available
Gun armament: none
Missile armament: none
Torpedo armament: probably six 533-mm (21-in) torpedo tubes (all bow) for? torpedoes
Anti-submarine armament: A/S torpedoes (above)
Electronics: one surface-search and navigation radar, various sonar systems, and one torpedo fire-control system
Propulsion: diesel-electric arrangement with ? diesels and ? electric motors delivering ?kW (?shp) to two shafts
Performance: not known
Complement: not known

Class
1. China (2)
2 boats

Remarks: Only two of this unsuccessful design were built for the North Sea Fleet which received both boats during the 1970s. Both this and the elderly 'Romeo' class will probably be replaced from the late 1980s with a new Chinese design.

'Näcken' class (Type A 14) patrol submarine

Sweden

Displacement: 1,030 tons surfaced and 1,125 tons dived
Dimensions: length 49·5m (162·4ft); beam 5·6m (18·4ft); draught 5·6m (18·4ft)
Gun armament: none
Missile armament: none
Torpedo armament: six 533-mm (21-in) tubes
Anti-submarine armament: two 400-mm (15·75-in) tubes for A/S torpedoes
Electronics: bow-mounted sonar
Propulsion: diesel-electric arrangement, with two diesels delivering 1,565 kW (2,100hp) to one electric motor delivering 1,100 kW (1,475hp) to one shaft
Performance: maximum speed 20 kts surfaced and submerged
Complement: 19

Class
1. Sweden (3)

Name	No.	Builders	Laid down	Commissioned
NÄCKEN	Näk	Kockums	Nov 1972	Apr 1980
NAJAD	Nad	Kockums	Sep 1973	June 1981
NEPTUN	Nep	Kockums	Mar 1974	Dec 1980

Remarks: The 'Näcken' class is a studied approach to the defence requirement of Sweden, and is designed solely for Baltic operations. The sonar is located in the bow, with the accommodation and machinery spaces abaft the control room and weapon spaces. The hull is based on the US 'Albacore' design, with a high beam-to-length ratio.

'Narhvalen' class patrol submarine

Denmark

Displacement: 420 tons surfaced and 450 tons dived
Dimensions: length 44·3m (145·3ft); beam 4·6m (15ft); draught 4·2m (13·8ft)
Gun armament: none
Missile armament: none
Torpedo armament: eight 533-mm (21-in) tubes (all bow)
Anti-submarine armament: none
Electronics: active and passive sonars
Propulsion: diesel-electric arrangment, with two Maybach (MTU) diesels delivering 1,120 kW (1,500bhp) and one electric motor delivering 1,120 kW (1,500bhp) to one shaft
Performance: maximum speed 12 kts surfaced and 17 kts submerged
Complement: 22

Class
1. Denmark (2)

Name	No.	Builders	Laid down	Commissioned
NARHVALEN	S 320	Royal Dockyard	Feb 1965	Feb 1970
NORDKAPEREN	S 321	Royal Dockyard	Mar 1966	Dec 1970

Remarks: The 'Narhvalen' class is based on the West German 'Type 205' class, modified to suit the particular requirements of the Royal Danish navy, which stress the coastal-protection role of small submarines. Reflecting the need for small size and low displacement, the 'Narhvalen' class carries no reload torpedoes, expended torpedoes being replaced between patrols. The Norwegian 'Type 207' is basically similar, though the Danish boats do not have or need the Norwegian boats' deep-diving capability.

'Oberon' and 'Porpoise' class patrol submarine

UK

Displacement: 1,610 tons standard, 2,030 tons surfaced and 2,410 tons dived
Dimensions: length 295·2 ft (90·0 m); beam 26·5 ft (8·1 m); draught 18 ft (5·5 m)
Gun armament: none
Missile armament: none
Torpedo armament: six 21-in (533-mm) tubes (all bow)
Anti-submarine armament: two 21-in (533-mm) tubes (both stern) for short A/S torpedoes carried as part of the total of 24 torpedoes
Electronics: one Type 1002 surface-search radar, one EMI Type 187 attack sonar, and one GEC Type 2007 long-range passive sonar
Propulsion: diesel-electric arrangement, with two Admiralty Standard Range diesels delivering 3,680 bhp (2,745 kW) and two electric motors delivering 6,000 shp (4,475 kW) to two shafts
Performance: maximum speed 12 kts surfaced and 17 kts submerged; range 10,350 miles (16,655 km) surfaced at cruising speed; diving depth 900 ft (275 m)
Complement: 7+62

Class

1. Australia (6)

Name	No.	Builders	Laid down	Com-missioned
OXLEY	S 57	Scotts Shipbuilding	July 1964	Apr 1967
OTWAY	S 59	Scotts Shipbuilding	June 1965	Apr 1968
ONSLOW	S 60	Scotts Shipbuilding	Dec 1967	Dec 1969
ORION	S 61	Scotts Shipbuilding	Oct 1972	June 1977
OTAMA	S 62	Scotts Shipbuilding	May 1973	Apr 1978
OVENS	S 70	Scotts Shipbuilding	June 1966	Apr 1969

2. Brazil (3)

Name	No.	Builders	Laid down	Com-missioned
HUMAITA	S 20	Vickers (Shipbuilding)	Nov 1970	June 1973
TONELERO	S 21	Vickers (Shipbuilding)	Nov 1971	Dec 1977
RIACHUELO	S 22	Vickers (Shipbuilding)	May 1973	Mar 1977

3. Canada (3)

Name	No.	Builders	Laid down	Com-missioned
OJIBWA	72	HM Dockyard Chatham	Sep 1962	Sep 1965
ONONDAGA	73	HM Dockyard Chatham	June 1964	June 1967
OKANAGAN	74	HM Dockyard Chatham	Mar 1965	June 1968

4. Chile (2)

Name	No.	Builders	Laid down	Com-missioned
O'BRIEN	22	Scott-Lithgow	Jan 1971	Apr 1976
HYATT	23	Scott-Lithgow	Jan 1972	Sep 1976

5. UK (13 'Oberon' class)

Name	No.	Builders	Laid down	Com-missioned
OBERON	S 09	HM Dockyard Chatham	Nov 1957	Feb 1961
ODIN	S 10	Cammell Laird & Co Ltd	Apr 1959	May 1962
ORPHEUS	S 11	Vickers (Shipbuilding)	Apr 1959	Nov 1960
OLYMPUS	S 12	Vickers (Shipbuilding)	Mar 1960	July 1962
OSIRIS	S 13	Vickers (Shipbuilding)	Jan 1962	Jan 1964
ONSLAUGHT	S 14	HM Dockyard Chatham	Apr 1959	Aug 1962
OTTER	S 15	Scotts Shipbuilding	Jan 1960	Aug 1962
ORACLE	S 16	Cammell Laird & Co Ltd	Apr 1960	Feb 1963
OCELOT	S 17	HM Dockyard Chatham	Nov 1960	Jan 1964
OTUS	S 18	Scotts Shipbuilding	May 1961	Oct 1963
OPOSSUM	S 19	Cammell Laird & Co Ltd	Dec 1961	June 1964
OPPORTUNE	S 20	Scotts Shipbuilding	Oct 1962	Dec 1964
ONYX	S 21	Cammell Laird & Co Ltd	Nov 1964	Nov 1967

6. UK (2 'Porpoise' class)

Name	No.	Builders	Laid down	Com-missioned
SEALION	S 07	Cammell Laird & Co Ltd	June 1958	July 1961
WALRUS	S 08	Scotts Shipbuilding	Feb 1958	Feb 1961

Now being phased out of service, the 'Porpoise' class was the precursor of the 'Oberon' class, and is here exemplified by the Sealion (S 07). Note the folded bow diving planes, which are extended into the horizontal position only when the boat is dived.

Remarks: The Australian boats, alternatively designated 'RAN Oberon' class, were ordered as four boats in 1963 and two additional units in 1971. They are similar in most respects to the British boats, but are currently being upgraded with Sperry Micropuffs passive ranging sonar, Krupp Atlas CSU3-41 attack sonar, Singer Librascope SFCS-RAN-Mk 1 fire-control system, and provision for Mk 48 torpedoes and tube-launched Sub-Harpoon anti-ship missiles. Four boats have already been modernized, with *Onslow* (S 61) and *Otama* (S 62) to be completed by late 1985. The Brazilian boats were ordered in 1969 (two units) and 1972 (one unit). They are similar to the British 'Oberons' but have the Vickers TIOS-B fire-control system. The Canadian boats are also similar to the British boats, but have more capable air-conditioning equipment and Canadian operational equipment and communications gear. As part of the SOUP (Submarine Operational Update Project) modernization the Canadian boats are being fitted with the Sperry Micropuffs passive ranging sonar and the Singer Librascope fire-control system; *Ojibwa* (72) and *Onondaga* (73) have already been modernized in this programme, with *Okanagan* (74) to follow by 1986. The Canadian boats carry the Mk 37C anti-submarine torpedo as their primary weapon. The two Chilean boats are similar to the British 'Oberon' class units, which will be phased out when the 'Type 2400' class boats begin to enter service in the 1990s.

'Quebec' class patrol submarine

USSR

Displacement: 450 tons surfaced and 530 tons dived
Dimensions: length 56·4 m (185 ft); beam 5·5 m (18 ft); draught 4·1 m (13·4 ft)
Gun armament: none
Missile armament: none
Torpedo armament: four 533-mm (21-in) tubes (all bow) for eight torpedoes
Anti-submarine armament: A/S torpedoes (see above)
Electronics: one 'Snoop Plate' surface-search radar, one 'Stop Light' electronic countermeasures system, one *Tamir* hull-mounted sonar, and one *Feniks* hull-mounted sonar
Propulsion: diesel-electric arrangment, with one diesel delivering 1,490 kW (2,000 bhp) and three electric motors delivering 1,490 kW (2,000 hp) to three shafts
Performance: maximum speed 17 kts surfaced and 16 kts submerged; range 13,000 km (8,080 miles) at cruising speed surfaced
Complement: 40

Class
1. USSR (16)
16 boats

Remarks: These boats were built at the Sudomekh yard in Leningrad starting in 1952, and of a planned total of 36 only 18 were completed. The type was the USSR's third patrol submarine design after World War II, and was intended for coastal operations. The surviving boats are now decidedly obsolete, and are thus being phased out of service or relegated to secondary tasks such as training.

'Romeo' class patrol submarine

USSR

Displacement: 1,400 tons surfaced and 1,800 tons dived
Dimensions: length 76·8m (251·9ft); beam 7·3m (23·9ft); draught 5·5m (18ft)
Gun armament: none
Missile armament: none
Torpedo armament: eight 533-mm (21-in) tubes (six bow and two stern) for 18 torpedoes
Anti-submarine armament: A/S torpedoes carried as part of the total above
Mines: 36 carried in place of torpedoes
Electronics: one 'Snoop Plate' surface-search radar, one 'Stop Light' electronic countermeasures system, one *Herkules* hull-mounted sonar, and one *Feniks* hull-mounted sonar
Propulsion: diesel-electric arrangement, with two diesels delivering 2,985kW (4,000bhp) and two electric motors delivering 2,985kW (4,000hp) to two shafts
Performance: maximum speed 17kts surfaced and 14kts submerged; range 29,650km (18,425 miles) at 10 kts surfaced; endurance 45 days
Complement: 54

Class
1. Bulgaria (2)

Name	No.
POBEDA	11
SLAVA	12

2. China (94)
94 boats (nos 126, 140, 142, 143, 153, 172, 175, 176, 208-212, 227-229, 245, 248, 249, 254, 267-270, 281-283, 291-3 and 64 others)

3. Egypt (10)
10 boats (nos 711, 722, 733, 744, 755 and 766 and four others)

4. North Korea (15)
15 boats

5. USSR (12)
12 boats

Remarks: Built at Górky between 1958 and 1961, the 'Romeo' class patrol submarine is an improved version of the 'Whiskey' class, with a hydrodynamically superior sail and improved sonar. Planned production was a prodigious 560, but only 20 were in actuality completed in the USSR thanks to the successful development of nuclear-powered boats. Several of the boats remaining in Soviet service are allocated to test programmes. Bulgaria's two 'Romeo' class boats were transferred from the USSR in 1972-73. By far the largest operator of the design is China, which received a few boats from the USSR in the early 1960s before establishing her own construction programme at Wuzhang in 1962, supplemented later by Guangzhou (Canton) and Jiangnan (Shanghai), with construction continuing at nine boats per year to replace time-expired earlier hulls and to make up for the failure of the 'Ming' class. Egypt received eight ex-Soviet boats during the 1960s and early 1970s, six of these being kept operational by cannibalization of the last two and supplemented by the delivery of two Chinese-built boats in early 1982. The North Korean boats comprise four ex-Chinese boats transferred in 1973 and 1974, and 11 indigenously-built boats produced up to 1982.

A 'Romeo' class patrol submarine of the Soviet navy runs on the surface.

'Sauro' class patrol submarine

Italy

Displacement: 1,455 tons surfaced and 1,630 tons dived
Dimensions: length 63.9m (210ft); beam 6·8m (22·5ft); draught 5·7m (18·9ft)
Gun armament: none
Missile armament: none
Torpedo armament: six 533-mm (21-in) tubes (all bow) for 12 torpedoes
Anti-submarine armament: A/S torpedoes carried as part of the strength above
Electronics: one SMA 3RM 20 surface-search and navigation radar, one IPD 70 hull-mounted active/passive sonar, one hull-mounted passive sonar, and extensive electronic countermeasures systems
Propulsion: diesel-electric arrangement, with three Fiat diesel generators supplying current to one electric motor delivering 2,720kW (3,650hp) to one shaft
Performance: maximum speed 11kts surfaced, 20kts submerged and 12kts submerged snorting; range 13,000km (6,080 miles) at cruising speed surfaced, or 23,150km (14,385 miles) at 4kts snorting, or 750km (465 miles) at 4kts submerged, or 38km (24 miles) at 20kts submerged; endurance 45 days; diving depth 300m (985ft)
Complement: 45, including 4 trainees

The Italian navy's patrol submarine Nazario Sauro (S 518) shows off her purposeful lines while moving at low speed on the surface.

Class
1. Italy (4+2)

Name	No.	Builders	Laid down	Commissioned
NAZARIO SAURO	S 518	Italcantieri	July 1974	Mar 1980
FECIA DI COSSATO	S 519	Italcantieri	Nov 1975	Mar 1980
LEONARDO DA VINCI	S 520	Italcantieri	June 1978	1982
GUGLIELMO MARCONI	S 521	Italcantieri	Oct 1979	Feb 1982

Remarks: Currently constituting the Italian navy's major long-range underwater strike force, the 'Sauro' class patrol submarines were built at Monfalcone in two pairs, of which the first was ordered in 1967, cancelled in 1968 and then reinstated in 1972, with the second pair ordered in 1976. Considerable problems were encountered with the battery system for the class, and this explains why the second boat, the *Fecia di Cossato* (S 519) was laid down more than one year later than her lead boat but commissioned slightly earlier, for the definitive CGA battery was proved in this boat and then fitted in the *Nazario Sauro* (S 518). The class has proved eminnently successful, and Italy plans to build another pair in the near future.

'Sava' class patrol submarine

Yugoslavia

Displacement: 965 tons dived
Dimensions: length 65·8m (215·8ft); beam 7·0m (22·9ft); draught 5·5m (18ft)
Gun armament: none
Missile armament: none
Torpedo armament: six 533-mm (21-in) tubes (all bow) for 16 torpedoes
Anti-submarine armament: A/S torpedoes carried as part of the strength above
Mines: 20 carried as an alternative to torpedoes
Electronics: surface-search radar, and sonar
Propulsion: diesel-electric arrangement

Performance: maximum speed 16·1kts submerged; diving depth 300m (985ft)
Complement: 35
Class
1. Yugoslavia (2)

Name	No.	Builders	Laid down	Commissioned
SAVA	831	S. and D.E. Factory	1975	1978
DRAVA	832	S. and D.E. Factory	—	1979

Remarks: Following Yugoslav practice for advanced weapons, the 'Sava' class patrol submarine was designed and built locally, but incorporates Soviet weapons, fire-control systems and sensors.

'Sjöormen' class (Type A11B) patrol submarine
Sweden

Displacement: 1,075 tons standard and 1,400 tons dived
Dimensions: length 51·0 m (167·3 ft); beam 6·1 m (20 ft); draught 5·8 m (19 ft)
Gun armament: none
Missile armament: none
Torpedo armament: four 533-mm (21-in) tubes (all bow)
Anti-submarine armament: two 406-mm (16-in) tubes (both stern) for A/S torpedoes
Electronics: surface-search radar, and sonar
Propulsion: diesel-electric arrangement with two Hedemora-Pielstick diesel generators supplying current to one Asea electric motor delivering 1,640 kW (2,200 bhp) to one shaft
Performance: maximum speed 15 kts surfaced and 20 kts submerged; endurance 21 days; diving depth 150 m (485 ft)
Complement: 23

Class
1. Sweden (5)

Name	No.	Builders	Laid down	Commissioned
SJÖORMEN	Sor	Kockums	1965	July 1968
SJÖLEJONET	Sle	Kockums	1966	Dec 1968
SJÖHUNDEN	Shu	Kockums	1966	June 1969
SJÖBJÖRNEN	Sbj	Karlskrona Varvet	1967	Feb 1969
SJÖHÄSTEN	Shä	Karlskrona Varvet	1966	Sep 1969

Remarks: Though designed and built in Sweden with Swedish equipment and armament, the 'Sjöormen' class of patrol submarine is based structurally on the 'Albacore'-hulled 'Barbel' class of the US Navy, with twin decks and advanced compartmentation to maximize use of internal volume. Compared with that the 'Barbel' class, the hull of the 'Sjöormen' class is of lighter construction as maximum diving depth is reduced to 150 m (490 ft) by the relative shallowness of the Baltic.

'Sutjeska' class patrol submarine
Yugoslavia

Displacement: 820 tons surfaced and 945 tons dived
Dimensions: length 60·0 m (196·8 ft); beam 6·8 m (22·3 ft); draught 4·9 m (16·1 ft)
Gun armament: none
Missile armament: none
Torpedo armament: six 533-mm (21-in) tubes (all bow)
Anti-submarine armament: none
Electronics: sonar
Propulsion: diesel-electric arrangement, with two Sulzer diesels and electric motors delivering 1,800 hp (1,345 kW) to two shafts
Performance: maximum speed 14 kts surfaced and 9 kts submerged; range 8,900 km (5,530 miles) at 8 kts surfaced
Complement: 38

Class
1. Yugoslavia (2)

Name	No.	Builders	Laid down	Commissioned
SUTJESKA	811	Uljanik Shipyard	1957	Sep 1960
NERETVA	812	Uljanik Shipyard	1957	1962

Remarks: Relatively little is known of the 'Sutjeska' class, the first patrol submarines to be designed and built in Yugoslavia. These are wholly unexceptional boats, and balance the propulsion system of American origins with armament, fire-control and sensor systems of Soviet origins. The Soviet items were fairly primitive in the original fit, but were extensively upgraded when the two boats were modernized. It seems likely that the two 'Sutjeska' class boats are approaching the end of their useful lives, and that they will shortly be relegated to training or the breaking-up yard.

'Tang' class patrol submarine
USA

Displacement: 2,050 tons surfaced and 2,700 tons dived
Dimensions: length 287 ft (87·4 m); beam 27·3 ft (8·3 m); draught 19 ft (6·2 m)
Gun armament: none
Missile armament: none
Torpedo armament: eight 21-in (533-mm) tubes (six bow and two stern)
Anti-submarine armament: A/S torpedoes
Electronics: one BPS-12 surface-search radar, one Raytheon/EDO/Honeywell BQS-4C active sonar, one BQR-8 passive sonar, one Sperry/Raytheon BQG-4 passive ranging sonar, all used in conjunction with the Mk 106 torpedo fire-control system, and acoustic countermeasures systems
Propulsion: diesel-electric arrangement, with three Fairbanks-Morse diesels and two electric motors delivering 5,600 hp (4,175 kW) to two shafts
Performance: maximum speed 15·5 kts surfaced and 16 kts submerged; range 12,650 miles (20,360 km) at 11 kts surfaced
Complement: 7+68

Class
1. Italy (2)

Name	No.	Builders	Laid down	Commissioned
LIVIO PIOMARTA	S 515	GD (EB Div)	Feb 1949	Aug 1952
ROMEO ROMEI	S 516	GD (EB Div)	June 1950	Mar 1952

2. Turkey (1)

Name	No.	Builders	Laid down	Commissioned
PIRIREIS	S 343	Portsmouth Navy Yard	Apr 1949	Oct 1951

3. USA (2)

Name	No.	Builders	Laid down	Commissioned
WAHOO	SS 565	Portsmouth Navy Yard	Oct 1949	May 1952
GUDGEON	SSAG 567	Portsmouth Navy Yard	May 1950	Nov 1952

Remarks: The 'Tang' class submarines, of which six were built in all, were the US Navy's response to lessons learned from examination of German U-boats captured at the end of World War II, resulting in a class with higher dived speed and lower submerged noise levels than its predecessors. Italy's two boats, which are scheduled for deletion by the end of 1984, were transferred in 1974 and 1973 respectively, and were later refitted at the Philadelphia Navy Yard. Turkey's single boat was acquired by loan for a five-year period in 1980 after the transfer to Iran of this and the two remaining US Navy boats had been cancelled after the fall of the Shah in 1979. Of the two US boats, the *Wahoo* (SS 565) is in reserve with the Atlantic Fleet, and the *Gudgeon* (SSAG 567) was used for acoustic research until being decommissioned in late 1983.

'Tango' class patrol submarine
USSR

Displacement: 3,000 tons surfaced and 3,700 tons dived
Dimensions: length 92·0 m (301·8 ft); beam 9·0 m (29·5 ft); draught 7·0 m (23 ft)
Gun armament: none
Missile armament: none
Torpedo armament: eight 533-mm (21-in) tubes
Anti-submarine armament: A/S torpedoes, and probably SS-N-15 missiles
Electronics: one 'Snoop Tray' surface-search radar, and sonar
Propulsion: diesel-electric arrangement, with three diesels delivering 4,475 kW (6,000 shp) and three electric motors delivering 4,475 kW (6,000 shp) to three shafts
Performance: maximum speed 15 kts surfaced and 16 kts submerged
Complement: 62

Class
1. USSR (18+2)
18+2 boats

Remarks: Still building at the rate of two boats per year at Gorky, the 'Tango' class patrol submarine is deployed only with the Black Sea and Baltic Fleets of the Soviet navy, mainly for operations in the Mediterranean. It is likely that they are armed with the SS-N-15 anti-submarine missile for highly potent anti-submarine operations in shallow waters. The continued building of the class to 20 units indicates that the USSR sees a worthwhile future for patrol boats.

'Toti' class patrol submarine

Italy

Displacement: 460 tons standard, 525 tons surfaced and 585 tons dived
Dimensions: length 46·2m (151·5ft); beam 4·7m (15·4ft); draught 4·0m (13·1ft)
Gun armament: none
Missile armament: none
Torpedo armament: four 533-mm (21-in) tubes for six torpedoes
Anti-submarine armament: A/S torpedoes carried as part of the total above
Electronics: one SMA 3RM 20/SMG surface-search and navigation radar, one IPD 64 bow-mounted active sonar, one IPD 64 stem-mounted passive sonar, one Velox hull-mounted passive ranging sonar, acoustic support measures, electronic countermeasures, and a computer fire-control system
Propulsion: diesel-electric arrangement, with two Fiat MB 820 N/I diesels and one electric motor delivering 1,640kW (2,200hp) to one shaft
Performance: maximum speed 14kts surfaced and 15kts submerged; range 5,550km (3,450 miles) at 5kts surfaced; diving depth 180m (590ft)
Complement: 4+22

The Italian coastal submarine Enrico Toti (S 506) reveals many of the features of the modern patrol boat: a highly streamlined hull/sail combination for low noise but good speed while submerged, the location of the IPD 64 active sonar in the bow dome for optimum performance in conjunction with the IPD 64 passive set in the stem, and the multiplicity of masts in the sail for the periscope, snort and various electronic/communication antennae.

Class

1. Italy (4)

Name	No.	Builders	Laid down	Com-missioned
ATTILIO BAGNOLINI	S 505	Italcantieri	Apr 1965	June 1968
ENRICO TOTI	S 506	Italcantieri	Apr 1965	Jan 1968
ENRICO DANDOLO	S 513	Italcantieri	Mar 1967	Sep 1968
LAZZARO MOCENIGO	S 514	Italcantieri	June 1967	Jan 1969

Remarks: The 'Toti' class was the first submarine design to be produced in Italy after World War II, and was seriously delayed by the imposition of a series of changes. As with the 'Sauro' class boats built later, the class was produced in two pairs.

'TR 1700' class patrol submarine

West Germany/Argentina

Displacement: 2,100 tons surfaced and 2,300 tons dived
Dimensions: length 65·0m (213·2ft); beam 7·3m (23·9ft); draught 6·5m (21·3ft)
Gun armament: none
Missile armament: none
Torpedo armament: six 533-mm (21-in) tubes (all bow) for 22 torpedoes
Anti-submarine armament: advanced A/S torpedoes carried as part of the total above
Electronics: surface-search radar, active sonar, passive sonar, intercept sonar, electronic countermeasures, and one Hollandse Signaalapparaten Sinbads torpedo fire-control system
Propulsion: diesel-electric arrangement, with four diesel generators supplying current to one electric motor delivering 6,600kW (8,850hp) to one shaft
Performance: maximum speed 13kts surfaced, 15kts snorting and 25kts submerged; range 27,800km (17,275 miles) at 5kts surfaced; diving depth 300m (985ft)
Complement: 26

Class

1. Argentina (0+3+3)
3 boats building and 3 on order

Remarks: Designed for long-range deep-water operations by Thyssen Nordseewerke, the TR 1700 class will be admirably suited to Argentina's maritime needs, and if financial considerations permit the full implementation of the programme, it seems that six boats might be in service by the end of the decade. However, a number of varying reports have been received about the programme, one saying that two boats would be built in West Germany at four by Astilleros Domecq Garcia at Tandanor in Argentina being gainsaid by a later revelation that three boats would be built in West Germany and another three in Argentina, and by a still later report that only four boats would be built, all of them in West Germany. However, even the partial implementation of the programme would give the Argentine navy a greatly enhanced long-range capability, for these boats are designed for high underwater burst speed for the rapid tracking of fast targets, and for great range.

'Type 205' class patrol submarine

West Germany

Displacement: 420 tons surfaced and 450 tons dived
Dimensions: length 43·9m (144ft); beam 4·6m (15·1ft); draught 4·3m (14·1ft)
Gun armament: none

Missile armament: none
Torpedo armament: eight 533-mm (21-in) tubes (all bow) for eight torpedoes
Anti-submarine armament: A/S torpedoes carried as part of the total above
Mines: up to 16 carried instead of torpedoes
Electronics: one Thomson-CSF Calypso surface-search and navigation radar, active sonar, passive sonar, and one Hollandse Signaalapparaten Mk 7 torpedo fire-control system
Propulsion: diesel-electric arrangement, with two Maybach (MTU) 820Db diesels delivering 895kW (1,200bhp) and one Siemens electric motor delivering 1,120kW (1,500bhp) to one shaft
Performance: maximum speed 10kts surfaced and 17kts submerged; diving depth 150m (490ft)
Complement: 4+18

Class

1. West Germany (6)

Name	No.	Builders	Laid down	Com-missioned
U1	S 180	Howaldtswerke	Feb 1965	June 1967
U2	S 181	Howaldtswerke	Sep 1964	Oct 1966
U9	S 188	Howaldtswerke	Dec 1964	Apr 1967
U10	S 189	Howaldtswerke	July 1965	Nov 1967
U11	S 190	Howaldtswerke	Apr 1966	June 1968
U12	S 191	Howaldtswerke	Sep 1966	Jan 1969

Remarks: The 'Type 205' class coastal submarine was the first underwater craft designed and built in West Germany after World War II, and is now beginning to show its age. The torpedo armament is loaded directly into the tubes through the bow caps, the stern being trimmed down to raise the caps clear of the water.

'Type 206' class patrol submarine
West Germany
Displacement: 450 tons surfaced and 500 tons dived
Dimensions: length 48·6m (159·4ft); beam 4·6m (15·1ft); draught 4·5m (14·8ft)
Gun armament: none
Missile armament: none
Torpedo armament: eight 533-mm (21-in) tubes (all bow) for eight torpedoes
Anti-submarine armament: A/S torpedoes carried as part of the total above
Mines: up to 20 carried instead of torpedoes, and up to 24 in external containers
Electronics: one Thomson-CSF Calypso surface-search and navigation radar, one active sonar, and one bow-mounted long-range passive panoramic sonar
Propulsion: diesel-electric arrangement, with two MTU diesel generators supplying current to one electric motor delivering 1,340kW (1,800hp) to one shaft
Performance: maximum speed 10kts surfaced and 17kts submerged; range 8,350km (5,190 miles) at 5kts surfaced
Complement: 4+18

Class
1. West Germany (18)

Name	No.	Builders	Laid down	Com-missioned
U 13	S 192	Howaldtswerke	Nov 1969	Apr 1973
U 14	S 193	Rheinstahl Nordseewerke	Sep 1970	Apr 1973
U 15	S 194	Howaldtswerke	May 1970	Apr 1974
U 16	S 195	Rheinstahl Nordseewerke	Apr 1971	Nov 1973
U 17	S 196	Howaldtswerke	Oct 1970	Nov 1973
U 18	S 197	Rheinstahl Nordseewerke	July 1971	Dec 1973
U 19	S 198	Howaldtswerke	Jan 1971	Nov 1973
U 20	S 199	Rheinstahl Nordseewerke	Feb 1972	May 1974
U 21	S 170	Howaldtswerke	Apr 1971	Aug 1974
U 22	S 171	Rheinstahl Nordseewerke	May 1972	July 1974
U 23	S 172	Rheinstahl Nordseewerke	Aug 1972	May 1975
U 24	S 173	Rheinstahl Nordseewerke	July 1972	Oct 1974
U 25	S 174	Howaldtswerke	Oct 1971	June 1974
U 26	S 175	Rheinstahl Nordseewerke	Nov 1972	Mar 1975
U 27	S 176	Howaldtswerke	Jan 1972	Oct 1974
U 28	S 177	Rheinstahl Nordseewerke	Jan 1972	Dec 1974
U 29	S 178	Howaldtswerke	Feb 1972	Nov 1974
U 30	S 179	Rheinstahl Nordseewerke	Apr 1973	Mar 1975

'Type 207' class patrol submarine
West Germany/Norway
Displacement: 370 tons standard and 435 tons dived
Dimensions: length 45·4m (149ft); beam 4·6m (15·1ft); draught 4·3m (14·1ft)
Gun armament: none
Missile armament: none
Torpedo armament: eight 533-mm (21-in) tubes (all bow) for eight torpedoes
Anti-submarine armament: A/S torpedoes carried as part of the total above
Electronics: sonar
Propulsion: diesel-electric arrangement, with two Maybach (MTU) 820 diesels powering generators supplying current to one electric motor delivering 1,270kW (1,700hp) to one shaft
Performance: maximum speed 10kts surfaced and 17kts submerged
Complement: 5+13

Class
1. Norway (14)

Name	No.	Builders	Laid down	Com-missioned
ULA	S 300	Rheinstahl Nordseewerke	1962	May 1965
UTSIRA	S 301	Rheinstahl Nordseewerke	1963	July 1965
UTSTEIN	S 302	Rheinstahl Nordseewerke	1962	Sep 1965
UTVAER	S 303	Rheinstahl Nordseewerke	1962	Dec 1965
UTHAUG	S 304	Rheinstahl Nordseewerke	1962	Feb 1966
SKLINNA	S 305	Rheinstahl Nordseewerke	1963	May 1966
SKOLPEN	S 306	Rheinstahl Nordseewerke	1963	Aug 1966
STADT	S 307	Rheinstahl Nordseewerke	1963	Nov 1966
STORD	S 308	Rheinstahl Nordseewerke	1964	Feb 1967
SVENNER	S 309	Rheinstahl Nordseewerke	1965	June 1967
KAURA	S 315	Rheinstahl Nordseewerke	1961	Feb 1965
KYA	S 317	Rheinstahl Nordseewerke	1961	June 1964
KOBBEN	S 318	Rheinstahl Nordseewerke	1961	Aug 1964
KUNNA	S 319	Rheinstahl Nordseewerke	1961	Oct 1964

Remarks: The 'Type 207' class is a development of the 'Type 205' with provision for greater diving depth and with superior sensors and armament, the latter including advanced wire-guided torpedoes.

'Type 209/1' class patrol submarine
West Germany
Displacement: 1,185 tons surfaced and 1,285 tons dived
Dimensions: length 55·9m (183·4ft); beam 6·3m (20·5ft); draught 5·5m (17·9ft)
Gun armament: none
Missile armament: none
Torpedo armament: eight 533-mm (21-in) tubes (all bow) with 14 torpedoes
Anti-submarine armament: A/S torpedoes carried as part of the strength above
Electronics: one surface-search radar, and hull-mounted sonar
Propulsion: diesel-electric arrangement, with four MTU 12V493 TY60 diesels powering four generators supplying current to one Siemens electric motor delivering 3,730kW (5,000hp) to one shaft
Performance: maximum speed 10kts surfaced and 22kts submerged
Complement: 32

The pennant number S 110 identifies this 'Type 209/1' class boat as the Glavkos, lead boat of the Greek 'Glavkos' class of eight submarines.

Remarks: In terms of sales success, the West German 'Type 209' class boat has proved the best patrol submarine since World War II, being adopted by many smaller navies for its combination of good performance, powerful armament and relatively low unit cost. The Argentine boats were assembled at Tandanor from shipped-over sections, while the Colombian boats were completed in West Germany. The Greek boats were delivered in two four-boat batches, the first four having a dived displacement of 1,210 tons. The Peruvian boats have a lower-powered electric motor, reducing submerged speed slightly. The seven boats building in Turkey are the first submarines built there, and the Venezuelan boats were built in Germany.

Class
1. Argentina (2 'Salta' class)

Name	No.	Builders	Laid down	Com-missioned
SALTA	S 31	Howaldtswerke	Apr 1970	Mar 1974
SAN LUIS	S 32	Howaldtswerke	Oct 1970	May 1974

2. Colombia (2)

Name	No.	Builders	Laid down	Com-missioned
PIJAO	SS 28	Howaldtswerke	Apr 1972	Apr 1975
TAYRONA	SS 29	Howaldtswerke	May 1972	July 1975

3. Greece (8 'Glavkos' class)

Name	No.	Builders	Laid down	Com-missioned
GLAVKOS	S 110	Howaldtswerke	Sep 1968	Nov 1971
NEREUS	S 111	Howaldtswerke	Jan 1969	Feb 1972
TRITON	S 112	Howaldtswerke	June 1969	Nov 1972
PROTEUS	S 113	Howaldtswerke	Oct 1969	Aug 1972
POSYDON	S 116	Howaldtswerke	Jan 1976	Mar 1979
AMPHITRITE	S 117	Howaldtswerke	Apr 1976	July 1979
OKEANOS	S 118	Howaldtswerke	Oct 1976	Nov 1979
PONTOS	S 119	Howaldtswerke	Jan 1977	Apr 1980

4. Peru (6)

Name	No.	Builders	Laid down	Com-missioned
CASMA	S 31	Howaldtswerke	July 1977	Dec 1980
ANTOFAGASTA	S 32	Howaldtswerke	Oct 1977	Feb 1981
PISAGUA	S 33	Howaldtswerke	Aug 1978	1983
CHIPANA	S 34	Howaldtswerke	Nov 1978	Sep 1982
ISLAY	S 45	Howaldtswerke	May 1971	Aug 1974
ARICA	S 46	Howaldtswerke	Nov 1971	Jan 1975

5. Turkey (5+1+6)

Name	No.	Builders	Laid down	Com-missioned
ATILAY	S 347	Howaldtswerke	Dec 1972	July 1975
SALDIRAY	S 348	Howaldtswerke	Jan 1973	Jan 1977
BATIRAY	S 349	Howaldtswerke	June 1975	July 1978
YILDIRAY	S 350	Howaldtswerke	May 1976	July 1981
TITIRAY	S 351	Gölcük Naval Yard	Mar 1980	1983
—	—	Gölcük Naval Yard	—	—

6. Venezuela (2)

Name	No.	Builders	Laid down	Com-missioned
SABALO	S 31	Howaldtswerke	May 1973	Aug 1976
CARIBE	S 32	Howaldtswerke	Aug 1973	Mar 1977

'Type 209/2' class patrol submarine

West Germany

Displacement: 1,285 tons surfaced and 1,390 tons dived
Dimensions: length 59·5m (195·1ft); beam 6·3m (20·5ft); draught 5·4m (17·9ft)
Gun armament: none
Missile armament: none
Torpedo armament: eight 533-mm (21-in) tubes (all bow) for 16 torpedoes
Anti-submarine armament: A/S torpedoes carried as part of the total above
Electronics: surface-search and navigation radar, and sonar
Propulsion: diesel-electric arrangement, with four MTU-Siemens diesel generators supplying current to one Siemens electric motor delivering 3,725kW (5,000shp) to one shaft
Performance: maximum speed 10kts surfaced and 21·5kts submerged
Complement: 33

Class

1. Chile (1+1)

Name	No.	Builders	Laid down	Com-missioned
THOMSON	—	Howaldtswerke	Nov 1980	1983
SIMPSON	—	Howaldtswerke	Nov 1980	1984

2. Ecuador (2)

Name	No.	Builders	Laid down	Com-missioned
SHYRI	S 11	Howaldtswerke	Aug 1974	Nov 1977
HUANCAVILCA	S 12	Howaldtswerke	Jan 1975	Mar 1978

3. Indonesia (3+1)

Name	No.	Builders	Laid down	Com-missioned
CAKRA	401	Howaldtswerke	Nov 1977	Mar 1981
NANGGALA	402	Howaldtswerke	Mar 1978	July 1981
—	403	Howaldtswerke	—	1983

Remarks: The 'Type 209/2' class patrol submarine is modelled on the 'Type 209/1', but has slightly greater displacement thanks to the lengthening of the hull, which permits the carriage of an extra pair of reload torpedoes and an increase in bunkerage for greater endurance. The two Chilean boats are both West German-built, as are the pair operated by the Ecuadorian navy. The Indonesian order, again being fulfilled entirely in West Germany, currently comprises four boats (the second pair of slightly larger dimensions than the first pair), with another two boats planned in the near future should financial considerations permit. Indonesia will then deploy one of the most powerful submarines arms in East Asia.

'Type 2400' class patrol submarine

UK

Displacement: 2,160 tons surfaced and 2,400 tons dived
Dimensions: length 230·5ft (70·25m); beam ?ft (?m); draught ?ft (?m)
Gun armament: none
Missile armament: Sub-Harpoon fired from the torpedo tubes
Torpedo armament: six 21-in (533-mm) tubes (all bow)
Anti-submarine armament: A/S torpedoes
Electronics: one Kelvin Hughes Type 1006 navigation and surface-search radar, one Thomson-CSF Argonaute (Type 2040) passive sonar, one Type 2019 Passive/Active Range and Intercept Sonar, one Type 2026 towed-array sonar, one Racal electronic support measures system, and one Ferranti/Gresham Lion AIO (Action Information Organization) system
Propulsion: diesel-electric arrangement, with one Paxman Valenta 16 RPA 200S diesel powering one GEC electric motor delivering 5,400shp (4,030kW) to one shaft
Performance: maximum speed 12kts surfaced, 10+ kts snorting and 20kts submerged; range 9,200+ miles (14,805+ km); diving depth 650+ ft (200+ m)
Complement: 7+13+24

Class

1. UK (0+10)
10 boats on order or planned

Remarks: First considered as a replacement for the elderly 'Oberon' class patrol submarine in the second half of the 1970s, the 'Type 2400' class proposed for the Royal Navy is currently planned as 10 large and highly capable boats. On the debit side, however, are the difficulty in fixing the final design, the increasing cost of the whole programme (which may lead to a reduction in the overall number of boats within the class) and the fairly large size of the proposed design (which will reduce its efficiency in shallow waters unsuitable for the Royal Navy's growing force of nuclear-powered fleet submarines). The first 'Type 2400' boats should be operational by the end of the decade.

'Uzushio' class patrol submarine

Japan

Displacement: 1,900 tons surfaced and 2,430 tons dived
Dimensions: length 72·0m (236·2ft); beam 9·9m (32·5ft); draught 7·5m (24·6ft)
Gun armament: none
Missile armament: none
Torpedo armament: six 21-in (533-mm) tubes (all amidships)
Anti-submarine armament: A/S torpedoes
Electronics: bow-mounted sonar
Propulsion: diesel-electric arrangement, with two Kawasaki/MAN V8V24/30 diesels delivering 2,535kW (3,400bhp) and one electric motor delivering 5,370kW (7,200hp) to one shaft
Performance: maximum speed 12kts surfaced and 20kts submerged; diving depth 200m (655ft)
Complement: 10+70

Remarks: American design influence is readily apparent in the teardrop design of the 'Uzushio' class boats, which also have bow-mounted sonar and outward-angled amidships torpedo tubes for an optimum balance of sensor and armament, the former occupying the primary position.

Class

1. Japan (7)

Name	No.	Builders	Laid down	Com-missioned
UZUSHIO	SS 566	Kawasaki	Sep 1968	Jan 1971
MAKISHIO	SS 567	Mitsubishi	June 1969	Feb 1972
ISOSHIO	SS 568	Kawasaki	July 1970	Nov 1972
NARUSHIO	SS 569	Mitsubishi	May 1971	Sep 1973
KUROSHIO	SS 570	Kawasaki	July 1972	Nov 1974
TAKASHIO	SS 571	Mitsubishi	July 1973	Jan 1976
YAESHIO	SS 572	Kawasaki	Apr 1975	Mar 1978

'Walrus' class patrol submarine

Netherlands

Displacement: 2,350 tons surfaced and 2,640 tons dived
Dimensions: length 67·0m (219·8ft); beam 8·4m (27·6ft); draught 7·0m (23ft)
Gun armament: none
Missile armament: none
Torpedo armament: six 533-mm (21-in) tubes (all bow)
Anti-submarine armament: A/S torpedoes
Electronics: one Decca navigation radar, Thomson-CSF sonar, and Hollandse Signaalapparaten SEWACO VIII data integration system
Propulsion: diesel-electric arrangement, with three SEMT-Pielstick diesels and one Holec electric motor delivering ?kW (?shp) to one shaft
Fuel: diesel oil
Performance: maximum speed 12kts surfaced and 20kts submerged

Complement: 49

Class

1. Netherlands (0+2)

Name	No.	Builders	Laid down	Com-missioned
WALRUS	S 802	Rotterdamse Droogdok Mij	Oct 1979	1986
ZEELEEUW	S 803	Rotterdamse Droogdok Mij	Sep 1981	1987

Remarks: Eventually planned to a total of four units, the 'Walrus' class patrol submarine is identical on the exterior to the 'Zwaardvis' class, but is designed of improved steel for greater diving depth. The use of a considerable degree of automation and a combined fire-control/electronic command system also permits a reduction in crew. Construction was delayed by two years in 1981 to permit alterations to be incorporated in the design.

'Whiskey' class patrol submarine
USSR

Displacement: 1,080 tons surfaced and 1,350 tons dived
Dimensions: length 76·0m (249·3ft); beam 6·5m (21·3ft); draught 4·9m (16·1ft)
Gun armament: none
Missile armament: none
Torpedo armament: four 533-mm (21-in) tubes (all bow) for 14 torpedoes
Anti-submarine armament: two 406-mm (16-in) A/S tubes (both stern)
Mines: up to 28 in place of the torpedoes
Electronics: one 'Snoop Plate' surface-search radar, one *Tamir* hull-mounted sonar, and one 'Stop Light' electronic countermeasures system
Propulsion: diesel-electric arrangement, with two diesels delivering 2,985kW (4,000bhp) and two electric motors delivering 2,015kW (2,700hp) to two shafts
Performance: maximum speed 18kts surfaced and 14kts submerged; range 24,000km (14,915 miles) at 8kts surfaced
Complement: 54

Class
1. Albania (3)
3 boats (nos 512, 514 and 516)

2. Cuba (1)
1 boat

3. Egypt (6)
6 boats (nos 415, 418, 421, 432, 455 and 477)

4. Indonesia (2)

Name	No.
PASOPATI	410
BRAMASTRA	412

5. North Korea (4)
4 boats

6. Poland (4)

Name	No.	Name	No.
ORZEL	292	**KONDOR**	294
SOKOL	293	**BIELIK**	295

7. USSR (130 'Whiskey' and 2 'Whiskey Canvas Bag' class)
130 'Whiskey' class boats (including 80 in reserve)
2 'Whiskey Canvas Bag' class boats

Remarks: Designed soon after World War II and showing strong signs of German design influence, the 'Whiskey' class patrol submarine was built in large numbers (about 240) between 1951 and 1957 at the Baltic Yard (Leningrad), Gorky, Komsomolsk and Nikolayev. All surviving boats are of the class originally designated 'Whiskey V'. Apart from the 130 standard boats (50 first-line and 80 reserve) available, the Soviet navy also deploys two of the 'Whiskey Canvas Bag' class radar pickets, each fitted with a sail-mounted 'Boat Sail' air-search radar. Only two of Albania's three 'Whiskey' class boats (two received in 1960 and the third expropriated in 1961) are now operational sea-going submarines. The single Cuban boat was delivered in 1979, and is probably used for training and as a charging station. Egypt's boats (delivered in 1957, 1958 and 1962) are of low serviceability, and one may have been cannibalized. Indonesia's 'Whiskey' class once numbered 14, but now amounts to two poor boats. North Korea and Poland have better-kept examples.

'Zulu IV' class patrol submarine
USSR

Displacement: 1,950 tons surfaced and 2,300 tons dived
Dimensions: length 90·0m (295·2ft); beam 7·4m (24·3ft); draught 6·1m (20ft)
Gun armament: none
Missile armament: none
Torpedo armament: 10 533-mm (21-in) tubes (six bow and four stern) for 24 torpedoes
Anti-submarine armament: A/S torpedoes carried as part of the total above
Mines: up to 40 in place of 20 torpedoes
Electronics: one 'Snoop Plate' surface-search radar, and one *Tamir* sonar
Propulsion: three diesels delivering 4,475kW (6,000bhp) and three electric motors delivering 3,730kW (5,000hp) to three shafts
Performance: maximum speed 18kts surfaced and 16kts submerged; range 37,000km (22,990 miles) at cruising speed surfaced
Complement: 75

Class
1. USSR (9)
9 boats including 5 in reserve

'Yuushio' class patrol submarine
Japan

Displacement: 2,200 tons
Dimensions: length 76·0m (249·3ft); beam 9·9m (32·5ft); draught 7·5m (24·6ft)
Gun armament: none
Missile armament: Sub-Harpoon underwater-to-surface missiles to be carried from SS 577 onwards
Torpedo armament: six 21-in (533-mm) tubes (all amidships)
Anti-submarine armament: A/S torpedoes
Electronics: one ZPS-4 surface-search radar, one ZQQ-4 bow sonar, and one SQS-36(J) fin sonar
Propulsion: two Kawasaki/MAN diesels delivering 2,910kW (3,900bhp) and one electric motor delivering 5,370kW (7,200bhp) to one shaft
Performance: maximum speed 12kts surfaced and 20kts submerged
Complement: 75

Class
1. Japan (5+1)

Name	No.	Builders	Laid down	Commissioned
YUUSHIO	SS 573	Mitsubishi	Dec 1976	Feb 1980
MOCHISHIO	SS 574	Kawasaki	May 1978	Mar 1981
SETOSHIO	SS 575	Mitsubishi	Apr 1979	Mar 1982
OKISHIO	SS 576	Kawasaki	Apr 1980	Mar 1983
NADASHIO	SS 577	Mitsubishi	Apr 1981	Mar 1984
—	SS 578	Kawasaki	Apr 1982	Mar 1985
—	SS 579	Mitsubishi	1983	1986
—	SS 580	—	1984	1987

Remarks: The 'Yuushio' class is an enlarged and upgraded version of the 'Uzushio' class patrol submarine.

'Zwaardvis' class patrol submarine
Netherlands

Displacement: 2,350 tons surfaced and 2,640 tons dived
Dimensions: length 66·2m (217·2ft); beam 10·3m (33·8ft); draught 7·1m (23·3ft)
Gun armament: none
Missile armament: none
Torpedo armament: six 21-in (533-mm) tubes (all bow) for 12 torpedoes
Anti-submarine armament: A/S torpedoes carried as part of the total above
Electronics: one Type 1001 surface-search radar, sonar, and one Hollandse Signaalapparaten WM-8 fire-control system
Propulsion: diesel-electric arrangement, with three diesel generators and one electric motor delivering 3,800kW (5,100hp) to one shaft
Performance: maximum speed 13kts surfaced and 20kts submerged
Complement: 8+60

Class
1. Netherlands (2)

Name	No.	Builders	Laid down	Commissioned
ZWAARDVIS	S 806	Rotterdamse Droogdok Mij	July 1966	Aug 1972
TIJGERHAAI	S 807	Rotterdamse Droogdok Mij	July 1966	Oct 1972

2. Taiwan (0+2)
2 boats on order

Remarks: The careful streamlining of the sail and teardrop hull gives the 'Zwaardvis' class good underwater performance despite a relatively low-powered electric motor. Taiwan has ordered two examples of the 'Zwaardvis (Improved)' class, but whether or not this order will be honoured (because of Chinese political pressure) remains to be seen; also uncertain is the degree to which the Taiwanese boats will differ from the Dutch originals.

As were other Western patrol submarine designs, the Dutch 'Zwaardvis' class was modelled on the US 'Barbel' design with important modifications for Dutch requirements. Noise-producing machinery is mounted on a sprung false deck.

'Clemenceau' class aircraft-carrier

France

Displacement: 27,310 tons normal and 32,780 tons full load
Dimensions: length 265·0m (869·4ft); beam 31·72m (104·1ft); draught 8·6m (28·2ft); flight deck length 257·0m (843·2ft) and width 29·5m (96·8ft)
Gun armament: eight 100-mm (3·9-in) L/55 DP in single mountings
Missile armament: none
Torpedo armament: none
Anti-submarine armament: none
Aircraft: 40 fixed-wing (20 Dassault-Breguet Super Etendards, 10 Vought F-8 Crusaders and 10 Dassault-Breguet Alizés) and four rotary-wing (two Aérospatiale Super Frelons and two Aérospatiale Alouette IIIs)
Armour: flight deck, hull sides and bulkheads in the area of the engine rooms and magazines, island and bridges
Electronics: one Thomson-CSF DRBV 50 surveillance radar, one Thomson-CSF DRBV 23B air-search radar, one Thomson-CSF DRBV 20C air-warning radar, two Thomson-CSF DRBI 10 height-finding radars, two Thomson-CSF DRBC 31 fire-control radars, two Thomson-CSF DRBC 32 fire-control radars, one Decca 1226 navigation radar, one NRBA landing radar, one SQS-503 sonar, one SENIT 2 combat information system, and comprehensive electronic countermeasures
Propulsion: six boilers supplying steam to two sets of Parsons geared turbines delivering 93,960kW (126,000shp) to two shafts
Performance: maximum speed 32kts; range 13,900km (8,635 miles) at 18kts or 6,500km (4,040 miles) at 32kts
Complement: 64+476+798

Class
1. France (2)

Name	No.	Builders	Laid down	Commissioned
CLEMENCEAU	R 98	Brest Naval Dockyard	Nov 1955	Nov 1961
FOCH	R 99	Chantiers de l'Atlantique	Feb 1957	July 1963

The mixed air group carried by the Foch (R 99) includes Dassault-Breguet Super Etendard strike fighters, Vought F-8 Crusader fighters and Dassault-Breguet Alizé anti-submarine aircraft. Also visible in this photograph (below the island) are some Aérospatiale Zéphyr butterfly-tail trainers.

Remarks: Apart from the USA and USSR, France is now the only country in the world to operate large aircraft-carriers for a multi-role air group of fixed-wing aircraft, complemented by helicopters. The design features an angled flight deck, two aircraft lifts, two steam catapults and two mirror landing aids. Both ships have been modernized and refitted to useful standards, and it is planned to keep the *Clemenceau* (R 98) in service until 1992 and the *Foch* (R 99) until 1998, each ship being replaced by a 'PA 88' class nuclear-powered carrier, which will be able to operate between 30 and 40 aircraft, two steam catapults being provided for fixed-wing types.

'Colossus' class aircraft-carrier

UK/Brazil

Displacement: 15,890 tons standard, 17,500 tons normal and 19,890 tons full load
Dimensions: length 695ft (211·8m); beam 80ft (24·4m); draught 24·5ft (7·5m); flight deck length 690ft (210·3m) and width 121ft (37·0m)
Gun armament: 10 40-mm Bofors L/60 AA in two Mk 2 quadruple mountings and one Mk 1 twin mounting
Missile armament: none
Torpedo armament: none
Anti-submarine armament: none
Aircraft: 20 (see Remarks)
Electronics: one Lockheed SPS-40B air-search radar, one SPS-4 surface-search radar, two General Electric SPS-8 combat-control radars, one Raytheon 1402 navigation radar and two SPG-34 gun fire-control radars
Propulsion: four Admiralty boilers supplying steam to two sets of Parsons geared turbines delivering 40,000shp (29,830kW) to two shafts

Performance: maximum speed 24kts; range 13,800 miles (22,210km) at 14kts or 7,140 miles (11,490km) at 23kts
Complement: 1,000 and an air group personnel strength of 300

Class
1. Argentina (1)

Name	No.	Builders	Laid down	Commissioned
VEINTICINCO DE MAYO	V2	Cammell Laird	Dec 1942	Jan 1945

2. Brazil (1)

Name	No.	Builders	Laid down	Commissioned
MINAS GERAIS	A 11	Swan, Hunter	Nov 1942	Jan 1945

Remarks: The *Minas Gerais* (A 11) carries some 20 aircraft, two lifts and one steam catapult; the Argentine *Veinticinco de Mayo* (V 2) differs in having Dutch electronics, up to 22 aircraft and a different look to the island and mast.

'Enterprise' class nuclear-powered multi-role aircraft-carrier

USA

Displacement: 75,700 tons standard and 89,600 full load
Dimensions: length 1,102ft (335·9m); beam 133ft (40·5m); draught 35·8ft (10·9m); flight deck width 252ft (76·8m)
Gun armament: three Phalanx Mk 15 20-mm close-in weapon systems, and three 20-mm Mk 68 mountings
Missile armament: three Mk 57 launchers for RIM-7 NATO Sea Sparrow surface-to-air missiles
Torpedo armament: none
Anti-submarine armament: none
Aircraft: about 84
Electronics: one Raytheon/Sylvania SPS-10 surface-search radar, one ITT/Gilfillan SPS-48C 3D air-search radar, one Raytheon SPS-49 air-search radar, one Westinghouse SPS-65 combined-search radar, one Westinghouse SPS-58 low-level air-search radar, three SPN series aircraft landing radars, three Raytheon Mk 91 missile fire-control systems, Naval Tactical Data system, OE-82 satellite communications antenna, URN-26 TACAN, four Mk 36 Super Chaffroc rapid-blooming overhead chaff systems, and one SLQ-29 ESM suite
Propulsion: eight pressurized-water cooled Westinghouse A2W reactors supplying steam to four sets of Westinghouse geared turbines delivering 280,000shp (208,795kW) to four shafts
Performance: maximum speed 35kts; range 460,600 miles (741,245km) at 20kts
Complement: 162+2,940, plus a carrier air wing complement of 304+2,323

Class
1. USA (1)

Name	No.	Builders	Laid down	Commissioned
ENTERPRISE	CVN 65	Newport News S.B.	Feb 1958	Nov 1961

The island of the Enterprise (CVN 65) has been altered radically since this 1976 photograph by alterations to the electronics suite.

Remarks: The *Enterprise* (CVN 65) was the world's second nuclear-powered surface warship, and the design was based on that of the highly successful 'Forrestal' class. She is to be extensively upgraded in 1993-95.

'Forrestal' class multi-role aircraft-carrier
USA

Displacement: 56,060 tons standard and 75,900 tons full load (CVs 59 and 60), or 60,000 tons standard and 79,300 tons full load (CVs 61 and 62)

Dimensions: length 1,086ft (331·0m) for CV59, 1,063ft (324·0m) for CV60, 1,071ft (326·4m) for CV 61 and 1,070ft (326·1m) for CV62; beam 129·5ft (39·5m); draught 37ft (11·3m); flight-deck width 252ft (76·8m)

Gun armament: to be fitted with three 20-mm Phalanx Mk 16 close-in weapon system mountings

Missile armament: two Mk 25 (CVs 59 and 60) or three Mk 29 (CVs 61 and 62) octuple launchers for RIM-7 Sea Sparrow surface-to-air missiles

Torpedo armament: none

Anti-submarine armament: none

Aircraft: about 70

Electronics: one Westinghouse SPS-58 low-angle air-search radar, one Raytheon/Sylvania SPS-10 surface-search radar, one ITT/Gilfillan SPS-48 3D air-search radar, one Raytheon SPS-49 air-search radar, one LN-66 navigation radar, two Mk 115 missile fire-control systems (CVs 59 and 60, to be replaced by three Mk 91 missile fire-control systems) or two Mk 91 missile fire-control systems (CVs 61 and 62), Naval Tactical Data System, URN-20 TACAN, OE-82 satellite communications antenna, three Mk 36 Super Chaffroc rapid-blooming overhead chaff launchers, and one SLQ-29 ESM suite

Propulsion: eight Babcock & Wilcox boilers supplying steam to four sets of Westinghouse geared turbines delivering 260,000shp (193,880kW) in CV 59 or 280,000shp (208,795kW) in CVs 60-62 to four shafts

Performance: maximum speed 33kts (CV 59) or 34kts (CVs 60-62); range 9,200 miles (14,805km) at 20kts or 4,600 miles (7,400km) at 30kts

Complement: 145+2,645, plus a carrier air wing complement of about 2,150

Class

1. USA (4)				Com-
Name	No.	Builders	Laid down	missioned
FORRESTAL	CV 59	Newport News S.B.	July 1952	Oct 1955
SARATOGA	CV 60	New York Navy Yard	Dec 1952	Apr 1956
RANGER	CV 61	Newport News S.B.	Aug 1954	Aug 1957
INDEPENDENCE	CV 62	New York Navy Yard	July 1955	Jan 1959

Remarks: The four units of the 'Forrestal' class were the first aircraft-carriers built specifically with jet aircraft operations in mind, and their design was delayed by the decision to incorporate the British-designed angled flight deck and steam catapult. Other notable features are the enclosed bow (the first on American carriers) for greater seaworthiness, an armoured flight deck, massive underwater protection, and internal compartmentation designed to mitigate the effects of nuclear as well as conventional damage. Apart from the four catapults and its angled flight deck, each ship has four deck-edge lifts (three to starboard and one to port). As built, a gun armament of eight 5-in (127-mm) guns in single mounts, but these were deleted as the BPMDS Sea Sparrow launchers were added; further improvement in point defence against aircraft and sea-skimmer missiles is planned with the addition of three 20-mm Mk 16 Phalanx CIWS mountings on each ship during its Service Life Extension Program refit: *Forrestal* (CV 59) in 1983-85, *Saratoga* (CV 60) in 1980-83, *Ranger* (CV 61) at an unknown future date, and *Independence* (CV 62) in 1985-87; *Ranger*'s SLEP slot has been reallocated to the *Kitty Hawk*. It is anticipated that the SLEP overhaul will increase each ship's service life by at least 30 years, possibly 45, and has been made necessary by the huge cost of building modern nuclear-powered carriers. The ships have proved extremely successful in service, and the basic design has proved the starting point for all American carrier designs since the early part of the 1950s.

Displaying her pennant number 59 on the side of the island and at the front of the flight deck, the conventionally-powered carrier Forrestal (CV 59) *completes a turn to starboard to bring her bows into the wind for aircraft launching, initially of a McDonnell Douglas F-4J fighter on the port catapult and of a Lockheed S-3A Viking anti-submarine aircraft on the starboard catapult. Other aircraft types visible on the flight deck provide ample evidence of the carrier's real multi-role capability: Grumman A-6 Intruder medium attack aircraft, Grumman EA-6 Prowler electronic warfare aircraft, Vought A-7 Corsair light attack aircraft and Sikorsky SH-3 Sea King anti-submarine helicopters. And apart from the pair of aircraft on the forward catapult, a pair of A-7 Corsairs can be seen on the waist catapults at the front of the angled flight deck.*

'Garibaldi' class light aircraft-carrier
Italy

Displacement: 10,100 tons standard and 13,370 tons full load

Dimensions: length 180·0m (590·4ft); beam 30·4m (99·7ft); draught 6·7m (22ft); flight-deck length 174·0m (570·7ft) and width 30·4m (99·7ft)

Gun armament: six 40-mm Breda L/70 AA in three twin mountings

Missile armament: two twin Teseo launchers for 10 Otomat Mk 2 surface-to-surface missiles, and two Albatros launchers for Aspide surface-to-air missiles

Torpedo armament: none

Anti-submarine armament: two triple ILAS 3 tube mountings for 324-mm (12·75-in) A 244S or 12·75-in (324-mm) Mk 46 A6S torpedoes, and helicopter-launched weapons (see below)

Aircraft: up to 18 Agusta-Sikorsky SH-3 Sea King helicopters

Electronics: one Selenia RAN 3L 3D radar, one Selenia RAT 31 medium-range air-search radar, one Selenia RAN 10S air-search radar, one SMA MM/SPS 702 combined air- and surface-search radar, three Selenia RTN 20X gun-control radars used in conjunction with the Dardo 40-mm fire-control system, two Selenia RTN 30X SAM-control radars used in conjunction with the ELSAG Argo NA30 Albatros fire-control system, one Selenia MM/SPN 703 navigation radar, one DE 1160 hull-mounted sonar, one IPN 10 data-processing system, two Breda SCLAR-D multi-role launchers, TACAN, and various electronic warfare systems

Propulsion: four General Electric/Fiat LM 2500 gas turbines delivering 59,655kW (80,000hp) to two shafts

Performance: maximum speed 30kts; range 13,000km (8,080 miles) at 20kts

Complement: 550 (accommodation is available for 825)

Class

1. Italy (1)				Com-
Name	No.	Builders	Laid down	missioned
GIUSEPPE GARIBALDI	C 551	Italcantieri	June 1981	1985

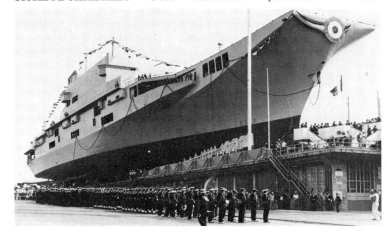

Remarks: Designed to replace the *Andrea Doria* and *Caio Duilio*, the *Giuseppe Garibaldi* (C 551) features extremely comprehensive offensive and defensive missile fits, excellent sensor fit and substantial anti-submarine capability.

'Hancock' class aircraft-carrier

USA

Displacement: 29,600 tons light, about 33,000 tons standard and 41,900 tons full load

Dimensions: length 899 ft (274·0 m); beam 103 ft (31·4 m); draught 31 ft (9·5 m); flight deck width 192 ft (58·5 m) for AVT 16 and 172 ft (52·4 m) for CVA 31

Gun armament: four 5-in (127-mm) L/38 DP in Mk 24 single mountings (CVA 31 only)

Missile armament: none

Torpedo armament: none

Anti-submarine armament: none

Aircraft: Between 70 and 80 for CVA 31, and none for AVT 16

Armour: 2·5/4-in (63·5/102-mm) belt, 2/5·3-in (51/134·6-mm) hangar deck, 1·5-in (38-mm) flight deck, and 1·5-in (38-mm) main deck

Electronics: one Raytheon/Sylvania SPS-10 surface-search radar, one General Electric SPS-30 3D air-search (CVA 31) or RCA SPS-12 air-search (AVT 16) radar, one Hughes/Westinghouse SPS-43 air-search radar, one SPN-10 navigation radar, one General Electric Mk 37 gun fire-control system (CVA 31 only), two General Electric Mk 56 gun fire-control systems, and URN-20 TACAN

Propulsion: eight Babcock & Wilcox boilers supplying steam to four sets of Westinghouse geared turbines delivering 150,000 shp (111,855 kW) to four shafts

Performance: maximum speed 30+ kts; range 20,725 miles (33,355 km) at 12 kts

Complement: 110+1,980, plus a carrier air wing complement of about 135+1,050 for CVA 31, and 75+1,365 for AVT 16

Class

1. USA (2)

Name	No.	Builders	Laid down	Commissioned
LEXINGTON	AVT 16	Bethlehem Steel Co	July 1941	Feb 1943
BON HOMME RICHARD	CVA 31	New York Navy Yard	Feb 1943	Nov 1944

Remarks: These two ships were built during World War II as 'Essex' class carriers, and have survived with good capability in a period of intense development in aircraft-carrier technology. They have now passed into a state of obsolescence, however, and only the *Lexington* (AVT 16) is retained in commission, and then only as a training carrier attached to the US Navy's main air training base at NAS Corpus Christi in Texas, providing fledgling aircrew with carrier operation experience without the need to pull a first-line carrier out of more profitable service. It is expected that the *Lexington* will be decommissioned in about 1990 and replaced by the *Coral Sea* (CV 43). Laid up in reserve are the *Bonne Homme Richard* and the essentially similar 'Intrepid' class *Oriskany* (CV 34).

'Independence' class light aircraft-carrier

USA

Displacement: 13,000 tons standard and 16,415 tons full load

Dimensions: length 623 ft (189·9 m); beam 71·5 ft (21·8 m); draught 26 ft (7·9 m); flight-deck length 545 ft (166·1 m) and width 108 ft (32·9 m)

Gun armament: 26 40-mm Bofors L/60 AA in two Mk 2 quadruple and nine Mk 1 twin mountings

Missile armament: none

Torpedo armament: none

Anti-submarine armament: none

Aircraft: seven fixed and 20 rotary-wing aircraft

Armour: 2/5-in (51/127-mm) belt, 2/3-in (51/76-mm) deck

Electronics: one Bendix SPS-6 air-search radar, one Lockheed SPS-40 air-search radar, one General Electric SPS-8 height-finding radar, one Raytheon/Sylvania SPS-10 surface-search radar, two navigation radars, two Mk 29 gun-control radars used in conjunction with two Mk 57 gun fire-control systems, two Mk 28 gun-control radars used in conjunction with two Mk 63 gun fire-control systems, URN-20 TACAN, and one WLR-1 electronic countermeasures system

Propulsion: four Babcock & Wilcox boilers supplying steam to four sets of General Electric geared turbines delivering 100,000 shp (74,570 kW) to four shafts

Performance: maximum speed 24 kts; range 8,300 miles (13,355 km) at 15 kts

Complement: 1,112 excluding air group personnel

Class

1. Spain (1)

Name	No.	Builders	Laid down	Commissioned
DÉDALO	R 01	New York Shipbuilding	Aug 1942	July 1943

Remarks: Converted while building from a cruiser, the *Dédalo* (R 01) has been extensively modernized to operate V/STOL fighters and assault helicopters, but is scheduled for replacement in 1986 by the new *Principe de Asturias* (R 11).

'Invincible' class light aircraft-carrier

UK

Displacement: 16,000 tons standard and 19,500 tons full load

Dimensions: length 677 ft (206·6 m); beam 90 ft (27·5 m); draught 24 ft (7·3 m); flight-deck length 550 ft (167·8 m) and width 105 ft (31·9 m)

Gun armament: two 20-mm Phalanx CIWS mountings, and two 20-mm AA

Missile armament: one twin launcher for 22 Sea Dart surface-to-air missiles

Torpedo armament: none

Anti-submarine armament: helicopter-launched weapons (see below)

Aircraft: five BAe Sea Harrier FRS.Mk 1 V/STOL aircraft and nine Westland Sea King HAS.Mk 2/5 helicopters

Electronics: one Marconi/Hollandse Signaalapparaten Type 1022 air-search radar, one Marconi Type 992R air-search radar, two Kelvin Hughes Type 1006 navigation radars, two Type 909 SAM-control radars used in conjunction with the two GWS 30 missile fire-control systems, one ADAWS 5 Action Data Automation Weapon System, one Plessey Type 2016 hull-mounted fleet escort sonar, one UAA-1 Abbey Hill ESM suite, and two Knebworth Corvus chaff launchers

Propulsion: four Rolls-Royce Olympus TM3B gas turbines delivering 112,000 shp (83,520 kW) to two shafts

Performance: maximum speed 28 kts; range 5,750 miles (9,250 km) at 15 kts

Complement: 131+265+604 plus 320 air group personnel

Class

1. UK (2+1)

Name	No.	Builders	Laid down	Commissioned
INVINCIBLE	R 05	Vickers (Shipbuilding) Ltd	July 1973	July 1980
ILLUSTRIOUS	R 06	Swan Hunter Ltd	Oct 1976	early 1983
ARK ROYAL	R 09	Swan Hunter Ltd	Dec 1978	1985

Remarks: After a lengthy gestation period in the 1960s, the 'Invincible' class was finally approved in the early 1970s as a successor to the Royal Navy's conventional aircraft-carriers, it having been decided that the construction of the proposed 'CVA 01' class was wholly outside the means (and also the political requirements) of the UK. Thus the Fleet Air Arm's seagoing fixed-wing air power was to be eliminated, and the 'Invincible' class of helicopter-carrying 'through-deck' cruiser produced to provide long-range anti-submarine capability. The whole programme was then delayed yet further by the need to revise the final design, and also by industrial problems. Political considerations again intruded to produce the announcement that the Royal Navy would receive only two of the planned three ships, and that the *Invincible* (R 05) was to be sold to Australia as a replacement for that country's carrier *Melbourne*. The Falklands War of 1982 led to a revision of this scheme, it being realised that three 'Invincible' class ships were needed by the Royal Navy. As completed, the units of the class have provision for a revived fixed-wing strength, in the form of BAe Sea Harrier multi-role aircraft. These can be fitted onto the existing pair of lifts, and are provided with take-off aid by the provision of a 'ski jump' lip to the flight deck (7° on the first two and 15° on the last). Point-defence weapons have also been increased considerably as a result of experience in the Falklands.

Looking like a cross between an aircraft-carrier and a cruiser, the Invincible *(R 05) shows off one of her BAe Sea Harrier multi-role fighters (on the low-angle ski-jump ramp), the Sea Dart twin launcher (forward of the flight deck) and the two Phalanx CIWS mountings (one in the bows and the other at the stern).*

'Jeanne d'Arc' class helicopter-carrier
France
Displacement: 10,000 tons standard and 12,365 tons full load
Dimensions: length 182·0m (597·1ft); beam 24·0m (78·7ft); draught 7·3m (24ft); flight-deck length 62·0m (203·4ft) and width 21·0m (68·9ft)
Gun armament: four 100-mm (3·9-in) L/55 DP in four single mountings
Missile armament: six container-launchers for six MM.38 Exocet surface-to-surface missiles
Torpedo armament: none
Anti-submarine armament: helicopter-launched weapons (see below)
Aircraft: up to eight Westland Lynx Mk 2 helicopters in a hangar under the flight deck
Capacity: up to 700 troops and associated equipment when used as a commando carrier
Electronics: one Thomson-CSF DRBV 22D air-search radar, one Thomson-CSF DRBV 50 combined air- and surface-search radar, one Thomson-CSF DRBI 10 height-finder radar, one Thomson-CSF DRBN 32 navigation radar, three Thomson-CSF DRBC 32A fire-control radars, one SQS-503 hull-mounted sonar, one SENIT 2 combat information system, and two Syllex eight-barrel chaff launchers
Propulsion: four boilers supplying steam to two sets of Rateau-Bretagne geared turbines delivering 29,825kW (40,000shp) to two shafts
Performance: maximum speed 26·5kts; range 11,125km (6,915 miles) at 15kts
Complement: 30+183+404 and up to 192 cadets

Class

Name	No.	Builders	Laid down	Commissioned
1. France (1)				
JEANNE D'ARC	R 97	Brest Naval Dockyard	July 1960	June 1964

'John F. Kennedy' class multi-role aircraft-carrier
USA
Displacement: 61,000 tons standard and 82,000 tons full load
Dimensions: length 1,052ft (320·7m); beam 130ft (39·6m); draught 35·9ft (10·9m); flight-deck width 252ft (76·9m)
Gun armament: three 20-mm Phalanx Mk 15 close-in weapon system mountings
Missile armament: three Mk 29 launchers for RIM-7 Sea Sparrow surface-to-air missiles
Torpedo armament: none
Anti-submarine armament: none
Aircraft: about 85
Electronics: one Raytheon/Sylvania SPS-10 surface-search radar, one Hughes/Westinghouse SPS-43 air-search radar, one Raytheon SPS-49 air-search radar, one Westinghouse SPS-58 air-search radar, one SPN-10 navigation radar, two SPN-42 landing radars, three Mk 91 missile fire-control systems, URN-20 TACAN, Naval Tactical Data System, several advanced electronic warfare systems, OE-82 satellite communications antenna, four Mk 36 Super Chaffroc rapid-blooming overhead chaff launchers, and one SLQ-29 ESM suite
Propulsion: eight Foster-Wheeler boilers supplying steam to four sets of Westinghouse geared turbines delivering 280,000shp (208,795kW) to four shafts
Performance: maximum speed 30+kts; range 9,200 miles (14,805km) at 20kts
Complement: 150+2,645, plus a carrier air wing complement of about 2,150

Class

Name	No.	Builders	Laid down	Commissioned
1. USA (1)				
JOHN F. KENNEDY	CV 67	Newport News S.B.	Oct 1964	Sep 1968

Remarks: The *John F. Kennedy* (CV 67) is similar in all essential respects to the 'Kitty Hawk' class, and was originally considered for nuclear propulsion.

'Kiev' class aircraft-carrier
USSR

Lead ship of her class, the Kiev is a remarkable achievement for her designers, combining missile types and aircraft in a potent tactical package.

Displacement: 36,000 tons standard and 42,000 tons full load
Dimensions: length 274·0m (898·7ft); beam 41·2m (135ft); draught 10·0m (32·8ft); overall width 50·0m (164ft) including flight deck and sponsons
Gun armament: four 76-mm (3-in) L/60 DP in two twin mountings, and eight 30-mm AA 'Gatling' mountings
Missile armament: four twin launchers for 16 SS-N-12 surface-to-surface missiles, two twin launchers for 72 SA-N-3 'Goblet' surface-to-air missiles, and two twin launchers for about 36 SA-N-4 surface-to-air missiles
Torpedo armament: two quintuple 533-mm (21-in) tube mountings
Anti-submarine armament: one twin SUW-N-1 launcher for 20 FRAS-1/SS-N-14 'Silex' missiles, two RBU 6000 12-barrel rocket-launchers, and helicopter-launched weapons (see below)
Aircraft: up to 32 are normally carried, a typical mixture being 12 Yakovlev Yak-36 'Forger-A' and one Yak-36 'Forger-B' fixed-wing aircraft, and 16 Kamov Ka-25 'Hormone-A' and three Ka-25 'Hormone-B' helicopters
Electronics: one 'Top Sail' 3D radar, one 'Top Steer' 3D radar, one 'Trap Door' SSM-control radar, two 'Head Light' SA-N-3 SAM-control radars, two 'Pop Group' SA-N-4 SAM-control radars, two 'Owl Screech' main armament gun-control radars, four 'Bass Tilt' AA gun-control radars, one 'Top Knot' aircraft-control radar, one 'Don Kay' navigation radar, two 'Palm Frond' navigation radars, two 'Don-2' navigation radars, one hull-mounted low-frequency sonar, one medium-frequency variable-depth sonar, and a most extensive electronic warfare suite including eight 'Side Globe', four 'Top Hat-A', four 'Top Hat-B', two 'Rum Tub', two 'Bell Clout' and two 'Cage Pot' antennae/housings
Propulsion: ? boilers supplying steam to four sets of geared turbines delivering 134,225kW (180,000shp) to four shafts
Performance: maximum speed 32kts; range 24,100km (14,975 miles) at 18kts or 7,400km (4,600 miles) at 30kts
Complement: 2,500 including air group personnel

Class

Name	Builders	Laid down	Commissioned
1. USSR (3+1)			
KIEV	Nikolayev South	Sep 1970	May 1975
MINSK	Nikolayev South	Dec 1972	Feb 1978
NOVOROSSIISK	Nikolayev South	Sep 1975	1982
KHARKOV	Nikolayev South	Dec 1978	1984

Remarks: The Soviet development of seagoing air power has been tardy, and its first steps (the helicopter carriers *Moskva* and *Leningrad*) were hesitant. However, with the development of the four-ship 'Kiev' class the Soviet navy has moved toward the main stream of naval air power development, each ship being able to carry a useful number of fixed- and rotary-wing aircraft for launch and recovery from the slightly angled flight deck. Two lifts are provided for movement of aircraft between the flight deck and hangar. Apart from its air component (whose fixed-wing Yakovlev Yak-36 'Forger' VTOL aircraft are of uncertain capability), each 'Kiev' class ship carries a comparatively prodigious anti-ship and anti-aircraft missile armament, together with effective anti-air point-defence gun armament and limited anti-submarine capability with rocket-launchers. Initially classed by the Soviets as anti-submarine cruisers, the 'Kiev' class ships are now designated tactical aviation cruisers, which reflects their capabilities far more neatly. The ships can be used for semi-independent long-range operations in peace, or for shorter-range integrated operations in war.

'Kitty Hawk' class multi-role aircraft-carrier
USA

The carrier **Kitty Hawk** *(CV 63) refuels the destroyer* **Goldsborough** *(DDG 20) during a deployment in the Pacific Ocean. Such UNREP (underway replenishment) is normally the task of the US Navy's vast support force of specialist ships, which are designed specifically to provide combatant ships with all they need, ranging from fuel and munitions to spare parts and frozen food. Evident on the* **Kitty Hawk's** *deck are some of her large aircraft complement: Vought A-7 Corsair light attack aircraft, Grumman A-6 Intruder medium attack aircraft, Grumman E-2 Hawkeye airborne warning and control aircraft, Lockheed S-3 Viking anti-submarine aircraft, Douglas A-3 Skywarrior electronic warfare and refuelling aircraft, Rockwell A-5 Vigilante reconnaissance aircraft, Sikorsky SH-3 Sea King anti-submarine helicopters and Boeing Vertol CH-46 Sea Knight utility helicopters.*

Displacement: 60,100 tons standard and 80,800 tons full load for CVs 63 and 64, or 60,300 tons standard and 78,500 tons full load for CV 66

Dimensions: length 1,046 ft (318·8m) for CVs 63 and 64, and 1,047·5 ft (319·3m) for CV 66; beam 130 ft (39·6m); draught 37 ft (11·3m); flight-deck width 252 ft (76·9m)

Gun armament: three 20-mm Phalanx Mk 15 close-in weapon system mountings

Missile armament: three Mk 29 octuple launchers for 24 RIM-7 Sea Sparrow surface-to-air missiles

Torpedo armament: none

Anti-submarine armament: air-dropped weapons (see below)

Aircraft: about 85

Electronics: one Hughes SPS-52 3D radar, one Hughes/Westinghouse SPS-43 air-search radar, one General Electric SPS-30 height-finding radar, one SPN-10 navigation radar, one SPN-42 navigation radar, two Mk 91 missile fire-control systems in CV 63, four Mk 76 missile-control radars in CV 64, three Mk 91 missile-control radars in CV 66, URN-20 TACAN, Naval Tactical Data System, several advanced electronic warfare systems, OE-82 satellite communications antenna, four Mk 36 Super Chaffroc rapid-blooming overhead chaff launchers, and one SLQ-29 ESM suite

Propulsion: eight Foster-Wheeler boilers supplying steam to four sets of Westinghouse geared turbines delivering 280,000 shp (208,795 kW) to four shafts

Performance: maximum speed 30+ kts; range 9,200 miles (14,805 km) at 20 kts or 4,600 miles (7,400 km) at 30 kts

Complement: 150+2,645, plus a carrier air wing complement of about 2,150

Class

1. USA (3)				
Name	No.	Builders	Laid down	Commissioned
KITTY HAWK	CV 63	New York S.B.	Dec 1956	Apr 1961
CONSTELLATION	CV 64	New York NY	Sep 1957	Oct 1961
AMERICA	CV 66	Newport News S.B.	Jan 1961	Jan 1965

Remarks: Designed as improved 'Forrestal' class carriers, the 'Kitty Hawk' and single 'John F. Kennedy' class ships were the US Navy's last fossil-fuelled carriers to be built. There are two catapults each on the bow and the angled flight deck, and four deck-edge lifts (one port and three starboard). Three 20-mm Mk 16 Phalanx CIWS mountings are being fitted on each ship, and service life extension program refits are planned for the *Kitty Hawk* (CV 63) in 1987-89, for the *Constellation* (CV 64) in 1989-1991, and for the *America* (CV 66) later.

'Majestic' class aircraft-carrier
UK

Displacement: 16,000 tons standard and 19,500 tons full load

Dimensions: length 700 ft (213·4m); beam 80 ft (24·4m); draught 24 ft (7·3m); flight-deck width 128 ft (39·0m)

Gun armament: seven 40-mm Bofors L/60 AA in single mountings

Missile armament: none

Torpedo armament: none

Anti-submarine armament: none

Aircraft: 22

Electronics: one Hollandse Signaalapparaten LW-05 air-search radar, one Hollandse Signaalapparaten ZW-06 surface-search radar, one Hollandse Signaalapparaten LW-10 and LW-11 tactical radars, and one Plessey Type 963 approach radar

Propulsion: four Admiralty boilers supplying steam to two sets of Parsons geared turbines delivering 40,000 shp (29,830 kW) to two shafts

Performance: maximum speed 24·5 kts; range 13,800 miles (22,210 km) at 14 kts and 7,150 miles (11,505 km) at 23 kts

Complement: 1,075

Class

1. India (1)				
Name	No.	Builders	Laid down	Commissioned
VIKRANT	R 11	Vickers-Armstrong Ltd	Oct 1943	Mar 1961

Remarks: The *Vikrant* has one catapult and two lifts, and was between 1979 and 1981 extensively refitted with Dutch electronics and with provision for an air group including BAe Sea Harrier and Dassault-Breguet Alizé fixed-wing aircraft.

'Midway' class multi-role aircraft-carrier
USA

Displacement: 51,000 tons standard and 62,200 tons full load for CV 41, or 52,500 tons standard and 62,200 tons full load for CV 43

Dimensions: length 979 ft (298·4m); beam 121 ft (36·9m); draught 35·3 ft (10·8m); flight-deck with 238 ft (72·5m)

Gun armament: three 20-mm Phalanx Mk 15 close-in weapon system mountings

Missile armament: (CV 41 only) two Mk 25 launchers for RIM-7 Sea Sparrow surface-to-air missiles

Torpedo armament: none

Anti-submarine armament: none

Aircraft: about 75

Armour: multi-layer protection afforded by thin armour on several decks

Electronics: one ITT/Gilfillan SPS-48C 3D radar (CV 41 only), one Westinghouse SPS-65V combined air- and surface-search radar (CV 41 only), one Hughes/Westinghouse SPS-43C air-search radar, one SPS-49 (CV 41) or General Electric SPS-30 (CV 43) air-search radar, one Raytheon/Sylvania SPS-10 surface-search radar (CV 43 only), one LN-66 navigation radar, one SPN-35A carrier-controlled approach radar (CV 41 only), one SPN-42 carrier-controlled approach radar (CV 41 only), one SPN-44 carrier-controlled approach radar (CV 41 only), one SPN-43A carrier-controlled approach radar (CV 43 only), two Mk 115 missile fire-control systems (CV 41 only), URN-20 TACAN, Naval Tactical Data System, OE-82 satellite communications antenna, one SLQ-29 ESM suite, and four Mk 36 Super Chaffroc rapid-blooming overhead chaff launchers

Propulsion: 12 Babcock & Wilcox boilers supplying steam to four sets of Westinghouse geared turbines delivering 212,000 shp (158,090 kW) to four shafts

Performance: maximum speed 30+ kts

Complement: 140+2,475 in CV 41 or 165+2,545 in CV 43, plus an air wing strength of about 1,800

Class

1. USA (2)				
Name	No.	Builders	Laid down	Commissioned
MIDWAY	CV 41	Newport News S.B.	Oct 1943	Sep 1945
CORAL SEA	CV 43	Newport News S.B.	July 1944	Oct 1947

Remarks: The oldest first-line carriers left in US Navy service, the two 'Midway' class multi-role carriers are survivors of the building programme instituted in World War II. Their size precludes the carriage of a full carrier air wing, however, and the two ships are thus allocated to slightly less significant roles.

'Nimitz' class nuclear-powered multi-role aircraft-carrier
USA

Displacement: 72,700 tons light, 81,600 tons standard and 91,485 tons full load (CVNs 68-70) or 96,350 tons full load (CVNs 71-73)

Dimensions: length 1,092ft (332·9m); beam 134ft (40·8m); draught 37ft (11·3m); flight-deck width 252ft (76·8m) for CVNs 68-70, or 257ft (78·4m) for CVNs 71-73

Gun armament: two (CVNs 68 and 69) or four (CVNs 70-73) 20-mm Phalanx Mk 15 close-in weapon system mountings

Missile armament: three Mk 29 launchers for 24 RIM-7 Sea Sparrow surface-to-air missiles (CVNs 68 and 69)

Torpedo armament: none

Anti-submarine armament: none

Aircraft: 90+

Electronics: one ITT/Gilfillan SPS-48B 3D radar, one Hughes/Westinghouse SPS-43A air-search radar, one Raytheon/Sylvania SPS-10F surface-search radar, two SPN-42 carrier aircraft-approach radars, one SPN-43 carrier aircraft-approach radar, one Applied Devices SPN-44 carrier aircraft-approach radar, one Litton LN-66 navigation radar, three Mk 115 SAM fire-control systems (CVNs 68 and 69) or four Mk 91 CIWS fire-control systems (CVNs 70-73), Naval Tactical Data System, URN-20 TACAN, OE-82 satellite communications antenna, and Mk 36 Super Chaffroc rapid-blooming overhead chaff launcher

Propulsion: two pressurized-water cooled nuclear reactors (Westinghouse A4W or General Electric A1G) supplying steam to four sets of geared turbines delivering 260,000shp (193,880kW) to four shafts

Performance: maximum speed 30+ kts

Complement: 3,300, and a carrier air wing strength of 3,000

Carrying only a couple of Sikorsky SH-3 Sea King helicopters, the nuclear-powered Carl Vinson (CV 70) undertakes her sea trials in January 1982. The vast flight deck area is vital not so much for flight operations as for the parking of aircraft which cannot be struck down into the internal hangarage.

Remarks: Undoubtedly the most powerful surface warships in the world, the planned eight units of the 'Nimitz' class will provide the US Navy with the core of its carrier task group strength from the 1990s onwards. Together with nuclear-powered escorts, these magnificent ships offer the possibility of high-speed long-range operations limited only by the aviation stores (fuel and munitions) and food that can be supplied by underway replenishment ships. The nuclear power-plant is remarkably efficient, permitting the use of only two reactors in comparison with the eight of the *Enterprise* (CVN 65). The normal fit of four catapults and four deck-edge lifts is retained, and Phalanx CIWS mountings are to be added.

Class
1. USA (3+3+2)

Name	No.	Builders	Laid down	Commissioned
NIMITZ	CVN 68	Newport News S.B.	June 1968	May 1975
DWIGHT D. EISENHOWER	CVN 69	Newport News S.B.	Aug 1970	Oct 1977
CARL VINSON	CVN 70	Newport News S.B.	Oct 1975	Feb 1982
THEODORE ROOSEVELT	CVN 71	Newport News S.B.	Oct 1981	1987
ABRAHAM LINCOLN	CVN 72	Newport News S.B.	—	1990
GEORGE WASHINGTON	CVN 73	Newport News S.B.	—	1990

'Principe de Asturias' class light aircraft-carrier
Spain

Displacement: 14,700 tons full load

Dimensions: length 195·1m (639·9ft); beam 24·7m (81ft); draught 9·1m (29·8ft); flight-deck length 175·0m (574ft) and width 32·0m (105ft)

Gun armament: four 20-mm Meroka 12-barrel close-in weapon system mountings

Missile armament: none

Torpedo armament: none

Anti-submarine armament: none

Aircraft: 17 V/STOL aircraft and helicopters

Electronics: one Hughes SPS-52D 3D radar, one Westinghouse SPS-55 surface-search radar, one ITT/Gilfillan SPN-35A air-control radar, four Meroka fire-control radars, one digital tactical data system, and URN-22 TACAN

Propulsion: two General Electric LM 2500 gas turbines delivering 46,000shp (34,300kW) to two shafts

Performance: maximum speed 26kts; range 13,900km (8,635 miles) at 20kts

Complement: 793 including air group personnel

Class
1. Spain (1)

Name	No.	Builders	Laid down	Commissioned
PRINCIPE DE ASTURIAS	R 11	Bazán	Oct 1979	1986

'Iowa' class battleship
USA

Displacement: 45,000 tons standard and 58,000 tons full load

Dimensions: length 887·2ft (270·4m); beam 108·2ft (33·0m); draught 38ft (11·6m)

Gun armament: nine 16-in (406-mm) L/50 in three triple mountings, 12 5-in (127-mm) L/38 DP in six Mk 38 twin mountings, and four 20-mm Phalanx Mk 15 close-in weapon system mountings

Missile armament: eight quadruple launchers for 32 BGM-109 Tomahawk cruise missiles, and four launchers for 16 RGM-84A Harpoon surface-to-surface missiles

Torpedo armament: none

Anti-submarine armament: helicopter-launched weapons (see below)

Aircraft: three or four helicopters on a platform aft

Armour: 13·5/1·62-in (343/41-mm) belt, 6-in (152-mm) decks, 17/7·25-in (432/184-mm) turrets, 17·3-in (439-mm) barbettes, and 17·5/7·25-in (445/184-mm) conning tower

Electronics: one Raytheon/Sylvania SPS-10 surface-search radar, one LN-66 search radar, one Raytheon SPS-49 air-search radar, two Mk 38 gun fire-control systems, four Mk 37 gun fire-control systems, one Mk 40 gun director, one Mk 51 gun director, eight Mk 36 Super Chaffroc launchers, one Raytheon SLQ-32 electronic warfare system, two WSC-3 satellite communications transceivers, and one Combat Engagement Center

Propulsion: eight Babcock & Wilcox boilers supplying steam to four sets of geared turbines (General Electric in BBs 61 and 63, Westinghouse in BBs 62 and 64) delivering 212,000shp (158,090kW) to four shafts

Performance: maximum speed 33kts; range 17,275 miles (27,800km) at 17kts

Complement: 1,571

Class
1. USA (2+2)

Name	No.	Builders	Laid down	Commissioned
IOWA	BB 61	New York Navy Yard	June 1940	Feb 1943
NEW JERSEY	BB 62	Philadelphia Navy Yard	Sep 1940	May 1943
MISSOURI	BB 63	New York Navy Yard	Jan 1941	June 1944
WISCONSIN	BB 64	Philadelphia Navy Yard	Jan 1941	Apr 1944

Remarks: The reactivation of possibly four 'Iowa' class battleships marks an extraordinary renaissance for the type, whose capabilities are needed as an interim measure pending the delivery of more aircraft-carriers to the US Navy. The initial modernization upgrades the electronics fit, provides medium- and long-range anti-ship capability with Harpoon and Tomahawk missiles, improves point defence with four Phalanx CIWS mountings, and adds an anti-submarine capability in the form of helicopters.

The Phase I-modernized New Jersey (BB 62) shows off her lines in April 1983.

'Brooklyn' class heavy cruiser
USA

Displacement: 10,000 tons standard and 13,500 tons full load
Dimensions: length 608·3ft (185·4m); beam 69ft (21·0m); draught 24ft (7·3m)
Gun armament: 15 6-in (152-mm) L/47 in five Mk 16 triple mountings, eight 5-in (127-mm) L/25 in Mk 27 single mountings, 28 40-mm Bofors L/60 AA in four Mk 2 quadruple and six Mk 1 twin mountings, and 24 20-mm Oerlikon AA in single and twin mountings
Missile armament: none
Torpedo armament: none
Anti-submarine armament: none
Aircraft: one Bell Model 205 JetRanger helicopter
Armour: 4/1·5-in (102/38-mm) belt, 3/2-in (76/51-mm) decks, 5/3-in (127/76-mm) turrets and 8-in (203-mm) conning tower

Electronics: one Raytheon/Sylvania SPS-10 surface-search and tactical radar, and one RCA SPS-12 air-search radar, and two Mk 34 gun fire-control systems for the main armament
Propulsion: eight Babcock & Wilcox boilers supplying steam to Parsons geared turbines delivering 100,000shp (74,570kW) to four shafts
Performance: maximum speed 32·5kts; range 14,1000km (8,760 miles) at 15kts
Complement: between 888 and 975 in peacetime

Class

1. Chile (1)				Com-
Name	No.	Builders	Laid down	missioned
O'HIGGINS	02	New York Navy Yard	Mar 1935	Sep 1937

'California' class nuclear-powered guided-missile cruiser
USA

The South Carolina (CGN 37) cruises quietly in the Indian Ocean during 1980.

Displacement: 9,560 tons standard and 11,100 tons full load
Dimensions: length 596ft (181·7m); beam 61ft (18·6m); draught 31·5ft (9·6m)
Gun armament: two 5-in (127-mm) L/54 DP in two Mk 42 single mountings, and (to be fitted) two Phalanx Mk 15 20-mm close-in weapons system mountings
Missile armament: two quadruple container-launchers for eight BGM-109 Tomahawk surface-to-surface missiles, two quadruple launchers for eight RGM-84A Harpoon surface-to-surface missiles, and two Mk 13 single launchers for 80 RIM-66C Standard MR surface-to-air missiles
Torpedo armament: none
Anti-submarine armament: one octuple Mk 16 launcher for RUR-5A ASROC missiles, and two triple Mk 32 tube mountings for 12·75-in (324-mm) Mk 46 A%S torpedoes
Electronics: one ITT/Gilfillan SPS-48 3D air-search radar, one Raytheon/Sylvania SPS-10 surface-search radar, one Lockheed SPS-40 air-search radar, four Raytheon SPG-51D missile-control radars used in conjunction with two Mk 74 missile fire-control systems, one Lockheed SPG-60 search-and-track radar and one

Lockheed SPQ-9A track-while-scan radar used in conjunction with the Mk 86 missile fire-control system, one Mk 11 weapons-direction system (to be replaced by Mk 13 weapons-direction system), one EDO/General Electric SQS-26CX bow-mounted 'bottom-bounce' sonar used in conjunction with the Mk 114 A/S weapons-direction system, Mk 6 Fanfare torpedo decoy system, URN-20 TACAN, Naval Tactical Data System, OE-82 satellite communications antenna, SRR-1 satellite communications receiver, WSC-3 satellite communication transceiver, one SIQ-32(V)3 ESM suite, and four Mk 36 Super Chaffroc rapid-blooming overhead chaff systems
Propulsion: two General Electric D2G pressurized-water cooled reactors supplying steam to two geared turbines delivering 60,000shp (44,740kW) to two shafts
Performance: maximum speed 30kts; nuclear core life about 700,000 miles (1,126,500km)
Complement: 28+512

Class

1. USA (2)				Com-
Name	No.	Builders	Laid down	missioned
CALIFORNIA	CGN 36	Newport News S.B.	Jan 1970	Feb 1974
SOUTH CAROLINA	CGN 37	Newport News S.B.	Dec 1970	Jan 1975

Remarks: Designed to constitute the primary area-defence escort of a nuclear-powered aircraft-carrier, the two units of the 'South Carolina' class were originally classified as nuclear-powered guided-missile frigates (DLGN), becoming nuclear-powered guided-missile cruisers in 1975. The ships proved very expensive to build, and this led to the cancellation of a proposed third unit. In US Navy terminology these are 'double-ended' ships, with missile armament at each end of the flush deck, separated by the superstructure and enclosed tower masts. The primary armament comprises Standard surface-to-air missiles launched from two Mk 13 single launchers and fed from under-deck magazines; there are four SPG-51 missile-control radars (two at each end of the ship), which permits the simultaneous engagement of four aircraft targets long before they come into attack range of the vulnerable carrier. Realizing the growing threat posed by Soviet surface combatants with their cruise missiles, the US Navy has recently upgraded the two 'California' class ships with eight Harpoon surface-to-surface missiles, while the submarine threat is countered (at least in part) by the provision of an octuple ASROC anti-submarine missile launcher. The one major tactical shortcoming of the class is lack of an embarked helicopter for longer-range anti-submarine operations, while the previous lack of point-defence capability has been rectified by the provision in each ship of two 20-mm Mk 15 Phalanx CIWS mountings. Command, control and communication systems are, like those of most other major US Navy warships, unexcelled anywhere in the world.

'Ceylon' heavy class cruiser
UK

Displacement: 8,780 tons standard and 11,110 tons full load
Dimensions: length 555·5ft (169·3m); beam 62ft (18·9m); draught 20·5ft (6·2m)
Gun armament: nine 6-in (152-mm) L/50 in three Mk 23 triple mountings, eight 4-in (102-mm) L/45 DP in four Mk 19 twin mountings, and 18 40-mm Bofors L/60 AA
Missile armament: none
Torpedo armament: none
Anti-submarine armament: none
Armour: 3·5-in (89-mm) sides, and 2-in (51-mm) deck and turrets
Electronics: one Type 960 air-search radar, one Type 277 search radar, one Type 293 search radar, one Type 284 gun-control radar, and one Type 275 gun-control radar

Propulsion: four Admiralty boilers supplying steam to Parsons geared turbines delivering 72,500shp (54,065kW) to four shafts
Performance: maximum speed 31·5kts; range 6,900 miles (11,105km) at 13kts or 2,300 miles (3,700km) at 31·5kts
Complement: 776

Class

1. Peru (1)				Com-
Name	No.	Builders	Laid down	missioned
CORONEL BOLOGNESI	CL 82	Alexander Stephen	Apr 1939	July 1943

Remarks: This ship is now totally obsolete.

'Colbert' class guided-missile heavy cruiser
France

Displacement: 8,500 tons standard and 11,300 tons full load

Dimensions: length 180·8 m (593·2 ft); beam 20·2 m (66·1 ft); draught 7·7 m (25·2 ft)

Gun armament: two 100-mm (3·9-in) L/55 DP in two single mountings, and 12 57-mm Bofors L/70 DP in six twin mountings

Missile armament: four container-launchers for four MM.38 Exocet surface-to-surface missiles, and one twin launcher for 48 Masurca surface-to-air missiles

Torpedo armament: none

Anti-submarine armament: none

Armour: 50/80-mm (2/3·15-in) belt, and 50-mm (2-in) deck

Electronics: one Thomson-CSF DRBV 50 combined air- and surface-search radar, one Thomson-CSF DRBV 23C air-search radar, one Thomson-CSF DRBV 20 air-warning radar, one Thomson-CSF DRBI 10D height-finder radar, two Thomson-CSF DRBR 51 SAM-control radars, one Thomson-CSF DRBC 32C 100-mm (3·9-in) gun-control radar, two Thomson-CSF DRBC 31 57-mm gun-control radars, one Decca RM 416 navigation radar, SENIT 1 combat information system, two Syllex chaff launchers, URN-20 TACAN, and one ESM suite

Propulsion: four Indret boilers supplying steam to two sets of CEM-Parsons geared turbines delivering 64,130 kW (86,000 shp) to two shafts

Performance: maximum speed 31·5 kts; range 7,400 km (4,600 miles) at 25 kts

Complement: 24+190+346

Remarks: In service as the flagship of the French Mediterranean fleet, the guided-missile cruiser *Colbert* (C 611) was built as a gun cruiser but modified to the standard described between 1970 and 1972. Apart from command, her primary function is area defence of a task group containing an aircraft-carrier in conjunction with the two 'Suffren' class missile ships. To this effect she has on her quarterdeck a twin launcher for 48 of the latest increased-range Masurca surface-to-air missiles, controlled by two DRBC 51 radars for the simultaneous engagement of two targets. The ship also has useful point-defence anti-air capability with her six twin 57-mm mountings, and anti-ship ability with Exocet missiles. She is expected to remain in service at least to 1995.

Class
1. France (1)

Name	No.	Builders	Laid down	Commissioned
COLBERT	C 611	Brest Naval Dockyard	Dec 1953	May 1959

'De Ruyter' class heavy cruiser
Netherlands

Displacement: 9,530 tons standard and 12,165 tons full load (*Almirante Grau*) or 9,850 tons standard and 12,250 tons full load (*Aguirre*)

Dimensions: length 190·3 m (624·5 ft) for *Almirante Grau* or 185·6 m (609 ft) for *Aguirre*; beam 17·3 m (56·7 ft); draught 6·7 m (22 ft)

Gun armament (*Almirante Grau*): eight 152-mm (6-in) L/53 DP in four twin mountings, eight 57-mm L/60 AA in four twin mountings, and eight 40-mm Bofors AA L/70 in two quadruple mountings

Gun armament (*Aguirre*): four 152-mm (6-in) L/53 DP in two twin mountings, six 57-mm L/60 AA in three twin mountings, and four 40-mm Bofors L/70 AA

Missile armament: none

Torpedo armament: none

Anti-submarine armament: helicopter-launched weapons (see below)

Aircraft: three Sikorsky SH-3D Sea King helicopters in a hangar aft (*Aguirre* only)

Armour: 76/102-mm (3/4-in) belt, and 20/25-mm (0·8/1-in) decks

Electronics: one Hollandse Signaalapparaten LW-01 air-search radar, one Hollandse Signaalapparaten DA-02 surface-search and target-indication radar, one Hollandse Signaalapparaten VI-01 height-finding radar (*Almirante Grau* only), one Hollandse Signaalapparaten ZW-01 surface-search and navigation radar, one Hollandse Signaalapparaten WM-25 search and main armament fire-control radar system, and one Hollandse Signaalapparaten WM-45 AA armament fire-control radar system

Propulsion: four Yarrow/Werkspoor boilers supplying steam to two sets of Parsons/de Schelde geared turbines delivering 63,385 kW (85,000 shp) to two shafts

Performance: maximum speed 32 kts

Complement: 49+904

Class
1. Peru (2)

Name	No.	Builders	Laid down	Commissioned
ALMIRANTE GRAU	CL 81	Wilton-Fijenoord	Sep 1939	Nov 1953
AGUIRRE	CL 84	Rotterdamse Droogdok	May 1939	Dec 1953

Remarks: The two 'De Ruyter' class gun cruisers were bought from The Netherlands in 1973, the *Aguirre* (CL 84) being modernized as a helicopter cruiser by 1976.

'Kirov' class nuclear-powered battle-cruiser
USSR

Displacement: 22,000 tons standard and 28,000 tons full load

Dimensions: length 250·0 m (820·2 ft); beam 28·5 m (93·5 ft); draught 10·0 m (32·8 ft)

Gun armament: two 100-mm (3·9-in) DP in single mountings, and eight 30-mm AA 'Gatling' mountings

Missile armament: 20 launch tubes for 20 SS-N-19 surface-to-surface missiles, 12 launch tubes for 96 SA-N-6 surface-to-air missiles, and two twin launchers for 36 SA-N-4 'Gecko' surface-to-air missiles

Torpedo armament: two quintuple 533-mm (21-in) tube mountings

Anti-submarine armament: one RBU 6000 12-barrel rocket-launcher, two RBU 1000 six-barrel rocket-launchers, one twin launcher for 16 SS-N-14 'Silex' anti-submarine missiles, and helicopter-launched weapons (see below)

Aircraft: three to five Kamov Ka-25 'Hormone' helicopters on a platform aft

Electronics: one 'Top Pair' 3D radar, one 'Top Steer' 3D radar, two 'Eye Bowl' SS-N-14 control radars, two 'Top Dome' SA-N-6 control radars, two 'Pop Group' SA-N-4 control radars, one 'Kite Screech' main armament control radar, four 'Bass Tilt' AA gun-control radars, three 'Palm Frond' navigation radars, hull-mounted sonar, variable-depth sonar, and a comprehensive electronic countermeasures suite including eight 'Side Globe', four 'Rum Tub' and two 'Round House' antennae/housings

Propulsion: two nuclear reactors and ? boilers supplying steam to ? sets of turbines delivering 119,300 kW (160,000 shp) to ? shafts

Performance: maximum speed 35 kts

Complement: 900

Class
1. USSR (1+1)

Name	Builders	Laid down	Commissioned
KIROV	Baltic Yard 189	June 1973	1981
—	Baltic Yard 189	1978	1983-84

Remarks: One of the most remarkable classes to have appeared in recent years, th 'Kirov' class battle-cruiser is designed for independent operations or for the screening of carrier groups. She thus has an extremely potent and varied mix of weapons and electronics, and nuclear propulsion for long range and high speed.

'Krasina' class guided-missile cruiser

USSR

Displacement: 11,000 tons standard and 13,000 tons full load

Dimensions: length 187·0m (613·5ft); beam 22·3m (73·2ft); draught 7·6m (25ft)

Gun armament: two 130-mm (5·12-in) L/70 in one twin mounting, and six 30-mm 'Gatling' type CIWS mountings

Missile armament: eight twin container-launchers for 16 SS-N-12 surface-to-surface missiles, eight vertical launch tubes for about 84 SA-N-6 surface-to-air missiles, and two twin launchers for 40 SA-N-4 surface-to-air missiles

Torpedo armament: two quadruple or quintuple tube mountings for dual-role anti-ship and anti-submarine torpedoes

Anti-submarine armament: two 12-barrel RBU 6000 launchers, and anti-submarine torpedoes (above)

Aircraft: one Kamov Ka-25 'Hormone-B' over-the-horizon targeting helicopter in a hangar aft

Electronics: one 'Top Pair' 3D radar, one 'Top Steer' 3D radar, three 'Palm Frond' navigation and surface-search radars, one 'Trap Door' type SSM-control radar, one 'Top Dome' SA-N-6 control radar, two 'Pop Group' SA-N-4 control radars, one 'Kite Screech' 130-mm (5·12-in) fire-control radar, three 'Bass Tilt' 30-mm fire-control radars, two 'Tee Plinth' IR surveillance systems, eight 'Side Globe' ECM fairings, four 'Rum Tub' ESM fairings, ? 'Bell' series ESM fairings, ? 'High Pole-B' IFF, two chaff launchers, one low-frequency hull sonar, and one medium-frequency variable-depth sonar

Propulsion: COGOG (COmbined Gas turbine Or Gas turbine) arrangement with four gas turbines delivering about 130,000kW (174,330shp) to two shafts

Performance: maximum speed 34 kts

Complement: about 600

Lead ship of a most impressive guided-missile cruiser class, the Slava has a highly effective sensor fit to complement her useful main gun armament and powerful missile complement, whose most dangerous offensive assets are the 16 SS-N-12 anti-ship missiles located in pairs to each side of the bridge structure. In the after end of the ship are the two types of SAM.

Class

1. USSR (2 + 1)

Name	Builders	Laid down	Commissioned
SLAVA	61 Kommuna Yard, Nikolayev	1976	1983
—	61 Kommuna Yard, Nikolayev	1978	1984
—	61 Kommuna Yard, Nikolayev	1979	1985

Remarks: Replacing the 'Kara' class on the slips at 61 Kommuna, the 'Krasina' class was at first known to NATO as the 'Black Com 1' class. Compared with the 'Kara' class, the 'Krasina' class has far less anti-submarine armament, and is designed principally as a scaled-down and conventionally-powered version of the 'Kirov' class battle-cruiser, optimized for the anti-ship and anti-air roles, the former being facilitated by the embarkation of a 'Hormone-B' mid-course guidance-update helicopter. Close air-defence is well provided by missiles and 'Gatling' type gun mountings.

'Long Beach' nuclear-powered guided-missile cruiser

USA

Displacement: 14,200 tons standard and 17,100 tons full load

Dimensions: length 721·2ft (219·9m); beam 73·2ft (22·3m); draught 29·7ft (9·1m)

Gun armament: two 5-in (127-mm) L/38 DP in Mk 30 single mountings, and two 20-mm Phalanx Mk 15 close-in weapon system mountings

Missile armament: two quadruple container-launchers for eight RGM-84A anti-ship missiles, two Mk 10 twin launchers for RIM-67B Standard-ER surface-to-air missiles

Torpedo armament: none

Anti-submarine armament: two triple Mk 32 tube mountings for 12·75-in (324-mm) Mk 46 A/S torpedoes, and one octuple launcher for RUR-5A ASROC missiles

Aircraft: provision for a helicopter on a platform aft

Electronics: one ITT/Gilfillan SPS-48 3D radar, one Raytheon SPS-49B air-search radar, one Raytheon/Sylvania SPS-10 surface-search radar, four SPG-55A SAM-control radars used in conjunction with the four Mk 76 missile fire-control systems, two SPG-49 gun-control radars used in conjunction with the two Mk 56 gun fire-control systems, one Sperry SPW-2 missile-guidance radar, one Mk 14 weapon direction system, one Sangamo SQS-23 hull-mounted long-range sonar, URN-20 TACAN, OE-82 satellite communications antenna, SRR-1 satellite communications receiver, WSC-3 satellite communications transceiver, and two Mk 36 Super Chaffroc rapid-blooming overhead chaff launchers

Propulsion: two pressurized-water cooled Westinghouse C1W nuclear reactors supplying steam to two sets of General Electric geared turbines delivering 80,000shp (59,655kW) to two shafts

Performance: maximum speed 36 kts

Complement: 79 + 1,081, plus flag accommodation for 10 + 58

Class

1. USA (1)

Name	No.	Builders	Laid down	Commissioned
LONG BEACH	CGN 9	Bethlehem Steel	Dec 1957	Sep 1961

Remarks: The *Long Beach* (CGN 9) was the world's first nuclear-powered surface combatant, and the first ship designed for the US Navy specifically as a cruiser since World War II. She was also the world's first warship to have a missile main armament. Despite her size, the ship is technically single-ended in her armament, though the armament forward of the superstructure includes two twin Mk 10 SAM launchers, used in conjunction with four SPG-55A radars for the simultaneous engagement of up to four targets. Located behind the bridge structure are the ASROC launcher and two 5-in (127-mm) gun mountings, the latter added in 1962-63. A large helicopter platform is provided over the stern, but no embarked aircraft is provided. Recently modernized and refurbished (and fitted with Harpoon anti-ship missiles), the *Long Beach* has the performance, size and communications to operate effectively as a flagship.

Long Beach (CGN 9) before her modernization with Phalanx and Harpoon mountings.

'Moskva' class helicopter cruiser
USSR

The helicopter cruiser Moskva shows off some of the class's distinctive features, including the area forward of the superstructure dedicated to anti-submarine and anti-aircraft missile armament, and the broad-beamed area aft of it as the helicopter platform. The under-deck hangar measures 67.0 by 25.0 m (219.8 by 82 ft), and is accessed by two lifts on the helicopter platform and another in the rear of the superstructure in a small hangar just forward of the helicopter platform. The stern also houses a variable-depth sonar.

Displacement: 16,500 tons standard and 20,000 tons full load
Dimensions: length 190.5 m (624.8 ft); beam 23.0 m (75.4 ft); draught 11.0 m (36.1 ft); flight-deck width 34.0 m (111.5 ft)
Gun armament: four 57-mm L/70 AA in two twin mountings
Missile armament: two twin launchers for 48 SA-N-3 'Goblet' surface-to-air missiles
Torpedo armament: none
Anti-submarine armament: one twin SUW-N-1 launcher for 20 FRAS-1 missiles, two RBU 6000 12-barrel rocket-launchers, and helicopter-launched weapons (see below)
Aircraft: 18 Kamov Ka-25 'Hormone-A' helicopters
Electronics: one 'Top Sail' 3D radar, one 'Head Net-C' 3D radar, two 'Head Light' SAM-control radars, two 'Muff Cob' AA gun-control radars, three 'Don-2' navigation radars, one low-frequency hull-mounted sonar, one medium-frequency variable-depth sonar, and an extensive electronics countermeasures suite including eight 'Side Globe' antennae/housings
Propulsion: four boilers supplying steam to two sets of geared turbines delivering 74,570 kW (100,000 shp) to two shafts
Performance: maximum speed 30 kts; range 16,675 km (10,360 miles) at 18 kts or 5,200 km (3,230 miles) at 30 kts
Complement: 840 excluding air group personnel

Class
1. USSR (2)

Name	Builders	Laid down	Commissioned
MOSKVA	Nikolayev South	1963	May 1967
LENINGRAD	Nikolayev South	1965	late 1966

Remarks: The 'Moskva' class marked a big step forward in Soviet maritime air power and anti-submarine capabilities, but was nonetheless something of a mixed blessing. For while anti-submarine and task group command problems were eased quite considerably by the availability of these two ships, their seakeeping qualities leave much to be desired and it was also realized as the ships were building that Soviet warships needed much enhanced anti-ship capability, perhaps even at the expense of the anti-submarine capability that had previously reigned supreme. Thus only two of a planned 20 units were built, the class being replaced on the slips of the 441 Nosenko Yard at Nikolayev South by the more capable 'Kiev' class aircraft-carriers, which combine the capabilities of the 'Moskva' class with an anti-ship armament, fixed-wing aircraft and a global intervention capacity.

'Sverdlov' class guided-missile heavy cruiser
USSR

Displacement: 16,000 tons standard and 17,500 tons full load
Dimensions: length 210.0 m (689 ft); beam 22.0 m (72.2 ft); draught 7.5 m (24.5 ft)
Gun armament: nine 152-mm (6-in) L/50 in three triple mountings, 12 100-mm (3.9-in) L/60 DP in six twin mountings, and 16 37-mm AA in eight twin mountings
Missile armament: one twin launcher for 30 SA-N-2 'Guideline' surface-to-air missiles
Torpedo armament: none
Anti-submarine armament: none
Mines: up to 150
Armour: 100/125-mm (3.9/4.9-in) belt, 40/50-mm (1.6/2-in) ends, 25/75-mm (1/3-in) decks, 125-mm (4.9-in) turrets and 150-mm (5.9-in) conning tower
Electronics: one 'Big Net' air-search radar, one 'Slim Net' air-search radar, one 'Low Sieve' surface-search radar, one 'Fan Song-E' missile-control radar, one 'Top Bow' main armament control radar, six 'Egg Cup' 152-mm (6-in) and 100-mm (3.9-in) gun-control radars, two 'Sun Visor' 100-mm (3.9-in) gun-control radars, one

Neptun navigation radar, and various electronic warfare systems
Propulsion: six boilers supplying steam to two sets of geared turbines delivering 82,025 kW (110,000 shp) to two shafts
Performance: maximum speed 32 kts; range 16,000 km (9,945 miles) at 18 kts or 4,600 km (2,860 miles) at 32 kts
Complement: about 70+940

Class
1. USSR (1)
Name
DZERZHINSKI

Remarks: Though now in reserve, the cruiser *Admiral Dzerzhinsky* is maintained in being for her partially effective SAM armament, the SA-N-2 launcher being fitted in 1962 at the expense of X turret. So far as is known, this was the only attempt at a naval installation of the large 'Guideline' SAM.

'Sverdlov' class command heavy cruiser
USSR

Displacement: 16,000 tons standard and 17,500 tons full load
Dimensions: length 210.0 m (689 ft); beam 22.0 m (72.2 ft); draught 7.5 m (24.5 ft)
Gun armament: six (*Admiral Senyavin*) or nine (*Zhdanov*) 152-mm (6-in) L/50 in two or three triple mountings, 12 100-mm (3.9-in) L/60 DP in six twin mountings, 32 37-mm AA in 16 twin mountings, and 16 (*Senyavin*) or eight (*Zhdanov*) 30-mm AA in eight or four twin mountings
Missile armament: one twin launcher for 18 SA-N-4 surface-to-air missiles
Torpedo armament: none
Anti-submarine armament: none
Aircraft: one Kamov Ka-25 'Hormone' helicopter on a platform aft (*Zhdanov*) or in a hangar aft (*Admiral Senyavin*)
Armour: 100/125-mm (3.9/4.9-in) belt, 40/50-mm (1.6/2-in) ends, 25/75-mm (1/3-in) decks, 125-mm (4.9-in) turrets and 150-mm (5.9-in) conning tower
Electronics: one 'Top Trough' air-search radar, one 'Low Sieve' surface-search radar, two 'Top Bow' main armament control radars, six 'Egg Cup' 152-mm (6-in)

and 100-mm (3.9-in) gun-control radars, two 'Sun Visor' 100-mm (3.9-in) gun-control radars, four (*Senyavin*) or two (*Zhdanov*) 'Drum Tilt' 30-mm gun-control radars, one 'Pop Group' SAM-control radar, one *Neptun* navigation radar
Propulsion: six boilers supplying steam to two sets of geared turbines delivering 82,025 kW (110,000 shp) to two shafts
Performance: maximum speed 32 kts; range 16,000 km (9,945 miles) at 18 kts or 4,600 km (2,860 miles) at 32 kts
Complement: about 70+940

Class
1. USSR (2)
Name
ADMIRAL SENYAVIN
ZHDANOV

Remarks: The accommodation and sensor fit of 'Sverdlov' class cruisers suits them to the command role, two conversions being effected in 1972-75.

'Sverdlov' class heavy cruiser

USSR

Displacement: 16,000 tons standard and 17,500 tons full load

Dimensions: length 210·0m (689ft); beam 22·0m (72·2ft); draught 7·5m (24·5ft)

Gun armament: 12 152-mm (6-in) L/50 in three triple mountings, 12 100-mm (3·9-in) L/60 DP in six twin mountings, 16 37-mm AA in eight twin mountings, and (*Oktyabrskaya Revolutsiya, Admiral Ushakov* and *Aleksandr Suvorov* only) 16 30-mm AA in eight twin mountings

Missile armament: none

Torpedo armament: none

Anti-submarine armament: none

Mines: up to 150

Armour: 100/125-mm (3·9/4·9-in) belt, 40/50-mm (1·6/2-in) ends, 25/75-mm (1/3-in) decks, 125-mm (4·9-in) turrets and 150-mm (5·9-in) conning tower

Electronics: one 'Big Net' or 'Knife Rest' or 'Top Trough' or 'Hair Net' or 'Slim Net' air-search radar, one 'Low Sieve' or 'High Sieve' surface-search radar, one 'Half Bow' target-indication radar, two 'Top Bow' 152-mm (6-in) gun-control radars, eight 'Egg Cup' 152-mm (6-in) and 100-mm (3·9-in) gun-control radars, two 'Sun Visor' 100-mm (3·9-in) gun-control radars, four 'Drum Tilt' 30-mm gun-control radars (*Oktyabrskaya Revolutsiya, Admiral Ushakov* and *Aleksandr Suvorov* only), and two *Neptun* or 'Don-2' navigation radars

Propulsion: six boilers supplying steam to two sets of geared turbines delivering 82,025kW (110,000shp) to two shafts

Performance: maximum speed 32kts; range 16,000km (9,945 miles) at 18kts or 4,600km (2,860 miles) at 32kts

Complement: about 70+940

Class

1. USSR (9)

Name

ADMIRAL LAZAREV
ADMIRAL USHAKOV
ALEKSANDR NEVSKY
ALEKSANDR SUVOROV
DMITRI POZHARSKI
MIKHAIL KUTUZOV
MURMANSK
OKTYABRSKAYA REVOLUTSIYA
SVERDLOV

Remarks: Like their guided-missile and command cruiser half-sisters, the nine 'Sverdlov' class gun cruisers were built at Leningrad, Nikolayev and Severodvinsk. It has originally been planned to build 24 of this class, epitomizing the Soviet navy's determination in the late 1940s to emerge from its wartime status as a coastal force, but from the late 1940s some 20 keels were laid down, 14 ships being launched from 1951 onwards, and only 14 being completed by the time the programme was terminated in 1957 with the realization that gun cruisers no longer served any real purpose in an era of nuclear-powered submarines and guided missiles. One unit was scrapped in 1961, and another transferred to Indonesia in 1962, and of the surviving nine basic cruisers eight are maintained in commission while the *Admiral Lazarev* is in reserve. Despite their age, these ships have the size and armour to resist anti-ship missiles, and their gun power would be most useful in amphibious landings.

'Andrea Doria' class guided-missile cruiser

Italy

Displacement: 5,000 tons standard and 6,500 tons full load

Dimensions: length 149·3m (489·8ft); beam 17·2m (56·4ft); draught 5·0m (16·4ft)

Gun armament: eight 76-mm (3-in) OTO-Melara L/62 in single mountings (only six guns on *Caio Duilio*)

Missile armament: one twin launcher for 40 RIM-67A Standard-ER surface-to-air missiles

Torpedo armament: none

Anti-submarine armament: two triple Mk 32 tube mountings for 12·75-in (324-mm) Mk 46 A/S torpedoes, and helicopter-launched torpedoes (see below)

Aircraft: four Agusta-Bell AB.212 ASW helicopters

Electronics: one Hughes SPS-52 3D air-search radar, one Lockheed SPS-40 long-range air-search radar, one SMA SPQ 2 navigation radar, two Sperry SPG-55C missile-control radars, four Selenia Orion RTN 10X radars as part of the ELSAG Argo/NA9 fire-control systems, SCLAR rocket-launcher systems for overhead chaff/flares and Sangamo SQS-23 long-range hull-mounted active sonar

Propulsion: four Foster-Wheeler boilers supplying steam to two double-reduction geared turbines (CNR in *Andrea Doria* and Ansaldo in *Caio Duilio*) delivering 44,740kW (60,000shp) to two shafts

Performance: maximum speed 31kts; range 9,250km (5,750 miles) at 17kts

Complement: 45+425

Class

1. Italy (2)

Name	No.	Builders	Laid down	Commissioned
ANDREA DORIA	C 553	Cantieri Navali Riuniti	May 1958	Feb 1964
CAIO DUILIO	C 554	Navalmeccanica	May 1958	Nov 1964

Remarks: The 'Andrea Doria' class represents Italian innovative capability at its best, combining many of the attributes of the guided-missile destroyer and helicopter cruiser on a hull of moderate displacement. The squeeze was a little too tight, and conditions for the four Agusta-Bell AB.212ASWs are cramped to the extent that operational efficiency suffers. (This was one of the reasons for the evolution of the 'Vittorio Veneto' class helicopter cruiser on a more generous displacement.) The helicopter platform measures 30·0 by 16·0 m (98·5 by 52·5ft), with a hangar in the after superstructure just forward of the helicopter platform. The two ships differ in sensor fit, and the *Caio Duilio* (C 554) has only six 76-mm (3-in) guns. In 1979-80 the *Caio Duilio* was refitted as a training ship for midshipmen, but would in emergencies be available in her original anti-submarine role. It is planned that both units of the 'Andrea Doria' should be replaced in the late 1980s by the highly capable 'Giuseppe Garibaldi' class light carrier currently being completed.

Visible in this photograph of the Italian helicopter cruiser Andrea Doria (C 553) are (fore to aft) the Mk 20 twin SAM launcher, the twin 76-mm (3-in) gun mountings flanking the forward SPG-55C SAM-control radar, another SPG-55C SAM-control radar, the SPS 768 long-range search radar (forward of the foremast) and the SPS-52 3D radar (on the mainmast) surmounted by the TACAN beacon. Also visible are the starboard units of the other three pairs of 76-mm (3-in) dual-purpose guns, which are most effective against fast attack craft and also moderately effective against subsonic aircraft thanks to the provision of four ELSAG Argo fire-control systems with Orion radars.

'Bainbridge' class nuclear-powered guided-missile cruiser
USA

Displacement: 7,600 tons standard and 8,592 tons full load
Dimensions: length 565ft (172·3m); beam 57·9ft (17·6m); draught 25·4ft (7·7m)
Gun armament: two 20-mm AA in a Mk 67 twin mounting
Missile armament: two quadruple launchers for RGM-84A Harpoon surface-to-surface missiles, and two Mk 10 twin launchers for 80 RIM-67B Standard-ER surface-to-air missiles
Torpedo armament: none
Anti-submarine armament: one octuple RUR-5A ASROC launcher and two triple Mk 32 tube mountings for 12·75-in (324-mm) Mk 44/46 torpedoes
Electronics: one Hughes SPS-52 3D air-search radar, one Raytheon/Sylvania SPS-10 surface-search radar, one Raytheon SPS-49 air-search radar, four Sperry/RCA SPG-55A fire-control radars used in conjunction with four Mk 76 missile fire-control systems, one Mk 11 weapons-direction system (to be replaced by Mk 14 weapons-direction system), URN-20 TACAN, Naval Tactical Data System, OE-82 satellite communications antenna, SSR-1 satellite receiver, WSC-1 satellite transceiver, one Sangamo SQS-23 long-range active sonar, four Mk 36 Super Chaffroc rapid-blooming overhead chaff system, and one SLQ-32(V)3 ESM suite
Propulsion: two General Electric D2G pressurized-water cooled reactors supplying steam to two geared turbines delivering 60,000shp (44,740kW) to two shafts
Performance: maximum speed 38 kts
Complement: 34+436, plus flag accommodation for 6+12

Class

1. USA (1)				
Name	No.	Builders	Laid down	Com-missioned
BAINBRIDGE	CGN 25	Bethlehem Steel Co	May 1959	Oct 1962

'Belknap' class guided-missile light cruiser
USA

Displacement: 6,570 tons standard and 7,900 tons full load
Dimensions: length 547ft (166·7m); beam 54·8ft (16·7m); draught 28·8ft (8·8m) to bottom of sonar dome and 19ft (5·8m) to keel
Gun armament: one 5-in (127-mm) L/54 in a Mk 42 mounting, and two 20-mm Phalanx Mk 15 close-in weapon system mountings
Missile armament: two quadruple launchers for eight RGM-84A Harpoon surface-to-surface missiles (except in *Jouett* and *Horne*), one Mk 10 twin launcher for 40 RIM-67B Standard SM-2 surface-to-air missiles, and (to be fitted) BGM-109 Tomahawk cruise missiles
Torpedo armament: none
Anti-submarine armament: two triple Mk 32 tube mountings for 12·75-in (324-mm) Mk 44/46 A/S torpedoes, and up to 20 RUR-5A ASROC missiles fired from the same Mk 10 launcher as the Standard SAMs
Aircraft: one Kaman SH-2F Seasprite helicopter
Electronics: one ITT/Gilfillan SPS-48 3D air-search radar, one Raytheon/Sylvania SPS-10 surface-search radar, one Raytheon SPS-49 (CGs 26-28 and 30) or Lockheed SPS-40 air-search radar, one Western Electric SPG-53F fire-control radar, two Sperry/RCA SPG-55D SAM fire-control radars, one SPG-53A gun fire-control radar, two Mk 76 missile fire-control systems, one Mk 68 gun fire-control system, one Mk 7 (CGs 26 and 27) or Mk 11 weapons-direction system (to be replaced by one Mk 14 weapons-direction system), one Mk 116 (CG 26) or Mk 114 A/S fire-control system, four Mk 28 Chaffroc (being replaced by Mk 36 Super Chaffroc) rapid-blooming overhead chaff systems, one SQS-53C (CG 26) or EDO/General Electric SQS-26 bow-mounted 'bottom-bounce' sonar, one Mk 6 Fanfare torpedo decoy system, Naval Tactical Data System, URN-20 TACAN, OE-82 satellite communications antenna, SRR-1 satellite communications receiver, WSC-3 satellite communications transceiver, and one SLQ-32(V)2 ESM suite
Propulsion: four boilers (Babcock & Wilcox in CGs 26-28 and 32-34, and Combustion Engineering in CGs 29-31) supplying steam to two sets of geared turbines (De Laval in CG 33 and General Electric in others) delivering 85,000shp (63,385kW) to two shafts
Performance: maximum speed 32·5kts
Complement: 31+387 (including squadron staff) or 520 (CG 26 including flag accommodation)

Just aft of the Mk 10 twin launcher on the foredeck of the Belknap (CG 26) is the raised top of the magazine from which the Standard or ASROC missiles are fed.

Class

1. USA (9)				
Name	No.	Builders	Laid down	Com-missioned
BELKNAP	CG 26	Bath Iron Works	Feb 1962	Nov 1964
JOSEPHUS DANIELS	CG 27	Bath Iron Works	Apr 1962	May 1965
WAINWRIGHT	CG 28	Bath Iron Works	July 1962	Jan 1966
JOUETT	CG 29	Puget Sound NY	Sep 1962	Dec 1966
HORNE	CG 30	San Francisco NY	Dec 1962	Apr 1967
STERETT	CG 31	Puget Sound NY	Sep 1962	Apr 1967
WILLIAM H. STANDLEY	CG 32	Bath Iron Works	July 1963	July 1966
FOX	CG 33	Todd Shipyard	Jan 1963	May 1966
BIDDLE	CG 34	Bath Iron Works	Dec 1963	Jan 1967

Remarks: The 'Belknap' class of guided-missile cruisers serve with the Atlantic and Pacific Fleets (three and six units respectively), and with the 'Leahy' class form the basis of US carrier task forces' escort capability. However, compared with the 'Leahy' class, the 'Belknap' class is a 'single-ended' design, and can thus engage only two aerial targets simultaneously. Additionally, the use of the Mk 10 launcher for SAMs and ASROC missiles has been found to limit the tactical flexibility of the design.

'Göta Lejon' class cruiser
Sweden

Displacement: 8,200 tons standard and 9,200 tons full load
Dimensions: length 182·0m (597ft); beam 16·5m (54ft); draught 6·6m (21·5ft)
Gun armament: seven 152-mm (6-in) L/53 DP on one triple and two twin mountings, four 57-mm Bofors L/60 AA, and 11 40-mm Bofors AA
Missile armament: none
Torpedo armament: two triple 533-mm (21-in) tube mountings
Anti-submarine armament: two depth-charge racks
Mines: 120 laid over the stern
Armour: 80/100-mm (3·15/3·94-in) belt, 40/60-mm (1·57/2·36-in) main deck, and 50/135-mm (1·97/5·3-in) turrets

Electronics: one Hollandse Signaalapparaten LW-03 air-search radar, one Type 277 search radar, one Type 293 tactical radar, one I-band fire-control radar
Propulsion: four Penhoët boilers supplying steam to two sets of De Laval geared turbines delivering 100,000shp (74,570kW) to two shafts
Performance: maximum speed 33 kts
Complement: 610

Class

1. Chile (1)				
Name	No.	Builders	Laid down	Com-missioned
LATORRE	04	Eriksberg Mek Verkstads	Sep 1943	Dec 1947

'Kara' class guided-missile cruiser
USSR

Displacement: 8,200 tons standard and 10,000 tons full load

Dimensions: length 173·2m (568ft); beam 18·0m (59ft); draught 6·7m (22ft)

Gun armament: four 76-mm (3-in) L/60 DP in two twin mountings, and four 30-mm AA 'Gatling' mountings

Missile armament: two quadruple container-launchers for eight SS-N-14 surface-to-underwater missiles, two twin launchers for 72 SA-N-3 'Goblet' surface-to-air missiles, and two twin launchers for 36 SA-N-4 'Gecko' SAMs; *Azov* has one SA-N-3 and one SA-N-6 system

Torpedo armament: two quintuple 533-mm (21-in) AS/ASW tube mountings

Anti-submarine armament: two RBU 6000 12-barrel rocket-launchers, two RBU 1000 six-barrel rocket-launchers, and helicopter-launched weapons (see below)

Aircraft: one Kamov Ka-25 'Hormone' helicopter in a hangar aft

Electronics: one 'Top Sail' 3D radar, one 'Head Net-C' 3D radar, two 'Don Kay' navigation radars, one 'Don 2' navigation radar, two 'Head Light' SA-N-3 missile-control radars (one 'Head Light' and one 'Top Dome' in *Azov*), two 'Pop Group' SA-N-4 missile-control radars, two 'Owl Screech' 76-mm gun-control radars, two 'Bass Tilt' 30-mm gun-control radars, hull-mounted sonar(s), variable-depth sonar, BAT-1 torpedo countermeasures system, one 'High Pole-A' IFF, one 'High Pole-B' IFF, two chaff launchers, and an extremely comprehensive electronic counter-measures and electronic support measures system comprising two 'Tee Plinth', eight 'Side Globe', two 'Bell Slam', one 'Bell Clout' and two 'Bell Tap' systems

Propulsion: COGOG (COmbined Gas turbine Or Gas turbine) arrangement, with two gas turbines delivering 17,900kW (24,000shp) and four gas turbines delivering 74,570kW (100,000shp) to two shafts

Performance: maximum speed 33kts; range 14,825km (9,210 miles) at 18kts or 3,700km (2,300 miles) at 32kts

Complement: 30+510

A 'Kara' class guided-missile cruiser under way.

Class
1. USSR (7)

Name	Builders	Laid down	Commissioned
NIKOLAYEV	Nikolayev North	1969	1971
OCHAKOV	Nikolayev North	1970	1973
KERCH	Nikolayev North	1971	1974
AZOV	Nikolayev North	1972	1975
PETROPAVLOVSK	Nikolayev North	1973	1976
TASHKENT	Nikolayev North	1974	1977
TALLINN	Nikolayev North	1975	1979

Remarks: The 'Kara' class was the first type of Soviet heavy cruiser built since the 'Sverdlov' class, and the seven ships of the class represent a formidable anti-submarine capability combined with long range and a mix of medium- and short-range surface-to-air missiles for area and point defence. The odd ship out is the *Azov*, which has been converted as a trials ship with the new SA-N-6 SAM missile system installed in place of the after SA-N-3 mounting and torpedo tubes.

'Kresta I' class guided-missile cruiser
USSR

Displacement: 6,140 tons standard and 7,500 tons full load

Dimensions: length 155·5m (510ft); beam 17·0m (55·7ft); draught 6·0m (19·7ft)

Gun armament: four 57-mm L/80 DP in two twin mountings, and (*Drozd* only) four 30-mm AA 'Gatling' mountings

Missile armament: two twin container-launchers for four SS-N-3B 'Shaddock' surface-to-surface missiles, and two twin launchers for 32 SA-N-1 'Goa' surface-to-air missiles

Torpedo armament: two quintuple 533-mm (21-in) AS/ASW tube mountings

Anti-submarine armament: two RBU 6000 12-barrel rocket-launchers, and two RBU 1000 six-barrel rocket-launchers

Aircraft: one Kamov Ka-25 'Hormone-B' helicopter in a hangar aft

Electronics: one 'Head Net-C' 3D radar, one 'Big Net' air-search radar, two 'Plinth Net' surface-search radars, one 'Scoop Pair' SSM-control radar, two 'Peel Group' SAM-control radars, two 'Muff Cob' main armament control radars, two 'Bass Tilt' AA gun-control radars (*Drozd* only), two 'Don-2' navigation radars, one 'High Pole-B' IFF, one hull-mounted sonar, and a comprehensive electronic counter-measures system with eight 'Side Globe' antennae/housings

Propulsion: four boilers supplying steam to two sets of geared turbines delivering 74,570kW (100,000shp) to two shafts

Performance: maximum speed 34kts; range 13,000km (8,080 miles) at 18kts or 3,700km (2,300 miles) at 32kts

Complement: 375

Class
1. USSR (4)

Name	No.	Builders	Laid down	Commissioned
ADMIRAL ZOZULYA	—	Zhdanov Yard	Sep 1964	1967
VLADIVOSTOK	017	Zhdanov Yard	1965	1968
VICE-ADMIRAL DROZD	298	Zhdanov Yard	1965	1968
SEVASTOPOL	—	Zhdanov Yard	1966	1969

Remarks: The 'Kresta I' class was designed to supplant the 'Kynda' class for anti-ship warfare, and was the first Soviet cruiser class designed with provision for an embarked over-the-horizon targeting helicopter, giving the units of the class the ability to operate effectively beyond the range of Soviet land-based aircraft.

'Kresta II' class guided-missile cruiser
USSR

Displacement: 6,000 tons standard and 7,800 tons full load

Dimensions: length 158·5m (520ft); beam 16·9m (55·45ft); draught 6·0m (19·7ft)

Gun armament: two twin 57-mm AA mountings and four 30-mm rotary-barrel AA cannon mountings

Missile armament: two quadruple container-launchers for eight SS-N-14 'Silex' anti-submarine missiles, and two twin launchers for 48 SA-N-3 'Goblet' SAMs

Torpedo armament: two quintuple 533-mm (21-in) AS/ASW tube mountings

Anti-submarine armament: SS-N-14 (see Missiles above), two 12-barrel RBU 6000 launchers and two six-barrel RBU 1000 launchers

Aircraft: one Kamov Ka-25 'Hormone-A' anti-submarine helicopter (hangar aft)

Electronics: one 'Top Sail' 3D air-search radar, one 'Head Net-C' 3D radar, two 'Don Kay' navigation radars, two 'Head Light' SAM control radars, two 'Muff Cob' 57-mm control radars, two 'Bass Tilt' 30-mm control radars, ECM suite with eight 'Side Globe' antennae, and one hull-mounted sonar

Propulsion: four water-tube boilers supplying steam to two sets of geared turbines, delivering 100,000shp (74,570kW) to two shafts

Performance: maximum speed 34kts; range 13,000km (8,080 miles) at 18kts or 3,250km (2,020 miles) at 32kts

Complement: 380-400

Class
1. USSR (10)

Name	Builders	Laid down	Commissioned
KRONSHTADT	Zhdanov Yard	1966	1969
ADMIRAL ISAKOV	Zhdanov Yard	1967	1970
ADMIRAL NAKHIMOV	Zhdanov Yard	1968	1971
ADMIRAL MAKAROV	Zhdanov Yard	1969	1972
MARSHAL VOROSHILOV	Zhdanov Yard	1970	1973
ADMIRAL OKTYABRSKY	Zhdanov Yard	1970	1973
ADMIRAL ISACHENKOV	Zhdanov Yard	1971	1974
MARSHAL TIMOSHENKO	Zhdanov Yard	1972	1975
VASILY CHAPAYEV	Zhdanov Yard	1973	1976
ADMIRAL YUMASCHEV	Zhdanov Yard	1974	1977

Remarks: The more numerous 'Kresta II' class is a development of the 'Kresta I' class reflecting the Soviet navy's increased concern with anti-submarine warfare during the mid-1960s. The main alterations are the replacement of the SS-N-3 anti-ship missile system with the SS-N-14 anti-submarine missile system, and the upgrading of the air-defence capability by the substitution of SA-N-3 launchers.

'Kynda' class guided-missile cruiser
USSR

Displacement: 4,400 tons standard and 5,700 tons full load

Dimensions: length 142·0m (465·8ft); beam 15·8m (51·8ft); draught 5·3m (17·4ft)

Gun armament: four 76-mm (3-in) L/60 DP in two twin mountings, and (in *Varyag*) four 30-mm 'Gatling' mountings

Missile armament: two quadruple container-launchers for 16 SS-N-3B 'Shaddock' surface-to-surface missiles, and one twin launcher for 22 SA-N-1 'Goa' surface-to-surface missiles

Torpedo armament: two triple 533-mm (21-in) AS/ASW tube mountings

Anti-submarine armament: two RBU 6000 12-barrel rocket-launchers

Aircraft: provision for one Kamov Ka-25 'Hormone' helicopter on a platform aft

Electronics: two 'Head Net-A' air-search radars or (in *Fokin*) one 'Head Net-A' air-search radar and one 'Head Net-C' 3D radar, or (in *Varyag*) two 'Head Net-C' 3D radars, two 'Plinth Net' surface-search radars (not in *Golorko*), two 'Scoop Pair' SSM-control radars, one 'Peel Group' SAM-control radar, two 'Owl Screech' gun-control radars, two 'Don-2' navigation radars, two 'Bass Tilt' 30-mm control radars (in *Varyag*), one 'High Pole-B' IFF, one hull-mounted sonar, and various electronic warfare systems

Propulsion: four boilers supplying steam to two sets of geared turbines delivering 74,570kW (100,000shp) to two shafts

Performance: maximum speed 34kts; range 11,125km (6,915 miles) at 15kts or 2,775km (1,725 miles) at 34kts

Complement: 390

*The **Admiral Golovko** was third of the four-strong 'Kynda' class.*

Class
1. USSR (4)

Name	Builders	Laid down	Com-missioned
GROZNY	Zhdanov Yard	1959	June 1962
ADMIRAL FOKIN	Zhdanov Yard	1960	Aug 1963
ADMIRAL GOLOVKO	Zhdanov Yard	1961	July 1964
VARYAG	Zhdanov Yard	1962	Feb 1965

Remarks: The 'Kynda' class was the USSR's first guided-missile cruiser class, and its units were optimized for anti-ship warfare in the role of destroyer flotilla leader. The missile armament is still useful, but reloading of the SS-N-3 tubes is slow, and long-range effectiveness is curtailed by lack of a helicopter.

'Leahy' class guided-missile cruiser
USA

Displacement: 5,670 tons standard and 7,800 tons full load

Dimensions: length 533ft (162·5m); beam 54·9ft (16·6m); draught 24·8ft (7·6m) to sonar dome

Gun armament: two 20-mm Phalanx Mk 15 close-in weapon system mountings

Missile armament: two quadruple container-launchers for eight RGM-84A Harpoon surface-to-surface missiles, and two Mk 10 twin launchers for 80 RIM-67B Standard-ER surface-to-air missiles

Torpedo armament: none

Anti-submarine armament: two triple Mk 32 tube mountings for 12·75-in (324-mm) Mk 46 A/S torpedoes, and one octuple launcher for RUR-5A ASROC missiles

Aircraft: provision for one Kaman SH-2F Seasprite on a platform aft

Electronics: one ITT/Gilfillan SPS-48A 3D radar, one Raytheon SPS-49 air-search radar, one Raytheon/Sylvania SPS-10 surface-search radar, two SPG-53F and two SPG-55B missile-control radars used in conjunction with four Mk 75 missile fire-control systems, one Mk 14 weapon direction system, one Sangamo SQS-23 bow-mounted sonar used in conjunction with the Mk 114 A/S fire-control system, Naval Tactical Data System, OE-82 satellite communications antenna, SRR-1 satellite communications receiver, WSC-3 satellite communications transceiver, URN-20 TACAN, four Mk 36 Super Chaffroc rapid-blooming overhead chaff launchers, and one SLQ-32(V)2 ESM suite

Propulsion: four boilers (Babcock & Wilcox in CGs 16-20 and Foster-Wheeler in the others) supplying steam to two sets of geared turbines (General Electric in CGs 16-18, De Laval in CGs 19-22, and Allis-Chalmers in CGs 23-24) delivering 85,000shp (63,385kW) to two shafts

Performance: maximum speed 32·7kts; range 9,200 miles (14,805km) at 20kts

Complement: 18+359 in CGs 16, 17, 21, and 23, or 32+381 in CGs 18-20, 22 and 24, plus flag accommodation for 6+18

*The 'Leahy' class cruiser **Harry E. Yarnell** (CG 17) in the harbour of Bath, Maine.*

Class
1. USA (9)

Name	No.	Builders	Laid down	Com-missioned
LEAHY	CG 16	Bath Iron Works	Dec 1959	Aug 1962
HARRY E. YARNELL	CG 17	Bath Iron Works	May 1960	Feb 1963
WORDEN	CG 18	Bath Iron Works	Sep 1960	Aug 1963
DALE	CG 19	New York S.B.	Sep 1960	Nov 1963
RICHMOND K. TURNER	CG 20	New York S.B.	Jan 1961	June 1964
GRIDLEY	CG 21	Puget Sound Bridge	July 1960	May 1963
ENGLAND	CG 22	Todd Shipyard	Oct 1960	Dec 1963
HALSEY	CG 23	San Francisco NY	Aug 1960	July 1963
REEVES	CG 24	Puget Sound NY	July 1960	May 1964

Remarks: The 'Leahy' class was the US Navy's first purpose-built guided-missile cruiser class, and was designed for the escort of fast carrier task groups, the 'double-ended' layout and combination of two SPG-53 and two SPG-55 SAM-control radars making possible the simultaneous engagement of four targets. Though the amidships ASROC launcher is effective, the class suffers from lack of an embarked anti-submarine helicopter. Good command facilities are provided.

'Sovremenny' class guided-missile cruiser
USSR

Displacement: 6,200 tons standard and 7,800 tons full load

Dimensions: length 156·0m (511·8ft); beam 17·3m (56·8ft); draught 6·5m (21·3ft)

Gun armament: four 130-mm (5·1-in) L/60 DP in two twin mountings, and four 30-mm AA in 'Gatling' mountings

Missile armament: two quadruple container-launchers for eight SS-N-22 anti-ship missiles, and two launchers for 48 SA-N-7 surface-to-air missiles

*The anti-ship **Sovremenny** is normally partnered by A/S 'Udaloy'.*

Torpedo armament: two twin 533-mm (21-in) AS/ASW tube mountings

Anti-submarine armament: two RBU 1000 six-barrel rocket-launchers

Aircraft: one Kamov Ka-25 'Hormone' helicopter in a hangar amidships

Electronics: one 'Top Steer' 3D radar, one 'Band Stand' SSM-control radar, six 'Front Dome' missile-control radars, one 'Kite Screech' main armament gun-control radar, two 'Bass Tilt' AA gun-control radars, three 'Palm Frond' navigation radars, extensive electronic countermeasures systems, and hull-mounted sonar

Propulsion: ? boilers supplying steam to two sets of turbo-pressurized turbines delivering 74,570kW (100,000shp) to two shafts

Performance: maximum speed 34kts

Complement: about 350

Class
1. USSR (4+2)

Name	Builders	Laid down	Com-missioned
SOVREMENNY	Zhdanov Yard	1976	Aug 1980
OTCHYANNY	Zhdanov Yard	1977	1982
—	Zhdanov Yard	1978	1983
—	Zhdanov Yard	1979	1984
—	Zhdanov Yard	1980	1985
—	Zhdanov Yard	1981	1986

'Ticonderoga' class guided-missile cruiser

USA

Displacement: 9,600 tons full load

Dimensions: length 566·8ft (172·8m); beam 55ft (16·8m); draught 31ft (9·5m)

Gun armament: two 5-in (127-mm) L/54 DP in two Mk 45 single mountings, and two 20-mm Phalanx Mk 15 close-in weapon system mountings

Missile armament: two octuple container-launchers for 16 RGM-84A Harpoon surface-to-surface missiles, and two Mk 26 twin launchers for up to 68 RIM-67B Standard surface-to-air missiles; from CG 49 onwards the ships will have two EX 41 vertical launchers in place of the Mk 26 launchers for up to 122 assorted missiles, and from CG 52 onwards the ships will have two Vertical Launch Systems each with 12 BGM-109 Tomahawk surface-to-surface cruise missiles

Torpedo armament: none

Anti-submarine armament: two triple Mk 32 tube mountings for 12·75-in (324-mm) Mk 46 A/S torpedoes, up to 20 RUR-5A ASROC missiles forming part of the total missile strength above and launched from the Mk 26 launchers, and helicopter-launched weapons (see below)

Aircraft: two Sikorsky SH-60B Seahawk helicopters in a hangar aft

Armour: 1-in (25-mm) over magazines

Electronics: two RCA SPY-1A phased-array pairs of long-range search, target-tracking and missile-control radars used in conjunction with the AEGIS Weapons Control System Mk 7 and four SPG-62 SAM-control radars, one Raytheon SPS-49 air-search radar, one Lockheed SPQ-9 track-while-scan radar used in conjunction with the Lockheed Mk 86 gun fire-control system, one Sangamo SQS-53 hull-mounted long-range active sonar and one SQR-15 Tactical Towed-Array Sonar used in conjunction with the Mk 116 underwater weapons fire-control system, OE-82 satellite communications antenna, SRR-1 satellite communications receiver, WSC-3 satellite communications receiver, one SLQ-32 ESM suite, and four Mk 36 Super Chaffroc rapid-blooming overhead chaff launchers

Propulsion: four General Electric LM 2500 gas turbines delivering 80,000shp (59,655kW) to two shafts

Performance: maximum speed 30+ kts

Complement: 33+327

Class

1. USA (2+9+14)

Name	No.	Builders	Laid down	Commissioned
TICONDEROGA	CG 47	Ingalls Shipbuilding	Jan 1980	Jan 1983
YORKTOWN	CG 48	Ingalls Shipbuilding	Oct 1981	July 1984
—	CG 49	Ingalls Shipbuilding	—	July 1985
—	CG 50	Ingalls Shipbuilding	—	Jan 1986
—	CG 51	Bath Iron Works	—	Jan 1986
—	CG 52	Ingalls Shipbuilding	—	July 1986
—	CG 53	Ingalls Shipbuilding	—	Feb 1987
—	CG 54-56	Ingalls Shipbuilding	—	Feb 1987
—	CG 57-59	Proposed FY 1985	—	—
—	CG 60-62	Proposed FY 1986	—	—
—	CG 63-65	Proposed FY 1987	—	—
—	CG 66-70	Proposed FY 1988	—	—

Remarks: The 'Ticonderoga' class guided-missile cruiser is one of the most significant classes to have appeared in US Navy service in recent years, and is based on a slightly stretched version of the hull and powerplant of the 'Spruance' class guided-missile destroyer. The key to the ships' importance is the AEGIS system fitted in each vessel: this combines the SPY-1A long-range radar (with four mechanically-fixed but electronically-scanning antennae, two on the forward superstructure and the other two on the after superstructure) for hemispherical detection, acquisition and tracking of multiple targets with the AEGIS Weapons Control System Mk 7 with its UYK-7 computers. In its definitive form this combination allows each 'Ticonderoga' class unit, entrusted with the task of co-ordinating a carrier task group's air defence, to analyse the relative threat posed by hundreds of possible aircraft and missiles (and ships) and then destroy the primary targets with its own missiles or with those of the other escorts, which are kept in the full picture by secure data-link. It is a truly formidable system, but also highly expensive. Future developments call for the upgrading of the AEGIS system wherever possible, and for the installation of Mk 41 vertical launchers in place of the current pair of Mk 26 twin launchers in CG 52 onwards. The vertical-launch system will handle the Tomahawk cruise missile as well as Standard SAMs.

Visible on the forward and starboard sides of the superstructure of the Ticonderoga (CG 47) are the two forward fixed antennae for the SPY-1A radar.

'Truxtun' class nuclear-powered guided-missile cruiser

USA

Displacement: 8,200 tons standard and 9,125 tons full load

Dimensions: length 564ft (171·9m); beam 58ft (17·7m); draught 31ft (9·4m)

Gun armament: one 5-in (127-mm) L/54 DP in one Mk 42 single mounting, and two 20-mm Phalanx Mk 15 close-in weapon system mountings

Missile armament: two quadruple container-launchers for eight RGM-84A Harpoon surface-to-surface missiles, and one Mk 10 twin launcher for up to 60 RIM-67B Standard-ER surface-to-air missiles

Torpedo armament: none

Anti-submarine armament: four Mk 32 tubes for 12·75-in (324-mm) Mk 46 A/S torpedoes, up to 20 RUR-5A ASROC missiles included in the total above for the Mk 10 launcher and launched from the Mk 10 launcher, and helicopter-launched weapons (see below)

Aircraft: one Kaman SH-2F Seasprite helicopter in a hangar aft

Electronics: one ITT/Gilfillan SPS-48 3D radar, one Lockheed SPS-40 air-search radar, one Raytheon/Sylvania SPS-10 surface-search radar, one SPG-53F gun-control radar used in conjunction with the Mk 68 gun fire-control system, two Sperry/RCA SPG-55B SAM-control radars used in conjunction with the two Mk 76 missile fire-control systems, one Mk 14 weapon direction system, one EDO/General Electric SQS-26 bow-mounted 'bottom-bounce' sonar, URN-20 TACAN, Naval Tactical Data System, OE-82 satellite communications antenna, SRR-1 satellite communications receiver, WSC-3 satellite communications transceiver, one SLQ-32(V)3 ESM suite, and four Mk 36 Super Chaffroc rapid-blooming overhead chaff launchers

Propulsion: two pressurized-water cooled General Electric D2G nuclear reactors supplying steam to two sets of geared turbines delivering 60,000shp (44,740kW) to two shafts

Performance: maximum speed 38 kts

Complement: 36+492, plus flag accommodation for 6+12

Class

1. USA (1)

Name	No.	Builders	Laid down	Commissioned
TRUXTUN	CGN 35	New York S.B.	June 1963	May 1967

The Truxtun (CGN 35) is a nuclear-powered version of the 'Belknap' class.

'Type 82' class guided-missile cruiser
UK

Displacement: 6,100 tons standard and 7,100 tons full load

Dimensions: length 507ft (154·5m); beam 55ft (16·8m); draught 23ft (7·0m) to sonar dome

Gun armament: one 4·5-in (114-mm) L/55 DP in one Mk 8 single mounting, and two 20-mm Oerlikon AA in two Mk 7 single mountings

Missile armament: one twin launcher for 40 Sea Dart surface-to-air missiles

Torpedo armament: none

Anti-submarine armament: one launcher for 40 Ikara missiles, one Limbo Mk 10 mortar, and helicopter-launched weapons (see below)

Aircraft: one Westland Wasp HAS.Mk 1 helicopter on a platform aft

Electronics: one Marconi Type 965 air-search radar with double AKE 2 array, one Marconi Type 992Q surface-search and target-indication radar, two Type 909 SAM-control radars, one Kelvin Hughes Type 1006 navigation radar, one Kelvin Hughes Type 162 hull-mounted side-looking classification sonar, one Type 170 hull-mounted short-range search and attack sonar, one Type 182 torpedo-decoy system, one Graseby Type 184 hull-mounted medium-range panoramic search and attack sonar, one Plessey/Ferranti ADAWS 2 action data automation weapon system used in conjunction with the GWS 30 Sea Dart and GWS 40 Ikara fire-control systems, one UAA-1 Abbey Hill ESM suite, two Knebworth Corvus chaff launchers and SCOT satellite communications antenna

The short-range air-defence capability of the Bristol (D 23) is currently being upgraded in the light of British experience in the Falklands campaign.

Propulsion: COSAG (COmbined Steam And Gas turbine) arrangement, with two boilers supplying steam to two sets of Admiralty Standard Range turbines delivering 30,000shp (22,370kW) and two Rolls-Royce Olympus TM1A gas turbines delivering 30,000shp (22,370kW) to two shafts

Performance: maximum speed 28kts; range 5,750 miles (9,255km) at 18kts

Complement: 29+378

Class

1. UK (1)				Com-
Name	No.	Builders	Laid down	missioned
BRISTOL	D 23	Swan Hunter Ltd	Nov 1967	Mar 1973

'Udaloy' class guided-missile cruiser
USSR

Displacement: 6,700 tons standard and 8,200 tons full load

Dimensions: length 162·0m (531·5ft); beam 19·3m (63·3ft); draught 6·2m (20·3ft)

Gun armament: two 100-mm (3·9-in) DP in single mountings, and four 30-mm AA in 'Gatling' mountings

Missile armament: two quadruple container-launchers for eight SS-N-14 surface-to-underwater and surface-to-surface missiles, and eight launchers for 48 SA-N-8 surface-to-air missiles

Torpedo armament: two quadruple 533-mm (21-in) AS/ASW tube mountings

Anti-submarine armament: two RBU 6000 12-barrel rocket-launchers, SS-N-14 missiles (see above), and helicopter-launched weapons (see below)

Aircraft: two Kamov Ka-27 'Helix-A' helicopters in two hangars aft

Electronics: two 'Strut Pair' air-search radars, two 'Eye Bowl' missile-control radars, one 'Kite Screech' main armament gun-control radar, two 'Bass Tilt' AA gun-control radars, three 'Palm Frond' navigation radars, two 'High Pole-B' IFF, bow-mounted sonar, variable-depth sonar, and extensive electronic counter-measures systems

Propulsion: COGOG (COmbined Gas turbine Or Gas turbine) arrangement, with four gas turbines delivering a total of about 70,000kW (93,870shp) to two shafts

Performance: maximum speed 35kts

Complement: about 350

Class

1. USSR (5+1)				Com-
Name	No.	Builders	Laid down	missioned
UDALOY	—	Yantar	1978	1980
VICE-ADMIRAL KULAKOV	—	Zhdanov Yard	1978	1981
—	—	Yantar	1979	1983
—	—	Zhdanov Yard	1979	1983
—	—	Zhdanov Yard	1980	1984
—	—	Zhdanov Yard	1981	1985

Remarks: The 'Udaloy' class is a potent successor to the 'Kresta II' class anti-submarine cruiser, and is designed to work with the 'Sovremenny' anti-ship class.

'Virginia' class nuclear-powered guided-missile cruiser
USA

Displacement: 8,625 tons standard and 10,400 tons full load

Dimensions: length 585ft (178·4m); beam 63ft (19·2m); draught 29·5ft (9·0m)

Gun armament: two 5-in (127-mm) L/54 DP in two Mk 45 single mountings, and two 20-mm Phalanx Mk 15 close-in weapon system mountings

Missile armament: two quadruple container-launchers for eight RGM-84A Harpoon surface-to-surface missiles, two Mk 26 twin launchers for a maximum of 50 RIM-67B Standard-MR surface-to-air missiles, and two quadruple launchers for eight BGM-109 Tomahawk surface-to-surface cruise missiles

Torpedo armament: none

Anti-submarine armament: two triple Mk 32 tube mountings for 12·75-in (324-mm) Mk 46 A/S torpedoes, up to 20 RUR-5A ASROC missiles launched from the Mk 26 launchers, and helicopter-launched weapons (see below)

Aircraft: two Sikorsky SH-60 Seahawk helicopters in a hangar aft

Electronics: one ITT-Gilfillan SPS-48A 3D radar, one Lockheed SPS-40B air-search radar, one Westinghouse SPS-55 surface-search radar, two Sperry/RCA SPG-51D SAM-control radars used in conjunction with the Mk 74 missile fire-control system, one Lockheed SPG-60D search and tracking radar and one Lockheed SPQ-9A track-while-scan radar used in conjunction with the Mk 86 fire-control system for the forward missile launcher and for gun fire, one Sangamo SQS-53A bow-mounted sonar used in conjunction with the Mk 116 underwater weapons fire-control system, one T Mk 6 Fanfare torpedo decoy system, Naval Tactical Data System, OE-82 satellite communications antenna, SSR-1 satellite

communications receiver, WSC-3 satellite communications transceiver, URN-20 TACAN, one SLQ-32(V)3 ESM suite, and four Mk 36 Super Chaffroc rapid-blooming overhead chaff launchers

Propulsion: two pressurized-water cooled General Electric D2G nuclear reactors supplying steam to two sets of geared turbines delivering 100,000shp (74,570kW) to two shafts

Performance: maximum speed 40kts

Complement: 27+445

Class

1. USA (4)				Com-
Name	No.	Builders	Laid down	missioned
VIRGINIA	CGN 38	Newport News S.B.	Aug 1972	Sep 1976
TEXAS	CGN 39	Newport News S.B.	Aug 1973	Sep 1977
MISSISSIPPI	CGN 40	Newport News S.B.	Feb 1975	Aug 1978
ARKANSAS	CGN 41	Newport News S.B.	Jan 1977	Oct 1980

Remarks: The 'Virginia' class guided-missile cruiser is a distinct improvement in comparison with the preceding 'California' class thanks to the provision of considerably higher speed (greater power on a better hull) combined with an enhanced weapon system. This latter centres on the use of Mk 26 twin launchers for Standard SAMs and ASROC anti-submarine missiles in place of two Mk 13 single launchers and a separate ASROC launcher. Also improved are the anti-submarine fire-control system and the highly advanced electronic warfare suite.

'Vittorio Veneto' class helicopter-cruiser

Italy

Displacement: 7,500 tons standard and 8,850 tons full load

Dimensions: length 179·6m (589ft); beam 19·4m (63·6ft); draught 6·0m (19·7ft)

Gun armament: eight 76-mm (3-in) L/62 DP in single mountings, and six 40-mm L/70 AA Breda Compact in three twin mountings

Missile armament: one Mk 10 twin launcher for about 40 RIM-67A Standard-ER surface-to-air missiles, and four Teseo container-launchers for four Otomat surface-to-surface missiles

Torpedo armament: none

Anti-submarine armament: two triple Mk 32 tube mountings for 12·75-in (324-mm) A/S torpedoes, and helicopter-launched weapons (see below)

Aircraft: up to nine Agusta (Bell) AB.212ASW helicopters on a flight deck aft

Electronics: one Hughes SPS-52C 3D radar, one Lockheed SPS-40 air-search radar, one Selenia MM/SM-702 surface-search radar, two Sperry/RCA SPG-55C SAM-control radars used in conjunction with the Aster fire-control system, four Selenia RTN 10X 76-mm (3-in) gun-control radars used in conjunction with four ELSAG Argo NA9 fire-control systems, two Selenia RTN 16X AA gun-control radars used in conjunction with two Dardo fire-control systems, one SMA 3RM 7 navigation radar, two SCLAR chaff launchers, URN-20 TACAN, one Abbey Hill ESM suite, and one Sangamo SQS-23 hull-mounted long-range sonar

Propulsion: four Ansaldo/Foster-Wheeler boilers supplying steam to two sets of Tosi geared turbines delivering 54,450kW (73,000shp) to two shafts

Performance: maximum speed 32kts; range 9,250km (5,750 miles) at 17kts

Complement: 50+500

Class

1. Italy (1)

Name	No.	Builders	Laid down	Commissioned
VITTORIO VENETO	C 550	Italcantieri	June 1965	July 1969

Vittorio Veneto (C 550) combines potent armament with good helicopter strength.

'Akizuki' class destroyer

Japan

Displacement: 2,300 tons standard and 2,890 tons full load

Dimensions: length 118·0m (387·1ft); beam 12·0m (39·4ft); draught 4·0m (13·1ft)

Gun armament: three 5-in (127-mm) L/54 in Mk 39 single mountings and four 3-in (76-mm) L/50 in two Mk 33 twin mountings

Missile armament: none

Torpedo armament: two quadruple 21-in (533-mm) Type 65 tube mountings

Anti-submarine armament: two triple Type 68 tube mountings and one Bofors Type 71 375-mm (14·76-in) four-barrel rocket-launcher

Electronics: one OPS-1 air-search radar, one OPS-15 surface-search radar, one Mk 34 fire-control radar used in conjunction with Mk 57 and Mk 63 gun fire-control systems, one Sangamo SQS-29 hull-mounted sonar and one OQA-1 variable-depth sonar

Propulsion: two Mitsubishi CE boilers supplying steam to two geared turbines (Escher-Weiss/Mitsubishi in *Akizuki* and Westinghouse in *Teruzuki*) delivering 33,555kW (45,000shp) to two shafts

Performance: maximum speed 32kts

Complement: 330

Class

1. Japan (2)

Name	No.	Builders	Laid down	Commissioned
AKIZUKI	DD 161	Mitsubishi	July 1958	Feb 1960
TERUZUKI	DD 162	Shin Mitsubishi	Aug 1958	Feb 1960

'Allen M. Sumner' class destroyer

USA/Argentina

Displacement: 2,200 tons standard and 3,320 tons full load

Dimensions: length 376·5ft (114·8m); beam 40·9ft (12·5m); draught 19ft (5·8m)

Gun armament: six 5-in (127-mm) L/38 in three twin Mk 38 mountings and four 3-in (76-mm) L/50 in two twin Mk 33 mountings

Missile armament: four MM.38 Exocet surface-to-surface missiles in single launchers

Torpedo armament: none

Anti-submarine armament: two triple ILAS 3 tube mountings for 12·75-in (324-mm) Whitehead A 244S A/S torpedoes, and two forward-firing Hedgehog mortars

Electronics: one Bendix SPS-6 air-search radar, one Raytheon/Sylvania SPS-10 surface-search radar, one Mk 56 gun fire-control radar operating in conjunction with Mk 35 radar, and one Sangamo SQS-30 hull-mounted active sonar operating in conjunction with Mk 105 A/S fire-control system

Propulsion: four Babcock & Wilcox boilers supplying steam to two geared turbines delivering 60,000shp (44,740kW) to two shafts

Performance: maximum speed 34kts; range 5,300 miles (8,530km) at 15kts or 1,140 miles (1,835km) at 31kts

Complement: 331

Class

1. Argentina (1)

Name	No.	Builders	Laid down	Commissioned
SEGUI	D 25	Federal S.B.	1944	Aug 1944

2. Brazil (1)

Name	No.	Builders	Laid down	Commissioned
MATO GROSSO	D 34	Federal S.B.	1944	Nov 1944

3. Taiwan (6)

Name	No.	Builders	Laid down	Commissioned
PO YANG	928	Bath Iron Works	1943	June 1944
YUEN YANG	944	Federal S.B. & D.D. Co	1943	June 1944
HUEI YANG	972	Federal S.B. & D.D. Co	1943	May 1944
HENG YANG	976	Bethlehem Steel Co	1943	June 1944
HSIANG YANG	986	Bethlehem Steel Co	1943	Apr 1944
HUA YANG	988	Bethlehem Steel Co	1944	Mar 1945

Remarks: The *Mato Grosso* (D 34) differs from the *Segui* (D 25) in having Sea Cat SAMs rather than Exocet anti-ship missiles, and Mk 32 anti-submarine torpedo tubes. The Taiwanese ships are basically similar to the Argentine vessel, but three carry Hsiung Feng (Gabriel) anti-ship missiles (one triple launcher in 988 and two twin launchers in 944 and 986). The radar fit also differs in detail, the Hsiung Feng-fitted ships having Selenia Orion RTN 10X missile-guidance systems. None of these ships would be able to tackle a modern warship, but local conditions render them all relatively useful. The Taiwanese, in particular, face only a very modest threat from China despite the total acrimony of their relationship.

The Mato Grosso (D 34) was bought from the USA in 1972, her four 'Allen M. Sumner (FRAM II)' class half-sisters following in 1973. The ship retains much of the appearance of the World War II destroyer she once was, with the exception mainly of the launcher for Sea Cat short-range surface-to-air missiles on the after deckhouse.

'Allen M. Sumner (FRAM II)' class destroyer
USA/Argentina

Displacement: 2,200 tons standard and 3,320 tons full load
Dimensions: length 376·5 ft (114·8 m); beam 40·9 ft (12·5 m); draught 19 ft (5·8 m)
Gun armament: six 5-in (127-mm) L/38 in three twin Mk 38 mountings
Missile armament: four MM.38 Exocet surface-to-surface missiles in single launchers
Torpedo armament: none
Anti-submarine armament: two triple ILAS 3 tube mountings for 12·75-in (324-mm) Whitehead A 244S A/S torpedoes, two forward-firing Hedgehog mortars and provision for a small A/S helicopter on a platform aft
Electronics: one Lockheed SPS-40 air-search radar, one Raytheon/Sylvania SPS-10 surface-search radar, one Mk 37 gun fire-control system operating in conjunction with Mk 25 radar, Sangamo SQS-30 hull-mounted active sonar, one Litton SQA-10 variable-depth sonar and one Mk 105 anti-submarine fire-control system
Propulsion: four Babcock & Wilcox boilers supplying steam to two geared turbines delivering 60,000 shp (44,740 kW) to two shafts
Performance: maximum speed 34 kts; range 5,300 miles (8,530 km) at 15 kts or 1,140 miles (1,835 km) at 31 kts
Complement: 291

Class
1. Argentina (2)

Name	No.	Builders	Laid down	Com-missioned
HIPOLITO BOUCHARD	D 26	Federal S.B.	1944	Sep 1944
PIEDRA BUENA	D 29	Bath Iron Works	1943	May 1944

2. Brazil (4)

Name	No.	Builders	Laid down	Com-missioned
SERGIPE	D 35	Bethlehem Steel	1944	Feb 1945
ALAGOAS	D 36	Bethlehem Steel	1944	June 1946
RIO GRANDE DO NORTE	D 37	Bethlehem Steel	1943	Mar 1945
ESPIRITO SANTO	D 38	Bethlehem Steel	1943	July 1944

3. Chile (2)

Name	No.	Builders	Laid down	Com-missioned
MINISTRO ZENTENO	16	Todd Pacific Shipyards	1944	Dec 1944
MINISTRO PORTALES	17	Federal S.B.	1943	May 1944

4. Colombia (1)

Name	No.	Builders	Laid down	Com-missioned
SANTANDER	D 03	Federal S.B.	1943	June 1944

5. Greece (1)

Name	No.	Builders	Laid down	Com-missioned
MIAOULIS	D 211	Federal S.B.	1943	Mar 1944

6. Iran (2)

Name	No.	Builders	Laid down	Com-missioned
BABR	61	Todd Pacific Shipyards	1943	Oct 1944
PALANG	62	Todd Pacific Shipyards	1944	Jan 1945

7. South Korea (2)

Name	No.	Builders	Laid down	Com-missioned
DAE GU	DD 917	Bath Iron Works	1944	Sep 1944
INCHON	DD 918	Federal S.B.	1943	Mar 1944

8. Turkey (1)

Name	No.	Builders	Laid down	Com-missioned
ZAFER	D 356	Federal S.B.	1944	Mar 1945

Remarks: The FRAM II modification programme was designed principally to enhance the anti-submarine capability of older US destroyers by the upgrading of sensors (provision of variable-depth sonar) and weapons (small helicopter and improved torpedoes). The Brazilian vessels have no Exocets, a different sonar fit and a combination of Westland Wasp helicopter and Mk 32 tubes; the Chilean and Colombian vessels are similar apart from having a different helicopter. Greece's one ship has an Alouette III helicopter and no anti-ship missiles. Iran's two ships are in reserve for lack of spares, but are fitted with provision for eight Standard SAMs on four launchers. The two South Korean ships each have a hangar and small helicopter, plus a Vulcan CIWS mounting. The Turkish ship is similar to the Greek ship, but has a 76-mm (3-in) OTO-Melara Compact DP for anti-aircraft and anti-FAC defence. All these ships are now elderly and obsolescent, and can at best be regarded only as second-line vessels even in less sophisticated theatres.

'Almirante' class guided-missile destroyer
Chile

Displacement: 2,730 tons standard and 3,300 tons full load
Dimensions: length 122·5 m (402 ft); beam 13·1 m (43 ft); draught 4·0 m (13·3 ft)
Gun armament: four 4-in (102-mm) L/60 in four single Mk(N)R mountings, and four 40-mm Bofors L/70 AA in single mountings
Missile armament: four container-launchers for MM.38 Exocet surface-to-surface missiles, and two quadruple surface-to-air missile launchers with 16 Sea Cat missiles
Torpedo armament: none
Anti-submarine armament: two triple Mk 32 tube mountings for 12·75-in (324-mm) Mk 44 A/S torpedoes, and two three-barrel Squid depth-charge mortars
Electronics: one Plessey AWS 1 air-search and target-indication radar
Propulsion: two Babcock & Wilcox boilers supplying steam to Parsons-Pametrada geared turbines delivering 54,000 shp (40,270 kW) to two shafts
Performance: maximum speed 34·5 kts; range 11,100 km (6,900 miles) at 16 kts
Complement: 17 + 249

Class
1. Chile (2)

Name	No.	Builders	Com-missioned
ALMIRANTE RIVEROS	18	Vickers-Armstrong Ltd	Dec 1960
ALMIRANTE WILLIAMS	19	Vickers-Armstrong Ltd	Mar 1960

'Amatsukaze' class guided-missile destroyer
Japan

Displacement: 3,050 tons standard and 4,000 tons full load
Dimensions: length 131·0 m (429·8 ft); beam 13·4 m (44 ft); draught 4·2 m (13·8 ft)
Gun armament: four 3-in (76-mm) L/50 in two Mk 33 twin mountings
Missile armament: one Mk 13 single launcher with 40 RIM-6B standard surface-to-air missiles
Torpedo armament: none
Anti-submarine armament: one Mk 16 octuple launcher for RUR-5A ASROC missiles, two triple Type 68 tube mountings for 12·75-in (324-mm) Mk 46 A/S torpedoes, and two Hedgehog Mk 15 mortars
Electronics: one Hughes SPS-39 3D air-search radar, one Westinghouse SPS-29 air-search radar, one OPS-16 surface-search radar, two Raytheon SPG-51C missile-control radars, one Mk 63 gun fire-control system and one Sangamo/General Electric SQS-23 long-range hull-mounted search sonar
Propulsion: two Ishikawajima/Foster-Wheeler boilers supplying steam to two Ishikawajima/General Electric geared turbines delivering 44,740 kW (60,000 shp) to two shafts
Performance: maximum speed 33 kts; range 12,975 km (8,065 miles) at 18 kts
Complement: 290

Class
1. Japan (1)

Name	No.	Builders	Laid down	Com-missioned
AMATSUKAZE	DD 163	Mitsubishi	Nov 1962	Feb 1965

'Anshan' class guided-missile destroyer
China

Displacement: 1,855 tons standard and 2,830 tons full load
Dimensions: length 112·8 m (370 ft); beam 10·2 m (33·5 ft); draught 4·0 m (13 ft)
Gun armament: four 130-mm (5·1-in) L/50 in single mountings, and eight 37-mm AA in four twin mountings
Missile armament: four Hai Ying Chinese-built derivatives of the SS-N-2 'Styx' surface-to-surface missile in two twin containers-launchers
Torpedo armament: none
Anti-submarine armament: two depth-charge racks
Electronics: one 'Knife Rest-A' air-search radar, one 'Square Tie' surface-search and fire-control radar, one *Neptun* navigation radar and one 'Ski Pole' IFF
Propulsion: three boilers supplying steam to two Tosi geared turbines delivering 35,800 kW (48,000 shp) to two shafts
Performance: maximum speed 32 kts; range 4,800 km (2,980 miles) at 19 kts
Complement: 200

Class
1. China (4)

Name	No.	Builders	Laid down	Com-missioned
ANSHAN	101	Nikolayev-Dalzavod	1935	1940
ZHANGZHUN	102	Nikolayev-Dalzavod	1936	1941
JILIN	103	Nikolayev-Komsomolsk	1936	1941
FUZHUN	104	Nikolayev-Komsomolsk	1935	1941

Remarks: Now nearing the end of their useful lives, the four 'Anshan' class destroyers are local modifications of ex-Soviet 'Gordy' class ships.

'Arleigh Burke' class guided-missile destroyer
USA
Displacement: 8,200 tons light and 8,500 tons full load
Dimensions: length 466ft (142·1m); beam 60ft (18·3m); draught 25ft (7·6m)
Gun armament: one 5-in (127-mm) L/54 DP in a Mk 45 mounting, and two 20-mm Mk 15 Phalanx CIWS mountings
Missile armament: two quadruple container-launchers for eight RGM-84A Harpoon anti-ship missiles, and two 45-cell Vertical-Launch Systems for 90 RUR-5A ASROC anti-submarine, RIM-66D Standard surface-to-air and BGM-109 Tomahawk anti-ship missiles
Torpedo armament: none
Anti-submarine armament: ASROC missiles in the VLS (above), two triple Mk 32 tube mountings for 14 12·75-in (324-mm) Mk 50 Barracuda A/S torpedoes, and helicopter-launched weapons (see below)
Aircraft: provision for one Sikorsky SH-60B Seahawk helicopter on a platform aft
Electronics: one RCA SPY-1D AEGIS air-search radar system, one Norden SPS-67 surface-search radar, three Westinghouse SPG-62 Standard-control radars used in conjunction with the Mk 99 missile fire-control system, one Seafire gun fire-control system, one Raytheon SLQ-32(V)2 ESM suite, two Mk 36 Super Chaffroc rapid-blooming overhead chaff launchers, one SQS-53C bow-mounted sonar, one SQR-19 towed-array sonar, Automatic Data Action System, TACAN, and one satellite-navigation system
Propulsion: four General Electric LM 2500 gas turbines delivering 100,000shp (74,570kW) to two shafts
Performance: maximum speed 32kts; range 5,750 miles (9,250km) at 20kts
Complement: 21+286

Class
1.USA (0+60)

Name	No.	Builders	Laid down	Commissioned
ARLEIGH BURKE	DDG51	—	—	1989
—	DDGs 52-54 Proposed FY 1985 programme			
—	DDGs 55-59 Proposed FY 1987 programme			
—	DDGs 60-111 Projected for future programmes			

Remarks: The 'Arleigh Burke' class of guided-missile destroyer is planned for service in the 1990s and onwards as a replacement for the 'Coontz' class guided-missile destroyers, 'Leahy' class guided-missile cruisers and 'Belknap' class guided-missile cruisers. The design is more akin to a cruiser in size and basic capability, and will be built entirely of steel with the exception of the funnels, which will be of aluminium. Some 130 tons of armour protection will protect vital spaces, and the ship will feature a 'collective protection system for defense against the fallout associated with NBC warfare', the first purpose-designed US warship to have such provision. The sensor and armament fit is particularly impressive, the SPY-1D radar being used in an AEGIS system with UYK-43B computers and advanced fire-control systems for the vertical-launch missiles. The use of the Seafire gun-control system, using a laser rangefinder, will make possible first-round hit capability with 5-in (127-mm) semi-active laser-guided shells. The anti-submarine fit of sensors and weapons is also particularly potent, especially with the new Mk 50 Barracuda torpedo.

'Audace' class guided-missile destroyer
Italy
Displacement: 3,950 tons standard and 4,560 tons full load
Dimensions: length 136·6m (448ft); beam 14·2m (46·6ft); draught 4·6m (15·1ft)
Gun armament: two 127-mm (5-in) OTO-Melara Compact L/54 DP in single mountings, and four 76-mm (3-in) OTO-Melara Compact L/62 DP in single mountings
Missile armament: one Mk 13 single launcher with 40 RIM-24 Tartar and RIM-66 Standard surface-to-air missiles
Torpedo armament: none
Anti-submarine armament: two triple ILRS 3 tube mountings for 12 12·75-in (324-mm) Mk 46 A/S torpedoes, two twin 533-mm (21-in) tube mountings for 12 A 184 A/S torpedoes, and helicopter-launched torpedoes (see below)
Aircraft: two Agusta-Bell AB.212ASW helicopters
Electronics: one Hughes SPS-52 3D air-search radar, two Raytheon SPG-51 radars for target tracking and missile guidance, one Selenia RAN 20S air-search radar, one SMA SPQ 2 surface-search radar, three Orion RTN 10X radars used in conjunction with the ELSAG Argo NA10 gun fire-control systems, two SCLAR launcher systems for overhead flares/chaff, and one CWE 610 sonar
Propulsion: four Foster-Wheeler boilers supplying steam to two double-reduction geared turbines (CNR in *Audace* and Ansaldo in *Ardito*) delivering 54,440kW (73,000shp) to two shafts
Performance: maximum speed 34kts; range 5,560km (3,455 miles) at 20kts
Complement: 30+350

Class
1. Italy (2+2 'Audace (improved)' class ships)

Name	No.	Builders	Laid down	Commissioned
ARDITO	D 550	Italcantieri	July 1968	Dec 1973
AUDACE	D 551	Cantieri Navali Riuniti	Apr 1968	Nov 1972

The Ardito (D 550) of the 'Audace' class carries a Mk 13 single SAM launcher on the forward extension of the twin-helicopter hangar, with twin SAM-control and single 3D radars forward of the launcher. Good gun armament is also carried.

Remarks: Essentially a much improved version of the 'Impavido' class, the 'Audace' class provided good anti-air and anti-submarine capabilities. The two 'Audace (Improved)' class ships planned will have upgraded helicopters and anti-ship missiles.

'Ayanami' class destroyer
Japan
Displacement: 1,700 tons standard and 2,500 tons full load
Dimensions: length 109·0m (357·6ft); beam 10·7m (35·1ft); draught 3·7m (12ft)
Gun armament: six 3-in (76-mm) L/50 DP in three Mk 33 twin mountings
Missile armament: none
Torpedo armament: none
Anti-submarine armament: two triple Type 68 tube mountings (DD 112) for 12·75-in (324-mm) Mk 46 A/S torpedoes, or two Mk 4 tubes (DDs 110 and 111) for Mk 32 A/S torpedoes, and two Hedgehog Mk 15 mortars
Electronics: one OPS-1 or OPS-2 air-search radar, one OPS-15 or OPS-16 surface-search radar, one Mk 34 fire-control radar for use in conjunction with Mk 57 and Mk 63 gun fire-control systems, one OQS-12 hull-mounted sonar and (DD 110) OQA-1 variable-depth sonar
Propulsion: two boilers supplying steam to two Mitsubishi/Escher-Weiss geared turbines delivering 26,100kW (35,000shp) to two shafts
Performance: maximum speed 32kts; range 11,100km (6,900 miles) at 18kts
Complement: 230

Class
1. Japan (7)

Name	No.	Builders	Laid down	Commissioned
AYANAMI	ASU 7004	Mitsubishi	Nov 1956	Feb 1958
ISONAMI	ASU 7005	Shin Mitsubishi	Dec 1956	Mar 1958
URANAMI	ASU 7006	Kawasaki	Feb 1957	Feb 1958
SHIKINAMI	ASU 7007	Mitsui	Dec 1956	Mar 1958
TAKANAMI	DD 110	Mitsui	Nov 1958	Jan 1960
OONAMI	DD 111	Ishikawajima	Mar 1959	Aug 1960
MAKINAMI	DD 112	Iino	Mar 1959	Oct 1960

Remarks: The oldest destroyer class still in service with the Japanese Maritime Self-Defense Force, the 'Ayanami' class now has little realistic anti-submarine value for lack of modern weapons and sensors, the two triple Type 68 tube mountings in the *Makinami* (DD 112) being useful only for self-defence, and the two Mk 4 tubes in the *Takinami* (DD 110) and *Oonami* (DD 111) using the obsolete Mk 32 torpedo. The obsolescence of the class has prompted the conversion of the first four ships (DDs 103 to 106) into training ships.

'Battle' class guided-missile destroyer
UK/Iran

Displacement: 2,325 tons standard and 3,360 tons full load

Dimensions: length 379ft (115·5m); beam 40·3ft (12·3m); draught 17·5ft (5·3m)

Gun armament: four 4·5-in (114-mm) L/45 in two Mk 4 twin mountings, and two 40-mm Bofors L/60 AA in single mountings

Missile armament: one quadruple launcher for eight Standard surface-to-air missiles, and one quadruple launcher for 16 Sea Cat surface-to-air missiles

Torpedo armament: none

Anti-submarine armament: one Squid three-barrel depth-charge mortar

Electronics: one Plessey AWS 1 air-search radar, one Plessey AWS 3 surface-search radar, one Contraves Sea Hunter gun fire-control radar, and one Decca RDL 1 electronic support measures system

Propulsion: two Admiralty boilers supplying steam to Parsons geared turbines delivering 50,000 shp (37,285 kW) to two shafts

Performance: maximum speed 31 kts; range 3,450 miles (5,550 km) at 20 kts

Complement: 270

Class

1. Iran (1)

Name	No.	Builders	Laid down	Commissioned
ARTEMIZ	51	Cammell Laird & Co Ltd	Nov 1943	Sep 1946

2. Pakistan (1)

Name	No.	Builders	Laid down	Commissioned
BADR	D 161	Swan, Hunter	Feb 1944	Dec 1946

Remarks: Though now probably unserviceable for lack of spares, the ex-British 'Battle' class destroyer *Artemiz* (51) is an interesting example of how elderly designs can be upgraded if sufficient funds are allocated, a modest but useful gun and anti-submarine armament being retained despite the addition of area-defence and point-defence surface-to-air missile systems. The ship was bought by Iran in 1967. Pakistan's *Badr* (D 161) was bought in 1956, and was modernized to a less ambitious standard as a standard gun destroyer with fairly substantial point-defence AA armament from seven 40-mm Bofors guns, four 21-in (533-mm) torpedo tubes, the same main armament and anti-submarine fits as the *Artemiz*

'Broadsword' class (Type 22) guided-missile destroyer
UK

Displacement: (F 88-91) 3,500 tons standard and 4,000 tons full load

Dimensions: (F 88-91) length 430ft (131·2m); beam 48·5ft (14·8m); draught 19·9ft (6·0m)

Dimensions: (F 92-95) length 471ft (143·6m) beam 48·5ft (14·8m); draught 19·9ft (6·0m)

Gun armament: two 40-mm Bofors L/60 AA in single mountings

Missile armament: four container-launchers for single MM.38 Exocet surface-to-surface missiles, and two sextuple launchers for Sea Wolf surface-to-air missiles

Torpedo armament: none

Anti-submarine armament: helicopter-launched torpedoes (see below), and (F 90 onwards) two triple STWS tube mountings for 12·75-in (324-mm) Mk 46 or Stingray A/S torpedoes

Aircraft: two Westland Lynx HAS.Mk 2 helicopters

Electronics: one Marconi Type 967 air-search radar, one Kelvin Hughes Type 968 air-search radar, one Kelvin Hughes Type 1006 navigation radar, two Type 910 missile-control radars as part of the GWS25 Sea Wolf fire-control system, one GWS50 Exocet fire-control system, one Type 2008 sonar, one Type 2016 sonar, SCOT satellite communication system, Computer-Assisted Action Information System and two Knebworth Corvus eight-barrel chaff launchers

Propulsion: COGOG (COmbined Gas turbine Or Gas turbine) arrangement, with two Rolls-Royce Olympus TM3B gas turbines delivering 56,000 bhp (41,760 kW) or two Rolls-Royce Tyne RM1A gas turbines delivering 8,500 bhp (6,340 kW) to two shafts

Performance: maximum speed 30 kts (on Olympus engines) or 18 kts (on Tyne engines); range 5,200 miles (8,370 km) at 18 kts on Tyne engines

Complement: 18+205, with a maximum of 290 possible

Class

1. UK (6+2+5)

Name	No.	Builders	Laid down	Commissioned
BROADSWORD	F 88	Yarrow (Shipbuilders) Ltd	Feb 1975	May 1979
BATTLEAXE	F 89	Yarrow (Shipbuilders) Ltd	Feb 1976	Mar 1980
BRILLIANT	F 90	Yarrow (Shipbuilders) Ltd	Mar 1977	May 1981
BRAZEN	F 91	Yarrow (Shipbuilders) Ltd	Aug 1978	July 1982
BOXER	F 92	Yarrow (Shipbuilders) Ltd	Nov 1979	1983
BEAVER	F 93	Yarrow (Shipbuilders) Ltd	June 1980	Aug 1984
BRAVE	F 94	Yarrow (Shipbuilders) Ltd	May 1982	1985
BLOODHOUND	F 95	Yarrow (Shipbuilders) Ltd	—	—

Remarks: Designed as successor to the widely admired 'Leander' class, the 'Type 22' or 'Broadsword' class guided-missile frigate has multi-role capability though optimized in present ships for anti-submarine operations. The first four units are 'Broadsword Batch 1' frigates, the following six ships being of the 'Broadsword Batch 2' type lengthened in the fore part of the ship and fitted with a more raked bow for better seakeeping qualities. The armament of Batch 1 and Batch 2 ships is similar, though from F 90 onwards the ships are each fitted with two triple STWS tube mountings for Mk 46 or Stingray anti-submarine torpedoes. The five 'Broadsword Batch 3' class ships to be built later in the decade are to somewhat different: though retaining the dimensions of the Batch 2 ships, they will have a COGAG propulsion arrangement with two Rolls-Royce Spey SM1A and two Rolls-Royce Tyne RM1A gas turbines, a gun armament of one 4·5-in (114-mm) Mk 8 and two twin 30-mm AA mountings, eight anti-ship missiles of an undetermined type, and the two sextuple launchers for Sea Wolf SAM already carried in the Batch 1 and Batch 2 ships. Displacement of the Batch 3 anti-ship frigates will be in the order of 4,200 tons standard and 4,700 tons full load.

The Boxer (F 92) is the lead ship of the 'Broadsword Batch 2' class, and her hull shows clear indications of the longitudinal stretch.

'C 65' class guided-missile destroyer
France

Displacement: 3,500 tons standard and 3,900 tons full load

Dimensions: length 127·0m (416·7ft); beam 13·4m (44ft); draught 5·8m (18·9ft)

Gun armament: two 100-mm (3·9-in) L/55 DP in single mountings

Missile armament: four container-launchers for single MM.38 Exocet surface-to-surface missiles

Torpedo armament: none

Anti-submarine armament: one launcher for 13 Malafon missiles, one quadruple 305-mm (12-in) mortar, and two launchers for 533-mm (21-in) L 5 torpedoes

Electronics: one Thomson-CSF DRBV 13 surveillance radar, one Thomson-CSF DRBV 22A air-search radar, one Thomson-CSF DRBC 32B gun fire-control radar, one Thomson-CSF DRBN 32 navigation radar, one CIT/ALCATEL DUBV 23 hull-mounted active search and attack sonar, one CIT/ALCATEL DUBV 43 variable-depth sonar, one SENIT 3 combat information system, and two Syllex eight-barrel chaff launchers

Propulsion: two boilers supplying steam to one double-reduction Rateau geared turbine delivering 21,365 kW (28,650 shp) to one shaft

Performance: maximum speed 27 kts; range 9,250 km (5,750 miles) at 18 kts

Complement: 15+89+125

The Aconit (D 609) was the prototype for the three 'F 67' class destroyers.

Class

1. France (1)

Name	No.	Builders	Laid down	Commissioned
ACONIT	D 609	Lorient Naval Dockyard	Jan 1966	Mar 1973

'C 70' class guided-missile destroyer (AA)

France

Displacement: 4,000 tons standard and 4,340 tons full load
Dimensions: length 139·0 m (456 ft); beam 14·0 m (45·9 ft); draught 5·7 m (18·7 ft)
Gun armament: one 100-mm (3·9-in) L/55 DP, and two 20-mm AA
Missile armament: four twin container-launchers for single MM.40 Exocet surface-to-surface missiles, one Mk 13 launcher for 40 RIM-66 Standard-MR surface-to-air missiles, and two Sadral point-defence surface-to-air missile systems
Torpedo armament: none
Anti-submarine armament: two tubes for 10 533-mm (21-in) L 5 torpedoes
Aircraft: one Aérospatiale SA 365F Dauphin helicopter on a platform aft
Electronics: one Thomson-CSF DRBJ 11 3D air-search radar, one Thomson-CSF DRBV 26 air-surveillance radar, one Thomson-CSF DRBC 32D fire-control radar, two Raytheon SPG-51C missile fire-control radars, one Thomson-CSF Vega weapons-direction system, one CSEE Panda fire-control director, one DUBA 25 hull-mounted sonar, one EBTF towed sonar, two ARB series ESM suites, one SENIT 6 combat information system, and two CSEE Dagaie and two Sagaie chaff launchers
Propulsion: four SEMT-Pielstick 18 PA6 BTC diesels delivering 31,620 kW (42,400 hp) to two shafts
Performance: maximum speed 30 kts; range 15,200 km (9,445 miles) at 17 kts or 9,250 km (5,750 miles) at 24 kts

Complement: 200

Class
1. France (0+2+2)

Name	No.	Builders	Laid down	Commissioned
—	—	Brest Naval Dockyard	1982	1987
—	—	Brest Naval Dockyard	1982	1988

Remarks: Using the same hull as the 'C 70' class anti-submarine destroyer, the 'C 70' anti-aircraft destroyer differs from its half-sister class in primary armament, sensors and propulsion. Two types of missile are carried for the anti-aircraft role, the Standard fired from the Mk 13 single launcher being designed for area-defence with the aid of two SPG-51C control radars, and the two Sadral short-range systems (mounted one on each side of the hangar) being provided for point-defence. The advanced MM.40 version of the Exocet anti-ship missile will be made the more effective by mid-course guidance from the Aerospatiale SA 365F Dauphin embarked helicopter, giving the ships a powerful secondary capability in the anti-ship role. The need for a mainmast structure for the DRBJ 11B 3D radar combines with the different uptake arrangement of the wholly diesel propulsion to give the 'C 70' AA version a totally different midships appearance to the 'C 70' AA version a totally different midships appearance to the 'C 70' ASW version, which also has a larger helicopter platform and hangar for two ASW helicopters. The second pair of 'C 70' AA destroyer should commission in 1990.

'C 70' class guided-missile destroyer (A/S)

France

Displacement: 3,830 tons standard and 4,170 tons full load
Dimensions: length 139·0 m (455·9 ft); beam 14·0 m (45·9 ft); draught 5·7 m (18·7 ft)
Gun armament: one 100-mm (3·9-in) L/55 DP, and two 20-mm AA
Missile armament: four container-launchers for eight MM.38 (MM.40 from D 642 onwards) Exocet surface-to-surface missiles, and one octuple launcher for 26 Crotale surface-to-air missiles
Torpedo armament: none
Anti-submarine armament: two tubes for 10 533-mm (21-in) L 5 torpedoes, and helicopter-launched Mk 46 A/S torpedoes (see below)
Aircraft: two Westland Lynx Mk 2 helicopters
Electronics: one Thomson-CSF DRBV 51 surveillance radar, one Thomson-CSF DRBV 26 air-search radar, one Thomson-CSF DRBC 32D fire-control radar, one Raytheon SPG-51C missile-control radar, two Decca RM 1226 navigation radars, one CIT/ALCATEL DUBV 23 hull-mounted active attack sonar, one CIT/ALCATEL DUBV 43 variable-depth sonar, one CSEE Panda optical fire-control director, one Thomson-CSF Vega weapon-direction system, one ABRB 17 ESM suite, one SENIT 4 combat information system, and two CSEE Dagaie and two Sagaie chaff launchers
Propulsion: CODOG (COmbined Diesel Or Gas turbine) arrangement, with two Rolls-Royce Olympus TM3B gas turbines delivering 52,000 bhp (38,775 kW) or two SEMT-Pielstick 16 PA6 CV280 diesels delivering 7,755 kW (10,400 bhp) to two shafts
Performance: maximum speed 30 kts on gas turbines or 21 kts on diesels; range 17,600 km (10,935 miles) at 18 kts on diesels
Complement: 15+90+111

Class
1. France (4+2+2)

Name	No.	Builders	Laid down	Commissioned
GEORGES LEYGUES	D 640	Brest Naval Dockyard	June 1974	Dec 1979
DUPLEIX	D 641	Brest Naval Dockyard	Oct 1975	June 1981
MONTCALM	D 642	Brest Naval Dockyard	Dec 1975	July 1982
JEAN DE VIENNE	D 643	Brest Naval Dockyard	Dec 1979	Dec 1983
—	D 644	Brest Naval Dockyard	Nov 1981	1985
—	D 645	Brest Naval Dockyard	Feb 1982	1986

Remarks: Planned as a class of eight, the 'C 70' ASW version will be divided into two four-ship sub-classes, the first four being 'C70/1' class ships as described above. The second quartet will be of the 'C70/2' type, with Flute ETBF towed-array sonar in place of the DUBV 43 variable-depth sonar of the 'C70/1' type, an improved version of the Crotale Naval SAM system to provide more range and anti-missile capability, the 100-mm (3·9-in) Creusot-Loire Compact DP gun, and Vampir infra-red surveillance equipment. Another modification will be the raising of the bridge structure, which has been found to be too low on current vessels. There is no doubt that these are highly capable ships, and though optimized for anti-submarine warfare still possess potent anti-aircraft and anti-ship capability. The seventh and eighth ships will commission by 1988.

The Georges Leygues (D 640) is seen during her sea trials.

'Carpenter (FRAM I)' class destroyer

USA

Displacement: 2,425 tons standard and 3,540 tons full load
Dimensions: length 390·5 ft (119·0 m); beam 41 ft (12·5 m); draught 20·9 ft (6·4 m)
Gun armament: two 5-in (127-mm) L/38 DP in one Mk 38 twin mounting
Missile armament: none
Torpedo armament: none
Anti-submarine armament: one octuple launcher for RUR-5A ASROC missiles, and two triple Mk 32 tube mountings for 12·75-in (324-mm) Mk 44 A/S torpedoes
Electronics: one Raytheon/Sylvania SPS-10 surface-search radar, one Lockheed SPS-40 air-search radar, one SPG-35 gun-control radar used in conjunction with the Mk 56 gun fire-control system, one Sangamo SQS-23 long-range hull-mounted active sonar used in conjunction with the Mk 144 A/S fire-control system, and one

Mk 1 target designation system
Propulsion: four Babcock & Wilcox boilers supplying steam to two General Electric geared turbines delivering 60,000 shp (44,740 kW) to two shafts
Performance: maximum speed 33 kts
Complement: 15+260

Class
1. Turkey (2)

Name	No.	Builders	Laid down	Commissioned
ALCITEPE	D 346	Bath Iron Works	Oct 1945	Nov 1949
ANITTEPE	DD 348	Consolidated Steel	July 1945	Dec 1949

'Charles F. Adams' class guided-missile destroyer
USA

Seen in this overhead view of the Charles F. Adams (DDG 2) are two 5-in (127-m) DP guns, the ASROC launcher (painted '2') and the Mk 11 twin Tartar launcher.

Displacement: 3,370 tons standard and 4,500 tons full load
Dimensions: length 437 ft (133·2 m); beam 47 ft (14·3 m); draught 20 ft (6·1 m)
Gun armament: two 5-in (127-mm) L/54 DP in two Mk 42 single mountings
Missile armament: two quadruple launchers for eight RGM-84A Harpoon surface-to-surface missiles, and (DDGs 2-14) one Mk 11 twin launcher for 42 RIM-24 Tartar surface-to-air missiles or (DDGs 15-24) one Mk 13 single launcher for 40 RIM-24 Tartar (being replaced by 40 RIM-66 Standard MR) surface-to-air missiles
Torpedo armament: none
Anti-submarine armament: one octuple launcher for RUR-5A ASROC missiles, and two triple Mk 32 tube mountings for 12·75-in (324-mm) Mk 46 A/S torpedoes
Electronics: one Hughes SPS-39A 3D air-search radar (being replaced by Hughes SPS-52 3D air-search radar), one Raytheon/Sylvania SPS-10 surface-search radar, one Lockheed SPS-40B (DDGs 2-14) or Westinghouse SPS-37 (DDGs 15-24) air-search radar, two Raytheon SPG-51C missile-control radars used in conjunction with the two Mk 74 missile fire-control systems, one Western Electric SPG-53A gun-control radar used in conjunction with the Mk 68 gun fire-control system, one Mk 4 weapon-direction system (being replaced by Mk 13 weapon-direction system), one Sangamo SQS-23 long-range active sonar (bow-mounted in DDGs 20-24 and hull-mounted in the others) used in conjunction with the Mk 111 (DDGs 2-15) or Mk 114 (DDGs 16-24) A/S fire-control system, one Mk 6 Fanfare torpedo decoy system, one OE-82 satellite communications antenna, SRR-1 satellite communications receiver, WSC-3 satellite communications transceiver, URN-20 TACAN, one WLR-6 and one ULQ-6B ECM systems, and two Mk 36 Super Chaffroc rapid-blooming overhead chaff launchers. A modernization programme for DDGs 17, 19, 20 and 22-24 is currently upgrading the electronic warfare suite with the ASMD (Anti-Ship Missile Defense) equipment which includes SLQ-31 and SLQ-32 electronic support measures items; replacing the SPS-40 with Lockheed SPS-40C or SPS-40D air-search radar as part of the SYS-1 Integrated Automatic Detection and Tracking System; substituting UYA-4 consoles for the original radar receivers in the Combat Information Center for real-time data-processing; installing the Mk 86 missile fire-control system, with Lockheed SPG-60 and Lockheed SPQ-9 radars, for joint operation of the gun and Standard missile armament; and fitting of two domes for Sperry SQQ-23 sonar
Propulsion: four boilers (Babcock & Wilcox in DDGs 2, 3, 7, 8, 10-13 and 20-22,
Combustion Engineering in DDGs 15-19, and Foster-Wheeler in DDGs 4-6, 9, 14 and 23-24) supplying steam to two geared turbines (General Electric in DDGs 2, 3, 7, 8, 10-13 and 15-22, and Westinghouse in DDGs 4-6, 9, 14 and 23-24) delivering 70,000 shp (52,200 kW) to two shafts
Performance: maximum speed 30 kts; range 6,900 miles (11,105 km) at 14 kts or 1,840 miles (2,960 km) at 30 kts
Complement: 24+330

Class
1. USA (23)

Name	No.	Builders	Laid down	Com-missioned
CHARLES F. ADAMS	DDG 2	Bath Iron Works	June 1958	Sep 1960
JOHN KING	DDG 3	Bath Iron Works	Aug 1958	Feb 1961
LAWRENCE	DDG 4	New York Shipbuilding	Oct 1958	Jan 1962
CLAUDE V. RICKETTS	DDG 5	New York Shipbuilding	May 1959	May 1962
BARNEY	DDG 6	New York Shipbuilding	May 1959	Aug 1962
HENRY B. WILSON	DDG 7	Defoe Shipbuilding Co	Feb 1958	Dec 1960
LYNDE McCORMICK	DDG 8	Defoe Shipbuilding Co	Apr 1958	June 1961
TOWERS	DDG 9	Todd Pacific Shipyards	Apr 1958	June 1961
SAMPSON	DDG 10	Bath Iron Works	Mar 1959	June 1961
SELLERS	DDG 11	Bath Iron Works	Aug 1959	Oct 1961
ROBISON	DDG 12	Defoe Shipbuilding Co	Apr 1959	Dec 1961
HOEL	DDG 13	Defoe Shipbuilding Co	June 1959	June 1962
BUCHANAN	DDG 14	Todd Pacific Shipyards	Apr 1959	Feb 1962
BERKELEY	DDG 15	New York Shipbuilding	June 1960	Dec 1962
JOSEPH STRAUSS	DDG 16	New York Shipbuilding	Dec 1960	Apr 1963
CONYNGHAM	DDG 17	New York Shipbuilding	May 1961	July 1963
SEMMES	DDG 18	Avondale Marine Ways Inc	Aug 1960	Dec 1962
TATTNALL	DDG 19	Avondale Marine Ways Inc	Nov 1960	Apr 1963
GOLDSBOROUGH	DDG 20	Puget Sound Bridge D.D.	Jan 1961	Nov 1963
COCHRANE	DDG 21	Puget Sound Bridge D.D.	July 1961	Mar 1964
BENJAMIN STODDERT	DDG 22	Puget Sound Bridge D.D.	June 1962	Sep 1964
RICHARD E. BYRD	DDG 23	Todd Pacific Shipyards	Apr 1961	Mar 1964
WADDELL	DDG 24	Todd Pacific Shipyards	Feb 1962	Aug 1964

Remarks: Designed on the same basic hull as the 'Forrest Sherman' class, and originally intended as continuations of the 'Hull' class, the 'Charles F. Adams' class was recast in the late 1950s as the US Navy's first custom-built guided-missile destroyer class for the outer escort ring of fast carrier task groups. The first 13 ships were fitted with the Mk 11 twin launcher, later units having the Mk 13 single launcher, though all ships can fire up to six missiles per minute regardless of launcher. From Fiscal Year 1980 it was planned to modernize the whole class with Harpoon surface-to-surface and Standard surface-to-air missiles, with considerably improved electronics suites at the same time, but the whole programme has been thrown into disarray by Congressional funding squabbles and altering operational requirements: some ships have thus been modernized to a certain degree (electronics and Harpoon missiles), while it seems likely that only DDGs 19, 20 and 22 will receive the full 'DDG Upgrade' modernization. These are still most capable ships, and are notable for their high levels of air-conditioned habitability. Though designed largely for area air-defence, the ships are also capable anti-submarine platforms.

'Charles F. Adams (Modified)' class (Type 103A) guided-missile destroyer
USA

Displacement: 3,370 tons standard and 4,500 tons full load
Dimensions: length 437 ft (133·2 m); beam 47 ft (14·3 m); draught 20 ft (6·1 m)
Gun armament: two 5-in (127-mm) L/54 DP in two Mk 42 single mountings (see Missile armament below)
Missile armament: two quadruple launchers for RGM-84A Harpoon surface-to-surface missiles are being fitted in place of the after 5-in (127-mm) gun, and one Mk 13 single launcher for 40 RIM-24 Tartar surface-to-air missiles
Torpedo armament: none
Anti-submarine armament: one octuple launcher for eight RUR-5A ASROC missiles, and two triple Mk 32 tube mountings for 12·75-in (324-mm) Mk 44/46 A/S torpedoes
Electronics: one Hughes SPS-52 3D air-search and target-designation radar, one Lockheed SPS-40 air-search radar, one Raytheon/Sylvania SPS-10 surface-search radar, two Raytheon SPG-51 missile-control radars used in conjunction with the Mk 74 missile fire-control system (being replaced by the Mk 86 missile fire-control system with Lockheed SPG-60 and Lockheed SPQ-9 radars), one Mk 68 gun fire-control system, one Sangamo SQS-23 long-range hull-mounted active sonar, URN-22 TACAN and SATIR I automatic data system
Propulsion: four Combustion Engineering boilers supplying steam to two geared
turbines delivering 70,000 shp (52,200 kW) to two shafts
Performance: maximum speed 30 kts; range 5,200 miles (8,370 km) at 20 kts
Complement: 19+319

Class
1. West Germany (3)

Name	No.	Builders	Laid down	Com-missioned
LÜTJENS	D 185	Bath Iron Works Corporation	Mar 1966	Mar 1969
MÖLDERS	D 186	Bath Iron Works Corporation	Apr 1966	Sep 1969
ROMMEL	D 187	Bath Iron Works Corporation	Aug 1967	May 1970

Remarks: Though they have an appearance modified somewhat from that of the US Navy's 'Charles F. Adams' class ships, the West German navy's 'Charles F. Adams (Modified)' class is similar in capability to the 'DDG Upgrade' programme ships, and is being further improved at the moment with two quadruple container-launchers for RGM-84A Harpoon anti-ship missiles in place of the after 5-in (127-mm) gun, improved Mk 86 fire-control system for the gun and Tartar missiles with digital computers in place of the present analog type, and numerous other modifications suiting the type yet further to operations in a European combat environment.

'Coontz' class guided-missile destroyer
USA

Displacement: 4,150-4,580 tons standard and 5,710-5,910 tons full load

Dimensions: length 512·5ft (156·3m); beam 52·5ft (16·0m); draught 23·4ft (7·1m)

Gun armament: one 5-in (127-mm) L/54 DP in a Mk 42 single mounting

Missile armament: two quadruple container-launchers for eight RGM-84A Harpoon surface-to-surface missiles, and one Mk 10 twin launcher for 40 RIM-66D Standard SM-2 surface-to-air missiles

Torpedo armament: none

Anti-submarine armament: one octuple launcher for RUR-5A ASROC missiles, and two triple Mk 32 tube mountings for 12·75-in (324-mm) Mk 46 torpedoes

Aircraft: provision for a helicopter on a platform aft

Electronics: ITT/Gilfillan SPS-48 3D air-search radar, one Raytheon/Sylvania SPS-10 surface-search radar, one Westinghouse SPS-37 air-search radar, one Western Electric SPG-53 gun-control radar used in conjunction with the Mk 68 fire-control system, two Sperry/RCA SPG-55B missile-control radars used in conjunction with the two Mk 76 missile fire-control systems, one Mk 11 weapon-control system (being replaced by the Mk 14 weapon-control system), one Sangamo SQS-23 long-range hull-mounted sonar used in conjunction with the Mk 111 AS weapon-control system, T-Mk 6 Fanfare torpedo decoy system, Mk 36 Super Chaffroc rapid-blooming overhead chaff system, URN-20 TACAN, Naval Tactical Data System, OE-82 satellite communications antenna, SRR-1 satellite communications receiver, and WSC-3 satellite communications transceiver

Propulsion: four boilers (Babcock & Wilcox in DDGs 40-46, and Foster-Wheeler in others) supplying steam to two geared turbines (Allis-Chalmers in DDGs 40-45, and De Laval in others) delivering 85,000shp (63,385kW) to two shafts

Performance: maximum speed 33kts; range 5,750 miles (9,255km) at 20kts

Complement: 21+356, plus provision for a flag staff of 7+12

The Coontz (DDG 40) shows off the type's appearance during 1975, unique amongst US Navy DDG types in having separate funnels and masts.

Class

1. USA (10)				Com-
Name	No.	Builders	Laid down	missioned
FARRAGUT	DDG 37	Bethlehem Steel Co	June 1957	Dec 1960
LUCE	DDG 38	Bethlehem Steel Co	Oct 1957	May 1961
MACDONOUGH	DDG 39	Bethlehem Steel Co	Apr 1958	Nov 1960
COONTZ	DDG 40	Puget Sound NY	Mar 1957	July 1960
KING	DDG 41	Puget Sound NY	Mar 1957	Nov 1960
MAHAN	DDG 42	San Francisco NY	July 1957	Aug 1960
DAHLGREN	DDG 43	Philadelphia NY	Mar 1958	Apr 1961
WILLIAM V. PRATT	DDG 44	Philadelphia NY	Mar 1958	Nov 1961
DEWEY	DDG 45	Bath Iron Works	Aug 1957	Dec 1959
PREBLE	DDG 46	Bath Iron Works	Dec 1957	May 1960

Remarks: Though currently rated as guided-missile destroyers, and originally commissioned as guided-missile frigates, they have much of the capabilities of the US Navy's 'single-ended' guided-missile cruisers, with a primary missile armament of long-range Terrier surface-to-air missiles operated from a Mk 10 twin launcher in conjunction with two SPG-55B missile-control radars within the context of an operational scenario controlled through the ship's Naval Tactical Data System. The class is named 'Coontz' for the first unit ordered specifically as a guided-missile vessel, the three ships before the *Coontz* (DDG 40) having been ordered as frigates, initially with two 5-in (127-mm) DP guns forward, though the B mount was replaced by an octuple ASROC launcher. Extensive use is made of aluminium in the superstructure to enhance stability by a reduction in weight. During the 1970s the ships were all modernized to enhance their anti-aircraft capability, extra superstructure accommodation being provided for the additional electronic systems, the sensors being upgraded to allow retrofitting of Standard surface-to-air missiles during the 1980s and other features being added to increase habitability and electrical power. The ships' primary anti-aircraft role is attested by the fact that though an ASROC launcher is carried there is no provision for an embarked anti-submarine helicopter, the platform aft being provided only with refuelling capability. The *Farragut* (DDG 37) is unique in the class in carrying eight reload rounds for the ASROC launcher, these being accommodated in a forward extension of the bridge structure just aft of the octuple launcher. The only ships not fitted with the two quadruple container-launchers for RGM-84A Harpoon anti-ship missiles are the *Luce* (DDG 38) and *King* (DDG 41), while other differences are the use of SPS-29E air-search radar in place of SPS-49 in the *Farragut, Luce* and *Mahan* (DDG 41), and the continued installation of Mk 28 Chaffroc launchers in the *Luce, Coontz* and *King*. Further improvement of the class is to be effected by the replacement of the Mk 11 weapon-control system by a Mk 14 system.

'County' class guided-missile destroyer
UK

Displacement: 6,200 tons standard and 6,800 tons full load

Dimensions: length 520·5ft (158·7m); beam 54ft (16·5m); draught 20·5ft (6·3m)

Gun armament: two 4·5-in (114-mm) L/45 DP in one Mk 6 twin mounting, and two 20-mm Oerlikon AA in single mountings

Missile armament: four container-launchers for MM.38 Exocet surface-to-surface missiles, one twin launcher for 36 Seaslug Mk 2 surface-to-air missiles, and two quadruple launchers for 32 Sea Cat surface-to-air missiles

Torpedo armament: none

Anti-submarine armament: two triple 12·75-in (324-mm) STWS tube mountings for 12 Mk 46 A/S torpedoes (Ds 19 and 20)

Aircraft: one Westland Wessex HAS.Mk 3 helicopter in a hangar aft

Electronics: one Marconi Type 965M air-search radar (with double AKE-2 array), one Marconi Type 992Q surveillance radar, one Type 278M height-finding radar, one Type 901 Seaslug-control radar, one Type 903 gun-control radar used in conjunction with the MRS3 gun fire-control system, two Type 904 Sea Cat-control radars used in conjunction with two GWS22 missile fire-control systems, one Decca Type 978 or Kelvin Hughes Type 1006 navigation radar, one Ferranti/Pye ADAWS 1 action data automation weapons system, one Type 176 hull-mounted panoramic sonar, one Type 177 hull-mounted medium-range panoramic sonar, one Type 182 torpedo-decoy system, one Type 192 hull-mounted sonar, one comprehensive ESM suite, and two Knebworth/Corvus chaff launchers

Propulsion: COSAG (COmbined Steam And Gas turbine) arrangement, with two Babcock & Wilcox boilers supplying steam to two sets of AEI geared turbines delivering 30,000shp (22,370kW) and four G.6 gas turbines delivering 30,000shp (22,370kW) to two shafts

Performance: maximum speed 30kts; range 4,000 miles (6,440km) at 28kts

Complement: 34+438

Class

1. Chile (1)				Com-
Name	No.	Builders	Laid down	missioned
PRAT	03	Swan Hunter Ltd	Mar 1966	Mar 1970

2. Pakistan (1)				Com-
Name	No.	Builders	Laid down	missioned
BABUR	C 84	Swan Hunter Ltd	Feb 1960	Nov 1963

3. UK (3)				Com-
Name	No.	Builders	Laid down	missioned
ANTRIM	D 18	Fairfield S.B. & Eng Co Ltd	Jan 1966	July 1970
GLAMORGAN	D 19	Vickers (Shipbuilding) Ltd	Sep 1962	Oct 1966
FIFE	D 20	Fairfield S.B. & Eng Co Ltd	June 1962	June 1966

'D 20' class destroyer

USA/Spain

Displacement: 2,080 tons standard, 2,750 tons normal and 3,050 tons full load
Dimensions: length 376·5ft (114·8m); beam 41·2ft (12·6m); draught 18ft (5·5m)
Gun armament (Ds 21 and 22): five 5-in (127-mm) L/38 DP in five Mk 30 single mountings, six 40-mm Bofors L/60 in three Mk 1 twin mountings, and six 20-mm Oerlikon AA in six Mk 4 single mountings
Gun armament (Ds 23 to 25): four 5-in (127-mm) L/38 DP in four Mk 30 single mountings and six 3-in (76-mm) L/50 in three Mk 33 twin mountings
Missile armament: none
Torpedo armament: three 21-in (533-mm) tubes (Ds 23, 24 and 25 only)
Anti-submarine armament: two triple Mk 32 tube mountings for 12·75-in (324-mm) torpedoes, two Mk 11 Hedgehog mortars, and one depth-charge rack (two in D 21)
Electronics: one Bendix SPS-6C air-search radar, one Raytheon/Sylvania SPS-10 surface-search radar, two Mk 37 radar-controlled main armament fire-control systems, (Ds 21 and 22) one Mk 56 AA armament fire-control system with Mk 35 radar or (Ds 23, 24 and 25) two Mk 63 DP armament fire-control systems with two SPG-34 radars, one Sangamo SQS-29 hull-mounted active or Sangamo/General Electric SQS-4 hull-mounted short-range sonar used in conjunction with the Mk 105 A/S weapon-control system, and (Ds 23, 24 and 25) one BLR-1 electronic support measures system
Propulsion: four Babcock & Wilcox boilers supplying steam to two sets of geared turbines (Westinghouse in D 21 and General Electric in others) delivering 60,000shp (44,740kW) to two shafts
Performance: maximum speed 35kts; range 5,750 miles (9,255km) at 15kts
Complement: 17+273

Class

1. Spain (5) Name	No.	Builders	Laid down	Com-missioned
LEPANTO	D 21	Gulf S.B.	June 1941	June 1943
ALMIRANTE FERRANDIZ	D 22	Gulf S.B.	June 1941	Sep 1943
ALMIRANTE VALDES	D 23	Bath Iron Works	Feb 1942	June 1943
ALCALA GALIANO	D 24	Todd Pacific	June 1943	June 1944
JORGE JUAN	D 25	Federal S.B.	May 1943	Dec 1943

Remarks: Now thoroughly overdue for deletion, the five Spanish 'D 60' class destroyers are basically US 'Fletcher' class ships loaned by the US Navy in the late 1950s (D 21 and D 22 in 1957, and D 23 in 1959) and early 1960s (D 24 and D 25 in 1960) and then bought by Spain in October 1972. The last two ships are of a later variant of the 'Fletcher' class, as indicated by their primary and secondary gun armaments, and the *Almirante Valdes* has been modified to this standard. It is hoped that all five will have been deleted by 1986 as the first 'Oliver Hazard Perry' class guided-missile frigates begin to come into service, though it is anticipated that their place will eventually be taken by a new class of destroyer to enter service in the late 1980s or early 1990s.

'D 60' class destroyer

USA/Spain

Displacement: 2,425 tons standard and 3,480 tons full load
Dimensions: length 390·5ft (119·0m); beam 40·9ft (12·4m); draught 19ft (5·8m)
Gun armament: four 5-in (127-mm) L/38 DP in two Mk 38 twin mountings
Missile armament: none
Torpedo armament: none
Anti-submarine armament: one octuple launcher for RUR-5A ASROC missiles, and two triple Mk 32 tube mountings for 12·75-in (324-mm) Mk 44 torpedoes
Aircraft: one Hughes Model 500 helicopter in a hangar aft
Electronics: one Lockheed SPS-40 (Ds 61 and 62) or Westinghouse SPS-37 (others) air-search radar, one Raytheon/Sylvania SPS-10 surface-search radar, one navigation radar, one Western Electric Mk 25 or Western Electric Mk 28 radar-controlled gun fire-control system, one Mk 37 radar-controlled gun fire-control system, one Sangamo SQS-23 hull-mounted long-range active sonar used in conjunction with the Mk 114 A/S weapon-control system, and electronic support measures
Propulsion: four Babcock & Wilcox boilers supplying steam to two sets of General Electric or Westinghouse geared turbines delivering 60,000shp (44,740kW) to two shafts
Performance: maximum speed 34kts; range 5,525 miles (8,890km) at 15kts
Complement: 17+257

The Gravina (D 62) is typical of the 'D 60' or 'Gearing (FRAM I)' class gun destroyers operated by the Spanish navy, modification including electronic support measures equipment and an ASROC launcher.

Class

1. Spain (5) Name	No.	Builders	Laid down	Com-missioned
CHURRUCA	D 61	Federal S.B.	1944	June 1945
GRAVINA	D 62	Consolidated Steel	1944	July 1945
MENDEZ NUÑEZ	D 63	Consolidated Steel	1945	Nov 1945
LANGARA	D 64	Consolidated Steel	1944	May 1945
BLAS DE LEZO	D 65	Bath Iron Works	1945	Nov 1945

Remarks: Operated under the Spanish designation 'D 60', these 'Gearing (FRAM I)' class destroyers were bought from the USA in 1978 after being transferred in 1972 (first pair) and 1975 (last three). The *Blas de Lezo* (D 65) differs from her sisters in having two forward gun mountings, no ASROC launcher and torpedo tube mountings alongside the after funnel.

'Daring' class guided-missile destroyer

UK

Displacement: 2,800 tons standard and 3,600 tons full load
Dimensions: length 390ft (118·9m); beam 43ft (13·1m); draught 18ft (5·5m)
Gun armament: four 4·5-in (114-mm) L/45 DP in two Mk 6 twin mountings, and four 40-mm Bofors AA L/60 in two Mk 5 twin mountings
Missile armament: eight container-launchers for MM.38 Exocet surface-to-surface missiles
Torpedo armament: none
Anti-submarine armament: one Squid projector
Aircraft: provision for a light helicopter on a platform aft
Electronics: one Plessey AWS 1 air-search radar, one combination air- and surface-search radar, and one Decca navigation radar
Propulsion: two Foster-Wheeler boilers supplying steam to two sets of English Electric geared turbines delivering 54,000shp (40,270kW) to two shafts
Performance: maximum speed 32kts; range 3,450 miles (5,550km) at 20kts
Complement: 297

Class

1. Peru (2) Name	No.	Builders	Laid down	Com-missioned
PALACIOS	DD 73	Yarrow (Shipbuilders) Ltd	Apr 1947	Mar 1954
FERRÉ	DD 74	Yarrow (Shipbuilders) Ltd	Sep 1946	Apr 1953

Remarks: Peru bought these two 'Daring' class destroyers from the UK in 1969, and from 1970 to 1973 they were modernized with an enclosed mast to support the Plessey AWS 1 radar and with the Exocet container-launchers replacing the Close-Range Blind Fire Director just forward of X turret. In 1975-76 both ships were again modified, this time with a helicopter platform instead of the Squid anti-submarine launcher. Since then the *Ferré* (DD 74) has again been modified, a helicopter hangar replacing X turret and two 40-mm Breda twin mountings replacing the earlier 40-mm Bofors mountings abreast the superstructure.

'Fletcher' class destroyer

USA/Greece

Displacement: 2,050 tons standard and 3,050 tons full load
Dimensions: length 376·5 ft (114·7 m); beam 39·5 ft (12·0 m); draught 18 ft (5·5 m)
Gun armament: four 5-in (127-mm) L/38 DP in four Mk 30 single mountings, six 3-in (76-mm) L/55 DP in three Mk 33 twin mountings, and 10 40-mm Bofors AA in two single and two quadruple mountings
Missile armament: none
Torpedo armament: one quintuple 21-in (533-mm) tube mounting
Anti-submarine armament: Hedgehog mortars, depth-charge racks, and side-launching racks for Mk 44 A/S torpedoes
Electronics: one Bendix SPS-6 air-search radar, one Raytheon/Sylvania SPS-10 surface-search radar, one Mk 25 gun-control radar as part of the General Electric Mk 37 main armament fire-control system, Mk 35 gun-control radar as part of the one Mk 56 and two Mk 63 secondary armament fire-control systems, two Mk 51 AA armament fire-control systems, and SQS-39 or SQS-43 hull-mounted sonar
Propulsion: four Babcock & Wilcox boilers supplying steam to two sets of General Electric geared turbines delivering 60,000 shp (44,740 kW) to two shafts
Performance: maximum speed 32 kts; range 6,900 miles (11,105 km) at 15 kts or 1,450 miles (2,335 km) at 32 kts
Complement: 250

Class

1. Argentina (1)

Name	No.	Builders	Laid down	Com-missioned
ALMIRANTE DOMECO GARCIA	D 23	Bath Iron Works	Oct 1942	May 1943

2. Brazil (5)

Name	No.	Builders	Laid down	Com-missioned
PARANA	D 29	Bethlehem Steel	May 1943	Jan 1944
PERNAMBUCO	D 30	Seattle-Tacoma S.B.	Apr 1942	Sep 1943
PIAUI	D 31	Federal S.B.	Mar 1943	Sep 1943
SANTA CATARINA	D 32	Bethlehem Steel	May 1943	Feb 1944
MARANHAO	D 33	Puget Sound Navy Yard	Aug 1943	Feb 1945

3. Chile (2)

Name	No.	Builders	Laid down	Com-missioned
BLANCO ENCALADA	14	Bath Iron Works	Mar 1943	Oct 1943
COCHRANE	15	Todd Pacific Shipyards	Jan 1944	Sep 1944

4. Greece (6)

Name	No.	Builders	Laid down	Com-missioned
ASPIS	D 06	Boston Navy Yard	Apr 1942	June 1943
VELOS	D 16	Boston Navy Yard	Feb 1941	May 1943
KIMON	D 42	Bath Iron Works	Aug 1942	Mar 1943
LONCHI	D 56	Boston Navy Yard	Apr 1942	July 1943
NEARCHOS	D 65	Federal S.B.	June 1942	Dec 1942
SFENDONI	D 85	Consolidated Steel	May 1941	Oct 1942

5. Mexico (1)

Name	No.	Builders	Laid down	Com-missioned
CUITLAHUAC	E 02	Consolidated Steel	July 1941	Feb 1943

6. South Korea (2)

Name	No.	Builders	Laid down	Com-missioned
CHUNG MU	DD 911	Bath Iron Works	Oct 1942	May 1943
PUSAN	DD 913	Federal S.B.	Mar 1943	Sep 1943

7. Spain (5)

See 'D 20' class

8. Taiwan (4)

Name	No.	Builders	Laid down	Com-missioned
KUN YANG	934	Bethleham Steel Co	Dec 1942	Dec 1943
CHING YANG	947	Bethlehem Steel Co	Jan 1942	Apr 1943
KWEI YANG	956	Bethlehem Steel Co	Nov 1942	Dec 1943
AN YANG	997	Bethlehem Steel Co	July 1942	May 1943

The Parana (D 29) is the lead ship of the Brazilian navy's group of five 'Fletcher' class destroyers, of which two are now believed to be in reserve.

Remarks: The 'Fletcher' class was the US Navy's most important fleet destroyer class of World War II, and served with particular distinction in the Pacific theatre, where its good range and excellent armament proved invaluable. The type was retained in service after World War II, but with the growth in importance of the late-war 'Allen M. Sumner' and 'Gearing' class gun destroyers, and of various post-war classes of gun and guided-missile destroyers, the ships of the 'Fletcher' class were released for export from the 1950s onwards, their capabilities suiting the ships more for South American, Mediterranean and Far Eastern navies than for the USA's major NATO allies of the period. At one time Argentina operated four 'Fletcher' class destroyers, which were handed over in 1962, 1963, 1971 and 1972, but of these only the *Almirante Domecq Garcia* (D 23) is still in service, having been recommissioned in 1981 after repairs to damage inflicted in a collision with the carrier *Vientincinco de Mayo*. There is little remarkable about the ship, which differs from the specification only in lacking the 40-mm Bofors guns and in having two triple Mk 32 tube mountings for anti-submarine torpedoes. Brazil's five 'Fletcher' class destroyers were received in 1961, 1961, 1967, 1968 and 1972 respectively. These ships each have a gun armament of five (four in D 30) 5-in (127-mm) DP and (Ds 29 and 32) 10 40-mm Bofors AA, an anti-submarine armament of two triple Mk 32 tube mountings (except in Ds 29 and 30), and a sonar fit of SQS-4, SQS-29 or SQS-34 sets. Chile's two ships were received in 1963, and approximate closely with the specification above apart from the fact that they lack the Bofors AA guns and have an anti-submarine fit of Hedgehogs, depth-charge throwers, depth-charge racks and side-launching torpedo racks. The largest current operator of the 'Fletcher' class is Greece, whose six ships are described in the specification above. The four ships received directly from the USA were *Aspis* (D 06), *Velos* (D 16), *Lonchi* (D 42) and *Sfendoni* (D 85), all of which were transferred in 1959 and bought by Greece in 1977. The *Kimon* (D 42) and *Nearchos* (D 65) were bought from West Germany in 1980 and 1981 respectively, together with two more ex-West German ships for cannibalization. Despite the relative obsolescence of the ships, all have been upgraded electronically while in Greek service. The one 'Fletcher' class destroyer operated by Mexico was transferred in 1970, and compared with the specification above lacks the 3-in (76-mm) secondary armament, has five 5-in (127-mm) guns, and has no provision for anti-submarine operations. South Korea currently deploys two 'Fletcher' class destroyers, these being transferred in 1963 and 1968 respectively, and then bought in 1977. They fit the specification above quite closely, but have five 5-in (127-mm) guns, no 3-in (76-mm) secondary guns, and an SQS-20 hull-mounted sonar. The current 'Fletcher' class destroyers that differ most from the norm are the quartet deployed by Taiwan. These were received in 1968, 1971, 1971 and 1967 respectively. These have a main armament of five 5-in (127-mm) guns, a secondary armament of four 3-in (76-mm) guns, and an AA battery consisting of two quadruple 40-mm (except 947) and six single 20-mm (except 947) guns plus one sextuple launcher for RIM-72B/C Sea Chaparral surface-to-air missiles (except 947). *Kun Yang* has been fitted for minelaying, and thus retains the original quintuple tube mounting for 21-in (533-mm) torpedoes, while the other three ships have two triple Mk 32 tube mountings for 12·75-in (324-mm) Mk 44/46 anti-submarine torpedoes. The sonar fit in these Taiwanese ships is SQS-50 in 934 and 956, SQS-40 in 947 and SQS-41 in 956. All the ships are fitted with BLR-1 or SLR-2 passive detection systems, and compared with other 'Fletcher' class destroyers have enlarged complements: 270 in 934 and 997, 279 in 947 and 261 in 956. These ships, in common with all other survivors of the 'Fletcher' class, are now well past their prime, and the provision of spares, even from extensive cannibalization, is presenting problems that must result in the demise of the class within a very few years.

'F 67' class guided-missile destroyer
France

Displacement: 4,580 tons standard and 5,745 tons full load
Dimensions: length 152·75m (501·1ft); beam 15·3m (50·2ft); draught 5·7m (18·7ft)
Gun armament: two 100-mm (3·9-in) L/55 DP in single mountings, and two 20-mm AA in single mountings
Missile armament: six container-launchers for MM.38 Exocet surface-to-surface missiles, and one octuple launcher for Crotale Naval surface-to-air missiles
Torpedo armament: none
Anti-submarine armament: one launcher for 13 Malafon missiles, and two launchers for 10 L 5 A/S torpedoes
Electronics: one Thomson-CSF DRBV 51 air- and surface-search radar, one Thomson-CSF DRBV 26 air-search radar, one Thomson-CSF DRBC 32D fire-control radar used in conjunction with the Thomson-CSF Vega sensor and weapon-control system, two Decca 1226 navigation radars, one CIT/ALCATEL DUBV 23 hull-mounted active search and attack sonar, one CIT/ALCATEL DUBV 43 variable-depth sonar, one SENIT 3 combat information system, and two Syllex chaff launchers (being replaced by CSEE Dagaie chaff launchers)
Propulsion: four boilers supplying steam to two sets of Rateau double-reduction geared turbines delivering 40,565kW (54,400shp) to two shafts
Performance: maximum speed 32kts; range 9,250km (5,750 miles) at 18kts or 3,500km (2,175 miles) at 30kts
Complement: 17+113+162

Class

1. France (3)				Com-
Name	No.	Builders	Laid down	missioned
TOURVILLE	D610	Lorient ND	Mar 1970	June 1974
DUGUAY-TROUIN	D611	Lorient ND	Feb 1971	Sep 1975
DE GRASSE	D612	Lorient ND	June 1972	Oct 1977

Remarks: Potent anti-submarine destroyers with good anti-ship and anti-aircraft capabilities, the three 'F 67' class destroyers serve with the French Atlantic Fleet, serving in turn as flagship of that force. The octuple Crotale Naval SAM launcher was fitted in place of the after 100-mm (3·9-in) gun during refits.

'Forrest Sherman' class destroyer
USA

Displacement: 2,800 to 3,000 tons standard and 3,960 to 4,200 tons full load
Dimensions: length 418ft (127·4m); beam 45ft (13·7m); draught 23ft (7·0m)
Gun armament: (DDs 942 and 944) three 5-in (127-mm) L/54 DP in three Mk 42 single mountings, or (DD 931 and others modified for improved anti-submarine capability) two 5-in (127-mm) L/54 DP in two Mk 42 single mountings
Missile armament: none
Torpedo armament: none
Anti-submarine armament: two triple Mk 32 tube mountings for 12·75-in (324-mm) Mk 46 A/S torpedoes, and (DDs 933, 937, 938, 940, 941 and 943) one octuple launcher for RUR-5A ASROC missiles
Electronics: one Raytheon/Sylvania SPS-10 surface-search radar, one Westinghouse SPS-37 or Lockheed SPS-40 air-search radar, one General Electric SPG-54A gun-control radar used in conjunction with the General Electric Mk 56 gun fire control system, one General Electric SPG-53E gun-control radar used in conjunction with the Naval Weapons Laboratory Mk 68 gun fire-control system, one Sangamo SQS-23 bow-mounted long-range active sonar and (modified ASW ships) one EDO SQS-35 variable-depth sonar used in conjunction with the Mk 114 A/S weapon-control system, one Mk 5 trget-designation system, one OE-82 satellite communications antenna, one SRR-1 satellite communications receiver, one WSC-3 satellite communications transceiver, and (unmodified ships) extensive electronic warfare systems
Propulsion: four boilers (Babcock & Wilcox in DDs 931, 933, 943 and 944, and Westinghouse in others) supplying steam to two sets of geared turbines (Westinghouse in DDs 931, 933, 937 and 938, and General Electric in others) delivering 70,000shp (52,200kW) to two shafts
Performance: maximum speed 33kts; range 5,200 miles (8,370km) at 20kts
Complement: 17+275, or (A/S modified vessels) 17+287

Class

1. USA (9)				Com-
Name	No.	Builders	Launched	missioned
FORREST SHERMAN	DD931	Bath Iron Works	Feb 1955	Nov 1955
BIGELOW	DD942	Bath Iron Works	Feb 1957	Nov 1957
MULLINNIX	DD944	Bethlem Steel	Mar 1957	Mar 1958
BARRY	DD933	Bath Iron Works	Oct 1955	Aug 1956
DAVIS	DD937	Bethlehem Steel	Mar 1956	Feb 1957
JONAS INGRAM	DD938	Bethlehem Steel	July 1956	July 1957
MANLEY	DD940	Bath Iron Works	Apr 1956	Feb 1957
DUPONT	DD941	Bath Iron Works	Sep 1956	July 1957
BLANDY	DD943	Bethlehem Steel	Dec 1956	Nov 1957

Remarks: These were the first fleet destroyers produced in the USA after World War II, and all have now been placed in reserve because of engineering problems. In the period from 1967 to 1971 six of the class (DDs 933, 937, 938, 940, 941 and 943) were extensively modified for enhanced anti-submarine capability, with an octuple ASROC launcher in place of one 5-in (127-mm) mount.

'Forrest Sherman (Converted)' class guided-missile destroyer
USA

Displacement: 2,5850 tons standard and 4,150 tons full load
Dimensions: length 418·ft 9127·5m); beam 44ft (13·4m); draught 20ft (6·1m)
Gun armament: one 5-in (127-mm) L/54 DP in a Mk 42 single mounting
Missile armament: one Mk 13 single launche for 40 RIM-24 Tartar surface-to-air missiles
Torpedo armament: none
Anti-submarine armament: two triple Mk 32 tube mountings for 12·75-in (324-mm) Mk 46 A/S torpedoes, and one octuple launcher for RUR-5A ASROC missiles
Electronics: one ITT/Gilfillan SPS-48 3D air-search radar, one Raytheon/Sylvania SPS-10 surface search radar, one Westinghouse SPS-37 air-search radar, one SPG-51C missile-control radar used in conjunction with the General Electric Mk 73 missile fire-control system, one SPG-53B gun-control radar used in conjunction with the Naval Weapons Laboratory Mk 68 gun fire-control system, one Mk 4 weapon-control system, one Sanagamo SQS-23 hull-mounted long-range active sonar used in conjunction with the Mk 114 A/S fire-control system, Naval Tactical Data System, URN-20 TACAN, one OE-82 satellite communications antenna, SRR-1 satellite communications receiver, and SWC-3 satellite communications transceiver
Propulsion: four boilers (Foster-Wheeler in DDG 31 and Babcock & Wilcox in DDG 32) suplying steam to two sets of Westinghouse geared turbines delivering 70,000shp (52,200kW) to two shafts
Performance: maximum speed 31kts; range 5,200 miles (8,370km) at 20kts
Complement: 22+315

Class

USA (2)				Com-
Name	No.	Builders	Launched	missioned
DECATUR	DDG31	Bethlehem Steel	Dec 1956	Dec 1956
JOHN PAUL JONES	DDG32	Bath Iron Works	May 1955	Apr 1956

Converted from a fleet destroyer into a guided-missile destroyer between 1965 and 1967, the John Paul Jones (DDG 32) has now been placed in reserve.

'Friesland' class destroyer

Netherlands

Displacement: 2,495 tons standard and 3,070 tons full load
Dimensions: length 116·0m (380·5ft); beam 11·7m (38·5ft); draught 5·2m (17ft)
Gun armament: four 120-mm (4·7-in) L/50 Bofors DP in two twin mountings, and four 40-mm Bofors L/70 in single mountings
Missile armament: none
Torpedo armament: none
Anti-submarine armament: two 375-mm (14·76-in) Bofors four-barrel rocket-launchers, and two depth-charge racks
Electronics: one Hollandse Signaalapparaten LW-03 air-search radar, one Hollandse Signaalapparaten DA-05 air- and surface-search radar, one Hollandse Signaalapparaten WM-45 gun-control radar system, one CWE 10-N hull-mounted sonar, and one PAE 1-N hull-mounted sonar
Propulsion: four Babcock & Wilcox boilers supplying steam to two sets of Werkspoor geared turbines delivering 44,740 kW (60,000 shp) to two shafts
Performance: maximum speed 36+ kts; range 7,400 km (4,600 miles) at 18 kts

Complement: 284

Class
1. Peru (7)

Name	No.	Builders	Laid down	Com-missioned
BOLOGNESI	DD 70	Dok en Werfmatschappij	Oct 1953	Oct 1957
CASTILLA	DD 71	Koninklijke Maatschappij	Feb 1954	Oct 1957
CAPITAN QUIÑONES	DD 76	Koninklijke Maatschappij	Nov 1953	Oct 1956
VILLAR	DD 77	Nederlandse Dok	Mar 1955	Aug 1958
GALVEZ	DD 78	Nederlandse Dok	Feb 1952	Sep 1956
DIEZ CANSECO	DD 79	Rotterdamse Droogdok	Jan 1954	Feb 1957
GUISE	DD 72	Nederlandse Dok	Jan 1954	Aug 1957

Remarks: The 'Friesland' class is a development of the 'Holland' class with greater displacement and performance, and represents a high point in gun destroyer development, the main armament being fully automatic and radar-controlled. The seven ships were all transferred in the early 1980s.

'Gearing (FRAM I)' class destroyer

USA/Greece

Displacement: 2,425 tons standard and 3,500 tons full load
Dimensions: length 390·5ft (119·0m); beam 41·2ft (12·6m); draught 19ft (5·8m)
Gun armament: four 5-in (127-mm) L/38 DP in two Mk 38 twin mountings, one 76-mm (3-in) L/62 DP OTO-Melara Compact, and one 40-mm Bofors L/60 AA
Missile armament: none
Torpedo armament: none
Anti-submarine armament: two triple Mk 32 tube mountings for 12·75-in (324-mm) Mk 44/46 A/S torpedoes, and one octuple launcher for RUR-5A ASROC missiles
Electronics: one Raytheon/Sylvania SPS-10 surface-search radar, one Westinghouse SPS-37 or Lockheed SPS-40 air-search radar, one Mk 25 or Mk 28 gun-control radar used in conjunction with the General Electric Mk 37 main armament fire-control system, one Selenia Orion 10X gun-control radar used in conjunction with the ELSAG Argo NA10 76-mm (3-in) gun fire-control system, and one Sangamo SQS-23 hull-mounted long-range active sonar
Propulsion: four Babcock & Wilcox boilers supplying steam to two sets of Westinghouse geared turbines delivering 60,000 shp (44,740 kW) to two shafts
Performance: maximum speed 32·5 kts; range 5,525 miles (8,890 km) at 15 kts
Complement: 16 + 253

Class
1. Brazil (2)

Name	No.	Builders	Com-missioned
MARCILIO DIAS	D 25	Consolidated Steel	Mar 1945
MARIZ e. BARROS	D 26	Consolidated Steel	Oct 1945

2. Ecuador (1)

Name	No.	Builders	Com-missioned
PRESIDENTE ELOY ALFARO	DD 01	Consolidated Steel	May 1946

3. Greece (6)

Name	No.	Builders	Com-missioned
KANARIS	D 212	Consolidated Steel	Sep 1945
KOUNTOURIOTIS	D 213	Bethlehem Steel	Mar 1946
SACHTOURIS	D 214	Bethlehem S.B.	Jan 1946
TOMPAZIS	D 215	Todd Pacific	May 1945
APOSTOLIS	D 216	Bath Iron Works	June 1945
KRIEZIS	D 217	Consolidated Steel	Feb 1946

4. Mexico (2)

Name	No.	Builders	Com-missioned
QUETZALCOATL	E 03	Bethlehem S.B.	Apr 1945
NETZAHUALCOYOTL	E 04	Bethlehem S.B.	May 1945

5. Pakistan (5)

Name	No.	Builders	Com-missioned
TARIQ	D 165	Federal S.B.	Jan 1946
TAIMUR	D 166	Todd Pacific	Mar 1949
TUGHRIL	D 167	Todd Pacific	Aug 1945
TIPPU SULTAN	D 168	Bethlehem S.B.	Apr 1946
ALAMGIR	D 169	Bethlehem S.B.	Dec 1946

6. South Korea (5)

Name	No.	Builders	Com-missioned
TAEJON	DD 919	Consolidated Steel	Apr 1946
KWANG JU	DD 921	Bath Iron Works	May 1945
KANG WON	DD 922	Federal S.B.	Sep 1945
KYONG KI	DD 923	Consolidated Steel	July 1945
JEONJU	—	Consolidated Steel	Mar 1945

7. Spain (5)
See 'D60' class

8. Taiwan (11)

Name	No.	Builders	Com-missioned
KAI YANG	915	Todd Pacific	Oct 1945
CHIEN YANG	921	Todd Pacific	Feb 1946
TE YANG	925	Bath Iron Works	July 1945
SHEN YANG	932	Bath Iron Works	Sep 1945
LIAO YANG	938	Bath Iron Works	May 1945
DANG YANG	966	Bethlehem Steel	Mar 1947
HAN YANG	978	Bath Iron Works	May 1945
LAO YANG	981	Todd Pacific	June 1946
LAI YANG	—	Bethlehem Steel	June 1946
CHAO YANG	912	Federal S.B.	July 1946
—	—	Consolidated Steel	Oct 1946

9. Turkey (7)

Name	No.	Builders	Com-missioned
YUCATEPE	D 345	Todd Pacific	June 1945
SAVAŞTEPE	D 348	Consolidated Steel	Dec 1945
KILIÇ ALI PAŞA	D 349	Consolidated Steel	Oct 1946
PIYALE PAŞA	D 350	Bath Iron Works	Nov 1945
M. FEVZI ÇAKMAK	D 351	Bethlehem Steel	Sep 1946
GAYRET	D 352	Todd Pacific	July 1946
ADATEPE	D 353	Bethlehem S.B.	June 1946

Remarks: Developed from the 'Allen M. Sumner' class with the same basic armament on a longer hull, the 'Gearing' class gun destroyer began to enter service in the closing stages of World War II, and was one of the destroyer mainstays of the US Navy in the late 1940s and 1950s before being handed on to the USA's allies as the US Navy re-equipped with more advanced ships. The technical description above applies specifically to the Greek ships, which have been considerably modified from the original standard with advanced anti-submarine sensors and armament, and (except Ds 215 and 216) a 76-mm (3-in) OTO-Melera Compact gun for AA and anti-FAC operations. Brazil's two ships are to a comparable standard, though lacking the Bofors AA gun, and can still operate a light anti-submarine helicopter (Westland Wasp) unlike the Greek ships, whose helicopter platform now accommodates the 76-mm (3-in) gun. The Greek ships were transferred during the 1970s and early 1980s (including two vessels for cannibalization), and the two Brazilian ships were handed over in 1973. Ecuador's sole ship was commissioned into the navy in 1980, and is similar to the Brazilian ships apart from its lack of an ASROC launcher. Mexico's two ships again lack an ASROC launcher, and were sold by the USA in 1982. Pakistan operates five 'Gearing' class destroyers with ASROC launchers, the first pair being bought in 1977, the second pair in 1980 and the last ship in 1982. South Korea's five 'Gearing (FRAM I)' class destroyers are closer to the American original in gun armament with six 5-in (127-mm) main weapons, with one twin 40-mm mounting for AA defence and no ASROC launcher, though the carriage of a single Aérospatiale Alouette III helicopter in the hangar aft provides longer-range anti-submarine defence; the first pair was bought in 1977, the third ship in 1978 and the last pair in 1981. Taiwan operates the largest force of 'Gearing (FRAM I)' class ships, all transferred between 1972 and 1981: these are all being fitted with three Hsiung Feng (Gabriel) anti-ship missiles and extra 40-mm guns to supplement four 5-in (127-mm) guns, two triple Mk 32 tube mountings and (except 915 and 966) one ASROC launcher. The Turkish ships are closely modelled on the Greek units.

'Gearing (FRAM II)' class destroyer

USA/South Korea

Displacement: 2,425 tons standard and 3,500 tons full load
Dimensions: length 390·5ft (119·0m); beam 41·2ft (12·6m); draught 19ft (5·8m)
Gun armament: six 5-in (127-mm) L/38 DP in three Mk 38 twin mountings, and two 40-mm Bofors L/60 AA in one twin mounting
Missile armament: four container-launchers for RGM-84A Harpoon surface-to-surface missiles
Torpedo armament: none
Anti-submarine armament: two triple Mk 32 tube mountings for 12·75-in (324-mm) Mk 44/46 A/S torpedoes, and two Mk 11 Hedgehog mortars
Aircraft: one light helicopter on a platform aft
Electronics: one Raytheon/Sylvania SPS-10 surface-search radar, one Lockheed SPS-40 air-search radar, one Mk 25 or Mk 28 gun-control radar used in conjunction with the General Electric Mk 37 gun fire-control system, and one Sangamo SQS-29 hull-mounted active sonar
Propulsion: four Babcock & Wilcox boilers supplying steam to two sets of General Electric geared turbines delivering 60,000shp (44,740kW) to two shafts
Performance: maximum speed 32·5kts; range 6,675 miles (10,740km) at 15kts
Complement: 280

Class

1. Argentina (1)				
Name	*No.*	*Builders*	*Laid down*	*Commissioned*
COMODORO PY	D 27	Consolidated Steel	Dec 1944	Apr 1945

2. Greece (1)				
Name	*No.*	*Builders*	*Laid down*	*Commissioned*
THEMISTOCLES	D 210	Bath Iron Works	May 1944	Dec 1944

3. South Korea (2)				
Name	*No.*	*Builders*	*Laid down*	*Commissioned*
CHUNG BUK	DD 915	Bath Iron Works	June 1944	Jan 1945
JEONG BUK	DD 916	Bath Iron Works	Sep 1944	Apr 1945

4. Taiwan (1)				
Name	*No.*	*Builders*	*Laid down*	*Commissioned*
FU YANG	963	Bath Iron Works	1945	Aug 1945

5. Turkey (2)				
Name	*No.*	*Builders*	*Laid down*	*Commissioned*
KOCATEPE	D 354	Bethlehem Steel	1944	June 1945
TINAZTEPE	D 355	Bethlehem Steel	1944	May 1947

Remarks: Argentina's single 'Gearing (FRAM II)' class destroyer was received in 1973, and is similar to the standard above apart from having Exocet anti-ship missiles in place of Harpoons and triple ILAS-3 anti-submarine tube mountings. Greece's *Themistocles* (D 210) is again similar, was received in 1971 and has provision for an Aérospatiale Alouette III helicopter. South Korea's two ships, received in 1972, are described above, and also have additional AA defence in the form of one 20-mm Vulcan CIWS mounting (*Chung Buk*) or one 30-mm Emerlec twin mounting (*Jeon Buk*). The Taiwanese *Fu Yang* (963) was received in 1971, and carries eight 40-mm Bofors AA guns and three Hsiung Feng (Gabriel) anti-ship missiles. The two Turkish ships were transferred in 1974 and 1972 respectively, and have a main armament of only four 5-in (127-mm) guns backed by a single 35-mm twin AA mounting.

*The **Perkins** (DD 877) is seen before her transfer as the Argentine **Py** (D 27).*

'Halland' class guided-missile destroyer

Sweden

Displacement: 2,800 tons standard and 3,400 tons full load
Dimensions: length 121·0m (397·2ft); beam 12·6m (41·3ft); draught 5·5m (18ft)
Gun armament: four 120-mm (4·7-in) L/50 DP in two twin mountings, two 57-mm Bofors L/50 AA in one twin mounting, and six 40-mm Bofors L/48 AA in six single mountings
Missile armament: one Mk 20 twin launcher for RB 08A surface-to-surface missiles
Torpedo armament: eight 533-mm (21-in) tubes in one quintuple and one triple mounting
Anti-submarine armament: two four-barrel Bofors 375-mm (14·76-in) rocket-launchers
Electronics: Philips Elektronikindustrier 9 LV 200 multi-role (air-search, surface-search and tracking) radar, Hollandse Signaalapparaten WM-20 fire-control radar, one search sonar and one attack sonar
Propulsion: two Penhöet/Motala-Verkstad boilers supplying steam to two sets of De Laval double-reduction geared turbines delivering 58,000bhp (43,250kW) to two shafts
Performance: maximum speed 35kts; range 5,500km (3,415 miles) at 20kts
Complement: 18+272

Class

1. Sweden (2)				
Name	*No.*	*Builders*	*Laid down*	*Commissioned*
HALLAND	J 18	Götaverken	1951	June 1955
SMÅLAND	J 19	Eriksberg Mek Verkstads	1951	Jan 1956

'Halland (Modified)' class destroyer

Sweden

Displacement: 2,650 tons standard and 3,300 tons full load
Dimensions: length 121·1m (397·2ft); beam 12·4m (40·7ft); draught 4·7m (15·4ft)
Gun armament: six 120-mm (4·7-in) L/50 DP in three twin mountings, and four 40-mm Bofors AA in single mountings
Missile armament: none
Torpedo armament: one quadruple 533-mm (21-in) tube mounting
Anti-submarine armament: one four-barrel Bofors 375-mm (14·76-in) rocket-launcher
Electronics: one Hollandse Signaalapparaten LW-03 air-search radar, one Hollandse Signaalapparaten DA-02 surface-search and target designation radar, and four Hollandse Signaalapparaten WM-20 fire-control radars
Propulsion: two Penhöet/Motala-Verkstad boilers supplying steam to two sets of De Laval double-reduction geared turbines delivering 55,000shp (41,015kW) to two shafts
Performance: maximum speed 25kts (D 05) or 32kts (D06); range 835km (520 miles) at 25kts
Complement: 21+227

Class

1. Colombia (2)				
Name	*No.*	*Builders*	*Laid down*	*Commissioned*
VEINTE DE JULIO	D 05	Kockums Mek Verkstads	Oct 1955	June 1958
SIETE DE AGOSTO	D 06	Götaverken	Nov 1955	Oct 1958

Remarks: Developed specifically for Colombia, the 'Halland (Modified)' class features a heavier main armament than the Swedish original, and also has no secondary armament and reduced AA defences. D 06 is in good condition (overhauled in the USA during 1974-75), while D 05 is due for deletion.

Veinte de Julio (D 05) carries a main armament of three twin 120-mm mountings.

'Hamburg' class (Type 101A) guided-missile destroyer
West Germany
Displacement: 3,340 tons standard and 4,680 tons full load
Dimensions: length 133·8 m (439 ft); beam 13·4 m (44 ft); draught 6·2 m (20·3 ft)
Gun armament: three 100-m (3·9-in) L/55 DP in single mountings, and eight 40-mm Breda AA in four twin mountings
Missile armament: two twin container-launchers for MM.38 Exocet surface-to-surface missiles
Torpedo armament: none
Anti-submarine armament: two four-barrel Bofors 375-mm (14·76-in) rocket-launchers, one quadruple 533-mm (21-in) tube mounting for A/S torpedoes, and two depth-charge throwers
Electronics: one Hollandse Signaalapparaten LW-02 air-search radar, one Hollandse Signaalapparaten DA-02 surface-search and target designation radar, one Decca navigation radar, two Hollandse Signaalapparaten WM-45 main armament fire-control radars, two Hollandse Signaalapparaten WM-45 AA armament fire-control radars, one Hollandse Signaalapparaten A/S fire-control

system used in conjunction with the ELAC 1BV hull-mounted sonar, one Breda SCLAR 20-tube chaff launcher, and extensive electronic countermeasures
Propulsion: four Wahodag boilers supplying steam to two sets of Wahodag geared turbines delivering 50,710 kW (68,000 shp) to two shafts
Performance: maximum speed 34 kts; range 11,125 km (6,915 miles) at 13 kts or 1,700 km (1,055 miles) at 34 kts
Complement: 19+249

Class
1. West Germany (4)

Name	No.	Builders	Laid down	Commissioned
HAMBURG	D 181	H. C. Stülcken	Jan 1959	Mar 1964
SCHLESWIG-HOLSTEIN	D 182	H. C. Stülcken	Aug 1959	Oct 1964
BAYERN	D 183	H. C. Stülcken	Sep 1960	July 1965
HESSEN	D 184	H. C. Stülcken	Feb 1961	Oct 1968

Remarks: Designed as general-purpose gun frigates optimized for anti-submarine warfare, the four units of the West German 'Hamburg' class were modernized extensively during the 1970s: the 100-mm (3·9-in) gun in X position was replaced by two twin container-launchers for MM.38 Exocet anti-ship missiles, the 40-mm Bofors AA guns were replaced by four 40-mm Breda twin AA mountings, a new Hollandse Signaalapparaten air-search radar was fitted, the five (three bow and two stern) fixed anti-ship torpedo tubes were removed, and two extra anti-submarine torpedo tubes were added. The West German navy hopes to keep these ships in service until the 1990s, which will entail further modification.

Visible forward of the bridge of the **Hamburg (D 181)** *are the two Bofors four-barrel anti-submarine rocket-launchers, plus two 100-mm (3·9-in) DP gun mountings.*

'Haruna' class guided-missile destroyer
Japan
Displacement: 4,700 tons standard and 6,300 tons full load
Dimensions: length 153·0 m (502 ft); beam 17·5 m (57·4 ft); draught 5·1 m (16·7 ft)
Gun armament: two 5-in (127-mm) L/54 DP in two Mk 42 single mountings, and two 20-mm Phalanx CIWS mountings
Missile armament: two quadruple container-launchers for eight RGM-84A Harpoon anti-ship missiles, and one octuple launcher for eight RIM-7 Sea Sparrow SAMs
Torpedo armament: none
Anti-submarine armament: two triple Mk 32 tube mountings for 12·75-in (324-mm) Mk 46 A/S torpedoes, one Mk 16 octuple launcher for 16 RUR-5A ASROC missiles, and helicopter-launched weapons (see below)
Aircraft: three Sikorsky SH-3 Sea King helicopters in a hangar aft
Electronics: one Hughes SPS-52 3D radar, one OPS-17 surface-search radar, two Type 72 gun fire-control radars, one Hollandse Signaalapparaten WM-25 missile-control radar, TACAN, one ESM suite, one OQS-3 hull sonar, and one SQS-3S (J) variable-depth sonar
Propulsion: ? boilers supplying steam to two sets of geared turbines delivering 52,200 kW (70,000 shp) to two shafts
Performance: maximum speed 32 kts
Complement: 364

Key features of the **Haruna (DD 141)** *are the large helicopter platform and associated hangar (large enough to handle three Mitsubishi-Sikorsky SH-3 anti-submarine helicopters), and the octuple ASROC launcher just forward of the bridge structure together with two 5-in (127-mm) DP gun mountings.*

Class
1. Japan (2)

Name	No.	Builders	Laid down	Commissioned
HARUNA	DD 141	Mitsubishi	Mar 1970	Feb 1973
HIEI	DD 142	Ishikawajima	Mar 1972	Nov 1974

'Hatsuyuki' class guided-missile destroyer
Japan
Displacement: 2,950 tons standard and 3,700 tons full load
Dimensions: length 126·0 m (413·3 ft); beam 13·6 m (44·6 ft); draught 8·5 m (27·9 ft)
Gun armament: one 76-mm (3-in) L/62 DP OTO-Melara Compact, and two 20-mm Phalanx close-in weapon system mountings
Missile armament: two quadruple launchers for eight RGM-84A Harpoon surface-to-surface missiles, and one octuple launcher for eight RIM-7 Sea Sparrow surface-to-air missiles
Torpedo armament: none
Anti-submarine armament: two triple Type 68 tube mountings for 12·75-in (324-mm) Mk 46 A/S torpedoes, one octuple launcher for 16 RUR-5A ASROC missiles, and helicopter-launched weapons (see below)
Aircraft: one Sikorsky SH-3 Sea King in a hangar aft
Electronics: one OPS-14B air-search radar, one OPS-18 surface-search radar, one FCS2 missile-control radar, one GFCS2 gun-control radar, one ECM suite, and one OQS-4 hull sonar
Propulsion: COGOG (COmbined Gas turbine Or Gas turbine) arrangement, with two Rolls-Royce Olympus TM3B gas turbines delivering 45,000 shp (33,555 kW) and two Rolls-Royce Tyne RM1C gas turbines delivering 10,680 shp (7,965 kW) to

two shafts
Performance: maximum speed 30 kts
Complement: 190

Class
1. Japan (5+4+3)

Name	No.	Builders	Laid down	Commissioned
HATSUYUKI	DD 122	Sumitomo	Mar 1979	Mar 1982
SHIRAYUKI	DD 123	Hitachi	Dec 1979	Feb 1983
MINEYUKI	DD 124	Mitsubishi	May 1981	Mar 1984
SAWAYUKI	DD 125	Ishikawajima Harima	Apr 1981	Feb 1984
HAMAYUKI	DD 126	Mitsui	Apr 1981	Jan 1984
—	DD 127	Ishikawajima Harima	Apr 1982	Jan 1985
—	DD 128	Sumitomo	Apr 1982	Mar 1985
—	DD 129	Hitachi	Oct 1983	1986
—	DD 130	Ishikawajima Harima	Oct 1983	1986

Remarks: The ships of the 'Hatsuyuki' class have very limited gun armament, but good anti-submarine armament plus anti-ship and anti-aircraft missiles and an effective sensor fit.

'Holland' class destroyer
Netherlands

Displacement: 2,215 tons standard and 2,765 tons full load
Dimensions: length 113·1m (371·1ft); beam 11·4m (37·5ft); draught 5·1m (16·8ft)
Gun armament: four 120-mm (4·7-in) L/50 DP in two twin mountings, and one 40-mm Bofors AA
Missile armament: none
Torpedo armament: none
Anti-submarine armament: two four-barrel Bofors 375-mm (14·76-in) rocket-launchers, and two depth-charge racks
Electronics: one Hollandse Signaalapparaten LW-03 air-search radar, one Hollandse Signaalapparaten DA-02 surface-search and target designation radar, one Hollandse Signaalapparaten ZW-01 surface-search radar, three Hollandse Signaalapparaten WM-45 fire-control system radars, and one Hollandse Signaal-apparaten hull-mounted sonar
Propulsion: four Babcock & Wilcox boilers supplying steam to two sets of Parsons/Werkspoor geared turbines delivering 33,555kW (45,000hp) to two shafts
Performance: speed 32kts; range 7,400km (4,600 miles) at 18kts
Complement: 247

Class
1. Peru (1)

Name	No.	Builders	Laid down	Com-missioned
GARCIA y GARCIA	DD 75	Rotterdamse Droogdok	Apr 1950	Dec 1954

'Hull' class destroyer
USA

Displacement: 2,800 to 3,000 tons standard and 3,960 to 4,200 tons full load
Dimensions: length 418ft (127·4m); beam 45ft (13·7m); draught 23ft (7·0m)
Gun armament: (DDs 945, 946 and 951) three 5-in (127-mm) L/54 DP in three Mk 42 single mountings, or (DDs 948 and 950, modified for improved anti-submarine capability) two 5-in (127-mm) L/54 DP in two Mk 42 single mountings
Missile armament: none
Torpedo armament: none
Anti-submarine armament: two triple Mk 32 tube mountings for 12·75-in (324-mm) Mk 46 A/S torpedoes, and (DDs 948 and 950) one octuple launcher for RUR-5A ASROC missiles
Electronics: one Raytheon/Sylvania SPS-10 surface-search radar, one Westinghouse SPS-37 or Lockheed SPS-40 air-search radar, one General Electric SPG-53A gun-control radar used in conjunction with the General Electric Mk 56 gun fire-control system, one General Electric SPG-53E gun-control radar used in conjunction with the Naval Weapons Laboratory Mk 68 gun fire-control system, one Sangamo SQS-23 bow-mounted long-range active sonar and (modified ASW ships) one EDO SQS-35 variable-depth sonar used in conjunction with the Mk 114 A/S weapon-control system, one Mk 5 target-designation system, one OE-82 satellite communications antenna, one SRR-1 satellite communications receiver, one WSC-3 satellite communications transceiver, and (unmodified ships) extensive electronic warfare systems
Propulsion: four Babcock & Wilcox boilers supplying steam to two sets of General Electric geared turbines delivering 70,000 shp (52,200kW) to two shafts
Performance: maximum speed 33kts; range 5,200 miles (8,370km) at 20kts
Complement: 17+275, or (A/S modified vessels) 17+287

Class
1. USA (5)

Name	No.	Builders	Launched	Com-missioned
HULL	DD 945	Bath Iron Works	Aug 1957	July 1958
EDSON	DD 946	Bath Iron Works	Jan 1958	Nov 1958
TURNER JOY	DD 051	Puget Sound Bridge	May 1958	Aug 1959
MORTON	DD 948	Ingalls Shipbuilding	May 1958	May 1959
RICHARD S. EDWARDS	DD 948	Puget Sound Bridge	May 1958	Feb 1959

*The **Hull (DD 945)** was used as trials ship for the 8-in (203-mm) Major Caliber Light Weight Gun, mounted in place of the forward 5-in (127-mm) mounting. The trials confirmed the overall value of the MCLWG, especially for enhanced shore bombardment capability, but the original 5-in (127-mm) mounting was replaced in February 1979 with the cancellation of the MCLWG programme for financial reasons.*

Remarks: The 'Hull' class is almost identical with the 'Forrest Sherman' class, but was designated separately because of its modified bow. Together with the 'Forrest Sherman' class, these ships were the first US warships to have more firepower aft than forward; but whereas the earlier units of the 'Forrest Sherman' class has the Mk 56 gun fire-control system forward and the Mk 86 system aft, this arrangement was reversed in all ships from DD 933 onwards, including all units of the 'Hull' class. Again in common with units of the 'Forrest Sherman' class, some of the 'Hull' class ships were modified between 1967 and 1971 as anti-submarine destroyers: an octuple ASROC launcher was fitted in place of the 5-in (127-mm) gun in X position, two triple Mk 32 tube mountings for self-defence anti-submarine torpedoes were located forward of the bridge structure, the deckhouse aft of the second funnel was increased in width to the full beam of the ship, and variable-depth sonar was added at the stern. It has been planned so to modify the whole class, but cost considerations meant that only DDs 948 and 950 were modified. With the exception of the *Edson* (DD 946), which is used for engine-room training with the Naval Reserve Force, all destroyers of the 'Hull' class have been placed in reserve because of increasing problems with their powerplants.

'Hull (Converted)' class guided-missile destroyer
USA

Displacement: 2,850 tons standard and 4,150 tons full load
Dimensions: length 418·4ft (127·5m); beam 44ft (13·4m); draught 20ft 20ft (6·1m)
Gun armament: one 5-in (127-mm) L/54 DP in a Mk 42 single mounting
Missile armament: one Mk 13 single launcher for 40 RIM-24 Tartar surface-to-air missiles
Torpedo armament: none
Anti-submarine armament: one triple Mk 32 tube mountings for 12·75-in (324-mm) Mk 46 A/S torpedoes, and one octuple launcher for RUR-5A ASROC missiles
Electronics: one ITT/Gilfillan SPS-48 3D air-search radar, one Raytheon/Sylvania SPS-10 surface-search radar, one Westinghouse SPS-37 air-search radar, one SPG-51C missile-control radar used in conjunction with the General Electric Mk 73 missile fire-control system one SPG-53B gun-control radar used in conjunction with the Naval Weapons Laboratory Mk 68 gun fire-control system, one Mk 4 weapon-control system, one Sanagamo SQS-23 hull-mounted long-range active sonar used in conjunction with the Mk 114 A/S fire-control system, Naval Tctical Data System, URN-20 TACAN, one OE-82 satellite communications antenna, SRR-1 satellite communications receiver, and SWC-3 satellite communications transceiver
Propulsion: four Babcock & Wilcox boilers supplying steam to two sets of General Electric geared turbines delivering 70,00shp (52,200kW) to two shafts
Performance: maximum speed 31kts; range 5,200 miles (8,370km) at20kts
Complement: 25+339

Class
1. USA (2)

Name	No.	Builders	Launched	Com-missioned
PARSONS	DDG 33	Ingalls Shipbuilding	Aug 1958	Oct 1959
SOMERS	DDG 34	Bath Iron Works	May 1958	Apr 1959

Remarks: Like the two 'Forrest Sherman (Converted)' class destroyers, the two 'Hull (Converted)' class guided-missile destroyers were produced between 1965 and 1968 at navy yards on the west coast of the USA. (The 'Forrest Sherman' class ships were converted on the east coast.) The transformation was radical, and involved the removal of all armament but the forward 5-in (127-mm) gun before the conversion proper could begin. This involved the addition of two lattice masts for the considerably increased radar fit and, as originally planned, the addition aft of one Mk 13 single launcher for Tartar launcher and facilities for DASH anti-submarine drone helicopters to complement the two triple Mk 32 anti-submarine tube mountings fitted forward of the bridge. The DASH concept lost favour with the US Navy, however, and the ships were completed with an octuple ASROC launcher instead of DASH facilities. Both ships were placed in reserve during 1982 because of the same powerplant problems as the rest of the 'Forrest Sherman' and 'Hull' force, but while the *Somers* (DDG 34) is to be kept in reserve for the Pacific Fleet, the *Parsons* (DDG 33) is to be scrapped.

'Impavido' class guided-missile destroyer

Italy

Displacement: 3,200 tons standard and 3,990 tons full load
Dimensions: length 131·3m (429·5ft); beam 13·6m (44·7ft); draught 4·5m (14·8ft)
Gun armament: two 5-in (127-mm) L/38 DP in one Mk 38 twin mounting, and four 76-mm (3-in) L/62 DP in single mountings
Missile armament: one Mk 13 single launcher for 40 RIM-66 Standard surface-to-air missiles
Torpedo armament: none
Anti-submarine armament: two triple Mk 32 tube mountings for 12·75-in (324-mm) Mk 46 A/S torpedoes
Aircraft: provision for a light helicopter on the platform aft

Electronics: one RCA SPS-12 air-search radar, one Hughes SPS-52B 3D air-search radar, one SMA SPQ 2 surface-search radar, two SPG-51B missile-control radars used in conjunction with two Raytheon Mk 73 missile fire-control systems, three Selenia Orion RTN 10X gun-control radars used in conjunction with the three ELSAG Argo NA10 gun fire-control systems, one SQS-23 hull-mounted sonar, one ESM suite and two Breda SCLAR 20-barrel chaff launcher systems
Propulsion: four Foster-Wheeler boilers supplying steam to two sets of Tosi geared turbines delivering 52,200kW (70,000shp) to two shafts
Performance: maximum speed 33kts; range 6,100km (3,790 miles) at 20kts or 2,775km (1,725 miles) at 30kts
Complement: 23+317

Class

| 1. Italy (2) | | | | Com- |
Name	No.	Builders	Laid down	missioned
IMPAVIDO	D 570	Cantieri Navali Riuniti	June 1957	Nov 1963
INTREPIDO	D 571	Italcantieri	May 1959	July 1964

Remarks: Precursors to the 'Audace' class, the two 'Impavido' class guided-missile destroyers are capable though limited anti-aircraft ships, but lack adequate anti-submarine capability as they have no embarked helicopter, or even provision for such a helicopter.

An indication of the age of the Impavido (D 570) is provided by her use of an American Mk 38 twin 5-in (127-mm) gun mounting.

'Iroquois' class destroyer

Canada

Displacement: 3,550 tons standard and 4,700 tons full load
Dimensions: length 426ft (129·8m); beam 50ft (15·2m); draught 15·5ft (4·7m)
Gun armament: one 5-in (127-mm) L/54 DP OTO-Melara Compact
Missile armament: two Raytheon quadruple launchers for 32 RIM-7 Sea Sparrow surface-to-air missiles
Torpedo armament: none
Anti-submarine armament: two triple Mk 32 tube mountings for 12·75-in (324-mm) Mk 46 torpedoes, one Mk NG 10 Limbo mortar, and helicopter-launched weapons (see below)
Aircraft: two Sikorsky CH-124 Sea King helicopters in a hangar amidships
Electronics: one SMA SPQ 2D surface-search and navigation radar, one SPS-501 long-range warning radar with Hollandse Signaalapparaten LW-03 antenna, two Hollandse Signaalapparaten WM-22 search and fire-control radar systems, one Canadian Westinghouse SQS-505 hull-mounted medium-range search and attack sonar, one Canadian Westinghouse SQS-505 variable-depth sonar, one Canadian Westinghouse SQS-501 bottomed-target classification sonar, one Litton CCS 280 automated data system, and URN-20 TACAN
Propulsion: COGOG (COmbined Gas turbine Or Gas turbine) arrangement, with two Pratt & Whitney FT4A2 gas turbines delivering 50,000shp (37,285kW) or two Pratt & Whitney FT12AH3 gas turbines delivering 7,400shp (5,520kW) to two shafts
Performance: maximum speed 29+ kts on main engines or 18kts on cruising engines; range 5,200 miles (8,370km) at 20kts
Complement: 20+225, plus an air unit of 7+33

Class

| 1. Canada (4) | | | | Com- |
Name	No.	Builders	Laid down	missioned
IROQUOIS	280	Marine Industries Ltd	Jan 1969	July 1972
HURON	281	Marine Industries Ltd	Jan 1969	Dec 1972
ATHABASKAN	282	Davies S.B. Co	June 1969	Nov 1972
ALGONQUIN	283	Davies S.B. Co	Sep 1969	Sep 1973

Features of the 'Iroquois' class well displayed by the Huron (281) are the large midships hangar for two Sikorsky CH-124 Sea King helicopters (with one such anti-submarine aircraft on the platform), the angled-out twin funnels, the closely grouped antennae for the radar systems (mostly of Dutch and Italian origins), and the 127-mm (5-in) OTO-Melara Compact main gun.

Remarks: Until the arrival of a new destroyer class (to permit retirement of the 'St Laurent' class frigates), the four 'Iroquois' or 'DD 280' class ships are the only destroyers in Canadian service, and are designed primarily for the anti-submarine role with helicopters as the basic weapon/sensor system in concert with limited shipborne weapons and good shipborne sensors. The helicopters are flown in conjunction with haul-down and deck-control systems to maximize the possibility of continued operations even under adverse weather conditions. Other features of the design are pre-wetting facility as part of the defence against nuclear fall-out and chemical weapons, an enclosed citadel, and retractable quadruple launchers (forward part of the superstructure) for Sea Sparrow surface-to-air point-defence missiles. The SQS-505 variable-depth sonar, with an 18-ft (5·5-m) towed body, has proved successful, but the improved capability of towed-array sonars are now clear and such a system has been specified for future Canadian destroyers.

'Japanese' class guided-missile destroyer

Japan

Displacement: 4,500 tons
Dimensions: length 150·0m (492·1ft); beam 16·4m (53·8ft); draught 4·7m (15·4ft)
Gun armament: two 5-in (127-mm) L/54 DP in two Mk 42 single mountings, and two 20-mm CIWS mountings
Missile armament: two quadruple container-launchers for eight RGM-84A Harpoon anti-ship missiles, and one Mk 13 single launcher for RIM-66 Standard surface-to-air missiles
Torpedo armament: none
Anti-submarine armament: one Mk 16 octuple launcher for RUR-5A ASROC missiles, and two triple Type 68 tube mountings for 12·75-in (324-mm) Mk 46 anti-submarine torpedoes
Aircraft: none
Electronics: one OPS-12 3D radar, one OPS-11 air-search radar, one OPS-28

surface-search radar, computer-assisted data-processing system, electronic warfare systems, and sonar
Propulsion: COGAG (COmbined Gas turbine And Gas turbine) arrangement, with two Rolls-Royce Olympus TM3B and two Rolls-Royce Spey SM1A gas turbines delivering ?shp (?kW) to two shafts
Performance: maximum speed 30+ kts

Class

| 1. Japan (0+2) | | | | Com- |
Name	No.	Builders	Laid down	missioned
—	DD 171	Mitsubishi	1983	1986
—	DD 172	Mitsubishi	1984	1988

Remarks: This new class provides more evidence of the Japanese Maritime Self-Defense Force's shift towards a more balanced type of ship.

'Kanin' class guided-missile destroyer

USSR

Displacement: 3,700 tons standard and 4,700 tons full load
Dimensions: length 139·0m (455·9ft); beam 14·7m (48·2ft); draught 5·0m (16·4ft)
Gun armament: eight 57-mm L/70 AA in two quadruple mountings, and eight 30-mm AA in four twin mountings
Missile armament: one twin launcher for 22 SA-N-1 'Goa' surface-to-air missiles
Torpedo armament: two quintuple 533-mm (21-in) AS/ASW tube mountings
Anti-submarine armament: three RBU 6000 12-barrel rocket-launchers
Aircraft: provision for one helicopter on a platform aft
Electronics: one 'Head Net-C' 3D radar, two 'Don Kay' navigation radars, one 'Peel Group' SAM-control radar, one 'Hawk Screech' 57-mm gun-control radar, two 'Drum Tilt' 30-mm gun-control radars, and one hull-mounted sonar
Propulsion: four boilers supplying steam to two sets of geared turbines delivering 59,655 kW (80,000 shp) to two shafts

Performance: maximum speed 34 kts; range 8,350 km (5,190 miles) at 16 kts or 2,050 km (1,275 miles) at 33 kts
Complement: 350
Class
1. USSR (8)

Name	Converting yard	Commissioned
BOYKY	Zhdanov Yard (five ships)	Zhdanov conversions 1968-72
DERZKY	and Pacific (three ships)	Pacific conversions 1974-78
GNEVNY		
GORDY		
GREMYASHCHY		
UPORNY		
ZHGUCHY		
ZORKY		

Remarks: The 'Kanin' class anti-aircraft destroyers were produced by a programme of modification from eight 'Krupny' class anti-ship destroyers, the alterations including the deletion of the two SS-N-1 anti-ship missile launchers and their replacement by a single twin launcher (aft) and an additional RBU 6000 anti-submarine rocket-launcher (foredeck), the enlargement of the helicopter platform, a different and longer bow (probably for a new bow-mounted sonar), the halving of the 57-mm armament, the enlarging of the bridge structure, the addition of new radars and, later, the addition of four 30-mm twin AA mountings.

A 'Kanin' class guided-missile destroyer shadows the British carrier Hermes *during 1973. Visible to starboard of the Soviet ship's after funnel are two of the four 30-mm AA mountings added for close-range air defence.*

'Kashin' class guided-missile destroyer

USSR

Displacement: 3,750 tons standard and 4,500 tons full load
Dimensions: length 143·3m (470·7ft); beam 15·8m (51·8ft); draught 4·7m (15·4ft)
Gun armament: four 76-mm (3-in) L/60 DP in two twin mountings
Missile armament: two twin launchers for 32 SA-N-1 'Goa' surface-to-air missiles
Torpedo armament: one quintuple 533-mm (21-in) AS/ASW tube mounting
Anti-submarine armament: two RBU 6000 12-barrel rocket-launchers, and two RBU 1000 six-barrel rocket-launchers
Electronics: either one 'Head Net-C' 3D radar and one 'Big Net' air-search radar or two 'Head Net-A' air-search radars, two 'Peel Group' missile-control radars, two 'Owl Screech' gun-control radars, two 'Don' navigation radars, 'High Pole-B' IFF, two 'Watch Dog' ECM systems, and hull-mounted sonar
Propulsion: four gas turbines delivering 70,095 kW (94,000 hp) to two shafts
Performance: maximum speed 35 kts; range 8,350 km (5,190 miles) at 18 kts or 2,600 km (1,615 miles) at 34 kts

Complement: 280
Class
1. USSR (13)

Name	Builders
KOMSOMOLETS UKRAINY	Nikolayev North
KRASNY-KAVKAZ	Nikolayev North
KRASNY-KRIM	Nikolayev North
OBRAZTSOVY	Zhdanov Yard
ODARENNY	Zhdanov Yard
PROVORNY	Nikolayev North
RESHITELNY	Nikolayev North
SKORY	Nikolayev North
SMETLIVY	Nikolayev North
SOOBRAZITELNY	Nikolayev North
SPOSOBNY	Nikolayev North
STEREGUSHCHY	Zhdanov Yard
STROGY	Nikolayev North

Remarks: The 'Kashin' class of anti-aircraft guided-missile destroyers was the world's first major warship design with all-gas turbine propulsion, and was possibly intended for AA escort of the contemporary 'Kynda' class anti-ship cruisers. The 'Kashin (Modified)' class programme was started in 1972 to provide some of the ships with improved anti-ship and anti-submarine capabilities by the lengthening of the hull to make possible the accommodation of SS-N-2C anti-ship missiles, a helicopter platform and variable-depth sonar. The Indian 'Kashin II' class is a further development of the 'Kashin (Modified)' class.

Photographed in 1982, the 'Kashin' class destroyer Obraztsovy *shows off the type's four funnels, separated by masts and the quintuple torpedo tube.*

'Kashin (Modified)' class guided-missile destroyer

USSR

Displacement: 3,950 tons standard and 4,750 tons full load
Dimensions: length 146·5m (480·6ft); beam 15·8m (51·8ft); draught 4·7m (15·4ft)
Gun armament: four 76-mm (3-in) L/60 DP in two twin mountings, and four 30-mm AA 'Gatling' mountings
Missile armament: two twin launchers for 32 SA-N-1 'Goa' surface-to-air missiles, and four container-launchers for four SS-N-2C 'Styx' surface-to-surface missiles
Torpedo armament: one quintuple 533-mm (21-in) AS/ASW tube mounting
Anti-submarine armament: two RBU 6000 12-barrel rocket-launchers, and helicopter-launched weapons (see below)
Aircraft: provision for one Kamov Ka-25 'Hormone' helicopter on a platform aft
Electronics: either one 'Head Net-C' 3D radar and one 'Big Net' air-search radar or two 'Head Net-A' air-search radars, two 'Peel Group' SAM-control radars, two

'Owl Screech' main armament gun-control radars, two 'Bass Tilt' AA gun-control radars, two 'Don Kay' or 'Don 2' navigation radars, one hull-mounted sonar, one variable-depth sonar, two ECM systems, and 'High Pole-B' IFF
Propulsion: four gas turbines delivering 70,095 kW (94,000 hp) to two shafts
Performance: maximum speed 35 kts; range 8,350 km (5,190 miles) at 18 kts or 2,600 km (1,615 miles) at 34 kts
Complement: 300
Class
1. USSR (6)

Name	Builders
OGNEVOY	Zhdanov Yard
SDERZHANNY	Nikolayev North
SLAVNY	Zhdanov Yard
SMELY	Nikolayev North
SMYSHLENNY	Nikolayev North
STROYNY	Nikolayev North

'Kashin II' class guided-missile destroyer
USSR

Displacement: 3,950 tons standard and 4,950 tons full load

Dimensions: length 146·5m (480·5ft); beam 15·8m (51·8ft); draught 4·8m (15·7ft)

Gun armament: two 76-mm (3-in) L/60 in one twin mounting, and eight 30-mm L/65 AA in four twin mountings

Missile armament: two twin launchers for 44 SA-N-1 'Goa' surface-to-air missiles, and four container-launchers for four SS-N-2C 'Styx' surface-to-surface missiles

Torpedo armament: one quintuple 533-mm (21-in) AS/ASW tube mounting

Anti-submarine armament: two RBU 6000 12-barrel rocket-launchers, and helicopter-launched weapons (see below)

Aircraft: provision for one Kamov Ka-25 'Hormone' helicopter on a platform aft

Electronics: one 'Head Net-C' 3D radar, one 'Big Net' air search radar, two 'Peel Group' SAM-control radars, one 'Owl Screech' main armament gun-control radar, two 'Drum Tilt' AA gun-control radars, two 'Don Kay' navigation radars, two 'High Pole-B' IFFs, hull-mounted sonar, and variable-depth sonar

Propulsion: four gas turbines delivering 71,585kW (96,000shp) to two shafts

Performance: maximum speed 35kts; range 8,350km (5,190 miles) at 18kts or 1,675km (1,040 miles) at 35kts

Complement: 320

Class
1. India (3+3)

Name	No.	Builders	Commissioned
RAJPUT	D 51	Nikolayev	1980
RANA	D 52	Nikolayev	1982
RANJIT	D 53	Nikolayev	1983

'Kidd' class guided-missile destroyer
USA

Displacement: 6,210 tons light and 9,200 tons full load

Dimensions: length 563ft (171·6m); beam 55ft (16·8m); draught 30ft (9·1m) to sonar dome

Gun armament: two 5-in (127-mm) L/54 DP in two Mk 45 single mountings, and two 20-mm Phalanx Mk 15 close-in weapon system mountings

Missile armament: two quadruple container-launchers for eight RGM-84A Harpoon surface-to-surface missiles, and two Mk 26 twin launchers for 52 RIM-67A Standard-ER surface-to-air missiles

Torpedo armament: none

Anti-submarine armament: two triple Mk 32 tube mountings for 12·75-in (324-mm) Mk 46 A/S torpedoes, 16 RUR-5A ASROC missiles (fired from the Mk 26 launchers), and helicopter-launched weapons (see below)

Aircraft: two Kaman SH-2F Seasprite helicopters in a hangar amidships

Electronics: one ITT/Gilfillan SPS-48C 3D radar, one Westinghouse SPS-55 surface-search and navigation radar, two Raytheon SPG-51D missile-control radars used in conjunction with two Mk 74 missile fire-control systems, one Lockheed SPG-60 search and tracking radar and one Lockheed SPQ-9 track-while-scan radar used in conjunction with two Lockheed Mk 86 gun fire-control systems, one SQS-53A hull-mounted sonar and one SQR-19 passive tactical towed-array sonar used in conjunction with the Singer Mk 116 A/S fire-control system, Automatic Data Action System, one Raytheon SLQ-32(V)2 ESM suite, and two Mk 36 Super Chaffroc rapid-blooming overhead chaff launchers

Propulsion: four General Electric LM 2500 gas turbines delivering 80,000shp (59,655kW) to two shafts

Performance: maximum speed 33kts; range 9,200 miles (14,805km) at 17kts or 3,800 miles (6,115km) at 30kts

Complement: 20+318

Class
1. USA (4)

Name	No.	Builders	Laid down	Commissioned
KIDD	DDG 993	Ingalls Shipbuilding	June 1978	May 1981
CALLAGHAN	DDG 994	Ingalls Shipbuilding	Oct 1978	Aug 1981
SCOTT	DDG 995	Ingalls Shipbuilding	Feb 1979	Oct 1981
CHANDLER	DDG 996	Ingalls Shipbuilding	May 1979	Mar 1982

Remarks: Though rated as guided-missile destroyers, the four ships of the 'Kidd' class are more akin to 'double-ended' guided-missile cruisers in terms of performance, capability and size. There is little doubt that they are the most powerful ships of their type in the world, combining excellent anti-ship, anti-submarine and anti-aircraft capabilities (both sensors and weapons) in a design of first-class habitability. It is interesting to note that the basic design is that of the 'Spruance' class, and it was at first intended to build the ASW-optimized 'Spruance' class ships to this standard, though financial considerations intervened to alter the scheme. These four units were laid down for Iran, but taken over for the US Navy after the emergence of the present regime in Iran. The class is unofficially known as the 'Ayatollah' class.

The Chandler (DDG 996) is the last unit of the 'Kidd' class.

'Kildin' class guided-missile destroyer
USSR

Displacement: 3,000 tons standard and 3,600 tons full load

Dimensions: length 126·5m (414·9ft); beam 13·0m (42·6ft); draught 4·9m (16·1ft)

Gun armament: 16 57-mm L/70 AA in four quadruple mountings

Missile armament: one launcher for six SS-N-1 'Scrubber' surface-to-surface missiles

Torpedo armament: two twin 533-mm (21-in) AS/ASW tube mountings

Anti-submarine armament: two RBU 2500 16-barrel rocket-launchers

Electronics: three 'Slim Net' surface-search radars, one 'Flat Spin' air-search radar, one 'Top Bow' missile-control radar, two 'Hawk Screech' gun-control radars, one 'Don-2' navigation radar, one 'Square Head' IFF, one 'High Pole-A' IFF, and one hull-mounted sonar

Propulsion: four boilers supplying steam to two sets of geared turbines delivering 53,690kW (72,000shp) to two shafts

Performance: maximum speed 35kts; range 8,350km (5,190 miles) at 16kts or 1,850km (1,150 miles) at 34kts

Complement: 300

Class
1. USSR (1)

Name	Builders
NEUDERZHIMY	Komsomolsk

Remarks: Based on the hull of the 'Kotlin' class destroyer, the 'Kildin' class has an SS-N-1 launcher in place of the after 130-mm (5·12-in) gun mounting.

'Kildin (Modified)' class guided-missile destroyer

USSR

Displacement: 3,000 tons standard and 3,600 tons full load
Dimensions: length 126·5m (414·9ft); beam 13·0m (42·6ft); draught 4·9m (16·1ft)
Gun armament: four 76-mm (3-in) L/60 DP in two twin mountings, and 16 57-mm L/70 AA in four quadruple mountings
Missile armament: four container-launchers for SS-N-2C 'Styx' surface-to-surface missiles
Torpedo armament: two twin 533-mm (21-in) AS/ASW tube mountings
Anti-submarine armament: two RBU 2500 16-barrel rocket-launchers
Electronics: one 'Head Net-C' 3D radar ('Strut Pair' air-search radar in *Bedovy*), one 'Owl Screech' main armament control radar, two 'Hawk Screech' AA gun-control radars, one 'Don-2' navigation radar, one 'Square Head' IFF, one 'High Pole-A' IFF, and one hull-mounted sonar

Propulsion: four boilers supplying steam to two sets of geared turbines delivering 53,690kW (72,000shp) to two shafts
Fuel: oil
Performance: maximum speed 35kts; range 8,350km (5,190 miles) at 16kts or 1,850km (1,150 miles) at 34kts
Complement: 300

Class
1. USSR (3)

Name	Builders
BEDOVY	Nikolayev
NEULOVIMY	Leningrad
PROZORLIVY	Nikolayev

'Kotlin' class destroyer

USSR

Displacement: 2,850 tons standard and 3,600 tons full load
Dimensions: length 127·5m (418·2ft); beam 12·9m (42·3ft); draught 4·6m (15·1ft)
Gun armament: four 130-mm (5·1-in) L/58 DP in two twin mountings, and 16 45-mm L/85 in four quadruple mountings
Missile armament: none
Torpedo armament: two quintuple 533-mm (21-in) tube mountings
Anti-submarine armament: two RBU 2500 16-barrel rocket-launchers, and six depth-charge throwers (except in *Svetly*)
Mines: 80
Aircraft: provision for one Kamov Ka-25 'Hormone' helicopter (*Svetly* only)
Electronics: one 'Slim Net' surface-search radar, one 'Sun Visor' main armament fire-control radar, two 'Egg Cup' main armament control radars, two 'Hawk Screech' AA gun-control radars, one 'Post Lamp' or 'Top Bow' fire-control radar, two 'Don' or *Neptun* navigation radars, 'High Pole-A' IFF, 'Square Head' IFF, and hull-mounted sonar

Propulsion: four boilers supplying steam to two sets of geared turbines delivering 53,690kW (72,000shp) to two shafts
Performance: maximum speed 36kts; range 8,350km (5,190 miles) at 15kts or 2,050km (1,275 miles) at 35kts
Complement: 285
Class
1. USSR (6)
Name
DALNEVOSTOCHNY KOMSOMOLETS
SPLESHNY
SPOKOINY
SVETLY
VESKY
VLIYATELNY

Remarks: Now obsolete, the 'Kotlin' class gun destroyers were developed from the 'Tallinn' class, and 32 were laid down in the 1950s.

'Kotlin (Modified)' class destroyer

USSR

Displacement: 2,850 tons standard and 3,600 tons full load
Dimensions: length 127·5m (418·2ft); beam 12·9m (42·3ft); draught 4·6m (15·1ft)
Gun armament: four 130-mm (5·1-in) L/58 DP in two twin mountings, eight 45-mm L/85 AA in two quadruple mountings, and four or eight 25-mm AA in two or four twin mountings
Missile armament: none
Torpedo armament: one quintuple 533-mm (21-in) tube mounting
Anti-submarine armament: two RBU 2500 16-barrel rocket-launchers, two RBU 600 six-barrel rocket-launchers, and six depth-charge throwers
Mines: 80
Electronics: one 'Slim Net' surface-search radar, one 'Sun Visor' main armament fire-control radar, two 'Egg Cup' main armament control radars, two 'Hawk Screech' AA gun-control radars, one 'Post Lamp' or 'Top Bow' fire-control radar, two 'Don' or *Neptun* navigation radars, 'High Pole-A' IFF, 'Square Head' IFF, and hull-mounted sonar
Propulsion: four boilers supplying steam to two sets of geared turbines delivering 53,690kW (72,000shp) to two shafts
Performance: maximum speed 36kts; range 8,350km (5,190 miles) at 15kts or 2,050km (1,275 miles) at 35kts
Complement: 285

Class
1. USSR (12)
Name
BLAGORODNY
BLESTYASHCHY
BURLIVY
BYVALY
MOSKOVSKY KOMSOMOLETS
NAPORISTY
PLAMENNY
SVEDUSHCHY
VDOKHNOVENNY
VOZMUSHCHENNY
VYDERZHANNY
VYZYVAYUSHCHY

Remarks: Modified in or shortly after 1962, these 12 ships have an extra deckhouse in place of the after quintuple torpedo tube mounting, two RBU 600 rocket-launchers aft, and two or four 25-mm twin AA mountings instead of two of the four 45-mm mountings. Two of these ships (and one 'Kotlin') are now in reserve.

'Luda' class guided-missile destroyer

China

Displacement: 3,250 tons standard and 3,750 tons full load
Dimensions: length 131·0m (429·8ft); beam 13·7m (45ft); draught 4·6m (15ft)
Gun armament: four 130-mm (5·1-in) L/50 in two twin mountings, eight 37-mm L/63 AA in four twin mountings, and 16 25-mm AA in eight twin mountings
Missile armament: two triple launchers for six SS-N-2C 'Styx' surface-to-surface missiles
Torpedo armament: none
Anti-submarine armament: two FQF 2500 A/S rocket-launchers, two or four depth-charge throwers, and two depth-charge racks
Electronics: one 'Cross Slot' air-search radar, 'Wasp Head' and 'Post Lamp' gun fire-control radars in nos 105-109 and 131-132, or 'Sun Visor-B' and 'Rice Lamp' gun fire-control radars (others), 'Square Tie' missile-control radar, *Neptun* navigation radar, one 'Square Head' IFF, and sonar
Propulsion: ? boilers supplying steam to two sets of geared turbines delivering 53,690kW (72,000shp) to two shafts

Performance: maximum speed 36kts; range 5,925km (3,680 miles) at 18kts
Complement: 215
Class
1. China (14+2)

Name	No.	Builders	Commissioned
—	105	Luda	1971
—	106	Luda	1972
—	107	Luda	1972
—	108	Luda	1973
—	109	Luda	1974
—	110	Luda	
—	111	Luda	—
—	131	Guangzhou	1974
—	132	Guangzhou	1974
—	161	Luda	1979
—	162	Guangzhou	1980
—	163	—	1980
—	164	—	1980
—	165	—	1981

'Meko 360' class guided-missile destroyer

West Germany/Nigeria

Displacement: 3,630 tons full load
Dimensions: length 125·6m (412ft); beam 15·0m (49·2ft); draught 4·3m (14·1ft)
Gun armament: one 127-mm (5-in) L/54 DP OTO-Melara Compact, and eight 40-mm Breda L/70 AA in four twin mountings
Missile armament: two quadruple container-launchers for eight Otomat surface-to-surface missiles, and one octuple launcher for 24 Aspide surface-to-air missiles
Torpedo armament: none
Anti-submarine armament: two triple Plessey tube mountings for 324-mm (12·75-in) A 244S A/S torpedoes, and helicopter-launched weapons (see below)
Aircraft: one helicopter in a hangar aft
Electronics: one Plessey AWS 5 surface-search radar, one Decca 1226 navigation radar, one Hollandse Signaalapparaten WM-25/STIR fire-control radar system, one Krupp-Atlas KAE 80 hull-mounted sonar, and two 105-mm (4·13-in) Breda SCLAR launchers
Propulsion: CODOG (COmbined Diesel Or Gas turbine) arrangement, with two

MTU 20V956 TB92 diesels delivering 7,455kW (10,000hp) and two Rolls-Royce Olympus TM3B gas turbines delivering 56,000hp (41,760kW) to two shafts
Fuel: diesel oil and kerosene
Performance: maximum speed 30·5kts on gas turbines; range 12,000km (7,455 miles) at cruising speed
Complement: 200

Class

1. Argentina (4)				Com-
Name	No.	Builders	Laid down	missioned
ALMIRANTE BROWN	D 10	Blohm und Voss	Sep 1980	1982
LA ARGENTINA	D 11	Blohm und Voss	Mar 1981	1983
HEROINA	D 12	Blohm und Voss	Aug 1981	1983
SARANDI	D 13	Blohm und Voss	Feb 1982	1984

2. Nigeria (1)				Com-
Name	No.	Builders	Laid down	missioned
ARADU	F 89	Blohm und Voss	Dec 1978	Sep 1981

Remarks: The 'Meko 360' class is the first fully modular design for a major warship in the world, the modular design of the armament, sensors and other key systems making replacement and updating a relatively simple matter of component replacement. The four Argentine ships differ somewhat from the earlier Nigerian ship, having a gas turbine propulsion system (two Rolls-Royce Olympus TM1Bs and two Rolls-Royce Tyne RM1Cs), provision for two Westland Lynx helicopters, eight MM.40 Exocet anti-ship missiles instead of Otomats, ILAS-3 rather than Plessey anti-submarine tube mountings, and a sensor fit that includes Hollandse Signaalapparaten DA-08A air- and surface-search radar, ZW-06 navigation radar, WM-25/STIR fire-control radars and Krupp-Atlas 80 hull-mounted sonar.

The Nigerian Aradu (F 89) shows off her neat lines, with the missiles grouped aft and four well-disposed 76-mm (3-in) guns for AA and anti-FAC use.

'Minegumo' class destroyer
Japan

The Minegumo (DD 116) is lead ship of her three-ship class.

Displacement: 2,050 tons standard and 2,150 tons full load
Dimensions: length 114·9m (377ft); beam 11·8m (38·7ft); draught 4·0m (13·1ft)
Gun armament: four 3-in (76-mm) L/50 DP in two Mk 33 twin mountings (DDs 116 and 117), or two 3-in (76-mm) L/50 DP in one Mk 33 twin mounting and one 76-mm (3-in) L/62 DP OTO-Melara Compact (DD 118)

Missile armament: none
Torpedo armament: none
Anti-submarine armament: two triple Type 68 tube mountings for 12·75in (324-mm) Mk 44/46 A/S torpedoes, one Mk 16 octuple launcher for RUR-5A ASROC missiles, and one Bofors Type 71 four-barrel rocket-launcher
Electronics: one OPS-11 air-search radar, one OPS-17 surface-search radar, two Mk 35 gun-control radars used in conjunction with Mk 56 and Mk 63 gun fire-control systems (DDs 116 and 117) or Type 2 gun fire-control system (DD 118), one OQS-3 hull-mounted sonar, and (DD 118 only) one SQS-35(J) variable-depth sonar
Propulsion: six Mitsubishi diesels delivering 19,760kW (26,500bhp) to two shafts
Performance: maximum speed 27kts; range 12,975km (8,065 miles) at 20kts
Complement: 210
Class

1. Japan (3)				Com-
Name	No.	Builders	Laid down	missioned
MINEGUMO	DD 116	Mitsui	Mar 1967	Aug 1968
NATSUGUMO	DD 117	Uraga	June 1967	Apr 1969
MURAKUMO	DD 118	Maizuru	Oct 1968	Aug 1970

Remarks: The 'Minegumo' class was designed to the same basic pattern as the 'Yamagumo' class with provision for DASH drone helicopters in place of the octuple ASROC launcher, which has now been fitted with the failure of DASH.

'Murasame' class destroyer
Japan

Displacement: 1,800 tons standard and 2,500 tons full load
Dimensions: length 108·0m (354·3ft); beam 11·0m (36ft); draught 3·7m (12·2ft)
Gun armament: three 5-in (127-mm) L/54 DP in three Mk 39 single mountings, and four 3-in (76-mm) L/50 DP in two Mk 33 twin mountings
Missile armament: none
Torpedo armament: none
Anti-submarine armament: two Mk 4 torpedo-launchers (DD 108) or two triple Type 68 tube mountings for 12·75-in (324-mm) Mk 44 A/S torpedoes (DDs 107 and 109), one Hedgehog rocket-launcher, and (DD 108 only) one Y-gun Mk 1 depth-charge projector and one depth-charge rack
Electronics: one OPS-1 air-search radar, one OPS-15 surface-search radar, Mk 34 gun-control radar used in conjunction with Mk 57 and Mk 63 gun fire-control systems, one Sangamo SQS-29 hull-mounted active sonar, and (DD 109 only) one OQA-1 variable-depth sonar
Propulsion: two boilers (Mitsubishi/Combustion Engineering in DD 107, and Ishikawajima/Foster-Wheeler in DDs 108 and 109) supplying steam to two sets of geared turbines (Mitsubishi in DD 107, and Ishikawajima in DDs 108 and 109)

delivering 22,370kW (30,000shp) to two shafts
Performance: maximum speed 30kts; range 11,125km (6,915 miles) at 18kts
Complement: 250
Class

1. Japan (3)				Com-
Name	No.	Builders	Laid down	missioned
MURASAME	DD 107	Mitsubishi	Dec 1957	Feb 1959
YUDACHI	DD 108	Ishikawajima	Dec 1957	Mar 1959
HARUSAME	DD 109	Uraga	June 1958	Dec 1959

'Perth' class guided-missile destroyer

USA/Australia

Displacement: 3,370 tons standard and 4,620 tons full load
Dimensions: length 440·8 ft (134·3 m); beam 47·1 ft (14·3 m); draught 20·1 ft (6·1 m)
Gun armament: two 5-in (127-mm) L/54 DP in two Mk 42 single mountings
Missile armament: one Mk 13 single launcher for 40 RIM-66 Standard SAMs.
Torpedo armament: none
Anti-submarine armament: two triple Mk 32 tube mountings for 12·75-in (324-mm) Mk 44/46 A/S torpedoes, and two single launchers for Ikara missiles
Electronics: one Hughes SPS-52B 3D radar, one Lockheed SPS-40C air-search radar, one Raytheon/Sylvania SPS-10F surface-search radar, one Kelvin Hughes Type 975 navigation radar, one SPG-53A gun-control radar used in conjunction with the Mk 68 gun fire-control system, one SPG-51C missile-control radar used in conjunction with the Mk 74 missile fire-control system, one Sangamo SQS-23F hull-mounted long-range active sonar, one UQC-1D sonar, one UQN-1 sonar, AIMS Mk 12 IFF, URN-20 TACAN, one Naval Combat Data System
Propulsion: four Foster-Wheeler boilers supplying steam to two sets of General Electric double-reduction geared turbines delivering 70,000 shp (52,200 kW) to two shafts
Performance: maximum speed 30+ kts; range 5,200 miles (8,370 km) at 15 kts or 2,300 miles (3,700 km) at 30 kts
Complement: 21+312

Class

1. Australia (3)

Name	No.	Builders	Laid down	Commissioned
PERTH	D 38	Defoe S.B. Co	Sep 1962	July 1965
HOBART	D 39	Defoe S.B. Co	Oct 1962	Dec 1965
BRISBANE	D 41	Defoe S.B. Co	Feb 1965	Dec 1967

Remarks: The 'Perth' class is the Australian version of the highly successful 'Charles F. Adams' class guided-missile destroyer, and form the 1st Destroyer Squadron. The Australian ships differ relatively little from their American counterparts, the most significant modification being the wide deckhouse between the funnels for the Ikara anti-submarine missile system. The ships were all upgraded between 1974 and 1979, with a future modernization from 1985 designed to add Harpoon anti-ship missiles as well as to upgrade the fire-control systems and Mk 13 missile launcher.

'Robert H. Smith' class destroyer/minelayer

USA

Displacement: 2,250 tons standard and 3,375 tons full load
Dimensions: length 376·5 ft (114·8 m); beam 40·9 ft (12·5 m); draught 19 ft (5·8 m)
Gun armament: six 5-in (127-mm) L/38 DP in three Mk 38 twin mountings, 12 40-mm Bofors L/60 AA in two Mk 1 twin and two Mk 2 quadruple mountings, and 11 20-mm AA
Missile armament: none
Torpedo armament: none
Anti-submarine armament: none
Mines: 80
Electronics: one Bendix SPS-6 air-search radar, one Raytheon/Sylvania SPS-10 surface-search radar, Mk 28 5-in (127-mm) gun-control radar used in conjunction with the Mk 37 gun fire-control system, and Mk 34 AA gun-control radar used in conjunction with the Mk 51 gun fire-control system
Propulsion: four Babcock & Wilcox boilers supplying steam to two sets of geared turbines delivering 60,000 shp (44,740 kW) to two shafts
Performance: maximum speed 34 kts; range 6,700 miles (10,780 km) at 15 kts
Complement: 274

Class

1. Turkey (1)

Name	No.	Builders	Laid down	Commissioned
MUAVENET	DM 357	Bethlehem Steel	1943	Sep 1944

'Roger de Lauria' class destroyer

Spain

Displacement: 3,010 tons standard and 3,785 tons full load
Dimensions: length 119·3 m (391·5 ft); beam 13·0 m (42·7 ft); draught 5·6 m (18·4 ft)
Gun armament: six 5-in (127-mm) L/38 DP in three Mk 38 twin mountings, and one 20-mm Meroka close-in weapon system mounting
Missile armament: provision for surface-to-air missile installation at a later date
Torpedo armament: two Mk 25 tubes for 21-in (533-mm) Mk 37 torpedoes
Anti-submarine armament: two triple Mk 32 tube mountings for 12·75-in (324-mm) Mk 44 A/S torpedoes, and helicopter-launched weapons (see below)
Aircraft: one Hughes Model 369HM helicopter on a platform aft
Electronics: one Lockheed SPS-40 air-search radar, one Raytheon/Sylvania SPS-10 surface-search radar, one Decca RM 426 navigation radar, one Mk 25 5-in (127-mm) gun-control radar used in conjunction with the Mk 37 gun fire-control system, one Mk 35 AA gun-control radar used in conjunction with the Mk 56 gun fire-control system, one Sangamo SQS-32C hull-mounted active sonar and one Litton SQA-10 variable-depth sonar both used in conjunction with the Mk 114 torpedo fire-control system, and electronic support measures
Propulsion: three boilers supplying steam to two sets of Rateau-Bretagne geared turbines delivering 44,740 kW (60,000 shp) to two shafts
Performance: maximum speed 28 kts; range 8,350 km (5,190 miles) at 15 kts
Complement: 20+298

Class

1. Spain (1)

Name	No.	Builders	Laid down	Commissioned
MARQUÉS DE LA ENSENADA	D 43	Bazán	Sep 1951	Sep 1970

'SAM Kotlin' class guided-missile destroyer

USSR

Displacement: 2,850 tons standard and 3,600 tons full load
Dimensions: length 127·5 m (418·2 ft); beam 12·9 m (42·3 ft); draught 4·6 m (15·1 ft)
Gun armament: two 130-mm (5·1-in) L/58 DP in one twin mounting, four 45-mm L/85 AA in one quadruple mounting (except *Bravy*, which has 12 45-mm L/85 AA in three quadruple mountings), and (*Nesokrushimy, Skrytny* and *Soznatelny*) eight 30-mm AA in four twin mountings
Missile armament: one twin launcher for 20 SA-N-1 'Goa' surface-to-air missiles
Torpedo armament: one quintuple 533-mm (21-in) AS/ASW tube mounting
Anti-submarine armament: two RBU 6000 rocket-launchers or (*Bravy* and *Skromny*) two RBU 2500 16-barrel rocket-launchers
Electronics: one 'Head Net-C' 3D radar or (*Bravy* only) one 'Head Net-A' air-search radar, one 'Peel Group' SAM-control radar, one 'Sun Visor' 130-mm gun-control radar, one 'Egg Cup' 130-mm gun-control radar, one 'Hawk Screech' 45-mm gun-control radar, two 'Drum Tilt' 30-mm gun-control radars (*Nesokrushimy, Skrytny* and *Soznatelny*), one or two 'Don Kay' or 'Don-2' navigation radars, one 'High Pole-B' IFF, and one hull-mounted high-frequency sonar
Propulsion: four boilers supplying steam to two sets of geared turbines delivering 53,690 kW (72,000 shp) to two shafts
Performance: maximum speed 36 kts; range 8,350 km (5,190 miles) at 15 kts or 2,000 km (1,245 miles) at 35 kts
Complement: 300

Class

1. Poland (1)

Name	No.
WARSZAWA	275

2. USSR (8)

Name
BRAVY
NAKHODCHIVY
NASTOYCHIVY
NESOKRUSHIMY
SKROMNY
SKRYTNY
SOZNATELNY
VOZBUZHDENNY

The Warszawa (275) is the Polish navy's largest warship.

'Sheffield' class (Type 42) guided-missile destroyer

UK

Displacement: 3,850 tons standard and 4,350 tons full load (Ds 86-92 and 108) or 4,775 tons standard and 5,350 tons full load (Ds 95-98)

Dimensions: (Ds 86-92 and 108) length 412 ft (125·6 m); beam 47 ft (14·3 m); draught 19 ft (5·8 m) to screws

Dimensions: (Ds 95-98) length 463 ft (141·1 m); beam 49 ft (14·9 m); draught 19 ft (5·8 m) to screws

Gun armament: one 4·5-in (114-mm) L/55 DP in one Mk 8 single mounting, four 20-mm Oerlikon AA, and two twin 30-mm AA

Missile armament: one twin launcher for 24 (Ds 86-92 and 108) or 40 (Ds 95-98) Sea Dart surface-to-air and surface-to-surface missiles

Torpedo armament: none

Anti-submarine armament: two triple tube mountings for 12·75-in (324-mm) Mk 46 A/S torpedoes, and helicopter-launched weapons (see below)

Aircraft: one Westland Lynx HAS.Mk 2 helicopter in a hangar aft

Electronics: one Marconi Type 965R air-search radar with double AKE 2 arrays (Ds 86-88) or one Marconi/Hollandse Signaalapparaten Type 1022 air-search radar (D 89 onwards), one Marconi Type 992Q surveillance and target indication radar, two Type 909 missile-control radars used in conjunction with the GWS 30 missile fire-control system, one Kelvin Hughes Type 1006 navigation and helicopter-control radar, one Graseby Type 184M hull-mounted medium-range panoramic search and attack sonar, one Kelvin Hughes Type 162M hull-mounted side-looking classification sonar, one Type 182 torpedo-decoy system, one Type 170B hull-mounted short-range search and attack sonar, one Ferranti/Plessey ADAWS 4 (ADAWS 8 in D95 on) action data automation weapon system, one UAA-1 Abbey Hill ESM suite, two SCOT satellite communication antennae, and two Knebworth Corvus chaff launchers

Propulsion: COGOG (COmbined Gas turbine Or Gas turbine) arrangement, with two Rolls-Royce Tyne RM1A gas turbines delivering 8,500 shp (6,340 kW) and two Rolls-Royce Olympus TM3B gas turbines delivering 56,000 shp (41,760 kW) to two shafts

Performance: maximum speed 29 kts on Olympus turbines or 18 kts on Tyne turbines; range 4,600 miles (7,400 km) at 18 kts or 750 miles (1,205 km) at 29 kts

Complement: 24 + 229, with a maximum accommodation of 312 possible

Class

1. UK (12)

Name	No.	Builders	Laid down	Commissioned
BIRMINGHAM	D 86	Cammell Laird	Mar 1972	Dec 1976
NEWCASTLE	D 87	Swan Hunter	Feb 1973	Mar 1978
GLASGOW	D 88	Swan Hunter	Apr 1974	May 1979
EXETER	D 89	Swan Hunter	July 1976	Sep 1980
SOUTHAMPTON	D 90	Vosper Thornycroft	Oct 1976	Oct 1981
NOTTINGHAM	D 91	Vosper Thornycroft	Feb 1978	1982
LIVERPOOL	D 92	Cammell Laird	July 1978	July 1982
MANCHESTER	D 95	Vickers (Shipbuilding)	May 1978	1982
GLOUCESTER	D 96	Vosper Thornycroft	Oct 1979	1984
EDINBURGH	D 97	Cammell Laird	Sep 1980	1984
YORK	D 98	Swan Hunter	Jan 1980	1984
CARDIFF	D 108	Vickers (Shipbuilding)	Nov 1972	Sep 1979

Remarks: Designed for the area defence of a Royal Navy task group, the 'Type 42' or 'Sheffield' class guided-missile destroyer was extensively blooded in the Falklands campaign of 1982, and found wanting in several important facets, notably damage-control and point defence against sea-skimmer missiles and low-level aircraft. The *Sheffield* and *Coventry* of this class were lost in the Falklands war, and urgent steps have been taken to improve the most serious defects, notably the addition of two twin 30-mm AA and two single 20-mm AA mountings at the cost of a reduction in boat strength. Further improvement will probably follow with the addition of a Hollandse Signaalapparaten/General Electric Goalkeeper CIWS mounting. The class has been produced in three batches, the first comprising the *Birmingham* (D 86), *Newcastle* (D 87), *Glasgow* (D 88) and much-delayed *Cardiff* (D 108); the second the *Exeter* (D 89), *Southampton* (D 90), *Nottingham* (D 91) and *Liverpool* (D 92); and the third the *Manchester* (D 95), *Gloucester* (D 96), *Edinburgh* (D 97) and *York* (D 98). The Batch 1 and Batch 2 ships are physically similar, though the Batch 2 ships have Type 1022 search radar instead of the Batch 1 ships' Type 965R. The Batch 3 ships are considerably different, with an increase in waterline length and beam of 42 ft (12·8 m) and 2 ft (0·61 m) respectively. This provides greater volume for advanced weapons (an additional 16 Sea Dart surface-to-air missiles, for instance) and also gives the hull better lines, raising speed by more than 1 kt despite an increase of 675 tons in full-load displacement. Extra anti-ship capability is provided for the class by the ability of the ships' Lynx helicopter to carry up to four Sea Skua anti-ship missiles.

The Glasgow (D 88) is a 'Sheffield Batch 1' class guided-missile destroyer. Visible are the single 4·5-in (114-mm) gun, twin Sea Dart launcher (with SAMs) and Lynx helicopter. Radars in evidence are the fore and aft domed Type 909s, tower mast Type 992, and Type 965R with twin AKE 2 arrays.

'Shirane' class destroyer

Japan

Displacement: 5,200 tons standard and 6,800 tons full load

Dimensions: length 159·0 m (521·5 ft); beam 17·5 m (57·5 ft); draught 5·3 m (17·5 ft)

Gun armament: two 5-in (127-mm) L/54 DP in two Mk 42 single mountings, and two 20-mm Phalanx close-in weapon system mountings

Missile armament: two quadruple container-launchers for eight RGM-84A Harpoon anti-ship missiles, and one octuple launcher for eight RIM-7 Sea Sparrow surface-to-air missiles

Torpedo armament: none

Anti-submarine armament: two triple Type 68 tube mountings for 12·75-in (324-mm) Mk 44/46 A/S torpedoes, one Mk 16 octuple launcher for 16 RUR-5A ASROC missiles, and helicopter-launched weapons (see below)

Aircraft: three Sikorsky SH-3 Sea King helicopeters in a hangar amidships

Electronics: one Hughes SPS-52B 3D search radar, one OPS-28 surface-search radar, two Type 72 gun-control radars, one Hollandse Signaalapparaten WM-25 missile-control radar, TACAN, one ESM suite, one OQS-101 hull-mounted sonar, one EDO SQS-35(J) variable-depth sonar, and one SQR-18 passive towed sonar

Propulsion: ? boilers supplying steam to two sets of geared turbines delivering 52,200 kW (70,000 shp) to two shafts

Performance: maximum speed 32 kts

Complement: 350

Class

1. Japan (2)

Name	No.	Builders	Laid down	Commissioned
SHIRANE	DD 143	Ishikawajima Harima	Feb 1977	Mar 1980
KURAMA	DD 144	Ishikawajima Harima	Feb 1978	Mar 1981

Seen during operations with one of its three Mitsubishi-Sikorsky SH-3 anti-submarine helicopters, the Shirane (DD 143) is a powerful single-role destroyer. The SAM launcher is located on the top of the hangar.

Remarks: The two 'Shirane' class ships are the most modern destroyers in service with the Japanese Maritime Self-Defense Force, and are optimized for anti-submarine warfare with ASROC and three helicopters for offensive operations and two triple Type 68 tube mountings for self-defence. The design is a modification of that of the 'Haruna' class, and of the two funnels the forward unit is set slightly to port and the after unit slightly to starboard of the centreline. It seems likely that provision will be made for RGM-84A Harpoon anti-ship missiles during mid-life refits.

'Skory' and 'Skory (Modified)' class destroyers
USSR

Displacement: 2,240 tons standard and 3,080 tons full load

Dimensions: length 120·5m (395·2ft); beam 11·9m (38·9ft); draught 4·6m (15·1ft)

Gun armament: four 130-mm (5·1-in) L/50 DP in two twin mountings, two 85-mm (3·3-in) L/55 DP in one twin mounting ('Skory' class), eight 37-mm AA in four twin mountings or seven 37-mm AA in seven single mountings ('Skory' class), four 25-mm AA in two twin mountings (some 'Skory' class), and ('Skory (Modified)' class only) five 57-mm AA in five single mountings

Missile armament: none

Torpedo armament: two ('Skory' class) or one ('Skory (Modified)' class) 533-mm (21-in) tube mountings

Anti-submarine armament: four depth-charge throwers ('Skory' class) or two RBU 2500 16-barrel rocket-launchers ('Skory (Modified)' class)

Mines: up to 80

Electronics: ('Skory' class) one 'High Sieve' surface-search radar, one 'Cross Bird' or 'Knife Rest' air-search radar, one 'Top Bow' or Half Bow' gun-control radar, one 'Post Lamp' target-designation radar, one or two 'Don-2' navigation radars, one 'High Pole-A' IFF, one 'Square Head' IFF, and one hull-mounted high-frequency sonar

Electronics: ('Skory (Modified)' class) one 'Slim Net' surface-search radar, one 'Top Bow' gun-control radar, two 'Hawk Screech' AA gun-control radars, one or two 'Don-2' navigation radars, one 'High Pole-A' IFF, one 'Square Head' IFF, and one hull-mounted high-frequency sonar

Propulsion: four boilers supplying steam to two sets of geared turbines delivering 44,740kW (60,000shp) to two shafts

Performance: maximum speed 33kts; range 7,225km (4,490 miles) at 13kts or 1,700km (1,055 miles) at 32kts

Complement: 280

Class

1. Egypt (4)

Name	No.
6 OCTOBER *	666
AL ZAFFER	822
DAMIET *	844
SUEZ	888

2. USSR (15 + 10 in reserve)

Name

BESSTRASHNY	**SOVERSHENNY**
BESSHUMNY *	**STATNY**
BEZBOYAZNENNY *	**STEPENNY**
BEZUDERZHNY	**STOYKY**
BEZUPRECHNY	**STREMITELNY**
BUYNY	**SUROVY**
OGNENNY *	**SVOBODNY**
OSTOROZHNY *	**VDUMCHIVY**
OSTRY	**VNIMATELNY**
OTCHETLIVY *	**VOLNY** *
OZHIVLENNY	**VRAZUMITELNY**
SERDITY	* 'Skory (Modified)' ships
SEREZNY	
SOLIDNY	

Remarks: Now thoroughly obsolescent, the 'Skory' class destroyers were built between 1949 and 1954 at Leningrad, Nikolayev and Severodvinsk, and of the planned total of 85 units only 75 were built as part of the Soviet navy's urgent development into a 'blue-water' force. The ships are classic gun destroyers, and numbers have declined steadily in recent years.

'Spruance' class guided-missile destroyer
USA

Displacement: 5,830 tons light and 7,810 tons full load

Dimensions: length 563·2ft (171·7m); beam 55·1ft (16·8m); draught 29ft (8·8m) to sonar dome

Gun armament: two 5-in (127-mm) L/54 DP in two Mk 45 single mountings, and two 20-mm Phalanx Mk 15 close-in weapon system mountings

Missile armament: two quadruple container-launchers for eight RGM-84A Harpoon surface-to-surface missiles (except in DDs 964 and 965), two quadruple container-launchers for eight BGM-109 Tomahawk surface-to-surface missiles (to be fitted in DDs 963, 964, 969, 973, 979, 984, 985, 988, 989 and 992), and one Mk 29 octuple launcher for 24 RIM-7 Sea Sparrow surface-to-air missiles

Torpedo armament: none

Anti-submarine armament: two triple Mk 32 tube mountings for 14 12·75-in (324-mm) Mk 46 A/S torpedoes, and one octuple launcher for 24 RUR-5A ASROC missiles

Aircraft: one Sikorsky SH-3 Sea King or two Kaman SH-2 Seasprite helicopters in a hangar aft

Electronics: one Lockheed SPS-40B air-search radar, one Westinghouse SPS-55 surface-search radar, one Lockheed SPG-60 search and track radar and one Lockheed SPQ-9A track-while-scan radar used in conjunction with the Lockheed Mk 86 gun fire-control system, one Mk 91 SAM fire-control system, one General Electric SQS-53 bow-mounted 'bottom-bounce' sonar used in conjunction with the Mk 116 underwater weapons fire-control system, one T Mk 6 Fanfare torpedo decoy system, URN-20 TACAN, Naval Tactical Data System, OE-82 satellite communications antenna, SRR-1 satellite communications receiver, WSC-3 satellite communications transceiver, Raytheon SLQ-32(V)2 ESM suite, and two Mk 36 Super Chaffroc rapid-blooming overhead chaff launchers

Propulsion: four General Electric LM 2500 gas turbines delivering 80,000shp (59,655kW) to two shafts

Performance: maximum speed 33kts; range 6,900 miles (11,105km) at 20kts

Complement: 24 + 272

Class

1. USA (31 + 1)

Name	No.	Builders	Laid down	Com-missioned
SPRUANCE	DD 963	Ingalls Shipbuilding	Nov 1972	Sep 1975
PAUL F. FOSTER	DD 964	Ingalls Shipbuilding	Feb 1973	Feb 1976
KINKAID	DD 965	Ingalls Shipbuilding	Apr 1973	July 1976
HEWITT	DD 966	Ingalls Shipbuilding	July 1973	Sep 1976
ELLIOTT	DD 967	Ingalls Shipbuilding	Oct 1973	Jan 1976
ARTHUR W. RADFORD	DD 968	Ingalls Shipbuilding	Jan 1974	Apr 1977
PETERSON	DD 969	Ingalls Shipbuilding	Apr 1974	July 1977
CARON	DD 970	Ingalls Shipbuilding	July 1974	Oct 1977
DAVID R. RAY	DD 971	Ingalls Shipbuilding	Sep 1974	Nov 1977
OLDENDORF	DD 972	Ingalls Shipbuilding	Dec 1974	Mar 1978
JOHN YOUNG	DD 973	Ingalls Shipbuilding	Feb 1975	May 1978
COMTE DE GRASSE	DD 974	Ingalls Shipbuilding	Apr 1975	Aug 1978
O'BRIEN	DD 975	Ingalls Shipbuilding	May 1975	Dec 1977
MERRILL	DD 976	Ingalls Shipbuilding	June 1975	Mar 1978
BRISCOE	DD 977	Ingalls Shipbuilding	July 1975	June 1978
STUMP	DD 978	Ingalls Shipbuilding	Aug 1975	Aug 1978
CONOLLY	DD 979	Ingalls Shipbuilding	Sep 1975	Oct 1978
MOOSBRUGGER	DD 980	Ingalls Shipbuilding	Nov 1975	Dec 1978
JOHN HANCOCK	DD 981	Ingalls Shipbuilding	Jan 1976	Mar 1979
NICHOLSON	DD 982	Ingalls Shipbuilding	Feb 1976	May 1979
JOHN RODGERS	DD 983	Ingalls Shipbuilding	Aug 1976	July 1979
LEFTWICH	DD 984	Ingalls Shipbuilding	Nov 1976	Aug 1979
CUSHING	DD 985	Ingalls Shipbuilding	Dec 1976	Sep 1979
HARRY W. HILL	DD 986	Ingalls Shipbuilding	Jan 1977	Nov 1979
O'BANNON	DD 987	Ingalls Shipbuilding	Feb 1977	Dec 1979
THORN	DD 988	Ingalls Shipbuilding	Aug 1977	Feb 1980
DEYO	DD 989	Ingalls Shipbuilding	Oct 1977	Mar 1980
INGERSOLL	DD 990	Ingalls Shipbuilding	Dec 1977	Apr 1980
FIFE	DD 991	Ingalls Shipbuilding	Mar 1978	May 1980
FLETCHER	DD 992	Ingalls Shipbuilding	Apr 1978	July 1980
HAYLER	DD 997	Ingalls Shipbuilding	Oct 1980	Mar 1983
—	DD 999	Proposed FY 1988 prog.	—	—

Remarks: The US Navy's most important anti-submarine destroyer force, the 'Spruance' class destroyers are designed for the escort of carrier task forces in conjunction with anti-aircraft cruisers. It is proposed to resume construction from FY88 to make good the gap left by the retirement of the 'Forrest Sherman' and 'Hull' classes, and existing ships will be extensively upgraded.

'Suffren' class guided-missile destroyer

France

Displacement: 5,090 tons standard and 6,090 tons full load
Dimensions: length 157·6m (517·1ft); beam 15·54m (51ft); draught 6·1m (20ft)
Gun armament: two 100-mm (3·9-in) L/55 DP in two single mountings, and four 20-mm AA in single mountings
Missile armament: four container-launchers for four MM.38 Exocet surface-to-surface missiles, and one twin launcher for 48 Masurca surface-to-air missiles
Torpedo armament: none
Anti-submarine armament: one single launcher for 13 Malafon missiles, and four launchers for L 5 A/S torpedoes
Electronics: one Thomson-CSF DRBI 23 3D air-surveillance and target-designation radar, one Thomson-CSF DRBV 50 air- and surface-search radar, one Thomson-CSF DRBN 32 navigation radar, two Thomson-CSF DRBR 51 SAM-control radars, one Thomson-CSF DRBC 32A gun-control radar, one CIT/Alcatel DUBV 23 hull-mounted active search and attack sonar, one CIT/Alcatel DUBV 43 variable-depth sonar, one SENIT 1 combat information system, TACAN, one ESM system, and two Dagaie chaff launchers
Propulsion: four boilers supplying steam to two sets of Rateau double-reduction geared turbines delivering 54,065kW (72,500shp) to two shafts
Performance: maximum speed 34kts; range 9,500km (5,905 miles) at 18kts or 4,450km (2,765 miles) at 29kts
Complement: 23+332

Class					
1. France (2)					Com-
Name	No.	Builders	Laid down	missioned
SUFFREN	D 602	Lorient Naval Dockyard	Dec 1962	July 1967
DUQUESNE	D 603	Brest Naval Dockyard	Nov 1964	Apr 1970

Indications of the capabilities of the 'Suffren' class are provided by this photograph of the Suffren (D 602), designed for the area protection of France's two aircraft-carriers against air and submarine threats: forward are two 100-mm (3·9-mm) DP guns with their associated DRBC 32A fire-control radar and domed DRBI 23 surveillance radar; amidships is the Malafon anti-submarine launcher with aircraft-type missile; and aft is the Masurca twin launcher with DRBR 51 radars. Since this 1976 photograph, Exocet SSMs have replaced the 30-mm AA guns.

'Type 47' class guided-missile destroyer (AA)

France

Displacement: 2,750 tons standard and 3,740 tons full load
Dimensions: length 128·5m (421·6ft); beam 12·96m (42·5ft); draught 6·3m (20·7ft)
Gun armament: six 57-mm L/60 DP in three twin mountings
Missile armament: one Mk 13 single launcher for 40 RIM-24B Tartar surface-to-air missiles
Torpedo armament: none
Anti-submarine armament: one 375-mm (14·76-in) six-barrel rocket-launcher, and two triple 550-mm (21·7-in) tube mountings for K 2 and L 3 A/S torpedoes
Electronics: one Thomson-CSF DRBV 20A air-search radar (D 622) or Thomson-CSF DRBV 22 air-search radar (Ds 625 and 630), one Hughes SPS-39A or SPS-39B 3D radar, two Raytheon SPG-51B SAM-control radars, one Thomson-CSF DRBV 31 surface-search and navigation radar, one DUBA 1 hull-mounted sonar, one CIT/ALCATEL DUBV 24 hull-mounted panoramic search and attack sonar, one SENIT 2 combat information system, and electronic warfare systems
Propulsion: four Indret boilers supplying steam to two sets of geared turbines delivering 46,980kW (63,000shp) to two shafts
Performance: maximum speed 32kts; range 9,250km (5,750 miles) at 18kts or 2,225km (1,385 miles) at 32kts
Complement: 17+83+177 in peace, or 24+83+216 in war

Class				
1. France (2)				Com-
Name	No.	Builders	Laid down	missioned
DUPETIT THOUARS	D 625	Brest Naval Dockyard	Mar 1952	Sep 1956
DU CHAYLA	D 630	Brest Naval Dockyard	July 1953	June 1957

The guided-missile destroyer Du Chayla (D 630) shows off some of her salient features, including (from bow to stern) the multi-barrel Bofors anti-submarine rocket-launcher, the forward 57-mm DP mounting, the DRBC 31 gun-control radar (above the bridge), the DRBV 22 air-search radar (head of foremast), the SPS 39 3D search radar (head of mainmast), the two SPG-51B Tartar-control radars and the Mk 13 Tartar SAM single launcher. Also visible is the starboard triple mounting (beside the forward funnel) for 550-mm (21·7-in) K 2 or L 3 torpedoes. Unlike their anti-submarine half-sisters, these two anti-aircraft destroyers are fitted with the SENIT combat information system, much enhancing their capabilities in modern naval actions.

'T 47' class destroyer (A/S)

France

Displacement: 2,750 tons standard and 3,900 tons full load
Dimensions: length 132·5m (434·6ft); beam 12·72m (41·7ft); draught 5·9m (19·4ft)
Gun armament: two 100-mm (3·9-in) L/55 DP in two single mountings, and two 20-mm AA
Missile armament: none
Torpedo armament: none
Anti-submarine armament: one launcher for 13 Malafon missiles, one 375-mm (14·76-in) six-barrel rocket-launcher, and two triple 550-mm (21·7-in) tube mountings for K 2 or L 3 A/S torpedoes
Electronics: one Thomson-CSF DRBV 22A air-search radar, one Thomson-CSF DRBV 50 combined air- and surface-search radar, two Thomson-CSF DRBC 32A main armament gun-control radars, one Thomson-CSF DRBN 32 navigation radar, one CIT/ALCATEL DUBV 23 hull-mounted active search and attack sonar, one CIT/ALCATEL DUBV 43 variable-depth sonar, and electronic warfare systems
Propulsion: four Indret boilers supplying steam to two sets of geared turbines delivering 46,980kW (63,000shp) to two shafts
Performance: maximum speed 32kts; range 9,250km (5,750 miles) at 18kts
Complement: 15+104+151

Class				
1. France (5)				Com-
Name	No.	Builders	Laid down	missioned
MAILLE BRÉZÉ	D 627	Lorient Naval Dockyard	Oct 1953	May 1957
VAUQUELIN	D 628	Lorient Naval Dockyard	Mar 1953	Nov 1956
D'ESTRÉES	D 629	Brest Naval Dockyard	May 1953	Mar 1957
CASABIANCA	D 631	F. C. Gironde	Oct 1953	May 1957
GUÉPRATTE	D 632	A. C. Bretagne	Aug 1953	June 1957

Remarks: The 'T 47' class destroyers were built as gun destroyers with a main armament of six 127-mm (5-in) guns. Between January 1968 and January 1971 five of the class were extensively modified for the anti-submarine role, internal alterations including the provision of air conditioning for all living spaces, the total replacement of electrical and electronic equipment, and the revision of damage-control features. Externally, the modification resulted in the removal of the whole of the original armament fit, which was then replaced by two 100-mm (3·9-in) DP guns and an anti-submarine fit of one Malafon missile launcher, one large rocket-launcher and two triple tube mountings for 550-mm (21·7-in) anti-submarine torpedoes. The class is currently allocated as three ships (*Maille Brézé, Vauquelin* and *Casabianca*) to the Atlantic Fleet and two (*D'Estrées* and *Guépratte*) to the Mediterranean Fleet. Further deliveries of the 'C 70' class anti-submarine destroyer will permit the gradual relegation of the 'T 47' class from 1985 onwards. Four other ships of the 'T 47' class were taken in hand between 1961 and 1965 for conversion into anti-aircraft guided-missile destroyers. Of these (*Kersaint, Bouvet, Dupetit Thouars* and *Du Chayla*) only two now remain in service, though they will be withdrawn as their missile systems (launchers and radars) are shifted into the new 'C 70' class of guided-missile destroyer, *Dupetit Thouars* in 1985 and *Du Chayla* in 1987. Additional AA capability is provided in these ships by a primary gun armament of six 57-mm DP guns in three twin mountings.

'T 53 (Modified)' class guided-missile destroyer

France

Displacement: 2,800 tons standard and 3,900 tons full load
Dimensions: length 132·8 m (435·7 ft); beam 12·7 m (41·7 ft); draught 5·4 m (17·7 ft)
Gun armament: one 100-mm (3·9-in) L/55
Missile armament: four container-launchers for four MM.38 Exocet surface-to-surface missiles
Torpedo armament: none
Anti-submarine armament: two launchers for eight L 5 A/S torpedoes, and helicopter-launched weapons (see below)
Aircraft: one Westland Lynx Mk 2 helicopter in a hangar aft
Electronics: one Thomson-CSF DRBV 22A air-search radar, one Thomson-CSF DRBV 51 combined air- and surface-search radar, one Thomson-CSF DRBC 32E gun-control radar, one Decca navigation radar, one Decca helicopter-control radar, one Thomson-CSF Vega fire-control system, one CIT/ALCATEL DUBV 23 hull-mounted active search and attack sonar, one CIT/ALCATEL DUBV 43 variable-depth sonar, one SENIT 2 combat information system, and two Knebworth Corvus chaff launchers
Propulsion: four Indret boilers supplying steam to two sets of Rateau geared turbines delivering 46,980 kW (63,000 shp) to two shafts
Performance: maximum speed 32 kts; range 9,250 km (5,750 miles) at 18 kts
Complement: 15+257

Class

1. France (1)

Name	No.	Builders	Laid down	Commissioned
DUPERRÉ	D 633	Lorient Naval Dockyard	Nov 1954	Oct 1957

'T 56' class destroyer

France

Displacement: 2,750 tons standard and 3,910 tons full load
Dimensions: length 132·8 m (435·7 ft); beam 12·7 m (41·7 ft); draught 5·4 m (17·7 ft)
Gun armament: two 100-mm (3·9-in) L/55 DP in two single mountings
Missile armament: none
Torpedo armament: none
Anti-submarine armament: one launcher for Malafon missiles, two triple 550-mm (21·7-in) tube mountings for K 2 and L 3 A/S torpedoes, and helicopter-launched weapons (see below)
Aircraft: one Aérospatiale Alouette III helicopter in a hangar aft
Electronics: one Thomson-CSF DRBV 50 combined air- and surface-search radar, one Thomson-CSF DRBV 22 air-search radar, one Thomson-CSF DRBC 32A gun-control radar, one Thomson-CSF DRBN 32 navigation radar, one CIT/ALCATEL DUBV 23 hull-mounted active search and attack sonar, one CIT/ALCATEL DUBV 43 variable-depth sonar, URN-22 TACAN, and electronic warfare systems
Propulsion: four Indret boilers supplying steam to two sets of Rateau geared turbines delivering 46,980 kW (63,000 shp) to two shafts
Performance: maximum speed 34 kts; range 9,250 km (4,750 miles) at 18 kts
Complement: 15+255

Class

1. France (1)

Name	No.	Builders	Laid down	Commissioned
LA GALISSONNIÈRE	D 638	Lorient Naval Dockyard	Nov 1958	July 1962

With the same hull and machinery as the 'T 47' and 'T 53' classes, the sole 'T 56' class ship, La Galissonnière (D 328) was built as an experimental anti-submarine ship, and was the first destroyer armed with the Malafon missile system. The sides of the hangar open outwards to form the helicopter platform.

'Tachikaze' class guided-missile destroyer

Japan

Displacement: 3,850 tons for DDs 168 and 169, or 3,900 tons for DD 170 standard and 4,800 tons full load
Dimensions: length 143·0 m (469·2 ft) for DDs 169 and 170, and 135·0 m (442·9 ft) for DD 168; beam 14·3 m (46·9 ft); draught 4·6 m (15 ft)
Gun armament: two 5-in (127-mm) L/54 DP in one Mk 42 twin mounting, and one 20-mm Phalanx CIWS mounting
Missile armament: two quadruple container-launchers for eight RGM-84A Harpoon surface-to-surface missiles (DD 170 only), and one Mk 13 single launcher for 40 RIM-66 Standard-MR surface-to-air missiles
Torpedo armament: none
Anti-submarine armament: two triple Type 68 tube mountings for 12·75-in (324-mm) Mk 44/46 A/S torpedoes, one Mk 16 octuple launcher for 16 RUR-5A ASROC missiles
Aircraft: none
Electronics: one Hughes SPS-52 3D radar, one OPS-11 air-search radar (DD 169 only), one OPS-17 surface-search radar, two Raytheon SPG-51C SAM-control radars, two Type 72 gun-control radars, one OQS-3 hull-mounted sonar, and one OLT-3 ESM suite
Propulsion: ? boilers supplying steam to two sets of Westinghouse geared turbines delivering 60,000 shp (44,740 kW) to two shafts
Performance: maximum speed 32 kts for DDs 169 and 170, and 33 kts for DD 168
Complement: 260 for DD 168, 250 for DD 169 and 270 for DD 170

Class

1. Japan (3)

Name	No.	Builders	Laid down	Commissioned
TACHIKAZE	DD 168	Mitsubishi	June 1973	Mar 1976
ASAKAZE	DD 169	Mitsubishi	May 1976	Mar 1979
SAWAKAZE	DD 170	Mitsubishi	Sep 1979	Mar 1983

Remarks: The 'Tachikaze' class is a dual-role destroyer type, with capability in the anti-submarine and anti-aircraft roles (Mk 13 SAM launcher aft and Mk 16 ASROC launcher forward). The *Sawakaze* (DD 170) is an improved version with anti-ship capability bestowed by the provision of two quadruple container-launchers for RGM-84 Harpoon surface-to-surface missiles.

'Takatsuki' class guided-missile destroyer

Japan

Displacement: 3,050 tons (DDs 164 and 165) or 3,100 tons (DDs 166 and 167) standard and 4,500 tons full load
Dimensions: length 136·0 m (446·2 ft); beam 13·4 m (44 ft); draught 4·4 m (14·5 ft)
Gun armament: two (one in DDs 164 and 165) 5-in (127-mm) L/54 DP in two (one) Mk 42 single mountings, and two 20-mm Phalanx CIWS mountings
Missile armament: (DDs 164 and 165 only) two quadruple container-launchers for eight RGM-84A Harpoon surface-to-surface missiles, and one octuple launcher for eight RIM-7 Sea Sparrow surface-to-air missiles
Torpedo armament: none
Anti-submarine armament: one Mk 16 octuple launcher for 16 RUR-5A ASROC missiles, one 375-mm (14·75-in) Bofors Type 71 four-barrel rocket-launcher, two triple Type 68 tube mountings for 12·75-in (324-mm) Mk 46 A/S torpedoes, and (DDs 166 and 167 only) helicopter-launched weapons (see below)
Aircraft: (DDs 166 and 167 only) provision for a helicopter on a platform aft
Electronics: one OPS-11B air-search radar, one OPS-17 surface-search radar, two Mk 56 fire-control radars, one Sangamo SQS-23 (DDs 164 and 165) or OQS-3 (DDs 166 and 167) hull-mounted sonar, one EDO SQS-35(J) variable-depth sonar (DDs 164 and 165 only), and one NOLR-1 or NOLQ-1 ESM suite
Propulsion: two Mitsubishi/Combustion Engineering boilers supplying steam to two sets of Mitsubishi/Westinghouse geared turbines delivering 44,760 kW (60,000 shp) to two shafts
Performance: maximum speed 32 kts; range 12,975 km (8,065 miles) at 20 kts
Complement: 270

Class

1. Japan (4)

Name	No.	Builders	Laid down	Commissioned
TAKATSUKI	DD 164	Ishikawajima Harima	Oct 1964	Mar 1967
KIKUZUKI	DD 165	Mitsubishi	Mar 1966	Mar 1968
MOCHIZUKI	DD 166	Ishikawajima Harima	Nov 1966	Mar 1969
NAGATSUKI	DD 167	Mitsubishi	Mar 1968	Feb 1970

Remarks: The 'Takatsuki' class was built for anti-submarine operations, and during the early 1980s the first two ships are being upgraded by the addition of Harpoon anti-ship and Sea Sparrow anti-aircraft missiles.

'Tromp' class guided-missile destroyer
Netherlands
Displacement: 3,900 tons standard and 4,580 tons full load
Dimensions: length 138·2m (453·3ft); beam 14·8m (48·6ft); draught 4·6m (15·1ft)

The Dutch guided-missile destroyer De Ruyter (F 806) provides anti-aircraft defence for the Royal Dutch navy's ASW Group II operating in the eastern Atlantic under NATO's auspices.

Gun armament: two 120-mm (4·7-in) L/50 DP in one twin mounting
Missile armament: eight container-launchers for 16 RGM-84A Harpoon surface-to-surface missiles, one Mk 13 single launcher for 40 RIM-24B Tartar surface-to-air missiles, and one octuple launcher for 16 RIM-7 Sea Sparrow surface-to-air missiles
Torpedo armament: none
Anti-submarine armament: two triple Mk 32 tube mountings for 12·75-in (324-mm) Mk 46 A/S torpedoes
Aircraft: one Westland Lynx helicopter in a hangar aft
Electronics: one Hollandse Signaalapparaten 3D-MITR 3D radar, one Hollandse Signaalapparaten WM-25 surface-search, gun-control and Sea Sparrow-control radar, two Raytheon SPG-51 Tartar-control radars, two Decca navigation radars, one CWE 610 hull-mounted sonar, one SEWACO I action-data system, one Daisy data-handling and underwater weapon fire-control system, and two Knebworth Corvus chaff launchers
Propulsion: COGOG (COmbined Gas turbine Or Gas turbine) arrangement, with two Rolls-Royce Tyne TM1 gas turbines delivering 8,000hp (5,965kW) and two Rolls-Royce Olympus TM3B gas turbines delivering 50,000hp (37,285kW) to two shafts
Performance: maximum speed 30kts; range 9,250km (5,750 miles) at 18kts
Complement: 34+267

Class
1. Netherlands (2)				Com-
Name	No.	Builders	Laid down	missioned
TROMP	F 801	Koninklijke Maatschappij	Sep 1971	Oct 1975
DE RUYTER	F 806	Koninklijke Maatschappij	Dec 1971	June 1976

'Type 42' class guided-missile destroyer
UK/Argentina
Displacement: 3,150 tons standard and 4,100 tons full load
Dimensions: length 410ft (125·0m); beam 47ft (14·3m); draught 19ft (5·8m) to screws
Gun armament: one 4·5-in (114-mm) L/55 DP in one Mk 8 single mounting, and two 20-mm Oerlikon AA in Mk 7 single mountings
Missile armament: four container-launchers for four MM.38 Exocet surface-to-surface missiles, and one twin launcher for 22 Sea Dart surface-to-air missiles
Torpedo armament: none
Anti-submarine armament: two triple ILAS 3 tube mountings for 324-mm (12·75-in) A244 A/S torpedoes, and helicopter-launched weapons (see below)
Aircraft: one Westland Lynx helicopter in a hangar aft
Electronics: one Marconi Type 965 air-search radar with twin AKE 2 arrays, one Marconi Type 992Q surface-search and target-indication radar, two Type 909 SAM-control radars, one Kelvin Hughes Type 1006 navigation and helicopter-control radar, one Kelvin Hughes Type 162 hull-mounted side-looking classification sonar, one Graseby Type 184 hull-mounted medium-range panoramic search and attack sonar, and one Plessey/Ferranti ADAWS 4 action data automation weapon system
Propulsion: COGOG (COmbined Gas turbine Or Gas turbine) arrangement, with two Rolls-Royce Tyne RM1A gas turbines delivering 8,500shp (6,340kW) and two Rolls-Royce Olympus TM3B gas turbines delivering 56,000shp (41,760kW) to two shafts
Performance: maximum speed 30kts; range 4,600 miles (7,400km) at 18kts
Complement: 300

Class
1. Argentina (2)				Com-
Name	No.	Builders	Laid down	missioned
HERCULES	D 1	Vickers (Shipbuilding)	June 1971	July 1976
SANTISIMA TRINIDAD	D 2	AFNE Rio Santiago	Oct 1971	July 1981

The Argentine destroyer Hercules has now been renumbered D 1.

'Vosper Thornycroft Mk 10' class guided-missile destroyer
UK/Brazil
Displacement: 3,200 tons standard and 3,800 tons full load
Dimensions: length 424ft (129·2m); beam 44·2ft (13·5m); draught 18·2ft (5·5m)
Gun armament: one (Fs 40, 41, 44 and 45) or two (Fs 42 and 43) 4·5-in (114-mm) L/55 DP in Vickers Mk 8 single mountings, and two 40-mm Bofors L/70 AA
Missile armament: two twin container-launchers for four MM.38 Exocet surface-to-surface missiles (Fs 42 and 43), and two triple launchers for Sea Cat surface-to-air missiles
Torpedo armament: none
Anti-submarine armament: one 375-mm (14·76-in) Bofors two-barrel rocket-launcher, two triple Plessey STWS 1 tube mountings for 12·75-in (324-mm) Mk 44/46 A/S torpedoes, one depth-charge rail, and (Fs 40, 41, 44 and 45) one launcher for 10 Ikara missiles, and helicopter-launched weapons (see below)
Aircraft: one Westland Lynx helicopter on a platform aft
Electronics: one Plessey AWS 2 air-search radar, one Hollandse Signaalapparaten ZW-06 surface-search radar, two Selenia Orion RTN 10X weapon-control and tracking radars, one tracking radar as part of the Branik control system for the Ikara A/S missile, Ferranti Computer-Assisted Action Information System, Decca electronic countermeasures equipment, one EDO 610E hull-mounted sonar, and (Fs 40, 41, 44 and 45) one EDO 700E variable-depth sonar
Propulsion: CODOG (COmbined Diesel Or Gas turbine) arrangement, with four MTU diesels delivering 11,750kW (15,760shp) or two Rolls-Royce Olympus TM3B gas turbines delivering 56,000bhp (41,760kW) to two shafts
Performance: maximum speed 30kts on gas turbines or 22kts on diesels; range 9,825km (6,105 miles) at 17kts on two diesels, or 7,775km (4,830 miles) at 19kts on four diesels, or 2,400km (1,490 miles) at 28kts on gas turbines; endurance 45 days
Complement: 21+179

Class
1. Brazil (6 'Niteroi' class)				Com-
Name	No.	Builders	Laid down	missioned
NITEROI	F 40	Vosper Thornycroft	June 1972	Nov 1976
DEFENSORA	F 41	Vosper Thornycroft	Dec 1972	Mar 1977
CONSTITUIÇÃO	F 42	Vosper Thornycroft	Mar 1974	Mar 1978
LIBERAL	F 43	Vosper Thornycroft	May 1975	Nov 1978
INDEPENDENCIA	F 44	Navyard	June 1972	Sep 1979
UNIÃO	F 45	Navyard	June 1972	Sep 1980

'Yamagumo' class destroyer

Japan

Displacement: 2,050 tons standard and 2,150 tons full load
Dimensions: length 114·9m (377ft); beam 11·8m (38·7ft); draught 4·0m (13·1ft)
Gun armament: four 3-in (76-mm) L/50 DP in two Mk 33 twin mountings
Missile armament: none
Torpedo armament: none
Anti-submarine armament: two triple Type 68 tube mountings for 12·75-in (324-mm) Mk 44/46 A/S torpedoes, one Mk 16 octuple launcher for RUR-5A ASROC missiles, and one Bofors Type 71 four-barrel rocket-launcher
Electronics: one OPS-11 air-search radar, one OPS-17 surface-search radar, two Mk 35 gun-control radars used in conjunction with Mk 56 and Mk 63 gun fire-control systems, one Sangamo SQS-23 hull-mounted sonar (DDs 113-115) or OQS-3 hull-mounted sonar (DDs 119-121), and SQS-35(J) variable-depth sonar (DDs 113, 114, 120 and 121)
Propulsion: six Mitsubishi diesels delivering 19,760kW (26,500bhp) to two shafts

Performance: maximum speed 27kts; range 12,975km (8,065 miles) at 20kts
Complement: 210

Class

1. Japan (6)

Name	No.	Builders	Laid down	Commissioned
YAMAGUMO	DD 113	Mitsui	Mar 1964	Jan 1966
MAKIGUMO	DD 114	Uraga	June 1964	Mar 1966
ASAGUMO	DD 115	Maizuru	June 1965	Aug 1967
AOKUMO	DD 119	Sumitomo	Oct 1970	Nov 1972
AKIGUMO	DD 120	Sumitomo	July 1972	July 1974
YUGUMO	DD 121	Sumitomo	Feb 1976	Mar 1978

Remarks: One of the larger anti-submarine destroyer classes in the Japanese Maritime Self-Defense Force, the 'Yamagumo' class was to have been larger, the *Yugumo* (DD 121) being planned as the lead ship of an improved sub-class with CODOG machinery for a speed of 32kts. The 'Hatsuyuki' class replaced this.

'Z' class destroyer

UK

Displacement: 1,730 tons standard and 2,575 tons full load
Dimensions: length 362·8ft (110·6m); beam 35·7ft (10·9m); draught 16ft (4·9m)
Gun armament: four 4·5-in (114-mm) L/45 DP in four single mountings, and six 40-mm Bofors L/60 AA
Missile armament: none
Torpedo armament: none
Anti-submarine armament: four depth-charge throwers
Electronics: one Type 960 air-search radar, one Type 293 tactical radar, and one fire-control radar system

Propulsion: two Admiralty boilers supplying steam to two sets of Parsons geared turbines delivering 40,000shp (29,830kW) to two shafts
Performance: maximum speed 31kts; range 3,225 miles (5,190km) at 20kts
Complement: 186

Class

1. Egypt (1)

Name	No.	Builders	Laid down	Commissioned
EL FATEH	833	Wm. Denny	May 1942	Jan 1943

'A 69' class guided-missile frigate

France

Displacement: 950 tons standard and 1,170 tons (or 1,250 tons in later ships) full load
Dimensions: length 80·0m (262·5ft); beam 10·3m (33·8ft); draught 5·3m (17·4ft) to sonar dome and 3·0m (9·8ft) to keel
Gun armament: one 100-mm (3·9-in) L/55 and two 20-mm AA
Missile armament: two (or four in F 792 and later ships) container-launchers for single MM.38 (or MM.40 in F 792 and later ships) Exocet surface-to-surface missiles
Torpedo armament: none
Anti-submarine armament: one Mk 54 sextuple 375-mm (14·76-in) rocket-launcher, and four tubes for 550-mm (21·65-in) L 3 or 533-mm (21-in) L 5 torpedoes
Electronics: one Thompson-CSF DRBV 51A air- and surface-search radar, one Thomson-CSF DRBN 32 navigation radar, one Thomson-CSF DRBC 32E fire-control radar, one Thomson-CSF DUBA 25 hull-mounted attack sonar, one Thomson-CSF Vega weapon-direction system, and two CSEE Dagaie chaff launchers
Propulsion: two SEMT-Pielstick PC2V diesels delivering 8,950kW (12,000bhp) to two shafts
Performance: maximum speed 24kts; range 8,340km (5,185 miles) at 15kts; endurance 15 days
Complement: 5+29+45

Class

1. Argentina (3)

Name	No.	Builders	Laid down	Commissioned
DRUMMOND	P 1	Lorient ND	Mar 1976	Nov 1978
GUERRICO	P 2	Lorient ND	Oct 1976	Nov 1978
GRANVILLE	P 3	Lorient ND	late 1978	June 1981

2. France (15+2)

Name	No.	Builders	Laid down	Commissioned
D'ESTIENNE D'ORVES*	F 781	Lorient ND	Sep 1972	Sep 1976
AMYOT D'INVILLE	F 782	Lorient ND	Sep 1973	Oct 1976
DROGOU*	F 783	Lorient ND	Oct 1973	Sep 1976
DÉTROYAT	F 784	Lorient ND	Dec 1974	May 1977
JEAN MOULIN	F 785	Lorient ND	Jan 1975	May 1977
QUARTIER MAITRE ANQUETIL*	F 786	Lorient ND	Aug 1975	Feb 1978
COMMANDANT DE PIMODAN*	F 787	Lorient ND	Sep 1975	May 1978
SECOND MAITRE LE BIHAN	F 788	Lorient ND	Nov 1976	July 1979
LIEUTENANT DE VAISSEAU LE HENAFF	F 789	Lorient ND	—	Feb 1980
LIEUTENANT DE VAISSEAU LAVALLÉE	F 790	Lorient ND	Nov 1977	Aug 1980
COMMANDANT L'HERMINIER	F 791	Lorient ND	May 1979	Dec 1981
PREMIER MAITRE L'HER	F 792	Lorient ND	July 1979	1981
COMMANDANT BLAISON	F 793	Lorient ND	Nov 1979	1982
ENSEIGNE DE VAISSEAU JACOUBET	F 794	Lorient ND	June 1980	1982
COMMANDANT DUCUING	F 795	Lorient ND	Oct 1980	1982
—	F 796	Lorient ND	Mar 1981	1983
—	F 797	Lorient ND	—	1984

*fitted with Exocet

The Commandant Blaison (F 793) is one of 10 'A 69' class frigates fitted with Exocet anti-ship missiles. Of these 10 ships, the four earliest are fitted for two single MM.38s, while the last six (including the Commandant Blaison) carry two twin MM.40 container-launchers, located just aft of the funnel. Other weapon items visible are the 100-mm (3·9-in) DP gun, the anti-submarine rocket-launcher above the after deckhouse, and the forward ends of the two starboard 533-mm (21-in) fixed torpedo tubes in the angle of the deckhouse. the radars are all grouped above the bridge and on the mast, and include DRBV 51A combined-search radar, DRBN 32 navigation radar and DRBC 32E fire-control radar. Other sensors include DUBA 25 hull-mounted sonar.

Remarks: Officially rated as corvettes, the French 'A 69' class frigates are designed for coastal anti-submarine operations, though 10 of the planned 18 ships have substantial anti-ship capability through the provision of Exocet surface-to-surface missile capability in all ships, though only those serving with the Mediterranean Fleet are actually fitted with the container-launchers. It is planned to upgrade all missile-carrying ships to MM.40 standard. The ships from *Premier Maitre L'Her* (F 792) onwards are fitted with two CSEE Dagaie chaff launchers, and earlier ships are receiving such launchers during the course of refits. The class has been found to possess excellent qualities of seaworthiness and economy, and this has promoted the use of the ships for a variety of alternative roles such as scouting, training and overseas deployments. Provision is made in the design for the accommodation of a troop detachment of one officer and 17 men.

'Almirante Clemente' class frigate

Venezuela

Displacement: 1,300 tons standard and 1,500 tons full load

Dimensions: length 99·1 m (325·1 ft); beam 10·84 m (35·6 ft); draught 3·7 m (12·2 ft)

Gun armament: two 76-mm (3-in) OTO-Melara Compact L/62 in single mountings, and two 40-mm AA in one twin mounting

Missile armament: none

Torpedo armament: none

Anti-submarine armament: two Hedgehog mortars, four depth-charge throwers and two depth-charge racks

Electronics: one Plessey AWS 1 air-search and target designation radar and one I-band fire-control radar

Propulsion: two Foster-Wheeler boilers supplying steam to two geared turbines delivering 17,900 kW (24,000 shp) to two shafts

Performance: maximum speed 32 kts; range 6,500 km (4,040 miles) at 15 kts

Complement: 12 + 150

Class

1. Venezuela (2)				Com-
Name	No.	Builders	Laid down	missioned
ALMIRANTE CLEMENTE	D 23	Ansaldo	May 1954	1956
GENERAL JOSÉ TRINIDAD MORAN	D 24	Ansaldo	May 1954	1956

Remarks: The two Venezuelan 'Almirante Clemente' class frigates are the survivors of a class of six such ships ordered from Italy in 1953. For their time the ships were particularly heavily armed, the gun armament comprising four 4-in (102-mm) DP guns in two twin mountings, four 40-mm Bofors AA guns in two twin mountings and eight 20-mm Oerlikon AA guns in four twin mountings. The two ships that survive were modernized by Cammell Laird and Plessey in the period from April 1968 to January 1976, the 4-in (102-mm) mountings being replaced by two 76-mm (3-in) OTO-Melara Compact mountings and the AA armament being reduced to a single 40-mm twin mounting and the radar fit being extensively altered.

'Almirante Pereira da Silva' class frigate

Portugal

Displacement: 1,450 tons standard and 1,950 tons full load

Dimensions: length 95·9 m (314·6 ft); beam 11·26 m (36·9 ft); draught 5·3 m (17·4 ft)

Gun armament: four 3-in (76-mm) L/50 in two twin mountings

Missile armament: none

Torpedo armament: none

Anti-submarine armament: two triple Mk 32 tube mountings for 12·75-in (324-mm) Mk 44 A/S torpedoes, and two four-barrel Bofors 375-mm (14·76-in) rocket launchers

Electronics: one Microlambda MLA 1b air-search radar, one Decca RM 316P navigation radar, one Decca Type 978 tactical radar, one SPG-34 gun fire-control radar, extensive electronic warfare suite, one Sangamo SQS-32A hull-mounted long-range search sonar, one Litton SQA-10 variable-depth sonar and one DUBA 3A attack sonar

Propulsion: two Foster-Wheeler boilers supplying steam to De Laval geared turbines delivering 14,915 kW (20,000 shp) to one shaft

Performance: maximum speed 27 kts; range 5,975 km (3,715 miles) at 15 kts

Complement: 12 + 154

Class

1. Portugal (3)				Com-
Name	No.	Builders	Laid down	missioned
ALMIRANTE PEREIRA DA SILVA	F 472	Estaleiros Navais	June 1962	Dec 1966
ALMIRANTE GAGO COUTINHO	F 473	Estaleiros Navais	Dec 1963	Nov 1967
ALMIRANTE MAGALHÃES CORREA	F 474	Estaleiros Navais	Aug 1965	Nov 1968

Remarks: The Portuguese 'Almirante Pereira da Silva' class is based on the US 'Dealey' class design, fairly extensively modified to suit Portuguese operational requirements. The class has been in service for nearly 20 years, and is ripe for replacement as maintenance is becoming difficult and the combined weapon/sensor fit is no longer adequate for Portugal's responsibilities within the NATO Atlantic requirement. Financial considerations at first dictated that the class be upgraded rather than replaced, but the emergence of NATO funding has permitted Portugal to undertake a new class of three modern frigates based on the Dutch 'Kortenaer' class, which will permit the retirement of the 'Almirante Pereira da Silva' class in the late 1980s. All three ships were built fairly rapidly with the use of prefabricated sections.

*The **Almirante Pereira da Silva** (F 472) is the lead ship of an obsolescent class.*

'Alpino' class frigate

Italy

Displacement: 2,000 tons standard and 2,700 tons full load

Dimensions: length 113·3 m (371·7 ft); beam 13·3 m (43·6 ft); draught 3·9 m (12·7 ft)

Gun armament: six 76-mm (3-in) L/62 DP in six single mountings

Missile armament: none

Torpedo armament: none

Anti-submarine armament: two triple Mk 32 tube mountings for 12·75-in (324-mm) Mk 44 A/S torpedoes, one Mk 113 semi-automatic depth-charge thrower, and helicopter torpedoes (see below)

Aircraft: two Agusta-Bell AB.212ASW helicopters

Electronics: one RCA SPS-12 surface-search radar, one SMA SPQ 2 search and navigation radar, three Orion gun fire-control radars as part of the Elsag/Argo 'O' control system, one SQS-43 hull-mounted sonar, one Litton SQA-10 variable-depth sonar, and one SCLAR overhead chaff/decoy/flare rocket system

Propulsion: CODAG (COmbined Diesel And Gas turbine) arrangement with four Tosi diesels delivering 12,525 kW (16,800 hp) and two Tosi-Metrovick gas turbines delivering 11,185 kW (15,000 hp) to two shafts

Performance: maximum speed 28 kts on diesels and gas turbines, or 20 kts on diesels; range 6,500 km (4,040 miles) at 18 kts

Complement: 13 + 150

Class

1. Italy (2)				Com-
Name	No.	Builders	Laid down	missioned
ALPINO	F 580	Cantieri Navali Riuniti	Feb 1963	Jan 1968
CARABINIERE	F 581	Cantieri Navali Riuniti	Jan 1965	Apr 1968

Remarks: The two 'Alpino' class frigates are moderately effective escort ships, though their light anti-aircraft armament would relegate them more to convoy than to fleet work in the event of major hostilities. The combination of two Agusta-Bell AB.212ASW helicopters, variable-depth and hull-mounted sonars and an automatically-loaded and trainable depth-charge mortar provides fairly useful anti-submarine capability.

*The **Carabiniere** (F 581) of the 'Alpino' class reveals some of her features, which include four beam- and two forward-mounted 76-mm (3-in) DP guns, the depth-charge mortar and, beside the latter, one of the two SCLAR launchers.*

'Amazon' class (Type 21) guided-missile frigate
UK

Displacement: 2,750 tons standard and 3,250+ tons full load
Dimensions: length 384ft (117·0m); beam 41·7ft (12·7m); draught 19·5ft (5·9m)
Gun armament: one 4·5-in (114-mm) L/55 in a single Mk 8 mounting, and two 20-mm Oerlikon cannon in single mountings
Missile armament: four MM.38 Exocet surface-to-surface missiles in single launchers, and one quadruple launcher for Sea Cat surface-to-air missiles (to be replaced by GWS25 Sea Wolf possibly during second refit)
Torpedo armament: none
Anti-submarine armament: two triple tube mountings for 12·75-in (324-mm) Mk 46 A/S torpedoes, and helicopter-launched torpedoes (see below)
Aircraft: one Westland Wasp HAS.Mk 1 or Westland Lynx HAS.Mk 2 helicopter

Electronics: one Marconi Type 992Q surveillance and target-indication radar, one Decca Type 978 navigation radar, two GWS24 Sea Cat control radars, two Selenia Orion RTN-10X WSA 4 gun fire-control systems, one Cossor Type 1010 IFF interrogator, one Plessey PTR 461 IFF transponder, SCOT satellite communications system, Computer-Assisted Action Information System, one Graseby Type 184M panoramic medium-range search and attack sonar, and one Kelvin Hughes Type 164M side-looking classification sonar
Propulsion: COGOG (COmbined Gas turbine Or Gas turbine) system, with two Rolls-Royce Olympus TM3B gas turbines delivering 56,000bhp (41,760kW) or two Rolls-Royce Tyne RM1A gas turbines delivering 8,500shp (6,340kW) to two shafts
Performance: maximum speed 30kts on Olympus turbines or 18kts on Tyne turbines; range 4,600 miles (7,400km) at 17kts or 1,380 miles (2,220km) at 30kts
Complement: 13+162, with a maximum of 192 possible
Class

1. UK (6)

Name	No.	Builders	Laid down	Commissioned
AMAZON	F 169	Vosper Thornycroft	Nov 1969	May 1974
ACTIVE	F 171	Vosper Thornycroft	July 1971	June 1977
AMBUSCADE	F 172	Yarrow (Shipbuilders)	Sep 1971	Sep 1975
ARROW	F 173	Yarrow (Shipbuilders)	Sep 1972	July 1976
ALACRITY	F 174	Yarrow (Shipbuilders)	Mar 1973	July 1977
AVENGER	F 185	Yarrow (Shipbuilders)	Oct 1974	July 1978

Remarks: The 'Amazon' or 'Type 21' class frigate was the first commercially-designed warship produced for the Royal Navy for many years, and was also the first British frigate class designed from the outset for gas turbine propulsion. The class has not proved altogether successful, additional ballast being required to maintain stability. Two of the class, the *Ardent* and *Antelope*, were sunk in the Falklands campaign of 1982. Of the others, the *Amazon* (F 169) and *Ambuscade* (F 172) are not fitted with Exocet missiles.

The Arrow (F 173) was the fifth of the 'Amazon' class to be built.

'Annapolis' class frigate
Canada

Displacement: 2,400 tons standard and 3,000 tons full load
Dimensions: length 371ft (113·1m); beam 42ft (12·8m); draught 14·4ft (4·4m)
Gun armament: two 3-in (76-mm) L/60 in one Mk 33 twin mounting
Missile armament: none

Torpedo armament: none
Anti-submarine armament: two triple Mk 32 tube mountings for 12·75-in (324-mm) Mk 44 A/S torpedoes, and one Limbo Mk 10 projector
Aircraft: one Sikorsky CH-124 Sea King helicopter
Electronics: one RCA SPS-12 air-search radar, one Raytheon/Sylvania SPS-10 surface-search radar, one Bell SPG-48 fire-control radar operating in conjunction with the Mk 69 gun fire-control radar, Type 501 bottom classification sonar, Type 502 Limbo-control sonar, Type 503 search sonar, Type 504 variable-depth sonar, SQS-10/11 sonar, URN-20 TACAN and Litton CCS-280 data system
Propulsion: two Babock & Wilcox boilers supplying steam to English Electric geared turbines delivering 30,000shp (22,370kW) to two shafts
Performance: maximum speed 28kts; range 5,475 miles (8,810km) at 14kts
Complement: 11+199
Class

1. Canada (2)

Name	No.	Builders	Laid down	Commissioned
ANNAPOLIS	265	Halifax Shipyards Ltd	July 1960	Dec 1964
NIPIGON	266	Marine Industries Ltd	Apr 1960	May 1964

Remarks: The Destroyer Life Extension Program has added Sea Sparrow SAMs, new air-search radar, new sonar and new electronic warfare systems to these two ships in the period 1982-4.

The Annapolis (265) is an impressively capable anti-submarine frigate.

'Atrevida' class frigate
Spain

Displacement: 1,030 tons standard and 1,135 tons full load
Dimensions: length 75·5m (247·8ft); beam 10·2m (33·5ft); draught 3·0m (9·8ft)
Gun armament: one 3-in (76-mm) L/50 in a Mk 22 single mounting and three 40-mm SP-48 L/60 AA in single mountings

Missile armament: none
Torpedo armament: none
Anti-submarine armament: two Hedgehog mortars, eight depth-charge mortars and two depth-charge racks
Mines: 20
Electronics: one Raytheon SPS-5B combined search radar and one QHBa sonar
Propulsion: two Sulzer diesels delivering 3,000bhp (2,235kW) to two shafts
Performance: maximum speed 18·5kts; range 14,825km (9,210 miles) at 10kts
Complement: 9+123

Class

1. Spain (4)

Name	No.	Builders	Laid down	Commissioned
ATREVIDA	PA 61	Bazán	June 1950	Aug 1954
PRINCESA	PA 62	Bazán	Mar 1953	Oct 1957
NAUTILUS	PA 64	Bazán	July 1953	Dec 1959
VILLA DE BILBAO	PA 65	Bazán	Mar 1953	Sep 1960

'Auk' class frigate

USA

Displacement: 890 tons standard and 1,250 tons full load
Dimensions: length 221·2ft (67·4m); beam 32·2ft (9·8m); draught 10·8ft (3·1m)
Gun armament: two 3-in (76-mm) L/50 DP in single mountings, four 40-mm Bofors AA in two twin mountings, and four 20-mm Oerlikon AA in two twin mountings
Missile armament: none
Torpedo armament: none
Anti-submarine armament: one triple Mk 32 tube mounting for 12·75-in (324-mm) Mk 44 A/S torpedoes, one Hedgehog mortar and depth charges
Electronics: one surface-search radar, one navigation radar and one sonar
Propulsion: diesel-electric arrangement, with General Motors diesels powering electric motors delivering 3,535 bhp (2,635 kW) to two shafts
Fuel: diesel oil
Performance: maximum speed 18 kts
Complement: about 110

Class

. Mexico (18)

Name	No.	Builders	Launched
LEANDRO VALLE	G-01	Pennsylvania S.Y.	July 1942
GUILLERMO PRIETO	G-02	Savannah Machine	July 1942
MARIANO ESCOBEDO	G-03	General Eng.	Jan 1943
PONCIANO ARRIAGA	G-04	General Eng.	Jan 1943
MANUEL DOBLADO	G-05	General Eng.	Feb 1943
SEBASTIAN L. DE TEJADA	G-06	General Eng.	Apr 1943
SANTOS DEGOLLADO	G-07	General Eng.	May 1943
IGNACIO DE LA LLAVE	G-08	Associated	Feb 1943
JUAN N. ALVARES	G-09	General Eng.	June 1943
MANUEL GUTIERREZ ZAMORA	G-10	Gulf S.B.	Aug 1944
VALENTIN G. FARIAS	G-11	General Eng.	Apr 1942
IGNACIO MANUEL ALTAMIRANO	G-12	John Mathis	Sept 1942
FRANCISCO ZARCO	G-13	Savannah Machine	Sept 1942
IGNACIO L. VALLARTA	G-14	Gulf S.B.	Apr 1942
JESUS G. ORTEGA	G-15	General Eng.	Jan 1943
MELCHOR OCAMPO	G-16	Gulf S.B.	Sept 1944
JUAN ALDAMA	G-18	Pennsylvania S.Y.	July 1942
HERMENEGILDO GALEANA	G-19	Winslow Marine	Nov 1942

2. Philippines (2)

Name	No.	Builders	Commissioned
RIZAL	PS 69	Savannah Machine	Aug 1945
QUEZON	PS 70	Associated S.B.	Feb 1944

3. South Korea (3)

Name	No.	Builders	Launched
SHIN SONG	PCE 711	Savannah Machine	Jan 1944
SUNCHON	PCE 712	American S.B. Co	Oct 1942
KOJE	PCE 713	Gulf S.B.	Sep 1943

4. Taiwan (3)

Name	No.	Builders	Commissioned
PING JIN	867	American S.B. Co	Nov 1942
WU SHENG	884	Savannah Machine	Apr 1945
CHU YUNG	896	American S.B. Co	Aug 1945

5. Uruguay (1)

Name	No.	Builders	Commissioned
COMANDANTE PEDRO CAMPBELL	4	Defoe B & M Works	Nov 1942

Remarks: The 'Auk' class, now widely used for patrol duties under the courtesy designation frigate, was produced in the USA during World War II as an ocean minesweeper force. However, its ships proved to have the endurance, seakeeping qualities and speed to serve as escorts in secondary theatres, and it is this latter capability that has maintained the type in service to the present. The specification applies in detail to the version in service with the navy of Taiwan, but is generally applicable to the 'Auk' class ships in service with other secondary naval forces. The largest operator of the type is the Mexican navy, which deploys 18 as patrol vessels and a single converted example as a survey vessel, the class being transferred as six ships in February 1973, four ships in April 1973 and nine ships in September 1973. The armament fit of the 18 patrol vessels is one 3-in (76-mm) L/50 gun, four 40-mm AA guns in two twin mountings, and two 20-mm AA guns in one twin mounting. The survey vessel *Mariano Matamoros* (H 01) is unarmed. The Philippines operate two 'Auk' class ships, again with their minesweeping gear removed. The ships were transferred in June 1965 and August 1967 respectively, and at that time received a second 3-in (76-mm) gun to complement one other 3-in (76-mm) L/50 gun, four 40-mm AA guns and four 20-mm AA guns, the two AA types disposed each in two twin mountings. The after 3-in (76-mm) gun has now been replaced by a helicopter platform, though no embarked helicopter is carried. The anti-submarine armament comprises one triple Mk 32 tube mounting, one Hedgehog mortar and depth charges. The three Taiwanese ships were transferred in 1965, 1965 and 1967, and one of them is fitted for minelaying. Uruguay's sole example was transferred in 1966 and is similar to the Filipino ships in armament fit.

The pennant number G-14 identifies this ex-US 'Auk' class minesweeper as the Mexican navy's Ignacio L. Vallarta *patrol ship.*

'Baleares' class (Type F70) guided-missile frigate

Spain

Displacement: 3,015 tons standard and 4,175 tons full load
Dimensions: length 133·6m (438ft); beam 14·3m (46·9ft); draught 4·7m (15·4ft)
Gun armament: one 5-in (127-mm) L/54 in a Mk 42 mounting, and (to be fitted) one Meroka AA and anti-missile point-defence system with two 20-mm Oerlikon R TG six-barrel cannon
Missile armament: one Mk 22 lightweight launcher for 16 RIM-24 Tartar or RIM-67 Standard ER surface-to-air missiles, and (to be fitted) four or eight launchers for RGM-84A Harpoon surface-to-surface missiles
Torpedo armament: none
Anti-submarine armament: one octuple RUR-5A ASROC launcher, four Mk 32 tubes for 12·75-in (324-mm) Mk 46 torpedoes, and two Mk 25 tubes for 19-in (484·5-mm) Mk 37 torpedoes; a maximum of 41 A/S torpedoes is carried
Electronics: one Hughes SPS-52A 3D air-search radar, one Raytheon/Sylvania SPS-10 surface-search radar, one Raytheon Marine Pathfinder navigation radar, one Raytheon SPG-51C missile-control radar used in conjunction with the Mk 74 missile-control system and Mk 73 missile-control director, one Western Electric SPG-53B gun/missile-control radar used in conjunction with the Mk 68 gun fire-control system, one Mk 114 torpedo-control system, one Sangamo SQS-23 long-range hull-mounted active sonar, one EDO SQS-35V variable-depth sonar, SRN-15A TACAN (F71 only), and WLR-1 electronic support measures (to be replaced by Elsag electronic support measures)
Propulsion: two V2M-type boilers supplying steam to one set of Westinghouse geared turbines delivering 35,000 shp (26,100 kW) to one shaft

Performance: maximum speed 28 kts; range 8,350 km (5,190 miles) at 20 kts
Complement: 15 + 241

Class

1. Spain (5)

Name	No.	Builders	Laid down	Commissioned
BALEARES	F 71	Bazán	Oct 1968	Sep 1973
ANDALUCIA	F 72	Bazán	July 1969	May 1974
CATALUÑA	F 73	Bazán	Aug 1970	Jan 1975
ASTURIAS	F 74	Bazán	Mar 1971	Dec 1975
EXTREMADURA	F 75	Bazán	Nov 1971	Nov 1976

Remarks: The Spanish navy's 'Baleares' class frigate is modelled on the US 'Knox' class but has a different SAM launcher (with few missiles), Mk 25 anti-submarine torpedo tubes, no helicopter facilities and revised sonar.

'Baptista de Andrade' class frigate
Portugal

Displacement: 1,250 tons standard and 1,380 tons full load
Dimensions: length 84·6m (277·5ft); beam 10·3m (33·8ft); draught 3·6m (11·8ft)
Gun armament: one 100-mm (3·9-in) L/55 DP and two 40-mm Bofors L/70 AA in single mountings
Missile armament: provision for two MM.38 Exocet surface-to-surface missiles
Torpedo armament: none
Anti-submarine armament: two triple Mk 32 tube mountings for 12·75-in (324-mm) Mk 44/46 torpedoes
Electronics: one Plessey AWS 2 air-search radar, one Decca TM 626 navigation radar, one Thomson-CSF Pollux fire-control radar used in conjunction with the CSEE Panda director, and one Diodon sonar

Propulsion: two SEMT-Pielstick PA6V-280 diesels delivering 8,170kW (10,960bhp) to two shafts
Performance: maximum speed 23·5kts; range 11,000km (6,835 miles) at 18kts
Complement: 107, plus provision for a marine detachment of 34 men

Class
1. Portugal (4)

Name	No.	Builders	Laid down	Commissioned
BAPTISTE DE ANDRADE	F 486	Bazán	1972	Nov 1974
JOAO ROBY	F 487	Bazán	1972	Mar 1975
AFONSO CERQUEIRA	F 488	Bazán	1973	June 1975
OLIVEIRA E. CARMO	F 489	Bazán	1972	Feb 1975

'Bear' class medium-endurance cutter
USA

Displacement: 1,780 tons full load
Dimensions: length 270ft (82·3m); beam 38ft (11·6m); draught 13·5ft (4·1m)
Gun armament: one 3-in (76-mm) L/62 in a Mk 75 mounting, and provision for one 20-mm close-in weapons system mounting
Missile armament: provision for RGM-84A Harpoon surface-to-surface missiles
Torpedo armament: none
Anti-submarine armament: helicopter-launched torpedoes
Aircraft: one Sikorsky HH-52A or Sikorsky SH-60B Sea Hawk helicopter
Electronics: one SPS-64(V) radar, Mk 92 weapon-control system, one SQR-19 Towed Array Sonar System, and Mk 36 Super Chaffroc rapid-blooming overhead chaff system
Propulsion: diesels delivering 7,000bhp (5,220kW) to two shafts
Performance: maximum speed 19·5kts; range 7,830 miles (12,600km) at 13·5kts
Complement: 13+82

Class
1. USA (6+7)

Name	No.	Builders	Commissioned
BEAR	WMEC 901	Tacoma B.B. Co	Aug 1982
TAMPA	WMEC 902	Tacoma B.B. Co	Dec 1982
HARRIET LANE	WMEC 903	Tacoma B.B. Co	Mar 1983
NORTHLAND	WMEC 904	Tacoma B.B. Co	June 1983
SPENCER	WMEC 905	Robert E. Derecktor Corporation	June 1984
SENECA	WMEC 906	Robert E. Derecktor Corporation	Oct 1984
ESCANABA	WMEC 907	Robert E. Derecktor Corporation	Jan 1985
TAHOMA	WMEC 908	Robert E. Derecktor Corporation	May 1985
— (ex-*Argus*)	WMEC 909	Robert E. Derecktor Corporation	Sep 1985
— (ex-*Tahoma*)	WMEC 910	Robert E. Derecktor Corporation	Jan 1986
— (ex-*Erie*)	WMEC 911	Robert E. Derecktor Corporation	May 1986
— (ex-*McCulloch*)	WMEC 912	Robert E. Derecktor Corporation	Sep 1986
— (ex-*Ewing*)	WMEC 913	Robert E. Derecktor Corporation	Jan 1987

'Bergamini' class frigate
ITALY

Displacement: 1,650 tons full load
Dimensions: length 94·0m (308·4ft); beam 11·4m (37·4ft); draught 3·2m (10·5m)
Gun armament: two 76-mm (3-in) L/62 DP OTO-Melara in single mountings
Missile armament: none
Torpedo armament: none
Anti-submarine armament: two triple Mk 32 tube mountings for 12·75-in (324-mm) Mk 44 A/S torpedoes, and one Mk 113 semi-automatic depth-charge mortar
Aircraft: one Agusta-Bell B.204B helicopter
Electronics: one RCA SPS-12 combined search radar, one SMA SPQ 2 search and navigation radar, one Selenia Orion 3 radar used in conjunction with the OG3 fire-control system, one SPR A radar interception set and one SQS-40 hull-mounted sonar
Propulsion: four Fiat CB/LR diesels delivering 11,930kW (16,000shp) to two shafts
Performance: maximum speed 24kts; range 5,500km (3,420 miles) at 18kts
Complement: 13+150

Class
1. Italy (2)

Name	No.	Builders	Laid down	Commissioned
VIRGINIO FASAN	F 594	Navalmeccanica	Mar 1960	Oct 1962
CARLO MARGOTTINI	F 595	Navalmeccanica	May 1957	May 1962

The **Virginio Fasan (F 594)** is one of two surviving 'Bergamini' class frigates.

'Berk' class frigate
Turkey

Displacement: 1,450 tons standard and 1,950 tons full load
Dimensions: length 95·15m (312·2ft); beam 11·82m (37·8ft); draught 4·4m (14·4ft)
Gun armament: two 3-in (76-mm) L/50 DP in single mountings
Missile armament: none
Torpedo armament: none
Anti-submarine armament: two triple Mk 32 tube mountings for 12·75-in (324-mm) A/S torpedoes, two Hedgehog Mk 11 mortars, and one depth-charge rack
Aircraft: provision for one helicopter on a platform aft
Electronics: one Lockheed SPS-40 air-search radar, one Raytheon/Sylvania SPS-10 surface-search radar, one SPG-34 fire-control radar used in conjunction with two Mk 63 gun fire-control systems, and one SQS-11 hull-mounted sonar
Propulsion: four Fiat-Tosi 3-016-RSS delivering 17,900kW (24,000bhp) to one shaft
Performance: maximum speed 25kts

Complement: not known

Class
1. Turkey (2)

Name	No.	Builders	Laid down	Commissioned
BERK	D 358	Gölcük Naval Yard	Mar 1967	July 1972
PEYK	D 359	Gölcük Naval Yard	Jan 1968	July 1975

Remarks: Evolved from the US 'Claud Jones' class design, the Turkish 'Berk' class frigates are the first major warships to be built in Turkey, and mark an important step in the process of modernizing the Turkish navy. It is clear, however, that both ships could benefit from a more modern fit of weapons and sensors, and from *better helicopter facilities. Nevertheless, the combination of local construction and imported design bodes well for the future of the hitherto neglected Turkish navy.*

'Black Swan' class frigate
UK/India

Displacement: 1,490 tons standard and 1,925 tons full load
Dimensions: length 299ft (91·2m); beam 37·5ft (11·4m); draught 8·6ft (2·6m)
Gun armament: four 4-in (102-mm) L/45 DP in two twin Mk 19 mountings, four 37-mm L/60 AA and two 20-mm AA
Missile armament: none
Torpedo armament: none
Anti-submarine armament: four depth-charge throwers and depth-charge racks
Electronics: navigation and search radar
Propulsion: two boilers supplying steam to two geared turbines delivering 36,000shp (26,845kW) to two shafts
Performance: maximum speed 19kts; range 3,900 miles (6,275km) at 12kts
Complement: 180

Class
1. Egypt (1)

Name	No.	Builders	Laid down	Commissioned
TARIQ	555	Yarrow (Shipbuilders) Ltd	Oct 1941	Jan 1943

2. India (1)

Name	No.	Builders	Laid down	Commissioned
KISTNA	F 46	Yarrow (Shipbuilders) Ltd	July 1942	Aug 1943

Remarks: Now very elderly, the 'Black Swan' class frigate was a World War II design, and the Indian ship, to which the specification applies, is now used only for training. The Egyptian ship was transferred in 1949, and differs from the *Kistna* in having six 4-in (102-mm) guns in three twin mountings; like the Indian vessel, the *Tariq* has little real operational significance because of its lack of modern sensors and armament.

'Brazilian' class guided-missile frigate
Brazil

Displacement: 1,900 tons full load
Dimensions: length 95·8m (314·2ft); beam 11·4m (37·4ft); draught 3·7m (12ft)
Gun armament: one 4·5-in (114-mm) L/55 in a Mk 8 single mounting, and two 40-mm Bofors 40-mm L/70 AA in two single mountings
Missile armament: two twin container-launchers for four Gabriel anti-ship missiles (possibly MM.40 Exocet anti-ship missiles)
Torpedo armament: none
Anti-submarine armament: two triple Mk 32 tube mountings for 12·75-in (324-mm) Mk 46 anti-submarine torpedoes, and helicoipter-launched weapons (see below)
Aircraft: one Westland Lynx Mk 2 helicopter in a hangar aft
Electronics: one search radar, one navigation radar, one fire-control radar, one Ferranti WSA420 fire-control system, one Ferranti CAAIS combat-information system, one hull-mounted medium-frequency sonar, one data-link system, one ECM system, and one Plessey Shield chaff/decoy launcher system
Propulsion: CODOG (COmbined Diesel Or Gas turbine) arrangement, with two MTU diesels delivering 2,570kW (3,450shp) and one General Electric LM 2500 gas turbine delivering 27,500shp (20,505kW) to two shafts
Performance: maximum speed 29kts on gas turbine or 15kts on diesels; range 7,400km (4,600 miles)
Complement: 120

Class
1. Brazil (0+4+8)

Remarks: Designed in Brazil with the aid of Marine Technik of West Germany, the new Brazilian frigate was ordered in February 1982, the first four units to be built by the Arsenal de Marinho do Rio de Janeiro (two ships) and private yards (two ships). The first ship is scheduled to commission in 1987, and the development of this important type of warship in South America for local construction is telling evidence of the fact that the naval arms race in that continent is becoming technologically more sophisticated, opening up the possibility of South American exports into markets up to now dominated by the products of the USA and Europe, and this Brazilian frigate would be an able competitor.

'Bremen' class (Type 122) guided-missile frigate
West Germany

Displacement: 3,415 tons full load
Dimensions: length 130·5m (428·1ft); beam 14·4m (48·5ft); draught 6·0m (19·7ft)
Gun armament: one 76-mm (3-in) L/62 DP OTO-Melara Compact, and one 105-mm (4·13-in) Breda 20-barrel rocket-launcher
Missile armament: two quadruple launchers for eight RGM-84A Harpoon surface-to-surface missiles, one eight-cell launcher for RIM-7 Sea Sparrow surface-to-air missiles, two multiple launchers for FIM-92 Stinger surface-to-air missiles, and (to be fitted) two launchers for RAM surface-to-air missiles
Torpedo armament: none
Anti-submarine armament: two twin Mk 32 tube mountings for 12·75-in (324-mm) Mk 44/46 A/S torpedoes, and helicopter-launched torpedoes
Aircraft: two Westland Lynx helicopters
Electronics: one Hollandse Signaalapparaten DA-08 air-search and target-indication radar, one Hollandse Signaalapparaten WM-25 surface-search and fire-control radar, one Hollandse Signaalapparaten ZW-06 surface-search radar, one SMA 3RM 20 surface-search radar, one Hollandse Signaalapparaten surveillance and target indicator radar, one SATIR fire-control system with fully automatic data processing, and Friedrich Krupp/Krupp-Atlas Elektronik DSQS-21 BZ hull-mounted active/passive sonar
Propulsion: CODOG (COmbined Diesel Or Gas turbine) arrangement, with two General Electric LM 2500 gas turbines delivering 51,600hp (38,480kW) or two MTU 20V-956-TB92 diesels delivering 7,755kW (10,400hp) to two shafts
Performance: maximum speed 30+ kts on gas turbines or 20kts on diesels; range 7,400km (4,600 miles) at 18kts
Complement: 203, with a maximum of 225 possible

Class
1. West Germany (4+2)

Name	No.	Builders	Laid down	Commissioned
BREMEN	F 207	Bremer Vulkan	July 1979	Apr 1982
NIEDERSACHSEN	F 208	AG Weser	Nov 1970	Oct 1982
RHEINLAND-PFALZ	F 209	Blohm und Voss	June 1980	Apr 1983
EMDEN	F 210	Thyssen Nordseewerke	June 1980	Oct 1983
KÖLN	F 211	Blohm und Voss	Dec 1980	Apr 1984
KARLSRUHE	F 212	Howaldtswerke	May 1981	Oct 1984

The Bremen (F 207) is lead ship of the West German navy's 'Bremen' or 'Type 122' class guided-missile frigate, designed to replace the now-deleted 'Fletcher' class destroyer and 'Köln' class frigate. Distinctive features of the design are (from bow to stern) the 76-mm (3-in) OTO-Melara Compact gun, the octuple Sea Sparrow SAM launcher, the Sea Sparrow control radar (above the bridge), the WM-25 fire-control radar (in the globe above the rear of the forward superstructure blocks, the DA-08 surveillance radar (above the forward end of the helicopter hangar) and the large hangar and flight deck for two Westland Lynx helicopters.

Remarks: The 'Bremen' or 'Type 122' guided-missile frigate has been developed from the Dutch 'Kortenaer' class design to meet the West German navy's specific requirements for a frigate able to operate in high-threat areas as an effective anti-ship and anti-submarine system. The air and underwater threats are countered effectively by surface-to-air missile systems (Sea Sparrow, Stinger and RAM-ASDM) and Mk 32 tube mountings, while offensive capability is bestowed by the eight Harpoon anti-ship missiles and the two well-equipped Lynx anti-submarine helicopters. The 76-mm (3-in) OTO-Melara Compact gun and WM-25 fire-control system provide useful defence against fast attack craft, moreover.

'Bronstein' class frigate

USA

Displacement: 2,360 tons standard and 2,650 tons full load

Dimensions: length 371·5 ft (113·2 m); beam 40·5 ft (12·34 m); draught 23 ft (7·0 m) to sonar dome

Gun armament: two 3-in (76-mm) L/50 DP in one Mk 33 twin mounting

Missile armament: none

Torpedo armament: none

Anti-submarine armament: one octuple launcher for RUR-5A ASROC missiles, two triple Mk 32 tube mountings for 12·75-in (324-mm) Mk 44/46 A/S torpedoes, and helicopter-launched torpedoes (see below)

Aircraft: provision for one Kaman SH-2F Seasprite helicopter on a platform aft

Electronics: one Raytheon/Sylvania SPS-10 surface-search radar, one Lockheed SPS-40 air-search radar, one SPG-35 fire-control radar used in conjunction with the Mk 56 gun fire-control system, one Mk 114 A/S fire-control system, one Mk 1 target-designation system, one EDO/General Electric SQS-26 bow-mounted 'bottom-bounce' sonar, one SQR-15 Towed Array Surveillance System sonar, one OE-82 satellite communications antenna and SRR-1 satellite communications antenna

Propulsion: two Foster-Wheeler boilers supplying steam to one De Laval geared turbine delivering 20,000 shp (14,915 kW) to one shaft

Performance: maximum speed 26 kts

Complement: 16+180

First of the US second-generation frigates, the Bronstein (FF 1037) and her sister ship may be regarded as prototypes for definitive classes such as the 'Garcia', 'Brooke' and 'Knox' classes, of which all use features pioneered or developed in the attractive 'Bronstein' class of frigate, of which one unit is attached each to the Pacific and Atlantic Fleets.

Class

1. USA (2)

Name	No.	Builders	Laid down	Com-missioned
BRONSTEIN	FF 1037	Avondale Shipyards	May 1961	June 1963
McCLOY	FF 1038	Avondale Shipyards	Sep 1961	Oct 1963

'Brooke' class guided-missile frigate

USA

Displacement: 2,645 tons standard and 3,425 tons full load

Dimensions: length 414·5 ft (126·3 m); beam 44·2 ft (13·47 m); draught 24·2 ft (7·4 m) to sonar dome and 15 ft (4·6 m) to keel

Gun armament: one 5-in (127-mm) L/38 DP in a Mk 30 mounting

Missile armament: one Mk 22 single launcher for 16 RIM-66 Standard-MR surface-to-air missiles

Torpedo armament: none

Anti-submarine armament: one octuple launcher for RUR-5A ASROC missiles, two triple Mk 32 tube mountings for 12·75-in (324-mm) Mk 44/46 A/S torpedoes, and helicopter-launched torpedoes (see below)

Aircraft: one Kaman SH-2F Seasprite helicopter

Electronics: one Hughes SPS-52 3D air-search radar, one Raytheon/Sylvania SPS-10 surface-search radar, one Raytheon SPG-51C missile-control radar used in conjunction with the Mk 74 missile fire-control system, one SPG-35 gun-control radar used in conjunction with the Mk 56 gun fire-control system, one EDO/General Electric SQS-26 bow-mounted 'bottom-bounce' sonar used in conjunction with the Mk 114 A/S fire-control system, one Mk 4 weapon-direction system, Mk 36 Super Chaffroc rapid-blooming overhead chaff system, one Raytheon SLQ-32 electronic support measures system, one OE-82 satellite communications antenna, SRR-1 satellite communications receiver, and WSC-3 satellite communications transceiver

Propulsion: two Foster-Wheeler boilers supplying steam to one geared turbine (Westinghouse in FFGs 1-3 and General Electric in FFGs 4-6) delivering 35,000 shp (26,100 kW) to one shaft

Performance: maximum speed 27·2 kts; range 4,600 miles (7,400 km) at 20 kts

Complement: 17+231

Class

1. USA (6)

Name	No.	Builders	Laid down	Com-missioned
BROOKE	FFG 1	Lockheed S.B.	Dec 1962	Mar 1966
RAMSEY	FFG 2	Lockheed S.B.	Feb 1963	June 1967
SCHOFIELD	FFG 3	Lockheed S.B.	Apr 1963	May 1968
TALBOT	FFG 4	Bath Iron Works	May 1964	Apr 1967
RICHARD L. PAGE	FFG 5	Bath Iron Works	Jan 1965	Aug 1967
JULIUS A. FURER	FFG 6	Bath Iron Works	July 1965	Nov 1967

Remarks: With the exception of their armament, the 'Brooke' class frigates are identical with the 'Garcia' class ships, though the substitution of a Mk 22 single SAM launcher for the after 5-in (127-mm) gun mounting changes the ships into useful guided-missile frigates, though the limited capacity of their SAM magazines makes the possibility of protracted operations problematical. Three of the class serve with the Pacific Fleet and the other three with the Atlantic Fleet. FFGs 4-6 have automatic reloading for their ASROC launchers.

'Campbell' class high-endurance cutter

USA

Displacement: 2,215 tons standard and 2,655 tons full load

Dimensions: length 327 ft (99·7 m); beam 41 ft (12·5 m); draught 15 ft (4·6 m)

Gun armament: one 5-in (127-mm) L/38 DP in a Mk 30 single mounting, two 40-mm Bofors AA and two 20-mm AA

Missile armament: none

Torpedo armament: none

Anti-submarine armament: provision for one forward-firing Hedgehog mortar and two triple Mk 32 tube mountings for 12·75-in (324-mm) Mk 44/46 A/S torpedoes

Electronics: one Sperry SPS-53 surface-search radar, one Westinghouse SPS-29 air-search radar, one Mk 52 gun fire-control system, and one EDO SQS-36A hull-mounted medium-range sonar

Propulsion: two Babcock & Wilcox boilers supplying steam to Westinghouse geared turbines delivering 6,200 shp (4,625 kW) to two shafts

Performance: maximum speed 19·8 kts; range 9,200 miles (14,805 km) at 10·5 kts or 4,600 miles (7,400 km) at 19 kts

Complement: 13+131

Class

1. USA (4)

Name	No.	Builders	Laid down	Com-missioned
BIBB	WHEC 31	Charleston Navy Yard	May 1935	Mar 1937
DUANE	WHEC 33	Philadelphia Navy Yard	May 1935	Aug 1936
INGHAM	WHEC 35	Philadelphia Navy Yard	May 1935	Sep 1936
TANEY	WHEC 37	Philadelphia Navy Yard	May 1935	Nov 1936

The Bibb (WHEC 31) is a member of one of the oldest classes serving with the US armed forces, and though fitted during the 1960s with an anti-submarine armament of one forward-firing Hedgehog mortar and two triple Mk 32 tube mountings for anti-submarine torpedoes, now have the limited gun armament of one 5-in (127-mm), two 40-mm and two 20-mm weapons.

'Canadian River' class frigate

Canada

Displacement: 1,400 tons standard and 2,125 tons full load

Dimensions: length 301·5ft (91·9m); beam 36·7ft (11·2m); draught 12ft (3·7m)

Gun armament: one 4-in (102-mm) L/45 DP in a Mk 23 single mounting, one 40-mm Bofors L/60 AA, and four 20-mm Oerlikon AA

Missile armament: none

Torpedo armament: none

Anti-submarine armament: none

Electronics: surface-search and navigation radar

Propulsion: two boilers supplying steam to triple-expansion engines delivering 5,500ihp (4,100kW) to two shafts

Fuel: oil 645 tons

Performance: maximum speed 20kts; range 4,850 miles (7,805km) at 12kts

Complement: 15+130 and up to 50 cadets

Class

1. Dominican Republic (1)

Name	No.	Builders	Laid down	Commissioned
MELLA	F 451	Davies S.B.	—	1944

Remarks: Transferred to the Dominican Republic in 1946, the Mella (F 451) has been considerably altered in appearance by the addition of extra deckhouses to transform the ship into a hybrid frigate/presidential yacht. When not used as a presidential yacht, the *Mella* is used as a naval staff headquarters.

'Cannon' class frigate

USA/Greece

Displacement: 1,240 tons standard and 1,900 tons full load

Dimensions: length 306ft (93·3m); beam 36·66ft (11·17m) draught 14ft (4·3m)

Gun armament: three 3-in (76-mm) L/50 DP in three Mk 22 single mountings, four 40-mm Bofors L/60 AA in two Mk 1 twin mountings, and 14 20-mm AA in seven twin mountings

Missile armament: none

Torpedo armament: none

Anti-submarine armament: one Hedgehog mortar, two Mk 32 tubes for 12·75-in (324-mm) Mk 44 A/S torpedoes, eight depth-charge throwers, and one depth-charge rack

Electronics: navigation radar, and Mk 29 radar with Mk 51 fire-control director in the Mk 52 fire-control system

Propulsion: diesel-electric arrangement, with four General Motors diesels powering two electric motors delivering 6,000bhp (4,475kW) to two shafts

Performance: maximum speed 19·25kts; range 10,350 miles (16,655km) at 12kts

Complement: 220

Class

1. Greece (4)

Name	No.	Builders	Laid down	Commissioned
AETOS	D 01	Tampa S.B.	Mar 1943	May 1944
IERAX	D 31	Tampa S.B.	Apr 1943	July 1944
LEON	D 54	Federal S.B.	Feb 1943	Aug 1943
PANTHIR	D 67	Federal S.B.	Sep 1943	Jan 1944

2. Philippines (2)

Name	No.	Builders	Laid down	Commissioned
DATU SIRATUNA	PF 77	Federal S.B.	Nov 1942	July 1943
RAJAH HUMABON	PF 78	Norfolk Navy Yard	Jan 1943	Aug 1943

3. Thailand (1)

Name	No.	Builders	Laid down	Commissioned
PIN KLAO	3	Western Pipe	1943	Sep 1943

4. Uruguay (2)

Name	No.	Builders	Laid down	Commissioned
URUGUAY	1	Federal S.B.	Dec 1942	July 1943
ARTIGAS	2	Federal S.B.	Aug 1943	Dec 1943

Remarks: The 'Cannon' class was designed in World War II as an escort destroyer, and was completed with only half the designed horsepower (and thus relatively low speed) in order to get the ships operational without loss of time when priority for diesel engines had been allocated to landing craft. The specification above refers to the Greek ships, which were transferred from the USA in two pairs during March 1951 and January 1951. At that time the torpedo armament of one triple 21-in (533-mm) tube mounting was removed, a later addition being the self-protection triple Mk 32 tube mounting. The Filipino ships were overhauled in South Korea before commissioning in 1980 and have different AA armament and no Mk 32 tubes. Thailand and Uruguay received their ships in 1959 and 1952.

'Casco' class frigate

USA

Displacement: 1,765 tons standard and 2,800 tons full load

Dimensions: length 311·6ft (95·0m); beam 41·1ft (12·5m); draught 13·5ft (4·1m)

Gun armament: one 5-in (127-mm) L/38 DP in a Mk 30 mounting, three 40-mm Bofors AA in one Mk 1 twin mounting and two Mk 3 single mountings, two 20-mm AA, six machine-guns, and two 81-mm mortars

Missile armament: none

Torpedo armament: none

Anti-submarine armament: none

Electronics: one Sperry SPS-53 surface-search radar, one SPA-34 air-search radar, and one Mk 26 gun-control radar used in conjunction with the Mk 52 gun fire-control system

Propulsion: two Fairbanks-Morse 38D8 diesels delivering 6,080bhp (4,535kW) to two shafts

Performance: maximum speed 18kts; range 9,200 miles (14,820km) at 17kts

Complement: 13+137

Class

1. Philippines (4)

Name	No.	Builders	Laid down	Commissioned
ANDRES BONIFACIO	PF 7	Lake Washington S.Y.	July 1941	Apr 1943
GREGORIO DE PILAR	PF 8	Lake Washington S.Y.	Feb 1943	May 1944
DIEGO SILANG	PF 9	Lake Washington S.Y.	June 1943	July 1944
FRANCISCO DAGOHOY	PF 10	Lake Washington S.Y.	July 1943	Oct 1944

Class

2. USA (1)

Name	No.	Builders	Laid down	Commissioned
UNIMAK	WHEC 379	Associated S.B.	Feb 1942	Dec 1943

Remarks: The 'Casco' class frigate was designed and built during World War II as the 'Barnegat' class seaplane tender for the US Navy. After the war the entire class was transferred to the US Coast Guard, which eventually classified the ships as high-endurance cutters. The four ships operated by the navy of the Philippines were originally transferred during 1971 and 1972 to the South Vietnamese navy, and thence to the Philippine navy in 1975. Two other ships of the class are owned by the Philippines for cannibalization. All operational ships are to be fitted with a helicopter platform aft, though not with supporting facilities of any kind. The US Coast Guard still maintains a single 'Casco' class cutter, the *Unimak* (WHEC 379) being the survivor of a class of 18, and having an armament of one 5-in (127-mm) and two 40-mm guns. Other of the class remain in service with the Ethiopian, Italian and Vietnamese navies for non-operational tasks such as training.

*The **Unimak (WHEC 379)** is to be retired in the mid-1980s, having served faithfully and long.*

'Centauro' class frigate

Italy

Displacement: 1,805 tons standard and 2,250 tons full load
Dimensions: length 103·1 m (338·4 ft); beam 12·0 m (39·5 ft); draught 3·8 m (12·6 ft)
Gun armament: three 76-mm (3-in) L/62 DP in three single mountings
Missile armament: none
Torpedo armament: none
Anti-submarine armament: two triple Mk 32 tube mountings for 12·75-in (324-mm) Mk 44/46 A/S torpedoes
Electronics: one Bendix SPS-6 air-search radar, one SMA SPQ 2 combined search and navigation radar, one Selenia Orion 3 gun-control radar used in conjunction with the OG3 gun fire-control system, one SQS-11 hull-mounted sonar, one EDO SQS-36 medium-range hull-mounted sonar, and one Elettronica SPR A radar interception system
Propulsion: two Foster-Wheeler boilers supplying steam to two double-reduction Tosi geared turbines delivering 16,400 kW (22,000 shp) to two shafts
Fuel: oil 300 tons
Performance: maximum speed 25 kts; range 5,560 km (3,455 miles) at 20 kts
Complement: 12 + 195

Class
1. Italy (2)

Name	No.	Builders	Laid down	Com-missioned
CENTAURO	F 554	Ansaldo	May 1952	May 1957
CIGNO	F 555	Cantieri Navali di Taranto	Feb 1954	Mar 1957

Remarks: The *Centauro* (F 554) is the sole survivor of class of four built in the mid-1950s for escort work. The ship is now obsolete, and will be deleted during the near future as the force of modern 'Maestrale' class frigates assumes the principal burden of smaller-ship anti-submarine warfare. One of the main failings of the 'Centauro' class was lack of helicopter facilities.

The frigate Cigno *(F 555) was deleted in 1983, but reveals the definitive look of this anti-submarine escort class, whose primary anti-submarine weapon was the three-barrel Menon mortar in a trainable turret. This weapon was loaded with the barrels vertical, the 160-kg (353-lb) bombs being fired at a fixed elevation of 45°, ranges between 400 and 900 m (437 and 984 yards) being obtainable by varying the quantity of gas permitted to enter the barrels from the three powder chambers. The* Centauro *is no longer fitted with the Menon mortar.*

'Charles Lawrence' and 'Crosley' class frigates

USA/Taiwan

Displacement: 1,400 tons standard and 2,130 tons full load
Dimensions: length 306 ft (93·3 m); beam 37 ft (11·3 m); draught 12·6 ft (3·8 m)
Gun armament: two 5-in (127-mm) L/38 in two Mk 30 single mountings, six 40-mm Bofors AA in three twin mountings, and four or eight 20-mm AA in four single or four twin mountings
Missile armament: none
Torpedo armament: none
Anti-submarine armament: two triple Mk 32 tube mountings for 12·75-in (324-mm) Mk 44 A/S torpedoes, two Hedgehog mortars and depth-charges
Electronics: Raytheon SPS-5 surface-search radar and RCA/General Electric Mk 26 fire-control system
Propulsion: two Foster-Wheeler boilers supplying steam to General Electric turbo-electric motors delivering 12,000 shp (8,950 kW) to two shafts
Performance: maximum speed 23·6 kts; range 5,750 miles (9,255 km) at 15 kts
Complement: 200

Class
1. Chile (3)

Name	No.	Builders	Laid down	Com-missioned
SERRANO	26	Consolidated Steel	1943	Jan 1945
ORELLA	27	Consolidated Steel	1943	Feb 1945
URIBE	29	Bethlehem S.B. Co	1942	June 1943

2. Ecuador (1)

Name	No.	Builders	Laid down	Com-missioned
MORAN VALVERDE	DD 02	Philadelphia Navy Yard	1943	Sep 1943

3. Mexico (4)

Name	No.	Builders	Laid down	Com-missioned
TEHUANTEPEC	B 05	Consolidated Steel	1943	Apr 1945
USUMACINTA	B 06	Consolidated Steel	1943	May 1945
COAHUILA	B 07	Bethlehem S.B. Co	1944	Mar 1945
CHIHUAHUA	B 08	Norfolk Navy Yard	1943	Oct 1943

4. South Korea (6)

Name	No.	Builders	Laid down	Com-missioned
KYONG NAM	DE 822	Defoe S.B. Co	1944	May 1945
AH SAN	DE 823	Bethlehem S.B. Co	1943	June 1945
UNG PO	DE 825	Bethlehem S.B. Co	1943	June 1945
KYONG PUK	DE 826	Charleston Navy Yard	1943	Jan 1944
JONNAM	DE 827	Charleston Navy Yard	1943	Mar 1944
CHI JU	DE 828	Charleston Navy Yard	1943	Apr 1945

5. Taiwan (9)

Name	No.	Builders	Laid down	Com-missioned
TIEN SHAN	615	Defoe S.B. Co	1944	June 1945
LU SHAN	821	Defoe S.B. Co	1942	Aug 1943
YU SHAN	826	Charleston Navy Yard	1943	Nov 1944
WEN SHAN	834	Bethlehem S.B. Co	1942	July 1943
FU SHAN	835	Charleston Navy Yard	1943	July 1944
CHUNG SHAN	845	Bethlehem S.B. Co	1943	Sep 1943
HUA SHAN	854	Defoe S.B. Co	1944	Apr 1945
TAI SHAN	878	Charleston Navy Yard	1943	Jan 1945
SHOU SHAN	893	Bethlehem S.B. Co	1944	Oct 1944

Remarks: The 'Charles Lawrence' and 'Crosley' class frigates are essentially similar, the 'Charles Lawrence' type being a 'Buckley' class escort destroyer modified into a high-speed transport with minimum external change and the 'Crosley' type being a more extensively altered high-speed transport version of the World War II 'Buckley' or 'Rudderow' class escort destroyers with a built-up midships section and provision for four LCVPs. Chile currently operates three 'Charles Lawrence' class frigates, all bought from the USA in 1966. These are fitted with SPS-4 combined air- and surface-search radar and each carry two LCUs. Ecuador's single 'Charles Lawrence' class frigate was received in 1967, and still serves in the high-speed transport role with provision for a maximum of 162 troops. Radar comprises SPS-6 and SPS-10 sets, and there is a small helicopter platform aft. Mexico operates one 'Charles Lawrence' (*Chihuahua*) and three 'Crosley' class ships, the first two received in 1963 and the second pair in 1969; these ships have SC combined-search radar and a commercial navigation radar. South Korea's force of two 'Charles Lawrence' (*Kyong Puk* and *Jonnam*) and four 'Crosley' class ships is still designed for the high-speed transport role, each fitted to carry 160 troops and four LCVPs; both classes have been fitted with a tripod mast. The largest operator of the two classes is Taiwan, which has three 'Charles Lawrence' (*Lu Shan, Wen Shan* and *Chung Shan*) and six 'Crosley' class ships. The specification above applies to these ships, which retain a vestigial troop-carrying capability with a normal complement of one LCVP per vessel.

'Chengdu' class guided-missile frigate

China

Displacement: 1,000 tons standard and 1,320 tons full load

Dimensions: length 91·5m (300·1ft); beam 10·1m (33·1ft); draught 3·2m (10·5ft)

Gun armament: three 100-mm (3·9-in) L/50 DP in three single mountings, 12 37-mm AA in six twin mountings, and four 14·5-mm (0·57-in) heavy machine-guns in two twin mountings

Missile armament: one twin launcher for two SS-N-2C 'Styx' surface-to-surface missiles

Torpedo armament: none

Anti-submarine armament: four depth-charge throwers

Mines: 50

Electronics: one 'Slim Net' surface-search radar, one *Neptun* navigation radar, one 'Sun-Visor-B' gun-control radar, one 'Square Tie' missile-control radar and one 'High Pole-A' IFF

Propulsion: two boilers supplying steam to two geared turbines delivering 14,915kW (20,000shp) to two shafts

Performance: maximum speed 28kts; range 3,700km (2,300 miles) at 10kts

Complement: 175

Class

1. China (4)

Name	No.	Builders	Laid down	Commissioned
GUILIN	508	Guangzhou	1955	1959
GUIYANG	505	Hutong	—	1958
KUNMING	506	Guangzhou	—	1959
CHENGDU	507	Hutong	1955	1958

'Chikugo' class frigate

Japan

Displacement: 1,470-1,500 tons standard and 1,700 tons full load

Dimensions: length 93·1m (305·5ft); beam 10·8m (35·5ft); draught 3·5m (11·5ft)

Gun armament: two 3-in (76-mm) L/50 DP in one Mk 33 twin mounting, and two 40-mm Bofors AA in one Mk 1 twin mounting

Missile armament: none

Torpedo armament: none

Anti-submarine armament: one octuple launcher for RUR-5A ASROC missiles, and two triple Type 68 tube mountings for 12·75-in (324-mm) Mk 44 torpedoes

Electronics: one OPS-14 air-search radar, one OPS-28 surface-search radar, one OPS-19 navigation radar, one Mk 33 radar used in conjunction with the Mk 1 gun fire-control system, one SQS-36 hull-mounted sonar and one SQS-35J variable-depth sonar

Propulsion: four diesels (Burmeister & Wain/Mitsui in DEs 215, 217, 218, 219, 221, 223 and 225, and Mitsubishi UEV 30/40N in others) delivering 11,930kW (16,000shp) to two shafts

Performance: maximum speed 25kts

Complement: 165

Class

1. Japan (11)

Name	No.	Builders	Laid down	Commissioned
CHIKUGO	DE 215	Mitsui	Dec 1968	July 1970
AYASE	DE 216	Ishikawajima Harima	Dec 1969	May 1971
MIKUMA	DE 217	Mitsui	Mar 1970	Aug 1971
TOKACHI	DE 218	Mitsui	Dec 1970	May 1972
IWASE	DE 219	Mitsui	Aug 1971	Dec 1972
CHITOSE	DE 220	Hitachi	Oct 1971	Aug 1973
NIYODO	DE 221	Mitsui	Sep 1972	Feb 1974
TESHIO	DE 222	Hitachi	July 1973	Jan 1975
YOSHINO	DE 223	Mitsui	Sep 1973	Feb 1975
KUMANO	DE 224	Hitachi	May 1974	Nov 1975
NOSHIRO	DE 225	Mitsui	Jan 1976	Aug 1977

Remarks: Well provided with sensors and electronic warfare systems, the 'Chikugo' class is the world's smallest warship type to carry the ASROC system.

The Mikuma (DE 217) was the third 'Chikugo' class frigate to be built.

'Claud Jones' class frigate

USA

Displacement: 1,450 tons standard and 1,750 tons full load

Dimensions: length 310ft (94·5m); beam 37ft (11·3m); draught 18ft (5·5m)

Gun armament: one 3-in (76-mm) L/50 DP in a Mk 34 mounting, two 37-mm AA in one twin mounting, two 25-mm AA in one twin mounting (341 and 342 only); or two 3-in (76-mm) L/50 DP in two Mk 34 single mountings and two 25-mm AA in one twin mounting (343 and 344 only)

Missile armament: none

Torpedo armament: none

Anti-submarine armament: two triple Mk 32 tube mountings for 12·75-in (324-mm) Mk 44 torpedoes and two Hedgehog mortars

Electronics: one Bendix SPS-6 air-search radar, one Raytheon/Sylvania SPS-10 surface-search radar, one Decca navigation radar, one Mk 70 gun fire-control system, and one Sangamo SQS-29/32 series hull-mounted sonar

Propulsion: four Fairbanks-Morse 38D81/8 diesels delivering 9,200hp (6,860kW) to one shaft

Performance: maximum speed 22kts

Complement: 15+160

Class

1. Indonesia (4)

Name	No.	Builders	Laid down	Commissioned
SAMADIKUN	341	Avondale Marine	Oct 1957	May 1959
MARTADINATA	342	American S.B. Co	Oct 1958	Nov 1959
MONGINSIDI	343	Avondale Marine	June 1957	Feb 1959
NGURAH RAI	344	American S.B. Co	Nov 1958	Mar 1960

Remarks: The first of these four 'Claud Jones' class frigates was transferred from the USA in 1973, the remaining three following in 1974. Despite their small size and limited armament, the 'Claud Jones' ships are well suited to the inter-island patrol requirements of the Indonesian navy, and all four ships were refitted in the Philippines between 1979 and 1982.

'Comandante João Belo' class frigate

Portugal

Displacement: 1,750 tons standard and 2,250 tons full load

Dimensions: length 103·7m (340·3ft); beam 11·7m (38·4m); draught 4·8m (15·7ft)

Gun armament: three 100-mm (3·9-in) L/55 DP in single mountings, and two 40-mm Bofors L/70 AA

Missile armament: none

Torpedo armament: none

Anti-submarine armament: two triple 533-mm (21-in) tube mountings for A/S torpedoes, and one quadruple 305-mm (12-in) mortar

Aircraft: provision being made for one helicopter during refit

Electronics: one Thomson-CSF DRBV 22A air-search radar, one Thomson-CSF DRBV 50 air/surface-search radar, one Decca RM 316 navigation radar, one Thomson-CSF DRBC 31D fire-control radar, one SQS-17A hull-mounted search sonar, and one DUBA 3A hull-mounted attack sonar

Propulsion: four SEMT-Pielstick diesels delivering 11,390kW (16,000bhp) to two shafts

Performance: maximum speed 25kts; range 13,900km (8,635km) at 15kts

Complement: 14+186

Class

1. Portugal (4)

Name	No.	Builders	Laid down	Commissioned
COMANDANTE JOÃO BELO	F 480	At et Ch de Nantes	Sep 1965	July 1967
COMANDANTE HERMENEGILDO CAPELO	F 481	At et Ch de Nantes	May 1966	Apr 1968
COMANDANTE ROBERTO IVENS	F 482	At et Ch de Nantes	Dec 1966	Nov 1968
COMANDANTE SACADURA CABRAL	F 483	At et Ch de Nantes	Aug 1967	July 1969

'Commandant Rivière' class guided-missile frigate
France

Displacement: 1,750 tons standard and 2,250 tons full load

Dimensions: length 103·0 m (337·9 ft); beam 11·5 m (37·7 ft); draught 4·3 m (14·1 ft)

Gun armament: two 100-mm (3·9-in) L/55 DP in single mountings, and two 30-mm AA

Missile armament: four container-launchers for MM.38 Exocet surface-to-surface missiles

Torpedo armament: none

Anti-submarine armament: two triple 533-mm (21-in) tube mountings for L3 or K2 torpedoes, and one quadruple 305-mm (12-in) mortar

Aircraft: provision for one light helicopter on a platform aft

Electronics: one Thomson-CSF DRBV 22A air-search radar, one Thomson-CSF DRBV 50 air/surface-search radar, one Thomson-CSF DRBC 32A gun-control radar, one Thomson-CSF DRBC 32C missile-control, one Thomson-CSF DRBN 32 navigation radar, one DUBA 3 hull-mounted sonar, one SQS-17 hull-mounted sonar, and two CSEE Dagaie chaff launchers

Propulsion: four SEMT-Pielstick diesels delivering 11,930 kW (16,000 bhp) to two shafts

Performance: maximum speed 25 kts; range 11,100 km (6,700 miles) at 10-12 kts

Complement: 10+61+96, and accommodation for a detachment of 80 troops who can be landed in two specially-carried LCPs

Class
1. France (9)

Name	No.	Builders	Laid down	Commissioned
VICTOR SCHOELCHER	F 725	Lorient ND	Oct 1957	Oct 1962
COMMANDANT BORY	F 726	Lorient ND	Mar 1958	Mar 1964
AMIRAL CHARNER	F 727	Lorient ND	Nov 1958	Dec 1962
DOUDART DE LAGRÉE	F 728	Lorient ND	Mar 1960	May 1963
BALNY	F 729	Lorient ND	Mar 1960	Feb 1970
COMMANDANT RIVIÈRE	F 733	Lorient ND	Apr 1957	Dec 1962
COMMANDANT BOURDAIS	F 740	Lorient ND	Apr 1959	Mar 1963
PROTET	F 748	Lorient ND	Sep 1961	May 1964
ENSEIGNE DE VAISSEAU HENRY	F 749	Lorient ND	Sep 1962	Jan 1965

Remarks: This well-balanced class of air-conditioned frigates is designed for worldwide operations, and as such each ship is fitted with command facilities.

'Courtney' class frigate
USA

Displacement: 1,450 tons standard and 1,915 tons full load

Dimensions: length 314·5 ft (95·9 m); beam 36·8 ft (11·2 m); draught 13·6 ft (4·1 m)

Gun armament: two 3-in (76-mm) L/50 DP in one Mk 33 twin mounting

Missile armament: none

Torpedo armament: none

Anti-submarine armament: two triple Mk 32 tube mountings for 12·75-in (324-mm) Mk 44 torpedoes, and one depth-charge rack

Aircraft: provision for one light helicopter on a platform aft

Electronics: one Bendix SPS-6 air-search radar, one Raytheon/Sylvania SPS-10 surface-search radar, and one Sangamo hull-mounted long-range active sonar

Propulsion: two Foster-Wheeler boilers supplying steam to one De Laval geared turbine delivering 20,000 shp (14,915 kW) to one shaft

Performance: maximum speed 25 kts; range 5,200 miles (8,370 km) at 15 kts

Complement: 11+150

Class
1. Colombia (1)

Name	No.	Builders	Commissioned
BOYACA	DE 16	New York Shipbuilding	Jan 1957

'Dealey' class frigate
USA

Displacement: 1,450 tons standard and 1,915 tons full load

Dimensions: length 314·5 ft (95·9 m); beam 36·8 ft (11·2 m); draught 13·6 ft (4·2 m)

Gun armament: four 3-in (76-mm) L/50 DP in two Mk 33 twin mountings

Missile armament: none

Torpedo armament: none

Anti-submarine armament: two triple Mk 32 tube mountings for 12·75-in (324-mm) Mk 44 torpedoes

Electronics: one Bendix SPS-6 air-search radar, one Raytheon/Sylvania SPS-10 surface-search radar, and two SPG-34 gun-control radars used in conjunction with the two Mk 63 gun fire-control systems

Propulsion: two Foster-Wheeler boilers supplying steam to one De Laval geared turbine delivering 20,000 shp (14,915 kW) to one shaft

Performance: maximum speed 25 kts; range 5,200 miles (8,370 km) at 15 kts

Complement: 11+150

Class
1. Uruguay (1)

Name	No.	Builders	Laid down	Commissioned
18 DE JULIO	3	Bath Iron Works	Oct 1952	June 1954

'Descubierta' class guided-missile frigate
Spain

Displacement: 1,235 tons standard and 1,480 tons full load

Dimensions: length 88·8 m (291·3 ft); beam 10·4 m (34 ft); draught 3·8 m (12·5 ft)

Gun armament: one 76-mm (3-in) L/62 DP OTO-Melara Compact, two 40-mm Breda L/70 AA in single mountings, and one 20-mm 12-barrel Meroka AA system

Missile armament: two quadruple launchers for eight RGM-84A Harpoon surface-to-surface missiles, and one Selenia Albatros octuple launcher system for 24 RIM-7 Sea Sparrow surface-to-air missiles

Torpedo armament: none

Anti-submarine armament: two triple Mk 32 tube mountings for 12·75-in (324-mm) Mk 46 torpedoes, and one 375-mm (14·76-in) Bofors twin rocket-launcher

Electronics: one Hollandse Signaalapparaten DA-05 air-search radar, one Hollandse Signaalapparaten DA-02 surface-search and target-designation radar, one Hollandse Signaalapparaten ZW-06 navigation and helicopter-control radar, one Hollandse Signaalapparaten WM-22/41 or WM-25 weapon-control system, one CSEE optical gun fire-control director, Raytheon 1160B hull-mounted sonar, Elettronica Beta electronic countermeasures system, one SEWACO integrated weapon-control, command and sensor system, and two chaff launchers

Propulsion: four MTU/Bazán 16V956 TB91 diesels delivering 13,425 kW (18,000 bhp) to two shafts

Performance: maximum speed 25·5 kts; range 7,400 km (4,600 miles) at 18 kts

Complement: 116, plus provision for a marine detachment of 30

Class
1. Egypt (2)

Name	No.	Builders	Laid down	Commissioned
—	—	Bazán	Oct 1979	1983
—	—	Bazán	Dec 1979	1983

2. Spain (6 'F30' class)

Name	No.	Builders	Laid down	Commissioned
DESCUBIERTA	F 31	Bazán	Nov 1974	Nov 1978
DIANA	F 32	Bazán	July 1975	June 1979
INFANTA ELENA	F 33	Bazán	Jan 1976	Apr 1980
INFANTA CRISTINA	F 34	Bazán	Sep 1976	Nov 1980
CAZADORA	F 35	Bazán	Dec 1977	July 1981
VENCEDORA	F 36	Bazán	May 1978	Jan 1982

'Descubierta (Modified)' class guided-missile frigate
Spain/Morocco
Displacement: 1,235 tons standard and 1,480 tons full load
Dimensions: length 88·8m (291·3ft); beam 10·4m (34ft); draught 3·8m (12·5ft)
Gun armament: one 76-mm (3-in) L/62 DP OTO-Melara Compact, and two 40-mm Breda L/70 AA in single mountings
Missile armament: four container-launchers for MM.40 Exocet surface-to-surface missiles, and one Selenia Albatros octuple launcher system for RIM-7 Sea Sparrow surface-to-air missiles
Torpedo armament: none
Anti-submarine armament: two triple Mk 32 tube mountings for 12·75-in (324-mm) Mk 44 torpedoes, and one 375-mm (14·76-in) Bofors twin rocket-launcher
Electronics: Hollandse Signaalapparaten LW-series air-search radar, Hollandse Signaalapparaten DA-series target-indication radar, Hollandse Signaalapparaten

ZW-series surface-search and navigation radar, Hollandse Signaalapparaten WM-20 series fire-control system, and SEWACO integrated weapon-control, command and sensor system
Propulsion: four MTU/Bazán 16V956 diesels delivering 11,930kW (16,000bhp) to two shafts
Performance: maximum speed 26kts; range 7,400km (4,600 miles) at cruising speed
Complement: 100

Class
1. Morocco (1)				Com-
Name	No.	Builders	Laid down	missioned
COLONEL ERRHAMANI	51	Bazán	March 1979	1982

'Durango' class frigate
Mexico
Displacement: 1,600 tons standard and 2,000 tons full load
Dimensions: length 78·2m (256·5ft); beam 11·2m (36·6ft); draught 3·1m (10·5ft)
Gun armament: two 4-in (102-mm) in single mountings, two 57-mm, and four 20-mm
Missile armament: none
Torpedo armament: none
Anti-submarine armament: none
Electronics: navigation radar

Propulsion: diesel-electric arrangement, with two Enterprise DMR-38 units delivering 5,000bhp (3,730kW) to two shafts
Performance: maximum speed 18kts; range 5,560km (3,455 miles) at 12kts
Complement: 24+125

Class
1. Mexico (1)				Com-
Name	No.	Builders	Laid down	missioned
DURANGO	B 01	Union Naval de Levante	1934	1938

Remarks: Built in Spain during the first half of the 1930s, the *Durango* is one of the oldest 'first-line' warships in the world, and was built as an armed transport for a military force of 20 officers and 450 men, which accounts in part for the vessel's slab-sided and high hull. As delivered to the Mexican navy the ship was powered by a geared turbine arrangement with Yarrow boilers and Parsons machinery, but this 6,500-shp (4,850-kW) arrangement was replaced in 1967 by the current diesel-electric system.

The Durango (B 01) has a decidedly obsolescent appearance despite her relatively new funnel structure, the imbalance of the appearance being highlighted by the two small latticed masts, the foremast supporting the antennae for the strictly limited sensor fit, which comprises only navigation radar. The ship is notable for its very short foredeck, the site for the 41-in (103-mm) gun that forms the ship's main armament. The 20-mm AA guns are grouped in beam pairs on the aft extensions of the bridge wings and on the deckhouse between the bridge structure and the funnel, with the two 57-mm guns just forward of the funnel.

'Edsall' class frigate
USA
Displacement: 1,200 tons standard and 1,850 tons full load
Dimensions: length 302·7ft (92·3m); beam 36·6ft (11·3m); draught 13ft (4·0m)
Gun armament: three 3-in (76-mm) L/50 DP in three Mk 22 single mountings, and eight 40-mm Bofors L/60 AA in one Mk 2 quadruple mounting and two Mk 1 twin mountings
Missile armament: none
Torpedo armament: none
Anti-submarine armament: none
Electronics: one Kelvin Hughes Type 14 radar, one Kelvin Hughes Type 17 radar, and one QCS-1 sonar

Propulsion: four Fairbanks-Morse 38D8 diesels delivering 6,000shp (4,475kW) to two shafts
Fuel: diesel oil
Performance: maximum speed 20kts; range 14,970 miles (24,090km) at 12kts
Complement: 15+201

Class
1. Mexico (1)			Com-
Name	No.	Builders	missioned
COMODORO MANUEL AZUETA	A 06	Brown S.B. Co	Aug 1943

Remarks: This ship is now well overdue for replacement.

'F 2000' class guided-missile frigate
Saudi Arabia/France
Displacement: 2,610 tons full load
Dimensions: length 115·0m (377·3ft); beam 12·5m (41ft); draught 4·7m (15·3ft)
Gun armament: one 100-m (3·9-in) L/55 DP, and four 40-mm Breda L/70 AA in two twin mountings
Missile armament: two quadruple launcher-containers for eight Otomat Mk 2 surface-to-surface missiles, and one quadruple launcher for 26 Crotale Naval surface-to-air missiles
Torpedo armament: none
Anti-submarine armament: four tubes for A/S torpedoes, and helicopter-launched weapons (see below)
Aircraft: one Aérospatiale SA 365F Dauphin 2 helicopter in a hangar aft
Electronics: one Thomson-CSF Sea Tiger combined air- and surface-search radar, one Thomson-CSF Castor II fire-control radar, one Thomson-CSF Sylosat navigation system, three CSEE Naja optronic fire-control directors, one Thomson-

CSF Tavitac tactical display system, one Thomson-CSF Diodon hull-mounted detection, tracking and attack sonar, one Sorel variable-depth sonar, two CSEE Dagaie chaff launchers, and one Thomson-CSF electronic countermeasures system
Propulsion: four SEMT-Pielstick 16PA6 BTC diesels delivering 26,250kW (35,200hp) to two shafts
Performance: maximum speed 30kts; range 12,000km (7,455km) at 18kts
Complement: 15+164

Class
1. Saudi Arabia (4)				Com-
Name	No.	Builders	Laid down	missioned
—	—	Lorient Naval Dockyard	Oct 1981	Mar 1984
—	—	CNIM	June 1982	—
—	—	CNIM	Dec 1982	—
—	—	CNIM	June 1983	—

'Fatahillah' class guided-missile frigate

Netherlands

Displacement: 1,200 tons standard and 1,450 tons full load
Dimensions: length 84·0m (275·6ft); beam 11·1m (36·4ft); draught 3·3m (10·7ft)
Gun armament: one 120-mm (4·7-in) L/46 DP, one 40-mm Bofors AA (361 and 362 only), and two 20-mm AA
Missile armament: four container-launchers for four MM.38 Exocet surface-to-surface missiles
Torpedo armament: none
Anti-submarine armament: one 375-mm (14·76-in) Bofors two-barrel rocket-launcher, two triple Mk 32 or ILAS 3 tube mountings for 12 Mk 44 12·75-in (324-mm) or 12 A 244S 324-mm (12·75-in) A/S torpedoes (361 and 362 only), and helicopter-launched weapons (363 only, see below)
Aircraft: one Nurtanio-MBB BO 105 helicopter in a hangar aft
Electronics: one Hollandse Signaalapparaten DA-05 combined air- and surface-search radar, one Decca AC 1229 navigation radar, one Hollandse Signaalapparaten WM-28 fire-control radar system, one Hollandse Signaalapparaten PHS 32 hull-mounted search and attack sonar, T Mk 6 Fanfare torpedo decoy system, and two Vickers Mk 4 chaff launchers
Propulsion: CODOG (COmbined Diesel Or Gas turbine) arrangement, with two MTU diesels delivering 4,475kW (6,000hp) and one Rolls-Royce Olympus TM3B gas turbine delivering 28,000hp (20,880kW) to two shafts

Performance: maximum speed 30kts; range 7,875km (4,895 miles) at 16kts
Complement: 89

Class
1. Indonesia (3)

Name	No.	Builders	Laid down	Commissioned
FATAHILLAH	361	Wilton-Fijenoord	Jan 1977	July 1979
MALAHAYATI	362	Wilton-Fijenoord	July 1977	Aug 1980
NALA	363	Wilton-Fijenoord	Jan 1978	late 1980

The Malahayati (362) has no provision for a helicopter in a hangar aft.

'Garcia' class frigate

USA

Displacement: 2,620 tons standard and 3,405 tons full load
Dimensions: length 414·5ft (126·3m); beam 44·2ft (13·5m); draught 24ft (7·3m)
Gun armament: two 5-in (127-mm) L/38 DP in two Mk 30 single mountings
Missile armament: none
Torpedo armament: none
Anti-submarine armament: two triple Mk 32 tube mountings for 12·75-in (324-mm) Mk 46 A/S torpedoes, and one octuple launcher for RUR-5A ASROC missiles
Aircraft: one Kaman SH-2F Seasprite helicopter in a hangar aft (except FFs 1048

The Davidson (FF 1045) of the 'Garcia' class has a balanced weapon/sensor fit.

and 1050)
Electronics: one Raytheon/Sylvania SPS-10 surface-search radar, one Lockheed SPS-40 air-search radar, one Mk 35 gun-control radar used in conjunction with the General Electric Mk 56 gun fire-control system, one Mk 1 target designation system, one EDO/General Electric SQS-26 bow-mounted 'bottom-bounce' sonar (SQS-26 AXR in FFs 1040, 1041, 1043, 1044 and 1045, and SQS-26 BR in FFs 1048, 1049, 1050 and 1051) used in conjunction with the Mk 114 A/S weapon-control system, T Mk 6 Fanfare torpedo decoy system, OE-82 satellite communications antenna, SRR-1 satellite communications receiver, WSC-3 satellite communications transceiver, and (FFs 1047 and 1049) Naval Tactical Data System
Propulsion: two Foster-Wheeler boilers supplying steam to one geared turbine (Westinghouse in FFs 1040, 1041, 1043, 1044 and 1045, and General Electric in the others) delivering 35,000shp (26,100kW) to one shaft
Performance: maximum speed 27·5kts
Complement: 13+226 (FFs 1040, 1041, 1043 and 1044) or 16+231 (other ships)

Class
1. USA (10)

Name	No.	Builders	Laid down	Commissioned
GARCIA	FF 1040	Bethlehem Steel	Oct 1962	Dec 1964
BRADLEY	FF 1041	Bethlehem Steel	Jan 1963	May 1965
EDWARD McDONNELL	FF 1043	Avondale	Apr 1963	Feb 1965
BRUMBY	FF 1044	Avondale	Aug 1963	Aug 1965
DAVIDSON	FF 1045	Avondale	Sep 1963	Dec 1965
VOGE	FF 1047	Defoe S.B. Co	Nov 1963	Nov 1966
SAMPLE	FF 1048	Lockheed S.B.	July 1963	Mar 1968
KOELSCH	FF 1049	Defoe S.B. Co	Feb 1964	June 1967
ALBERT DAVID	FF 1050	Lockheed S.B.	Apr 1964	Oct 1968
O'CALLAHAN	FF 1051	Defoe S.B. Co	Feb 1964	July 1968

'Glover' class frigate

USA

Displacement: 2,645 tons standard and 3,425 tons full load
Dimensions: length 414·5ft (126·3m); beam 44·2ft (13·5m); draught 24ft (7·3m)
Gun armament: one 5-in (127-mm) L/38 DP in a Mk 30 single mounting
Missile armament: none
Torpedo armament: none
Anti-submarine armament: two triple Mk 32 tube mountings for 12·75-in (324-mm) Mk 46 A/S torpedoes, one octuple launcher for RUR-5A ASROC missiles, and helicopter-launched weapons (see below)
Aircraft: provision for one Kaman SH-2F Seasprite helicopter on a platform aft
Electronics: one Raytheon/Sylvania SPS-10 surface-search radar, one Lockheed SPS-40 air-search radar, one SPG-35 gun-control radar used in conjunction with the General Electric Mk 56 gun fire-control system, one Mk 1 target designation system, one EDO/General Electric SQS-26 AXR bow-mounted 'bottom-bounce' sonar and one EDO SQS-35 variable-depth sonar used in conjunction with the Singer Mk 114 A/S fire-control system, OE-82 satellite communications antenna, and SRR-1 satellite communications receiver
Propulsion: two Foster-Wheeler boilers supplying steam to one Westinghouse geared turbine delivering 35,000shp (26,100kW) to one shaft
Performance: maximum speed 27kts
Complement: 248

Class
1. USA (1)

Name	No.	Builders	Laid down	Commissioned
GLOVER	FF 1098	Bath Iron Works	July 1963	Nov 1965

'Godavari' class guided-missile frigate

India

Displacement: 3,850 tons full load

Dimensions: length 414·6 ft (126·4 m); beam 47·6 ft (14·5 m); draught 29·5 ft (9·0 m)

Gun armament: one 76-mm (3-in) L/62 DP OTO-Melara Compact, and two 30-mm AA 'Gatling' mountings

Missile armament: two container-launchers for SS-N-2B 'Styx' surface-to-surface missiles, and one SA-N-4 surface-to-air missile

Torpedo armament: none

Anti-submarine armament: two triple ILAS 3 tube mountings for 324-mm (12·75-in) Whitehead A 244S A/S torpedoes, and helicopter-launched weapons (see below)

Aircraft: two Westland Sea King Mk 42/42A helicopters in a hangar aft

Electronics: one 'Head Net-C' 3D air-search radar, one Hollandse Signaal-apparaten LW-05 air-search radar, one Decca Type 978 navigation radar, one 'Pop Group' SAM-control radar, two 'Drum Tilt' AA gun-control radars, and one hull-mounted Graseby Type 184 medium-range panoramic search and attack sonar

Propulsion: two gas turbines delivering 30,000 hp (22,370 kW) to two shafts

Performance: maximum speed 27 kts; range 5,200 miles (8,370 km) at 12 kts

Complement: 250

Class

1. India (3+3)

Name	No.	Builders	Laid down	Commissioned
GODAVARI	F 51	Mazagon Docks Ltd	1978	1983
GANGA	—	Mazagon Docks Ltd	1981	1984
GOMATI	—	Mazagon Docks Ltd	1980	1984

'Grisha I' and 'Grisha III' class guided-missile frigates

USSR

Displacement: 950 tons standard and 1,100 tons full load

Dimensions: length 72·0 m (236·2 ft); beam 10·0 m (32·8 ft); draught 3·7 m (12·1 ft)

Gun armament: two 57-mm L/80 DP in one twin mounting, and ('Grisha III' only) one 30-mm AA Gatling mounting

Missile armament: one twin launcher for SA-N-4 surface-to-air missiles

Torpedo armament: two twin 533-mm (21-in) tube mountings

Anti-submarine armament: two 12-barrel RBU-6000 rocket-launchers

Mines: fitted with two tracks for minelaying

Electronics: one 'Strut Curve' air-search radar, one Don-2 navigation radar, one 'Pop Group' SAM-control radar, one 'Muff Cob' gun-control radar in 'Grisha I' or one 'Bass Tilt' gun-control radar in 'Grisha III', 'High Pole-A' IFF, hull-mounted sonar, and variable-depth sonar

Propulsion: CODAG (COmbined Diesel And Gas turbine) arrangement, with two diesels delivering 11,930 kW (16,000 shp) and one gas turbine delivering 17,900 kW (24,000 shp) to three shafts

Performance: maximum speed 36 kts; range 3,700 km (2,300 miles) at 20 kts or 925 km (575 miles) at 30 kts

Complement: 80

Class

1. USSR (15 'Grisha I' + 31 'Grisha III')

15 'Grisha I'

31 'Grisha III'

The 'Grisha I' class is distinguishable by its lack of an after 30-mm CIWS mounting fitted in the 'Grisha III' class, which also has different fire-control radars. The KGB-operated 'Grisha II' class has two twin 57-mm gun mountings.

'Hamilton' and 'Hero' class high-endurance cutters

USA

Displacement: 2,715 tons standard and 3,050 tons full load

Dimensions: length 378 ft (115·2 m); beam 42·8 ft (13·1 m); draught 20 ft (6·1 m)

Gun armament: one 5-in (127-mm) L/38 in a Mk 30 single mounting, two 40-mm Bofors AA, and two 20-mm Phalanx Mk 16 close-in weapon system mountings

Missile armament: none

Torpedo armament: none

Anti-submarine armament: two triple Mk 32 tube mountings for 12·75-in (324-mm) Mk 46 A/S torpedoes

Aircraft: one Sikorsky HH-52A or Sikorsky HH-3F Pelican helicopter on a platform aft

Electronics: one Westinghouse SPS-29 air-search radar, one SPS-64 surface-search radar, one SPG-35 gun fire-control radar used in conjunction with the General Electric Mk 56 gun fire-control system, and one EDO SQS-38 hull-mounted medium-range sonar

Propulsion: CODOG (COmbined Diesel Or Gas turbine) arrangement, with two Fairbanks-Morse diesels delivering 7,000 bhp (5,220 kW) and two Pratt & Whitney FT4A gas turbines delivering 36,000 shp (26,845 kW) to two shafts

Performance: maximum speed 29 knots on gas turbines and 20 kts on diesels; range 16,000 miles (25,750 km) at 11 kts on diesels or 2,750 miles (4,425 km) at 29 kts on gas turbines

Complement: 15 + 149

Class

1. USA (12)

Name	No.	Builders	Laid down	Commissioned
HAMILTON	WHEC 715	Avondale Shipyards	Jan 1965	Feb 1967
DALLAS	WHEC 716	Avondale Shipyards	Feb 1966	Oct 1967
MELLON	WHEC 717	Avondale Shipyards	July 1966	Dec 1967
CHASE	WHEC 718	Avondale Shipyards	Oct 1966	Mar 1968
BOUTWELL	WHEC 719	Avondale Shipyards	Dec 1966	June 1968
SHERMAN	WHEC 720	Avondale Shipyards	Feb 1967	Aug 1968
GALLATIN	WHEC 721	Avondale Shipyards	Apr 1967	Dec 1968
MORGENTHAU	WHEC 722	Avondale Shipyards	July 1967	Feb 1969
RUSH	WHEC 723	Avondale Shipyards	Oct 1967	July 1969
MUNRO	WHEC 724	Avondale Shipyards	Feb 1970	Sep 1971
JARVIS	WHEC 725	Avondale Shipyards	Sep 1970	Dec 1971
MIDGETT	WHEC 726	Avondale Shipyards	Apr 1971	Mar 1972

Remarks: This class of high-endurance cutters, named for treasury secretaries and USCG heroes, was the largest gas turbine-powered US warship class until the advent of the 'Spruance' class. A class of 36 was planned, but only these 12 multi-role ships were built.

'Hunt' class (Type 1) frigate

UK

Displacement: 1,000 tons standard and 1,490 tons full load

Dimensions: length 280 ft (85·4 m); beam 29 ft (8·8 m); draught 7·5 ft (2·3 m)

Gun armament: four 4-in (102-mm) L/45 in two Mk 19 twin mountings, two 37-mm L/63 AA, and two 25-mm AA in a twin mounting

Missile armament: none

Torpedo armament: none

Anti-submarine armament: two depth-charge throwers

Electronics: surface-search/navigation radar, and sonar

Propulsion: two Admiralty boilers supplying steam to two Parsons geared turbines delivering 19,000 shp (14,170 kW) to two shafts

Performance: maximum speed 25 kts; range 2,300 miles (3,700 km) at 12 kts

Complement: 133

Class

1. Egypt (1)

Name	No.	Builders	Laid down	Commissioned
PORT SAID	525	Yarrow (Shipbuilders) Ltd	Dec 1939	Dec 1940

'Hvidbjørnen' class frigate

Denmark
Displacement: 1,345 tons standard and 1,650 tons full load
Dimensions: length 72·6 m (238·2 ft); beam 11·6 m (38 ft); draught 5·0 m (16·4 ft)
Gun armament: one 76-mm (3-in) DP
Missile armament: none
Torpedo armament: none
Anti-submarine armament: depth-charges
Aircraft: one Westland Lynx helicopter in a hangar aft
Electronics: one AWS-1 air-search radar, one CWS-2 surface-search radar, one NWS-1 tactical radar, and one PMS-26 hull-mounted sonar
Propulsion: four General Motors 16-567C diesels delivering 6,400 bhp (4,770 kW) to one shaft

Performance: maximum speed 18 kts; range 11,125 km (6,915 miles) at 13 kts
Complement: 73

Class

1. Denmark (4)

Name	No.	Builders	Laid down	Com-missioned
HVIDBJØRNEN	F 348	Aarhus Flydedok	June 1961	Dec 1962
VAEDDEREN	F 349	Aalborg Vaerft	Oct 1961	Mar 1963
INGOLF	F 350	Svendborg Vaerft	Dec 1961	July 1963
FYLLA	F 351	Aalborg Vaerft	July 1962	July 1963

Remarks: These ships are designed more for fishery protection in northern waters than for modern war.

'Hvidbjørnen (Modified)' class frigate

Denmark
Displacement: 1,970 tons full load
Dimensions: length 74·7 m (245 ft); beam 12·2 m (40 ft); draught 5·3 m (17·4 ft)
Gun armament: one 76mm (3-in) DP
Missile armament: none
Torpedo armament: none
Anti-submarine armament: none
Aircraft: one Westland Lynx helicopter in a hangar aft
Electronics: one AWS-1 air-search radar, one CWS-2 surface-search radar, one NWS-1 tactical radar, one NWS-2 navigation radar, and one PMS-26 hull-mounted sonar
Propulsion: three Burmeister & Wain Alpha diesels delivering 5,550 kW (7,440 bhp) to one shaft
Performance: maximum speed 18 kts; range 11,125 km (6,915 miles) at 13 kts
Complement: 59

Class

1. Denmark (1)

Name	No.	Builders	Laid down	Com-missioned
BESKYTTEREN	F 340	Aalborg Vaerft	Dec 1974	Feb 1976

Remarks: Like its half-sister 'Hvidbjornen' class, the sole 'Hvidbjornen (Modified)' class frigate is more an offshore patrol and fishery protection vessel than a true warship, designed and constructed specifically for navigation in icy waters, though the provision of modest armament and appropriate sensors gives the ships a limited combat potential.

'Ibn Khaldoum' class frigate

Yugoslavia/Iraq
Displacement: 1,850 tons full load
Dimensions: length 96·7 m (317·3 ft); beam 11·2 m (36·7 ft); draught 4·5 m (14·8 ft)
Gun armament: one 57-mm DP, one 40-mm AA, and eight 20-mm AA
Missile armament: fitted for but not with four container-launchers for four MM.38 Exocet surface-to-surface missiles
Torpedo armament: none
Anti-submarine armament: two tubes for A/S torpedoes, and one A/S rocket-launcher
Aircraft: one light helicopter on a platform aft
Electronics: surface-search/navigation radar, and sonar
Propulsion: CODOG (COmbined Diesel Or Gas turbine) arrangement, with two MTU 16V956 TB91 diesels delivering 5,595 kW (7,500 shp) and one Rolls-Royce Olympus TM3B gas turbine delivering 22,300 hp (16,630 kW) to two shafts
Performance: maximum speed 26 kts on gas turbines and 20 kts on diesels; range

7,400 km (4,600 miles) at cruising speed
Complement: 93 and up to 100 cadets/trainees

Class

1. Indonesia (1)

Name	No.	Builder	Com-missioned
HADJAR DEWANTORO	364	Yugoslavia	Oct 1981

2. Iraq (1)

Name	No.	Builder	Com-missioned
IBN KHALDOUM	—	Yugoslavia	Mar 1981

Remarks: Though rated as frigates, these trim ships carry only light armament and are in reality training vessels, though capable of secondary anti-submarine and escort roles in times of crisis.

'Ishikari' class guided-missile frigate

Japan
Displacement: 1,290 tons
Dimensions: length 85·0 m (278·8 ft); beam 10·6 m (34·7 ft); draught 5·9 m (19·2 ft)
Gun armament: one 76-mm (3-in) L/62 DP OTO-Melara Compact
Missile armament: two quadruple launchers for eight RGM-84A Harpoon surface-to-surface missiles
Torpedo armament: none
Anti-submarine armament: two triple Type 68 tube mountings for 12·75-in (324-mm) Mk 44/46 A/S torpedoes, and one 375-mm (14·76-in) Bofors four-barrel rocket-launcher
Electronics: OPS-28 surface-search and OPS-19 navigation radars
Propulsion: CODOG (COmbined Diesel Or Gas turbine) arrangement, with one Rolls-Royce Olympus TM3B gas turbine delivering 22,500 shp (16,780 kW) or one 6 DRV diesel delivering 3,500 kW (4,700 shp) to two shafts
Performance: maximum speed 25 kts
Complement: 90

Class

1. Japan (1)

Name	No.	Builders	Laid down	Com-missioned
ISHIKARI	DE 226	Mitsui	May 1979	Mar 1981

Remarks: The sole 'Ishikari' class frigate was authorized in 1977 as a development type, Japan having designed no frigates since the 'Chikugo' class in the mid-1960s. The type has proved moderately successful, the lessons learned being incorporated in the design of the 'Yubari' class, which is slightly larger and provided with more power. The CODOG propulsion arrangement provides high burst speeds coupled with long endurance at cruising speed.

'Isuzu' class frigate
Japan
Displacement: 1,490 tons standard and 1,700 tons full load
Dimensions: length 94·0m (308·3ft); beam 10·4m (34·2ft); draught 3·5m (11·5ft)
Gun armament: four 3-in (76-mm) L/50 DP in two Mk 33 twin mountings
Missile armament: none
Torpedo armament: one quadruple 21-in (533-mm) tube mounting
Anti-submarine armament: two triple Type 68 tube mountings for 12·75-in (324-mm) Mk 44/46 A/S torpedoes, one 375-mm (14·76-mm) Bofors four-barrel rocket-launcher, one Mk 1 Y-gun depth-charge thrower, and (DEs 211 and 214) one depth-charge rack
Electronics: one OPS-1 air-search radar, one OPS-16 surface-search radar, Mk 34 gun-control radar used in conjunction with the Mk 63 gun fire-control system, one Sangamo SQS-29 hull-mounted sonar, and (DEs 212 and 213) one OQA-1 variable-depth sonar
Propulsion: four diesels (Mitsubishi in DEs 212 and 213, and Mitsui in DEs 211 and 214) delivering 11,930kW (16,000hp) to two shafts
Performance: maximum speed 25kts
Complement: 180

Visible on the stern of the Mogami (DE 212) is the OQA-1 variable-depth sonar, which gives the ship useful submarine-detection capability.

Class

1. Japan (4)				
Name	No.	Builders	Laid down	Commissioned
ISUZU	DE 211	Mitsui	Apr 1960	July 1961
MOGAMI	DE 212	Mitsubishi	Aug 1960	Oct 1961
KITAKAMI	DE 213	Ishikawajima Harima	June 1962	Feb 1964
OOI	DE 214	Maizuru	June 1962	Jan 1964

'Jacob van Heemskerck' class guided-missile frigate
Netherlands
Displacement: about 3,750 tons full load
Dimensions: length 130·5m (428·1ft); beam 14·6m (47·9ft); draught 4·3m (14·1ft)
Gun armament: one 30-mm Hollandse Signaalapparaten/General Electric Goalkeeper close-in weapon system mounting
Missile armament: one Mk 13 single launcher for ? RIM-66B Standard-MR surface-to-air missiles, two quadruple container-launchers for eight RGM-84A Harpoon anti-ship missiles, and one octuple Sea Sparrow surface-to-air missile launcher
Torpedo armament: none
Anti-submarine armament: two twin Mk 32 tube mountings for 12·75-in (324-mm) Mk 46 anti-submarine torpedoes
Aircraft: none
Electronics: one Hollandse Signaalapparaten LW-08 air-search radar, one Hollandse Signaalapparaten DA-05 surface-search radar, one Hollandse Signaalapparaten ZW-06 navigation radar, three Hollandse Signaalapparaten STIR fire-control radars, one SEWACO II data-information and cocmmand system, one Daisy data-handling system, various electronic warfare systems including Ramses ECM, two Knebworth Corvus chaff launchers, and SQS-509 sonar
Propulsion: COGOG (COmbined Gas turbine Or Gas turbine) arrangement, with two Rolls-Royce Olympus TM3B gas turbines delivering 50,000shp (37,285kW) and two Rolls-Royce Tyne RM1C gas turbines delivering 8,000shp (5,965kW) to two shfts
Performance: maximum speed 30kts; range 8,700km (5,405 miles) at 16kts
Complement: 176

Class

1. The Netherlands (0+2)				
Name	No.	Builders	Laid down	Commissioned
JACOB VAN HEEMSKERCK	F 812	Koninklijke Maatschappij	Jan 1981	1985
WITTE DE WITH	F 813	Koninklijke Maatschappij	Dec 1981	1986

Remarks: These two ships are replacements for the 'Kortenaer' class *Pieter Florisz* (F 812) and *Witte de With* (F 813) sold to Greece while building in mid-1980 and mid-1981 respectively. The opportunity was taken to improve the capability of the Royal Dutch navy with two variants of the 'Kortenaer' class, retaining the same basic hull and machinery, but optimized for the air-defence and task group command roles rather than anti-submarine warfare. To this end all provision for helicopters has been removed, the volume thus vacated being used for the Mk 13 launcher and its Standard surface-to-air missiles in the medium-range air-defence role. Short-range and point-defence capabilities are provided by the Sea Sparrow and Goalkeeper systems respectively, while self-defence against submarine attack is provided by the Mk 32 tubes. As on the 'Kortenaer' class ships, long-range anti-ship capability is provided by the eight Harpoon surface-to-surface missiles. Extra accommodation is provided for a task group commander and his staff, and it is planned that when completed the ships will be allocated to ASW Group I in the Atlantic and to ASW Group III in the English Channel area, complementing the anti-aircraft destroyer *Tromp* in the former group and providing command and anti-aircraft facilities for the latter group.

'Jiangdong' class guided-missile frigate
China
Displacement: 1,570 tons standard and 2,000 tons full load
Dimensions: length 103·2m (338·5ft); beam 10·2m (38·5ft); draught 3·1m (10·2ft)
Gun armament: two 100-mm (3·9-in) L/56 DP in one twin mounting, and eight 37-mm AA in four twin mountings
Missile armament: two twin launchers for surface-to-air missiles
Torpedo armament: none
Anti-submarine armament: two RBU 1200 five-barrel rocket-launchers, two depth-charge throwers, and two depth-charge racks
Electronics: air-search radar, surface-search radar, missile-control radar, gun-control radar, navigation radar, and sonar
Propulsion: two diesels delivering 11,930kW (16,000shp) to two shafts
Performance: maximum speed 25·5kts; range 7,400km (4,600 miles) at 15kts
Complement: 190

Class

1. China (2+3)				
Name	No.	Builders	Laid down	Commissioned
ZHONGDONG	531	Hutong	1971	1977
—	532	Hutong	1972	—

'Jianghu' class guided-missile frigate
China
Displacement: 1,570 tons standard and 2,000 tons full load
Dimensions: length 103·2m (338·5ft); beam 10·2m (38·5ft); draught 3·1m (10·2ft)
Gun armament: two 100-mm (3·9-in) L/56 DP in one twin mounting, and 12 37-mm AA in six twin mountings
Missile armament: two twin launchers for SS-N-2B 'Styx' surface-to-surface missiles
Torpedo armament: none
Anti-submarine armament: two RBU 1200 five-barrel rocket-launchers, four depth-charge throwers, and two depth-charge racks
Mines: fitted with racks for minelaying
Electronics: air-search radar, surface-search radar, missile-control radar, gun-control radar, navigation radar, and sonar
Propulsion: two diesels delivering 11,930kW (16,000shp) to two shafts
Performance: maximum speed 25·5kts; range 7,400km (4,600 miles) at 15kts
Complement: 195

Class

1. China (14+3)				
Name	No.	Builders	Laid down	Commissioned
—	510	Shanghai	1974	1976
—	511	Shanghai	1974	1976
—	512	Shanghai	1974	1976
—	513	Shanghai	1975	1977
—	514	Shanghai	1976	1978
—	515	Shanghai	1976	1978
—	516	Shanghai	1977	1979
—	517	Shanghai	1978	1980
—	518	Shanghai	1979	1981

plus 533, 551 and three others

'Jiangnan' class frigate
China
Displacement: 1,350 tons standard and 1,600 tons full load
Dimensions: length 90·8 m (297·8 ft); beam 10·0 m (32·8 ft); draught 3·9 m (12·8 ft)
Gun armament: three 100-mm (3·9-in) L/56 DP in three single mountings, eight 37-mm AA in four twin mountings, and four 12·7-mm (0·5-in) heavy machine-guns in two twin mountings
Missile armament: none
Torpedo armament: none
Anti-submarine armament: two RBU 1200 five-barrel rocket-launchers, four depth-charge throwers, and two depth-charge racks
Mines: believed to possess minelaying capability
Electronics: one 'Ball Gun' surface-search radar, one 'Wok Won' gun-control radar, one *Neptun* navigation radar, and sonar

Propulsion: four diesels delivering 17,900 kW (24,000 shp) to two shafts
Performance: maximum speed 28 kts
Complement: 175

Class
1. China (5)

Name	No.	Builders	Laid down	Commissioned
—	509	Jiangnan	1965	1967
—	501	Jiangnan	1965	1967
—	502	Jiangnan	1966	1968
—	503	Guangzhou	1966	1968
—	504	Guangzhou	1967	1969

Remarks: The class is similar to the Soviet 'Riga' class.

'João Coutinho' class frigate
Portugal
Displacement: 1,205 tons standard and 1,380 tons full load
Dimensions: length 84·6 m (277·5 ft); beam 10·3 m (33·8 ft); draught 3·6 m (11·8 ft)
Gun armament: two 3-in (76-mm) L/50 DP in one Mk 34 twin mounting, and two 40-mm Bofors L/70 AA in one twin mounting
Missile armament: none
Torpedo armament: none
Anti-submarine armament: one Hedgehog rocket-launcher, two depth-charge throwers, and two depth-charge racks

Electronics: one Microlambda MLA 1B air-search radar, one Decca TM 626 navigation radar, one SPG-34 gun-control radar used in conjunction with the Mk 63 gun fire-control system, one Mk 51 AA gun fire-control system, and one QCU-2 hull-mounted sonar
Propulsion: two SEMT-Pielstick PA6V-280 diesels delivering 8,175 kW (10,960 kW) to two shafts
Performance: maximum speed 24·5 kts; range 10,925 km (6,790 miles) at 18 kts
Complement: 9+91, and provision for a Marine detachment of 34
Class
1. Portugal (6)

Name	No.	Builders	Laid down	Commissioned
ANTONIO ENES	F 471	Bazán	Apr 1968	June 1971
JOÃO COUTINHO	F 475	Blohm und Voss	Sep 1968	Mar 1970
JACINTO CANDIDO	F 476	Blohm und Voss	Apr 1968	June 1970
GENERAL PEREIRA D'EÇA	F 477	Blohm und Voss	Oct 1968	Oct 1970
AUGUSTO DE CASTILHO	F 484	Bazán	Aug 1968	Nov 1970
HONORIO BARRETO	F 485	Bazán	July 1968	Apr 1971

Remarks: Modelled closely on the French 'Commandant Rivière' class design, the 'Joao Coutinho' class has different armament and sensors, and has proved highly successful in Portuguese service. It is therefore planned to modernize the class when finances permit in the late 1980s and early 1990s.

'Joseph Hewes' or 'Knox (Modified)' class guided-missile frigate
USA
Displacement: 3,010 tons standard and 4,200 tons full load
Dimensions: length 438 ft (133·5 m); beam 46·8 ft (14·3 m); draught 24·8 ft (7·8 m) to sonar dome
Gun armament: one 5-in (127-mm) L/54 in a Mk 42 single mounting, and (to be fitted) one 20-mm Phalanx Mk 15 close-in weapon system mounting
Missile armament: two quadruple container-launchers for eight RGM-84A Harpoon surface-to-surface missiles in FFs 1080-1097, and one Mk 25 launcher for RIM-7 Sea Sparrow surface-to-air missiles in FFs 1078-1083 (all Sea Sparrow installations to be replaced by Phalanx CIWS installations)
Torpedo armament: none
Anti-submarine armament: four Mk 32 tubes for 12·75-in (324-mm) Mk 46 A/S torpedoes, one octuple launcher for RUR-5A ASROC missiles, and helicopter-launched weapons (see below)

Almost identical with the 'Knox' class frigates but built under cover from large prefabricated modules, the Brewton (FF 1086) and her sisters constitute the 'Joseph Hewes' class of anti-submarine frigates.

Aircraft: one Kaman SH-2F Seasprite helicopter in a hangar aft
Electronics: one Raytheon/Sylvania SPS-10 surface-search radar, one Lockheed SPS-40 air-search radar, one SPG-53A gun-control radar used in conjunction with the Mk 68 gun fire-control system, one Mk 115 missile fire-control system, one Mk 1 target designation system, one EDO/General Electric SQS-26 CX bow-mounted sonar and EDO SQS-35 variable-depth sonar used in conjunction with the Mk 114 A/S fire-control system, OE-82 satellite communications antenna, SRR-1 satellite communications receiver, and WSC-3 satellite communications transceiver
Propulsion: two Combustion Engineering boilers supplying steam to one Westinghouse geared turbine delivering 35,000 shp (26,100 kW) to one shaft
Performance: maximum speed 27 kts; range 4,600 miles (7,400 km) at 20 kts
Complement: 22+261
Class
1. USA (20)

Name	No.	Builders	Laid down	Commissioned
JOSEPH HEWES	FF 1078	Avondale	May 1969	Apr 1971
BOWEN	FF 1079	Avondale	July 1969	May 1971
PAUL	FF 1080	Avondale	Sep 1969	Aug 1971
AYLWIN	FF 1081	Avondale	Nov 1969	Sep 1971
ELMER MONTGOMERY	FF 1082	Avondale	Jan 1970	Oct 1971
COOK	FF 1083	Avondale	Mar 1970	Dec 1971
McCANDLESS	FF 1084	Avondale	June 1970	Mar 1972
DONALD B. BEARY	FF 1085	Avondale	July 1970	July 1972
BREWTON	FF 1086	Avondale	Oct 1970	July 1972
KIRK	FF 1087	Avondale	Dec 1970	Sep 1972
BARBEY	FF 1088	Avondale	Feb 1971	Nov 1972
JESSE L. BROWN	FF 1089	Avondale	Apr 1971	Feb 1973
AINSWORTH	FF 1090	Avondale	June 1971	Mar 1973
MILLER	FF 1091	Avondale	Aug 1971	June 1973
THOMAS C. HART	FF 1092	Avondale	Oct 1971	July 1973
CAPODANNO	FF 1093	Avondale	Oct 1971	Nov 1973
PHARRIS	FF 1094	Avondale	Feb 1972	Jan 1974
TRUETT	FF 1095	Avondale	Apr 1972	June 1974
VALDEZ	FF 1096	Avondale	June 1972	July 1974
MOINESTER	FF 1097	Avondale	Aug 1972	Nov 1974

'King' class frigate
Argentina
Displacement: 915 tons standard and 1,030 tons full load
Dimensions: length 77·0m (252·7ft); beam 8·8m (29ft); draught 2·3m (7·5ft)
Gun armament: three 4-in (102-mm) DP in single mountings, and four 40-mm Bofors L/70 AA in one twin and two single mountings
Missile armament: none
Torpedo armament: none
Anti-submarine armament: four depth-charge throwers
Electronics: navigation radar
Propulsion: two Werkspoor diesels delivering 1,865kW (2,500bhp) to two shafts
Performance: maximum speed 18kts; range 11,125km (6,915 miles) at 12kts
Complement: 100

Class
1. Argentina (2)			Com-
Name	No.	Builders	missioned
MURATURE	P 20	Rio Santiago Naval Yard	Apr 1945
KING	P 21	Rio Santiago Naval Yard	Nov 1946

Remarks: Though carrying the 'P' designator used for Argentine frigates, this pair of elderly ships is used for training of cadets and also for offshore patrol. Neither ship possesses any real naval value in modern terms, as the class lacks sensors and anti-submarine armament, and it is expected that the two units will be replaced by locally-built training/patrol ships of about the same displacement when finances permit.

'Knox' class guided-missile frigate
USA
Displacement: 3,010 tons standard and 3,875 tons full load
Dimensions: length 438ft (133·5m); beam 46·8ft (14·3m); draught 24·8ft (7·8m) to sonar dome
Gun armament: one 5-in (127-mm) L/54 in a Mk 42 single mounting, and (to be fitted) one 20-mm Phalanx Mk 15 close-in weapon system mounting
Missile armament: two quadruple container-launchers for eight RGM-84A Harpoon surface-to-surface missiles in FFs 1053-1062, 1064, 1066, 1067 and 1069-1077, and one Mk 25 launcher for RIM-7 Sea Sparrow surface-to-air missiles in FFs 1052-1069 and 1071-1077, or one Mk 29 launcher for RIM-7 Sea Sparrow surface-to-air missiles in FF 1070 (all Sea Sparrow installations to be replaced by Phalanx CIWS installations)
Torpedo armament: none
Anti-submarine armament: four Mk 32 tubes for 12·75-in (324-mm) Mk 46 A/S torpedoes, one octuple launcher for RUR-5A ASROC missiles, and helicopter-launched weapons (see below)
Aircraft: one Kaman SH-2F Seasprite helicopter in a hangar aft
Electronics: one Raytheon/Sylvania SPS-10 surface-search radar, one Lockheed SPS-40 air-search radar, one SPG-53A gun-control radar used in conjunction with the Mk 68 gun fire-control system, one Mk 115 missile fire-control system, one Mk 1 target designation system, one EDO/General Electric SQS-26 CX bow-mounted sonar and EDO SQS-35 variable-depth sonar used in conjunction with the Mk 114 A/S fire-control system, OE-82 satellite communications antenna, SRR-1 satellite communications receiver, and WSC-3 satellite communications transceiver
Propulsion: two boilers (Babcock & Wilcox in FFs 1056, 1057, 1061, 1063, 1065, 1072, 1073, 1075 and 1077, and Combustion Engineering in the others) supplying steam to one Westinghouse geared turbine delivering 35,000shp (26,100kW) to one shaft
Performance: maximum speed 27kts; range 4,600 miles (7,400km) at 20kts
Complement: 22+261

Class
1. USA (26)				Com-
Name	No.	Builders	Laid down	missioned
KNOX	FF 1052	Todd Pacific	Oct 1965	Apr 1969
ROARK	FF 1053	Todd Pacific	Feb 1966	Nov 1969
GRAY	FF 1054	Todd Pacific	Nov 1966	Apr 1970
HEPBURN	FF 1055	Todd Pacific	June 1966	July 1969
CONNOLE	FF 1056	Avondale	Mar 1967	Aug 1969
RATHBURNE	FF 1057	Lockheed S.B.	Jan 1968	May 1970
MEYERKORD	FF 1058	Todd Pacific	Sep 1966	Nov 1969
W. S. SIMS	FF 1059	Avondale	Apr 1967	Jan 1970
LANG	FF 1060	Todd Pacific	Mar 1967	Mar 1970
PATTERSON	FF 1061	Avondale	Oct 1967	Mar 1970
WHIPPLE	FF 1062	Todd Pacific	Apr 1967	Aug 1970
REASONER	FF 1063	Lockheed S.B.	Jan 1969	July 1971
LOCKWOOD	FF 1064	Todd Pacific	Nov 1967	Dec 1970
STEIN	FF 1065	Lockheed S.B.	June 1970	Jan 1972
MARVIN SHIELDS	FF 1066	Todd Pacific	Apr 1968	Apr 1971
FRANCIS HAMMOND	FF 1067	Todd Pacific	July 1967	July 1970
VREELAND	FF 1068	Avondale	Mar 1968	June 1970
BAGLEY	FF 1069	Lockheed S.B.	Sep 1970	May 1972
DOWNES	FF 1070	Todd Pacific	Sep 1968	Aug 1971
BADGER	FF 1071	Todd Pacific	Feb 1968	Dec 1970
BLAKELY	FF 1072	Avondale	June 1968	July 1970
ROBERT E. PEARY	FF 1073	Lockheed S.B.	Dec 1970	Sep 1972
HAROLD E. HOLT	FF 1074	Todd Pacific	May 1968	Mar 1971
TRIPPE	FF 1075	Avondale	July 1968	Sep 1970
FANNING	FF 1076	Todd Pacific	Dec 1968	July 1971
OUELLET	FF 1077	Avondale	Jan 1969	Dec 1970

Remarks: A large class of dedicated anti-submarine escorts, the 'Knox' class ships have reload ASROC missiles in a magazine under the bridge, and telescoping hangars for their single Kaman SH-2 LAMPS helicopter.

'Köln' class (Type 120) frigate
West Germany
Displacement: 2,100 tons standard and 2,700 tons full load
Dimensions: length 109·9m (360·5ft); beam 11·0m (36·1ft); draught 5·1m (16·7ft)
Gun armament: two 100-mm (3·9-in) L/55 DP in single mountings, and six 40-mm Bofors AA in two single and two twin mountings
Missile armament: none
Torpedo armament: none
Anti-submarine armament: four 533-mm (21-in) tubes for A/S torpedoes, two 375-mm (14·76-in) Bofors four-barrel rocket-launchers, and two depth-charge throwers
Mines: can carry 80 for laying over the stern
Electronics: one Hollandse Signaalapparaten ZW-series surface-search and navigation radar, one Hollandse Signaalapparaten DA-02 target-designation radar, two Hollandse Signaalapparaten WM-45 main armament fire-control systems, two Hollandse Signaalapparaten WM-45 AA armament fire-control systems, one PAE/CWE hull-mounted sonar used in conjunction with the Hollandse Signaalapparaten A/S fire-control system, and one Hollandse Signaalapparaten WM-9 torpedo fire-control system
Propulsion: CODAG (COmbined Diesel And Gas turbine arrangement), with four MAN diesels delivering 8,950kW (12,000bhp) and two Brown-Boveri gas turbines delivering 17,895kW (24,000bhp) to two shafts
Performance: maximum speed 28kts with gas turbines and 18kts on diesels; range 1,675km (1,040 miles) at 28kts
Complement: 17+193

Class
1. Turkey (2)				Com-
Name	No.	Builders	Laid down	missioned
GAZI OSMAN PASA	D 370	H. C. Stülcken Sohn	Dec 1958	Dec 1962
—	—	H. C. Stülcken Sohn	Apr 1958	Oct 1961

2. West Germany (4)				Com-
Name	No.	Builders	Laid down	missioned
KÖLN	F 220	H. C. Stülcken Sohn	Dec 1957	Apr 1961
AUGSBURG	F 222	H. C. Stülcken Sohn	Oct 1958	Apr 1962
LÜBECK	F 224	H. C. Stülcken Sohn	Oct 1959	July 1963
BRAUNSCHWEIG	F 225	H. C. Stülcken Sohn	July 1960	June 1964

The Lübeck (F 224) is one of four 'Köln' class frigates forming West Germany's 2nd Frigate Squadron, the class being reduced by transfers.

'Koni' class guided-missile frigate

USSR

Displacement: 1,700 tons standard and 2,000 tons full load

Dimensions: length 95·0 m (311·6 ft); beam 12·0 m (39·3 ft); draught 4·2 m (13·7 ft)

Gun armament: four 76-mm (3-in) L/60 DP in two twin mountings, and four 30-mm AA in two twin mountings

Missile armament: one twin launcher for SA-N-4 surface-to-air missiles

Torpedo armament: none

Anti-submarine armament: two RBU 6000 12-barrel rocket-launchers

Electronics: one 'Strut Curve' air-search radar, one 'Pop Group' SAM-control radar, one 'Owl Screech' main armament control radar, one 'Drum Tilt' AA gun-control radar, and hull-mounted sonar

Propulsion: CODAG (COmbined Diesel And Gas turbine) arrangement, with two diesels delivering 8,950 kW (12,000 shp) and one gas turbine delivering 13,425 kW (18,000 shp) to three shafts

Performance: maximum speed 28 kts on gas turbine and 22 kts on diesels; range 3,700 km (2,300 miles) at 14 kts

Complement: 110

Class

1. Algeria (2)

Name	No.
MURAT REIS	901
RAIS KELLICEN	—

2. Cuba (1)

Name	No.
MARIEL	350

3. East Germany (2)

Name	No.	Builders	Commissioned
ROSTOCK	141	Leningrad	July 1978
BERLIN	142	Leningrad	May 1979

4. USSR (1)

Name	No.
DELFIN	—

5. Yugoslavia (1)

Name	No.
SPLIT	R 31

The USSR retains a single example of the 'Koni Type I' frigate for the training of crews for the type's export customers, who find the type a useful escort type with limited anti-aircraft and anti-submarine capability. Mounted at the forward edge of the bridge superstructure are the two 12-barrel RBU 6000 anti-submarine rocket-launchers. The short foredeck accommodates one of the two twin 76-mm (3-in) gun mountings.

Remarks: The small numbers of 'Koni' class frigates produced in the USSR for export fall into two basically similar types, the 'Koni Type I' and 'Koni Type II', the latter being distinguishable by the deckhouse filling the area between the after superstructure and funnel, presumably for air-conditioning equipment in vessels intended for hot-climate operations. Algeria operates two 'Koni Type II' frigates, received in December 1980 and April 1982. Cuba's single 'Koni Type II' frigate was received in August 1981, and it is possible that another such vessel was received in the first half of 1984. East Germany was the first recipient of 'Koni' class frigates, her two 'Koni Type I' ships being received in June 1978 and April 1979. The final operator of the class is Yugoslavia, which took delivery of two 'Koni Type I' frigates in March 1980 and December 1982. The class is fitted with the SA-N-4 surface-to-air missile system in the after deckhouse, the launcher being a retractable unit covered by a circular hatch cover. It is possible that the type was designed as a successor to the 'Riga' class, and that for unknown reasons it proved unsuitable for Soviet service, compelling the retention of the obsolescent 'Riga' class frigates.

'Kortenaer' class guided-missile frigate

Netherlands

Displacement: 3,050 tons standard and 3,630 tons full load

Dimensions: length 130·5 m (428·1 ft); beam 14·4 m (47·2 ft); draught 6·2 m (20·3 ft) to the screws

Gun armament: one 76-mm (3-in) L/62 DP OTO-Melara Compact, and one 40-mm Bofors AA (to be replaced by Hollandse Signaalapparaten close-in cannon system)

Missile armament: two quadruple container-launchers for eight RGM-84A Harpoon surface-to-surface missiles, and one Mk 29 launcher for RIM-7 Sea Sparrow surface-to-air missiles

Torpedo armament: none

Anti-submarine armament: two twin Mk 32 tube mountings for 12·75-in (324-mm) Mk 46 A/S torpedoes, and helicopter-launched weapons (see below)

Aircraft: two Westland Lynx helicopters in a hangar aft

Electronics: one Hollandse Signaalapparaten LW-08 long-range air-search radar, one Hollandse Signaalapparaten ZW-06 surface-search and navigation radar, one Hollandse Signaalapparaten DA-series surface-search and target-designation radar, one Hollandse Signaalapparaten WM-25 fire-control system, one Hollandse Signaalapparaten STIR surveillance target indicator radar, one Canadian Westinghouse SQS-505 bow-mounted medium-range search and attack sonar, one Hollandse Signaalapparaten SEWACO II data-processing system, one Ramses electronic countermeasures system, one Daisy data-handling system, and two Knebworth Corvus chaff launchers

Propulsion: COGOG (COmbined Gas turbine Or Gas turbine) arrangement, with two Rolls-Royce Olympus TM3B gas turbines delivering 50,000 shp (37,285 kW) or two Rolls-Royce Tyne RM1C gas turbines delivering 8,000 shp (5,965 kW) to two shafts

Performance: maximum speed 30 kts; range 8,700 km (5,405 miles) on Tynes at 16 kts

Complement: 167

Class

1. Greece (2+1+2)

Name	No.	Builders	Laid down	Commissioned
ELLI	F 450	Koninklijke Maatschappij	July 1977	Oct 1981
LIMNOS	F 451	Koninklijke Maatschappij	June 1978	1982

2. The Netherlands (10)

Name	No.	Builders	Laid down	Commissioned
KORTENAER	F 807	Koninklijke Maatschappij	Apr 1975	Oct 1978
CALLENBURGH	F 808	Koninklijke Maatschappij	June 1975	July 1979
VAN KINSBERGEN	F 809	Koninklijke Maatschappij	Sep 1975	Apr 1980
BANCKERT	F 810	Koninklijke Maatschappij	Feb 1976	Oct 1980
PIET HEYN	F 811	Koninklijke Maatschappij	Apr 1977	Apr 1981
ABRAHAM CRIJNSSEN	F 816	Koninklijke Maatschappij	Oct 1978	late 1982
PHILIPS VAN ALMONDE	F 823	Dok en Werfmaatschappij	Oct 1977	Dec 1981
BLOYS VAN TRESLONG	F 824	Dok en Werfmaatschappij	Apr 1978	late 1982
JAN VAN BRAKEL	F 825	Koninklijke Maatschappij	Nov 1979	spring 1983
PIETER FLORISZ	F 826	Koninklijke Maatschappij	Jan 1981	early 1984

Remarks: The 'Kortenaer' class is an excellent and versatile anti-submarine frigate design with useful anti-ship capability. The after 76-mm (3-in) gun is being removed in Dutch ships as the Goalkeeper CIWS mounting becomes available, and habitability is promoted by the extensive use of automation, which has reduced the crew from the 200 originally intended. The Greek ships (whose locally-built sisters appear to be in a construction limbo) have AB.212ASW helicopters, and a fire-control suite reduced to one WM-25 and one STIR equipment.

'Krivak I' and 'Krivak II' class guided-missile frigates

USSR

Displacement: 3,000 tons standard and 3,800 tons full load
Dimensions: length 122·5 m (401·8 ft); beam 14·0 m (45·9 ft); draught 4·7 m (15·4 ft)
Gun armament: four 76-mm (3-in) L/60 DP in two twin mountings ('Krivak I') or two 100-mm (3·9-in) L/56 DP in two single mountings ('Krivak II')
Missile armament: two twin launchers for SA-N-4 surface-to-air missiles
Torpedo armament: two quadruple 533-mm (21-in) tube mountings
Anti-submarine armament: one quadruple launcher for SS-N-14 'Silex' A/S missiles, and two RBU 6000 12-barrel rocket-launchers
Electronics: one 'Head Net-C' 3D radar, two 'Eye Bowl' SS-N-14 control radars, two 'Pop Group' SAM-control radars, one 'Owl Screech' gun-control radar, one 'Don Kay' navigation radar, one 'Don-2' navigation radar, one 'High Pole-B' IFF, one hull-mounted sonar, one variable-depth sonar, and electronic warfare systems
Propulsion: four gas turbines delivering 53,690 kW (72,000 shp) to two shafts
Performance: maximum speed 32 kts; range 7,400 km (4,600 miles) at 15 kts or 2,775 km (1,725 miles) at 32 kts
Complement: 220

Armament of the 'Krivak I' class escort frigate includes two twin 76-mm (3-in) guns and two SA-N-4 launchers aft, and one quadruple SS-N-14 launcher forward.

Class

1. USSR (32+?)

Name	No.	Builders
BDITELNY	—	Zhdanov/Kaliningrad
BODRY	—	Zhdanov/Kaliningrad
DRUZHNY	—	Zhdanov/Kaliningrad
LENINGRADSKY KOMSOMOLETS	—	Zhdanov/Kaliningrad
LETUCHY	—	Zhdanov/Kaliningrad
PYLKY	—	Zhdanov/Kaliningrad
RAZUMNY	—	Zhdanov/Kaliningrad
RAZYASHCHY	—	Zhdanov/Kaliningrad
RETIVY	—	Zhdanov/Kaliningrad
SILNY	—	Zhdanov/Kaliningrad
STOROZHEVOY	—	Zhdanov/Kaliningrad
SVIREPY	—	Zhdanov/Kaliningrad
ZADORNY	—	Zhdanov/Kaliningrad
ZHARKI	—	Zhdanov/Kaliningrad
BEZZAVETNY	—	Kamysch-Burun
BUZUKORIZNENNY	—	Kamysch-Burun
DOSTOYNY	—	Kamysch-Burun
DOBLESTNY	—	Kamysch-Burun
DEYATELNY	—	Kamysch-Burun
LADNY	—	Kamysch-Burun
plus one other		
BESSMENNY*	—	Kaliningrad
GORDELIVY*	—	Kaliningrad
GROMKY*	—	Kaliningrad
GROZYASHCHY*	—	Kaliningrad
NEUKROTIMY*	—	Kaliningrad
PYTLIVY*	—	Kaliningrad
RAZYTELNY*	—	Kaliningrad
REVNOSTNY*	—	Kaliningrad
REZKY*	—	Kaliningrad
REZVY*	—	Kaliningrad
RYANY*	—	Kaliningrad

*'Krivak II' class

'Leander (Batch 1)' class frigate

UK

Displacement: 2,450 tons standard and 2,860 tons full load
Dimensions: length 372 ft (113·4 m); beam 41 ft (12·5 m); draught 18 ft (5·5 m) to screws
Gun armament: two 40-mm Bofors L/60 AA in two single mountings
Missile armament: two quadruple launchers for Sea Cat surface-to-air missiles
Torpedo armament: none
Anti-submarine armament: one Ikara A/S weapon system, and one Limbo three-barrel mortar
Aircraft: one Westland Lynx HAS.Mk 2 or Westland Wasp HAS.Mk 1 helicopter in a hangar aft
Electronics: one Plessey Type 994 combined air- and surface-search radar, one Decca Type 978 navigation radar, two Type 903 SAM-control radars used in conjunction with one Sperry MRS 3/GWS 22 missile fire-control system, and one GWS 40 Ikara-control system linked to Type 170 hull-mounted short-range search and attack sonar, one Graseby Type 184 hull-mounted medium-range panoramic search and attack sonar and one EMI Type 199 variable-depth sonar, one Computer-Assisted Action Information System, and two Knebworth Corvus chaff launchers
Propulsion: two Babcock & Wilcox boilers supplying steam to two sets of White-English Electric double-reduction geared turbines delivering 30,000 shp (22,370 kW) to two shafts
Performance: maximum speed 28 kts; range 4,600 miles (7,400 km) at 15 kts
Complement: 19+238

Class

1. UK (8)

Name	No.	Builders	Laid down	Conversion, completed
AURORA	F 10	John Brown	June 1961	Mar 1976
EURYALUS	F 15	Scotts Shipbuilding	Nov 1961	Mar 1976
GALATEA	F 18	Swan Hunter Ltd	Dec 1961	Sep 1974
ARETHUSA	F 38	J. Samuel White	Sep 1962	Apr 1977
NAIAD	F 39	Yarrow (Shipbuilders)	Oct 1962	July 1975
DIDO	F 104	Yarrow (Shipbuilders)	Dec 1959	Oct 1978
LEANDER	F 109	Harland & Wolff Ltd	Apr 1959	Dec 1972
AJAX	F 114	Cammell Laird	Oct 1959	Sep 1973

'Leander (Batch 2)' class guided-missile frigate

UK

Displacement: 2,450 tons standard and 3,200 tons full load
Dimensions: length 372 ft (113·4 m); beam 41 ft (12·5 m); draught 19 ft (5·8 m)
Gun armament: two 40-mm Bofors L/60 AA in two single mountings
Missile armament: four container-launchers for four MM.38 Exocet surface-to-surface missiles, and three quadruple launchers for Sea Cat surface-to-air missiles
Torpedo armament: none
Anti-submarine armament: two triple Mk 32 tube mountings for 12·75-in (324-mm) Mk 44/46 A/S torpedoes
Aircraft: one Westland Lynx HAS.Mk 2 or Westland Wasp HAS.Mk 1 helicopter in a hangar aft
Electronics: one Marconi Type 965 air-search radar with single AKE array, one Plessey Type 994 combined air- and surface-search radar, one Decca Type 978 navigation radar, two Type 903 SAM-control radars used in conjunction with one Sperry MRS 3/GWS 22 missile fire-control system, one Graseby Type 184 hull-mounted medium-range panoramic search and attack sonar, and two Knebworth Corvus chaff launchers
Propulsion: two Babcock & Wilcox boilers supplying steam to two sets of White-English Electric double-reduction geared turbines delivering 30,000 shp (22,370 kW) to two shafts
Performance: maximum speed 28 kts; range 4,600 miles (7,400 km) at 15 kts
Complement: 20+203

Class

1. New Zealand (2)

Name	No.	Builders	Laid down	Commissioned
WAIKATO	F 55	Harland & Wolff	Jan 1964	Sep 1966
SOUTHLAND	F 104	Yarrow (Shipbuilders)	Dec 1959	Sep 1963

2. UK (8)

Name	No.	Builders	Laid down	Conversion, completed
CLEOPATRA	F 28	HM Dockyard Devonport	June 1963	Nov 1975
SIRIUS	F 40	HM Dockyard Portsmouth	Aug 1963	Oct 1977
PHOEBE	F 42	Alexander Stephen	June 1963	Apr 1977
MINERVA	F 45	Vickers-Armstrong	July 1963	Mar 1979
DANAE	F 47	HM Dockyard Devonport	Dec 1964	Sep 1980
JUNO	F 52*	John I. Thornycroft	July 1964	—
ARGONAUT	F 56	Hawthorn Leslie	Nov 1964	Mar 1980
PENELOPE	F 127	Vickers-Armstrong	Mar 1961	Mar 1981

*training ship

'Leander (Batch 3)' or 'Broad-beam Leander' class frigate
UK

The **Canterbury** *(F 421) is a fine example of the 'Leander (Batch 3)' class in its original form with a 4·5-in (114-mm) gun mounting forward, triple Mk 32 tubes on the beams, and a quadruple Sea Cat launcher above the Westland Wasp hangar.*

Displacement: 2,500 tons standard and 2,960 tons full load
Dimensions: length 372 ft (113·4 m); beam 43 ft (13·1 m); draught 18 ft (5·5 m) to screws
Gun armament: (unconverted ships) two 4·5-in (114-mm) L/45 DP in one Mk 6 twin mounting and two 20-mm AA in single mountings, or (converted ships) two 40-mm Bofors AA in single mountings
Missile armament: (unconverted ships) one quadruple launcher for Sea Cat surface-to-air missiles, or (converted ships) four container-launchers for four MM.38 Exocet surface-to-surface missiles, and one sextuple launcher for Sea Wolf surface-to-air missiles
Torpedo armament: none
Anti-submarine armament: (unconverted ships) one Limbo three-barrel mortar, or (converted ships) two triple Mk 32 tube mountings for 12·75-in (324-mm) Mk 44/46 A/S torpedoes
Aircraft: one Westland Lynx HAS.Mk 2 helicopter in a hangar aft
Electronics: one Marconi Type 965 air-search radar with single AKE array, one Plessey Type 994 combined air- and surface-search radar (unconverted ships) or one combined Marconi Type 967 air-search radar and one Kelvin-Hughes Type 968 surface-search radar unit (converted ships), one GWS 25 SAM fire-control system, one Type 170 hull-mounted short-range search and attack sonar and one Type 177 hull-mounted medium-range panoramic search and attack sonar (unconverted ships) or one Type 2016 hull-mounted sonar (converted ships), SCOT satellite communications system, and two Knebworth Corvus chaff launchers
Propulsion: two Babcock & Wilcox boilers supplying steam to two sets of White-English Electric double-reduction geared turbines delivering 30,000 shp (22,370 kW) to two shafts
Performance: maximum speed 28 kts; range 4,600 miles (7,400 km) at 15 kts
Complement: 19+241

Class

1. Chile (2)
Name	No.	Builders	Laid down	Com-missioned
CONDELL	06	Yarrow (Shipbuilders)	June 1971	Dec 1973
ALMIRANTE LYNCH	07	Yarrow (Shipbuilders)	Dec 1971	May 1974

2. India (6)
Name	No.	Builders	Laid down	Com-missioned
HIMGIRI	F 32	Mazagon Docks Ltd	1967	Nov 1974
NILGIRI	F 33	Mazagon Docks Ltd	Oct 1966	June 1972
UDAYGIRI	F 35	Mazagon Docks Ltd	Jan 1973	Feb 1977
DUNAGIRI	F 36	Mazagon Docks Ltd	Sep 1970	Feb 1976
VINDHYAGIRI	F 38	Mazagon Docks Ltd	1975	1980
TARAGIRI	F 41	Mazagon Docks Ltd	1974	Sep 1979

3. New Zealand (2)
Name	No.	Builders	Laid down	Com-missioned
CANTERBURY	F 421	Yarrow (Shipbuilders)	Apr 1969	Oct 1971
WELLINGTON	F 69	Vickers-Armstrong Ltd	Oct 1966	Oct 1969

4. UK (9)
Name	No.	Builders	Laid down	Conversion, completed
ACHILLES	F 12	Yarrow (Shipbuilders)	Dec 1967	—
DIOMEDE	F 16	Yarrow (Shipbuilders)	Jan 1968	—
ANDROMEDA	F 57*	HM Dockyard	May 1966	Dec 1980
HERMIONE	F 58*	Alexander Stephen	Dec 1965	Jan 1983
JUPITER	F 60*	Yarrow (Shipbuilders)	Oct 1966	July 1983
APOLLO	F 70	Yarrow (Shipbuilders)	May 1969	—
SCYLLA	F 71*	HM Dockyard	May 1967	Sep 1983
ARIADNE	F 72	Yarrow (Shipbuilders)	Nov 1969	—
CHARYBDIS	F 75*	Harland & Wolff Ltd	Jan 1967	June 1982

*conversion

Remarks: The 'Leander' class has been one of the most successful Western frigate designs since World War II, being built extensively in the UK and India, and forming the basis for the Dutch 'Van Speijk' and Indian 'Godavari' classes. The design was a development of the 'Type 12' class. The 'Leander (Batch 1)' class is distinguished by the fact that it is optimized for anti-submarine warfare with variable-depth sonar and Ikara missile system. The 'Leander (Batch 2)' class is itself divided into two groups, designated 'Leander (Batch 2)' when fitted with four MM.38 Exocets, three quadruple Sea Cat SAM launchers and an anti-submarine fit of three triple STWS tube mountings and Type 184 sonar; and 'Leander (Batch 2 TA)' when fitted with four MM.38 Exocets, two quadruple Sea Cat SAM launchers and an anti-submarine fit of two triple STWS tube mountings and Type 2024 towed-array (TA) sonar. The 'Leander (Batch 3)' class is also divided into two groups, the 'Leander (Batch 3)' ships having one quadruple Sea Cat SAM launcher, and an anti-submarine fit of Type 2016 sonar and a Limbo mortar; and the 'Leander (Batch 3 Converted)' ships having four MM.38 Exocets, one Sea Wolf sextuple launcher, and an anti-submarine fit of Type 2016 sonar and two triple STWS tube mountings. The gun armament also differs between classes, the more so as close-in AA weapons are augmented in the light of experience in the Falklands campaign. Chile's two ships each have four MM.38 Exocets, one quadruple Sea Cat launcher with 16 SAMs, two triple Mk 32 tube mountings, one 4·5-in (114-mm) twin gun mounting and no variable-depth sonar; it is believed that Chile is interested in acquiring another two 'Leander' class frigates. The Indian ships differ from the British standard quite considerably, with a telescopic hangar for an Aérospatiale Alouette III helicopter (Westland Sea King in Fs 38 and 41, which also lack the telescopic hangar) two quadruple Sea Cat launchers with 32 SAMs (one launcher only in Fs 33 and 34), and (in Fs 38 and 41) an anti-submarine armament of two triple ILAS 3 tube mountings plus one 375-mm (14·76-in) Bofors rocket-launcher. Fs 33 and 34 have a single GWS 22 SAM-control system, the other possessing two Hollandse Signaalapparaten WM-44 systems. It is believed that Fs 38 and 41 are each to receive two SS-N-2 anti-ship missile launchers. The New Zealand ships are fairly close to their British equivalents, the standard fit being two 4·5-in (114-mm) guns, one quadruple Sea Cat launcher and two triple Mk 32 tube mountings; *Southland* has no 4·5-in (114-mm) guns, two quadruple Sea Cat launchers and Ikara anti-submarine missiles. *Wellington* may receive Harpoon anti-ship missiles, it is believed.

'Leopard' class (Type 41) frigate
UK

Displacement: 2,250 tons standard and 2,515 tons full load
Dimensions: length 339·8 ft (103·6 m); beam 40 ft (12·2 m); draught 16 ft (4·9 m)
Gun armament: two 4.5-in (114-mm) L/45 DP in one Mk 6 twin mounting, and two 40-mm Bofors L/60 AA in single mountings
Missile armament: none
Torpedo armament: none
Anti-submarine armament: one Squid three-barrel mortar
Electronics: one Type 960 air-search radar, one Type 293 surface-search and tactical radar, one Type 275 gun-control radar, one Decca Type 978 navigation radar, and sonar
Propulsion: eight Admiralty Standard Range diesels delivering 14,400 bhp (10,740 kW) to two shafts
Performance: maximum speed 24 kts; range 8,625 miles (13,880 km) at 16 kts
Complement: 210

Class

1. Bangladesh (2)
Name	No.	Builders	Laid down	Com-missioned
ABU BAKR	F 15	John Brown	Aug 1953	Mar 1957
ALI HAIDER	F 17	Wm. Denny & Bros Ltd	Nov 1953	Dec 1959

2. India (3)
Name	No.	Builders	Laid down	Com-missioned
BRAHMAPUTRA	F 31	John Brown	1956	Mar 1958
BEAS	F 37	Vickers-Armstrong Ltd	1957	May 1960
BETWA	F 39	Vickers-Armstrong Ltd	1957	Dec 1960

'Lupo' class guided-missile frigate

Italy

Displacement: 2,210 tons standard and 2,500 tons full load

Dimensions: length 113·2m (371·3ft); beam 11·3m (37·1ft); draught 3·7m (12·1ft)

Gun armament: one 127-mm (5-in) L/54 DP OTO-Melara Compact, and four 40-mm Breda AA in two twin mountings

Missile armament: eight container-launchers for eight Otomat Mk 2 surface-to-surface missiles, and one octuple launcher for RIM-7 Sea Sparrow surface-to-air missiles

Torpedo armament: none

Anti-submarine armament: two triple Mk 32 tube mountings for 12·75-in (324-mm) Mk 44/46 A/S torpedoes, and helicopter-launched weapons (see below)

Aircraft: one helicopter in a hangar aft

Electronics: one Selenia RAN 10S (MM/SPS 774) air-search radar, one SMA SPQ 2F surface-search radar, one SMA 3RM 20 navigation radar, two ELSAAG Argo NA 10 AA fire-control systems with Selenia Orion RTN 10X radars, one Selenia IPN 10 tactical data display system, one Raytheon DE 1160B hull-mounted sonar, and two SCLAR chaff launchers

Propulsion: CODOG (COmbined Diesel Or Gas turbine) arrangement, with two General Motors diesels delivering 5,815kW (7,800hp) or two Fiat/General Electric LM-2500 gas turbines delivering 37,285kW (50,000hp) to two shafts

Performance: maximum speed 35kts on gas turbines or 21kts on diesels; range 8,000km (4,970miles) at 16kts on diesels

Complement: 16+169

Class

1. Iraq (0+4)

Name	No.	Builders	Laid down	Com-missioned
—	—	CNR, Ancona	Mar 1982	1985
—	—	CNR, Ancona	Sept 1982	1986
—	—	CNR, Ancona	Mar 1983	1986
—	—	CNR, Ancona	Sept 1983	1987

2. Italy (4)

Name	No.	Builders	Laid down	Com-missioned
LUPO	F 564	Cantieri Navali Riuniti	Oct 1974	Sep 1977
SAGITTARIO	F 565	Cantieri Navali Riuniti	Feb 1976	Nov 1978
PERSEO	F 566	Cantieri Navali Riuniti	Feb 1977	Mar 1980
ORSA	F 567	Cantieri Navali Riuniti	Aug 1977	Mar 1980

3. Peru (2+2)

Name	No.	Builders	Laid down	Com-missioned
MELITON CARVAJAL	F 51	Cantieri Navali Riuniti	Aug 1974	Feb 1979
MANUEL VILLAVICENCIO	F 52	Cantieri Navali Riuniti	Oct 1976	June 1979
MONTERO	F 53	SIMAC Peru	1978	Jan 1984
—	—	SIMAC Peru	1979	—

4. Venezuela (6)

Name	No.	Builders	Laid down	Com-missioned
MARISCAL SUCRE	F 21	Cantieri Navali Riuniti	Nov 1976	May 1980
ALMIRANTE BRION	F 22	Cantieri Navali Riuniti	June 1977	Mar 1981
GENERAL URDANETA	F 23	Cantieri Navali Riuniti	Jan 1978	Aug 1981
GENERAL SOUBLETTE	F 24	Cantieri Navali Riuniti	Aug 1978	Dec 1981
GENERAL SALOM	F 25	Cantieri Navali Riuniti	Nov 1978	Feb 1982
JOSÉ FELIX RIBAS	F 26	Cantieri Navali Riuniti	Aug 1979	Oct 1982

Remarks: The 'Lupo' class has not proved altogether successful in Italian service despite its formidable armament. The design originated from a requirement for an escort frigate with useful anti-ship capability, but experience has shown that too much was sought in slightly too small a hull with adverse effects on aspects such as seakeeping qualities and habitability. This has prompted the Italians to develop the larger 'Maestrale' class fleet frigate with marginally improved armament in a larger hull. However, the 'Lupo' design has proved highly attractive to overseas buyers, who see the virtues of the powerful armament as outweighing the design's defects. Iraq ordered four ships of the class in February 1981, these being closely similar to the Italian baseline ships apart from having a fixed rather than telescopic hangar, which in turn restricts SAM capacity to the eight Aspide missiles in the octuple launcher above the hangar. (The Italian ships, it should be noted, can fire either the Aspide or the generally-similar RIM-7 Sea Sparrow point-defence surface-to-air missile.) In comparison with the Iraqi ships, the Peruvian vessels (two delivered from Italy, one built in Peru and a fourth under construction in Peru) retain the telescopic hangar, but alterations include manual rather than powered reloading of the octuple SAM launcher, and the 40-mm mountings are located higher than in the Italian ships. The largest force of 'Lupo' class frigates is that owned by Venezuela, whose six ships are very similar to the Italian units apart from their fixed hangars (making impossible the stowage of reload rounds for the octuple SAM launcher, SQS-29 hull-mounted sonar, and two triple ILAS 3 tube mountings for Whitehead A 244S anti-submarine.

Clearly visible in this illustration of the Lupo (F 564) at speed are the helicopter platform with the associated telescopic hangar in the extended position, the octuple SAM launcher above the hangar roof and, along the port beam one of the two 40-mm Breda Compact AA mountings, two pairs of Otomat anti-ship missile launchers as part of the Teseo system and, between the paired launchers one of the two triple Mk 32 tube mountings. Just visible forward of the bridge is the 127-mm (5-in) OTO-Melara Compact gun. The two SCLAR launchers are located one to each beam just in front of the bridge.

'M' class guided-missile frigate

Netherlands

Displacement: 2,650 tons

Dimensions: length 111·8m (366·7ft); beam 13·8m (45·3ft); draught 4·0m (13·1ft)

Gun armament: one 76-mm (3-in) L/62 DP OTO-Melara Compact, and one 30-mm Hollandse Signaalapparaten/General Electric Goalkeeper CIWS mounting

Missile armament: two quadruple container-launchers for eight RGM-84A Harpoon anti-ship missiles, and one octuple launcher for ? Sea Sparrow SAMs

Torpedo armament: none

Anti-submarine armament: two twin Mk 32 tube mountings for 12·75-in (324-mm) Mk 46 anti-submarine torpedoes, and helicopter-launched weapons (see below)

Aircraft: one helicopter in a hangar aft

Electronics: one Hollandse Signaalapparaten DA-08 combined air- and surface-search radar, one Hollandse Signaalapparaten ZW-06 surface warning and helicopter-control radar, Hollandse Signaalapparaten WM-25 fire-control radar, SEWACO II command system, several ECM and ESM systems, two chaff launchers, one torpedo decoy system, and one Hollandse Signaalapparaten PHS 36 hull-mounted search and attack sonar

Propulsion: CODOG (COmbined Diesel Or Gas turbine) arrangement, with one Rolls-Royce Olympus gas turbine delivering 28,000shp (20,880kW) and two diesel engines delivering 8,400bhp (6,265kW) to two shafts

Performance: maximum speed 28kts on gas turbine or 21kts on diesels; range 7,400km (4,600 miles) at 19kts

Complement: 80

Class

1. The Netherlands (0+5)

five ships to be built from late in the 1980s

Remarks: This is a most interesting design, intended as far superior replacements for the obsolescent 'Wolf' class corvette currently being withdrawn from service. A high degree of automation is planned to permit effective operations with a remarkably small crew, and it is probable that funds for construction will become available after 1987, permitting deliveries to begin in the 1990s. The 'M' class design groups both guns forward of the bridge (the 76-mm/3-in weapon in front of the CIWS mounting) with the missile and torpedo armament in the after portion of the ship as four Harpoon launchers on each side of the funnel, the SAM launcher on the hangar roof, and the twin Mk 32 tube mountings in the sides of the deckhouse just forward of the hangar.

'Mackenzie' class frigate

Canada

Displacement: 2,380 tons standard and 2,880 tons full load

Dimensions: length 366ft (111·6m); beam 42ft (12·8m); draught 13·5ft (4·1m)

Gun armament: four 3-in (76-mm) L/50 DP in one Mk 6 and one Mk 33 twin mountings

Missile armament: none

Torpedo armament: none

Anti-submarine armament: two Limbo Mk 10 three-barrel mortars, and side-launchers for Mk 43 A/S torpedoes

Electronics: one Raytheon/Sylvania SPS-10 surface-search radar, one RCA SPS-12 air-search radar, one Bell SPG-48 gun-control radar used in conjunction with the Mk 69 gun fire-control system, one Canadian Westinghouse SQS-501 bottom classification sonar, one Canadian Westinghouse SQS-502 mortar-control sonar, one Canadian Westinghouse SQS-503 search sonar, and one SQS-10 hull-mounted sonar

Propulsion: two Babcock & Wilcox boilers supplying steam to two sets of English Electric geared turbines delivering 30,000shp (22,370kW) to two shafts

Performance: maximum speed 28kts; range 3,150 miles (5,070km) at 14kts

Complement: 11+199

The pennant number 263 identifies the 'Mackenzie' class ship as the Yukon.

Class

1. Canada (4)

Name	No.	Builders	Laid down	Commissioned
MACKENZIE	261	Vickers	Dec 1958	Oct 1962
SASKATCHEWAN	262	Victoria Machinery	July 1959	Feb 1963
YUKON	263	Burrard D.D.	Oct 1959	May 1963
QU'APPELLE	264	Davie S.B.	Jan 1960	Sep 1963

Remarks: The four 'Mackenzie' class frigates are officially classified as destroyers, and have between 1982 and 1985 been undergoing the Destroyer Life Extension Program refit to maintain them in service up to 1993. The design is unusual for the use of two different 3-in (76-mm) gun mountings, and also for the large stern accommodating a well for two Mk 10 Limbo mortars, the primary short-range anti-submarine armament.

'Maestrale' class guided-missile frigate

Italy

Displacement: 2,500 tons standard and 3,040 tons full load

Dimensions: length 122·7m (405ft); beam 12·9m (42·5ft); draught 8·4m (27·4ft) to screws

Gun armament: one 127-mm (5-in) L/54 DP OTO-Melara Compact, and four 40-mm Breda L/70 AA in two twin mountings

The Maestrale (F 570) under way at moderate speed.

Remarks: Developed from the 'Lupo' design, the 'Maestrale' class is an excellent fleet anti-submarine frigate, her extra size in comparison with the 'Lupo' class permitting more comfortable accommodation, better seakeeping, a fixed hangar and variable-depth sonar.

Missile armament: four container-launchers for four Otomat Mk 2 surface-to-surface missiles, and one quadruple launcher for Aspide surface-to-air missiles

Torpedo armament: two 533-mm (21-in) tubes for A 184 wire-guided anti-ship and anti-submarine torpedoes

Anti-submarine armament: two triple Mk 32 tube mountings for 12·75-in (324-mm) Mk 44/46 A/S torpedoes, and helicopter-launched weapons (see below)

Aircraft: two Agusta-Bell AB.212ASW helicopters in a hangar aft

Electronics: one Selenia RAN 10S (MM/SPS 774) air-search radar, one Selenia MM/SPS 702 surface-search radar, one Selenia MM/SPN 703 navigation radar, one Selenia RM20 missile-control radar used in conjunction with the Selenia Albatros SAM fire-control system, two Selenia RM20 gun-control radars used in conjunction with the two Selenia/ELSAG Dardo AA gun fire-control systems, one Raytheon DE 1164 variable-depth sonar, and two SCLAR chaff launchers

Propulsion: CODOG (COmbined Diesel Or Gas turbine) arrangement, with two General Motors 230 diesels delivering 11,000hp (8,200kW) or two Fiat/General Electric LM 2500 gas turbines delivering 50,000shp (37,285kW) to two shafts

Performance: maximum speed 32kts on gas turbines and 21kts on diesels; range 11,125km (6,915 miles) at 16kts

Complement: 24+208

Class

1. Italy (6+2)

Name	No.	Builders	Laid down	Commissioned
MAESTRALE	F 570	Cantieri Navali Riuniti	Mar 1978	Feb 1982
GRECALE	F 571	Cantieri Navali Riuniti	Mar 1979	Sep 1982
LIBECCIO	F 572	Cantieri Navali Riuniti	Aug 1979	Sep 1982
SCIROCCO	F 573	Cantieri Navali Riuniti	Feb 1980	Jan 1983
ALISEO	F 574	Cantieri Navali Riuniti	Aug 1980	June 1983
EURO	F 575	Cantieri Navali Riuniti	Apr 1981	Dec 1983
ESPERO	F 576	Cantieri Navali Riuniti	1981	1984
ZEFFIRO	F 577	Cantieri Navali Riuniti	1982	1984

'Makut Rajakumarn' class frigate

UK/Thailand

Displacement: 1,650 tons standard and 1,900 tons full load

Dimensions: length 320ft (97·6m); beam 36ft (11·0m); draught 18·1ft (5·5m)

Gun armament: one 4·5-in (114-mm) L/55 in a Mk 8 single mounting, and two 40-mm Bofors L/60 AA in two single mountings

Missile armament: one quadruple launcher for Sea Cat surface-to-air missiles

Torpedo armament: none

Anti-submarine armament: one Limbo Mk 10 three-barrel rocket-launcher, one depth-charge rack, and two depth-charge throwers

Electronics: one Hollandse Signaalapparaten LW-04 air-search radar, one Decca 626 navigation radar, one Hollandse Signaalapparaten WM-22 gun fire-control radar system, one Hollandse Signaalapparaten WM-44 SAM fire-control radar system, one Type 170B hull-mounted short-range search and attack sonar, one Kelvin Hughes Type 162 hull-mounted side-looking classification sonar, one

Plessey MS 27 hull-mounted lightweight search and attack sonar, and one Hollandse Signaalapparaten combat information system

Propulsion: CODOG (COmbined Diesel Or Gas turbine) arrangement, with one Crossley-Pielstick 12PC2V diesel delivering 6,000bhp (4,475kW) and one Rolls-Royce Olympus TM3B gas turbine delivering 23,125shp (17,245kW) to two shafts

Performance: maximum speed 26kts on gas turbine and 18kts on diesel; range 5,750 miles (9,250km) at 18kts on diesel and 1,380 miles (2,220km) at 26kts on gas turbine

Complement: 16+124

Class

1. Thailand (1)

Name	No.	Builders	Laid down	Commissioned
MAKUT RAJAKUMARN	7	Yarrow (Shipbuilders)	Jan 1970	May 1973

'Meko 140' class guided-missile frigate

West Germany/Argentina

Displacement: 1,470 tons standard and 1,700 tons full load

Dimensions: length 91·2m (299·1ft); beam 12·0m (39·4ft); draught 3·3m (10·8ft)

Gun armament: one 76-mm (3-in) L/62 DP OTO-Melara Compact, and four 40-mm AA in two Breda Compact twin mountings

Missile armament: two twin container-launchers for four MM.40 Exocet anti-ship missiles

Torpedo armament: none

Anti-submarine armament: two triple ILAS 3 tube mountings for 324-mm (12·75-in) Whitehead A 244S anti-submarine torpedoes, and helicopter-launched weapons (see below)

Aircraft: one Westland Lynx helicopter in a telescopic hangar aft

Electronics: one Hollandse Signaalapparaten DA-05 air-search radar, one Decca surface-search radar, one Decca navigation radar, Hollandse Signaalapparaten WM-20 series fire-control radar, several electronic warfare systems, two CSEE Dagaie chaff launchers, and one Krupp-Atlas hull-mounted sonar

Propulsion: two Pielstick 16PC2-5V400 diesels delivering 20,000 shp (14,915 kW) to two shafts

Performance: maximum speed 27 kts; range 7,400 km (4,600 miles) at 18 kts

Complement: 100

Class
1. Argentina (2+4)

Name	No.	Builders	Laid down	Commissioned
ESPORA	P 4	AFNE Rio Santiago	Apr 1981	1983
ROSALES	P 5	AFNE Rio Santiago	Feb 1982	1984
SPIRO	P 6	AFNE Rio Santiago	—	—

'Mirka I' and 'Mirka II' class frigate

USSR

Displacement: 950 tons standard and 1,100 tons full load

Dimensions: length 81·0m (275·7ft); beam 9·1m (29·9ft); draught 3·0m (9·8ft)

Gun armament: four 76-mm (3-in) L/60 DP in two twin mountings

Missile armament: none

Torpedo armament: one quintuple 406-mm (16-in) tube mounting in 'Mirka I' and two quintuple 406-mm (16-in) tube mountings in 'Mirka II'

Anti-submarine armament: four RBU 6000 12-barrel rocket-launchers in 'Mirka I' and two RBU 6000 12-barrel rocket-launchers in 'Mirka II'

Electronics: one 'Slim Net' surface-search radar, one 'Strut Curve' air-search radar, one 'Hawk Screech' gun fire-control radar system, one 'Don-2' navigation radar, two 'Square Head' IFF, one 'High Pole B' IFF, one hull-mounted sonar, and one dunking sonar

Propulsion: CODOG (COmbined Diesel Or Gas turbine) arrangement, with two diesels delivering 8,950 kW (12,000 hp) and two gas turbines delivering 22,370 kW (30,000 hp) to two shafts

Performance: maximum speed 36 kts; range 4,650 km (2,890 miles) at 20 kts

Complement: 98

Class
1. USSR (18)
9 'Mirka I' class ships
9 'Mirka II' class ships

A 'Mirka II' class frigate is seen in the Mediterranean.

'Najin' class frigate

North Korea

Displacement: 1,500 tons

Dimensions: length 100·0m (328·1ft); beam 10·0m (32·8ft); draught 2·7m (8·9ft)

Gun armament: two 100-mm (3·9-in) L/56 DP in two single mountings, four 57-mm AA in two twin mountings, four 25-mm AA in two twin mountings, and eight 14·5-mm (0·57-in) heavy machine-guns in four twin mountings

Missile armament: none

Torpedo armament: one triple 533-mm (21-in) tube mounting

Anti-submarine armament: two RBU 1200 five-barrel rocket-launchers, two depth-charge mortars, and two depth-charge racks

Mines: about 30

Electronics: one 'Skin Head' surface-search radar, one 'Pot Head' surface-search radar, one 'Ski Pole' IFF, one hull-mounted sonar, and one variable-depth sonar

Propulsion: two diesels delivering 11,185 kW (15,000 bhp) to two shafts

Performance: maximum speed 26 kts; range 7,400 km (4,600 miles) at 14 kts

Complement: 180

Class
1. North Korea (4)

Name	No.	Builders	Laid down	Commissioned
—	3025	—	1971	1973
—	3026	—	—	1975
—	3027	—	—	1976
—	—	—	1976	1979

'Niels Juel' class guided-missile frigate

Denmark

Displacement: 1,320 tons full load

Dimensions: length 84·0m (275·5ft); beam 10·3m (33·8ft); draught 3·1m (10·2ft)

Gun armament: one 76-mm (3-in) L/62 DP OTO-Melara Compact

Missile armament: two quadruple container-launchers for eight RGM-84A Harpoon surface-to-surface missiles, and one octuple launcher for RIM-7 Sea Sparrow surface-to-air missiles (and to be fitted with the General Dynamics RAM surface-to-air point-defence missile system once the missile is ready for service)

Torpedo armament: none

Anti-submarine armament: four Mk 32 tubes for 12·75-in (324-mm) Mk 44/46 A/S torpedoes

Electronics: one Plessey AWS 5 tactical radar, one Skanter Mk 009 radar, one Philips Electroniksindustrier 9GR 600 multi-function radar, two Selenia RTN-10 fire-control radars, one Philips Elektroniksindustrier surface-search radar, one Philips Elektroniksindustrier combat information system and SSM-control system, and sonar

Propulsion: CODOG (COmbined Diesel Or Gas turbine) arrangement, with one MTU 20V956 TB92 diesel delivering 3,355 kW (4,500 hp) or one General Electric LM 2500 gas turbine delivering 18,400 shp (13,720 kW) to two shafts

Performance: maximum speed 28 kts on gas turbine or 20 kts on diesel; range 4,625 km (2,875 miles) at 18 kts

Complement: 90

Class
1. Denmark (3)

Name	No.	Builders	Laid down	Commissioned
NIELS JUEL	F 354	Aalborg Vaerft	Oct 1976	Aug 1980
OLFERT FISCHER	F 355	Aalborg Vaerft	Dec 1978	Oct 1981
PETER TORDENSKIOLD	F 356	Aalborg Vaerft	Dec 1979	Apr 1982

'Obuma' class frigate

Netherlands/Nigeria

Displacement: 1,725 tons standard and 2,000 tons full load
Dimensions: length 109·8 m (360·2 ft); beam 11·3 m (37 ft); draught 3·5 m (11·5 ft)
Gun armament: two 4-in (102-mm) L/45 DP in a Mk 19 twin mounting, and four 40-mm Bofors AA in single mountings
Missile armament: none
Torpedo armament: none
Anti-submarine armament: one Squid three-barrel rocket-launcher

Electronics: one Plessey AWS 4 surface-search radar, and one Type 293 radar
Propulsion: four MAN diesels delivering 11,930 kW (16,000 bhp) to two shafts
Performance: maximum speed 26 kts; range 6,500 km (4,040 miles) at 15 kts
Complement: 216

Class

1. Nigeria (1)

Name	No.	Builders	Laid down	Com-missioned
OBUMA	F 87	Wilton-Fijenoord	Apr 1964	Sep 1965

'Oliver Hazard Perry' or 'FFG 7' class guided-missile frigate

USA

Displacement: 3,605 tons full load
Dimensions: length 445 ft (135·6 m); beam 45 ft (13·7 m); draught 24·5 ft (5·7 m) to sonar dome
Gun armament: one 76-mm (3-in) L/62 DP OTO-Melara Compact in a Mk 75 single mounting, and one 20-mm Phalanx Mk 15 close-in weapon system mounting
Missile armament: one Mk 13 single launcher for 40 RGM-84A Harpoon surface-to-surface and RIM-66 Standard-MR surface-to-air missiles
Torpedo armament: none
Anti-submarine armament: two triple Mk 32 tube mountings for 12·75-in (324-m) Mk 46 A/S torpedoes, and helicopter-launched weapons (see below)
Aircraft: two Kaman SH-2F Seasprite helicopters in a hangar aft (to be replaced from 1986 onwards by Sikorsky SH-60B Sea Hawk helicopters which require a lengthening of the ships by 8 ft/2·4 m by an increase in the rearward angle of the transom to produce an overall length of 453 ft (138 m)
Electronics: one Raytheon SPS-49 long-range air-search radar, one Westing-house SPS-55 surface-search and navigation radar, one Lockheed SPG-60 modified with STIR (surveillance target indicator radar) for weapons control, one Mk 13 weapon direction system, one Mk 92 (Hollandse Signaalapparaten WM-28) weapon-control system, one Raytheon SQS-56 hull-mounted medium-range sonar, one SQR-19 towed-array sonar, one T Mk 6 Fanfare torpedo-decoy system, one Raytheon SLQ-32 electronic countermeasures system, two OE-82 satellite communications antennae, one SRR-1 satellite communications receiver, and one WSC-3 satellite communications transceiver
Propulsion: two General Electric LM 2500 gas turbines delivering 41,000 shp (30,575 kW) to one shaft
Performance: maximum speed 29 kts; range 5,200 miles (8,370 km) at 20 kts
Complement: 11+153, and an air unit strength of 46

Class

1. Australia (3+1+6)

Name	No.	Builders	Laid down	Com-missioned
ADELAIDE	F 01	Todd Pacific	July 1977	Nov 1980
CANBERRA	F 02	Todd Pacific	Mar 1978	Mar 1981
SYDNEY	F 03	Todd Pacific	Jan 1980	Jan 1983
DARWIN	F 04	Todd Pacific	July 1981	May 1984

2. Spain (0+3+2)

Name	No.	Builders	Laid down	Com-missioned
—	F 81	Bazán	1983	1985
—	F 82	Bazán	1983	1986
—	F 83	Bazán	1984	1987

3. USA (35+10+5)

Name	No.	Builders	Laid down	Com-missioned
OLIVER HAZARD PERRY	FFG 7	Bath Iron Works	June 1975	Dec 1977
McINERNEY	FFG 8	Bath Iron Works	Nov 1977	Nov 1979
WADSWORTH	FFG 9	Todd Pacific	July 1977	Feb 1980
DUNCAN	FFG 10	Todd Pacific	Apr 1977	May 1980
CLARK	FFG 11	Bath Iron Works	July 1978	May 1980
GEORGE PHILIP	FFG 12	Todd Pacific	Dec 1977	Oct 1980
SAMUEL ELIOT MORISON	FFG 13	Bath Iron Works	Dec 1978	Oct 1980
SIDES	FFG 14	Todd Pacific	Aug 1978	May 1981
ESTOCIN	FFG 15	Bath Iron Works	Apr 1979	Jan 1981
CLIFTON SPRAGUE	FFG 16	Bath Iron Works	Sep 1979	Mar 1981
JOHN A. MOORE	FFG 19	Todd Pacific	Dec 1978	Nov 1981
ANTRIM	FFG 20	Todd Pacific	June 1978	Sep 1981
FLATLEY	FFG 21	Bath Iron Works	Nov 1979	June 1981
FAHRION	FFG 22	Todd Pacific	Dec 1978	Jan 1982
LEWIS B. PULLER	FFG 23	Todd Pacific	May 1979	Apr 1982
JACK WILLIAMS	FFG 24	Bath Iron Works	Feb 1980	Sep 1981
COPELAND	FFG 25	Todd Pacific	Oct 1979	Aug 1982
GALLERY	FFG 26	Bath Iron Works	May 1980	Dec 1981
MAHLON S. TISDALE	FFG 27	Todd Pacific	Mar 1980	Nov 1982
BOONE	FFG 28	Todd Pacific	Mar 1979	May 1982
STEPHEN W. GROVES	FFG 29	Bath Iron Works	Sep 1980	Apr 1982
REID	FFG 30	Todd Pacific	Oct 1980	Feb 1983
STARK	FFG 31	Todd Pacific	Aug 1979	Oct 1982
JOHN L. HALL	FFG 32	Bath Iron Works	Jan 1981	June 1982
JARRETT	FFG 33	Todd Pacific	Feb 1981	1983
AUBREY FITCH	FFG 34	Bath Iron Works	Apr 1981	1982
UNDERWOOD	FFG 36	Bath Iron Works	July 1981	1983
CROMMELIN	FFG 37	Todd Pacific	May 1980	1983
CURTS	FFG 38	Todd Pacific	July 1981	1983
DOYLE	FFG 39	Bath Iron Works	Oct 1981	1983
HALYBURTON	FFG 40	Todd Pacific	Sep 1980	1983
McCLUSKY	FFG 41	Todd Pacific	Oct 1981	1984
KLAKRING	FFG 42	Bath Iron Works	Mar 1982	1983
THACH	FFG 43	Todd Pacific	Mar 1982	1984
DE WERT	FFG 45	Bath Iron Works	June 1982	1983
RENTZ	FFG 46	Todd Pacific	Sep 1982	1984
NICHOLAS	FFG 47	Bath Iron Works	Sep 1982	1984
VANDERGRIFT	FFG 48	Todd Pacific	Oct 1981	1984
ROBERT G. BRADLEY	FFG 49	Bath Iron Works	Dec 1982	1984
TAYLOR	FFG 50	Bath Iron Works	1983	1984
GARY	FFG 51	Todd Pacific	1982	1985
CARR	FFG 52	Todd Pacific	1982	1985
HAWES	FFG 53	Bath Iron Works	1983	1985
FORD	FFG 54	Todd Pacific	1983	1985
—	FFG 55	Bath Iron Works	1984	1985
—	FFG 56	Bath Iron Works	1984	1985
—	FFG 57	Todd Pacific	1984	1986
—	FFG 58	Todd Pacific	1984	1986
—	FFG 59	Todd Pacific	1985	1987
—	FFG 60	Todd Pacific	1985	1987

The Curts (FFG 38) is in every way typical of the 'Oliver Hazard Perry' class.

Remarks: The 'Oliver Hazard Perry' class is one of the most significant frigate classes in the world, and is a balanced design for anti-submarine, anti-ship and anti-aircraft deployment. The planned 10 Australian ships are in all essential respects similar to the US class, while the much-delayed Spanish ships will have SQS-56 towed-array sonar and the Meroka close-in weapon system. In American ships the SQR-19 towed-array sonar is fitted only from FFG 36 onwards, the 8 ft (2·4 in) longer stern also permitting an improved helicopter haul-down system.

'Oslo' class guided-missile frigate

Norway

Displacement: 1,450 tons standard and 1,745 tons full load
Dimensions: length 96·6m (317ft); beam 11·2m (36·7ft); draught 5·3m (17·4m) to screws
Gun armament: four 3-in (76-mm) L/50 DP in two Mk 33 twin mountings
Missile armament: six container-launchers for six Penguin surface-to-surface missiles, and one octuple launcher for RIM-7 Sea Sparrow surface-to-air missiles
Torpedo armament: none
Anti-submarine armament: two triple Mk 32 tube mountings for 12·75-in (324-mm) Mk 44/46 A/S torpedoes, and one Terne system with one six-barrel rocket-launcher
Electronics: one Thomson-CSF DRBV 22 air-search radar, one Decca TM 1226 navigation radar, one Hollandse Signaalapparaten WM-22 fire-control system, one EDO SQS-36 hull-mounted medium-range sonar, and one Terne III Mk 3 sonar system

Propulsion: two Babcock & Wilcox boilers supplying steam to one set of De Laval/Ljungstrom double-reduction geared turbines delivering 14,915 kW (20,000 shp) to one shaft
Performance: maximum speed 25 kts; range 8,350 km (5,190 miles) at 15 kts
Complement: 11 + 140

Class
1. Norway (5)

Name	No.	Builders	Laid down	Commissioned
OSLO	F 300	Marinens Hovedverft	1963	Jan 1966
BERGEN	F 301	Marinens Hovedverft	1964	June 1967
TRONDHEIM	F 302	Marinens Hovedverft	1963	June 1966
STAVANGER	F 303	Marinens Hovedverft	1965	Dec 1967
NARVIK	F 304	Marinens Hovedverft	1964	Nov 1966

'Peder Skram' class guided-missile frigate

Denmark

Displacement: 2,030 tons standard and 2,720 tons full load
Dimensions: length 112·6m (396·ft); beam 12·0m (39·5ft); draught 3·6m (11·8ft)
Gun armament: two 5-in (127-mm) L/38 DP in one Mk 38 twin mounting, and four 40-mm Bofors L/60 AA in single mountings
Missile armament: two quadruple container-launchers for eight RGM-84A Harpoon surface-to-surface missiles, and one quadruple launcher for 16 RIM-7 Sea Sparrow surface-to-air missiles
Torpedo armament: two twin 533-mm (21-in) tube mountings
Anti-submarine armament: two depth-charge racks, and A/S torpedoes launched from the tubes above
Electronics: two CWS-3 combined air- and surface-search radars, one NWS-1 tactical radar, one NWS-2 navigation radar, three CGS-1 fire-control radars, and one Plessey PMS 26 lightweight hull-mounted search and attack sonar
Propulsion: CODOG (COmbined Diesel Or Gas turbine) arrangement, with two General Motors 16-567D diesels delivering 4,800 hp (3,580 kW) and two Pratt & Whitney PWA GG 4A-3 gas turbines delivering 44,000 hp (32,810 kW) to two shafts
Performance: maximum speed 32·5 kts on gas turbines or 16·5 kts on diesels
Complement: 115

Class
1. Denmark (2)

Name	No.	Builders	Laid down	Commissioned
PEDER SKRAM	F 352	Helsingörs J. & M.	Sep 1964	May 1966
HERLUF TROLLE	F 353	Helsingörs J. & M.	Dec 1964	Apr 1967

Remarks: Despite their small size, the two 'Peder Skram' class frigates are well-balanced anti-ship and anti-submarine vessels admirably suited to the operational requirements of the Royal Danish navy.

*The **Peder Skram** (F 352) leads her sister **Herluf Trolle** (F 353).*

'Petya I', 'Petya I (Modified)', 'Petya II' and 'Petya II (Modified)' class frigates

USSR

Displacement: 950 tons standard and 1,100 tons full load
Dimensions: length 82·3m (270ft); beam 9·1m (29·9ft); draught 3·2m (10·5ft)
Gun armament: four 76-mm (3-in) L/60 DP in two twin mountings
Missile armament: none
Torpedo armament: none
Anti-submarine armament: four RBU 2500 16-barrel rocket-launchers ('Petya I' and 'Petya I (Modified)' classes) or two RBU 6000 12-barrel rocket-launchers ('Petya II' and 'Petya II (Modified)' classes), one ('Petya I' and 'Petya I (Modified)' classes) or two ('Petya II' and 'Petya II (Modified)' classes) quintuple 406-mm (16-in) tube mountings for A/S torpedoes, and two depth-charge racks
Electronics: one 'Slim Net' ('Petya I' and 'Petya I (Modified)' classes) or 'Strut Curve' ('Petya II' and 'Petya II (Modified)' classes) search radar, one 'Hawk Screech' gun-control radar, one Neptun ('Petya I' class) or 'Don-2' ('Petya I (Modified)', 'Petya II' and 'Petya II (Modified)' classes) navigation radar, two 'Square Head' and one 'High Pole-B' ('Petya I' and 'Petya I (Modified)' classes) or one 'High Pole-B' ('Petya II' and 'Petya II (Modified)' classes) IFF, and ('Petya I (Modified)' and 'Petya II (Modified)' class only) one variable-depth sonar
Propulsion: CODAG (COmbined Diesel And Gas turbine) arrangement, with one diesel delivering 4,475 kW (6,000 hp) and two gas turbines delivering 22,370 kW (30,000 hp) to three shafts
Performance: maximum speed 35 kts; range 7,400 km (4,600 miles) at 20 kts or 925 km (575 miles) at 35 kts
Complement: 98

Class
1. India (12 'Petya II')

Name	No.		Name	No.
ARNALA	P 68		**KADMATH**	P 78
ANDROTH	P 69		**KILTAN**	P 79
ANJADIP	P 73		**KAVARATTI**	P 80
ANDAMAN	P 74		**KATCHAL**	P 81
AMINI	P 75		**KANJAR**	P 82
KAMORTA	P 77		**AMINDIVI**	P 83

2. Syria (2 'Petya I')
2 'Petya I' class ships (nos 12 and 14)

3. USSR (7 'Petya I', 11 'Petya I (Modified)', 25 'Petya II' and 1 'Petya II (Modified)')
7 'Petya I' class ships
11 'Petya I (Modified)' class ships
25 'Petya II' class ships
1 'Petya II (Modified)' class ship

4. Vietnam (4 'Petya I')
4 'Petya I' class ships

Remarks: Built at Kaliningrad between 1960 and 1972, the 'Petya' class has been developed into four sub-classes, the two primary types being differentiated by their anti-submarine weapons, and the modified types within these types by provision for towed-array sonar.

'PF 103' class frigate
USA

Displacement: 900 tons standard and 1,135 tons full load
Dimensions: length 275 ft (83·8 m); beam 33 ft (10·1 m); draught 10 ft (3·0 m)
Gun armament: two 3-in (76-mm) L/50 DP in two Mk 34 single mountings, and two 40-mm Bofors AA in a twin mounting

The Kahnamuie has now been renumbered 84 in the Iranian republican navy

Remarks: All the ships are similar, the Iranian units having two 23-mm AA guns.

Missile armament: none
Torpedo armament: none
Anti-submarine armament: two triple Mk 32 tube mountings for 12·75-in (324-mm) Mk 44 A/S torpedoes, and one Hedgehog rocket-launcher
Electronics: one Bendix SPS-6 air-search radar, and one SPG-34 gun-control radar used in conjunction with the Mk 63 gun fire-control system
Propulsion: two Fairbanks-Morse diesels delivering 6,000 bhp (4,475 kW) to two shafts
Performance: maximum speed 20 kts
Complement: 150
Class

1. Iran (4)

Name	No.	Builders	Laid down	Commissioned
BAYANDOR	81	Levingstone Shipbuilding	Aug 1962	May 1964
NAGHDI	82	Levingstone Shipbuilding	Sep 1962	July 1964
MILANIAN	83	Levingstone Shipbuilding	May 1967	Feb 1969
KAHNAMUIE	84	Levingstone Shipbuilding	June 1967	Feb 1969

2. Thailand (2)

Name	No.	Builders	Laid down	Commissioned
TAPI	5	American S.B. Co	Apr 1970	Nov 1971
KHIRIRAT	6	Norfolk S.B. & D.D. Co	Feb 1972	Aug 1974

'Pizarro (Modernized)' class frigate
Spain

Displacement: 1,925 tons standard and 2,230 tons full load
Dimensions: length 95·3 m (312·5 ft); beam 12·0 m (39·5 ft); draught 5·4 m (17·7 ft)
Gun armament: two 5-in (127-mm) L/38 DP in two Mk 30 single mountings, and four 40-mm Bofors L/70 AA in single mountings
Missile armament: none
Torpedo armament: none
Anti-submarine armament: two Hedgehog rocket-launchers, two side-launching racks for six A/S torpedoes, eight depth-charge mortars, and two depth-charge racks
Electronics: one Raytheon SPS-5B surface-search radar, one Microlambda MLA 1B surface-search radar, one Decca TM 626 navigation radar, one Mk 29 gun-control radar used in conjunction with the Mk 52 gun fire-control system, and QHB-a hull-mounted sonar
Propulsion: two Yarrow boilers supplying steam to two sets of Parsons geared turbines delivering 6,000 shp (1,475 kW) to two shafts
Performance: maximum speed 18·5 kts; range 5,575 km (3,465 miles) at 15 kts
Complement: 16 + 239
Class

1. Spain (1)

Name	No.	Builders	Laid down	Commissioned
VICENTE YAÑEZ PINZON	PA 41	Bazán	Sep 1943	Aug 1949

'President' class frigate
UK/South Africa

Displacement: 2,380 tons standard and 2,800 tons full load
Dimensions: length 370 ft (112·8 m); beam 41·1 ft (12·5 m); draught 17·3 ft (5·3 m)
Gun armament: two 4·5-in (114-mm) L/50 DP in a Mk 6 twin mounting, and two 40-mm Bofors L/70 AA
Missile armament: none
Torpedo armament: none
Anti-submarine armament: two triple Mk 32 tube mountings for 12·75-in (324-mm) Mk 44 A/S torpedoes, and one Limbo three-barrel mortar
Aircraft: one Westland Wasp helicopter on a platform aft
Electronics: one Thomson-CSF Jupiter air-search radar, one Type 293 combined air- and surface-search radar, one ELSAG Argo NA9 fire-control system, one Type 177 hull-mounted medium-range panoramic sonar, and one Type 174 hull-mounted sonar
Propulsion: two Babcock & Wilcox boilers supplying steam to two sets of double-reduction geared turbines delivering 30,000 shp (22,370 kW) to two shafts
Performance: maximum speed 29 kts; range 5,200 miles (8,370 km) at 12 kts
Complement: 13 + 190

Class

1. South Africa (2)

Name	No.	Builders	Laid down	Commissioned
PRESIDENT PRETORIUS	F 145	Yarrow (Shipbuilders)	Nov 1960	Mar 1964
PRESIDENT STEYN	F 147	Alexander Stephen	May 1960	Apr 1963

'Purga' class frigate
USSR

Displacement: 2,250 tons standard and 5,000 tons full load
Dimensions: length 97·0 m (318·2 ft); beam 15·0 m (49·2 ft); draught 7·0 m (23 ft)
Gun armament: four 100-mm (3·9-in) DP in single mountings
Missile armament: none
Torpedo armament: none
Anti-submarine armament: none
Electronics: one 'Slim Net' surface-search radar, one 'High Sieve' surface-search radar, one 'Cross Bird' air-search radar, one 'Sun Visor' gun-control radar, one 'Wasp Head' gun-control radar, one *Neptun* navigation radar
Propulsion: two diesels delivering 5,965 kW (8,000 hp) to two shafts
Performance: maximum speed 16 kts; range 18,500 km (11,495 miles) at 12 kts
Complement: 250
Class
1. USSR (1)
1 ship

'Rahmat' class frigate
UK/Malaysia

Displacement: 1,250 tons standard and 1,600 tons full load
Dimensions: length 308 ft (93·9 m); beam 34·1 ft (10·4 m); draught 14·8 ft (4·5 m)
Gun armament: one 4·5-in (114-mm) L/45 in a Mk 8 single mounting, and two 40-mm Bofors AA in single mountings
Missile armament: one quadruple launcher for Sea Cat surface-to-air missiles
Torpedo armament: none
Anti-submarine armament: one Limbo Mk 10 three-barrel rocket-launcher
Aircraft: provision for a light helicopter on a hatch over the Limbo well
Electronics: one Hollandse Signaalapparaten LW-02 air-search radar, one Hollandse Signaalapparaten WM-22 gun-control radar system, and one Hollandse Signaalapparaten WM-44 SAM-control radar system
Propulsion: CODOG (COmbined Diesel Or Gas turbine) arrangement, with one Rolls-Royce Olympus TM1B gas turbine delivering 19,500 hp (14,545 kW) and one Pielstick-Crosley diesel delivering 3,850 hp (2,870 kW) to two shafts
Performance: maximum speed 26 kts on gas turbine and 16 kts on diesel; range 6,900 miles (11,105 km) at 16 kts
Complement: 140
Class
1. Malaysia (1)

Name	No.	Builders	Laid down	Commissioned
RAHMAT	F 24	Yarrow (Shipbuilders) Ltd	Feb 1966	Mar 1971

'Reliance' class medium-endurance cutter
USA
Displacement: 950 tons standard and 1,007 tons full load

Dimensions: length 210·5ft (64·2m); beam 34ft (10·4m); draught 10·5ft (3·2m)

Gun armament: one 3-in (76-mm) L/50 DP in a Mk 34 single mounting, and two 40-mm Bofors AA

Missile armament: none

Torpedo armament: none

Anti-submarine armament: none

Aircraft: one Sikorsky HH-52A helicopter on a platform aft

Electronics: one SPS-64 surface-search radar

Propulsion: two Alco 251B diesels delivering 5,000 bhp (3,730 kW) to two shafts

Performance: maximum speed 16kts; range 7,000 miles (11,265km) at 13kts (WTR 615 and WMECs 616-619) or at 14 kts (WMECs 620-630); endurance 15 days

Complement: 7+54

Class
1. USA (16)

Name	No.	Builders	Commissioned
RELIANCE	WTR 615*	Todd Shipyards	June 1964
DILIGENCE	WMEC 616	Todd Shipyards	Aug 1964
VIGILANT	WMEC 617	Todd Shipyards	Oct 1964
ACTIVE	WMEC 618	Christy Corporation	Sep 1966
CONFIDENCE	WMEC 619	U.S. Coast Guard	Feb 1966
RESOLUTE	WMEC 620	American S.B. Co	Dec 1966
VALIANT	WMEC 621	American S.B. Co	Oct 1967
COURAGEOUS	WMEC 622	American S.B. Co	Apr 1968
STEADFAST	WMEC 623	American S.B. Co	Sep 1968
DAUNTLESS	WMEC 624	American S.B. Co	June 1968
VENTUROUS	WMEC 625	U.S. Coast Guard	Aug 1968
DEPENDABLE	WMEC 626	American S.B. Co	Nov 1968
VIGOROUS	WMEC 627	American S.B. Co	May 1969
DURABLE	WMEC 628	U.S. Coast Guard	Dec 1967
DECISIVE	WMEC 629	U.S. Coast Guard	Aug 1968
ALERT	WMEC 630	American S.B. Co	Aug 1969

*training ship

Remarks: Designated medium-endurance cutters, the ships of the 'Reliance' class are designed for the primary role of search-and-rescue, with a high bridge and provision for a Sikorsky HH-52A helicopter as required.

'Restigouche (Improved)' class frigate
Canada
Displacement: 2,390 tons standard and 2,900 tons full load

Dimensions: length 371ft (113·1m); beam 42ft (12·8m); draught 14·1ft (4·3m)

Gun armament: two 3-in (76-mm) L/70 in one Mk 6 twin mounting

Missile armament: none

Torpedo armament: none

Anti-submarine armament: one Limbo Mk 10 three-barrel mortar, and one octuple launcher for ASROC missiles

Electronics: one RCA SPS-12 air-search radar, one Raytheon/Sylvania SPS-10 surface-search radar, one SPG-48 gun-control radar, one Sperry Mk 2 navigation radar, one Canadian Westinghouse SQS-501 bottom classification sonar, one Canadian Westinghouse SQS-505 hull-mounted medium-range search and attack sonar, and one Canadian Westinghouse SQS-505 variable-depth sonar

Propulsion: two Babcock & Wilcox boilers supplying steam to two sets of English Electric geared turbines delivering 30,000 shp (22,370 kW) to two shafts

Performance: maximum speed 28kts; range 5,475 miles (8,810km) at 14kts

Complement: 13+201

Class
1. Canada (4)

Name	No.	Builders	Laid down	Commissioned
GATINEAU	236	Davie S.B.	Apr 1953	Feb 1959
RESTIGOUCHE	257	Vickers	July 1953	June 1958
KOOTENAY	258	Burrard D.D.	Aug 1952	Mar 1959
TERRA NOVA	259	Victoria Machinery	Nov 1952	June 1959

The Terra Nova (259) reveals the slick features of the 'Restigouche (Improved)' class of frigates, with anti-submarine armament aft and gun armament forward.

Remarks: Officially rated as destroyers, the 'Restigouche (Improved)' class frigates were evolved in the late 1960s and early 1970s by the elimination of the after 3-in (76-mm) twin mount and one Limbo mortar to provide space for an ASROC launcher and variable-depth sonar. A lattice foremast also relaced the tower-and-pole type of the basic 'Restigouche' class, whose three units are now in reserve, for the carriage of additional radars. The Destroyer Life Extension Program to be completed by 1986 will add new radar for service up to 1994.

'Rhein' class frigate/depot ship
West Germany
Displacement: 2,370 tons standard and 2,890 tons full load (As 55 and 56) or 2,940 tons full load (others)

Dimensions: length 98·4m (322·8ft) for As 55 and 56 or 98·2m (322·1ft) for the others; beam 11·8m (38·8ft); draught 4·4m (14·4ft)

Gun armament: two 100-mm (3·9-in) L/55 DP in two single mountings (except As 55 and 56), and four 40-mm Bofors AA in two twin mountings (As 55 and 56) or four single mountings (others)

Missile armament: none

Torpedo armament: none

Anti-submarine armament: none

Electronics: one Hollandse Signaalapparaten DA-02 air-search radar, one Hollandse Signaalapparaten ZW-01 surface-search radar, one navigation radar, two Hollandse Signaalapparaten WM-45 gun-control radar systems, and one hull-mounted sonar

Propulsion: Six diesels (Mercedes-Benz in As 55 and 56, and Maybach in others) delivering 10,740 kW (14,400 hp) to two shafts; As 54, 55, 56, 65 and 67 have diesel-electric drive delivering 8,500 kW (11,400 bhp) to two shafts

Performance: maximum speed 20·5 kts; range 3,000 km (1,865 miles) at 15kts

Complement: 114 in As 55 and 56; 125 in As 54, 65 and 67; 163 in As 61 and 68; and 153 in the others

Class
1. West Germany (10)

Name	No.	Builders	Launched	Commissioned
LAHN	A 55	Flender	Nov 1961	Mar 1964
LECH	A 56	Flender	May 1962	Dec 1964
RHEIN	A 58	Schliekerwerft	Feb 1959	Nov 1961
ELBE	A 61	Schliekerwerft	May 1960	Apr 1962
MAIN	A 63	Lindenau	July 1960	June 1963
SAAR	A 65	Norderwerft	Mar 1961	May 1963
NECKAR	A 66	Lürssen	June 1961	Dec 1963
MOSEL	A 67	Schliekerwerft	Dec 1960	June 1963
WERRA	A 68	Lindenau	Mar 1963	Sep 1964
DONAU	A 69	Schlichting	Nov 1960	May 1964

Remarks: The *Saar* (A 65) and *Mosel* (A 67) are minesweeper depot ships, the *Lahn* (A 55) and *Lech* (A 56) have no 100-mm (3·9-in) guns and are submarine depot ships, and the others support FAC squadrons. Three others have been transferred: the *Weser* to Greece in 1975 and the *Rühr* and *Iser* to Turkey in 1976 and 1982.

The Elbe (A 61) reveals the frigate-like lines of this West German depot class, which can be used for escort work with their fore and aft armaments of 100-mm (3·9-in) DP guns and 40-mm AA guns.

'Riga' class frigate

USSR

Displacement: 1,000 tons standard and 1,320 tons full load

Dimensions: length 91·5 m (300·1 ft); beam 10·1 m (33·1 ft); draught 3·2 m (10·5 ft)

Gun armament: three 100-mm (3·9-in) L/50 DP in three single mountings, four 37-mm AA in two twin mountings, and (some ships) four 25-mm AA in two twin mountings

Missile armament: none

Torpedo armament: one twin or triple 533-mm (21-in) tube mounting

Anti-submarine armament: two RBU 2500 16-barrel rocket-launchers, two depth-charge racks, and (some ships) four depth-charge throwers

Mines: 50

Electronics: one 'Slim Net' surface-search radar, one 'Sun Visor-B' 100-mm gun-control radar, one 'Wasp Head' AA gun-control radar, one *Neptun* or 'Don-2' navigation radar, two 'Square Head' IFF, one 'High Pole' IFF, one hull-mounted high-frequency sonar, and (some ships) one dipping sonar

Propulsion: two boilers supplying steam to two geared turbines delivering 14,915 kW (20,000 shp) to two shafts

Performance: maximum speed 28 kts; range 3,700 km (2,300 miles) at 15 kts or 1,300 km (810 miles) at 27 kts

Complement: 175

Class	
1. Bulgaria (2)	
Name	*No.*
DRUZKI	15
SMELI	16
2. Finland (1)	
Name	*No.*
HÄMEENMÄA	02
3. Indonesia (2)	
Name	*No.*
JOS SUDARSO	351
LAMBUNG MANGKURAT	357

4. USSR (47)

Name
ARCHANGELSKY KOMSOMOLETS
ASTRAKHANSKY KOMSOMOLETS
BARS
BARSUK
BOBR
IRKUTSKY KOMSOMOLETS
KOBCHIK
KOMSOMOLETS GRUZY
KOMSOMOLETS LITVY
KRASNODARSKY KOMSOMOLETS
KUNITSA
LEOPARD
PANTERA
ROSOMOKHA
RYS
SOVETSKY AZERBAYDZHAN
SOVETSKY DAGESTAN
SOVETSKY TURKMENISTAN
TUMAN
VOLK
VORON
plus 26 others

Remarks: Built between 1952 and 1959, the 'Riga' class frigate was designed as successor to the 'Kola' class, and is a useful but unexceptional gun class. Exports amounted to 16 (two to Bulgaria in 1957-58, four to East Germany in 1956-59, two to Finland in 1964 and eight to Indonesia in 1962-65), though only five of these now remain in service. The Finnish ship *Hämeenmäa* (02) is now used as a minelayer (50 mines) and has an extra 30-mm twin mounting (*left*).

'River' class frigate

Australia

Displacement: 2,100 tons standard and 2,700 tons full load

Dimensions: length 370 ft (112·8 m); beam 41 ft (12·5 m); draught 17·3 ft (5·3 m) to screws

Gun armament: two 4·5-in (114-mm) L/45 DP in one Mk 6 twin mounting

Missile armament: one quadruple launcher for Sea Cat surface-to-air missiles

Torpedo armament: none

Anti-submarine armament: one Limbo (Australia) Mk 10 three-barrel mortar, and one launcher for Ikara missiles

Electronics: one Hollandse Signaalapparaten LW-02 air-search radar, one Westinghouse SPS-55 surface-search radar (Ds 45-49 only, replacing Type 293 surface-search radar) or one Hollandse Signaalapparaten SGR-301 surface-search and navigation radar (Ds 50 and 53), one Decca Type 978 navigation radar (Ds 45-49), one Hollandse Signaalapparaten WM-22 fire-control system (Ds 50 and 53, and being fitted in earlier ships as a replacement for MRS 3 fire-control radars), one Kelvin Hughes Type 162 hull-mounted side-looking classification sonar, one Type 170 hull-mounted short-range search and attack sonar, one Type 177 hull-mounted medium-range panoramic search sonar, one Type 185 hull-mounted sonar, and (after modernization) one Mulloka hull-mounted sonar

Propulsion: two Babcock & Wilcox boilers supplying steam to two sets of double-reduction geared turbines delivering 30,000 shp (22,370 kW) to two shafts

Performance: maximum speed 30 kts; range 3,900 miles (6,275 km) at 12 kts

Complement: 13+237 (Ds 45-49) or 13+234 (Ds 50 and 53)

Class

1. Australia (6)

Name	No.	Builders	Laid down	Commissioned
YARRA	D 45	HMA Naval Dockyard	Apr 1957	July 1961
PARRAMATTA	D 46	Cockatoo Island Dockyard	Jan 1957	July 1961
STUART	D 48	Cockatoo Island Dockyard	Mar 1959	June 1963
DERWENT	D 49	HMA Naval Dockyard	June 1958	Apr 1964
SWAN	D 50	HMA Naval Dockyard	Aug 1965	Jan 1970
TORRENS	D 53	Cockatoo Island Dockyard	Aug 1965	Jan 1971

Remarks: The class is based on the 'Leander' class.

'River' class frigate

UK

Displacement: 1,490 tons standard and 2,215 tons full load

Dimensions: length 301·5 ft (91·9 m); beam 36·5 ft (11·1 m); draught 14·2 ft (4·3 m)

Gun armament: one 4-in (102-mm) L/45 DP, four 37-mm AA in two twin Mk 5 mountings, and six 20-mm AA

Missile armament: none

Torpedo armament: none

Anti-submarine armament: four depth-charge throwers

Electronics: surface-search and navigation radar

Propulsion: two Admiralty boilers supplying steam to triple-expansion engines delivering 5,500 ihp (4,100 kW) to two shafts

Performance: maximum speed 18 kts; range 8,850 miles (14,245 km) at 12 kts

Complement: 110

Class

1. Egypt (1)

Name	No.	Builders	Laid down	Commissioned
RASHID	511	Smith's Dock Co Ltd	July 1941	May 1942

'Rothesay' class (Modified Type 12) frigate
UK

Displacement: 2,380 tons standard and 2,800 tons full load

Dimensions: length 370ft (112·8m); beam 41ft (12·5m); draught 17·3ft (5·3m)

Gun armament: two 4·5-in (114-mm) L/45 in one Mk 6 twin mounting

Missile armament: one quadruple launcher for Sea Cat surface-to-air missiles

Torpedo armament: none

Anti-submarine armament: one Limbo three-barrel mortar, and helicopter-launched weapons (see below)

Aircraft: one Westland Wasp HAS.Mk 1 helicopter in a hangar aft

Electronics: one Plessey Type 994 surface-search radar, one Type 978 navigation radar, one Sperry MRS 3 gun fire-control system, one GWS 20 optical director for Sea Cat system, one Type 174 hull-mounted sonar, one Type 170 hull-mounted short-range search and attack sonar, and one Kelvin Hughes Type 162 hull-mounted side-looking classification sonar

Propulsion: two Babcock & Wilcox boilers supplying steam to two sets of Admiralty Standard Range double-reduction geared turbines delivering 30,000shp (22,370kW) to two shafts

Performance: maximum speed 30kts; range 5,200 miles (8,370km) at 12kts

Complement: 15+220

Class

1. New Zealand (1)

Name	No.	Builders	Laid down	Commissioned
OTAGO	F 111	John I. Thornycroft Ltd	1957	June 1960

2. UK (2)

Name	No.	Builders	Laid down	Commissioned
YARMOUTH	F 101	John Brown	Nov 1957	Mar 1960
PLYMOUTH	F 126	HM Dockyard	July 1958	May 1961

Remarks: Developed from the 'Whitby' or 'Type 12' class frigate, the 'Rothesay' or 'Type 12 (Modified)' class frigate was evolved in the mid-1950s as an anti-submarine warfare type. The class was modernized between 1966 and 1972, one of the two Limbo mortars being replaced by a Sea Cat SAM launcher and facilities for a small helicopter. The *Otago* (F 111) of the Royal New Zealand navy was ordered as the British Hastings but transferred while building. She resembles the British ships in all essential respects, but has two triple Mk 32 tube mountings for anti-submarine protection. Her sister ship *Taranaki* was deleted in 1983. The British ships are obsolete, and are being phased out as new-build frigates come into commission. A sister ship, the *Londonderry* (F 108) has no combat potential, being unarmed and fitted out as a trials vessel for the Admiralty Surface Weapons Establishment. Extra AA guns are being fitted in others.

'Rudderow' class frigate
USA

Displacement: 1,450 tons standard and 2,000 tons full load

Dimensions: length 306ft (93·3m); beam 37ft (11·3m); draught 14ft (4·3m)

Gun armament: two 5-in (127-mm) L/38 DP in two Mk 30 single mountings, four 40-mm Bofors AA in two twin mountings, and four 20-mm AA in single mountings

Missile armament: none

Torpedo armament: none

Anti-submarine armament: two triple Mk 32 tube mountings for 12·75-in (324-mm) Mk 44 A/S torpedoes, one Hedgehog rocket-launcher, and 36 depth charges

Mines: 20

Electronics: one Bendix SPS-6C air-search radar, one Raytheon SPS-5D surface-search radar, and one hull-mounted sonar

Propulsion: two Foster-Wheeler boilers supplying steam to two General Electric turbo-electric drives delivering 12,000shp (8,950kW) to two shafts

Performance: maximum speed 24kts; range 6,000 miles (9,655km) at 12kts

Complement: about 200

Class

1. South Korea (1)

Name	No.	Builders	Laid down	Commissioned
CHUNG NAM	DE 821	Defoe Shipbuilding Co	Oct 1943	June 1944

2. Taiwan (1)

Name	No.	Builders	Laid down	Commissioned
TAI YUAN	PN 959	Bethlehem Steel Co	Oct 1943	Mar 1944

Remarks: Formerly US navy escort destroyers, these two 'Rudderow' class frigates are nearing the end of their useful lives. The South Korean ship was transferred in 1963, and has no 20-mm guns.

'St Laurent' class frigate
Canada

Displacement: 2,260 tons standard and 3,050 tons full load

Dimensions: length 366ft (111·6m); beam 42ft (12·8m); draught 14ft (4·3m)

Gun armament: two 3-in (76-mm) L/50 DP in one Mk 33 twin mounting

Missile armament: none

Torpedo armament: none

Anti-submarine armament: two triple Mk 32 tube mountings for 12·75-in (324-mm) Mk 44/46 A/S torpedoes, one Limbo Mk 10 three-barrel mortar, and helicopter-launched weapons (see below)

Aircraft: one Sikorsky CH-124 Sea King helicopter in a hangar amidships

Electronics: one RCA SPS-12 air-search radar, one Raytheon/Sylvania SPS-10 surface-search radar, one Sperry Mk 2 navigation radar, one SPG-48 gun-control radar used in conjunction with the Mk 69 gun fire-control system, URN-20 TACAN, one Canadian Westinghouse SQS-501 hull-mounted bottom classification sonar, one Canadian Westinghouse SQS-503 hull-mounted sonar, and one Canadian Westinghouse SQS-504 variable-depth sonar

Propulsion: two Babcock & Wilcox boilers supplying steam to two sets of English Electric geared turbines delivering 30,000shp (22,370kW) to two shafts

Performance: maximum speed 28kts; range 5,250 miles (8,450km) at 12kts

Complement: 16+197, plus an air unit strength of 7+13

Class

1. Canada (6)

Name	No.	Builders	Laid down	Commissioned
SAGUENAY	206	Halifax Shipyards Ltd	Apr 1951	Dec 1956
SKEENA	207	Burrard D.D. & Shipbuilding	June 1951	Mar 1957
OTTAWA	229	Vickers	June 1951	Nov 1956
MARGAREE	230	Halifax Shipyards Ltd	Sep 1951	Oct 1957
FRASER	233	Yarrows Ltd	Dec 1951	June 1957
ASSINIBOINE	234	Marine Industries Ltd	May 1952	Aug 1956

Remarks: The class was modernized to carry the Sea King helicopter in the 1960s, one 3-in (76-mm) twin gun mounting and one Limbo mortar being sacrificed. An extensive refit is being provided to prolong service life to 1990.

'Salisbury' class (Type 61) frigate
UK

Displacement: 2,170 tons standard and 2,410 tons full load

Dimensions: length 339·8ft (103·6m); beam 40ft (12·2m); draught 15·5ft (4·7m) to screws

Gun armament: two 4·5-in (114-mm) L/45 in one Mk 6 twin mounting, and two 40-mm Bofors L/60 AA in two Mk 9 single mountings

Missile armament: none

Torpedo armament: none

Anti-submarine armament: one Squid three-barrel mortar

Electronics: one Marconi Type 965 long-range air-search radar with twin AKE 2 array, one Type 993 surface-search radar, one Type 278M height-finding radar, one Type 986 air-warning and air-direction radar, one Type 978 navigation radar, one Type 275 gun-control radar used in conjunction with the Mk 6M gun fire-control director, one Type 174 hull-mounted sonar, and one Type 164B hull-mounted sonar

Propulsion: eight Admiralty Standard Range 1 diesels delivering 14,400bhp (10,740kW) to two shafts

Performance: maximum speed 24kts; range 8,650 miles (13,920km) at 16kts

Complement: 14+223

Class

1. Bangladesh (2)

Name	No.	Builders	Laid down	Commissioned
UMAR FAROOQ	F 16	Hawthorn Leslie Ltd	Aug 1953 Apr 1958	Nov 1955

Remarks: The *Umar Farooq* (F 16) is now the only 'Salisbury' class frigate left, and was transferred from the Royal Navy in December 1976.

'Savage' class frigate
USA

Displacement: 1,590 tons standard and 1,850 tons full load
Dimensions: length 306 ft (93·3 m); beam 36·6 ft (11·2 m); draught 14 ft (4·3 m)
Gun armament: two 3-in (76-mm) L/50 DP in two Mk 34 single mountings, two 20-mm AA, and five 0·5-in (12·7-mm) heavy machine-guns
Missile armament: none
Torpedo armament: none
Anti-submarine armament: two triple Mk 32 tube mountings for 12·75-in (324-mm) Mk 44 A/S torpedoes, and one Hedgehog Mk 15 rocket-launcher
Electronics: one Raytheon/Sylvania SPS-10 surface-search, one Westinghouse SPS-28 air-search radar, one SPG-34 gun-control radar used in conjunction with the Mk 63 gun fire-control system for the forward gun, one Mk 51 gun fire-control system for the after gun, and one Sangamo SQS-31 hull-mounted active sonar
Propulsion: two Fairbanks-Morse diesels delivering 3,400 bhp (2,535 kW) to two shafts

Performance: maximum speed 20 kts; range 13,250 miles (21,325 km) at 11 kts
Complement: about 170

Class
1. Philippines (1)

Name	No.	Builders	Commissioned
RAJAH LAKANDULA	PF 4	Brown S.B. Co	Sep 1943

2. Tunisia (1)

Name	No.	Builders	Commissioned
PRESIDENT BOURGUIBA	E 7	Consolidated Steel Corporation	Nov 1943

3. Vietnam (1)

Name	No.	Builders	Commissioned
TRAN KHANH DU	—	Consolidated Steel Corporation	Jan 1944

'Tacoma' class frigate
USA

Displacement: 1,445 tons standard
Dimensions: length 304 ft (92·7 m); beam 37·5 ft (11·4 m); draught 13·7 ft (4·2 m)
Gun armament: three 3-in (76-mm) L/50 in three Mk 34 single mountings, two 40-mm Bofors AA, and nine 20-mm AA
Missile armament: none
Torpedo armament: none
Anti-submarine armament: two triple Mk 32 tube mountings for 12·75-in (324-mm) Mk 44 A/S torpedoes, and eight depth-charge throwers
Electronics: one Raytheon SPS-5 or Raytheon/Sylvania SPS-10 surface-search radar, one Bendix SPS-6 air-search radar, and one Mk 51 gun-control radar system

Propulsion: two boilers supplying steam to two sets of triple-expansion engines delivering 5,500 ihp (4,105 kW) to two shafts
Performance: maximum speed 18 kts; range 8,300 miles (13,355 km) at 12 kts
Complement: 180

Class
1. Thailand (2)

Name	No.	Builders	Laid down	Commissioned
TAHCHIN	1	Consolidated Steel Corporation	Apr 1943	Oct 1943
PRASAE	2	Consolidated Steel Corporation	Aug 1943	Feb 1944

Remarks: Now used mainly for training, the two 'Tacoma' class frigates of the Thai navy were acquired from the USA in 1951.

'Type 41/61' class frigate
UK/Malaysia

Displacement: 2,300 tons standard and 2,520 tons full load
Dimensions: length 339·3 ft (103·5 m); beam 40 ft (12·2 m); draught 16 ft (4·9 m) to screws
Gun armament: one 100-mm (3·9-in) L/55 DP, and two 40-mm Bofors AA in single mountings
Missile armament: none
Torpedo armament: none
Anti-submarine armament: one Limbo Mk 10 three-barrel rocket-launcher
Electronics: one Plessey AWS 1 air-search radar, one Type 170 hull-mounted short-range search and attack sonar, and one Type 176 hull-mounted sonar
Propulsion: eight Admiralty Standard Range diesels delivering 14,400 shp (10,740 kW) to two shafts
Performance: maximum speed 24 kts; range 5,525 miles (8,890 km) at 15 kts
Complement: 210
Class
1. Malaysia (1)

Name	No.	Builders	Laid down	Commissioned
HANG TUAH	F 76	Yarrow (Shipbuilders)	1965	May 1973

Remarks: Based on the 'Salisbury' and 'Leopard' classes, this hybrid was ordered by Ghana, eventually received by the Royal Navy and transferred in 1977. The ship is particularly lightly armed, and thus suited to training and patrol.

'Type FS 1500' class guided-missile frigate
West Germany

Displacement: 1,500 tons standard and 1,800 tons full load
Dimensions: length 90·0 m (295·2 ft); beam 11·3 m (37·1 ft); draught 3·4 m (11·2 ft)

The Almirante Padilla (51) is the lead ship of the Colombian navy's force of four 'Type FS 1500' class guided-missile frigates to an impressive design.

Gun armament: one 76-mm (3-in) L/62 DP OTO-Melara Compact, two 40-mm Breda L/70 AA in a twin mounting, and two 30-mm Oerlikon AA in a twin mounting
Missile armament: two quadruple container-launchers for eight MM.40 Exocet surface-to-surface missiles
Torpedo armament: none
Anti-submarine armament: two triple Mk 32 tube mountings for 12·75-in (324-mm) Mk 44/46 A/S torpedoes, and helicopter-launched weapons (see below)
Aircraft: one helicopter in a hangar aft
Electronics: COMING
Propulsion: four MTU 20V1163 TB62 diesels delivering 11,635 kW (15,600 hp) to two shafts
Fuel: diesel oil
Performance: maximum speed 26·5 kts; range 9,250 km (5,750 miles) at 18 kts
Complement: 90
Class
1. Colombia (4)
three ships commissioned in 1983 with a fourth under construction

2. Malaysia (2+2)
2 on order with 2 more to follow

'Ulsan' class guided-missile frigate
South Korea
Displacement: 1,600 tons standard and 1,940 tons full load

Dimensions: length 102·0m (334·6ft); beam 11·5m (37·7ft); draught 3·6m (11·8ft)

Gun armament: two 76-mm (3-in) L/62 DP OTO-Melara Compact in two single mountings, and eight 30-mm AA in four Emerson twin mountings

Missile armament: two quadruple container-launchers for eight RGM-84A Harpoon surface-to-surface missiles

Torpedo armament: none

Anti-submarine armament: two Mk 32 tubes for 12·75-in (324-mm) Mk 44/46 A/S torpedoes, and depth charges

Electronics: search and navigation radars

Propulsion: CODOG (COmbined Diesel Or Gas turbine) arrangement, with two MTU 16V538 diesels delivering 5,370kW (7,200hp) and two General Electric LM 2500 gas turbines delivering 46,000hp (34,300kW) to two shafts

Performance: maximum speed 35 kts

Complement: 123

Class

1. South Korea (1)

Name	No.	Builders	Laid down	Commissioned
ULSAN	FF 951	Hyundai Shipyard	—	Jan 1981

'Van Speijk' class guided-missile frigate
Netherlands
Displacement: 2,255 tons standard and 2,735 tons full load

Dimensions: length 113·4m (372ft); beam 12·5m (41ft); draught 5·5m (18ft)

Gun armament: one 76-mm (3-in) L/62 DP OTO-Melara Compact

Missile armament: two quadruple container-launchers for eight RGM-84A Harpoon surface-to-surface missiles, and two quadruple launchers for Sea Cat surface-to-air missiles

Torpedo armament: none

Anti-submarine armament: two triple Mk 32 tube mountings for 12·75-in (324-mm) Mk 44/46 A/S torpedoes, and helicopter-launched weapons (see below)

Aircraft: one Westland Lynx helicopter in a hangar aft

Electronics: one Hollandse Signaalapparaten LW-03 air-search radar, one Hollandse Signaalapparaten DA-05 combined air- and surface-search and target-indication radar, one Kelvin Hughes surface-search and navigation radar, one Hollandse Signaalapparaten WM-45 gun fire-control radar system, one Hollandse Signaalapparaten WM-44 SAM fire-control radar system, one CWE-610 hull-mounted sonar, one Type 170B hull-mounted short-range search and attack sonar, one Kelvin Hughes Type 162 hull-mounted side-looking classification sonar, one PDE-700 variable-depth sonar, one SEWACO V data integration system, Daisy data-processing system, and various electronic countermeasures systems

Propulsion: two Babcock & Wilcox boilers supplying steam to two sets of Werkspoor/English Electric double-reduction geared turbines delivering 22,370kW (30,000shp) to two shafts

Performance: maximum speed 30 kts; range 8,350km (5,190 miles) at 12 kts

Complement: 175

Class

1. Netherlands (6)

Name	No.	Builders	Laid down	Commissioned
VAN SPEIJK	F 802	Nederlandse Dok	Oct 1963	Feb 1967
VAN GALEN	F 803	Koninklijke Maatschappij	July 1963	Mar 1967
TJERK HIDDES	F 804	Nederlandse Dok	June 1964	Aug 1967
VAN NES	F 805	Koninklijke Maatschappij	July 1963	Aug 1967'
ISAAC SWEERS	F 814	Nederlandse Dok	May 1965	May 1968
EVERTSEN	F 815	Koninklijke Maatschappij	July 1965	Dec 1967

'Vosper Thornycroft Mk 5' guided-missile frigate
UK/Iran
Displacement: 1,110 tons standard and 1,400 tons full load

Dimensions: length 310ft (94·4m); beam 36·3ft (11·1m); draught 14ft (4·3m) to screws

Gun armament: one 4·5-in (114-mm) L/55 DP in one Mk 8 single mounting, and two 35-mm Oerlikon L/90 AA in one twin mounting

Missile armament: one quintuple container-launcher for five Sea Killer surface-to-surface missiles, and one triple launcher for nine Sea Cat surface-to-air missiles

Torpedo armament: none

Anti-submarine armament: one Limbo Mk 10 three-barrel mortar

Electronics: one Plessey AWS 1 air-search radar, two Contraves Sea Hunter surface-search radars and associated systems for gun and missile fire control, one Type 170 hull-mounted short-range search and attack sonar, one Type 174 hull-mounted sonar, and one Racal-Decca RDL 1 electronic support measures system

Propulsion: CODOG (COmbined Diesel Or Gas turbine) arrangement, with two Paxman Ventura diesels delivering 3,800shp (2,835kW) or two Rolls-Royce Olympus TM3B gas turbines delivering 46,000shp (34,300kW) to two shafts

Performance: maximum speed 39 kts; range 3,700 miles (5,955km) at 17 kts

Complement: 125

Class

1. Iran (4 'Saam' class)

Name	No.	Builders	Laid down	Commissioned
SAAM	71	Vosper Thornycroft Ltd	May 1967	May 1971
ZAAL	72	Vickers (Shipbuilding) Ltd	Mar 1968	Mar 1971
ROSTAM	73	Vickers (Shipbuilding) Ltd	Dec 1967	June 1972
FARAMARZ	74	Vosper Thornycroft Ltd	July 1968	Feb 1972

'Vosper Thornycroft Mk 7' class guided-missile frigate
UK/Libya
Displacement: 1,325 tons standard and 1,625 tons full load

Dimensions: length 330ft (100·6m); beam 36ft (11·0m); draught 11·2ft (3·4m)

Gun armament: one 4·5-in (114-mm) L/55 DP in a Mk 8 single mounting, two 40-mm Bofors L/70 AA in single mountings, and two 35-mm Oerlikon L/90 AA in a twin mounting

Missile armament: four container-launchers for four Otomat surface-to-surface missiles, and four Albatros launchers for Aspide surface-to-air missiles

Torpedo armament: none

Anti-submarine armament: two triple ILAS 3 tube mountings for 324-mm (12·75-in) A 244S A/S torpedoes

Electronics: one Selenia RAN-series air-search radar, one Selenia RAN-series surface-search radar, one Selenia Orion RTN-series fire-control radar used in conjunction with the ELSAG Argo NA-series fire-control system, and one Thomson-CSF Diodon hull-mounted sonar

Propulsion: CODOG (COmbined Diesel Or Gas turbine) arrangement, with two Paxman Ventura diesels delivering 3,500bhp (2,610kW) and two Rolls-Royce Olympus TM2A gas turbines delivering 46,400shp (34,600kW) to two shafts

Performance: maximum speed 37·5 kts on gas turbines; range 6,550 miles (10,540km) at 17 kts

Complement: not known

Class

1. Libya (1)

Name	No.	Builders	Laid down	Commissioned
DAT ASSAWARI	F 01	Vosper Thornycroft Ltd	Sep 1968	Feb 1973

Remarks: The 'Vosper Thornycroft Mk 7' class frigate is an interesting exercise in the packaging of a powerful and varied armament into a relatively small hull. The missile and anti-submarine armament (together with most of the sensor suite) is of Italian origin, and the ship is currently undergoing a lengthy refit in Italy, the process being delayed by a fire in 1980.

'Whitby' class (Type 12) guided-missile frigate

UK/India

Displacement: 2,145 tons standard and 2,545 tons full load (F 40) or 2,555 tons full load (F 43)

Dimensions: length 369·8 ft (112·7 m); beam 41 ft (12·5 m); draught 17·8 ft (5·4 m) to screws

Gun armament: four 40-mm Bofors AA in one twin and two single mountings

Missile armament: two container-launchers for two SS-N-2 'Styx' surface-to-surface missiles

Torpedo armament: none

Anti-submarine armament: two Limbo three-barrel mortars

Electronics: one Type 277 tactical radar, one Type 993 tactical radar, one 'Square Tie' missile-control radar, one fire-control radar system, one Kelvin Hughes Type 162 hull-mounted side-looking classification sonar, one Type 170 hull-mounted short-range search and attack sonar, and one Type 174 hull-mounted sonar

Propulsion: two Babcock & Wilcox boilers supplying steam to two sets of English Electric geared turbines delivering 30,000 shp (22,370 kW) to two shafts

Performance: maximum speed 30 kts; range 5,200 miles (8,370 km) at 12 kts

Complement: 11+220

Class
1. India (2)

Name	No.	Builders	Laid down	Com-missioned
TALWAR	F 40	Cammell Laird & Co Ltd	1957	1960
TRISHUL	F 43	Harland & Wolff Ltd	1957	1960

'Wielingen' class guided-missile frigate

Belgium

Displacement: 1,880 tons light and 2,285 tons full load

Dimensions: length 106·4 m (349 ft); beam 12·3 m (40·3 ft); draught 5·6 m (18·4 ft)

Gun armament: one 100-mm (3·9-in) L/55 DP, and provision for one close-in weapon system mounting

Missile armament: four container-launchers for four MM.38 Exocet surface-to-surface missiles, and one octuple launcher for RIM-7 Sea Sparrow surface-to-air missiles

Torpedo armament: two launchers for L 5 torpedoes

Anti-submarine armament: one 375-mm (14·76-in) Le Creuset-Loire six-barrel rocket-launcher

Electronics: one Hollandse Signaalapparaten DA-05 combined air- and surface-search radar, one Raytheon TM 1645 navigation radar, one Hollandse Signaal-apparaten WM-25 fire-control radar system, one CSEE Panda optical director, one Hollandse Signaalapparaten SEWACO IV data automation system, one ELCOS 1 radar-warning receiver, one Westinghouse SQS-505A hull-mounted medium-range search and attack sonar, one Nixie torpedo decoy system, and two Mk 36 Super Chaffroc rapid-blooming overhead chaff launchers

Propulsion: CODOG (COmbined Diesel Or Gas turbine) arrangement, with two Cockerill CO-240 diesels delivering 4,475 kW (6,000 bhp) and one Rolls-Royce Olympus TM3B gas turbine delivering 28,000 bhp (20,880 kW) to two shafts

Performance: maximum speed 29 kts on gas turbine and 20 kts on diesels; range 8,350 km (5,190 miles) at 18 kts on diesels

Complement: 15+145

Class
1. Belgium (4)

Name	No.	Builders	Laid down	Com-missioned
WIELINGEN	F 910	Boelwerf	Mar 1974	Jan 1978
WESTDIEP	F 911	Cockerill	Sep 1974	Jan 1978
WANDELAAR	F 912	Boelwerf	Mar 1975	Oct 1978
WESTHINDER	F 913	Cockerill	Dec 1975	Oct 1978

The Wielingen (F 910) has gun and rocket armament forward, and missiles aft.

Remarks: Designed by the Belgian navy and built in Belgium, the 'Wielingen' class marks a departure for the Belgian navy, which has hitherto been a coastal defence force. The type currently features two twin container-launchers for MM.38 Exocet anti-ship missiles on the after deckhouse, a position originally envisaged for the CIWS mounting when this latter is selected and fitted. The decision is likely to go to the Signaal/General Electric Goalkeeper system.

'Yubari' class guided-missile frigate

Japan

Displacement: 1,400 tons

Dimensions: length 91·0 m (298·6 ft); beam 10·8 m (35·4 ft); draught 3·5 m (11·5 ft)

Gun armament: one 76-mm (3-in) L/62 DP OTO-Melara Compact

Missile armament: two quadruple container-launchers for eight RGM-84A Harpoon surface-to-surface missiles

Torpedo armament: none

Anti-submarine armament: one 375-mm (14·76-in) Bofors four-barrel rocket-launcher, and two triple Type 68 tube mountings for 12·75-in (324-mm) Mk 44/46 A/S torpedoes

Electronics: search/navigation radars, and sonar

Propulsion: CODOG (COmbined Diesel Or Gas turbine) arrangement, with one 6 DRV diesel delivering 3,505 kW (4,700 shp) and one Rolls-Royce Olympus TM3B gas turbine delivering 22,500 shp (16,780 kW) to two shafts

Fuel: diesel oil and kerosene

Performance: maximum speed 26 kts

Complement: 98

Class
1. Japan (2)

Name	No.	Builders	Laid down	Com-missioned
YUBARI	DE 227	Sumitomo	Feb 1981	Mar 1983
YUBETSU	DE 228	Hitachi	Feb 1982	Mar 1984

Remarks: A multi-role frigate design evolved from the experimental 'Ishikari' class, the 'Yubari' class is currently planned at just two units, though three of a 'Yubari (Modified)' class are planned as part of the 1983-87 five-year construction programme.

When completely equipped, the Yubari (DE 227) will have two quadruple container-launchers for Harpoon anti-ship missiles right at the stern, with a CIWS gun mounting aft of the funnel. Visible here are the port triple Type 68 tube mounting just forward of the funnel, the chaff launchers on the beams forward of the mast, and the gun and A/S rocket-launcher forward of the bridge.

'Admirable' class corvette

USA

Displacement: 650 tons standard and 945 tons full load
Dimensions: length 184·5 ft (56·24 m); beam 33 ft (10·06 m); draught 9·8 ft (3·0 m)
Gun armament: one 3-in (76-mm) L/50, two twin 40-mm Bofors AA mountings and two twin 20-mm Oerlikon AA mountings
Missile armament: none
Torpedo armament: none
Anti-submarine armament: one Hedgehog mortar, two depth-charge throwers and two depth-charge racks
Electronics: navigation radar
Propulsion: two General Motors diesels delivering 1,710 shp (1,275 kW) to two shafts
Performance: maximum speed 14·8 kts; range 4,950 miles (7,965 km) at 10 kts
Complement: 80-95

Class

1. Burma (1)

Name	No.	Builders	Commissioned
YAN GYI AUNG	PCE 42	Willamette Iron & Steel Co	1944

2. Dominican Republic (2)

Name	No.	Builders	Commissioned
PRESTOL BOTELLO	BM 454	Associated S.B.	Aug 1943
TORTUGUERO	BM 455	Associated S.B.	Aug 1943

3. Mexico (16)

Name	No.	Builder
D 01	01	USA
D 02	02	USA
D 03	03	USA
D 04	04	USA
D 05	05	USA
D 06	06	USA
D 10	10	USA
D 11	11	USA
D 12	12	USA
D 13	13	USA
D 14	14	USA
D 15	15	USA
D 16	16	USA
D 17	17	USA
D 18	18	USA
D 19	19	USA

4. Philippines (1)

Name	No.	Builders	Commissioned
MAGAT SALAMAT	PS 20	Winslow Marine Railway & S.B. Co	1944

5. Vietnam (2)

Name	No.	Builders
— (ex-USS Prowess)	—	Gulf S.B.
— (ex-USS Sentry)	—	Gulf S.B.

'Albatros' class corvette

Italy

Displacement: 800 tons standard and 950 tons full load
Dimensions: length 76·3 m (250·3 ft); beam 9·65 m (31·66 ft); draught 2·8 m (9·2 ft)
Gun armament: two 40-mm Bofors L/70 AA in single mountings
Missile armament: none
Torpedo armament: none
Anti-submarine armament: two Hedgehog Mk II mortars, two depth-charge throwers, one depth-charge rack and two triple Mk 32 tube mountings for 12·75-in (324-mm) A/S torpedoes
Electronics: one SMA SPQ 2 combined navigation and surface-search radar, and one QCU 2 hull-mounted sonar
Propulsion: two Fiat diesels delivering 3,880 kW (5,200 bhp) to two shafts
Performance: maximum speed 19 kts; range 9,250 km (5,750 miles) at 18 kts
Complement: 99

Class

1. Italy (4)

Name	No.	Builders	Laid down	Commissioned
AQUILA	F 542	Breda Marghera	July 1953	Oct 1956
ALBATROS	F 543	Navalmeccanica	1953	June 1955
ALCIONE	F 544	Navalmeccanica	1953	Oct 1955
AIRONE	F 545	Navalmeccanica	1953	Dec 1955

Remarks: Italy is now the only operator of this obsolescent class, funded by the USA as three ships for Italy, four for Denmark and one for The Netherlands; the Dutch ship was transferred to Italy as the *Aquila* (F 542) in October 1961.

'Assad' class guided-missile corvette

Italy/Libya

Displacement: 670 tons full load
Dimensions: length 61·7 m (202·4 ft); beam 9·3 m (30·5 ft); draught 2·2 m (7·6 ft)
Gun armament: one 76-mm (3-in) L/62 DP OTO-Melara Compact, and two 35-mm Oerlikon L/90 AA in one twin mounting
Missile armament: four container-launchers for four Otomat surface-to-surface missiles
Torpedo armament: none
Anti-submarine armament: two triple ILAS-3 tube mountings for 324-mm (12·75-in) A 244S A/S torpedoes
Mines: up to 16
Electronics: one Selenia RAN 11L/X combined air- and surface-search radar, one Decca TM 1226 navigation radar, one Selenia Orion RTN 10X fire-control radar used in conjunction with the ELSAG NA 10 fire-control system, one Selenia IPN 10 command and control system, and one Thomson-CSF Diodon hull-mounted search and attack sonar
Propulsion: four MTU 16V956 TB91 diesels delivering 13,425 kW (18,000 shp) to four shafts
Performance: maximum speed 34 kts; range 8,150 km (5,065 miles) at 14 kts
Complement: 58

Class

1. Ecuador (6)

Name	No.	Builders	Commissioned
ESMERALDAS	CM 11	CNR Muggiano	1982
MANABI	CM 12	CNR Ancona	1982
LOS RIOS	CM 13	CNR Muggiano	1982
EL ORO	CM 14	CNR Ancona	1983
GALAPAGOS	CM 15	CNR Muggiano	1983
LOJA	CM 16	CNR Ancona	1983

2. Iraq (1+5)

Name	No.	Builders	Commissioned
HUSSA EL HUSSAIR	F 210	CNR	1984

3. Libya (4)

Name	No.	Builders	Commissioned
ASSAD EL TADJER	412	Cantieri del Muggiano	Sep 1979
ASSAD EL TOUGOUR	413	Cantieri del Muggiano	Feb 1980
ASSAD AL KHALI	414	Cantieri del Muggiano	Sep 1980
ASSAD AL HUDUD	415	Cantieri del Muggiano	Sep 1980

Remarks: Originally designated the 'Wadi' class when first ordered by Libya in 1974, this class was redesignated the 'Assad' class during 1982-83 and has been ordered in useful numbers by two Arab countries (Iraq and Libya) and in a half-sister form by Ecuador. The Libyan standard is detailed above, and it is believed that the Iraqi ships will be essentially similar, though two of the six, namely the *Hussa el Hussair* (F 210) and the other unit building at CNR at Muggiano, have provision for a light helicopter in a telescopic hangar aft in place of four of the Otomat launchers, which in other ships total six for an increase of two in comparison with the Libyan ships. Another modification is the use of a 40-mm Breda Compact twin AA mounting in place of the 35-mm Oerlikon twin AA mounting of the Libyan ships; this Breda mounting is not fitted in helicopter ships, though these retain the quadruple Albatros launcher for eight Aspide SAMs that also differentiates the Iraqi ships from those of Libya.

The Libyan Assad al Tadjer (412) is seen while undergoing builder's trials in 1978 while still bearing the original name Wadi M'Ragh of the 'Wadi' class. The Otomat anti-ship launchers are now fitted forward of the 35-mm guns.

'Badr' class guided-missile corvette
USA
Displacement: 732 tons standard and 815 tons full load
Dimensions: length 245ft (74·7m); beam 31·5ft (9·6m); draught 14·6ft (4·5m)
Gun armament: one 76-mm (3-in) L/62 DP OTO-Melara Compact, two 20-mm Phalanx close-in weapon system mountings, and two 40-mm grenade-launchers
Missile armament: two quadruple container-launchers for eight RGM-84A Harpoon surface-to-surface missiles
Torpedo armament: none
Anti-submarine armament: two triple Mk 32 tube mountings for 12·75-in (324-mm) Mk 46 A/S torpedoes
Electronics: one Westinghouse SPS-55 surface-search radar, one Lockheed SPS-40B air-search radar, one Mk 92 fire-control radar system, and one Raytheon SQS-56 hull-mounted medium-range sonar
Propulsion: CODOG (COmbined Diesel Or Gas turbine) arrangement, with two MTU diesels delivering 2,980 kW (4,000 hp) and one General Electric LM 2500 gas turbine delivering 23,000 bhp (17,150 kW) to two shafts
Performance: maximum speed 30 kts on gas turbine and 16 kts on diesels
Complement: 7+51

Class
1. Saudi Arabia (4)			Com-
Name	No.	Builders	missioned
BADR	612	Tacoma B.B. Co	Nov 1980
AL YARMOOK	614	Tacoma B.B. Co	May 1981
HITTEEN	616	Tacoma B.B. Co	Aug 1981
TABUK	618	Tacoma B.B. Co	Nov 1981

Remarks: These are small but potent missile-armed ships of good performance, and are well conceived in terms of the multi-threat environment of Saudi-Arabia's confined water naval environment.

'Bouchard' class corvette
Argentina
Displacement: 450 tons standard, 620 tons normal and 650 tons full load
Dimensions: length 60·0m (196·9ft); beam 7·2m (23·5ft); draught 2·6m (8·5ft)
Gun armament: four 40-mm Bofors AA and two machine-guns
Missile armament: none
Torpedo armament: none
Anti-submarine armament: none
Electronics: navigation radar
Propulsion: two MAN diesels delivering 1,490 kW (2,000 bhp) to two shafts
Performance: maximum speed 16 kts; range 11,125 km (6,915 miles) at 12 kts
Complement: 70

Class
1. Paraguay (3)			Com-
Name	No.	Builders	missioned
NANAWA	M 1	Rio Santiago Naval Yard	May 1937
CAPITAN MEZA	M 2	Hansen and Puccini	May 1939
TENIENTE FARINA	M 3	Rio Santiago Naval Yard	July 1938

'Cherokee' class patrol vessel
USA/Argentina
Displacement: 1,235 tons standard and 1,675 tons full load
Dimensions: length 205ft (62·5m); beam 38·5ft (11·7m); draught 17ft (5·2m)
Gun armament: six 40-mm Bofors L/60 AA in two twin and two single mountings
Missile armament: none
Torpedo armament: none
Anti-submarine armament: none
Electronics: one navigation radar
Propulsion: four diesels powering an electric motor delivering 3,000 hp (2,240 kW) to one shaft
Performance: maximum speed 16 kts
Complement: 85

Class
1. Argentina (2)			Com-
Name	No.	Builders	missioned
COMMANDANTE GENERAL IRIGOYEN	A 1	Charleston S.B.	Mar 1945
FRANCISCO DE GURRUCHAGA	A 3	Charleston S.B.	June 1945

2. Chile (1)			Com-
Name	No.	Builders	missioned
SERGENTO ALDEA	63	Charleston S.B.	Jan 1944

3. Colombia (3)			Com-
Name	No.	Builders	missioned
SEBASTIAN DE BELAL CALZAR	RM 73	Charleston S.B.	July 1943
RODRIGO DE BASTIDAS	RM 74	Charleston S.B.	Apr 1944
BAHIA SOLANO	RM 76	Charleston S.B.	June 1944

Remarks: The 'Cherokee' class was designed to provide the US Navy with a major class of ocean-going tugs, for use particularly in the Pacific in the rescue of major fleet units disabled by enemy action far from base. Many of the 'Cherokee' class remain in service in their original or other non-combatant roles, while those listed above have been transformed into useful patrol craft for secondary purposes. Argentina received her two ships in 1961, Chile her single example in 1971 and Colombia her four ships in 1979. The Chilean ship has one 3-in (76-mm) and two 20-mm guns, while the Colombian vessels have just the 3-in (76-mm) weapon.

'Cohoes' class corvette
USA
Displacement: 650 tons standard and 855 tons full load
Dimensions: length 162·3ft (49·5m); beam 33·8ft (10·3m); draught 11·7ft (3·6m)
Gun armament: two 3-in (76-mm) in single mountings, and three 20-mm AA in single mountings
Missile armament: none
Torpedo armament: none
Anti-submarine armament: none
Electronics: one navigation radar
Propulsion: one Busch Sulzer diesel-electric arrangement delivering 1,200 shp (895 kW) to one shaft
Fuel: diesel oil
Performance: maximum speed 12 kts
Complement: 48

Class
1. Dominican Republic (3)			Com-
Name	No.	Builders	missioned
CAMBIASO	P 207	Marietta Manufacturing Co	Apr 1945
SEPARACION	P 208	Marine S.B. Co	Apr 1945
CALDERAS	P 209	Leatham D Smith S.B. Co	Mar 1945

Remarks: The 'Cohoes' class was built as a netlayer force in World War II, and while ships of the type are used for non-combatant duties by Uruguay and Venezuela, the Dominican Republic's three units serve as patrol vessels.

'De Cristofaro' class corvette
Italy
Displacement: 850 tons standard and 1,020 tons full load
Dimensions: length 80·2m (263·2ft); beam 10·3m (33·7ft); draught 2·7m (9ft)
Gun armament: two 76-mm (3-in) L/62 DP in two single mountings
Missile armament: none
Torpedo armament: none
Anti-submarine armament: two triple Mk 32 tube mountings for 12·75-in (324-mm) Mk 44/46 torpedoes, and one Mk 113 semi-automatic depth-charge thrower
Electronics: one SMA SPQ 2 surface-search radar, and one Selenia Orion 3 gun-control radar used in conjunction with the two OG3 gun fire-control systems, and two EDO SQS-36 sonars (one hull-mounted and one variable-depth) used in conjunction with the ELSAG DLB 1 anti-submarine fire-control system
Propulsion: two Fiat 3012 RSS diesels delivering 6,265 kW (8,400 bhp) to two shafts
Performance: maximum speed 23 kts; range 7,400 km (4,600 miles) at 16 kts
Complement: 8+123

Class
1. Italy (3)				Com-
Name	No.	Builders	Laid down	missioned
UMBERTO GROSSO	F 541	Ansaldo	Oct 1962	Apr 1966
LICIO VISINTINI	F 546	CRDA Monfalcone	Sep 1963	Aug 1966
SALVATORE TODARO	F 550	Ansaldo	Oct 1962	Apr 1966

'Deidre' and 'P 22' class patrol vessel

Eire

Displacement: 1,020 tons
Dimensions: length 213·7 ft (65·2 m); beam 34·1 ft (10·5 m); draught 14 ft (4·4 m)
Gun armament: one 40-mm Bofors AA, and two 20-mm Oerlikon AA in single mountings
Missile armament: none
Torpedo armament: none
Anti-submarine armament: none

Electronics: two Decca navigation radars, and one Simrad SU hull-mounted sonar
Propulsion: two SEMT-Pielstick diesels delivering 3,580 kW (4,800 bhp) to one shaft
Performance: maximum speed 18 kts; range 7,775 miles (12,515 km) at 12 kts
Complement: 5+41

Class

1. Eire (4)

Name	No.	Builders	Commissioned
DEIRDRE	FP 20	Verolme	May 1972
EMER	P 21	Verolme	Jan 1978
AOIFE	P 22	Verolme	Oct 1979
AISLING	P 23	Verolme	May 1980

Remarks: The *Deidre* (FP 20) was the first Eire-built ship for Irish naval service, and is slightly different from the other three vessels, which are officially the 'P 22' class, to which the specification above applies. The *Deidre* displaces 972 tons, has a length of 184·3 ft (56·2 m) between perpendiculars, and is capable of 18 kts on the 4,200 bhp (3,130 kW) delivered by her two British Polar diesels. Her armament comprises a single 40-mm gun.

Seen here in the form of the Emer (P 21), *lead ship of her type, the 'P 22' class and the sole unit of the earlier 'Deidre' class were the first warships designed and built in Eire, though their appearance confirms that seakeeping qualities and the other attributes of offshore patrol and fishery protection have played a larger part in th design than any purely naval virtues. The primary armament is a single 40-mm Bofors AA gun, which can also operate effectively against small craft, and this is fitted forward of the bridge behind a three-sided spray shield. The provision of hull-mounted sonar gives the ships a submarine-detection capability, though helicopters would have to be called in for a 'kill'.*

'Nanuchka I' and 'Nanuchka III' class guided-missile corvettes

USSR

Displacement: 780 tons standard and 900 tons full load
Dimensions: length 60·0 m (196·8 ft); beam 12·2 m (40 ft); draught 3·1 m (10·2 ft)
Gun armament: two 57-mm L/70 AA in one twin mounting ('Nanuchka I') or one 76-mm (3-in) L/59 DP ('Nanuchka III'), and ('Nanuchka III' only) one 30-mm AA in a 'Gatling' mounting
Missile armament: two triple container-launchers for six SS-N-9 surface-to-surface missiles, and one twin launcher for 18 SA-N-4 surface-to-air missiles
Torpedo armament: none
Anti-submarine armament: none
Electronics: one 'Band Stand' surface-search radar, one 'Peel Pair' and one 'Spar Stump' surface-search and navigation radars, two 'Fish Bowl' fire-control radars, one 'Muff Cob' 57-mm gun-control radar ('Nanuchka I') or one 'Bass Tilt' gun-

control radar ('Nanuchka III'), one 'Band Stand' SSM-control radar and one 'Pop Group' SAM-control radar in large dome, one 'Don' navigation radar, one 'High Pole-B' IFF, one 'Square Head' IFF, and various electronic warfare systems
Propulsion: three diesels delivering 17,895 kW (24,000 shp) to three shafts
Performance: maximum speed 34 kts; range 8,350 km (5,190 miles) at 15 kts or 2,400 km (1,490 miles) at 33 kts
Complement: 70

Class

1. Algeria (2)

Name	No.	Builder	Commissioned
RAS HAMIDOU	801	USSR	July 1980
SALAH REIS	802	USSR	Feb 1981
REIS ALI	802	USSR	May 1982
—	803	USSR	Jan 1983

2. India (3+0+3)

Name	No.	Builder	Commissioned
VIJAY DURG	K 71	USSR	Mar 1977
SINDHU DURG	K 72	USSR	—
HOS DURG	K 73	USSR	—

3. Libya (2+2)

Name	No.	Builder	Commissioned
EAN MARA	416	USSR	Oct 1981
EAN EL GAZALA	417	USSR	Feb 1983
—	—	USSR	—
—	—	USSR	—

4. USSR (17 'Nanuchka I' and 5+1 'Nanuchka III' class)
17 'Nanuchka I' plus others on order
5+1 'Nanuchka III'

Remarks: The 'Nanuchka' classes are extremely powerful coastal vessels built in the Pacific and at Petrovsky from 1969. The Indian ships differ mainly in having four SS-N-2B anti-ship missiles in place of the longer-range SS-N-9s.

'Nawarat' class corvette

Burma

Displacement: 400 tons standard and 450 tons full load
Dimensions: length 163 ft (49·7 m); beam 26·8 ft (8·2 m); draught 5·8 ft (1·8 m)
Gun armament: two 25-pdr (88-mm) QF, and two 40-mm Bofors AA in single mountings
Missile armament: none
Torpedo armament: none
Anti-submarine armament: none
Electronics: one navigation radar

Propulsion: two Paxman-Ricardo diesels delivering 1,160 bhp (865 kW) to two shafts
Performance: maximum speed 12 kts
Complement: 43

Class

1. Burma (2)

Name	No.	Builders	Commissioned
NAGAKYAY	—	Government Dockyard	Dec 1960
NAWARAT	—	Government Dockyard	Apr 1960

'P 31' class patrol vessel

Eire

Displacement: 1,800 tons
Dimensions: length 265 ft (80·8 m); beam 39·4 ft (12·0 m); draught 13·8 ft (4·2 m)
Gun armament: one 57-mm Bofors, and two 20-mm AA in a twin mounting
Missile armament: none, but provision for SAMs
Torpedo armament: none
Anti-submarine armament: none, but provision for A/S tubes
Aircraft: one Aérospatiale Alouette III helicopter
Electronics; surface-search/navigation radar

Propulsion: two Ruston 12RKCM diesels delivering 6,640 bhp (4,950 kW) to two shafts
Performance: maximum speed 20+ kts; range 8,000+ miles (12,875+ km) at 15 kts
Complement: 85

Class
1. Eire (0+2)
2 ships on order

'Parchim' class corvette

East Germany

Displacement: 1,200 tons full load
Dimensions: length 73·0 m (239·4 ft); beam 9·7 m (31·8 ft); draught 3·8 m (12·5 ft)
Gun armament: two 57-mm L/80 AA in a twin mounting, and two 30-mm AA in a twin mounting
Missile armament: two launchers for SA-N-5 surface-to-air missiles
Torpedo armament: none
Anti-submarine armament: two RBU 6000 12-barrel rocket-launchers, four 406-mm (16-in) tubes for A/S torpedoes, and depth charges
Mines: fitted with rails for minelaying
Electronics: one 'Strut Curve' air-search radar, one 'Muff Cob' gun-control radar, one 'High Pole-B' IFF, one 'Cross Loop-B' IFF, and hull-mounted sonar
Propulsion: CODAG (COmbined Diesel And Gas turbine) arrangement, with two diesels and one gas turbine delivering ? kW (? hp) to three shafts
Performance: maximum speed about 36 kts
Complement: 80

Class
1. East Germany (9+9)

Name	No.	Builders	Commissioned
WISMAR	241	Peenewerft	Apr 1981
PARCHIM	242	Peenewerft	1981
BAD DOBERAN	243	Peenewerft	1981
BUETZOW	244	Peenewerft	1981
—	245	Peenewerft	1981

Plus seven others

Remarks: The 'Parchim' class is modelled on the Soviet 'Grisha' class, and is a capable escort class with good anti-aircraft capability. The building rate is about three per year, indicating perhaps 12 in service by early 1984.

'PCE 827' class corvette

USA

Displacement: 640 tons standard and 855 tons full load
Dimensions: length 184·5 ft (56·3 m); beam 33·1 ft (10·1 m); draught 9·5 ft (2·9 m)
Gun armament: one 3-in (76-mm) L/50 DP, and six 40-mm Bofors AA in single or twin mountings
Missile armament: none
Torpedo armament: none
Anti-submarine armament: two Mk 32 tubes for 12·75-in (324-mm) Mk 44 A/S torpedoes
Electronics: navigation radar
Propulsion: two General Motors diesels delivering 2,000 bhp (1,490 kW) to two shafts
Performance: maximum speed 15 kts
Complement: 90 to 100

Class
1. Burma (1)

Name	No.	Builders	Commissioned
YAN TAING AUNG	PCE 41	Willamette Iron & Steel	Aug 1943

2. Philippines (7)

Name	No.	Builders	Commissioned
MIGUEL MALVAR	PS 19	Pullman Car Co	May 1944
SULTAN KUDARAT	PS 22	Willamette Iron & Steel	Oct 1943
DATU MARIKUDO	PS 23	Pullman Car Co	June 1944
CEBU	PS 28	Albina E and M Works	July 1944
NEGROS OCCIDENTAL	PS 29	Albina E and M Works	Mar 1944
PANGASINAN	PS 31	Willamette Iron & Steel	June 1944
ILOILO	PS 32	Willamette Iron & Steel	Jan 1945

Remarks: These are ex-US submarine-chasers and rescue craft used as corvettes.

'Saar 5' class guided-missile corvette

Israel

Displacement: 850 tons
Dimensions: length 77·2 m (253·2 ft); beam 8·8 m (28·9 ft); draught 4·2 m (13·8 ft) to screws
Gun armament: two 76-mm (3-in) L/62 DP OTO-Melara Compact in two single mountings, and six 30-mm AA in three twin mountings
Missile armament: four container-launchers for four surface-to-surface missiles (probably a combination of RGM-84A Harpoon and Gabriel Mk 2 missiles)
Torpedo armament: none
Anti-submarine armament: one 375-mm (14·76-in) Bofors three-barrel rocket-launcher, two triple Mk 32 tube mountings for 12·75-in (324-mm) Mk 44/46 A/S torpedoes, and helicopter-launched weapons (see below)

Aircraft: one light helicopter in a hangar amidships
Electronics: extensive radar, sonar and ESM fit
Propulsion: CODAG (COmbined Diesel And Gas turbine) arrangement, with two MTU diesels delivering 2,980 kW (4,000 hp) and one General Electric LM 2500 gas turbine delivering 24,000 bhp (17,895 kW) to two shafts
Performance: maximum speed 42 kts on gas turbines and 25 kts on diesels; range 8,350 km (5,190 miles) at cruising speed on diesels
Complement: 45

Class
1. Israel (0+2+?)
2 ships building and ? on order

'Sleipner' class corvette

Norway

Displacement: 600 tons standard and 780 tons full load
Dimensions: length 69·0 m (227·8 ft); beam 8·0 m (26·2 ft); draught 2·4 m (8·2 ft)
Gun armament: one 3-in (76-mm) L/50 DP in one Mk 34 single mounting, and one 40-mm Bofors AA
Missile armament: none
Torpedo armament: none
Anti-submarine armament: two triple Mk 32 tube mountings for 12·75-in (324-mm) Mk 44/46 A/S torpedoes, and one Terne six-barrel rocket-launcher
Electronics: one Decca TM 1229 surface-search and navigation radar, one Decca Type 202 navigation radar, one TVT-300 gun fire-control system, one EDO

SQS-36 hull-mounted medium-range sonar, and one Terne III Mk 3 hull-mounted Terne-control sonar
Propulsion: four Maybach (MTU) diesels delivering 6,710 kW (9,000 bhp) to two shafts
Performance: maximum speed 20+ kts
Complement: 62

Class
1. Norway (2)

Name	No.	Builders	Laid down	Commissioned
SLEIPNER	F 310	Nylands Verksted Shipyard	1963	Apr 1965
AEGER	F 311	Akers	1964	Mar 1967

'Sotomoyo' class patrol ship

USA

Displacement: 690 tons standard and 800 tons full load

Dimensions: length 143 ft (43·6 m); beam 33·9 ft (10·3 m); draught 13 ft (4·0 m)

Gun armament: one 40-mm Bofors AA, and two 20-mm AA in single mountings

Missile armament: none

Torpedo armament: none

Anti-submarine armament: none

Electronics: one navigation radar

Propulsion: diesel-electric arrangement delivering 1,500 bhp (1,120 kW) to one shaft

Performance: maximum speed 12·5 kts; range 19,000 miles (30,575 km) at 8 kts

Complement: 49

Class

1. Argentina (3)

Name	No.	Builders	Commissioned
YAMANA	A 6	Levingstone Shipbuilding Co	Jan 1943
ALFEREZ SOBRAL	A 9	Levingstone Shipbuilding Co	Apr 1945
COMODORO SOMELLERA	A 10	Levingstone Shipbuilding Co	Dec 1944

2. Chile (2)

Name	No.	Builders	Commissioned
LIENTUR	60	Levingstone Shipbuilding Co	Sep 1944
LAUTARO	62	Levingstone Shipbuilding Co	June 1943

'Tarantul I' and 'Tarantul II' class guided-missile corvettes

USSR

Displacement: 550 tons full load

Dimensions: length 56·5 m (185·3 ft); beam 10·5 m (34·4 ft); draught 2·0 m (6·6 ft)

Gun armament: one 76-mm (3-in) DP, and two 30-mm AA in two 'Gatling' mountings

Missile armament: two twin container-launchers for four SS-N-2C 'Styx' surface-to-surface missiles in 'Tarantul I' class, or for four SS-N-22 surface-to-surface missiles in 'Tarantul II' class, and one quadruple launcher for SA-N-5 surface-to-air missiles

Torpedo armament: none

Anti-submarine armament: none

Electronics: one 'Band Stand' air-search radar ('Tarantul II' class only), one 'Cheese Cake' surface-search radar, one 'Bass Tilt' AA gun-control radar, one 'Spin Trough' navigation radar, one 'High Pole' IFF, and one 'Square Head' IFF

Propulsion: CODAG (COmbined Diesel And Gas turbine) arrangement, with one diesel delivering 1,490 kW (2,000 shp) and two gas turbines delivering 22,370 kW (30,000 shp) to three shafts

Performance: maximum speed 36 kts

Complement: 50

Class

1. USSR (4+3)

4 ships plus 3 on order

'Thetis' class (Type 420) corvette

West Germany

Displacement: 730 tons full load

Dimensions: length 69·7 m (228·7 ft); beam 8·5 m (27 ft); draught 4·2 m (14 ft)

Gun armament: two 40-mm Breda L/70 AA in one twin mounting

Missile armament: none

Torpedo armament: none

Anti-submarine armament: one 375-mm Bofors four-barrel rocket-launcher, and one quadruple 533-mm (21-in) tube mounting for A/S torpedoes

Electronics: one Kelvin Hughes 14/9 radar, one TRS-N radar, and one ELAC 1BV hull-mounted sonar

Propulsion: two MAN diesels delivering 5,070 kW (6,800 bhp) to two shafts

Performance: maximum speed 19·5 kts

Complement: 4+60

Class

1. West Germany (5)

Name	No.	Builders	Commissioned
THETIS	P 6052	Rolandwerft	July 1961
HERMES	P 6053	Rolandwerft	Dec 1961
NAJADE	P 6054	Rolandwerft	May 1962
TRITON	P 6055	Rolandwerft	Nov 1962
THESEUS	P 6056	Rolandwerft	Aug 1963

'Turunmaa' class corvette

Finland

Displacement: 660 tons standard and 770 tons full load

Dimensions: length 74·1 m (243·1 ft); beam 7·8 m (25·6 ft); draught 2·4 m (7·9 ft)

Gun armament: one 120-mm (4·7-in) L/46 DP, two 40-mm Bofors AA in single mountings, and two 23-mm AA in one twin mounting

Missile armament: none

Torpedo armament: none

Anti-submarine armament: two RBU-series rocket-launchers, and two depth-charge racks

Electronics: one Hollandse Signaalapparaten WM-22 surface-search and gun-control radar, and one navigation radar

Propulsion: CODOG (COmbined Diesel Or Gas turbine) arrangement, with three Mercedes-Benz (MTU) diesels delivering 2,240 kW (3,000 bhp) and one Rolls-Royce Olympus TM1A gas turbine delivering 15,000 hp (11,185 kW) to three shafts

Performance: maximum speed 35 kts on gas turbine and 17 kts on diesels

Complement: 70

Class

1. Finland (2)

Name	No.	Builders	Laid down	Commissioned
TURUNMAA	03	Wärtsilä	Mar 1967	Aug 1968
KARJALA	04	Wärtsilä	Mar 1967	Oct 1968

'Vosper Mk 1' class corvette

UK/Ghana

Displacement: 440 tons standard and 500 tons full load

Dimensions: length 177 ft (53·9 m); beam 28·5 ft (8·7 m); draught 13 ft (4·0 m)

Gun armament: one 4-in (102-mm) L/40 DP in a Mk 23 single mounting, and one 40-mm Bofors AA

Missile armament: none

Torpedo armament: none

Anti-submarine armament: one Squid three-barrel depth-charge mortar

Electronics: one Plessey AWS 1 air-search radar, one Decca 45 navigation radar, and one Type 164 hull-mounted sonar

Propulsion: two Maybach/Bristol Siddeley diesels delivering 7,100 bhp (5,295 kW) to two shafts

Performance: maximum speed 20 kts; range 3,350 miles (5,390 km) at 14 kts

Complement: 6+48

Class

1. Ghana (2 'Kromantse' class)

Name	No.	Builders	Commissioned
KROMANTSE	F 17	Vosper Ltd	July 1964
KETA	F 18	Vickers (Shipbuilding) Ltd	May 1965

'Vosper Mk 1B' class corvette

UK/Libya

Displacement: 440 tons standard and 500 tons full load
Dimensions: length 177·3 ft (54·0 m); beam 28·5 ft (8·7 m); draught 13 ft (4·0 m) to screws
Gun armament: one 4-in (102-mm) L/40 in a Mk 23 single mounting, and two 40-mm Bofors AA in single mountings
Missile armament: none
Torpedo armament: none
Anti-submarine armament: none
Electronics: one surface-search radar, and one navigation radar
Propulsion: two Paxman Ventura 16 YJCM diesels delivering 3,800 bhp (2,835 kW) to two shafts
Performance: maximum speed 18 kts; range 3,350 miles (5,390 km) at 14 kts
Complement: 5+58

Class

1. Libya (1)				
Name	No.	Builders	Laid down	Commissioned
TOBRUK	C 01	Vosper Ltd	—	Apr 1966

'Vosper Thornycroft Mk 3' class corvette

UK/Nigeria

Displacement: 500 tons standard and 650 tons full load
Dimensions: length 202 ft (61·6 m); beam 31 ft (9·5 m); draught 11·3 ft (3·5 m)
Gun armament: two 4-in (102-mm) L/45 DP in a Mk 19 twin mounting, two 40-mm Bofors AA in single mountings, and two 20-mm Oerlikon AA
Missile armament: none
Torpedo armament: none
Anti-submarine armament: none
Electronics: one Plessey AWS 1 air-search radar, one Decca TM 626 navigation radar, one Hollandse Signaalapparaten WM-22 fire-control radar system, and one Plessey MS 22 hull-mounted sonar
Propulsion: two MAN V24/30-B diesels delivering 5,965 kW (8,000 bhp) to two shafts
Performance: maximum speed 22 kts; range 3,450 miles (5,550 km) at 14 kts
Complement: 8+59

Class

1. Nigeria (2)				
Name	No.	Builders	Laid down	Commissioned
DORINA	F 81	Vosper Thornycroft Ltd	Jan 1970	June 1972
OTOBO	F 82	Vosper Thornycroft Ltd	Sep 1970	Nov 1972

'Vosper Thornycroft Mk 9' class corvette

UK/Nigeria

Displacement: 850 tons full load
Dimensions: length 226 ft (69·0 m); beam 31·5 ft (9·6 m); draught 9·8 ft (3·0 m)
Gun armament: one 76-mm (3-in) L/62 DP OTO-Melara Compact, one 40-mm Bofors L/70 AA, and two 20-mm Oerlikon AA
Missile armament: one triple launcher for 12 Sea Cat surface-to-air missiles
Torpedo armament: none
Anti-submarine armament: one 375-mm (14·76-in) Bofors two-barrel rocket-launcher
Electronics: one Plessey AWS 2 surface-search radar, one Decca TM 1226 navigation radar, one Hollandse Signaalapparaten WM-24 fire-control radar system, and one Plessey PMS 26 hull-mounted sonar
Propulsion: four MTU 20V956 TB92 diesels delivering 13,125 kW (17,600 shp) to two shafts
Performance: maximum speed 27 kts; range 2,550 miles (4,105 km) at 14 kts
Complement: 90

Class

1. Nigeria (2)				
Name	No.	Builders	Laid down	Commissioned
ERIN'MI	F 83	Vosper Thornycroft Ltd	Oct 1975	Jan 1980
ENYIMIRI	F 84	Vosper Thornycroft Ltd	Feb 1977	July 1980

'Wolf' class corvette

USA/Netherlands

Displacement: 870 tons standard and 975 tons full load
Dimensions: length 56·2 m (184·5 ft); beam 10·3 m (33·7 ft); draught 2·9 m (9·5 ft)
Gun armament: one 3-in (76-mm) L/50 DP, four 40-mm Bofors AA, and two 20-mm AA
Missile armament: none
Torpedo armament: none
Anti-submarine armament: one Hedgehog rocket-launcher, two (four in Fs 821 and 822) depth-charge throwers, and two depth-charge racks
Electronics: one Kelvin Hughes navigation radar, and one QCU-2 hull-mounted sonar
Propulsion: two General Motors diesels delivering 1,800 bhp (1,345 kW) to two shafts

Performance: maximum speed 15 kts; range 7,975 km (4,955 miles) at 10 kts
Complement: 78

Class

1. Netherlands (6)			
Name	No.	Builders	Commissioned
WOLF	F 817	Avondale Marine Ways	Mar 1954
FRET	F 818	General Shipbuilding	May 1954
HERMELIJN	F 819	General Shipbuilding	Aug 1954
VOS	F 820	General Shipbuilding	Dec 1954
PANTER	F 821	Avondale Marine Ways	June 1954
JAGUAR	F 822	Avondale Marine Ways	June 1954

'Al Mansur' class fast attack craft (missile)

Oman/UK

Displacement: 166 tons standard and 185 tons full load
Dimensions: length 123 ft (37·5 m); beam 22·5 ft (6·9 m); draught 6 ft (2·2 m)
Gun armament: two 40-mm Breda L/70 AA in one twin mounting
Missile armament: two single container-launchers for two MM.38 Exocet surface-to-surface missiles
Torpedo armament: none
Anti-submarine armament: none
Electronics: one Decca 1229 navigation and surface-search radar, one

Laurence-Scott optical director, and one Sperry Sea Archer fire-control system
Propulsion: two Paxman Ventura 16RP200 diesels delivering 4,800 bhp (3,580 kW) to two shafts
Performance: maximum speed 25 kts; range 3,800 miles (6,115 km) at 15 kts
Complement: 4+24
Class

1. Oman (2)

Name	No.	Builders	Commissioned
AL MANSUR	B 2	Brooke Marine	Mar 1973
AL NEJAH	B 3	Brooke Marine	May 1973

'Al Siddiq' class fast attack craft (missile)

Saudi Arabia/USA

Displacement: 385 tons full load
Dimensions: length 190·5 ft (58·1 m); beam 26·5 ft (8·1 m); draught 11 ft (3·4 m)
Gun armament: one 76-mm (3-in) L/62 DP OTO-Melara Compact, two 20-mm Phalanx close-in weapon system mountings, two 20-mm AA, and one 81-mm mortar
Missile armament: two twin container-launchers for four RGM-84A Harpoon surface-to-surface missiles
Torpedo armament: none
Anti-submarine armament: none
Electronics: one Westinghouse SPS-55 surface-search radar, one Lockheed SPS-40B air-search radar, and one Mk 92 fire-control radar system
Propulsion: CODOG (COmbined Diesel Or Gas turbine) arrangement, with two MTU diesels delivering 2,985 kW (4,000 hp) and one General Electric LM 2500 gas

turbine delivering 23,000 bhp (17,150 kW) to two shafts
Performance: maximum speed 38 kts on gas turbine and 15·5 kts on diesels
Complement: 5+33

Class

1. Saudi Arabia (9)

Name	No.	Builders	Commissioned
AL SIDDIQ	511	Peterson Builders Inc	Dec 1980
AL FAROUQ	513	Peterson Builders Inc	June 1981
ABDUL AZIZ	515	Peterson Builders Inc	Aug 1981
FAISAL	517	Peterson Builders Inc	Nov 1981
KAHLID	519	Peterson Builders Inc	Jan 1982
AMYR	521	Peterson Builders Inc	June 1982
TARIQ	523	Peterson Builders Inc	Aug 1982
OQBAH	525	Peterson Builders Inc	Oct 1982
ABU OBAIDAH	527	Peterson Builders Inc	Dec 1982

'Al Wafi' class fast attack craft (gun)

Oman/UK

Displacement: 135 tons standard and 155 tons full load
Dimensions: length 123 ft (37·5 m); beam 22·5 ft (6·9 m); draught 6 ft (2·2 m)

Gun armament: one 76-mm (3-in) L/62 DP OTO-Melara Compact, and one 20-mm Oerlikon AA
Missile armament: none
Torpedo armament: none
Anti-submarine armament: none
Electronics: one Decca 1226 navigation radar, one Decca 1229 navigation radar, one Laurence-Scott optical director, and one Sperry Sea Archer fire-control system
Propulsion: two Paxman Ventura 16RP200 diesels delivering 4,800 bhp (3,580 kW) to two shafts
Performance: maximum speed 25 kts; range 3,800 miles (6,115 km) at 15 kts
Complement: 3+24
Class

1. Oman (4)

Name	No.	Builders	Commissioned
AL WAFI	B 4	Brooke Marine	Mar 1977
AL FULK	B 5	Brooke Marine	Mar 1977
AL MUJAHID	B 6	Brooke Marine	July 1977
AL JABBAR	B 7	Brooke Marine	Oct 1977

'Algerian' class fast attack craft (missile)

Algeria

Displacement: about 200 tons
Dimensions: length 40·0 m (131·2 ft); beam 7·0 m (23 ft); draught 1·8 m (5·9 ft)
Gun armament: two 76-mm (3-in) L/62 DP OTO-Melara Compact in a twin mounting
Missile armament: two container-launchers for two Otomat surface-to-surface missiles
Torpedo armament: none

Anti-submarine armament: none
Electronics: surface-search and navigation radar
Propulsion: two diesels delivering 8,200 kW (11,000 bhp) to two shafts
Fuel: diesel oil
Performance: maximum speed 32 kts
Complement: 18

Class
1. Algeria (4)
4 craft building

'Arzana' class fast attack craft (patrol)

UK

Displacement: 110 tons standard and 175 tons full load
Dimensions: length 110 ft (33·5 m); beam 21 ft (6·m); draught 6·6 ft (2·0 m)
Gun armament: two 30-mm A32 AA in one twin mounting, and one 20-mm A41 AA

Torpedo armament: none
Anti-submarine armament: none
Electronics: one Decca TM 1626 navigation radar
Propulsion: two Paxman diesels delivering 5,400 hp (4,025 kW) to two shafts
Performance: maximum speed 30 kts; range 2,075 miles (3,340 km) at 14 kts
Complement: 26

Class
1. united Arab emirates (6)

Name	No.	Builders	Commissioned
ARZANA	P 1101	Vosper Thornycroft Ltd	June 1975
ZURARA	P 1102	Vosper Thornycroft Ltd	Aug 1975
MURBAN	P 1103	Vosper Thornycroft Ltd	Sep 1075
AL GHULLAN	P 1104	Vosper Thornycroft Ltd	Sep 1975
RADOOM	P 1105	Vosper Thornycroft Ltd	July 1976
GHANADHAH	P 1106	Vosper Thornycroft Ltd	July 1976

'Asheville' class fast attack craft (missile)

USA/South Korea

Displacement: 225 tons standard and 245 tons full load
Dimensions: length 164·5 ft (50·1 m); beam 23·8 ft (7·3 m); draught 9·5 ft (2·9 m)
Gun armament: one 3-in (76-mm) L/50 in a Mk 34 mounting, one 40-mm Bofors L/60 AA in a Mk 3 mounting and four 0·5-in (12·7-mm) heavy machine-guns in two twin mountings
Missile armament: one twin launch container for two Standard surface-to-air missiles
Torpedo armament: none
Anti-submarine armament: none
Electronics: navigation radar and one Western Electric SPG-50 radar in conjunction with the Mk 63 gun fire-control system
Propulsion: CODOG (COmbined Diesel Or Gas turbine) arrangement with two Cummins diesels delivering 1,450 bhp (1,080 kW) or one General Electric gas turbine delivering 13,300 shp (9,920 kW) to two shafts
Performance: maximum speed 16 kts on diesels and 40+ kts on gas turbine; range 1,950 miles (3,140 km) at 16 kts or 375 miles (605 km) at 37 kts
Complement: 3+22

Class

1. South Korea (1)

Name	No.	Builders	Commissioned
PAEK KU 51	PGM 351	Tacoma B.B. Co	Apr 1970

2. Turkey (2)

Name	No.	Builders	Commissioned
YILDIRIM	P 338	Peterson Builders Inc	Sep 1969
BORA	P 339	Peterson Builders Inc	Oct 1969

3. USA (4)

Name	No.	Builders	Commissioned
TACOMA	PG 92	Tacoma B.B. Co	July 1969
WELCH	PG 93	Peterson Builders Inc	Sep 1969
BEACON	PG 99	Peterson Builders Inc	Nov 1969
GREEN BAY	PG 101	Peterson Builders Inc	Dec 1969

Remarks: Turkey's two units have no missiles and are used for patrol. The USA has left four of the original 17 craft (all of which survive, most in non-combatant roles), though these are slated for transfer and have no missiles.

'Babochka' class fast attack hydrofoil (patrol)

USSR

Displacement: 400 tons full load
Dimensions: length 50·0 m (164 ft); beam 8·5 m (27·9 ft); draught 2·0 m (6·6 ft)
Gun armament: two 30-mm AA Gatling mountings
Missile armament: none
Torpedo armament: none
Anti-submarine armament: two quadruple tube mountings for 406-mm (16-in) A/S torpedoes

Electronics: navigation radar, search radar and 'Bass Tilt' gun fire-control radar
Propulsion: three Kuznetsov NK-12 gas turbines delivering 26,845 kW (36,000 hp) to three shafts
Performance: maximum speed 50 kts
Complement: 45

Class

1. USSR (1)
one craft

'Constitucion' class fast attack craft (missile/gun)

UK

Displacement: 170 tons
Dimensions: length 121 ft (36·9 m); beam 23·3 ft (7·1 m); draught 6 ft (1·8 m)
Gun armament: one 76-mm (3-in) L/62 DP OTO-Melara Compact (Ps 12, 14 and 16 only), and one 40-mm Breda L/70 AA (all)

Missile armament: two container-launchers for two Otomat surface-to-surface missiles (Ps 12, 14 and 16 only)
Torpedo armament: none
Anti-submarine armament: none
Electronics: one SMA SPQ 2D surface-search radar, and one Selenia Orion RTN 10X fire-control radar used in conjunction with the ELSAG Argo NA10 fire-control system
Propulsion: two MTU diesels delivering 5,370 kW (7,200 hp) to two shafts
Performance: maximum speed 31 kts; range 2,500 km (1,555 miles) at 16 kts
Complement: 3+14

Class

1. Venezuela (6)

Name	No.	Builders	Laid down	Commissioned
CONSTITUCION	P 11	Vosper Thornycroft Ltd	Jan 1973	Aug 1974
FEDERACIÓN	P 12*	Vosper Thornycroft Ltd	Aug 1973	Mar 1975
INDEPENDENCIA	P 13	Vosper Thornycroft Ltd	Feb 1973	Sep 1974
LIBERTAD	P 14*	Vosper Thornycroft Ltd	Sep 1973	June 1975
PATRIA	P 15	Vosper Thornycroft Ltd	Mar 1973	Jan 1975
VICTORIA	P 16*	Vosper Thornycroft Ltd	Mar 1974	Sep 1975

*fitted with missiles

'Cormoran' class fast attack craft (missile)

Spain/Morocco

Displacement: 410 tons full load
Dimensions: length 57·4 m (188·3 ft); beam 7·6 m (24·9 ft); draught 2·7 m (8·9 ft)
Gun armament: one 76-mm (3-in) L/62 DP OTO-Melara Compact, and one 40-mm Breda L/70 AA
Missile armament: four container-launchers for MM.40 Exocet surface-to-surface missiles
Torpedo armament: none
Anti-submarine armament: none
Electronics: one Hollandse Signaalapparaten ZW-06 search radar, one Hollandse Signaalapparaten Wm-20 fire-control radar, and one CSEE director system
Propulsion: two MTU/Bazán 16V356 T1391 diesel delivering 6,000 kW (8,045 bhp) to two shafts
Performance: maximum speed 36 kts; range 4,650 km (2,890 miles) at 15 kts
Complement: 41

Class

1. Morocco (4)

Name	No.	Builders	Commissioned
EL KHATABI	35	Bazán	July 1981
COMMANDNT BOUTOUBA	35	Bazán	Nov 1981
COMMANDANT EL HARTY	37	Bazán	Feb 1982
COMMANDANT AZOUGGARGH	38	Bazán	Aug 1982

'CPIC' class fast attack craft (patrol)
USA
Displacement: 71 tons full load
Dimensions: length 100ft (30·5m); beam 18·5ft (5·6m); draught 6ft (1·8m)
Gun armament: two 30-mm AA in an Emerlec twin mounting, and one 20-mm AA
Missile armament: surface-to-surface missiles may be carried
Torpedo armament: none
Anti-submarine armament: none
Electronics: one surface-search and navigation radar
Propulsion: three Avco Lycoming gas turbines delivering 6,750 shp (5,035 kW) to three shafts; there are also two Volvo auxiliary diesels delivering 375 kW (500 hp)
Performance: maximum speed 45 kts
Complement: 11
Class
1. South Korea (6)

Name	No.	Builders	Commissioned
KILURKI 11	PKM 211	Tacoma B.B. Co	1975
KILURKI 12	PKM 212	Korea Tacoma International	1979
KILURKI 13	PKM 213	Korea Tacoma International	1979
KILURKI 15	PKM 215	Korea Tacoma International	1979
KILURKI 71	PKM 271	Korea Tacoma International	1979
KILURKI 72	PKM 272	Korea Tacoma International	1979

'Dvora' class fast attack craft (missile)
Israel

The 'Dvora' class craft are currently the world's smallest FAC(M)s.

Displacement: 47 tons
Dimensions: length 21·6m (70·8ft); beam 5·5m (18ft); draught 1·0m (3·3ft)
Gun armament: two 20-mm Oerlikon AA in single mountings, and two machine-guns
Missile armament: two single container-launchers for IAI Gabriel surface-to-surface missiles
Torpedo armament: none
Anti-submarine armament: none
Electronics: one Decca 926 surface-search and navigation radar
Propulsion: two MTU 12V331 TC81 diesels delivering ? kW (? hp) to two shafts
Performance: maximum speed 36 kts; range 1,300 km (810 miles) at 27 kts
Complement: 10
Class
1. Israel (2)
2 craft

2. Taiwan (26+4)
26 craft (plus 4 on order)

'Flagstaff 2' class fast attack hydrofoil (missile)
USA/Israel
Displacement: 91·5 tons
Dimensions: length 84ft (25·6m); beam 21·3ft (6·5m); draught 5ft (1·6m)
Gun armament: four 30-mm AA in two twin mountings, with the possibility of replacing one such mounting with a single 76-mm (3-in) L/62 DP OTO-Melara Compact
Missile armament: four container-launchers for IAI Gabriel or RGM-84A Harpoon surface-to-surface missiles
Torpedo armament: none
Anti-submarine armament: none
Electronics: surface-search and navigation radars
Propulsion: one gas turbine for foilborne operation and two diesels for hullborne operation
Performance: maximum speed 52 kts
Complement: not known
Class
1. Israel (2+10)
2 craft (plus 10 on order)

Despite considerable development problems, the Shimrit (M 161) was accepted in 1982, with construction of a further 11 units being undertaken in Israel.

'Guacolda' class fast attack craft (torpedo)
West Germany
Displacement: 119 tons standard and 134 tons full load
Dimensions: length 36·0m (118·1ft); beam 5·6m (18·4ft); draught 2·2m (7·2ft)
Gun armament: two 40-mm Bofors AA in single mountings
Missile armament: none
Torpedo armament: four 533-mm (21-in) tubes
Anti-submarine armament: none
Electronics: surface-search and navigation radar
Propulsion: two Mercedes-Benz diesels delivering 3,580 kW (4,800 bhp) to two shafts
Performance: maximum speed 32 kts; range 2,775 km (1,725 miles) at 15 kts or 1,300 km (810 miles) at 30 kts
Complement: 20
Class
1. Chile (4)

Name	No.	Builders	Commissioned
GUACOLDA	80	Bazán	1965
FRESIA	81	Bazán	1965
QUIDORA	82	Bazán	1966
TEGUALDA	83	Bazán	1966

2. Ecuador (3 'Manta' class)

Name	No.	Builders	Commissioned
MANTA	LT 41 (ex-LT 91)	Lürssen	June 1971
TULCAN	LT 42 (ex-LT 92)	Lürssen	Apr 1971
NUEVO ROCAFUERTE	LT 43 (ex-LT 93)	Lürssen	June 1971

Remarks: The Chilean 'Guacolda' and Ecuadorian 'Manta' classes are basically similar in design and construction, though the use in the Ecuadorian class of three MTU diesels delivering 6,705 kW (8,990 bhp) to three shafts increases speed to 35 kts. As originally delivered, the 'Manta' class had two 21-in (533-mm) tubes, though these may now have been removed, leaving the primary armament as four single container-launchers for four Gabriel 2 anti-ship missiles. The gun armament comprises two 30-mm cannon in an Emerlec twin mounting for AA and anti-FAC defence. The electronic fit was extensively revised in 1980. Unlike the 'Guacolda' class, which was built in Spain by Bazan, the 'Manta' class was produced at Vegesack by the parent company, Lürssen, for delivery in the early 1970s.

'Hainan' class fast attack craft (patrol)

China

Displacement: 375 tons standard and 400 full load
Dimensions: length 58·8m (192·9ft); beam 7·2m (23·6ft); draught 2·2m (7·2ft)
Gun armament: four 57-mm L/70 in two mountings, and four 25-mm AA in two twin mountings
Missile armament: none
Torpedo armament: none
Anti-submarine armament: four five-barrel RBU 1200 rocket-launchers, two depth-charge throwers and two depth-charge racks
Mines: fitted for minelaying
Electronics: one 'Pot Head' or 'Skin Head' surface-search radar, one fire-control radar and one navigation radar
Propulsion: four diesels delivering 6,550kW (8,800shp) to four shafts
Performance: maximum speed 30·5kts; range 2,400km (1,490 miles) at 15kts
Complement: 69

Class
1. Bangladesh (1+?)
1 craft plus ? on order

2. China (28)
28 craft

3. North Korea (6)
6 craft

4. Pakistan (4)

Name	No.
BALUCHISTAN	P 155
SIND	P 159
PUNJAB	—
SAHAD	—

'Hauk' class fast attack craft (missile)

Norway

Displacement: 120 tons standard and 155 tons full load
Dimensions: length 36·5m (119-7ft); beam 6·2m (20·3ft); draught 3·6m (11·8ft)
Gun armament: one 40-mm Bofors AA, and one 20-mm Oerlikon AA
Missile armament: six container-launchers for Penguin Mk 2 surface-to-surface missiles

The Hauk (P 986) shows off the similarity of the 'Hauk' class to the earlier 'Snögg' class, which it resembles apart from the provision for six rather than four Penguin missiles, and the use of a more advanced fire-control system.

Torpedo armament: two 533-mm (21-in) tubes
Anti-submarine armament: none
Electronics: one Kongsberg Vapenfabrikk MSI-805 missile-control system
Propulsion: two Maybach (MTU) MB 872A diesels delivering 5,220kW (7,000hp) to two shafts
Performance: maximum speed 34kts; range 815km (505 miles) at 34kts
Complement: 22

Class
1. Norway (14)

Name	No.	Builders	Commissioned
HAUK	P 986	Bergens Mek Verksteder	Aug 1977
ØRN	P 987	Bergens Mek Verksteder	Jan 1979
TERNE	P 988	Bergens Mek Verksteder	Mar 1979
TJELD	P 989	Bergens Mek Verksteder	May 1979
SKARV	P 990	Bergens Mek Verksteder	July 1979
TEIST	P 991	Bergens Mek Verksteder	Sep 1979
JO	P 992	Bergens Mek Verksteder	Nov 1979
LOM	P 993	Bergens Mek Verksteder	Jan 1980
STEGG	P 994	Bergens Mek Verksteder	Mar 1980
FALK	P 995	Bergens Mek Verksteder	Apr 1980
RAVN	P 996	Westamarin A/S	May 1980
GRIBB	P997	Westamarin A/S	July 1980
GEIR	P 998	Westamarin A/S	Sep 1980
ERLE	P 999	Westamarin A/S	Dec 1980

'Helsinki' class fast attack craft (gun)

Finland

Displacement: 280 tons standard and 300 tons full load
Dimensions: length 45·0m (147·6ft); beam 8·9m (29·2ft); draught 3·0m (9·9ft)
Gun armament: one 57-mm Bofors L/70 AA, and two 23-mm AA in a twin mounting
Missile armament: none
Torpedo armament: none
Anti-submarine armament: none
Electronics: Philips Elektroniksindustrier 9 LV 225 radar fire-control system
Propulsion: three MTU 16V538 TB92 diesels delivering 8,200kW (11,000shp) to three shafts
Performance: maximum speed 30kts
Complement: 30

Class
1. Finland (1+7)

Name	No.	Builders	Commissioned
HELSINKI	60	—	Sep 1981

Remarks: The 'Helsinki' class FAC(G) is a good example of the success achieved by Finland in developing indigenous weapon systems with considerable imported content, for into a hull of Finnish design and construction are fitted Swedish electronics, West German diesels, Swedish main gun armament and Soviet AA gun armament. It is anticipated that 12 may eventually be built as the complement of three four-craft squadrons, and it is more than likely that anti-ship missile armament will be added. The Bofors 57-mm gun is a dedicated surface-to-surface weapon accommodated within a plastic turret.

'Huchuan' class fast attack hydrofoil (torpedo)

China

Displacement: 39 tons standard and 45 tons full load
Dimensions: length 21·8m (71·5ft); beam 5·0m (16·6ft) over foils; draught 1·0m (3·3ft) hullborne
Gun armament: four 14·5-mm (0·57-in) heavy machine-guns in two twin mountings
Missile armament: none
Torpedo armament: two 533-mm (21-in) tubes
Anti-submarine armament: none
Electronics: one 'Skin Head' surface-search radar
Propulsion: three M50 diesels delivering 2,685kW (3,600hp) to three shafts
Performance: maximum speed 55kts foilborne; range 925km (575 miles) at cruising speed
Complement: 12-15

Class
1. Albania (32)
32 craft

2. China (130)
130 craft

3. Pakistan (4)
4 craft

4. Romania (19)
19 craft (VT 51-69)

5. Tanzania (4)
4 craft

6. Zaire (4)
4 craft

'Hugin' class fast attack craft (missile)
Sweden
Displacement: 120 tons standard and 150 tons full load
Dimensions: length 36·6m (120ft); beam 6·3m (20·7ft); draught 1·7m (5·6ft)
Gun armament: one 57-mm Bofors L/70 AA
Missile armament: six container-launchers for RB 15 surface-to-surface missiles
Torpedo armament: none

Anti-submarine armament: none
Mines: fitted for minelaying
Electronics: one Philips Elektronikindustrier 9 LV 200 Mk 2 surface-search and fire-control system radar, one Skanter Mk 009 navigation radar, and one Simrad SQ 3D/SF hull-mounted sonar
Propulsion: two Maybach (MTU) 20V672 TY90 diesels delivering 5,370 kW (7,200 bhp) to two shafts
Performance: maximum speed 36 kts
Complement: 3+19

The Swedish Hugin (P 151) is seen on trials before the installation of her six Penguin anti-ship missiles, later to be replaced by Swedish RB 15 weapons.

Class
1. Sweden (16 'Hugin' and 1 'Jägaren' class)

Name	No.	Builders	Commissioned
HUGIN	P 151	Bergens Mek Verksteder	July 1978
MUNIN	P 152	Bergens Mek Verksteder	July 1978
MAGNE	P 153	Bergens Mek Verksteder	Oct 1978
MODE	P 154	Westamarin A/S	Jan 1979
VALE	P 155	Westamarin A/S	Apr 1979
VIDAR	P 156	Westamarin A/S	Aug 1979
MJÖLNER	P 157	Westamarin A/S	Oct 1979
MYSING	P 158	Westamarin A/S	Feb 1980
KAPAREN	P 159	Bergens Mek Verksteder	Aug 1980
VÄKTAREN	P 160	Bergens Mek Verksteder	Sep 1980
SNAPPHANEN	P 161	Bergens Mek Verksteder	Jan 1980
SPEJAREN	P 162	Bergens Mek Verksteder	Mar 1980
STYRBJÖRN	P 163	Bergens Mek Verksteder	June 1980
STARKODDER	P 164	Bergens Mek Verksteder	Aug 1981
TORDÖN	P 165	Bergens Mek Verksteder	Oct 1981
TIRFING	P 166	Bergens Mek Verksteder	Jan 1982
JÄGAREN	P 150	Bergens Mek Verksteder	Nov 1972

'Jaguar' class fast attack craft (torpedo)
West Germany
Displacement: 160 tons standard and 190 tons full load
Dimensions: length 42·5m (139·4ft); beam 7·2m (23·4ft); draught 2·4m (7·9ft)
Gun armament: two 40-mm Bofors L/70 AA in single mountings
Missile armament: none
Torpedo armament: four 533-mm (21-in) tubes
Anti-submarine armament: none
Mines: four mines can be carried if two torpedo tubes are removed
Electronics: navigation radar
Propulsion: four Maybach (MTU) diesels delivering 8,950 kW (12,000 bhp) to four shafts
Performance: maximum speed 42 kts
Complement: 39

Class
1. Greece (6)

Name	No.	Builders	Commissioned
HESPEROS	P 50	Lürssen	1958
KENTAUROS	P 52	Lürssen	1958
KYKLON	P 53	Lürssen	1958
LELAPS	P 54	Lürssen	1958
SKORPIOS	P 55	Lürssen	1958
TYFON	P 56	Lürssen	1958

2. Saudi Arabia (3)

Name	No.	Builders	Commissioned
DAMMAM	—	Lürssen	1969
KHABAR	—	Lürssen	1969
MACCAH	—	Lürssen	1969

The pennant number of the ex-West German 'Jaguar' class FAC(T) Tyfon of the Greek navy is now P 56. The six craft were transferred in 1976-77.

3. Turkey (4)

Name	No.	Builders	Commissioned
TUFAN	P 331	Lürssen	1962
MIZRAK	P 333	Lürssen	1962
KALKAN	P 335	Lürssen	1959
KARAYEL	P 336	Lürssen	1962

Remarks: The six Greek craft are supported by three other ex-West German craft transferred for cannibalization. The Turkish force was once seven operational and three spare craft, three of the former being deleted in 1982.

'Jerong' class fast attack craft (gun)
Malaysia
Displacement: 255 tons full load
Dimensions: length 44·9m (147·3ft); beam 7·0m (23ft); draught 2·5m (8·3ft)
Gun armament: one 57-mm Bofors L/60 DP, and one 40-mm Bofors L/70 AA
Missile armament: none
Torpedo armament: none
Anti-submarine armament: none
Electronics: navigation radar, and one CSEE Naja optronic fire-director
Propulsion: three Maybach/Mercedes Benz diesels delivering 7,380 kW (9,900 bhp) to three shafts
Performance: maximum speed 32 kts; range 3,700 km (2,300 miles) at 15 kts
Complement: 41

Class
1. Malaysia (6)

Name	No.	Builders	Commissioned
JERONG	P 3505	Hong Leong-Lürssen	Mar 1976
TODAK	P 3506	Hong Leong-Lürssen	June 1976
PAUS	P 3507	Hong Leong-Lürssen	Aug 1976
YU	P 3508	Hong Leong-Lürssen	Nov 1976
BAUNG	P 3509	Hong Leong-Lürssen	Jan 1977
PARI	P 3510	Hong Leong-Lürssen	Mar 1977

Remarks: The 'Jerong' class has adequate performance and range for patrol and the support of FAC(M)s with its powerful 57-mm Bofors gun, though the former role is the raison d'etre for the class as a replacement for the 'Kedah' class.

'Kartal' class fast attack craft (missile and torpedo)

West Germany/Turkey

Displacement: 160 tons standard and 180 tons full load
Dimensions: length 42·8m (140·5ft); beam 7·1m (23·5ft); draught 2·2m (7·2ft)
Gun armament: two 40-mm Bofors L/70 AA in single mountings
Missile armament: four container-launchers for Penguin Mk 2 surface-to-surface missiles
Torpedo armament: four 533-mm (21-in) tubes
Anti-submarine armament: none
Electronics: Hollandse Signaalapparaten WM-28 fire-control radar
Propulsion: four Maybach (MTU) 16V538 diesels delivering 8,950 kW (12,000 bhp) to four shafts
Performance: maximum speed 42 kts
Complement: 39

Class 1. Turkey (9)			
Name	No.	Builders	Commissioned
DENIZKUSU	P 321	Lürssen	1967
ATMACA	P 322	Lürssen	1967
SAHIN	P 323	Lürssen	1967
KARTAL	P 324	Lürssen	1967
MELTEM	P 325	Lürssen	1968
PELIKAN	P 326	Lürssen	1968
ALBATROS	P 327	Lürssen	1968
ŞIMŞEK	P 328	Lürssen	1968
KASIRGA	P 329	Lürssen	1967

'Komar' class fast attack craft (missile)

USSR

Displacement: 68 tons standard and 75 tons full load
Dimensions: length 26·8m (87·9ft); beam 6·2m (20·3ft); draught 1·5m (4·9ft)
Gun armament: two 25-mm AA in a twin mounting, or two twin 25-mm AA in 'Hegu' class
Missile armament: two container-launchers for SS-N-2A 'Styx' surface-to-surface missiles
Torpedo armament: none
Anti-submarine armament: none
Electronics: one 'Square Tie' surface-search radar, one 'Dead Duck' IFF, and one 'High Pole-A' IFF
Propulsion: four M50 diesels delivering 3,580 kW (4,800 bhp) to four shafts
Performance: maximum speed 40 kts; range 740 km (460 miles) at 30 kts
Complement: 19

Class
1. Algeria (6)
6 craft (nos 671, 672, 673, 674, 675 and 676)
2. China (2+95 'Hegu' class)
2 craft plus 95 locally-built 'Hegu' class craft
3. Cuba (10+4)
10 craft plus 4 craft on order
4. Egypt (4)
4 craft
5. North Korea (10+10 'Sohung' class)
10 craft plus 10 locally-built 'Sohung' class craft
6. Syria (6)
6 craft (nos 41, 42, 43, 44, 45 and 46)

'La Combattante I' class fast attack craft (missile)

France

Displacement: 180 tons standard and 202 tons full load
Dimensions: length 45·0m (147·8ft); beam 7·35m (24·1ft); draught 2·45m (8·ft)
Gun armament: two 40-mm Bofors AA in two single mountings
Missile armament: one quadruple launcher for SS.12 surface-to-surface missiles
Torpedo armament: none
Anti-submarine armament: none
Electronics: surface-search/navigation radar

Propulsion: two SEMT-Pielstick diesels delivering 2,865 kW (3,840 bhp) to two shafts
Performance: maximum speed 28 kts; range 3,700 km (2,300 miles) at 12 kts
Complement: 3+22

Class 1. France (1)			
Name	No.	Builders	Commissioned
LA COMBATTANTE	P 730	C.M.N. Cherbourg	Mar 1964

'La Combattante II' class fast attack craft (missile and torpedo)

France/Greece

Displacement: 234 tons standard and 255 tons full load
Dimensions: length 47·0m (154·2ft); beam 7·1m (23·3ft); draught 2·5m (8·2ft)
Gun armament: four 35-mm Oerlikon L/95 AA in two twin mountings
Missile armament: four container-launchers for MM.38 Exocet surface-to-surface missiles
Torpedo armament: two 533-mm (21-in) tubes
Anti-submarine armament: none
Electronics: one Thomson-CSF Triton surface-search and navigation radar, and one Thomson-CSF Pollux SSM-control radar
Propulsion: four MTU 872 diesels delivering 8,950 kW (12,000 bhp) to four shafts

Performance: maximum speed 36·5 kts; range 3,700 km (2,300 miles) at 15 kts or 1,575 km (980 miles) at 25 kts
Complement: 4+36

Class 1. Greece (4)			
Name	No.	Builders	Commissioned
ANTHIPOPLOIARHOS ANNINOS	P 14	C. M. de Normandie	June 1972
IPOPLOIARHOS ARLIOTIS	P 15	C. M. de Normandie	Apr 1972
IPOPLOIARHOS KONIDIS	P 16	C. M. de Normandie	July 1972
IPOPLOIARHOS BATSIS	P 17	C. M. de Normandie	Dec 1971

'La Combattante II/Kaman' class fast attack craft (missile)

France/Iran

Displacement: 234 tons standard and 275 tons full load
Dimensions: length 47·0m (154·2ft); beam 7·1m (23·3ft); draught 1·9m (6·2ft)
Gun armament: one 76-mm (3-in) L/62 DP OTO-Melara Compact, and one 40-mm Bofors L/70 AA
Missile armament: four container-launchers for RGM-84A Harpoon surface-to-surface missiles
Torpedo armament: none
Anti-submarine armament: none
Electronics: one Hollandse Signaalapparaten WM-28 tactical and fire-control radar
Propulsion: four MTU 16V538 TB91 diesels delivering 10,740 kW (14,400 bhp) to four shafts
Performance: maximum speed 34·5 kts; range 3,700 km (2,300 miles) at 15 kts or 1,300 km (810 miles) at 33·7 kts
Complement: 31

Class 1. Iran (12 'Kaman' class)			
Name	No.	Builders	Commissioned
KAMAN	P 221	C.M. de Normandie	Aug 1977
ZOUBIN	P 222	C.M. de Normandie	Sep 1977
KHADANG	P 223	C.M. de Normandie	Mar 1978
PEYKAN	P 224	C.M. de Normandie	Mar 1978
JOSHAN	P 225	C.M. de Normandie	Mar 1978
FALAKHON	P 226	C.M. de Normandie	Mar 1978
SHAMSHIR	P 227	C.M. de Normandie	Mar 1978
GORZ	P 228	C.M. de Normandie	Aug 1978
GARDOUNEH	P 229	C.M. de Normandie	Sep 1978
KHANJAR	P 230	C.M. de Normandie	Aug 1981
HEYZEH	P 231	C.M. de Normandie	Aug 1981
TABARZIN	P 232	C.M. de Normandie	Aug 1981

Remarks: The 12 'Kaman' class ships represent potentially one of the most powerful strike forces available to the Iranian navy, but lack missiles.

'La Combattante IIG' class fast attack craft (missile)

France/Libya
Displacement: 311 tons full load
Dimensions: length 49·0 m (160·7 ft); beam 7·1 m (23·3 ft); draught 2·0 m (6·6 ft)
Gun armament: one 76-mm (3-in) L/62 DP OTO-Melara Compact, and two 40-mm Breda L/70 AA in a twin mounting
Missile armament: four container-launchers for Otomat surface-to-surface missiles
Torpedo armament: none
Anti-submarine armament: none
Electronics: one Thomson-CSF Triton surface-search radar and one Thomson-CSF Castor fire-control radar linked in a Thomson-CSF Vega fire-control system, and one CSEE Panda gunnery director
Propulsion: four MTU 20V538 TB91 diesels delivering 13,425 kW (18,000 shp) to four shafts

Performance: maximum speed 39 kts; range 2,960 km (1,840 miles) at 15 kts
Complement: 27

Class
1. Libya (10)

Name	No.	Builders	Com-missioned
BEIR GRASSA	518	C.M.N. Cherbourg	1980
BEIR GZIR	522	C.M.N. Cherbourg	1981
BEIR GTIFA	524	C.M.N. Cherbourg	1981
BEIR GLULUD	526	C.M.N. Cherbourg	1980
BEIR ALGANDULA	528	C.M.N. Cherbourg	1982
BEIR KTITAT	532	C.M.N. Cherbourg	1982
BEIR ALKRARIM	534	C.M.N. Cherbourg	1982
BEIR ALKARDMEN	536	C.M.N. Cherbourg	1982
BEIR ALKUR	538	C.M.N. Cherbourg	1982
BEIR ALKUESAT	542	C.M.N. Cherbourg	1982

'La Combattante III' class fast attack craft (missile and torpedo)

France/Greece
Displacement: 360 tons standard and 425 tons full load for P 20 to P 23, and 330 tons standard and 430 tons full load for P 24 to P 29

The Antiploiarhos Laskos (P 20) is lead craft of the 10-strong 'La Combattante III' class of Greek navy fast attack craft. The primary armament comprises four MM.38 Exocet anti-ship missiles in two angled pairs, the gun armament features two 76-mm (3-in) OTO-Melara Compact guns (fore and aft) and four 30-mm cannon in two twin mountings (amidships), and there are also two 533-mm (21-in) torpedo tubes. Ps 24 to 29 have six Penguin missiles in place of the Exocets.

Dimensions: length 56·0 m (183·7 ft); beam 7·9 m (25·9 ft); draught 2·5 m (8·2 ft)
Gun armament: two 76-mm (3-in) L/62 DP OTO-Melara Compact in two single mountings, and four 30-mm AA in two Emerlec twin mountings
Missile armament: four container-launchers for MM.38 Exocet surface-to-surface missiles in P 20 to P 23, and six container-launchers for Penguin Mk 2 surface-to-surface missiles in P 24 to P 29
Torpedo armament: two 533-mm (21-in) tubes
Anti-submarine armament: none
Electronics: one Thomson-CSF Triton surface-search and navigation radar, one Thomson-CSF Vega II SSM fire-control system with Thomson-CSF Castor and Thomson-CSF Pollux tracking radars, and two CSEE Panda optical fire directors
Propulsion: four MTU MD 20V538 TB91 diesels delivering 13,425 kW (18,000 bhp) to four shafts
Performance: maximum speed 35·7 kts; range 3,700 km (2,300 miles) at 15 kts or 1,300 km (810 miles) at 32·6 kts
Complement: 5+37

Class
1. Greece (10)

Name	No.	Builders	Com-missioned
ANTIPLOIARHOS LASKOS	P 20	C.M. de Normandie	Apr 1977
PLOTARHIS BLESSAS	P 21	C.M. de Normandie	July 1977
IPOPLOIARHOS MIKONIOS	P 22	C.M. de Normandie	Feb 1978
IPOPLOIARHOS TROUPAKIS	P 23	C.M. de Normandie	Nov 1977
SIMEOFOROS KAVALOUDIS	P 24	Hellenic Shipyards	July 1980
ANTHIPOPLOIARHOS KOSTAKOS	P 25	Hellenic Shipyards	Sep 1980
IPOPLOIARHOS DEYIANNIS	P 26	Hellenic Shipyards	Dec 1980
SIMEOFOROS XENOS	P 27	Hellenic Shipyards	Mar 1981
SIMEOFOROS SIMITZOPOULOS	P 28	Hellenic Shipyards	June 1981
SIMEOFOROS STARAKIS	P 29	Hellenic Shipyards	Oct 1981

'La Combattante III' fast attack craft (missile)

France/Tunisia
Displacement: 395 tons standard and 425 tons full load
Dimensions: length 56·0 m (183·7 ft); beam 8·2 m (26·9 ft); draught 2·2 m (7·2 ft)
Gun armament: one 76-mm (3-in) L/62 DP OTO-Melara Compact, two 40-mm Breda L/70 AA in a twin mounting, and two 30-mm Oerlikon AA
Missile armament: eight container-launchers for MM.40 Exocet surface-to-surface missiles
Torpedo armament: none
Anti-submarine armament: none
Electronics: navigation and fire-control radars, one CSEE Sylosat navigation system, two CSEE Naja optronic directors, and one CSEE Dagaie chaff launcher
Propulsion: five MTU 20V538 TB93 diesels delivering 14,390 kW (19,300 hp) to four shafts
Performance: maximum speed 38·5 kts; range 3,700 km (2,300 miles) at 15 kts or 1,300 km (810 miles) at 33 kts
Complement: 42

Class
1. Tunisia (0+3)
3 craft on order

'La Combattante IIIB' class fast attack craft (missile)

France/Nigeria
Displacement: 385 tons standard and 430 tons full load
Dimensions: length 56·2 m (184·4 ft); beam 7·6 m (24·9 ft); draught 2·1 m (7 ft)
Gun armament: one 76-mm (3-in) L/62 DP OTO-Melara Compact, two 40-mm Breda L/70 AA in a twin mounting, and four 30-mm AA in Emerlec twin mountings
Missile armament: four container-launchers for MM.38 Exocet surface-to-surface missiles
Torpedo armament: none
Anti-submarine armament: none
Electronics: one Thomson-CSF fire-control radar, and two CSEE Panda optical directors
Propulsion: four MTU 16V956 TB92 diesels delivering 14,915 kW (20,000 shp) to four shafts
Performance: maximum speed 41 kts; range 3,700 km (2,300 miles) at 15 kts
Complement: 42

Class
1. Nigeria (3)

Name	No.	Builders	Com-missioned
SIRI	P 181	C.M.N. Cherbourg	Feb 1981
AYAM	P 182	C.M.N. Cherbourg	June 1981
EKUN	P 183	C.M.N. Cherbourg	Sep 1981

'La Combattante IIIM' class fast attack craft (missile)
France/Qatar
Displacement: 345 tons standard and 395 tons full load
Dimensions: length 56·0 m (183·7 ft); beam 8·2 m (26·9 ft); draught 2·2 m (7·2 ft)
Gun armament: one 76-mm (3-in) L/62 DP OTO-Melara Compact, two 40-mm Breda L/70 AA in a twin mounting, and two 30-mm Oerlikon AA in a twin mounting
Missile armament: eight container-launchers for MM.40 Exocet surface-to-surface missiles
Torpedo armament: none
Anti-submarine armament: none

Electronics: navigation and fire-control radar, two CSEE Panda directors and one CSEE Dagaie chaff launcher
Propulsion: five MTU 20V538 TB93 diesels delivering 14,390 kW (19,300 hp) to four shafts
Performance: maximum speed 38·5 kts
Complement: 6+35
Class
1. Qatar (0+3)
3 craft on order

'Lazaga' class fast attack craft (missile)
Spain
Displacement: 275 tons standard and 400 tons full load
Dimensions: length 58·1 m (190·6 ft); beam 7·6 m (24·9 ft); draught 2·6 m (8·5 ft)
Gun armament: one 76-mm (3-in) L/62 DP OTO-Melara Compact, one 40-mm Breda-Bofors L/70 AA, and two 20-mm Oerlikon GK 204 AA
Missile armament: one quadruple container-launcher for RGM-84A Harpoon surface-to-surface missiles
Torpedo armament: none
Anti-submarine armament: provision for two triple Mk 32 tube mountings for 12·75-in (324-mm) Mk 46 A/S torpedoes, and depth-charge racks
Electronics: one Hollandse Signaalapparaten WM-22 surface-search and target-indication radar, one Raytheon navigation radar, one CSEE optical director, one ELAC hull-mounted sonar, electronic countermeasures suite, and IFF

Propulsion: two MTU-Bazán MA15 TB91 diesels delivering 5,965 kW (8,000 bhp) to two shafts
Performance: maximum speed 30 kts; range 11,300 km (7,020 miles) at 17 kts
Complement: 4+30

Class
1. Spain (6)

Name	No.	Builders	Commissioned
LAZAGA	PC 01	Lürssen	July 1975
ALSEDO	PC 02	Bazán	Feb 1977
CADARSO	PC 03	Bazán	July 1976
VILLAMIL	PC 04	Bazán	Apr 1977
BONIFAZ	PC 05	Bazán	July 1977
RECALDE	PC 06	Bazán	Dec 1977

'Libelle' class fast attack craft (torpedo)
East Germany
Displacement: 30 tons
Dimensions: length 18·0 m (59·1 ft); beam 5·0 m (16·4 ft); draught 1·0 m (3·3 ft)
Gun armament: two 23-mm AA in one twin mounting
Missile armament: none
Torpedo armament: two stern-launching 533-mm (21-in) weapons
Anti-submarine armament: none

Electronics: one surface-search and navigation radar
Propulsion: three diesels delivering 2,685 kW (3,600 hp) to three shafts
Performance: maximum speed 40 kts
Complement: not known
Class
1. East Germany (31)
31 craft (**KARL BAIER** and 30 others)

'Lürssen FPB 38' class fast attack craft (gun)
West Germany
Displacement: 188 tons half load
Dimensions: length 38·5 m (126·3 ft); beam 7·0 m (23 ft); draught 2·2 m (7·2 ft)
Gun armament: two 40-mm Bofors L/70 AA in a twin mounting
Missile armament: none
Torpedo armament: none
Anti-submarine armament: none
Mines: up to ?
Electronics: one navigation and surface-search radar, and one CSEE Lynx

optical director used in conjunction with the Philips Elektronikindustrier 9LV 100 optronic fire-control system
Propulsion: two diesels delivering 6,710 kW (9,000 hp) to two shafts
Performance: maximum speed 32 kts; range 2,050 km (1,275 miles) at 16 kts
Complement: not known

Class
1. Bahrain (2)

Name	No.	Builders	Commissioned
AL RIFFA	—	Lürssen	Aug 1981
HOWAR	—	Lürssen	Nov 1981

'Lürssen FPB 45' class fast attack craft (missile)
West Germany/Ecuador
Displacement: 255 tons
Dimensions: length 45·0 m (147·6 ft); beam 7·0 m (23 ft); draught 2·5 m (8·1 ft)
Gun armament: one 76-mm (3-in) OTO-Melara Compact, and two 35-mm Oerlikon L/90 AA in a twin mounting
Missile armament: four container-launchers for four MM.38 Exocet surface-to-surface missiles
Torpedo armament: none
Anti-submarine armament: none
Electronics: one navigation radar, and one Thomson-CSF Vega fire-control system with Triton and Pollux radars
Propulsion: four MTU diesels delivering 10,440 kW (14,000 hp) to four shafts

Performance: maximum speed 40 kts; range 2,900 km (1,800 miles) at 16 kts
Complement: 35
Class
1. Ecuador (3)

Name	No.	Builders	Commissioned
QUITO	LM 31	Lürssen	July 1976
GUAYAQUIL	LM 32	Lürssen	Dec 1977
CUENCA	LM 33	Lürssen	July 1977

2. Ghana (2)

Name	No.	Builders	Commissioned
DZATA	P 26	Lürssen	July 1980
SEBO	P 27	Lürssen	July 1980

'Lürssen PB 57' class fast attack craft (gun)
West Germany
Displacement: 376 tons full load
Dimensions: length 58·1 m (190·6 ft); beam 7·6 m (25 ft); draught 2·8 m (9·2 ft)
Gun armament: one 76-mm (3-in) L/62 DP OTO-Melara Compact, and one 40-mm Bofors AA
Missile armament: none
Torpedo armament: none
Anti-submarine armament: none
Electronics: one surface-search radar, one navigation radar, and one Thomson-

CSF Canopus fire-control system
Propulsion: three MTU diesels delivering 8,500 kW (11,400 hp) to three shafts
Performance: maximum speed 00 kts
Complement: 60

Class
1. Ghana (2)

Name	No.	Builders	Commissioned
ACHIMOTA	P 28	Lürssen	1980
YOGAGA	P 29	Lürssen	1980

'Lürssen FPB 57' class fast attack craft (missile)

West Germany/Nigeria

Displacement: 410 tons full load

Dimensions: length 58·1 m (190·6 ft); beam 7·6 m (24·9 ft); draught 2·7 m (8·9 ft)

Gun armament: one 76-mm (3-in) L/62 DP OTO-Melara Compact, and two 40-mm Breda L/70 AA and two twin Emerlec 30-mm mountings

Missile armament: four launchers for four Otomat anti-ship missiles

Torpedo armament: none

Anti-submarine armament: none

Electronics: one Hollandse Signaalapparaten WM-28 fire-control radar system

Propulsion: four MTU 16V956 TB92 diesels delivering 15,000 kW (20,115 shp) to two shafts

Performance: maximum speed 42 kts; range 2,400 km (1,490 miles) at 30 kts

Complement: 40

Class

1. Kuwait (2)

2 craft

2. Nigeria (3)

Name	No.	Builders	Commissioned
EKPE	P 178	Lürssen	Aug 1981
DAMISA	P 179	Lürssen	Aug 1981
AGU	P 180	Lürssen	Aug 1981

3. Singapore (3)

3 craft built by Singapore Shipbuiling

4. Turkey (5)

Name	No.	Builders	Commissioned
DOGAN	P 340	Lürssen	June 1977
MARTI	P 341	Taşkizak Naval Yard	July 1978
TAYFUN	P 342	Taşkizak Naval Yard	July 1979
VOLKAN	P 343	Taşkizak Naval Yard	July 1980
GURBET	P 344	Taşkizak Naval Yard	1983

Remarks: Largest standard-hull type produced by Lürssen, perhaps the world's foremost designer of fast attack craft, the 'Lürssen FBP 57' serves with three navies as a missile craft. The specification applies to the Nigerian craft, but all three sub-types are similar in size and propulsion. The Kuwaiti duo have 13,400 kW (17,970 shp) for 36 kts, and the armament of four MM.40 Exocet anti-ship missiles, one 76-mm (3-in) gun and one 40-mm Breda twin mounting has a Philips Elektronikindustrier 9LV 228 fire-control system. The Turkish craft differ in having eight RGM-84A Harpoon anti-ship missiles in two quadruple container-launchers and a secondary gun armament of one 35-mm twin mounting. Singapore's three craft are FAC(G)s with one 76-mm and two 40-mm guns.

'Lürssen TNC 45' class fast attack craft (missile)

West Germany/UAE

Displacement: 230 tons

Dimensions: length 45·0 m (147·6 ft); beam 7·0 m (23 ft); draught 2·3 m (7·5 ft)

Gun armament: one 76-mm (3-in) L/62 DP OTO-Melara Compact, and two 40-mm Breda AA in a twin mounting

Missile armament: four container-launchers for four MM.40 Exocet surface-to-surface missiles

Torpedo armament: none

Anti-submarine armament: none

Electronics: one Philips Elektronikindustrier 9LV 200 Mk 2 surface-search and tracking radar, one Decca navigation radar, one CSEE Panda optical director, one Decca Cutlass electronic countermeasures system, and one CSEE Dagaie chaff launcher

Propulsion: four MTU diesels delivering 10,740 kW (14,400 hp) to four shafts

Performance: maximum speed 40 kts

Complement: 40

Class

1. Argentina (2)

Name	No.	Builders	Commissioned
INTREPIDA	P 85	Lürssen	July 1974
INDOMITA	P 86	Lürssen	Dec 1974

2. Bahrain (0+2)

2 craft on order

3. Indonesia (2)

Name	No.	Builders	Commissioned
BERUANG	652	Lürssen	1959
HARIMAU	654	Lürssen	1960

4. Kuwait (6)

6 craft

5. Singapore (6)

Name	No.	Builders	Commissioned
SEA WOLF	P 76	Lürssen	1972
SEA LION	P 77	Lürssen	1972
SEA DRAGON	P 78	Singapore Shipbuilding & Engineering	1974
SEA TIGER	P 79	Singapore Shipbuilding & Engineering	1974
SEA HAWK	P 80	Singapore Shipbuilding & Engineering	1975
SEA SCORPION	P 81	Singapore Shipbuilding & Engineering	1975

6. Thailand (3)

Name	No.	Builders	Commissioned
PRABPARAPAK	1	Singapore Shipbuilding & Engineering	July 1976
HANHAK SATTRU	2	Singapore Shipbuilding & Engineering	Nov 1976
SUPHAIRIN	3	Singapore Shipbuilding & Engineering	Feb 1977

7. United Arab Emirates (6)

Name	No.	Builders	Commissioned
BANI YAS	4501	Lürssen	Nov 1980
MURBAN	4502	Lürssen	Nov 1980
RADOOM	4503	Lürssen	July 1981
SHAHEEN	4504	Lürssen	July 1981
SAQR	4505	Lürssen	Sep 1981
TAREF	4506	Lürssen	Sep 1981

Remarks: The 'Lürssen TNC 45' is one of the most successful FAC classes yet developed, the specification above applying to the variant in service with the United Arab Emirates. Argentina's two craft were delivered as FAC(G/T)s with one 76-mm and two 40-mm guns and two 533-mm (21-in) torpedo tubes; they are currently being converted to carry Otomat anti-ship missiles. Bahrain's two craft carry four Exocets, one 76-mm (3-in) gun and one twin 40-mm mounting apiece, and have WM-28 fire-control; both craft were delivered from Lürssen by 1984. Indonesia's two craft are FAC(T)s comparable to the West German 'Jaguar' class with four 533-mm (21-in) tubes. Kuwait has accepted all six craft from Lürssen, these having four MM.40 Exocets apiece, plus one 76-mm (3-in) gun and one twin 40-mm mounting plus Philips Elektronikindustrier 9LV 228 fire-control. Singapore's craft have WM-28 fire-control for five Gabriel missiles (one triple and two single launchers), and the gun armament is one 57-mm and one 40-mm gun. The Thai craft are essentially similar to the Singapore navy's six craft.

The layout of Bahrain's 'Lürssen TNC-45' class craft is evident in this example under trial in West Germany: 76-mm (3-in) gun forward, twin 40-mm mounting aft and missile launchers amidships.

'Matka' class fast attack hydrofoil (missile)

USSR

Displacement: 200 tons standard and 230 tons full load
Dimensions: length 39·9m (130·9ft); beam 8·0m (26·2ft); draught 1·8m (5·9ft)
Gun armament: one 76-mm (3-in), and one 30-mm AA in a 'Gatling' mounting
Missile armament: two container-launchers for two SS-N-2C 'Styx' surface-to-surface missiles
Torpedo armament: none
Anti-submarine armament: none

Electronics: one 'Cheese Cake' surface-search radar, one 'Bass Tilt' fire-control radar, one 'High Pole-B' IFF, one 'Square Head' IFF, and chaff launchers
Propulsion: three M503A diesels delivering 8,950kW (12,000hp) to three shafts
Performance: maximum speed 42kts
Complement: 30
Class
1. USSR (17)
17 craft

'Mod' class fast attack craft (missile)

Israel/South Africa

Displacement: 430 tons full load
Dimensions: length 204ft (62·2m); beam 25ft (7·8m); draught 8ft (2·4m)
Gun armament: two 76-mm (3-in) L/62 DP OTO-Melara Compact in single mountings, two 20-mm AA in single mountings, and four 0·5-in (12·7-mm) heavy machine-guns in twin mountings
Missile armament: six container-launchers for six Skorpioen (Gabriel Mk II) surface-to-surface missiles
Torpedo armament: none
Anti-submarine armament: none
Electronics: surface-search radar and ECM suite
Propulsion: four Maybach diesels delivering 8,950kW (12,000hp) to four shafts
Performance: maximum speed 32kts; range 4,200 miles (6,760km) at cruising

speed or 1,725 miles (2,775km) at 30kts
Complement: 47
Class
1. South Africa (8+1+3)

Name	No.	Builders	Commissioned
JAN SMUTS	P 1561	Haifa Shipyard	Sep 1977
P. W. BOTHA	P 1562	Haifa Shipyard	Dec 1977
FREDERIC CRESWELL	P 1563	Haifa Shipyard	May 1978
JIM FOUCHÉ	P 1564	Sandock Austral	Dec 1978
FRANS ERASMUS	P 1565	Sandock Austral	July 1979
OSWALD PIROW	P 1566	Sandock Austral	Mar 1980
HENDRIK MENTZ	P 1567	Sandock Austral	Sep 1982
KOBIE COETZEE	P 1568	Sandock Austral	Mar 1983
—	P 1569	Sandock Austral	—

'Mol' class fast attack craft (torpedo)

USSR

Displacement: 160 tons standard and 200 tons full load
Dimensions: length 39·0m (127·9ft); beam 8·1m (26·6ft); draught 1·8m (5·9ft)
Gun armament: four 30-mm AA in two twin mountings
Missile armament: none
Torpedo armament: four 533-mm (21-in) tubes
Anti-submarine armament: 12 depth charges
Electronics: one 'Pot Drum' surface-search radar, one 'Drum Tilt' fire-control radar, one 'High Pole-B' IFF, and one 'Square Head' IFF
Propulsion: three M504 diesels delivering 11,185kW (15,000hp) to three shafts

Performance: maximum speed 36kts; range 2,300km (1,430 miles) at 14kts
Complement: 3+22
Class
1. Ethiopia (2)
2 craft
2. Somalia (4)
4 craft
3. Sri Lanka (1)

Name	No.
SAMUDRA DEVI	P 3250

'MV 400' class fast attack craft (gun)

Italy/Thailand

Displacement: 450 tons full load
Dimensions: length 60·4m (198·2ft); beam 8·8m (28·9ft); draught 4·5m (14·75ft)
Gun armament: two 76-mm (3-in) L/62 DP OTO-Melara Compact in two single mountings, and two 40-mm AA in one Breda Compact twin mounting
Missile armament: provision for anti-ship missiles in the future
Torpedo armament: none
Anti-submarine armament: none
Electronics: one Hollandse Signaalapparaten WM-22/61 tactical radar, one SMA 3RM navigation radar, one Lirod 8 electro-optical fire-control system, and four

Hycor Mk 135 chaff launchers
Propulsion: three MTU 20V538T B92 diesels delivering 11,175kW (14,985hp) to three shafts
Performance: maximum speed 30kts; range 4,600km (2,860 miles) at 18kts
Complement: 45
Class
1. Thailand (3)

Name	No.	Builders	Commissioned
CHON BURI	1	CN Breda (Venice)	Dec 1982
SONGKHLA	2	CN Breda (Venice)	Jan 1983
PHUKET	3	CN Breda (Venice)	May 1983

'October' class fast attack craft (missile)

Egypt

Displacement: 82 tons full load
Dimensions: length 25·5m (84ft); beam 6·1m (20ft); draught 1·3m (5ft)
Gun armament: four 30-mm AA in two twin mountings
Missile armament: two container-launchers for two Otomat surface-to-surface missiles
Torpedo armament: none
Anti-submarine armament: none
Electronics: one Marconi S810 surface-search radar, and one Marconi/Sperry Sapphire missile-control radar
Propulsion: four CRM 18D/S2 diesels delivering 4,025kW (5,400hp) to four shafts
Performance: maximum speed 40kts; range 750km (465 miles) at 30kts
Complement: 20
Class
1. Egypt (6)
6 craft (nos 207, 208, 209, 210, 211 and 212)

Remarks: The 'October' class FAC(M) is an interesting hybrid, combining the hull of the Soviet 'Komar' class with armament and electronics of Western European manufacture. The armament is relatively light, this being necessitated by the small size and displacement of the class, but in conjunction with high speed and manoeuvrability this still gives the Egyptian craft good capability for coastal operations. The craft were built in Alexandria between 1975 and 1976.

The primary armament of the 'October' class is the pair of Otomat anti-ship missiles located one on each side of the superstructure, but a potent AA and anti-FAC capability is bestowed by the twin 30-mm cannon mountings supplied by the UK, though these lack any form of protection. Located as high as possible for maximum range are the Marconi S 810 surface-search radar and the Marconi/Sperry Sapphire fire-control radar. These craft were refitted in the UK by Vosper Thornycroft between 1979 and 1981.

'Osa I' and 'Osa II' class fast attack craft (missile)

USSR

Displacement: 165 tons standard and 210 tons full load
Dimensions: length 39·0m (127·9ft); beam 7·8m (25·6ft); draught 1·8m (5·9ft)
Gun armament: four 30-mm L/65 AA in two twin mountings
Missile armament: four container-launchers for four SS-N-2A 'Styx' ('Osa I') or SS-N-2C 'Styx' ('Osa II') surface-to-surface missiles, and (on some craft) one quadruple launcher for SA-N-5 surface-to-air missiles
Torpedo armament: none
Anti-submarine armament: none
Electronics: one 'Square Tie' surface-search radar, one 'Drum Tilt' gun-control radar, one 'High Pole' IFF, and two 'Square Head' IFFs
Propulsion: three diesels (M503A in 'Osa I' and M504 in 'Osa II') delivering 8,950kW (12,000bhp) in 'Osa I' and 11,185kW (15,000bhp) in 'Osa II' to three shafts
Performance: maximum speed 38kts in 'Osa I' and 40kts in 'Osa II'; range 1,500km (930 miles) at 30kts or 925km (575 miles) at 35kts
Complement: 30

The 'Osa I' class was built in the USSR during the early 1980s specifically for coastal defence with the SS-N-2A anti-ship missile, whose container-launchers are seen in the photograph. The improved 'Osa II' class followed in the late 1960s.

Class

1. Algeria (3 'Osa I' and 9 'Osa II')
3 'Osa I' class craft
9 'Osa II' class craft

2. Benin (2 'Osa I')
2 'Osa I' class craft

3. Bulgaria (3 'Osa I' and 1 'Osa II')
3 'Osa I' class craft
1 'Osa II' class craft

4. China (115)
115 Soviet and locally-built 'Huangfen' class craft

5. Cuba (5 'Osa I' and 13 'Osa II')
5 'Osa I' class craft
13 'Osa II' class craft

6. East Germany (15 'Osa I')
Name
ALBERT GAST
ALBIN KOBIS
ANTON SAFEKOW*
AUGUST LUTTGENS
FRIEDRICH SCHULZE*
FRITZ GAST
HEINRICH DORRENBACH
JOSEF SCHARES
KARL MESBERG
MAX REICHPIETSCH
OTTO TOST
PAUL EISENSCHNEIDER
PAUL WIECZOREK
RICHARD SORGE
RUDOLF EGELHOFER
*training craft

7. Egypt (8 'Osa I')
8 'Osa I' class craft (nos 301, 312, 323, 341, 356, 378, 389 and 390)

8. Ethiopia (3 'Osa II')
3 'Osa II' class craft

9. India (8 'Osa I' and 8 'Osa II')

Name	No.
VEER	K 82
VIDYUT	K 83
VIJETA	K 84
VINASH	K 85
NIPAT	K 86
NASHAT	K 87
NIRBHIK	K 88
NIRGHAT	K 89
*PRACHAND	K 90
*PRALAYA	K 91
*PRATAP	K 92
*PRABAL	K 93
*CHAPAL	K 94
*CHAMAK	K 95
*CHATAK	K 96
*CHARAG	K 97

*'Osa II' craft

10. Iraq (4 'Osa I' and 8 'Osa II')

Name	No.
HAZIRANI*	—
KANUN ATH-THANI*	6
NISAN*	7
TAMUZ*	17
SA'D	—
KHALID IBN	—
AL WALID	—

Plus 5 others
*'Osa I' craft

11. Libya (12 'Osa II')
12 'Osa II' class craft (nos 952, 953, 954, 955, 956 and seven others)

12. North Korea (8 'Osa I' + 8 'Soju')
8 'Osa I' and 8 locally-built 'Soju' class craft

13. Poland (13 'Osa I')
13 'Osa I' craft (nos 421-433)

14. Romania (5 'Osa I')
5 'Osa I' craft (nos 194-198)

15. Somalia (2 'Osa II')
2 'Osa II' class craft

16. South Yemen (6 'Osa II')
6 'Osa II' class craft

17. Syria (6 'Osa I' and 6 'Osa II')
6 'Osa I' class craft (nos 21-26)
6 'Osa II' class craft

18. USSR (70 'Osa I' and 50 'Osa II')
70 'Osa I' class craft
50 'Osa II' class craft

19. Vietnam (8 'Osa II')
8 'Osa II' class craft

20. Yugoslavia (10 'Osa I')

Name	NO.
MITAR ACEV	RC 301
VLADO BAGAT	RC 302
PETAR DRAPŠIN	RC 303
STEVO FILIPOVIĆ	RC 304
ŽIKICA JOVANOVIĆ-ŠPANAC	RC 305
NIKOLA MARTINOVIĆ	RC 306
JOSIP MAŽAR SOSA	RC 307
KARLO ROJC	RC 308
FRANC ROZMAN-STANE	RC 309
VELIMIR ŠKORPIK	RC 310

'P 4' class fast attack craft (torpedo)

USSR

Displacement: 22 tons standard and 25 tons full load
Dimensions: length 19·0m (62·3ft); beam 3·3m (10·8ft); draught 1·0m (3·3ft)
Gun armament: two 14·5-mm (0·57-in) heavy machine-guns in a twin mounting
Missile armament: none
Torpedo armament: two 457-mm (18-in) tubes
Anti-submarine armament: none
Electronics: one 'Skin Head' surface-search radar, one 'High Pole' IFF, and one 'Dead Duck' IFF
Propulsion: two M50 diesels delivering 1,790kW (2,400bhp) to two shafts
Performance: maximum speed 42kts; range 760km (475 miles) at 30kts
Complement: 12

A 'P 4' class fast attack craft (torpedo) of the North Korean navy.

Class

1. Albania (12)
12 craft (nos 111, 115, 304 and nine others)

2. Benin (2)
2 craft

3. Bulgaria (4)
4 craft

4. China (60)
60 craft

5. Cuba (12)
12 craft

6. Egypt (4)
4 craft

7. North Korea (12)
12 craft

8. North Yemen (4)
4 craft

9. Romania (6)
6 craft (nos 87-92)

10. Syria (8)
8 craft

11. Tanzania (4)
4 craft (nos JW 981-984)

12. Zaire (3)
3 craft

'P 6' class fast attack craft (torpedo)

USSR
Displacement: 64 tons standard and 73 tons full load
Dimensions: length 26·0 m (85·3 ft); beam 6·1 m (20 ft); draught 1·5 m (4·9 ft)
Gun armament: four 25-mm AA in two twin mountings
Missile armament: none
Torpedo armament: two 533-mm (21-in) tubes

Anti-submarine armament: none
Electronics: one 'Pot Head' surface-search radar, one 'High Pole-A' IFF, and one 'Dead Duck' IFF
Propulsion: four M50 diesels delivering 3,580 kW (4,800 hp) to four shafts
Performance: maximum speed 45 kts; range 1,125 km (700 miles) at 30 kts
Complement: 15

Class
1. Algeria (4)
4 craft (nos 631-634)
2. China (65)
65 craft
3. Cuba (6)
6 craft
4. Egypt (20)
20 craft
5. Equatorial Guinea (1)
1 craft
6. Guinea (4)
4 craft
7. Guinea-Bissau (1)
1 craft

8. Iraq (12)
Name
AL ADRISI
AL BAHI
AL SHAAB
AL TAMI
ALEF
IBN SAID
LAMAKI
RAMADAN
SHULAB
TAMUR
TĀREQ BEN ZAID
Plus one other

9. North Korea (64 'P 6' and 8 'Sinpo')
64 'P 6' class craft
8 'Sinpo' class craft
10. Somalia (4)
4 craft
11. South Yemen (2)
2 craft (nos 111 and 112)
12. Tanzania (3)
3 craft

'P 400' class fast attack craft (missile)

France
Displacement: 425 tons full load
Dimensions: length 54·0 m (177·2 ft); beam 8·0 m (26·25 ft); draught 2·6 m (8·5 ft)
Gun armament: one 40-mm AA, and one 20-mm AA
Missile armament: two single container-launchers for two MM.38 Exocet anti-ship missiles
Torpedo armament: none
Anti-submarine armament: none
Electronics: surface-search and navigation radars
Propulsion: two Alsthorn-Atlantique diesels delivering 6,560 kW (8,800 hp) to two shafts

Performance: maximum speed 26 kts; range 7,400 km (4,600 miles) at 15 kts
Complement: 3 + 10 + 11

Class
1. France (0 + 4 + 4)
four craft building and a further four ordered from CMN Cherbourg

Remarks: Designed for coastal patrol with limited anti-ship capability, the 'P 400' class is currently under review, though the first craft started trials early in 1984.

'Patra' class fast attack craft (missile)

France
Displacement: 115 tons standard and 130 tons full load
Dimensions: length 37·0 m (121·4 ft); beam 5·5 m (18 ft); draught 1·6 m (5·2 ft)
Gun armament: one 40-mm Bofors AA, and one 12·7-mm (0·5-in) heavy machine-gun
Missile armament: six SS.12 surface-to-surface missiles
Torpedo armament: none
Anti-submarine armament: none
Electronics: navigation radar
Propulsion: two AGO V12 CZSHR diesels delivering 2,985 kW (4,000 hp) to two shafts
Performance: maximum speed 26 kts; range 3,250 km (2,020 miles) at 10 kts or 1,400 km (870 miles) at 20 kts
Complement: 1 + 17

Class
1. France (4)

Name	No.	Builders	Commissioned
TRIDENT	P 670	Auroux	Dec 1976
GLAIVE	P 671	Auroux	Apr 1977
ÉPÉE	P 672	C.M.N. Cherbourg	Oct 1976
PERTUISANE	P 673	C.M.N. Cherbourg	Jan 1977

2. Ivory Coast (2)

Name	No.	Builders	Commissioned
L'ARDENT	—	Auroux	Oct 1978
L'INTREPIDE	—	Auroux	Oct 1978

Remarks: The craft of the Ivory Coast navy are similar to the French units apart from possessing a missile armament of four MM.40 Exocet anti-ship missiles.

'Pauk' class fast attack craft (patrol)

USSR
Displacement: 700 tons full load
Dimensions: length 57·0 m (1870 ft); beam 10·5 m (34·4 ft); draught 2·0 m (6·6 ft)
Gun armament: one 76-mm (3-in) L/59 DP, and one 30-mm AA in a 'Gatling' mounting
Missile armament: one quadruple launcher for SA-N-5 surface-to-air missiles
Torpedo armament: none
Anti-submarine armament: two RBU 1200 five-barrel rocket-launchers, and four 406-mm (16-in) tubes for A/S torpedoes
Electronics: one 'Plank Shave' combined air- and surface-search radar, one 'Bass Tilt' gun-control radar, electronic warfare systems, IFF, and variable-depth sonar

Propulsion: two diesels delivering 8,950 kW (12,000 hp) to two shafts
Performance: maximum speed 26 kts
Complement: about 80

Class
1. USSR (10 + ?)
10 craft plus ? on order

Remarks: Designed to replace the 'Poti' class, the 'Pauk' class is evidently based on the 'Tarantul' class missile corvette, but optimized for anti-submarine warfare with a longer stern for variable-depth sonar. The first was commissioned in 1979, and production continues on a steady basis.

'Pegasus' class fast attack hydrofoil (missile)
USA
Displacement: 240 tons full load

Dimensions: length 132·9ft (40·5m) with foils extended and 145·3ft (44·3m) with foils retracted; beam 47·5ft (14·5m) with foils extended and 28·2ft (8·6m) with foils

The Taurus (PHM 3) rides high on her three-point foils.

retracted; draught 23·2ft (7·1m) with foils extended and 7·5ft (2·3m) with foils retracted

Gun armament: one 76-mm (3-in) L/62 DP OTO-Melara Compact in a Mk 75 single mounting

Missile armament: two twin container-launchers for four RGM-84A Harpoon surface-to-surface missiles

Torpedo armament: none

Anti-submarine armament: none

Electronics: one SMA 3TM20-H2 navigation radar, one Mk 94 (PHM 1) or Mk 92 (others) fire-control radar system, and one Mk 34 Chaffroc rapid-blooming overhead chaff launcher

Propulsion: two MTU 8V331 TC81 diesels delivering 1,195kW (1,600bhp) to two waterjets for hullborne operation, and one General Electric LM 2500 gas turbine delivering 18,000shp (13,425kW) to Aerojet waterjets for foilborne operation

Performance: maximum speed 48kts foilborne and 12kts hullborne; range 1,950 miles (3,140km) at 9kts and 800 miles (1,285km) at 40kts

Complement: 4+17

Class
1. USA (6)			Commissioned
Name	No.	Builders	
PEGASUS	PHM 1	Boeing Co	July 1977
HERCULES	PHM 2	Boeing Co	July 1982
TAURUS	PHM 3	Boeing Co	Oct 1981
AQUILA	PHM 4	Boeing Co	Dec 1981
ARIES	PHM 5	Boeing Co	Apr 1982
GEMINI	PHM 6	Boeing Co	June 1982

'Perdana' class fast attack craft (missile)
France/Malaysia
Displacement: 234 tons standard and 265 tons full load

Dimensions: length 47·0m (154·2ft); beam 7·0m (23·1ft); draught 3·9m (12·8ft)

Gun armament: one 57-mm Bofors L/70, and one 40-mm Bofors L/70 AA

Missile armament: two container-launchers for two MM.38 Exocet surface-to-surface missiles

Torpedo armament: none

Anti-submarine armament: none

Electronics: one Thomson-CSF Triton surface-search radar, and one Thomson-CSF Pollux fire-control radar both used in conjunction with a Thomson-CSF Vega weapon-control system

Propulsion: three MTU MB 870 diesels delivering 6,050kW (10,800hp) to three shafts

Performance: maximum speed 36·5kts; range 1,500km (930 miles) at 25kts

Complement: 5+30

Class
1. Malaysia (4)			Commissioned
Name	No.	Builders	
PERDANA	P 3501	C.M. de Normandie	Dec 1972
SERANG	P 3502	C.M. de Normandie	Jan 1973
GANAS	P 3503	C.M. de Normandie	Feb 1973
GANYANG	P 3504	C.M. de Normandie	Mar 1973

'Poti' class fast attack craft (patrol)
USSR
Displacement: 500 tons standard and 580 tons full load

Dimensions: length 60·0m (196·8ft); beam 8·0m (26·2ft); draught 2·8m (9·2ft)

Gun armament: two 57-mm L/80 DP in one twin mounting

Missile armament: none

Torpedo armament: none

Anti-submarine armament: two RBU 6000 12-barrel rocket-launchers, and four 406-mm (16-in) tubes for A/S torpedoes

Electronics: one 'Strut Curve' air-search radar, one 'Spin Trough' navigation radar, one 'Muff Cob' gun-control radar, one 'High Pole-B' IFF, and one hull-mounted high-frequency sonar

Propulsion: CODAG (COmbined Diesel And Gas turbine) arrangement, with two M503A diesels delivering 5,965kW (8,000shp) and two gas turbines

delivering 22,370kW (30,000shp) to two shafts

Performance: maximum speed 35kts; range 11,125km (6,915 miles) at 10kts, or 4,800km (2,985 miles) at 16kts, or 925km (575 miles) at 34kts

Complement: 80

Class
1. Bulgaria (3)	3. USSR (62)
3 craft (nos 33, 34 and 35)	62 craft
2. Romania (3)	
3 craft (nos V 31, V 32 and V 33)	

Remarks: The 'Poti' class was built between 1961 to 1968 especially for the coastal anti-submarine role, in which it was moderately successful though only in conditions of friendly air superiority as it lacked adequate AA armament.

'PR 72M' and 'PR 72S' class attack craft (gun)
France
Displacement: 375 tons standard and 445 tons full load

Dimensions: length 57·5m (188·8ft); beam 7·6m (25ft); draught 2·1m (7·1ft)

Gun armament: one 76-mm (3-in) L/62 DP OTO-Melara Compact, and one 40-mm Breda L/70

Missile armament: provision for MM.38/MM.40 Exocet surface-to-surface missiles

Torpedo armament: none

Anti-submarine armament: none

Electronics: one Thomson-CSF Triton surface-search radar, and one Thomson-CSF Pollux tracking radar both integrated with the Thomson-CSF Vega weapon-control system

Propulsion: four AGO diesels delivering 8,235kW (11,040hp) to four shafts

Performance: maximum speed 28kts; range 4,650km (2,890 miles) at 16kts

Complement: 5+48

Class
1. Morocco (2+2)			Commissioned
Name	No.	Builders	
OKBA	33	Société Française de Constructions Navales	Dec 1976
TRIKI	34	Société Française de Constructions Navales	July 1977

2. Senegambia (1)			Commissioned
Name	No.	Builders	
NJAMBUUR	—	Société Française de Constructions Navales	1982

Remarks: The Moroccan 'PR 72M' and Senegambian 'PR 72S' classes are closely similar, though the single Senegambian vessel is slightly heavier in its displacement, and is dimensionally slightly larger with a length of 58·7m (192·5ft) for a deeper draught on the same beam. The armament differs slightly more, the Senegambian vessel having two 76-mm (3-in) L/62 DP OTO-Melara and two 20-mm F2 guns plus no provision for missiles. The electronics suite is also less capable than that of the Moroccan vessels.

'PR 72P' class fast attack craft (missile)

France

Displacement: 470 tons standard and 560 tons full load
Dimensions: length 64·0m (210ft); beam 8·4m (27·4ft); draught 1·6m (5·2ft)
Gun armament: one 76-mm (3-in) L/62 DP OTO-Melara Compact, two 40-mm Breda L/70 AA in a twin mounting, and two 20-mm Oerlikon AA
Missile armament: four container-launchers for four MM.38 Exocet surface-to-surface missiles
Torpedo armament: none
Anti-submarine armament: none
Electronics: one Thomson-CSF Triton surface-search radar, and one Thomson-CSF Castor II weapon-control radar both used in conjunction with the Thomson-CSF Vega weapon fire-control system, one Decca TM 1226 navigation radar, and one CSEE Panda director
Propulsion: four SACM/AGO 240 V16 diesels delivering 16,404kW (22,000shp) to four shafts
Performance: maximum speed 34kts; range 4,625km (2,875 miles) at 16kts
Complement: 36

Class

1. Peru (6)			
Name	No.	Builders	Commissioned
VELARDE	P 21	Société Française de Constructions Navales	July 1980
SANTILLANA	P 22	Société Française de Constructions Navales	July 1980
DE LOS HEROS	P 23	Société Française de Constructions Navales	Nov 1980
HERRERA	P 24	Société Française de Constructions Navales	Feb 1981
LARREA	P 25	Société Française de Constructions Navales	June 1981
SANCHEZ CARRION	P 26	Société Française de Constructions Navales	Sep 1981

Remarks: The 'PR 72P' class is a scaled-up version of the 'PR 72M' and 'PR 72S' classes, the additional size and displacement making possible the carriage of effective DP and AA gun armaments in addition to the four single container-launchers for Exocet anti-ship missiles. Considerably greater power provides much enhanced speed despite the greater displacement. The hulls were built in two places, those of Ps 21, 23 and 25 by Lorient Naval Yard, while those of Ps 22, 24 and 26 were built at Villeneuve-la-Garonne. The sensor fit is good by Latin American standards.

'President' class fast attack craft (missile)

France/Gabon

Displacement: 150 tons
Dimensions: length 42b1.0m (138ft); beam 7b1.7m (25·3ft); draught 1b1.9m (6·5ft)
Gun armament: one 40-mm Bofors AA, and one 20-mm AA
Missile armament four SS.12M surface-to-surface missiles
Torpedo armament: none
Anti-submarine armament: none

Electronics: one navigation radar
Propulsion: three MTU 20V672 TY90 diesels delivering 7,050kW (9,450hp) to three shafts
Performance: maximum speed 38·5kts; range 2,780km (1,725 miles) at 15kts
Complement: 3+17

Class

1. Gabon (1)			
Name	No.	Builders	Commissioned
PRESIDENT EL HADJ OMAR BONGO	P 10	Ch. N. de l'Esterel	Aug 1978

'PSMM Mk 5' class fast attack craft (missile)

USA/South Korea

Displacement: 250 tons full load
Dimensions: length 165ft (50·3m); beam 24ft (7·3m); draught 9·5ft (2·9m)
Gun armament: one 3-in (76-mm) L/50 DP in a Mk 34 mounting, one 40-mm AA, and two 0·5-in (12·7-mm) machine-guns
Missile armament: four Standard launchers for eight RGM-84A Harpoon surface-to-surface missiles
Torpedo armament: none
Anti-submarine armament: none
Electronics: surface-search/navigation radar
Propulsion: six Avco Lycoming TF35 gas turbines delivering 16,800hp (12,535kW) to two shafts
Performance: maximum speed 40+ kts; range 2,750 miles (4,425km) at 18kts
Complement: 5+27

Class

1. Indonesia (4+4)			
Name	No.	Builders	Commissioned
RENCONG	621	Tacoma B.B. Co	Oct 1979
MANDAU	622	Tacoma B.B. Co	Oct 1979
BADIK	623	Tacoma B.B. Co	1980
KERIS	624	Tacoma B.B. Co	1980

2. Philippines (3)
3 craft

3. South Korea (8)			
Name	No.	Builders	Commissioned
PAEK KU 52	PGM 352	Tacoma B.B. Co	Mar 1975
PAEK KU 53	PGM 353	Tacoma B.B. Co	Mar 1975
PAEK KU 55	PGM 355	Tacoma B.B. Co	Feb 1976
PAEK KU 56	PGM 356	Tacoma B.B. Co	Feb 1976
PAEK KU 57	PGM 357	Tacoma B.B. Co	1977
PAEK KU 58	PGM 358	Tacoma B.B. Co	1977
PAEK KU 59	PGM 359	Tacoma B.B. Co	1977
PAEK KU 61	PGM 361	Tacoma B.B. Co	1978

4. Taiwan (2+2)			
Name	No.	Builders	Commissioned
LUNG CHIANG	PGG 581	Tacoma B.B. Co	1979
SUI CHIANG	PGG 582	China Shipbuilding Corporation	1979

Remarks: The Indonesian boats each have four Exocets, a 57-mm Bofors and a 40-mm Bofors gun, and Dutch electronics; the Filipino craft are essentially similar. Taiwan's craft have two Hsiung Fen missiles, a 76-mm (3-in) gun and twin 35-mm guns.

'Province' class fast attack craft (missile)

UK/Oman

Displacement: about 420 tons full load

The Dhofar (B 8) is the lead craft of the three-strong and highly potent 'Province' class, and is seen here on trials before the installation of the missile units.

Dimensions: length 186ft (56·7m); beam 26·9ft (8·2m); draught 8·9ft (2·7m)
Gun armament: one 76-mm (3-in) L/62 DP OTO-Melara Compact, and two 40-mm Breda L/70 AA in a twin mounting
Missile armament: two triple container-launchers for six MM.40 Exocet surface-to-surface missiles
Torpedo armament: none
Anti-submarine armament: none
Electronics: Plessey AWS 4 search radar, and Sperry Sea Archer fire-control system
Propulsion: four Paxman Valenta diesels delivering 18,200hp (13,570kW) to four shafts
Performance: maximum speed 40kts
Complement: 59, including 19 passengers/trainees

Class

1. Oman (2+1)			
Name	No.	Builders	Commissioned
DHOFAR	B 8	Vosper Thornycroft Ltd	1982
AL SHARQIYAH	B 9	Vosper Thornycroft Ltd	1983
AL BATNAH	B 10	Vosper Thornycroft Ltd	1984

'Ratcharit' class fast attack craft (missile)

Thailand/Italy
Displacement: 235 tons standard and 270 tons full load
Dimensions: length 49·8m (163·4ft); beam 7·5m (24·6ft); draught 2·3m (7·5ft)
Gun armament: one 76-mm (3-in) L/62 DP OTO-Melara Compact, and one 40-mm Breda L/70 AA
Missile armament: four container-launchers for four MM.38 Exocet surface-to-surface missiles
Torpedo armament: none
Anti-submarine armament: none
Electronics: one navigation radar, and one Hollandse Signaalapparaten WM-20

series fire-control radar system
Propulsion: three MTU diesels delivering 10,065kW (13,500hp) to three shafts
Performance: maximum speed 37kts; range 3,700km (2,300 miles) at 15kts
Complement: 45

Class
| 1. Thailand (3) | | | Com- |
Name	No.	Builders	missioned
RATCHARIT	4	C. N. Breda	Aug 1979
WITTHAYAKHOM	5	C. N. Breda	Nov 1979
UDOMDET	6	C. N. Breda	Feb 1980

'Ramadan' class fast attack craft (missile)

UK/Egypt
Displacement: 312 tons
Dimensions: length 170·6ft (52·0m); beam 25ft (7·6m); draught 6·6ft (2·0m)
Gun armament: one 76-mm (3-in) L/62 DP OTO-Melara Compact, and two 40-mm Breda L/70 AA in a twin mounting
Missile armament: four container-launchers for four Otomat surface-to-surface missiles
Torpedo armament: none
Anti-submarine armament: none
Electronics: one Marconi S 820 surface-search radar, one Marconi/Sperry Sapphire gun fire-control system, and one Ferranti Computer-Assisted Action Information System

Propulsion: four MTU diesels delivering 12,790kW (17,150hp) to four shafts
Performance: maximum speed 40kts; range 3,700km (2,300 miles) at 16kts
Complement: 40

Class
| 1. Egypt (6) | | | Com- |
Name	No.	Builders	missioned
RAMADAN	561	Vosper Thornycroft Ltd	1981
KHYBER	562	Vosper Thornycroft Ltd	1982
EL KADESSEYA	563	Vosper Thornycroft Ltd	1982
EL YARMOUK	564	Vosper Thornycroft Ltd	1982
HETTEIN	565	Vosper Thornycroft Ltd	1982
BADR	566	Vosper Thornycroft Ltd	1982

'Saar 2' class fast attack craft (missile)

Israel
Displacement: 220 tons standard and 250 tons full load
Dimensions: length 45·0m (147·6ft); beam 7·0m (23ft); draught 2·5m (8·2ft)
Gun armament: between one and three 40-mm Breda AA in single mountings
Missile armament: between two and eight Gabriel surface-to-surface missiles (in two single and two triple container-launchers) depending on the gun armament fitted, the two triple missile container-launchers being trainable units installed on the ring mountings for the two after 40-mm mountings
Torpedo armament: none
Anti-submarine armament: up to four Mk 32 tubes for 12·75-in (324-mm) Mk 46 A/S torpedoes if no triple missile container-launchers are carried
Electronics: one Thomson-CSF Neptune surface-search radar, one Selenia Orion RTN-10X fire-control radar system, comprehensive electronic countermeasure systems, and one EDO 780 variable-depth sonar
Propulsion: four Maybach 871 diesels delivering 10,065kW (13,500bhp) to four shafts
Performance: maximum speed 40+ kts; range 4,625km (2,875 miles) at 15kts, or 2,965km (1,840 miles) at 20kts, or 1,850km (1,150 miles) at 30kts
Complement: between 35 and 40

Class
| 1. Israel (6) | | | Com- |
Name	No.	Builders	missioned
MIVTACH	311	Chantiers de Normandie	1968
MIZNAG	312	Chantiers de Normandie	1968
MIFGAV	313	Chantiers de Normandie	1968
EILATH	321	Chantiers de Normandie	1968
HAIFA	322	Chantiers de Normandie	1968
AKKO	323	Chantiers de Normandie	1968

As delivered to Israel in 1969, this 'Saar' class FAC was a 'Saar 1' class FAC(G) with an armament of three 40-mm guns (one forward of the bridge and two aft). She was subsequently modified to the 'Saar 2' configuration illustrated, with one 40-mm gun and a maximum of eight Gabriel anti-ship missiles (two in single fixed container-launchers forward of the bridge and six in two triple container-launchers on trainable mountings installed on the rings for the previously-fitted after 40-mm guns). The Israeli craft are fitted with advanced radar and fire-control systems, plus indigenously-developed electronic warfare systems.

Remarks: The 'Saar 2' class retains anti-submarine capability, the provision of sonar making possible effective use of the four Mk 46 torpedoes that can be shipped.

'Saar 3' class fast attack craft (missile)

Israel
Displacement: 220 tons standard and 250 tons full load
Dimensions: length 45·0m (147·6ft); beam 7·0m (23ft); draught 2·5m (8·2ft)
Gun armament: one 76-mm (3-in) L/62 DP OTO-Melara Compact, and up to two 40-mm Breda AA in single mountings
Missile armament: between two and eight Gabriel surface-to-surface missiles (in two single and two triple container-launchers) depending on the gun armament fitted, the two triple missile container-launchers being trainable units installed on the ring mountings for the two after 40-mm mountings
Torpedo armament: none
Anti-submarine armament: none
Electronics: one Thomson-CSF Neptune surface-search radar, one Selenia Orion RTN-10X fire-control radar system, one EDO 780 variable-depth sonar, and comprehensive electronic countermeasure systems
Propulsion: four Maybach 871 diesels delivering 10,065kW (13,500bhp) to four shafts

Performance: maximum speed 40+ kts; range 4,625km (2,875 miles) at 15kts, or 2,965km (1,840 miles) at 20kts, or 1,850km (1,150 miles) at 30kts
Complement: between 35 and 40

Class
| 1. Israel (6) | | | Com- |
Name	No.	Builders	missioned
SAAR	331	Chantiers de Normandie	1969
SOUFA	332	Chantiers de Normandie	1969
GAASH	333	Chantiers de Normandie	1969
HEREV	341	Chantiers de Normandie	1969
HANIT	342	Chantiers de Normandie	1969
HETZ	343	Chantiers de Normandie	1969

Remarks: Like the 'Saar 2' class designed in West Germany but built in France for political reasons, the 'Saar 3' class features more powerful gun armament (single 76-mm/3-in gun forward instead of a 40-mm weapon) but has no anti-submarine capability. Standard missile fit is six Gabriels in two triple units aft.

'Saar 4' class fast attack craft (missile)

Israel

Displacement: 415 tons standard and 450 tons full load
Dimensions: length 58·0m (190·6ft); beam 7·6m (25ft); draught 2·4m (8ft)
Gun armament: two 76-mm (3-in) L/62 DP OTO-Melara Compact in single mountings, and two 20-mm Oerlikon AA
Missile armament: four container-launchers for four RGM-84A Harpoon surface-to-surface missiles, and five container-launchers for five Gabriel Mk 2 surface-to-surface missiles
Torpedo armament: none
Anti-submarine armament: none
Aircraft: one light helicopter on a platform aft (*Tarshish* only, which has thus lost its after 76-mm/3-in gun)
Electronics: one Thomson-CSF Neptune surface-search radar, one Selenia Orion RTN-10X fire-control radar system, one Elta MN-53 electronic support measures system, four large and 72 small chaff launchers, and (except in *Yaffo*) one ELAC hull-mounted sonar
Propulsion: four Maybach 871 diesels delivering 10,440kW (14,000hp) to four shafts
Performance: maximum speed 32kts; range 7,400km (4,600 miles) at 17·5kts or 3,075km (1,910 miles) at 30kts
Complement: 45

Class

1. Chile (2)

Name	No.	Builders	Commissioned
CASMA	—	Haifa Shipyard	Mar 1974
CHIPANA	—	Haifa Shipyard	Oct 1973

2. Israel (8)

Name	No.	Builders	Commissioned
RESHEF	—	Haifa Shipyard	Apr 1973
KIDON	—	Haifa Shipyard	Sep 1974
TARSHISH	—	Haifa Shipyard	Mar 1975
YAFFO	—	Haifa Shipyard	Apr 1975
NITZHON	—	Haifa Shipyard	Mar 1979
KOMEMIUT	—	Haifa Shipyard	Oct 1979
ATSMOUT	—	Haifa Shipyard	Nov 1979
MOLEDET	—	Haifa Shipyard	mid-1980

Remarks: A logical development of the 'Saar 2' and 'Saar 3' classes, the 'Saar 4' class developed in Israel carries an extremely powerful blend of anti-ship missiles in the form of medium-range Gabriels and long-range Harpoons, plus two of the useful OTO-Melara Compact 76-mm (3-in) guns and a comprehensive suite of Israeli-produced sensors and electronic warfare systems. The *Tarshish* has a helicopter platform in place of the after gun, paving the way for such an installation in the first units of the 'Saar 4.5' class.

'Saar 4·5' class fast attack craft (missile)

Israel

Displacement: 488 tons
Dimensions: length 61·7m (202·4ft); beam 7·6m (25ft); draught 2·5m (8·2ft)
Gun armament: one 40-mm Breda AA (to be replaced by a 30-mm PCM 30 mounting), two 20-mm Oerlikon AA, and four 0·5-in (12·7-mm) heavy machine-guns
Missile armament: four container-launchers for four RGM-84A Harpoon surface-to-surface missiles, four container-launchers for four Gabriel Mk 2 surface-to-surface missiles, and a surface-to-air missile system on the hangar roof
Torpedo armament: none
Anti-submarine armament: helicopter-launched weapons (see below)
Aircraft: one Bell Model 205 helicopter in a hangar amidships
Electronics: one Thomson-CSF Neptune surface-search radar, one Selenia Orion RTN-10X fire-control radar system, one Elta MN-53 electronic support measures system, four large and 72 small chaff launchers, and one ELAC hull-mounted sonar
Propulsion: four Maybach 871 diesels delivering 10,440kW (14,000hp) to four shafts
Performance: maximum speed 31kts
Complement: 53

Class

1. Israel (4+2)

Name	No.	Builders	Commissioned
ALIA	—	Haifa Shipyard	end 1980
GEOULA	—	Haifa Shipyard	mid-1981
ROMACH	—	Haifa Shipyard	late 1981
KESHET	—	Haifa Shipyard	mid-1982

Remarks: Evolved from the 'Saar 4' class, the 'Saar 4.5' class was designed to provide extra long-range punch for the Israeli navy by the carriage of an embarked helicopter for mid-course missile guidance and for anti-submarine operations. However, the helicopter installation proved only moderately successful and was thus fitted only in the *Alia* and *Geoula*, later ships having a 76-mm (3-in) OTO-Melara Compact gun and four extra Gabriel launchers in the helicopter facility's place. It is believed that a Phalanx CIWS mounting has been added forward of the superstructure in all units of the class.

'Shanghai Types II, III and IV' class fast attack craft (gun)

China

Displacement: 120 tons standard and 155 tons full load
Dimensions: length 39·0m (128ft); beam 5·5m (18ft); draught 1·7m (5·6ft)
Gun armament: four 37-mm L/63 AA in two twin mountings and four 25-mm L/80 AA in two twin mountings for Type II, or two 57-mm L/70 AA in one twin mounting and one 25-mm L/80 AA for Types III and IV; some craft have a twin 75-mm Type 56 recoilless rifle installation
Missile armament: none
Torpedo armament: none
Anti-submarine armament: eight depth charges
Mines: up to 10
Electronics: one 'Skin Head' or 'Pot Head' surface-search radar, one hull-mounted sonar, and (in some craft) one variable-depth sonar
Propulsion: four diesels delivering 3,580kW (4,800bhp) to four shafts
Performance: maximum speed 30kts; range 1,500km (930 miles) at 17kts
Complement: 25

Class

1. Albania (6 'Shanghai II')
6 craft (nos 101-106)

2. Bangladesh (4 'Shanghai II')

Name
SHAHEED DAULAT
SHAHEED FARID
SHAHEED MOHIBULLAH
SHAHEED AKHTARUDDIN

3. Cameroon (2 'Shanghai II')
2 craft

4. China (305 'Shanghai II, III and IV')
305 craft

5. Congo (3 'Shanghai II')
3 craft

6. Guinea (6 'Shanghai II')
6 craft (nos P733-P736 and two others)

7. North Korea (8 'Shanghai II')
8 craft

8. Pakistan (12 'Shanghai II')

Name	No.
QUETTA	P 141
LAHORE	P 142
MARDAN	P 143
GILGIT	P 144
PISHIN	P 145
SUKKUR	P 147
SEHWAN	P 148
BAHAWALPUR	P 149
BANNU	P 154
KALAT	P 156
LARKANA	P 157
SAHIWAL	P 160

9. Romania (20 'Shanghai II')
20 craft

10. Sierra Leone (2 'Shanghai II')
2 craft (nos 002 and 003)

11. Sri Lanka (7 'Sooraya' or 'Shanghai II' class)

Name
BALAWATHA
DAKSAYA
JAGATHA
RAKSHAKA
RANAKAMI
SOORAYA
WEERAYA

12. Tanzania (6 'Shanghai II')
6 craft (nos JW 9861-9866)

13. Tunisia (2 'Shanghai II')

Name	No.
GAFSAH	305
AMILCARE	—

14. Zaire (4 'Shanghai II')
4 craft (nos 101-104)

'Shershen' class fast attack craft (torpedo)

USSR

Displacement: 145 tons standard and 175 tons full load
Dimensions: length 36·0m (118·1ft); beam 7·7m (25·3ft); draught 1·5m (4·9ft)
Gun armament: four 30-mm L/65 AA in two twin mountings
Missile armament: none
Torpedo armament: four 533-mm (21-in) tubes
Class

1. Angola (4)
4 craft

2. Bulgaria (6)
6 craft (nos 24-29)

3. Cape Verde (2)
2 craft

4. Congo (1)
1 craft

5. East Germany (18)

Name	No.
WILLI BANSCH	811
MAX ROSCHER	812
ARVID HARNACK	813
BERNARD BÄSTLEIN	814
FRITZ BEHN	815
WILHELM FLORIN	831
ERICH KUTTNER	832
ARTHUR BECKER	833
FRITZ HECKERT	834
ERNST SCHNELLER	836
EDGAR ANDRE	851
JOSEF ROEMER	852
ERNST GRUBER	853
HEINZ KAPELLE	854
ADAM KUCKHOFF	855
RUDOLF BREITSCHEID	S814*
FIETE SCHULZE	S815*
BRUNO KÜHN	S816*

*training craft

6. Egypt (6)
6 craft (nos 310, 321, 332, 343, 354 and 365)

Anti-submarine armament: 12 depth charges
Electronics: one 'Pot Drum' surface-search radar, one 'Drum Tilt' gun-control radar, one 'High Pole-A' IFF, and one 'Square Head' IFF
Propulsion: three M503A diesels delivering 8,950kW (12,000bhp) to three shafts
Performance: maximum speed 47kts; range 1,500km (930 miles) at 30kts
Complement: 23

7. Guinea (2)
2 craft

8. Guinea-Bissau (2)
2 craft

9. North Korea (4)
4 craft

10. USSR (30)
30 craft

11. Vietnam (8)
8 craft

12. Yugoslavia (15)

Name	No.
TOPCIDER	TC 211
PIONIR	TC 214
JADRAN	TC 216
CRVENA ZVIJEZDA	TC 220
BIOKOVAK	TC 221
PARTIZAN II	TC 222
IVAN	—
KORNAT	—
PARTIZAN	—
PROLETER	—
STRELJKO	—

Plus 4 others

'Snögg' class fast attack craft (missile and torpedo)

Norway

Displacement: 100 tons standard and 125 tons full load

The Rapp (P 981) of the 'Snögg' class shows off her powerful armament of four Penguin missiles, four 533-mm (21-in) torpedoes and a single 40-mm gun.

Dimensions: length 36·5m (119·8ft); beam 6·2m (20·5ft); draught 1·3m (5ft)
Gun armament: one 40-mm Bofors AA
Missile armament: four container-launchers for four Penguin surface-to-surface missiles
Torpedo armament: four 533-mm (21-in) tubes
Anti-submarine armament: none
Electronics: one surface-search and navigation radar
Propulsion: two Maybach (MTU) diesels delivering 5,370kW (7,200bhp) to two shafts
Performance: maximum speed 32kts; range 1,000km (620 miles) at 32kts
Complement: 18
Class

1. Norway (6)

Name	No.	Builders	Commissioned
SNÖGG	P 980	Båtservice	1970
RAPP	P 981	Båtservice	1970
SNAR	P 982	Båtservice	1970
RASK	P 983	Båtservice	1971
KVIKK	P 984	Båtservice	1971
KJAPP	P 985	Båtservice	1971

'Søløven' class fast attack craft (torpedo)

Denmark

Displacement: 95 tons standard and 120 tons full load
Dimensions: length 30·3m (99·4ft); beam 8·0m (26·2ft); draught 2·5m (8·2ft)
Gun armament: two 40-mm Bofors AA in single mountings
Missile armament: none

The Søhunden (P 514) and her sisters are currently in reserve but being refitted.

Torpedo armament: four 533-mm (21-in) tubes (only two tubes if after gun is enclosed)
Anti-submarine armament: none
Electronics: one NWS 1 surface-search and navigation radar
Propulsion: CODOG (COmbined Diesel Or Gas turbine) arrangement, with two General Motors 6V-71 diesels delivering 300bhp (225kW) and three Bristol Siddeley Proteus gas turbines delivering 12,750shp (9,510kW) to three shafts
Performance: maximum speed 54kts on gas turbines or 10kts on diesels; range 740km (460 miles) at 46kts
Complement: 24
Class

1. Denmark (6)

Name	No.	Builders	Commissioned
SØLØVEN	P 510	Vosper Ltd	Feb 1965
SØRIDDEREN	P 511	Vosper Ltd	Feb 1965
SØBJORNEN	P 512	Royal Dockyard	Oct 1965
SØHESTEN	P 513	Royal Dockyard	June 1966
SØHUNDEN	P 514	Royal Dockyard	Dec 1966
SØULVEN	P 515	Royal Dockyard	May 1967

'Sparviero' class fast attack hydrofoil (missile)

Italy

Displacement: 62·5 tons
Dimensions: length 24·6m (80·7ft) foilborne and 23·0m (75·4ft) for hull; beam 12·1m (39·7ft) foilborne and 7·0m (22·9ft) for hull; draught 4·4m (14·4ft) hullborne and 1·6m (5·2ft) for hull
Gun armament: one 76-mm (3-in) L/62 DP OTO-Melara Compact
Missile armament: two single container-launchers for two Otomat surface-to-surface missiles (P 420) or two single container-launchers for two Otomat Mk 2 surface-to-surface missiles (others)
Torpedo armament: none
Anti-submarine armament: none
Electronics: one Selenia Orion RTN 10X missile-control radar used in conjunction with the ELSAG NA-10 fire-control system
Propulsion: CODOG (COmbined Diesel Or Gas turbine) arrangement, with one diesel delivering 119kW (160bhp) to a retractable propeller for hullborne propulsion, and one Rolls-Royce Proteus gas turbine delivering 4,500bhp (3,355kW) to a waterjet pump for foilborne propulsion
Performance: maximum speed 50kts foilborne in calm sea or 8kts hullborne; range 2,225km (1,385 miles) at 8kts or 740km (460 miles) at 45kts
Complement: 2+8

Extremely compact but with considerable power, the Sparviero (P 420) packs a considerable offensive missile and gun punch, is handy and fast, and can operate effectively in sea conditions that would seriously degrade the overall performance of displacement-type FACs. The Sparviero was essentially a prototype, and was exhaustively evaluated over a considerable period before the rest of the class was ordered.

Class 1. Italy (7)			
Name	No.	Builders	Commissioned
SPARVIERO	P 420	Alinavi	July 1974
NIBBIO	P 421	Cantieri Navali Riuniti	Nov 1980
FALCONE	P 422	Cantieri Navali Riuniti	Aug 1981
ASTORE	P 423	Cantieri Navali Riuniti	1981
GRIFONE	P 424	Cantieri Navali Riuniti	1982
GHEPPIO	P 425	Cantieri Navali Riuniti	1982
CONDOR	P 426	Cantieri Navali Riuniti	1983

'Spica-M' class fast attack craft (missile)

Sweden/Malaysia

Displacement: 240 tons
Dimensions: length 43·6m (142·6ft); beam 7·1m (23·3ft); draught 2·4m (7·4ft)
Gun armament: one 57-mm Bofors AA, and one 40-mm Bofors AA
Missile armament: four container-launchers for four MM.38 Exocet surface-to-surface missiles
Torpedo armament: none
Anti-submarine armament: none
Electronics: one Philips Elektroniksindustrier 9GR 600 surface-search radar, one Decca navigation radar, one Philips Elektronikindustrier 9LV 200 Mk 2 weapon control system, and one LME laser ranger and TV tracker for the AA armament

Propulsion: three MTU diesels delivering 8,055kW (10,800hp) to three shafts
Performance: maximum speed 34·5kts; range 3,425km (2,130 miles) at 14kts
Complement: 6+34

Class 1. Malaysia (4)			
Name	No.	Builders	Commissioned
HANDALAN	P 3511	Karlskrona Varvet	Aug 1979
PERKASA	P 3512	Karlskrona Varvet	Aug 1979
PENDEKAR	P 3513	Karlskrona Varvet	Aug 1979
GEMPITA	P 3514	Karlskrona Varvet	Aug 1979

'Spica I' class (T 121) fast attack craft (torpedo and missile)

Sweden

Displacement: 185 tons standard and 215 tons full load
Dimensions: length 42·7m (140·1ft); beam 7·1m (23·3ft); draught 2·6m (8·5ft)
Gun armament: one 57-mm Bofors L/70
Missile armament: it is possible that the craft will each receive an armament of four or eight container-launchers for four or eight RB 15 surface-to-surface missiles in place of two or four torpedo tubes
Torpedo armament: six 533-mm (21-in) tubes for six torpedoes
Anti-submarine armament: none
Electronics: one Hollandse Signaalapparaten WM-22 radar fire-control system for guns and torpedoes
Propulsion: three Bristol Siddeley Proteus gas turbines delivering 12,720shp

(9,485kW) to three shafts
Performance: maximum speed 40kts
Complement: 7+21

Class 1. Sweden (6)			
Name	No.	Builders	Commissioned
SPICA	T 121	Götaverken	1966
SIRIUS	T 122	Götaverken	1966
CAPELLA	T 123	Götaverken	1966
CASTOR	T 124	Karlskrona Varvet	1967
VEGA	T 125	Karlskrona Varvet	1967
VIRGO	T 126	Karlskrona Varvet	1967

'Spica II' class (T 131) fast attack craft (torpedo and missile)

Sweden

Displacement: 190 tons
Dimensions: length 43·6m (143ft); beam 7·1m (23·3ft); draught 2·4m (7·4ft)
Gun armament: one 57-mm Bofors L/70
Missile armament: it is possible that the craft will each receive an armament of four or eight container-launchers for four or eight RB 15 surface-to-surface missiles in place of two or four torpedo tubes
Torpedo armament: six 533-mm (21-in) tubes for six wire-guided torpedoes
Anti-submarine armament: none
Electronics: one Philips Elektronikindustrier 9LV 200 combined air- and surface-search radar, and one chaff launcher
Propulsion: three Bristol Siddeley Proteus gas turbines delivering 12,900bhp (9,620kW) to three shafts
Performance: maximum speed 40·5kts
Complement: 27

Class 1. Sweden (12)			
Name	No.	Builders	Commissioned
NORRKÖPING	T 131	Karlskrona Varvet	May 1973
NYNÄSHAMN	T 132	Karlskrona Varvet	Sep 1973
NORRTÄLJE	T 133	Karlskrona Varvet	Feb 1974
VARBERG	T 134	Karlskrona Varvet	June 1974
VÄSTERÅS	T 135	Karlskrona Varvet	Oct 1974
VÄSTERVIK	T 136	Karlskrona Varvet	Jan 1975
UMEÅ	T 137	Karlskrona Varvet	May 1975
PITEÅ	T 138	Karlskrona Varvet	Sep 1975
LULEÅ	T 139	Karlskrona Varvet	Nov 1975
HALMSTAD	T 140	Karlskrona Varvet	Apr 1976
STRÖMSTAD	T 141	Karlskrona Varvet	Sep 1976
YSTAD	T 142	Karlskrona Varvet	Jan 1976

'Stenka' class fast attack craft (patrol)

USSR

Displacement: 170 tons standard and 210 tons full load
Dimensions: length 39·0m (127·9ft); beam 7·8m (25·6ft); draught 1·8m (5·9ft)
Gun armament: four 30-mm L/65 AA in two twin mountings
Missile armament: none
Torpedo armament: none
Anti-submarine armament: four 406-mm (16-in) tubes for A/S torpedoes, and two depth-charge racks

Electronics: one 'Pot Drum' surface-search radar, one 'Muff Cob' gun-control radar, one 'High Pole' IFF, two 'Square Head' IFF, and one dipping sonar
Propulsion: three M503A diesels delivering 8,950kW (12,000shp) to three shafts
Performance: maximum speed 36kts
Complement: 30

Class
1. USSR (90)
90 craft

'Stockholm' class fast attack craft (missile)

Sweden

Displacement: 310 tons
Dimensions: length 50·0m (164ft); beam 7·5m (24·6ft); draught 2·0m (6·6ft)
Gun armament: one 57-mm Bofors L/70 in a single mounting, and one 40-mm Bofors L/70 AA in a single mounting
Missile armament: six container-launchers for six RB 15 anti-ship missiles
Torpedo armament: two 533-mm (21-in) tubes for two Type 61 wire-guided anti-ship torpedoes
Anti-submarine armament: two 400-mm (15·75-in) Type 42 wire-guided anti-submarine torpedoes as an alternative to the two Type 61 torpedoes (see above)
Electronics: one Ericsson Sea Giraffe surface-search and surveillance radar, one Philips Elektronikindustrier 9LV 200 fire-control radar system, one Saab-Scania EWS 905 electronic countermeasures system, and one variable-depth sonar
Propulsion: CODAG (COmbined Diesel And Gas turbine) arrangement, with two MTU 16V396 TB93 diesels delivering 3,130kW (4,200shp) and one gas turbine delivering 4,475kW (6,000shp) to three shafts

Performance: maximum speed 32kts on all engines, and 20kts on diesels alone
Complement: 30

Class
1. Sweden (2)

Name	No.	Builders	Commissioned
STOCKHOLM	R 11	Karlskrona Varvet	1984
MALMO	R 12	Karlskrona Varvet	1984

Remarks: Evolved from the 'Spica II' class, the 'Stockholm' class has been designed to provide the Royal Swedish navy with two capable yet versatile flotilla leaders for the 16 'Hugin' and 12 'Spica II' class fast attack craft (missile). In common with other Swedish warships, the 'Stockholm' class design has provision for minelaying, an important factor in Swedish defence plans. The armament is nicely balanced, with missiles or torpedoes available for anti-ship operations, a different type of torpedo for anti-submarine operations, and guns for protection against other FACs and low-flying aircraft.

'Storm' class fast attack craft (missile)

Norway

Displacement: 100 tons standard and 125 tons full load
Dimensions: length 36·5m (119·8ft); beam 6·2m (20·5ft); draught 1·5m (5ft)
Gun armament: one 76-mm (3-in) Bofors L/50 DP, and one 40-mm Bofors AA
Missile armament: six container-launchers for six Penguin surface-to-surface missiles
Torpedo armament: none
Anti-submarine armament: none
Electronics: one Hollandse Signaalapparaten WM-20 radar fire-control system for guns and missiles
Propulsion: two Maybach·MB 872A diesels delivering 5,370kW (7,200bhp) to two shafts
Performance: maximum speed 32kts
Complement: 4+9+13

Class
1. Norway (19)

Name	No.	Builders	Commissioned
STORM	P 960	Bergens Mek Verksteder	1968
BLINK	P 961	Bergens Mek Verksteder	1965
GLIMT	P 962	Bergens Mek Verksteder	1966
SKJOLD	P 963	Westermoen	1966
TRYGG	P 964	Bergens Mek Verksteder	1966
KJEKK	P 965	Bergens Mek Verksteder	1966
DJERV	P 966	Westermoen	1966
SKUDD	P 967	Bergens Mek Verksteder	1966
ARG	P 968	Bergens Mek Verksteder	1966
STEIL	P 969	Westermoen	1967
BRANN	P 970	Bergens Mek Verksteder	1967
TROSS	P 971	Bergens Mek Verksteder	1967
HVASS	P 972	Westermoen	1967
TRAUST	P 973	Bergens Mek Verksteder	1967
BROTT	P 974	Bergens Mek Verksteder	1967
ODD	P 975	Westermoen	1967
BRASK	P 977	Bergens Mek Verksteder	1967
ROKK	P 978	Westermoen	1968
GNIST	P 979	Bergens Mek Verksteder	1968

The Brann (P970) of the Royal Norwegian navy's 'Storm' class shows the salient features of this fast attack craft (missile) design. Only 20 of a planned 23 craft were built, and the Pil (P 976) was deleted in 1982, leaving an in-service strength of 19 craft. From forward aft, the most notable features are the 76-mm (3-in) Bofors gun suitable for the engagement of surface targets only, the WM-20 series fire-control radar in a radome atop the short lattice mast, the 40-mm Bofors AA guns, and the container-launchers for six Penguin anti-ship missiles. These missiles were added from 1970, when the craft were already in service, and have enhanced the capability of the class to an enormous degree. Not all the craft carry a full complement of missiles all the time.

'Tuima' class fast attack craft (missile)

Finland

Displacement: 165 tons standard and 210 tons full load
Dimensions: length 39·0m (127·9ft); beam 8·1m (26·5ft); draught 1·8m (5·9ft)
Gun armament: four 30-mm AA in two twin mountings
Missile armament: four container-launchers for four SS-N-2A 'Styx' surface-to-surface missiles
Torpedo armament: none
Anti-submarine armament: none
Electronics: surface-search/navigation radar
Propulsion: three M504 diesels delivering 11,185kW (15,000hp) to three shafts

Performance: maximum speed 40kts; range 1,500km (930 miles) at 30kts
Complement: 30

Class
1. Finland (4)

Name	No.	Builder
TUIMA	11	USSR/Finland
TUISKU	12	USSR/Finland
TUULI	14	USSR/Finland
TYRSKY	15	USSR/Finland

'Turya' class fast attack hydrofoil (torpedo)
USSR

Displacement: 190 tons standard and 250 tons full load
Dimensions: length 39·3m (128·7ft); beam 7·8m (25·6ft); draught 1·8m (5·9ft)
Gun armament: two 57-mm L/70 AA in one twin mounting, and two 25-mm AA in one twin mounting
Missile armament: none
Torpedo armament: four 533-mm (21-in) tubes for four torpedoes
Anti-submarine armament: A/S torpedoes

Electronics: one 'Pot Drum' surface-search radar, one 'Muff Cob' 57-mm gun-control radar, one 'High Pole' IFF, one 'Square Head' IFF, and one dipping sonar
Propulsion: three M504 diesels delivering 11,185kW (15,000shp) to three shafts
Performance: maximum speed 45kts foilborne
Complement: 30

Class
1. Cuba (6)	2. USSR (30)
6 craft	30 craft

'Type A' and 'Type B' class fast attack craft (gun)
UK/Singapore

Displacement: 100 tons standard and 130 tons full load
Dimensions: length 109·6ft (33·5m); beam 21ft (6·4m); draught 5·6ft (1·8m)
Gun armament: one 40-mm Bofors AA, and one 20-mm Oerlikon AA in 'Type A'; one 76-mm (3-in) Bofors DP, and one 20-mm Oerlikon AA in 'Type B'
Missile armament: none
Torpedo armament: none
Anti-submarine armament: none
Electronics: one navigation radar and ('Type B') one Hollandse Signaalapparaten WM-26 fire-control radar
Propulsion: two Maybach (MTU) 16V538 diesels delivering 5,370kW (7,200bhp) to two shafts
Performance: maximum speed 32kts; range 1,250 miles (2,010km) at 15kts
Complement: between 19 and 22

Class

1. Singapore (3 'Type A')
Name	No.	Builders	Commissioned
INDEPENDENCE	P 69	Vosper Thornycroft Ltd	July 1970
FREEDOM	P 70	Vosper Thornycroft Private Ltd	Jan 1971
JUSTICE	P 72	Vosper Thornycroft Private Ltd	Apr 1971

2. Singapore (3 'Type B')
Name	No.	Builders	Commissioned
SOVEREIGNTY	P 71	Vosper Thornycroft Ltd	Feb 1971
DARING	P 73	Vosper Thornycroft Private Ltd	Sep 1971
DAUNTLESS	P 74	Vosper Thornycroft Private Ltd	1971

Remarks: These two classes differ only in armament and sensors. The lead boat of each type was built in the UK, the others being delivered from local sources.

'Type 143' class fast attack craft (missile)
West Germany

Displacement: 295 tons standard and 390 tons full load
Dimensions: length 57·5m (188·6ft); beam 7·6m (24·9ft); draught 2·5m (8·2ft)
Gun armament: two 76-mm (3-in) L/62 DP OTO-Melara Compact in two single mountings
Missile armament: four container-launchers for four MM.38 Exocet surface-to-surface missiles, and (to be fitted in place of the after 76-mm/3-in gun) one launcher for RAM-ASMD surface-to-air missiles when the type's development is complete
Torpedo armament: two 533-mm (21-in) tubes for wire-guided torpedoes
Anti-submarine armament: none
Electronics: one Hollandse Signaalapparaten WM-27 surface-search and weapon-control radar system, one SMA 3RM 20 navigation radar, and one AGIS data system
Propulsion: four MTU 16V956 diesels delivering 11,930kW (16,000hp) to four shafts
Performance: maximum speed 35+ kts; range 2,400km (1,490 miles) at 30kts
Complement: 40
Remarks: The 'Type 143' and 'Type 143A' are very similar. The after 76-mm (3-in) guns are being shifted into the 'Type 143A' boats to make way for the RAM point-defence missile system (to be fitted in the 'Type 143A' boats). Otherwise the 'Type 143A' boats are 0·2m (0·66ft) longer and lack torpedo armament, though they are fitted for minelaying. 'Type 143B' distinguishes modified 'Type 143' craft.

Class

1. West Germany (10 'Type 143')
Name	No.	Builders	Commissioned
ALBATROSS	P 6111	Lürssen	Nov 1976
FALKE	P 6112	Lürssen	Apr 1976
GEIER	P 6113	Lürssen	June 1976
BUSSARD	P 6114	Lürssen	Aug 1976
SPERBER	P 6115	Kröger	Sep 1976
GREIF	P 6116	Lürssen	Nov 1976
KONDOR	P 6117	Kröger	Dec 1976
SEEADLER	P 6118	Lürssen	Mar 1977
HABICHT	P 6119	Kröger	Dec 1977
KORMORAN	P 6120	Lürssen	July 1977

2. West Germany (10 'Type 143A')
Name	No.	Builders	Commissioned
GEPARD	P 6121	AEG Telefunken/Lürssen	1982
PUMA	P 6122	AEG Telefunken/Lürssen	1982
HERMELIN	P 6123	AEG Telefunken/Kröger	1983
NERZ	P 6124	AEG Telefunken/Lürssen	1983
ZOBEL	P 6125	AEG Telefunken/Lürssen	1983
FRETTCHEN	P 6126	AEG Telefunken/Lürssen	1983
DACHS	P 6127	AEG Telefunken/Lürssen	1984
OZELOT	P 6128	AEG Telefunken/Lürssen	1984
WIESEL	P 6129	AEG Telefunken/Kröger	1984
HYÄNE	P 6130	AEG Telefunken/Kröger	1984

'Type 148' class fast attack craft (missile)
West Germany

Displacement: 235 tons standard and 265 tons full load
Dimensions: length 47·0m (154·2ft); beam 7·0m (23ft); draught 2·1m (6·9ft)
Gun armament: one 76-mm (3-in) L/62 DP OTO-Melara Compact, and one 40-mm Bofors AA
Missile armament: four container-launchers for four MM.38 Exocet surface-to-surface missiles
Torpedo armament: none
Anti-submarine armament: none
Electronics: one Thomson-CSF Triton combined air- and surface-search and target-designation radar, and one Thomson-CSF Pollux tracking radar, both used in conjunction with a Thomson-CSF Vega fire-control system, and one SMA 3RM 20 navigation radar
Propulsion: four MTU MD 872 diesels delivering 8,950kW (12,000bhp) to four shafts
Performance: maximum speed 35+ kts; range 1,125km (700 miles) at 30kts
Complement: 4+26
Remarks: Built of steel (the 'Type 143' and 'Type 143A' having wooden hulls on aluminium frames), the 'Type 148' class was built in France (excepting Lürssen-built Ps 6146, 6148, 6150, 6152, 6154, 6156, 6158 and 6160) for completion at Cherbourg.

Class

1. West Germany (20)
Name	No.	Builders	Commissioned
TIGER	P 6141	C. M. de Normandie	Oct 1972
ILTIS	P 6142	C. M. de Normandie	Jan 1973
LUCHS	P 6143	C. M. de Normandie	Apr 1973
MARDER	P 6144	C. M. de Normandie	June 1973
LEOPARD	P 6145	C. M. de Normandie	Aug 1973
FUCHS	P 6146	C. M. de Normandie	Oct 1973
JAGUAR	P 6147	C. M. de Normandie	Nov 1973
LÖWE	P 6148	C. M. de Normandie	Jan 1974
WOLF	P 6149	C. M. de Normandie	Feb 1974
PANTHER	P 6150	C. M. de Normandie	Mar 1974
HÄHER	P 6151	C. M. de Normandie	June 1974
STORCH	P 6152	C. M. de Normandie	July 1974
PELIKAN	P 6153	C. M. de Normandie	Sep 1974
ELSTER	P 6154	C. M. de Normandie	Nov 1974
ALK	P 6155	C. M. de Normandie	Jan 1975
DOMMEL	P 6156	C. M. de Normandie	Feb 1975
WEIHE	P 6157	C. M. de Normandie	Apr 1975
PINGUIN	P 6158	C. M. de Normandie	May 1975
REIHER	P 6159	C. M. de Normandie	June 1975
KRANICH	P 6160	C. M. de Normandie	Aug 1975

'Waspada' class fast attack craft (missile)
Singapore/Brunei
Displacement: 150 tons full load
Dimensions: length 121ft (36·9m); beam 23·5ft (7·2m); draught 6ft (1·8m)
Gun armament: two 30-mm Oerlikon GCM-BO1 AA in one twin mounting, and two 0·5-in (12·7-mm) heavy machine-guns
Missile armament: two container-launchers for two MM.38 Exocet surface-to-surface missiles
Torpedo armament: none
Anti-submarine armament: none
Electronics: one Decca TM 1229 navigation radar, one Decca ranging radar used with an optical fire director, and one Sperry Sea Archer missile fire-control system

Propulsion: two MTU 12V538 TB91 diesels delivering 6,710kW (9,000bhp) to two shafts
Performance: maximum speed 32kts; range 1,400 miles (2,255km) at 14kts
Complement: 4+20

Class
1. Brunei (3)

Name	No.	Builders	Com-missioned
WASPADA	P 02	Vosper Singapore	1978
PEJUANG	P 03	Vosper Singapore	1979
SETERIA	P 04	Vosper Singapore	1979

'Willemoes' class fast attack craft (missile)
Denmark
Displacement: 260 tons full load
Dimensions: length 46·0m (150·9ft); beam 7·4m (24ft); draught 2·5m (8·2ft)
Gun armament: one 76-mm (3-in) L/62 DP OTO-Melara Compact
Missile armament: two quadruple container-launchers for eight RGM-84A Harpoon surface-to-surface missiles
Torpedo armament: two 533-mm (21-in) tubes for two torpedoes
Anti-submarine armament: none
Electronics: one surface-search radar, one NWS-3 navigation radar, and one Philips Elektroniksindustrier 9LV 200 fire-control radar system
Propulsion: CODOG (COmbined Diesel Or Gas turbine) arrangement, with two General Motors 8V-71 diesels delivering 1,600bhp (1,195kW) and three Rolls-Royce Proteus gas turbines delivering 12,750bhp (9,510kW) to three shafts
Performance: maximum speed 38kts on gas turbines and 12kts on diesels
Complement: 6+19

Class
1. Denmark (10)

Name	No.	Builders	Com-missioned
BILLE	P 540	Frederikshavn Vaerft	Oct 1976
BREDAL	P 541	Frederikshavn Vaerft	Jan 1977
HAMMER	P 542	Frederikshavn Vaerft	Apr 1977
HUITFELD	P 543	Frederikshavn Vaerft	June 1977
KRIEGER	P 544	Frederikshavn Vaerft	Sep 1977
NORBY	P 545	Frederikshavn Vaerft	Nov 1977
RODSTEEN	P 546	Frederikshavn Vaerft	Feb 1978
SEHESTED	P 547	Frederikshavn Vaerft	May 1978
SUENSON	P 548	Frederikshavn Vaerft	Aug 1978
WILLEMOES	P 549	Frederikshavn Vaerft	June 1976

The Willemoes (P 549) is lead craft of the capable 'Willemoes' class.

'Blue Ridge' class amphibious command ship
USA

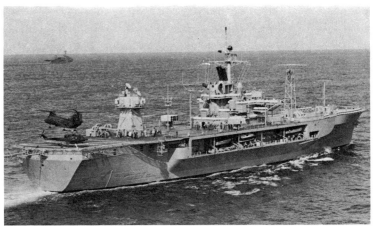

The Mount Whitney (LCC 20) of the 'Blue Ridge' class shows off the type's lines during an Atlantic deployment in 1980. The hull and propulsion are modelled on those of the 'Iwo Jima' class amphibious assault ship, bestowing almost identical performance, while the flight deck can still accommodate a helicopter despite the proliferation of communication and navigation antennae, whose locations have an adverse effect on the weapons' arcs of fire. The Mk 25 SAM launchers are located on the port and starboard beams abaft the island superstructure.

Displacement: 19,100 tons full load
Dimensions: length 620ft (189·0m); beam 82ft (25·0m); draught 29ft (8·8m)
Gun armament: four 3-in (76-mm) L/50 DP in two Mk 33 twin mountings, and (to be fitted) two Phalanx Mk 16 20-mm close-in weapons system mountings
Missile armament: two Mk 25 basic point-defense missile system launchers for RIM-7 Sea Sparrow surface-to-air missiles
Torpedo armament: none
Anti-submarine armament: none
Aircraft: provision for a utility helicopter
Electronics: ITT/Gilfillan SPS-48 3D air-search radar, one Raytheon/Sylvania SPS-10 surface-search radar, one Lockheed SPS-40 air-search radar, two Mk 115 missile fire-control systems, URN-20 TACAN, OE-82 satellite communications antenna, SRR-1 satellite communications receiver, WSR-3 satellite communications transceiver, Naval Tactical Data System, Amphibious Command Information System and Naval Intelligence Processing System
Propulsion: two Foster-Wheeler boilers supplying steam to one General Electric geared turbine delivering 22,000shp (16,405kW) to one shaft
Performance: maximum speed 23kts; range 15,000 miles (24,140km) at 16kts
Complement: 40+680, plus command staff of 200+500

Class
1. USA (2)

Name	No.	Builders	Laid down	Com-missioned
BLUE RIDGE	LCC 19	Philadelphia NY	Feb 1967	Nov 1970
MOUNT WHITNEY	LCC 20	Newport News S.B.	Jan 1969	Jan 1971

Remarks: Though nominally amphibious command ships, the two 'Blue Ridge' class ships serve as fleet flagships.

'Fearless' class assault ship

UK

Displacement: 11,060 tons standard, 12,120 full load and 16,950 tons flooded down
Dimensions: length 520ft (158·5m); beam 80ft (24·4m); draught 20·5ft (6·2m) normal and 32ft (9·8m) flooded down
Gun armament: two 40-mm Bofors L/70 AA in two single mountings
Missile armament: four quadruple launchers for Sea Cat surface-to-air missiles
Torpedo armament: none
Anti-submarine armament: none
Aircraft: five Westland Wessex HU.Mk 5 helicopters on a platform aft

Capacity: the well deck can accommodate four LCM(9)s, which can be supplemented in the ship-to-shore role by four LCVPs carried in davits; typical internal load is 15 main battle tanks, seven 3-ton trucks and 20 Land Rovers; normal troop accommodation is 400, but up to 700 can be carried in austere conditions
Electronics: one Plessey Type 994 combined air- and surface search radar, one Decca Type 978 navigation radar, one Computer-Assisted Action Information System, and two Knebworth Corvus chaff launchers
Propulsion: two Babcock & Wilcox boilers supplying steam to two sets of English Electric geared turbines delivering 22,000shp (16,405kW) to two shafts
Performance: maximum speed 21kts; range 5,750 miles (9,250km) at 20kts
Complement: 580

Class

1. UK (2)				
Name	No.	Builders	Laid down	Com-missioned
FEARLESS	L 10	Harland & Wolff	July 1962	Nov 1965
INTREPID	L 11	John Brown & Co (Clydebank)	Dec 1962	Mar 1967

Remarks: The two 'Fearless' class assault ships were to have been scrapped during the 1980s until their vital role in the Falklands campaign of 1982 earned them a fully justified reprieve. Each ship is fitted out as the HQ unit for a naval assault group and landing brigade, though the capacity of each ship is somewhat short of a brigade of infantry (see above). Though landing ships possess greater payload capability, the virtue of the assault ship lies with its speed, seakeeping and range, all factors of paramount significance in the Falklands campaign.

Evident in this illustration of the Fearless (L 10) under way are the large array of antennae for communications (long- and short-range) and navigation, the two port-side LCVPs, the starboard bridge-wing 40-mm Bofors AA gun, two quadruple Sea Cat SAM launchers forward of the bridge, two Wessex helicopters on the flight deck above the flooding dock, and stern crane.

'Iwo Jima' class amphibious assault ship

USA

Displacement: 18,000 tons full load for LPHs 2, 3 and 7, or 18,300 tons full load for LPHs 9 and 10, or 17,705 tons full load for LPH 11, or 17,515 tons full load for LPH 12
Dimensions: length 602·3ft (183·7m); beam 84ft (25·6m); draught 26ft (7·9m); flight-deck width 104ft (31·7m)
Gun armament: four 3-in (76-mm) L/50 DP in two Mk 33 twin mountings, and (to be fitted) two 20-mm Phalanx Mk 16 close-in weapon system mountings
Missile armament: two Mk 25 launchers for RIM-7 Sea Sparrow surface-to-air missiles
Torpedo armament: none
Anti-submarine armament: none
Aircraft: 20 Boeing Vertol CH-46 Sea Knight helicopters, or 11 Sikorsky CH-53 Sea Stallion helicopters, or a mixture of the two, and (with a reduction in helicopter strength) four BAe/McDonnell Douglas AV-8A Harrier aircraft
Capacity: accommodation is provided for a US Marine Corps battalion landing team (144+1,602) plus its equipment, guns and vehicles; this accommodation amounts to 4,300 sq ft (400 m²) for vehicles and 37,400 sq ft (3,475 m²) for palleted stores, plus bulk storage for 6,500 US gal (24,605 litres) of vehicle fuel and 405,000 US gal (1,533,090 litres) of helicopter fuel
Electronics: one Raytheon/Sylvania SPS-10 surface-search radar, one Lockheed SPS-40 air-search radar, one SPN-10 navigation radar, two Mk 63 gun fire-control systems, two Mk 115 missile fire-control systems, URN-20 TACAN, OE-82 satellite

communications antenna, SRR-1 satellite communications receiver, WSC-3 satellite communications transceiver, advanced electronic warfare equipment, and one Mk 36 Super Chaffroc rapid-blooming overhead chaff launcher
Propulsion: two boilers (Babcock & Wilcox in LPH 9 and Combustion Engineering in others) supplying steam to one geared turbine (De Laval in LPH 10, General Electric in LPH 12, and Westinghouse in others) delivering 22,000shp (16,405kW) to one shaft
Performance: maximum speed 23kts
Complement: 47+562

Class

1. USA (7)				
Name	No.	Builders	Laid down	Com-missioned
IWO JIMA	LPH 2	Puget Sound NY	Apr 1959	Aug 1961
OKINAWA	LPH 3	Philadelphia NY	Apr 1960	Apr 1962
GUADALCANAL	LPH 7	Philadelphia NY	Sep 1961	July 1963
GUAM	LPH 9	Philadelphia NY	Nov 1962	Jan 1965
TRIPOLI	LPH 10	Ingalls Shipbuilding	June 1964	Aug 1966
NEW ORLEANS	LPH 11	Philadelphia NY	Mar 1966	Nov 1968
INCHON	LPH 12	Ingalls Shipbuilding	Apr 1968	June 1970

Remarks: The seven 'Iwo Jima' class amphibious assault ships are allocated three to the Pacific and four to the Atlantic, and were the first ships in the world designed specifically for the delivery of amphibious assault force by helicopter. Each ship carries a US Marine Corps battalion landing team together with its weapons, vehicles etc, as well as a reinforced assault helicopter squadron. Trials have also confirmed the ships' ability to operate AV-8 V/STOL close-support aircraft, which can offer the landing battalion very powerful air support in areas outside conventional aircraft's operational radius. From 1986 the class will begin a Service Life Extension Program to add 15 years to the proposed 30-year life of each vessel, the programme being designed to upgrade systems where relevant as well as to improve survivability and to modernize machinery and living spaces.

The Iwo Jima (LPH 2), under way in the Atlantic during 1978, shows off her carrier-like appearance, with a complement of nine Boeing Vertol CH-46, four Sikorsky CH-53 and numbers of smaller helicopters visible. Two large deck-edge elevators provide access to the large internal hangar even for the largest helicopters. The SAM launchers are on the port quarter and forward of the bridge.

'Tarawa' class amphibious assault ship

USA

Displacement: 39,300 tons full load

Dimensions: length 820 ft (249·9 m); beam 106 ft (32·3 m); draught 26 ft (7·9 m)

Gun armament: three 5-in (127-mm) L/54 DP in three Mk 45 single mountings, six 20-mm AA in six Mk 67 single mountings, and (to be fitted) two 20-mm Phalanx Mk 16 close-in weapon system mountings

Missile armament: two Mk 25 launchers for RIM-7 Sea Sparrow surface-to-air missiles (to be removed when CIWS is fitted)

Torpedo armament: none

Anti-submarine armament: none

Aircraft: up to 19 Sikorsky CH-53 Sea Stallion or 26 Boeing Vertol CH-46 Sea Knight helicopters, and (by a reduction in embarked helicopter strength) a small number of BAe/McDonnell Douglas AV-8A Harrier aircraft

Capacity: apart from two full length hangar decks under the flight deck, there is a docking well measuring 268 ft (81·7 m) in length and 78 ft (23·8 m) in width to accommodate four LCU 1610 type landing craft, other landing capability being provided by six LCM(6) craft; vehicle accommodation area is 33,730 sq ft (3,135 m²), and stowage volume for palleted stores is 116,900 cu ft (3,310 m³); liquid storage is provided for 10,000 US gal (37,855 litres) of vehicle fuel and 400,000 US gal (1,514,160 litres) of helicopter fuel; troop accommodation is provided for a reinforced battalion of US Marines totalling 1,703 officers and men

Electronics: one Hughes SPS-52 3D radar, one Lockheed SPS-40 air-search radar, one Raytheon/Sylvania SPS-10 surface-search radar, one ITT/Gilfillan SPN-35 navigation radar, one Lockheed SPG-60 search and tracking radar and one Lockheed SPQ-9A track-while-scan radar both used in conjunction with the four Lockheed Mk 86 gun fire-control systems, two Mk 115 missile fire-control systems, URN-22 TACAN, Integrated Tactical Amphibious Warfare Data System, OE-82 satellite communications antenna, SRR-1 satellite communications receiver, WSC-3 satellite communications transceiver, several electronic warfare systems, and Mk 36 Super Chaffroc rapid-blooming overhead chaff launchers

Propulsion: two Combustion Engineering boilers supplying steam to two sets of Westinghouse geared turbines delivering 140,000 shp (104,400 kW) to two shafts

Performance: maximum speed 24 kts; range 11,500 miles (18,505 km) at 20 kts

Complement: 90+812

Class

1. USA (5)				
Name	No.	Builders	Laid down	Commissioned
TARAWA	LHA 1	Ingalls Shipbuilding	Nov 1971	May 1976
SAIPAN	LHA 2	Ingalls Shipbuilding	July 1972	Oct 1977
BELLEAU WOOD	LHA 3	Ingalls Shipbuilding	Mar 1973	Sep 1978
NASSAU	LHA 4	Ingalls Shipbuilding	Aug 1973	July 1979
PELELIU	LHA 5	Ingalls Shipbuilding	Nov 1976	May 1980

Remarks: The 'Tarawa' class is a general-purpose amphibious assault ship design with a docking well and landing craft as well as assault helicopters.

'Alligator' class landing ship tank

USSR

Displacement: 3,400 tons standard and 4,500 tons full load

Dimensions: length 114·0 m (374 ft); beam 15·5 m (50·85 ft); draught 4·5 m (14·76 ft)

Gun armament: two 57-mm AA in one twin mounting, two shore-bombardment rocket systems (Types 3 and 4) and four 25-mm AA in two twin mountings (Type 4)

Missile armament: two SA-N-5 surface-to-air missile launchers (some)

Torpedo armament: none

Anti-submarine armament: none

Capacity: 1,700 tons; handled with the aid of two 5-ton cranes (Type 1) or one 15-ton crane (Types 2, 3 and 4); ramps are built into the bow and stern for roll-on/roll-off operations; Naval Infantry units are normally embarked

Electronics: one 'Don 2' or 'Spin Trough' navigation radar and one 'Muff Cob' gun fire-control radar

Propulsion: two diesels delivering 6,710 kW (9,000 bhp) to two shafts

Performance: maximum speed 18 kts; range 20,000 km (12,425 miles) at 15 kts

Complement: 100

The Nikolai Vilkov *is an 'Alligator Type 4' class landing ship tank similar to the Type 3 (with shore-bombardment rocket-launchers) apart from extra AA guns.*

Class		
1. USSR (14)	Type 1: four units	Type 3: six units
	Type 2: two units	Type 4: two units

'Anchorage' class landing ship dock

USA

Displacement: 8,600 tons light and 13,600 tons full load

Dimensions: length 553·3 ft (168·6 m); beam 84 ft (25·6 m); draught 20 ft (6·1 m)

Gun armament: six 3-in (76-mm) L/50 in three Mk 33 twin mountings, and (to be fitted) two 20-mm Mk 16 close-in weapons system mountings

Missile armament: none

Torpedo armament: none

Anti-submarine armament: none

Aircraft: provision for a helicopter platform aft

Capacity: the docking well in the stern measures 430 ft (131·1 m) in length and 50 ft (15·25 m) in width, and accommodates three LCUs, or 29 LCM(6)s or many LVTs; there is deck space for one LCM, with one LCPL and one LCVP on davits; there are two 50-ton cranes for the handling of freight

Electronics: one Raytheon/Sylvania SPS-10 surface-search radar, one Lockheed SPS-40 air-search radar, one OE-82 satellite communications antenna, one SRR-1 receiver, one WSC-3 transceiver, and (to be fitted) one Mk 36 Super Chaffroc rapid-blooming overhead chaff system

Propulsion: two Foster-Wheeler boilers supplying steam to De Laval geared turbines delivering 24,000 shp (17,895 kW) to two shafts

Performance: maximum speed 22 kts; maximum sustained speed 20 kts

Complement: 21+376, plus 28+348 troops

Class

1. USA (5)			
Name	No.	Builders	Commissioned
ANCHORAGE	LSD 36	Ingalls Shipbuilding	Mar 1969
PORTLAND	LSD 37	General Dynamics	Oct 1970
PENSACOLA	LSD 38	General Dynamics	Mar 1971
MOUNT VERNON	LSD 39	General Dynamics	May 1972
FORT FISHER	LSD 40	General Dynamics	Dec 1972

'Austin' class amphibious transport dock

USA

Displacement: 10,000 tons light, and 15,900 tons (LPD 4-6), or 16,550 tons (LPD 7-10), or 16,900 tons (AGF 11 and LPD 12-13), or 17,000 tons (LPD 14-15) full load
Dimensions: length 570ft (173·8m); beam 100ft (30·5m); draught 23ft (7·0m)
Gun armament: two 3-in (76-mm) L/50 DP in one Mk 33 twin mounting, and (to be fitted) two 20-mm Phalanx Mk 16 close-in weapons system mountings
Missile armament: none
Torpedo armament: none
Anti-submarine armament: none

The Coronado (AGF 11) is specially fitted as a Persian Gulf command ship.

Aircraft: up to six Boeing Vertol CH-46 Sea Knight helicopters
Capacity: the docking well measures 395ft (120·4m) in length and 50ft (15·24m) in width, and can accommodate one LCU and three LCM(6)s, or nine LCM(6)s, or four LCM(8)s, or 28 LVTs; freight is handled by two forklifts, six cranes and one elevator
Electronics: one Raytheon/Sylvania SPS-10 surface-search radar, one Lockheed SPS-40 air-search radar, URN-20 TACAN, OE-82 satellite communications antenna, SRR-1 satellite receiver and WSC-3 satellite transceiver, and (to be fitted) Mk 36 Super Chaffroc rapid-blooming overhead chaff system
Propulsion: two Foster-Wheeler (Babcock & Wilcox in LPD 5 and LPD 12) boilers supplying steam to two De Laval geared turbines delivering 24,000 shp (17,895 kW) to two shafts
Performance: maximum speed 21 kts
Complement: 27+446, and provision for 930 troops in LPD 4-6 and LPD 14-15, or for 840 troops in LPD 7-10, AGF 11 and LPD 12-13, which have flag accommodation for about 90

Class

1. USA (12)			Com-
Name	*No.*	*Builders*	*missioned*
AUSTIN	LPD 4	New York Navy Yard	Feb 1965
OGDEN	LPD 5	New York Navy Yard	June 1965
DULUTH	LPD 6	New York Navy Yard	Dec 1965
CLEVELAND	LPD 7	Ingalls Shipbuilding Corporation	Apr 1967
DUBUQUE	LPD 8	Ingalls Shipbuilding Corporation	Sep 1967
DENVER	LPD 9	Lockheed S.B. & Construction Co	Oct 1968
JUNEAU	LPD 10	Lockheed S.B. & Construction Co	July 1969
CORONADO	AGF 11	Lockheed S.B. & Construction Co	May 1970
SHREVEPORT	LPD 12	Lockheed S.B. & Construction Co	Dec 1970
NASHVILLE	LPD 13	Lockheed S.B. & Construction Co	Feb 1970
TRENTON	LPD 14	Lockheed S.B. & Construction Co	Mar 1971
PONCE	LPD 15	Lockheed S.B. & Construction Co	July 1971

'Batral' class landing ship medium

France

Displacement: 750 tons standard and 1,410 tons full load
Dimensions: length 80·0m (262·4ft); beam 13·0m (42·6ft); draught 3·0m (9·84ft) maximum
Gun armament: two 40-mm Bofors AA in single mountings, one 81-mm mortar and two 12·7-mm (0·5-in) heavy machine-guns in single mountings
Missile armament: none
Torpedo armament: none
Anti-submarine armament: none
Aircraft: provision for one helicopter on a platform aft
Capacity: up to 380 tons, including troops and up to 12 vehicles, offloaded with the aid of a 10-ton derrick, and transported in one LCVP and one LCPS
Electronics: one Decca navigation radar and two hull-mounted sonars
Propulsion: two diesels delivering 2,685 kW (3,600 hp) to two shafts

The Champlain (L 9030) is designed for the transport of an assault company.

Performance: maximum speed 16 kts; range 8,350 km (5,190 miles) at 13 kts
Complement: 4+35, plus accommodation for 5+15+118 troops in the first French pair and for 188 troops in the second French pair

Class

1. Chile (2)			Com-
Name	*No.*	*Builders*	*missioned*
MAIPO	91	Asmar	1981
RANCAGUA	92	Asmar	1982
2. France (4+2)			Com-
Name	*No.*	*Builders*	*missioned*
CHAMPLAIN	L 9030	Brest Naval Dockyard	Oct 1974
FRANCIS GARNIER	L 9031	Brest Naval Dockyard	June 1974
DUMONT D'URVILLE	L 9032	Chantiers de Normandie	1983
JACQUES CARTIER	L 9033	Chantiers de Normandie	1983
—	—	Chantiers de Normandie	1982
—	—	Chantiers de Normandie	
3. Ivory Coast (1)			Com-
Name	*No.*	*Builders*	*missioned*
ELEPHANT	—	Dubigeon	Feb 1977
4. Morocco (3)			Com-
Name	*No.*	*Builders*	*missioned*
DAOUD BEN AICHA	—	Dubigeon	May 1977
AHMED ES SAKALI	—	Dubigeon	Sep 1977
ABOU ABDALLAH EL AYACHI	—	Dubigeon	Mar 1978
5. Panama (2)			Com-
Name	*No.*	*Builders*	*missioned*
—	—	Chantiers de la Manche	—
—	—	Chantiers de la Manche	—

'BDC' class landing ship tank

France

Displacement: 1,400 tons standard and 4,225 tons full load
Dimensions: length 102·1m (335ft); beam 15·5m (50·9ft); draught 3·2m (10·5ft)
Gun armament: one twin-barrel 120-mm (4·7-in) mortar, three 40-mm Bofors AA, and one 20-mm AA
Missile armament: none
Torpedo armament: none
Anti-submarine armament: none
Aircraft: two Aérospatiale Alouette III helicopters in a hangar amidships (Ls 9007 and 9009 only)
Capacity: normal troop accommodation is 170, though this can be increased to 335 in austere conditions and to 807 in emergencies; ship-to-shore transport is provided by four LCVPs; up to 1,800 tons of freight can be accommodated
Electronics: navigation radar

Propulsion: two SEMT-Pielstick 16PA1 diesels delivering 1,490 kW (2,000 bhp) to two shafts
Performance: maximum speed 11 kts; range 34,250 km (21,285 miles) at 10 kts
Complement: 6+69

Class

1. France (5)			Com-
Name	*No.*	*Builders*	*missioned*
ARGENS	L 9003	Ch. de Bretagne	June 1960
BIDASSOA	L 9004	Ch. Seine Maritime	Oct 1961
TRIEUX	L 9007	Ch. de Bretagne	Mar 1960
DIVES	L 9008	Ch. Seine Maritime	Apr 1961
BLAVET	L 9009	Ch. de Bretagne	Jan 1961

Remarks: These are very useful long-range ships.

'De Soto County' class landing ship tank
USA
Displacement: 4,165 tons light and 7,100 tons full load
Dimensions: length 445ft (135·6m); beam 62ft (18·9m); draught 17·5ft (5·3m)
Gun armament: six 3-in (76-mm) L/50 DP in three Mk 33 twin mountings
Missile armament: none
Torpedo armament: none
Anti-submarine armament: none
Aircraft: provision for a helicopter on the platform amidships
Capacity: the lower tank deck is 288ft (87·8m) in length, and can accommodate 23 medium tanks or other vehicles up to 75 tons in weight; troop accommodation is 30+604; and liquid storage is provided for 170,000 US gal (643,520 litres) of diesel or jet fuel and 7,000 US gal (26,500 litres) of vehicle fuel; entry and egress are effected through the bow door, and other landing capability is provided by four LCVPs carried in davits, and one LCU and two pontoons carried on deck
Electronics: navigation radar
Propulsion: six diesels (Fairbanks-Morse or Cooper Bessemer) delivering 13,700bhp (10,215kW) to two shafts
Performance: maximum speed 16·5kts
Complement: 15+173

The Grado (L 9890) has a vehicle-landing raft attached to her port side.

Class

1. Brazil (1)

Name	No.	Builders	Commissioned
DUQUE DE CAXAIS	G26	Avondale Shipyards	Nov 1957

2. Italy (2)

Name	No.	Builders	Commissioned
GRADO	L9890	Avondale Shipyards	1957
CAORLE	L9891	Newport News S.B.	1957

3. Mexico (1)

Name	No.	Builders	Commissioned
(ex-USS *Lorain County*)	—	American S.B.	Oct 1959

4. USA (2)

Name	No.	Builders	Commissioned
SUFFOLK COUNTY	LSTT 1173	Boston Navy Yard	Aug 1957
WOOD County	LSTT 1178	American S.B.	Aug 1959

'Frösch' class landing ship tank
East Germany
Displacement: 1,950 tons standard and 4,000 tons full load
Dimensions: length 91·0m (298·4ft); beam 11·0m (36·1ft); draught 2·8m (9·2ft)
Gun armament: four 57-mm L/70 AA in two twin mountings, four 30-mm L/65 AA in two twin mountings, and (in some ships) one rocket-launcher system
Missile armament: none
Torpedo armament: none
Anti-submarine armament: none
Mines: provision for laying through stern doors
Capacity: 800 tons including 12 tanks
Electronics: one 'Strut Curve' long-range air-search radar, one 'Square Head' surface search radar, one TSR 333 navigation radar, two 'Muff Cob' 57-mm fire-control radars, two 'Drum Tilt' 30-mm fire-control radars, and numerous other electronic systems
Propulsion: two diesels delivering ?kW (?hp) to two shafts
Performance: maximum speed 18kts
Complement: not known

Class

1. East Germany (12)

Name	No.
COTTBUS	614
EBERSWALDEZ	—
EISENHÜTTEN STADT	—
FRANKFURT AM ODER	—
HETTSTADT	—
HOYERS WERDE	634
LÜBBEN	—
NEUBRANDENBURG	—
SCHWERIN	—
SEIGER	631

Plus 2 others

'Ivan Rogov' class landing ship dock
USSR

*The **Ivan Rogov** heralds the emergence of a potent long-range amphibious assault capability for the USSR, each ship being able to transport a full battalion of Naval Infantry with its vehicles and other equipment. The bow ramp offers beaching capability, while the well makes offshore operations a simple matter. Good AA protection by SAMs and guns is provided.*

Displacement: 14,000 tons full load
Dimensions: length 159·0m (521·6ft); beam 24·5m (80·2ft); draught 6·5m (21·2ft)
Gun armament: two 76-mm (3-in) L/60 DP in one twin mounting, four 30-mm AA 'Gatling' mountings, and one 40-barrel BM-21 rocket-launcher
Missile armament: one twin launcher for SA-N-4 surface-to-air missiles
Torpedo armament: none
Anti-submarine armament: none
Aircraft: three to five Kamov Ka-25 'Hormone' helicopters on a platform forward and in a hangar aft
Capacity: the dock is some 76·0m (249·3ft) long, and the vessel is designed to carry a Naval Infantry battalion of 522 men with up to 40 tanks; the docking well can accommodate two 'Lebed' class hovercraft and one 'Ondatra' class LCM, though this reduces tank capacity to 20
Electronics: one 'Head Net-C' 3D radar, one 'Owl Screech' main armament fire-control radar, two 'Bass Tilt' AA fire-control radars, one 'Pop Group' SAM fire-control radar, one 'Don Kay' navigation radar, and one 'High Pole' IFF
Propulsion: two gas turbines delivering 33,555kW (45,000shp) to two shafts
Performance: maximum speed 26kts; range 18,500km (11,500 miles) at 12kts
Complement: 400

Class

1. USSR (2)

Name	Builders	Commissioned
IVAN ROGOV	Kaliningrad	1978
ALEKSANDR NIKOLAEV	Kaliningrad	1982

'LSM 1' class landing ship medium
USA

Displacement: 1,095 tons full load

Dimensions: length 203·5 ft (62·0 m); beam (34·6 ft (10·5 m); draught 8·5 ft (2·6 m)

Gun armament: two 40-mm Bofors in a twin mounting, and a varying number of 20-mm AA, though this can be and is variable in a number of navies depending on role and theatre

Missile armament: none

Torpedo armament: none

Anti-submarine armament: none

Capacity: 900 tons maximum or 740 tons for beaching at a draught of 3·4 ft (1·04 m)

Electronics: one surface-search and navigation radar

Propulsion: two Fairbanks-Morse or General Motors diesels delivering 2,800 bhp (2,090 kW) to two shafts

Performance: maximum speed 12 kts

Complement: about 60

Class
1. **China** 14 ex-US ships for minelaying and as support ships
2. **Dominican republic** 1 ex-US ship
3. **Ecuador** *2 ex-US ships*
4. **Greece** 5 ex-US ships
5. **Israel** 3 ex-US ships
6. **Paraguay** 1 ex-US ship used as a light forces tender
7. **Peru** 2 ex-US ships
8. **Philippines** 4 ex-US ships
9. **South Korea** 8 ex-US ships, one of them used as a minelayer support ship
10. **Thailand** 3 ex-US ships
11. **Turkey** 5 ex-US ships used as coastal minelayers
12. **Venezuela** 1 ex-US ship used as a transport
13. **Vietnam** ex-US ships

'LST 1-1152' class landing ship tank
USA

Displacement: 1,655 tons standard and 3,640 tons full load

Dimensions: length 328 ft (100·0 m); beam 50 ft (15·2 m); draught 14 ft (4·3 m)

Gun armament: a variety of armaments is carried, typical installations being up to 10 40-mm Bofors AA in two twin and six single mountings, or two 3-in (76-mm) and six 40-mm Bofors AA

Missile armament: none

Torpedo armament: none

Anti-submarine armament: none

Capacity: 1,875 tons maximum or 446 tons for bleaching at designed draught

Electronics: surface-search and navigation radar

Propulsion: two General Motors diesels delivering 1,700 bhp (1,270 kW) to two shafts

Fuel: diesel oil

Performance: maximum speed 11·6 kts; range 6,900 miles (11,105 km) at 9 kts

Complement: between 100 and 125

Class
1. **Brazil** 1 ex-US ship
2. **Chile** 2 ex-US ships
3. **China** 15 ex-US ships, plus others if taken out of commercial service
4. **Ecuador** 1 ex-US ship
5. **Greece** 5 ex-US ships
6. **Indonesia** 9 ex-US ships, some with Soviet armament now fitted
7. **Malaysia** 2 ex-US ships used as light forces tenders
8. **Mexico** 2 ex-US ships used as rescue vessels
9. **Peru** 3 ex-US ships
10. **Philippines** 24 ex-US ships
11. **Singapore** 6 ex-US ships
12. **South Korea** 8 ex-US ships
13. **Taiwan** 21 ex-US ships
14. **Thailand** 5 ex-US ships
15. **Turkey** 2 ex-US ships with an alternative minelaying role
16. **Vietnam** 3 ex-US ships

The 'LST 1-1152' class Ikaria (L 154) of the Greek navy is seen carrying the Sifnos (L 150), an 'LCU 501' class landing craft, utility.

'Newport' class landing ship tank
USA

Displacement: 8,450 tons full load

Dimensions: length 522·3 ft (159·2 m) hull; beam 69·5 ft (21·2 m); draught 17·5 ft (5·3 m)

Gun armament: four 3-in (76-mm) L/50 DP in two Mk 33 twin mountings, and two 20-mm Phalanx Mk 16 close-in weapon system mountings

Missile armament: none

Torpedo armament: none

Anti-submarine armament: none

Capacity: there is a payload area of 19,000 sq ft (1,765 m²) for a vehicle stowage of 500 tons, vehicles exiting over a 75-ton capacity 112-ft (34·1-m) derrick-supported bow ramp or, if amphibious, through a stern gate; each LST can also carry four sections of pontoon causeway, and the troop capacity is 20+400

Electronics: one Raytheon/Sylvania SPS-10 surface-search radar, one Mk 36 Super Chaffroc rapid-blooming overhead chaff launcher, OE-82 satellite communications antenna, and one WSC-3 satellite communications transceiver

Propulsion: six diesels (General Motors in LSTs 1179-1181, and Alco in LSTs 1182-1198) delivering 16,000 bhp (11,930 kW) to two shafts

Performance: maximum speed 20 kts; range 2,875 miles (4,625 km) at cruising speed

Complement: 14+211

Class

1. USA (20)			
Name	*No.*	*Builders*	*Commissioned*
NEWPORT	LST 1179	Philadelphia NY	June 1969
MANITOWOC	LST 1180	Philadelphia NY	Jan 1970
SUMTER	LST 1181	Philadelphia NY	June 1970
FRESNO	LST 1182	National Steel & S.B.	Nov 1969
PEORIA	LST 1183	National Steel & S.B.	Feb 1970
FREDERICK	LST 1184	National Steel & S.B.	Apr 1970
SCHENECTADY	LST 1185	National Steel & S.B.	June 1970
CAYUGA	LST 1186	National Steel & S.B.	Aug 1970
TUSCALOOSA	LST 1187	National Steel & S.B.	Oct 1970
SAGINAW	LST 1188	National Steel & S.B.	Jan 1971
SAN BERNARDINO	LST 1189	National Steel & S.B.	Mar 1971
BOULDER	LST 1190	National Steel & S.B.	June 1971
RACINE	LST 1191	National Steel & S.B.	July 1971
SPARTANBURG COUNTY	LST 1192	National Steel & S.B.	Sep 1971
FAIRFAX COUNTY	LST 1193	National Steel & S.B.	Oct 1971
LA MOURE COUNTY	LST 1194	National Steel & S.B.	Dec 1971
BARBOUR COUNTY	LST 1196	National Steel & S.B.	Feb 1972
HARLAN COUNTY	LST 1196	National Steel & S.B.	Apr 1972
BARNSTABLE COUNTY	LST 1197	National Steel & S.B.	May 1972
BRISTOL COUNTY	LST 1198	National Steel & S.B.	Aug 1972

The Newport (LST 1179) shows off the type's derrick-and-ramp bow for high speeds.

'Polnochny' class landing ship medium

USSR

Displacement: (Type A) 780 tons standard and 800 tons full load; (Type B) 790 tons standard and 850 tons full load; and (Type C) 700 tons standard and 1,150 tons full load

Dimensions: (Type A) length 73·0m (239·5ft), beam 8·5m (27·9ft) and draught 1·8m (5·8ft); (Type B) length 76·0m (249·3ft), beam 8·5m (27·9ft) and draught 1·8m (5·8ft); and (Type C) length 82·0m (269ft), beam 10·0m (32·8ft) and draught 1·8m (5·8ft)

Gun armament: (Type A) two 140-mm (5·5-in) rocket-launchers, and two 14·5-mm (0·57-in) machine-guns, or two 25-mm AA or two 30-mm AA; (Type B) two 140-mm (5·5-in) rocket-launchers, and two or four 30-mm AA in one or two twin mountings; and (Type C) two 140-mm (5·5-in) rocket-launchers, and four 30-mm AA in twin mountings

Missile armament: some ships have four launchers for 32 SA-N-5 surface-to-air missiles

Torpedo armament: none

Anti-submarine armament: none

Capacity: 350 tons, including up to six tanks

Electronics: (Type A) one 'Don-2' or 'Spin Trough' navigation radar, and (ships with 30-mm cannon) one 'Drum Tilt' gun-control radar; (Type B) one 'Don-2' or 'Spin Trough' navigation radar, and one 'Drum Tilt' gun-control radar; and (Type C) one 'Don-2' navigation radar, and one 'Drum Tilt' gun-control radar

Propulsion: two diesels delivering 2,980kW (4,000shp) in Types A and B, and 3,730kW (5,000shp) in Type C to two shafts

Performance: maximum speed 18kts (Types A and B) or 20kts (Type C)

Complement: 40

There are three variants of the 'Polnochny' class, the ship illustrated being of Type A. The class was built in Poland between 1963 and 1972, all with bow ramps.

Class
1. Algeria (1 Type A)	**6. India** (2 Type A and 4 Type C+?)	**10. Somalia** (1 Type A)
2. Angola (3 Type B)	**7. Iraq** (4 Type C)	**11. South Yemen** (1 Type B)
3. Cuba (3 Type B)	**8. Libya** (3 Type C)	**12. USSR** (50 ships)
4. Egypt (3 Type A)	**9. Poland** (23 ships)	**13. Vietnam** (3 Type B)
5. Ethiopia (1 Type C)		

'PS 700' class landing ship tank

France/Libya

Displacement: 2,800 tons full load

Dimensions: length 99·5m (326·4ft); beam 15·6m (51·2ft); draught 2·4m (7·9ft)

Gun armament: one 81-mm mortar, and six 40-mm Breda L/70 AA in three twin mountings

Missile armament: none

Torpedo armament: none

Anti-submarine armament: none

Aircraft: one Aérospatiale Alouette III helicopter on a platform aft

Capacity: up to 11 tanks, and up to 240 troops

Electronics: one navigation radar, and one CSEE Panda director

Propulsion: two SEMT-Pielstick diesels delivering 3,980kW (5,340hp) to two shafts

Performance: maximum speed 15·4kts; range 7,400km (4,600 miles) at 14kts

Complement: 35

Class
1. Libya (2)

Name	No.	Builders	Commissioned
IBN OUF	132	C.N.I.M.	Mar 1977
IBN HARISSA	134	C.N.I.M.	Mar 1978

'Raleigh' class amphibious transport dock

USA

Displacement: 8,040 tons light and 13,600 tons full load

Dimensions: length 521·8ft (159·1m); beam 100ft (30·5m); draught 22ft (6·7m)

Gun armament: six 3-in (76-mm) L/50 DP in three Mk 33 twin mountings, and two 20-mm Phalanx Mk 16 close-in weapon system mountings

Missile armament: none

Torpedo armament: none

Anti-submarine armament: none

Aircraft: up to six Boeing Vertol CH-46 Sea Knight helicopters on a platform aft

Capacity: the docking well measures 168ft (51·2m) in length and 50ft (15·2m) in width, large enough to accommodate one LCU and three LCM(6)s, or four LCM(8)s, or 20 LVTs; further ship-to-shore capability is provided by two LCM(6)s or four LCPLs launched by crane; troop capacity is 143+996

Electronics: one Raytheon/Sylvania SPS-10 surface-search radar, one Lockheed SPS-40 air-search radar, one Mk 56 gun fire-control system, two Mk 51 gun fire-control systems, OE-82 satellite communications antenna, SRR-1 satellite communications receiver, WSC-3 satellite communications transceiver, and Mk 36 Super Chaffroc rapid-blooming overhead chaff launcher

Propulsion: two Babcock & Wilcox boilers supplying steam to two sets of De Laval geared turbines delivering 24,000shp (17,895kW) to two shafts

Performance: maximum speed 21kts

Complement: 30+460

Class
1. USA (3)

Name	No.	Builders	Laid down	Commissioned
RALEIGH	LPD 1	New York Navy Yard	June 1960	Sep 1962
VANCOUVER	LPD 2	New York Navy Yard	Nov 1960	May 1963
LA SALLE	AGF 3	New York Navy Yard	Apr 1962	Feb 1964

The Raleigh (LPD 1) was the first of her type, combining features from amphibious transports and cargo ships. La Salle has been converted into a small command ship.

'Ropucha' class landing ship tank

USSR

Displacement: 3,450 tons standard and 4,400 tons full load

Dimensions: length 110·0m (360·9ft); beam 14·5m (47·6ft); draught 3·6m (11·5ft)

Gun armament: four 57-mm AA in two twin mountings

Missile armament: none

Torpedo armament: none

Anti-submarine armament: none

Capacity: COMING

Electronics: one 'Strut Curve' long-range air-search radar, one 'Muff Cob' gun-control radar, one 'Don-2' navigation radar, and one 'High Pole-B' IFF

Propulsion: four diesels delivering 7,455kW (10,000shp) to two shafts

Performance: maximum speed 17kts

Complement: 95

Class
1. South Yemen (1)
1 ship

2. USSR (13)
13 ships

'Sir Bedivere' class logistic landing ship

UK

Displacement: 3,270 tons light and 5,675 tons full load
Dimensions: length 412·1 ft (125·1 m); beam 59·8 ft (19·6 m); draught 13 ft (4·3 m)
Gun armament: two 40-mm Bofors AA in two single mountings
Missile armament: none
Torpedo armament: none
Anti-submarine armament: none

The Australian Tobruk (L 50) is a heavy-lift development of the 'Sir Bedivere' class, displacing 5,800 tons and able to lift 500 troops or 1,300 tons of freight.

Aircraft: provision for helicopters on a platform aft
Capacity: the troop accommodation is 340, or 534 in austere conditions; the beaching cargo capacity is 340 tons, and included in this total may be 16 main battle tanks, 34 mixed vehicles, 120 tons of petroleum products and 30 tons of ammunition; other loads can include 20 helicopters, and payload is handled by three cranes; landing craft may be carried in place of lifeboats
Electronics: navigation radar
Propulsion: two Mirrlees Blackstone diesels delivering 9,400 bhp (7,010 kW) to two shafts
Performance: maximum speed 17 kts; range 9,200 miles (14,805 km) at 15 kts
Complement: 18+50

Class

1. Australia (1)

Name	No.	Builders	Laid down	Commissioned
TOBRUK	L 50	Carrington Slipways	Feb 1978	Apr 1981

2. UK (5)

Name	No.	Builders	Laid down	Commissioned
SIR BEDIVERE	L 3004	Hawthorn Leslie	Oct 1965	May 1967
SIR GERAINT	L 3027	Alexander Stephen	June 1965	July 1967
SIR LANCELOT	L 3029	Fairfield S.B.	Mar 1962	Jan 1964
SIR PERCIVALE	L 3036	Hawthorn Leslie	Apr 1966	Mar 1968
SIR TRISTRAM	L 3505	Hawthorn Leslie	Feb 1966	Sept 1967

'TCD' class landing ship dock

France

Displacement: 5,800 tons light and 8,500 tons full load
Dimensions: length 149·0 m (488·9 ft); beam 23·0 m (75·4 ft); draught 5·4 m (17·7 ft) normal and 8·7 m (28·5 ft) flooded down
Gun armament: two 120-mm (4·7-in) mortars and four 40-mm Bofors AA
Missile armament: none
Torpedo armament: none
Anti-submarine armament: none
Aircraft: the main helicopter platform can accommodate three Aérospatiale SA 321 Super Frelon or 10 SA 318 Alouette III helicopters, while the portable platform aft can accommodate one Super Frelon or three Alouette IIIs
Capacity: the well deck measures 120·0 m (393·7 ft) in length and 14·0 m (45·9 ft) in width, and can accommodate two EDIC landing craft tanks (each loaded with 11 tanks) or 18 loaded LCM(6)s for the direct-assault role, in which case troop accommodation is 343; in the logistics role a freight load of 1,500 tons can be carried; typical loads are one 400-ton ship, or 12 50-ton barges, or 120 AMX-13 light tanks, or 84 amphibious tractors, or 340 Jeeps, or 18 Super Frelons, or 80 Alouette IIIs; there are two 35-ton cranes for freight
Electronics: one Thomson-CSF DRBN 32 navigation radar, and (L 9021 only) one SQS-17 hull-mounted sonar
Propulsion: two SEMT-Pielstick diesels delivering 6,415 kW (8,600 bhp) to two shafts
Performance: maximum speed 17 kts; range 16,675 km (10,360 miles) at 15 kts
Complement: 238

Class

1. France (2)

Name	No.	Builders	Laid down	Commissioned
OURAGAN	L 9021	Brest Naval Dockyard	June 1962	June 1965
ORAGE	L 9022	Brest Naval Dockyard	June 1966	Apr 1968

'Terrebonne Parish' class landing ship tank

USA

Displacement: 2,590 tons standard and 5,800 tons full load
Dimensions: length 384 ft (117·1 m); beam 55 ft (16·8 m); draught 17 ft (5·2 m)
Gun armament: six 3-in (76-mm) L/50 DP in three Mk 27 twin mountings
Missile armament: none
Torpedo armament: none
Anti-submarine armament: none
Capacity: up to 10 M48 main battle tanks or 17 LVTP amphibious tractors, plus a maximum of 395 men who can be moved ashore with the aid of four embarked landing craft
Electronics: one Raytheon/Sylvania SPS-10 surface-search radar, one navigation radar, two Western Electric SPG-34 gun-control radars used in conjunction with two Mk 63 gun fire-control systems
Propulsion: four General Motors diesels delivering 6,000 bhp (4,475 kW) to two shafts
Performance: maximum speed 15 kts; range 17,275 miles (27,800 km) at 9 kts
Complement: 116

Class

1. Greece (2)

Name	No.	Builders	Commissioned
INOUSE	L 104	Bath Iron Works	Mar 1953
KOS	L 116	Christy Corporation	Sep 1954

2. Spain (3)

Name	No.	Builders	Commissioned
VELASCO	L 11	Bath Iron Works	Nov 1952
MARTIN ALVAREZ	L 12	Christy Corporation	June 1954
CONDE DE VENADITO	L 13	Bath Iron Works	Sep 1953

3. Turkey (2)

Name	No.	Builders	Commissioned
ERTUĞRUL	L 401	Christy Corporation	1954
SERDAR	L 402	Christy Corporation	1954

The Greek Kos (L 116) shows off the definitive configuration of the bow-door LST developed during World War II, with superstructure and machinery aft to leave as much space as possible for tank accommodation in the midships and bow sections. Note the stern anchor, a substantial type dropped as the ship approaches the beach so that the unladen vessel can be kedged off when required. The gun armament in the bow is raised to leave access to the offloading ramp inside the bow doors, a design feature that limited maximum speed and led to the derrick-and-ramp design for a 20-kt cruising speed.

Remarks: Greece's two 'Terrebonne Parish' LSTs were acquired in 1977 and refitted in Greek yards. Spain's ships, to which the specification applies, were received in 1971 (two ships) and 1972 (one ship). Turkey's two ships are, like the two Greek units, generally similar to the Spanish vessels, and were received in 1973 and 1974, and are the largest of an extensive LST force.

'Thomaston' class landing ship dock
USA

Displacement: 6,880 tons light and 12,000 tons full load
Dimensions: length 510ft (155·5m); beam 84ft (25·6m); draught 19ft (5·8m)
Gun armament: six 3-in (76-mm) L/50 DP in three Mk 33 twin mountings
Missile armament: none
Torpedo armament: none
Anti-submarine armament: none
Aircraft: provision for helicopters on an optional platform over the docking well
Capacity: the docking well measures 391ft (119·2m) in length and 48ft (14·6m) in width, large enough to accommodate 21 LCM(6) landing craft, or three LCUs and six LCMs, or 50 LVTP amphibious tractors, with another 30 LVTPs housed on the mezzanine and upper decks; troop capacity is 340
Electronics: one Bendix SPS-6 air-search radar, one Raytheon/Sylvania SPS-10 surface-search radar, OE-82 satellite communications antenna, SRR-1 satellite communications receiver, WSC-3 satellite communications transceiver, and one Mk 36 Super Chaffroc rapid-blooming overhead chaff launcher (except LSD 28)
Propulsion: two Babcock & Wilcox boilers supplying steam to two sets of General Electric geared turbines delivering 24,000shp (17,895kW) to two shafts
Performance: maximum speed 22·5kts; range 11,500+ miles (18,505+ km) at cruising speed
Complement: 21+379

Class
1. USA (8)

Name	No.	Builders	Commissioned
THOMASTON	LSD 28	Ingalls Shipbuilding Corporation	Sep 1954
PLYMOUTH ROCK	LSD 29	Ingalls Shipbuilding Corporation	Nov 1954
FORT SNELLING	LSD 30	Ingalls Shipbuilding Corporation	Jan 1955
POINT DEFIANCE	LSD 31	Ingalls Shipbuilding Corporation	Mar 1955
SPIEGEL GROVE	LSD 32	Ingalls Shipbuilding Corporation	June 1956
ALAMO	LSD 33	Ingalls Shipbuilding Corporation	Aug 1956
HERMITAGE	LSD 34	Ingalls Shipbuilding Corporation	Dec 1956
MONTICELLO	LSD 35	Ingalls Shipbuilding Corporation	Mar 1957

A stern view of the Spiegel Grove (LSD 32) of the 'Thomaston' class reveals the size of the well deck, which is wide enough to accommodate a 165-ton Bell JEFF-B amphibious assault landing hovercraft during the latter's trials in 1980. The improved LCAC derivative has been ordered against a requirement for 108 units.

'Whidbey Island' class landing ship dock
USA

Displacement: 11,125 tons light and 15,725 tons full load
Dimensions: length 609ft (185·6m); beam 84ft (25·6m); draught 20·5ft (6·3m)
Gun armament: two 20-mm Phalanx Mk 16 close-in weapon system mountings
Missile armament: none
Torpedo armament: none
Anti-submarine armament: none
Aircraft: provision for Sikorsky CH-53 Sea Stallion helicopters and BAe/McDonnell Douglas AV-8A Harrier fixed-wing aircraft on the flight deck aft
Capacity: the well deck measures 440ft (134·1m) in length and 50ft (15·2m) in width, and ship-to-shore transport capability is provided by four Amphibious Air-Cushion Vehicles (LCACs) or 26 LCM(6)s; including four loaded LCACs in the well deck, there is a total of 12,500sqft (1,161·25m²) of vehicle area, and up to 5,000cuft (141·6m³) of palletized freight can be accommodated; troop capacity is 338
Electronics: one Raytheon SPS-49 air-search radar, one Norden SPS-67 surface-search radar, one Litton LN-66 navigation radar, OE-82 satellite communications antenna, SSR-1 satellite communications receiver, WSC-3 satellite communications transceiver, Mk 36 Super Chaffroc rapid-blooming overhead chaff launcher, and Raytheon SLQ-32(V) electronic warfare system
Propulsion: four Colt-Pielstick 16PC2V diesels delivering 34,000bhp (25,355kW) to two shafts
Performance: maximum speed 20+ kts
Complement: 19+337

Class
1. USA (2+10)

Name	No.	Builders	Laid down	Commissioned
WHIDBEY ISLAND	LSD 41	Lockheed S.B.	Aug 1981	Nov 1984
—	LSD 42	Lockheed S.B.	Aug 1982	Dec 1985
—	LSD 43	Proposed FY 1983	—	—
—	LSD 44	Proposed FY 1984	—	—
—	LSD 45-46	Proposed FY 1985	—	—
—	LSD 47-48	Proposed FY 1986	—	—
—	LSD 49-50	Proposed FY 1987	—	—
—	LSD 51-52	Proposed FY 1988	—	—

'Avenger' class mine countermeasures vessel
USA

An artist's impression of the Avenger (MCM 1) reveals the modern lines of the class, designed to replace the obsolete 'Aggressive' and 'Acme' classes.

Displacement: 1,040 tons full load
Dimensions: length 210ft (64·0m); beam 44·3ft (13·5m); draught 10·5ft (3·2m)
Gun armament: two 0·5-in (12·7-mm) heavy machine-guns
Missile armament: none
Torpedo armament: none
Anti-submarine armament: none
Electronics: one Westinghouse SPS-55 surface-search radar, and SQQ-30 sonar
Propulsion: four Waukesha diesels delivering power to two shafts
Performance: maximum speed 14kts
Complement: 5+57

Class
1. USA (0+1+20)

Name	No.	Builders	Commissioned
AVENGER	MCM 1	Peterson Builders Inc	1985
—	MCM 2	Approved in FY 1983 programme	—
—	MCM 3-6	Proposed in FY 1984 programme	—
—	MCM 7-10	Proposed in FY 1985 programme	—
—	MCM 11-21	Proposed future programmes	—

'Aggressive' and 'Dash' class ocean minesweepers/minehunters

USA

Displacement: 620 tons light and 735 tons full load
Dimensions: length 172ft (52·4m); beam 36ft (11·0m); draught 13·6ft (4·2m)
Gun armament: one 40-mm Bofors Mk 3 AA
Missile armament: none
Torpedo armament: none
Anti-submarine armament: none
Electronics: navigation radar and General Electric SQQ-14 minehunting and classification sonar
Propulsion: four Packard or Waukesha diesels delivering 2,280bhp (1,700kW) to two shafts
Performance: maximum speed 14kts; range 3,450 miles (5,550km) at 10kts
Complement: 5+67

Class

1. Belgium (7)

Name	No.	Builders	Laid down	Commissioned
J. E. VAN HAVERBEKE	M 902	Peterson Builders Inc	Mar 1959	Nov 1960
A. F. DUFOUR	M 903	Bellingham S.Y.	Feb 1954	Sep 1955
DE BROUWER	M 904	Bellingham S.Y.	Apr 1954	Nov 1955
BREYDEL	M 906	Tacoma B.B. Co	Nov 1954	Jan 1956
ARTEVELDE	M 907	Tacoma B.B. Co	Oct 1953	Dec 1955
G. TRUFFAUT	M 908	Tampa S.B. Co	Feb 1955	Sep 1956
F. BOVESSE	M 909	Tampa S.B. Co	Apr 1954	Dec 1956

2. France (10)

Name	No.	Builder	Commissioned
OUISTREHAM	M 610	USA	Mar 1957
ALENÇON	M 612	USA	Jan 1955
BERNEVAL	M 613	USA	Aug 1954
CANTHO	M 615	USA	Oct 1955
DOMPAIRE	M 616	USA	May 1955
GARIGLIANO	M 617	USA	Oct 1954
MYTHO	M 618	USA	May 1955
VINH LONG	M 619	USA	Oct 1955
BERLAIMONT	M 620	USA	Sep 1956
BACCARAT	M 623	USA	Nov 1956

3. Italy (4)

Name	No.	Builders	Commissioned
SALMONE	M 5430	Martinolich S.B. Co	June 1956
STORIONE	M 5431	Martinolich S.B. Co	Feb 1956
SGOMBRO	M 5432	Tampa Marine Corporation	May 1957
SQUALO	M 5433	Tampa Marine Corporation	June 1957

4. The Netherlands (1)

Name	No.	Builders	Commissioned
ONBEVREESD	A 855	Astoria Marine Construction Co	Sep 1954

5. Spain (4)

Name	No.	Builders	Commissioned
GUADALETE	M 41	Colbert BW	Dec 1953
GUADALMEDINA	M 42	Wilmington BW	July 1954
GUADALQUIVIR	M 43	Tacoma B.B. Co	Feb 1956
GUADIANA	M 44	Burgess Boat Co	Nov 1954

The Sgombro (M 5432) of the Italian navy is typical of the 'Aggressive' class of ocean minesweepers, which are built on wooden hulls with stainless-steel machinery for the lowest possible magnetic signature.

6. USA (23)

Name	No.	Builders	Commissioned
CONSTANT	MSO 427		Sep 1954
DASH*	MSO 428		Aug 1953
DETECTOR*	MSO 429		Jan 1954
DIRECT*	MSO 430		July 1954
DOMINANT*	MSO 431		Nov 1954
ENGAGE	MSO 433		June 1954
ENHANCE	MSO 437		Apr 1955
ESTEEM	MSO 438		Sep 1955
EXCEL	MSO 439		Feb 1955
EXPLOIT	MSO 440		Mar 1954
EXULTANT	MSO 441		June 1954
FEARLESS	MSO 442		Sep 1954
FIDELITY	MSO 443		Jan 1955
FORTIFY	MSO 446		July 1954
ILLUSIVE	MSO 448		Nov 1953
IMPERVIOUS	MSO 449		July 1954
IMPLICIT	MSO 455		Mar 1954
INFLICT	MSO 456		May 1954
PLUCK	MSO 464		Aug 1954
CONQUEST	MSO 488		July 1955
GALLANT	MSO 489		Sep 1955
LEADER	MSO 490		Nov 1955
PLEDGE	MSO 492		Apr 1956

*decommissioned FY 1983

Remarks: Originally designated the 'Agile' class, this type was built during the 1950s to the total of 93 units, many of them being transferred later to the USA's European allies. The seven Belgian vessels were transferred between 1955 and 1960 from the USA (five ships) and in 1966 from Norway (two ships). France received her 10 ships in three batches during 1953, and of these a group of five (Ms 615, 616, 617, 618 and 619) have been modernized for minehunting with DUBM 21A sonar and PAP 104 mine destructors; the other have been refitted. Italy's four ships were transferred in 1956-57. The Netherlands received four of the class, but only one remains in first-line service, in this instance as a mine-countermeasures support ship. The four ships currently operated by Spain were transferred from the USA in 1971 (three ships) and 1972 (one ship), all being bought outright in 1974; they have SPS-5C surface-search and navigation radar and an armament of one 20-mm twin AA mounting. Of the surviving US Navy ships, three are active with the Atlantic Fleet, the others operating with the reserves.

'Circé' class minehunter

France

Displacement: 465 tons standard, 495 tons normal and 510 tons full load
Dimensions: length 50·9m (167ft); beam 8·9m (29·2ft); draught 3·4m (11·15ft)
Gun armament: one 20-mm AA
Missile armament: none
Torpedo armament: none
Anti-submarine armament: none
Electronics: one navigation radar, one DUBM 20 minehunting sonar and two PAP wire-guided detonation sleds
Propulsion: one MTU diesel delivering 1,340kW (1,800bhp) to one shaft
Performance: maximum speed 15kts; range 5,560km (3,455 miles) at 12kts
Complement: 4+15+29

Class

1. France (5)

Name	No.	Builders	Launched	Commissioned
CYBÈLE	M 712	C.M. de Normandie	Jan 1972	Sep 1972
CALLIOPE	M 713	C.M. de Normandie	Nov 1971	Sep 1972
CLIO	M 714	C.M. de Normandie	June 1971	May 1972
CIRCÉ	M 715	C.M. de Normandie	Dec 1970	May 1972
CERES	M 716	C.M. de Normandie	Aug 1972	Mar 1973

The Cybèle (M 712) is built of laminated wood, and has two propulsion systems (one for conventional movement and the other for minehunting). The latter comprises two small and quiet propellers (at the base of the single main rudder) driven by 195-kW (260-hp) electric motors for a speed of 7kts and extreme manoeuvrability.

'Krogulec' class ocean minesweeper
Poland

Designed largely for Baltic operations, Poland's 'Krogulec' minesweeper class is epitomized by the Zuraw (623), with a 25-mm twin mounting forward of the bridge.

Displacement: 500 tons
Dimensions: length 58·0m (190·3ft); beam 7·5m (24·6ft); draught 2·5m (8·2ft)
Gun armament: six 25-mm AA in three twin mountings
Missile armament: none
Torpedo armament: none
Anti-submarine armament: none
Electronics: surface-search radar, and navigation radar
Propulsion: ? diesels delivering ?kW (?hp) to two shafts
Performance: maximum speed 16 kts
Complement: not known
Class

1. Poland (12)

Name	No.	Builders	Commissioned
ORLIK	613	Stocznia	1964
KROGULEC	614	Stocznia	1963
JASTRAB	615	Stocznia	1964
KORMORAN	616	Stocznia	1963
CZAJKA	617	Stocznia	1964
ALBATROS	618	Stocznia	1965
PELIKAN	619	Stocznia	1965
TUKAN	620	Stocznia	1966
KANIA	621	Stocznia	1966
JASKOLKA	622	Stocznia	1966
ZURAW	623	Stocznia	1967
CZALPA	624	Stocznia	1967

'Landsort' class mine countermeasures vessel
Sweden

Displacement: 340 tons standard
Dimensions: length 47·5m (155·8ft); beam 9·6m (31·5ft); draught 2·2m (7·3ft)
Gun armament: one 40-mm Bofors L/48 AA
Missile armament: none
Torpedo armament: none
Anti-submarine armament: none
Electronics: one Philips Elektronikindustrier/Racal-Decca 9MJ 400 radar navigation system, one Thomson-CSF 2022 minehunting sonar, and control equipment for one catamaran magnetic/acoustic minesweeper unit
Propulsion: four TAMD 120B diesels delivering 940kW (1,260hp) to two shafts
Performance: maximum speed 14 kts
Complement: 12 + 12

Class
1. Sweden (0+6)
6 craft on order

'MHCAT' class minehunter
Australia

Displacement: about 170 tons
Dimensions: length 101·7ft (30·9m); beam 29·5ft (9·0m); draught 6·6ft (2·0m)
Gun armament: none
Missile armament: none
Torpedo armament: none
Anti-submarine armament: none
Electronics: navigation radar, one Krupp Atlas DSQS-11H minehunting sonar used as part of the containerized mission package (sonar, tactical data system, navigation system and mine-destructor control system for the PAP 104 submersible that lays demolition charges beside the mine)
Propulsion: two Poyaud diesel-generator sets delivering power to two propeller/steering units
Performance: maximum speed 10 kts
Complement: 2 + 11
Class
1. Australia (0+2+4)
two craft building with the possibility of four more to be ordered

Remarks: This is an experimental catamaran design for stability and good deck area.

'Natya I' and 'Natya II' class ocean minesweepers
USSR

Displacement: 650 tons standard and 950 tons full load
Dimensions: length 61·0ft (200·1ft); beam 10·0m (32·8ft); draught 3·5m (11·5ft)
Gun armament: four 30-mm AA in two twin mountings, and four 25-mm AA in two twin mountings
Missile armament: none
Torpedo armament: none

Photographed from a British frigate, a Soviet 'Natya I' class ocean minesweeper displays the type's basic similarity to other comparable vessels, with a large quarterdeck for the stowage and working of the sweeping gear. The 30-mm mounts are on the centreline fore and aft, the 25-mm mountings being staggered amidships.

Anti-submarine armament: two RBU 1200 five-barrel rocket-launchers ('Natya I' only)
Electronics: one 'Drum Tilt' gun-control radar, one 'Don-2' navigation radar, one 'High Pole-B' IFF, and two 'Square Head' IFF
Propulsion: two diesels delivering 5,965kW (8,000shp) to two shafts
Performance: maximum speed 20 kts
Complement: 50
Class

1. India (6)

Name	No.	Builder	Commissioned
PONDICHERRY	M 61	USSR	1978
PORBANDAR	M 62	USSR	1978
BEDI	M 63	USSR	1979
BHAVNAGAR	M 64	USSR	1979
ALLEPPEY	M 65	USSR	1980
RATNAGIRI	M 66	USSR	1980

2. Libya (4)

Name	No.	Builder	Commissioned
RAS EL GELAIS	111	USSR	1981
RAS HADAD	113	USSR	1981
RAS AL HAMMAN	115	USSR	1983
RAS AL FALLUGA	117	USSR	1983

3. USSR (34 'Natya I' and 1 'Natya II' class)
34 'Natya I' class ships
1 'Natya II' class ship

'T 43' and 'T 43 (Modified)' class ocean minesweepers

USSR

Displacement: 500 tons standard and 580 tons full load ('T 43' class) or 600 tons ('T 43 (Modified)' class)

Dimensions: length 58·0m (190·2ft) for 'T 43' class and 60·0m (196·8ft) for 'T 43 (Modified)' class; beam 8·4m (27·6ft); draught 2·1m (6·9ft)

Gun armament: two 37-mm AA in one twin mounting, two 25-mm AA in one twin mounting, and ('T 43 (Modified)' class only) four heavy machine-guns in two twin mountings

Missile armament: none

Torpedo armament: none

Anti-submarine armament: two depth-charge throwers

Mines: up to 20

Electronics: one 'Ball End' surface-search radar, one *Neptun* navigation radar, one 'High Pole-A' IFF, and one 'Square Head' IFF

Propulsion: two Type 9D diesels delivering 1,640kW (2,200bhp) to two shafts

Performance: maximum speed 14kts; range 5,550km (3,450 miles) at 10kts

Complement: 65

A 'T 43' class ocean minesweeper of the Soviet navy.

Class

1. Albania (2 'T 43')
2 ships (nos 152 and 342)

2. Algeria (2 'T 43')
2 ships (nos M521 and M522)

3. Bulgaria (2 'T 43')
2 ships (nos 48 and 49)

4. China (23 'T 43')
23 ships (nos 341, 342, 364·

5. Egypt (6 'T 43')

Name
ASSIUT
BAHAIRA
CHARKIEH
DAKHLIA
GHARBIA
SINAI

6. Indonesia (4 'T 43')

Name	No.
PULAO RANI	701
PULAO RATEWO	702
PULAO RORBAS	704
PULAO RAJA	705

7. Iraq (2 'T 43')

Name	No.
AL YARMOUK	465
AL KADISIA	467

8. Poland (4 'T 43' and 8 'T 43 (Modified)' class)

Name	No.
ZUBR	601*
TUR	602*
LOS	603*
DZIK	604*
BIZON	605
BOBR	606
ROZMAK	607
DELFIN	608
FOKA	609
MORS	610
RYS	611
ZBIK	612

* 'T 43' clas ships

9. Syria (1 'T 43')

Name
YARMOUK

10. USSR (65 'T 43' and 11 'T 43/AGR')
65 'T 43' class ships
11 'T 43/AGR' class ships

Remarks: More than 200 'T 43' class ocean minesweepers were built in several Soviet yards between 1948 and 1957, and an additional 12 were built at Stocznia for the Polish navy. A large number of 'T 43' class ships were converted to other roles (salvage, diver support etc), including 11 Soviet and one Polish ship into 'T 43/AGR' class radar pickets with a tripod foremast and pole mainmast for 'Big Net', or 'Knife Rest' or 'Squat Eye' air-search radars.

'Tripartite' class minehunter

Belgium/France/Netherlands

Displacement: 510 tons standard and 544 tons full load

Dimensions: length 49·1m (161ft); beam 8·9m (29·2ft); draught 2·5m (8·2ft)

Gun armament: one 20-mm AA

Missile armament: short-range missile system perhaps to be retrofitted

Torpedo armament: none

Anti-submarine armament: none

Electronics: automatic navigation radar system; automatic data-processing system, Thomson-CSF DUBM 21A IBIS mine countermeasures sonar, and two PAP-104 minehunting systems

Propulsion: one Werkspoor diesel delivering 1,700kW (2,280shp) to one shaft; there are also two 88-kW (118-shp) auxiliary engines

Performance: maximum speed 15kts (or 7kts on auxiliary motors); range 5,500km (3,420 miles) at 12kts; endurance 15 days

Complement: between 29 and 40

Class

1. Belgium (0+10+5)
10 ships building and 5 projected

2. France (4+6+5)

Name	No.	Builders	Commissioned
ERIDAN	M641	Lorient ND	1982
CASSIOPÉE	M642	Lorient ND	1983
ANDROMÈDE	M643	Lorient ND	1984
—	M644	Lorient ND	1985
—	M645	Lorient ND	1985

3. The Netherlands (5+10)

Name	No.	Builders	Commissioned
ALKMAAR	850	Van der Giessen-de Noord-Alblasserdam	1983
DELFZIJL	851	Van der Giessen-de Noord-Alblasserdam	1983
DORDRECHT	852	Van der Giessen-de Noord-Alblasserdam	1983
HAARLEM	853	Van der Giessen-de Noord-Alblasserdam	1983
HARLINGEN	854	Van der Giessen-de Noord-Alblasserdam	1984
HELLEVOETSLUIS	855	Van der Giessen-de Noord-Alblasserdam	1985
MAASSLUIS	856	Van der Giessen-de Noord-Alblasserdam	1985
MAKKUM	857	Van der Giessen-de Noord-Alblasserdam	1985
MIDDELBURG	858	Van der Giessen-de Noord-Alblasserdam	1986
SCHEVENINGEN	859	Van der Giessen-de Noord-Alblasserdam	1986
SCHIEDAM	860	Van der Giessen-de Noord-Alblasserdam	1987
URK	861	Van der Giessen-de Noord-Alblasserdam	1987
ZIERIKZEE	862	Van der Giessen-de Noord-Alblasserdam	1988
VLAARDINGEN	863	Van der Giessen-de Noord-Alblasserdam	1988
WILLEMSTAD	864	Van der Giessen-de Noord-Alblasserdam	1989

Remarks: The 'Tripartite' class of minehunters is of great importance in the naval affairs of Western Europe, this basically homogeneous class of 45 vessels providing advanced mine detection and destruction capability. The hulls are of a standard GRP design, to be built at yards in each country, Belgium then delivering the electrical installations for all 45 ships, France the minehunting and destroying gear plus some of the electronics, and The Netherlands the propulsion system.

'Yurka' class ocean minesweeper

USSR

Displacement: 400 tons standard and 460 tons full load

Dimensions: length 52·0m (170·6ft); beam 9·3m (30·5ft); draught 2·0m (6·6ft)

Gun armament: four 30-mm AA in two twin mountings

Missile armament: none

Torpedo armament: none

Anti-submarine armament: none

Mines: up to 10

Electronics: one 'Don-2' navigation radar, one 'Drum Tilt' fire-control radar, two 'Square Head' IFF, and one 'High Pole-B' IFF

Propulsion: two diesels delivering 2,985kW (4,000bhp) to two shafts

Performance: maximum speed 18kts; range 2,000km (1,245 miles) at 18kts

Complement: 45

Class

1. Egypt (4)

Name	No.	Name	No.
GIZA	690	**QENA**	696
ASWAN	695	**SOHAG**	699

2. USSR (49)
49 ships

3. Vietnam (1)
1 ship

'Adjutant' class coastal minehunter/minesweeper
USA

Displacement: 330 tons light and 390 tons full load
Dimensions: length 144 ft (43·9 m); beam 27·9 ft (8·5 m); draught 8 ft (2·4 m)
Gun armament: one 40-mm Bofors AA
Missile armament: none
Torpedo armament: none
Anti-submarine armament: none
Electronics: navigation radar and Plessey Type 193 hull-mounted sonar
Propulsion: two General Motors diesels delivering 880 shp (657 kW) to two shafts
Performance: maximum speed 13·5 kts; range 3,400 miles (5,470 km) at 10·5 kts
Complement: 4+17+19

The pennant number 5510 identifies this 'Adjutant' class coastal mine-sweeper as the Larice of the Italian navy. Features of the design are the high bow and deck line carried aft as far as the break behind the tall bridge structure, the armament of two 20-mm cannon, the low funnel for the exhaust of the twin diesel engines, and the after portion of the ship devoted to the minesweeping gear (paravanes, winches, cable drums and lifting equiment) for the ship's primary mission. Less evident are the wooden hull and non-magnetic metal fixtures and fittings, all designed to keep the magnetic signature of the ship as small as possible for protection against magnetic-influence mines. Like other navies, that of Italy has found the type of use in ancillary roles (survey, diver support etc) as the ships are retired from first-line minesweeping duties.

Class

1. Belgium (6)

Name	No.	Builders	Com-missioned
STAVELOT*	M 928	Boelwerf	July 1955
ROCHEFORT*	M 930	Beliard	Nov 1955
NIEUWPOORT*	M 932	Beliard	Jan 1956
KOKSIJDE*	M 933	Beliard	Nov 1955
VERVIERS	M 934	Boston, USA	June 1956
VEURNE	M 935	Boston, USA	Aug 1956

*in reserve

2. Denmark (7)

Name	No.	Builder
AARØSUND	M 571	USA
EGERNSUND	M 573	USA
GRØNSUND	M 574	USA
GULDBORGSUND	M 575	USA
OMØSUND	M 576	USA
ULVSUND	M 577	USA
VILSUND	M 578	USA

3. Fiji (3)

Name	No.	Builders	Com-missioned
KIKAU	204	Bellingham SY	Feb 1956
KULA	205	Bellingham SY	June 1955
KIRO	206	Bellingham SY	July 1955

4. France (7)

Name	No.	Builder	Com-missioned
PIVOINE	M 633	USA	—
RÉSÉDA	M 635*	USA	—
ACACIA	M 638*	USA	June 1953
AZALÉE	M 668*	USA	Oct 1953
CYCLAMEN	M 674*	USA	May 1954
EGLANTINE	M 675*	USA	Aug 1954
GLYCINE	M 679	USA	Oct 1954

*in reserve

5. Greece (14)

Name	No.	Builder	
ATALANTI	M 202	USA	
ANTIOPI	M 205	USA	
FAEDRA	M 206	USA	
THALIA	M 210	USA	
NIOVI	M 254	USA	
ALKYON	M 211	Peterson Builders Inc	Dec 1968
KLIO	M 213	Peterson Builders Inc	Aug 1968
AVRA	M 214	Peterson Builders Inc	Oct 1968
PLEIAS	M 240	Peterson Builders Inc	June 1967
KICHLI	M 241	Peterson Builders Inc	July 1964
KISSA	M 242	Peterson Builders Inc	Sep 1964
AIGLI	M 246	Tacoma B.B. Co	Jan 1965
DAFNI	M 247	Peterson Builders Inc	Sep 1964
AEDON	M 248	Peterson Builders Inc	Oct 1964

6. Iran (3)

Name	No.	Builders	Com-missioned
SHAHROKH	301	Bellingham S.Y.	1960
SIMORGH	302	Tacoma B.B. Co	1962
KARKAS	303	Peterson Builders Inc	1959

7. Italy (9)

Name	No.	Builder
CASTAGNO	M 5504*	USA
CEDRO	M 5505*	USA
FRASSSINO	M 5508*	USA
GELSO	M 5509*	USA
LARICE	M 5510	USA
NOCE	M 5511	USA
OLMO	M 5512	USA
PLATANO	M 5516*	USA
MANDORLO	M 5519*	USA

*minehunters

8. Norway (10 'Sauda' class)

Name	No.	Builders	Com-missioned
SAUDA	M 311	Hodgeson Bros, Gowdy & Stevens	Aug 1953
SIRA	M 312	Hodgeson Bros, Gowdy & Stevens	Nov 1955
TANA	M 313*	Hodgeson Bros, Gowdy & Stevens	1954
ALTA	M 314	Hodgeson Bros, Gowdy & Stevens	1954
OGNA	M 315	Båtservice	Mar 1955
VOSSO	M 316	Skaaluren Skibsbyggeri	Mar 1955
GLOMMA	M 317	Hodgeson Bros, Gowdy & Stevens	1954
TISTA	M 331	Forende Båtbyggeriex	Apr 1955
KVINA	M 332	Båtservice	July 1955
UTLA	M 334	Båtservice	Nov 1955

*minehunter

9. Pakistan (6)

Name	No.	Builder
MAHMOOD	M 160	USA
MOMIN	M 161	USA
MUBARAK	M 162	USA
MUJAHID	M 164	USA
MUKHTAR	M 165	USA
MOSHAL	M 167	USA

The Egernsund (M 573) of the Royal Danish navy is similar to the Italian ships, but has a 40-mm Bofors gun, extended bulwarks and a revised sweeping arrangement.

10. Singapore (2)

Name	No.	Builders
JUPITER	M 101	
MERCURY	M 102	

11. South Korea (8)

Name	No.	Builders	Commissioned
KUM SAN	MSC 551	Peterson Builders Inc	1959
KO HUNG	MSC 552	Peterson Builders Inc	1959
KUM KOK	MSC 553	Peterson Builders Inc	1959
NAM YANG	MSC 555	Peterson Builders Inc	1963
NA DONG	MSC 556	Peterson Builders Inc	1963
SAM CHOK	MSC 557	Peterson Builders Inc	1968
YONG DONG	MSC 558	Peterson Builders Inc	1975
OK CHEON	MSC 559	Peterson Builders Inc	1975

12. Spain (6)

Name	No.	Builders	Commissioned
JUCAR	M 21	Bellingham S.Y.	June 1956
EBRO	M 22	Bellingham S.Y.	Dec 1958
DUERO	M 23	Tampa Marine Corporation	Jan 1959
TAJO	M 24	Tampa Marine Corporation	July 1959
GENIL	M 25	Tacoma B.B. Co.	Sep 1959
ODIEL	M 26	Tampa Marine Corporation	Oct 1959

13. Taiwan (13)

Name	No.	Builder	Commissioned
YUNG CHOU	423	USA	July 1959
YUNG CHING	432	USA	1955
YUNG CHENG	441	USA	1955
YUNG AN	449	USA	June 1955
YUNG JU	457	USA	Apr 1965
YUNG SUI	462	USA	1954
YUNG LO	469	USA	June 1960
YUNG SHAN	476	USA	1954
YUNG NIEN	479	USA	Dec 1958
YUNG FU	482	USA	1953
YUNG JEN	485	USA	1953
YUNG HSIN	488	USA	Mar 1965
YUNG CHI	497	USA	1955

14. Thailand (4)

Name	No.	Builders	Commissioned
LADYA	5	Peterson Builders Inc	Dec 1963
BANGEKO	6	Dorchester S.B.	July 1965
TADINDENG	7	Tacoma B.B. Co	Aug 1965
DONCHEDI	8	Peterson Builders Inc	Sep 1965

15. Tunisia (2)

Name	No.	Builders	Commissioned
HANNIBAL	—	Stephen Bros	May 1953
SOUSSE	—	Harbor B.B. Co	Mar 1953

16. Turkey (12)

Name	No.	Builders
SEYMEN	M 507	Hiltebrant D.D.
SELÇUK	M 508	Stephen Bros
SEYHAN	M 509	South Coast Co
SAMSUN	M 510	Bellingham S.Y.
SINOP	M 511	Bellingham S.Y.
SURMENE	M 512	Bellingham S.Y.
SEDDULBAHIR	M 513	Bellingham S.Y.
SILIFKE	M 514	Dorchester S.B.
SAROS	M 515	Dorchester S.B.
SIGACIK	M 516	Peterson Builders Inc
SAPANCA	M 517	Peterson Builders Inc
SARIYER	M 518	Peterson Builders Inc

17. Uruguay (1)

Name	No.	Builder	Commissioned
RIO NEGRO	13	USA	1954

Remarks: All similar and originally built as the 'AMS' or 'MSC' type, the coastal minesweepers of the classes now known as the 'Adjutant', 'Bluebird', 'MSC 268', 'MSC 294' and 'Redwing' classes were built in the USA during the 1950s for transfer to the USA's primary overseas allies. The 'Adjutant' class is described above, and the other classes differ significantly only in their length and propulsion: the 'Bluebird' class is of 145·3 ft (44·3 m) length, 360 ton full-load displacement and 1,760 bhp (1,310 kW) for 12 kts; the 'MSC 268' and 'MSC 294' classes resemble each other and have a length of 145·4 ft (44·3 m), a full-load displacement of 370 tons and 1,200 bhp (895 kW) for 14 kts; and the 'Redwing' class has a length of 144 ft (43·9 m), a full-load displacement of 470 tons and 1,760 bhp (1,310 kW) for 12 kts. Countries operating the basic 'Adjutant' class are Belgium (whose minehunters have Plessey Type 193 sonar), Denmark, France, Greece (Ms 202, 205, 206, 210 and 254), Italy, Norway (whose minehunters have Thomson-CSF Ibis III sonar), Pakistan, Spain (whose ships have UQS-1 sonar), Taiwan, Tunisia and Turkey; some of these are 'MSC 268' and 'MSC 294' class ships now to approximate 'Adjutant' class standard. The 'Bluebird' class is used only by Thailand. The 'MSC 268' and 'MSC 294' classes are in service with Greece, Iran, Pakistan, South Korea, Spain, Taiwan and Turkey. And the 'Redwing' class is employed by Fiji and Singapore. It is hard to imagine that these ships will be retained for their original purposes for much longer, especially in European waters, and it is likely that they will be scrapped or, like the single Uruguayan 'Adjutant' class vessel, relegated to secondary tasks such as survey, support for other classes or patrol.

'Agave' class coastal minesweeper/minehunter
USA/ITALY

Displacement: 375 tons standard and 405 tons full load

Dimensions: length 43·9 m (144 ft); beam 7·8 m (25·6 ft); draught 2·6 m (8·5 ft)

Gun armament: one twin 20-mm AA mounting

Missile armament: none

Torpedo armament: none

Anti-submarine armament: none

Electronics: navigation radar

Propulsion: two diesels delivering 895 kW (1,200 bhp) to two shafts

Performance: maximum speed 13·5 kts; range 4,600 km (2,860 miles) at 10 kts

Complement: 5+33

Class
1. Italy (14)

Name	No.	Builder	Commissioned
BAMBU	M 5521	Italy	
EBANO	M 5522	Italy	
MANGO	M 5523*	Italy	
MOGANO	M 5524	Italy	
PALMA	M 5525*	Italy	
SANDALO	M 5527	Italy	
AGAVE	M 5531	Italy	
ALLORO	M 5532	Italy	
EDERA	M 5533	Italy	
GELSOMINO	M 5535	Italy	
GIAGGIOLO	M 5536	Italy	
LOTO	M 5538*	Italy	
TIMO	M 5540	Italy	
VISCHIO	M 5542	Italy	

*minehunters

The Italian-built 'Agave' class is modelled on the 'Adjutant' class from the USA, and is seen here in the form of the Palma (M 5525), whose conversion into a minehunter was completed in 1981. In evidence are the two port-side paravanes, the tall bridge structure for the easier spotting of surfaced mines, and the tarpaulined 20-mm Oerlikon twin AA/mine-destroying cannon mounting forward of the bridge. The hunter conversion removed the conventional sweeping gear.

'Arkö' class coastal minesweeper

Sweden

Displacement: 285 tons standard and 300 tons full load
Dimensions: length 44·4m (145·6ft); beam 7·5m (24·6ft); draught 3·0m (9·9ft)
Gun armament: one 40-mm L/48
Missile armament: none
Torpedo armament: none
Anti-submarine armament: none
Electronics: one navigation radar
Propulsion: two Mercedes-Benz (MTU) diesels delivering 1,195kW (1,600bhp) to two shafts
Performance: maximum speed 14·5kts
Complement: 25

Class

1. Sweden (10)			Com-
Name	No.	Builders	missioned
ARKÖ	M 57	Karlskrona Varvet	1958
SPÅRÖ	M 58	Hälsingborg	1958
KARLSÖ	M 59	Karlskrona Varvet	1958
IGGÖ	M 60	Hälsingborg	1961
STYRSÖ	M 61	Karlskrona Varvet	1962
SKAFTÖ	M 62	Hälsingborg	1962
ASPÖ	M 63	Karlskrona Varvet	1962
HASSLÖ	M 64	Hälsingborg	1962
NÄMDÖ	M 67	Karlskrona Varvet	1964
BLIDÖ	M 68	Hälsingborg	1964

'Dokkum' class coastal minesweeper/minehunter

Netherlands

Displacement: 373 tons standard and 453 tons full load
Dimensions: length 45·7m (149·8ft); beam 8·5m (28ft); draught 2·0m (6·6ft)
Gun armament: two 40-mm Bofors AA in single mountings
Missile armament: none
Torpedo armament: none
Anti-submarine armament: none
Electronics: one Hollandse Signaalapparaten ZW-series surface-search and navigation radar, and (minehunters only) one Plessey Type 193 minehunting sonar
Propulsion: two MAN/Fijenoord diesels delivering 1,865kW (2,500bhp) to two shafts
Performance: maximum speed 16kts; range 4,630km (2,875 miles) at 10kts
Complement: between 27 and 36 depending on role

Remarks: The 'Dokkum' class units modified to minehunting have Plessey Type 193 sonar, and the other units have been extensively refitted in the 1970s.

Class

1. The Netherlands (15)			Com-
Name	No.	Builder	missioned
DOKKUM	M 801*	Netherlands	1955-56
HOOGEZAND	M 802	Netherlands	1955-56
NAALDWIJK	M 809	Netherlands	1955-56
ABCOUDE	M 810	Netherlands	1955-56
DRACHTEN	M 812	Netherlands	1955-56
OMMEN	M 813	Netherlands	1955-56
GIETHOORN	M 815	Netherlands	1955-56
VENLO	M 817	Netherlands	1955-56
DRUNEN	M 818*	Netherlands	1955-56
NAARDEN	M 823	Netherlands	1955-56
HOOGEVEEN	M 827	Netherlands	1955-56
STAPHORST	M 828*	Netherlands	1955-56
SITTARD	M 830	Netherlands	1955-56
GEMERT	M 841	Netherlands	1955-56
VEERE	M 842*	Netherlands	1955-56

*minehunters

'Hatsushima' class coastal minesweeper

Japan

Displacement: 440 tons standard
Dimensions: length 55·0m (180·4ft); beam 9·4m (30·8ft); draught 2·5m (8·2ft)
Gun armament: one 20-mm Oerlikon AA
Missile armament: none
Torpedo armament: none
Anti-submarine armament: none
Electronics: navigation radar
Propulsion: two diesels delivering 1,075kW (1,440bhp) to two shafts
Performance: maximum speed 14kts
Complement: 45

Class

1. Japan (11+4)			Com-
Name	No.	Builders	missioned
HATSUSHIMA	MSC 649	Nippon Steel Tube Co (Isogo)	Mar 1979
NINOSHIMA	MSC 650	Hitachi	Dec 1979
MIYAJIMA	MSC 651	Nippon Steel Tube Co (Isogo)	Jan 1980
ENOSHIMA	MSC 652	Nippon Steel Tube Co (Isogo)	Dec 1980
UKISHIMA	MSC 653	Hitachi	Nov 1981
OOSHIMA	MSC 654	Hitachi	Nov 1981
NIJIMA	MSC 655	Nippon Steel Tube Co (Isogo)	Nov 1981
YAKUSHIMA	MSC 656	Nippon Steel Tube Co (Isogo)	Nov 1982
NARUSHIMA	MSC 657	Hitachi	Nov 1982
—	MSC 658	—	1983
—	MSC 659	—	1983

'Hunt' class coastal minesweeper/minehunter

UK

Displacement: 615 tons standard and 725 tons full load
Dimensions: length 197ft (60·0m); beam 32·8ft (10·0m); draught 8·2ft (2·5m)
Gun armament: one 40-mm Bofors AA
Missile armament: none
Torpedo armament: none
Anti-submarine armament: none
Electronics: navigation radar, and Type 2093 hull-mounted sonar
Propulsion: two Ruston-Paxman 9-59K Deltic diesels delivering 3,800bhp (2,835kw) to two shafts
Performance: maximum speed 16kts; range 1,725 miles (2,775km) at 12kts
Complement: 6+39

Class

1. UK (6+5)			Com-
Name	No.	Builders	missioned
BRECON	M 29	Vosper Thornycroft Ltd	Mar 1980
LEDBURY	M 30	Vosper Thornycroft Ltd	June 1981
CATTISTOCK	M 31	Vosper Thornycroft Ltd	June 1982
COTTESMORE	M 32	Yarrow, Glasgow	Mar 1983
BROCKLESBY	M 33	Vosper Thornycroft Ltd	Feb 1983
MIDDLETON	M 34	Yarrow, Glasgow	June 1984
DULVERTON	M 35	Vosper Thornycroft Ltd	Sep 1983
—	M 36	Vosper Thornycroft Ltd	1986
CHIDDINGFOLD	M 37	Vosper Thornycroft Ltd	Aug 1984
—	M 38	Vosper Thornycroft Ltd	1987
HURWORTH	M 39	Vosper Thornycroft Ltd	1986

The Ledbury (M 30) is the second unit of the 'Hunt' class, whose primary 'weapon' is a pair of French PAP 104 mine-destructor sleds.

Remarks: The 'Hunt' class witnesses the Royal Navy's tardy realization of the obsolescence of the 'Ton' class. The ships are undoubtedly capable, combining sweeping and hunting capability in an excellent GRP hull, but are being built in small numbers and too slowly.

'Kondor II' class coastal minesweeper

East Germany

Displacement: 245 tons standard and 310 tons full load
Dimensions: length 49·0m (160·8ft); beam 7·0m (23ft); draught 2·0m (6·6ft)
Gun armament: six 25-mm AA in three twin mountings
Missile armament: none
Torpedo armament: none
Anti-submarine armament: none
Electronics: surface-search radar, and navigation radar
Propulsion: two diesels delivering 2,980kW (4,000bhp) to two shafts
Performance: maximum speed 21kts
Complement: 20 to 24

Class
1. East Germany (31)

Name	No.	Builders
ALTENBURG	—	Peenewerft
BANSIN	—	Peenewerft
BERNAU	—	Peenewerft
BITTERFELD	—	Peenewerft
BOLTENHAGEN	—	Peenewerft
DESSAU	—	Peenewerft
EILENBURG	—	Peenewerft
FREIBERG	—	Peenewerft
GENTHIN	—	Peenewerft
GRANSEE	—	Peenewerft
GREIZ	—	Peenewerft
GRIMMA	—	Peenewerft
GUBEN	—	Peenewerft
JÜTERBOG	—	Peenewerft
KAMENZ*	—	Peenewerft
KLÜTZ	—	Peenewerft
KYRITZ	—	Peenewerft
NEURUPPIN	—	Peenewerft
ORANIENBURG	—	Peenewerft
PRITZWALK	—	Peenewerft
RATHENOW	—	Peenewerft
RIESA	—	Peenewerft
ROBEL	—	Peenewerft
ROSSLAU	—	Peenewerft
SCHÖNEBECK	—	Peenewerft
STRALSUND*	—	Peenewerft
STRASBURG	—	Peenewerft
TANGERHÜTTE	—	Peenewerft
WILHELM PIECKSTADT	—	Peenewerft
WITTSTOCK	—	Peenewerft
ZERBST	—	Peenewerft

*training vessel

'Lerici' class minehunter

Italy/Malaysia

Displacement: 470 tons standard and 500 tons full load
Dimensions: length 49·9m (163·7ft); beam 9·6m (31·5ft); draught 2·6m (8·6ft)
Gun armament: one 40-mm Bofors AA
Missile armament: none
Torpedo armament: none
Anti-submarine armament: none
Electronics: SMA 3ST 7 navigation radar, one CGE-Fiat SQQ 14 minehunting sonar, and two PAP 104 minehunting/destroying vehicles

Propulsion: one GMT 230B diesel delivering 1,840hp (1,370kW) to one shaft or to two Hunting thrust jets
Performance: maximum speed 15kts on propeller and 7kts on thrust jets; range 4,625km (2,875miles) at 12kts; endurance 10 days
Complement: 40

Class
1. Italy (0+4+6)
4 vessels building and 6 projected

2. Malaysia (0+4)
4 ships on order

'Lindau' class coastal minesweeper/minehunter

West Germany

Displacement: 365 tons standard and 463 tons full load (minehunters) or 465 tons full load (minesweepers)
Dimensions: length 47·1m (154·5ft); beam 8·3m (27·2ft); draught 3·0m (9·8ft) for minehunters and 2·8m (9·2ft) for minesweepers
Gun armament: one 40-mm Bofors L/70 AA
Missile armament: none
Torpedo armament: none
Anti-submarine armament: none
Electronics: one navigation radar, and (minehunters) one Plessey Type 193M minehunting sonar and two PAP 104 minehunting/destroying sleds, or (minesweepers) three remotely-controlled Troika vehicles, each displacing 99 tons and powered by one 333-kW (446-hp) MWM D602 diesel for a speed of 10kts

The **Fulda** *(M 1086) is of the 'Lindau' class minehunting variant.*

Propulsion: two Maybach (MTU) diesels delivering 2,980kW (4,000bhp) to two shafts
Performance: maximum speed 16·5kts; range 1,575km (980miles) at 16·5kts
Complement: 5+38 for minehunters, or 4+40 for minesweepers

Class
1. West Germany (18)

Name	No.	Builders	Commissioned
GÖTTINGEN	M 1070	Burmester	May 1958
KOBLENZ	M 1071	Burmester	July 1958
LINDAU	M 1072	Burmester	Apr 1958
SCHLESWIG	M 1073*	Burmester	Oct 1958
TÜBINGEN	M 1074	Burmester	Sep 1958
WETZLAR	M 1075	Burmester	Aug 1958
PADERBORN	M 1076*	Burmester	Dec 1958
WEILHEIM	M 1077	Burmester	Jan 1959
CUXHAVEN	M 1078	Burmester	Mar 1959
DÜREN	M 1079*	Burmester	Apr 1959
MARBURG	M 1080	Burmester	June 1959
KONSTANZ	M 1081*	Burmester	July 1959
WOLFSBURG	M 1082*	Burmester	Oct 1959
ULM	M 1083*	Burmester	Nov 1959
FLENSBURG	M 1084	Burmester	Dec 1959
MINDEN	M 1085	Burmester	Jan 1960
FULDA	M 1086	Burmester	Mar 1960
VÖLKLINGEN	M 1087	Burmester	May 1960

*Troika ships

'MSC 322' class coastal minesweeper/minehunter

USA

Displacement: 320 tons standard and 407 tons full load
Dimensions: length 153ft (46·6m); beam 26·9ft (8·2m); draught 8·2ft (2·5m)
Gun armament: two 20-mm AA in a twin mounting
Missile armament: none
Torpedo armament: none
Anti-submarine armament: none
Electronics: one Westinghouse SPS-55 surface-search radar, and one General Electric SQQ-14 hull-mounted minehunting and classification sonar
Propulsion: two Waukesha diesels delivering 1,200hp (895kW) to two shafts

Performance: maximum speed 13kts
Complement: 4+39

Class
1. Saudi Arabia (4)

Name	No.	Builders	Commissioned
ADDRIYAH	MSC 412	Peterson Builders Inc	July 1978
AL QUYSUMAH	MSC 414	Peterson Builders Inc	Aug 1978
AL WADEEAH	MSC 416	Peterson Builders Inc	Sep 1979
SAFWA	MSC 418	Peterson Builders Inc	Oct 1979

'Sasha' class coastal minesweeper

USSR
Displacement: 250 tons standard and 280 tons full load
Dimensions: length 45·1m (147·9ft); beam 6·1m (20ft); draught 2·0m (6·6ft)
Gun armament: one 57-mm AA, and four 25-mm AA in two twin mountings
Missile armament: none
Torpedo armament: none
Anti-submarine armament: none
Electronics: one 'Ball End' surface-search and navigation radar, one 'High Pole'
IFF, and one 'Dead Duck' IFF
Propulsion: two diesels delivering 1,640kW (2,200bhp) to two shafts
Performance: maximum speed 18kts
Complement: 25

Class
1. USSR (15)
15 ships

'Schütze' class (Type 340/341) coastal minesweeper

West Germany
Displacement: 305 tons full load
Dimensions: length 47·4m (155·5ft); beam 7·0m (22·9ft); draught 2·2m (7·2ft)
Gun armament: one 40-mm Bofors AA
Missile armament: none
Torpedo armament: none
Anti-submarine armament: none
Electronics: one TRS-N navigation radar
Propulsion: two Maybach or Mercedes-Benz (MTU) diesels delivering 3,355kW
(4,500bhp) to two shafts
Performance: maximum speed 24kts; 3,700km (2,300 miles) at 13kts
Complement: 4+32

The Herkules (M 1095) typifies the now-obsolescent 'Schütze' class. The
'Aratu' class in Brazilian service is basically similar, and can undertake the
same types of acoustic, magnetic and wire sweeping.

Class
1. Brazil (6 'Aratu' class)

Name	No.	Builders	Commissioned
ARATU	M 15	Abeking und Rasmussen	May 1971
ANHATOMIRIM	M 16	Abeking und Rasmussen	Nov 1971
ATALAIA	M 17	Abeking und Rasmussen	Dec 1972
ARACATUBA	M 18	Abeking und Rasmussen	Dec 1972
ABROLHOS	M 19	Abeking und Rasmussen	Apr 1975
ALBARDÃO	M 20	Abeking und Rasmussen	July 1975

2. West Germany (21)

Name	No.	Builders	Commissioned
CASTOR	M 1051	Abeking und Rasmussen	1962
POLLUX	M 1054	Abeking und Rasmussen	1961
SIRIUS	M 1055	Abeking und Rasmussen	1961
RIGEL	M 1056	Abeking und Rasmussen	1962
REGULUS	M 1057	Abeking und Rasmussen	1962
MARS	M 1058	Abeking und Rasmussen	1960
SPICA	M 1059	Abeking und Rasmussen	1961
SKORPION	M 1060	Abeking und Rasmussen	1963
SCHÜTZE	M 1062	Abeking und Rasmussen	1959
WAAGE	M 1063	Abeking und Rasmussen	1962
DENEB	M 1064	Schürenstedt	1961
JUPITER	M 1065	Schürenstedt	1961
ATAIR	M 1067	Schlichting	1961
WEGA	M 1069	Abeking und Rasmussen	1963
PERSEUS	M 1090	Schlichting	1961
PLUTO	M 1092	Schürenstedt	1960
NEPTUN	M 1093	Schlichting	1960
WIDDER	M 1094	Schürenstedt	1960
HERKULES	M 1095	Schlichting	1960
FISCHE	M 1096	Abeking und Rasmussen	1960
GEMMA	M 1097	Abeking und Rasmussen	1960

'Sonya' class coastal minesweeper/minehunter

USSR
Displacement: 350 tons standard and 400 tons full load
Dimensions: length 47·5m (155·8ft); beam 8·0m (26·2ft); draught 2·0m (6·6ft)
Gun armament: two 30-mm AA in a twin mounting, and two 25-mm AA in a twin
mounting
Missile armament: none
Torpedo armament: none
Anti-submarine armament: none
Electronics: one 'Don-2' navigation radar, one 'High Pole-B' IFF, and two 'Square
Head' IFF
Propulsion: two diesels delivering 1,790kW (2,400shp) to two shafts
Performance: maximum speed 18kts
Complement: 43

Class
1. Cuba (2)
2 ships

2. USSR (42)
42 ships

'Takami' and 'Kasado' class coastal minesweepers

Japan
Displacement: 380 tons standard and 490 tons full load ('Takami' class) or 340 tons
standard and 450 tons full load ('Kasado' class)
Dimensions: length 46·0m (150·9ft); beam 8·5m (28ft); draught 2·3m (7·5ft)
Gun armament: one 20-mm AA
Missile armament: none
Torpedo armament: none
Anti-submarine armament: none
Electronics: one OPS-4 or OPS-9 surface-search and navigation radar
Propulsion: two diesels delivering 895kW (1,200hp) to two shafts
Performance: maximum speed 14kts
Complement: 43

Class
1. Japan (22)

Name	No.	Builders	Commissioned
MINASE	MSC 627	Nippon Steel Tube Co	Mar 1967
IBUKI	MSC 628	Hitachi	Feb 1968
KATSURA	MSC 629	Nippon Steel Tube Co	Feb 1968
TAKAMI	MSC 630	Hitachi	Dec 1969
IOU	MSC 631	Nippon Steel Tube Co	Jan 1970
MIYAKE	MSC 632	Hitachi	Nov 1970
UTONE	MSC 633	Nippon Steel Tube Co	Sep 1970
AWAJI	MSC 634	Hitachi	Mar 1971
TOUSHI	MSC 635	Nippon Steel Tube Co	Mar 1971
TEURI	MSC 636	Hitachi	Mar 1972
MUROTSU	MSC 637	Nippon Steel Tube Co	Mar 1972
TASHIRO	MSC 638	Hitachi	July 1973
MIYATO	MSC 639	Nippon Steel Tube Co	Aug 1973
TAKANE	MSC 640	Hitachi	Aug 1974
MUZUKI	MSC 641	Nippon Steel Tube Co	Aug 1974
YOKOSE	MSC 642	Hitachi	Dec 1975
SAKATE	MSC 643	Nippon Steel Tube Co	Dec 1975
OUMI	MSC 644	Hitachi	Nov 1976
FUKUE	MSC 645	Nippon Steel Tube Co	Nov 1976
OKITSU	MSC 646	Hitachi	Sep 1977
HASHIRA	MSC 647	Nippon Steel Tube Co (Isogo)	Mar 1978
IWAI	MSC 648	Hitachi	Mar 1978

1st three 'Kasado' class

'Ton' class coastal minesweeper/minehunter

UK

Displacement: 360 tons standard and 440 tons full load
Dimensions: length 153ft (46·3m); beam 27·7ft (8·5m); draught 8·2ft (2·5m)
Gun armament: one 40-mm Bofors AA
Missile armament: none
Torpedo armament: none
Anti-submarine armament: none
Electronics: one Kelvin Hughes Type 1006 navigation radar, and (minehunters) one Plessey Type 193 hull-mounted minehunting sonar
Propulsion: two diesels (Mirrlees JVSS 12 in M 1141 and 1158, and Napier Deltic 18A-7C in others) delivering 2,500bhp (1,865kW) to two shafts
Performance: maximum speed 15kts; range 2,875 miles (4,625km) at 12kts
Complement: 29 in minesweepers, and 5+33 in minehunters

Class

1. Argentina (6)

Name	No.	Builders	Commissioned
NEUQUEN	M 1	John I. Thornycroft Ltd	1968
RIO NEGRO	M 2	J. S. Doig Ltd	1968
CHUBUT	M 3	Fleetlands Shipyards Ltd	1968
TIERRA DEL FUEGO	M 4	White's Shipyard Ltd	1968
CHACO	M 5	Richards	1968
FORMOSA	M 6	Camper & Nicholson's	1968

2. Eire (3)

Name	No.	Builders	Commissioned
GRÁINNE	CM 10	John I. Thornycroft Ltd	1955
BANBA	CM 11	Camper & Nicholson's	1953
FÓLA	CM 12	John I. Thornycroft Ltd	1956

3. France (5 'Sirius' class)

Name	No.	Builders	Commissioned
CAPRICORNE	M 737	C.M.N. Cherbourg	July 1958
PHÉNIX	M 749	C.M.N. Cherbourg	Dec 1956
CAPELLA	M 755	C.M.N. Cherbourg	May 1956
CÉPHÉE	M 756	C.M.N. Cherbourg	June 1956
VERSEAU	M 757	C.M.N. Cherbourg	Sep 1956

4. India (4)

Name	No.	Builders	Commissioned
CUDDALORE	M 90	J. S. Doig Ltd	1955
CANNAMORE	M 91	Fleetlands Shipyard Ltd	1956
KARWAR	M 92	Camper & Nicholson's	1956
KAKINADA	M 93	Dorset Yacht Co Ltd	1955

5. Portugal (4 'Sao Roque' class)

Name	No.	Builders	Commissioned
SÃO ROQUE	M 401	CUF Shipyard	June 1956
RIBEIRA GRANDE	M 402	CUF Shipyard	Feb 1957
LAGOA	M 403	CUF Shipyard	Aug 1956
ROSARIO	M 404	CUF Shipyard	Feb 1956

6. South Africa (10)

Name	No.	Builders	Commissioned
JOHANNESBURG	M 1207	White's Shipyard Ltd	1958
KIMBERLEY	M 1210	Dorset Yacht Co Ltd	1958
PORT ELIZABETH	M 1212	Harland & Wolff Ltd	1958
MOSSELBAAI	M 1213	Harland & Wolff Ltd	1959
WALVISBAAI	M 1214	Harland & Wolff Ltd	1959
EAST LONDON	M 1215	Cook Welton and Gemmell	1958
WINDHOEK	M 1498	John I. Thornycroft Ltd	1959
DURBAN	M 1499	Camper & Nicholson's	1957
PRETORIA	P 1556	Goole Shipbuilding Co	1954
KAAPSTAD	P 1557	Cook Welton and Gemmell	1954

7. Turkey (4 'MCB' class)

Name	No.	Builders	Commissioned
TRABZON	M 530	Davie S.B. Co	1958
TERME	M 531	Davie S.B. Co	1958
TIREBOLU	M 532	Davie S.B. Co	1958
TEKIRDAG	M 533	Davie S.B. Co	1958

8. UK (28)

Name	No.	Builders	Commissioned
BILDESTON	M 1110	J. S. Doig Ltd	Apr 1953
BRERETON	M 1113	Richards	July 1954
BRINTON	M 1114	Cook Welton and Gemmell	Mar 1954
BRONINGTON	M 1115	Cook Welton and Gemmell	June 1954
BOSSINGTON	M 1133	John I. Thornycroft Ltd	Dec 1956
GAVINTON	M 1140	J. S. Doig Ltd	July 1954
HUBBERSTON	M 1147	Fleetlands Shipyards Ltd	Oct 1955
IVESTON	M 1151	Philip & Sons Ltd	June 1955
KEDLESTON	M 1153	William Pickersgill & Son	July 1955
KELLINGTON	M 1154	William Pickersgill & Son	Nov 1955
KIRKLISTON	M 1157	Harland & Wolff Ltd	Aug 1954
MAXTON	M 1165	Harland & Wolff Ltd	Feb 1957
NURTON	M 1166	Harland & Wolff Ltd	Aug 1957
SHERATON	M 1181	White's Shipyard Ltd	Aug 1956
ALFRISTON	M 1103	John I. Thornycroft Ltd	Mar 1954
BICKINGTON	M 1109	White's Shipyard Ltd	May 1954
CRICHTON	M 1124	J. S. Doig Ltd	Apr 1954
CUXTON	M 1125	Camper & Nicholson's	1953
HODGESTON	M 1146	Fleetlands Shipyards Ltd	Dec 1954
POLLINGTON	M 1173	Camper & Nicholson's	Sep 1958
SHAVINGTON	M 1180	White's Shipyard Ltd	Mar 1956
UPTON	M 1187	John I. Thornycroft Ltd	July 1956
WALKERTON	M 1188	John I. Thornycroft Ltd	Jan 1958
WOTTON	M 1195	Philip & Sons Ltd	June 1957
SOBERTON	M 1200	Fleetlands Shipyards Ltd	Sep 1957
STUBBINGTON	M 1204	Camper & Nicholson's	July 1957
LEWISTON	M 1208	Herd & Mackenzie	June 1960
CROFTON	M 1216	John I. Thornycroft Ltd	Aug 1958

First 14 minehunters; *large patrol craft

10. Yugoslavia (4)

Name	No.	Builders	Commissioned
VUKOV KLANAC	M 151	A. Normand	Sep 1957
PODGORA	M 152	A. Normand	Sep 1957
BLITVENICA	M 153	A. Normand	Sep 1957
GRADAC	M 161	Mali Losinj SY	1960

Remarks: Between 1953 and 1960, some 118 'Ton' class coastal minesweepers were built to incorporate lessons learned in the Korean War. Early units had Mirrlees Blackstone diesels, while later ships were fitted with Napier Deltic diesels of lighter weight. All minehunter conversions have Deltics and active rudders as well as Type 193 minehunting sonar. In 1967 Argentina bought six ex-British ships, and in 1968 the last pair was converted for minehunting. Australia bought six ex-British ships in 1961, and of these three remain in service, the first pair as minehunters. Eire's three ships were bought in 1971 and are used for patrol. France built a number of the class under the local designation 'Sirius' class, and of these just five remain in service as minesweepers with SEMT-Pielstick diesels, while three were transferred to Yugoslavia in 1957 as hunters with Type 193M sonar; a fourth of this 'Vukov Klanac' class was built locally. India's four ships were acquired in 1956 and are in reserve. The Portuguese ships were built locally, and are engined by Mirrlees Blackstone. Of the 10 ships received by South Africa in the second half of the 1950s, six are used as minesweepers, *Kimberley* and *Port Elizabeth* are hunters, and *Pretoria* and *Kaapstad* have a primary patrol role. The four Turkish ships are part of the 20-strong Canadian 'Bay' class, similar in most respects to the 'Ton' class. The British ships are being phased out slowly as more advanced vessels become available, the first 14 of the 28 above being hunters. Three of the hunters and six of the sweepers are used for reserve training, and another five are used as large patrol craft in Hong Kong. Additionally, seven of the British minesweeper variant are used for coastal patrol in connection with fishery protection, though unlike the ships in Hong Kong, which have only vestigial sweeping capability, the UK-based ships retain full sweeping capacity. Some 21 of the British 'Ton' class ships have a frigate-type enclosed bridge, only seven retaining the original semi-enclosed type with lattice mast.

The Kirkliston (M 1157) is a 'Ton' class minehunter, and one of the sub-variant with fully-enclosed bridge. The hull is mahogany over aluminium frames, and much non-magnetic material is used.

'Vanya' and 'Vanya (Modified)' class coastal minesweepers/minehunters

USSR

Displacement: 200 tons standard and 245 tons full load
Dimensions: length 40·0m (131·2ft); beam 7·3m (23·9ft); draught 1·8m (5·9ft)
Gun armament: two 30-mm AA in one twin mounting ('Vanya' class) or two 25-mm AA in one twin mounting ('Vanya (Modified)' class)
Missile armament: none
Torpedo armament: none
Anti-submarine armament: none
Mines: up to 5
Electronics: one 'Don-2' navigation radar ('Vanya' class) or 'Don Kay' navigation radar ('Vanya (Modified)' class), and one 'Square Head' IFF ('Vanya' class) or 'High Pole-B' IFF ('Vanya (Modified)' class)
Propulsion: two diesels delivering 1,640kW (2,200bhp) to two shafts
Performance: maximum speed 18kts; range 2,000km (1,245 miles) at 18kts
Complement: 30

Class
1. Bulgaria (4 'Vanya')
4 ships (nos 36-39)

2. Syria (2 'Vanya')
2 ships

3. USSR (69 'Vanya' and 3 'Vanya (Modified)' class)
69 'Vanya' class ships
3 'Vanya (Modified)' class ships

Remarks: Built between 1961 and 1973, the Soviet 'Vanya' class is based on a wooden hull, and the type is suitable for both minesweeping and minehunting. The type is designed largely for the protection of the Soviet navy's main operational bases, as indicated by the designation *bazovy tralshchik*, or base minesweeper. The three 'Vanya (Modified)' class ships are intended as leaders for the 10 'Ilyusha' class inshore minesweepers, and differ from the standard 'Vanya' class in having a forward extension to the bridge, 25-mm instead of 30-mm twin AA mountings, two boats stowed on the quarterdeck, and an extra lattice mast being added at the midships break. In this form the ship is able to control by radio an unmanned 'Ilyusha' class sweeper, which otherwise has a crew of 10. Transfers of the 'Vanya' class have been few: Bulgaria received four of the type in 1970 (two ships) and 1971 (two ships), while Syria was the recipient of two 'Vanya' class sweepers in December 1972. An unusual feature of the design is its lack of a funnel, exhaust gases being piped out through holes in the ships' sides. The class was probably designed as successor to the 'Sasha' class, of which some 10 now remain in the Soviet inventory for secondary sweeping tasks.

'Vegesack' class coastal minesweeper

France

Displacement: 360 tons standard and 380 tons full load
Dimensions: length 47·3m (155·1ft); beam 8·6m (28·2ft); draught 2·9m (9·5ft)
Gun armament: two 20-mm AA in one twin mounting
Missile armament: none
Torpedo armament: none
Anti-submarine armament: none
Electronics: one navigation radar
Propulsion: two Mercedes-Benz (MTU) 820Eb diesels delivering 1,120kW (1,500bhp) to two shafts
Performance: maximum speed 15kts
Complement: 40

Class
1. Turkey (6)

Name	No.	Builders	Commissioned
KARAMÜRSEL	M 520	Amiot	1960
KEREMPE	M 521	Amiot	1960
KILIMLI	M 522	Amiot	1960
KOZLU	M 523	Amiot	1960
KUŞADASI	M 524	Amiot	1960
KEMER	M 525	Amiot	1960

Remarks: These ships were built in France for the West German navy, but were placed in reserve by the West German navy in 1963. In the middle 1960s the poor minesweeping resources of the Turkish navy prompted their transfer, the first five in 1975-76, and the last in 1979.

'Wilton' class coastal minesweeper

UK

Displacement: 450 tons full load
Dimensions: length 153ft (46·3m); beam 28·8ft (8·8m); draught 8·5ft (2·5m)
Gun armament: one 40-mm Bofors in a Mk 7 single mounting
Missile armament: none
Torpedo armament: none
Anti-submarine armament: none
Electronics: one Kelvin Hughes Type 975 surface-search radar, one Type 955M radar, and one Plessey Type 193M hull-mounted minehunting sonar
Propulsion: two English Electric Deltic 18-7A diesels delivering 3,000bhp (2,235kW) to two shafts
Performance: maximum speed 16kts; range 2,650 miles (4,265km) at 13kts
Complement: 5+32

Class
1. UK (1)

Name	No.	Builders	Commissioned
WILTON	M 1116	Vosper Thornycroft Ltd	July 1973

Remarks: The *Wilton* (M 1116) was the world's first GRP warship, and was ordered in 1970. The design is similar to that of the 'Ton' class, and the ship is in fact fitted with reconditioned machinery from the scrapped 'Ton' class *Derriton*.

'Zhenya' class coastal minesweeper

USSR

Displacement: 220 tons standard and 330 tons full load
Dimensions: length 42·7m (140·1ft); beam 7·6m (25ft); draught 1·8m (6ft)
Gun armament: two 30-mm AA in one twin mounting
Missile armament: none
Torpedo armament: none
Anti-submarine armament: none
Mines: up to six
Electronics: one 'Don-2' navigation radar, two 'Square Head' IFF, and one 'High Pole-B' IFF
Propulsion: two diesels delivering 1,790kW (2,400shp) to two shafts
Performance: maximum speed 18kts
Complement: 40

Class
1. USSR (3)
3 ships

Remarks: The 'Zhenya' class represents an early Soviet attempt at the design and construction of a GRP minesweeper, the ships of the class being built in the early 1970s at Leningrad as a slightly enlarged modified version of the 'Vanya' class, from which it differs mainly in its construction and in having a conventional funnel for the engine exhaust gases. And in comparison with the 'Vanya' class, the 30-mm twin mount is moved farther forward from the bridge to provide deck area for the fire-control system. There were apparently problems with the GRP hull, for only three units were completed out of a considerably larger number originally envisaged, and its place appears to have been taken by the wooden-hulled 'Sonya' class, which is still in production.

A powerful anti-submarine destroyer with useful anti-aircraft capability, the 'Broadsword' or 'Type 22' class guided-missile destroyer is exemplified here by the lead ship of the class, HMS *Broadsword* (F 88). The primary anti-submarine weapon is the Westland Lynx helicopter, one of the two carried being seen on the platform over the stern. Above the hangar is the after of the two sextuple Sea Wolf missile launchers, and to starboard of the funnel structure is a triple Mk 32 anti-submarine torpedo launcher. Easily distinguished electronic features are the after Type 910 Sea Wolf radar just forward of the launcher, the combined Type 967 and Type 968 surveillance radars on top of the foremast, and the forward Type 910 radar above the bridge. Forward of the breakwater on the forecastle is the starboard twin container-launcher for MM.38 Exocet surface-to-surface missiles.

The most modern class of guided-missile frigate in US service is the 'FFG 7' or 'Oliver Hazard Perry' class, of which a total of 50 is planned. Three early examples of the Atlantic Fleet are seen here, namely the USS *Oliver Hazard Perry* (FFG 7), the USS *Antrim* (FFG 20) and the USS *Jack Williams* (FFG 24). Salient features of the pre-fabricated design are the high bow, the massive and blocky superstructure, and the helicopter platform at the stern. Also discernible with little difficulty are the Mk 13 single launcher for Standard and Harpoon missiles (forward of the superstructure), the globe mounting for the antenna of the Mk 92 (Americanized WM-28) weapon-control system (above the bridge), and the parabolic antenna for the AN/SPS-49 long-range search radar (just aft of the Mk 92 globe). Between the mast and the low stack assembly are the antenna for the STIR (modified AN/SPG-60) weapon-control system and the Mk 75 76-mm (3-in) gun. Space and weight are reserved above the hangar for a Mk 15 Phalanx CIWS mounting.

Above: The Royal Australian Navy has also adopted the 'Oliver Hazard Perry' design, and the second RAN unit is HMAS *Canberra* (F 02), which shows off to advantage the type's high, slab-sided superstructure.

A 'Vosper Mk 9' class frigate of the Nigerian navy, *Erin'Omi* (F 83) is a compact but well-balanced design showing how much can be achieved on a relatively small displacement. Located forward is the 76-mm (3-in) OTO-Melara Compact gun, while other armament includes a twin-barrel Bofors anti-submarine rocket-launcher just forward of the bridge, a Bofors 40-mm AA gun on the superstructure right aft, and a triple Sea Cat surface-to-air missile launcher on the stern. The aftermost antenna is for the Plessey AWS 2 search radar, while the globe houses the antenna for the WM-24 fire-control system.

Above: The 'Kortenaer' class guided-missile frigate *Van Kinsbergen* (F 809) unleashes a RIM-7 Sea Sparrow surface-to-air missile from the octuple launcher just forward of the bridge. Other armament is a 76-mm (3-in) OTO-Melara Compact gun, a 40-mm Bofors AA gun (to be replaced by the Signaal/General Electric Goalkeeper CIWS when this becomes available), eight Harpoon surface-to-surface missiles just aft of the tower foremast, two twin Mk 32 anti-submarine torpedo tube mountings in the after deckhouse, and two Westland Lynx anti-submarine helicopters.

Although not apparent in this head-on view, which emphasizes the 76-mm (3-in) OTO-Melara Compact gun, the main punch of the West German 'Type 143A' class fast attack craft lies with the four MM.38 Exocet surface-to-surface missiles towards the stern. The globe above the bridge accommodates the antenna for the WM-27 fire-control system.

A Penguin surface-to-surface missile is launched from one of the six container-launchers for the Mk 2 version of this IR-homing weapon carried by the 'Hauk' class fast attack craft *Terne* (P 988) of the Royal Norwegian navy.

Virtual sisters of the Israeli 'Saar 4' class, the South African 'Mod' class fast attack craft carries two 76-mm (3-in) OTO-Melara Compact guns (one forward and one aft) and six individual Skorpioen surface-to-surface missiles. The secondary armament comprises two 20-mm cannon and two twin 0.5-in (12.7-mm) machine guns.

The first of a new class of five fast attack craft (gun), HMS *Peacock* (P 239) is designed for guard duty in Hong Kong, and is indicative of the British lack of interest in high-speed missile-armed attack craft, for the type is capable of barely 25 kts and has an armament of only one 76-mm (3-in) OTO-Melara Compact gun.

Obsolescent but still a force to be feared is the Soviet navy's 'Osa II' class of fast attack craft, of which some 50 are in service. Each is armed with four container-launchers for SS-N-2C 'Styx' surface-to-surface missiles and two twin 30-mm mountings, the latter controlled via the 'Drum Tilt' radar visible behind the mast, which supports the 'Square Tie' search radar.

Under test before delivery, this group of Swift 105-ft (32-m) large patrol craft was destined for Ethiopia, but only P 201 to P 204 were delivered before the imposition of a US embargo on arms supplies to Ethiopia. Visible on the deck of the nearest craft are the circular deck openings for the planned armament of two twin 30-mm Emerlec mountings. With limited armament and negligible electronics (only Decca RM 916 navigation radar), these craft are suitable solely for coastal patrol.

More punch is packed by the Egyptian 'October' class, which has two twin 35-mm A 32 cannon mountings (one forward and the other aft) and two container-launchers for Otomat surface-to-surface missiles. In this photograph of an 'October' class craft under trial, the Otomats have not been shipped, though the starboard support structure for the container can be seen.

The 'Spica I' or 'T 121' class fast attack craft of the Royal Swedish navy are effective coastal defence vessels, with a powerful 57-mm Bofors gun and six tubes for 533-mm (21-in) wire-guided anti-ship torpedoes. The WM-22 radar-directed fire-control system is used with the gun and the torpedoes.

No great speed or offensive capability is available to or required by the Royal Australian Navy's 'Fremantle' class large patrol craft, seen here in the form of the lead craft HMAS *Fremantle* (P 203).

Largest craft in the Honduran navy are two of these Swift 105-ft (32-m) fast attack craft (patrol), which can achieve 32 kts on two MTU diesels.

Above: Delivered to the US Navy in 1982, the Bell-Halter surface-effect ship (SES) weighs 128 tons and is a hybrid air-cushion vehicle with solid sidewalls formed by the catamaran hulls of the vessel. Though only an experimental vessel, the type points almost certainly to the future of mine-countermeasures, assault landing and patrol vessels with its combination of high speed and long range.

Below: The USS *Hercules* (PHM 2) is the second unit of the agile and speedy 'Pegasus' class fast attack hydrofoil (missile). The Mk 92 (Americanized WM-28) radar-directed fire-control system is used for the Mk 75 (OTO-Melara Compact) 76-mm (3-in) gun and for the four RGM-84A Harpoon surface-to-surface missiles. The trestle for the port twin container-launcher unit for the Harpoon can be seen above the port hydrofoil leg at the stern.

Although they carry a relatively light armament (one 76-mm/3-in OTO-Melara Compact gun and two Otomat Mk 2 surface-to-surface missiles) in comparison with conventional fast attack craft (missile), the units of the Italian 'Sparviero' class have a considerable advantage in speed and agility, and can maintain their speed in conditions that would hamper displacement-hull craft. Seen here is the *Nibbio* (P 421), lead craft of the production class for which the *Sparviero* (P 420) was the prototype.

The pennant number M461 identifies this 'Tripartite' type minehunter as *Eridan*, the lead ship of the French 'Eridan' class version of the standard French/Belgian/Dutch minehunter. This is an important class of some 45 ships and, though there are detail differences, all will have French minehunting gear, Belgian electrical systems and Dutch propulsion in nationally-produced hulls.

Left: Mine warfare has for many years been a Russian and Soviet speciality, yet the Western alliance has let itself fall disastrously behind in this potentially decisive naval regime. One of the current mainstays of NATO is the US-designed MSO type dating from the 1950s. Such a mine-sweeper is here seen taking on fuel at sea.

Lead craft of the 'Flagstaff 2' class fast attack hydrofoil, the Israeli *Shimrit* (M 161) was built by Grumman Lantana, and carries the interesting missile armament of four Harpoon and four Gabriel surface-to-surface missiles.

Defence against aircraft and air-launched missiles has assumed a massive importance among modern navies during the 1970s and early 1980s, particularly with the threat of saturation air and missile attacks on major surface task groups becoming more likely. Gunfire, especially from rapid-fire cannon, offers the chance of 'last-ditch' defence, but longer-range protection rests with the missile. Among the best of medium/long-range surface-to-air missiles is the Standard SM-1, seen (*below*) after launch from the 'Coontz' class destroyer USS *Farragut* (DDG 37). Short/medium-range defence is well entrusted in many Western navies to the RIM-7 Sea Sparrow, the surface-launch version of the AIM-7 Sparrow air-to-air missile. Lightweight launchers for this important weapon have made it possible to provide SAM defence for all types of surface vessel, and a Sea Sparrow is seen (*left*) during launch from the USS *Camden* (AOE 2), one of four 'Sacramento' class fast combat support ships.

Startling enough in itself, the re-emergence of the battleship in the US Navy is also notable for the type's highly capable and diverse weapon fit. Here the USS *New Jersey* (BB 62) fires a BGM-109 Tomahawk long-range anti-ship missile during her work-up trials off the California coast in 1982.